MAX ZERWICK
AND
MARY GROSVENOR

A GRAMMATICAL ANALYSIS
OF THE
GREEK NEW TESTAMENT

VOL. II
EPISTLES — APOCALYPSE

ROME
BIBLICAL INSTITUTE PRESS
1979

If I had been a priest I should have made a thorough study of Hebrew and Greek so as to understand the thought of God as he has vouchsafed to express it in our human language.

Sᴛ Tʜᴇʀᴇsᴀ ᴏғ ᴛʜᴇ Cʜɪʟᴅ Jᴇsᴜs

Original title: Max Zerwick, S.I., *Analysis philologica Novi Testamenti graeci*. 3rd edition. Scripta Pontificii Instituti Biblici, 107. Rome 1966. Pontifical Biblical Institute.

Translated, revised, and adapted by Mary Grosvenor in collaboration with the author.

PRINTED IN ITALY

TYPIS PONTIFICIAE UNIVERSITATIS GREGORIANAE - ROMAE

EXTRACT FROM PREFACE TO VOL. I

Despite the decline in the study of Latin and Greek, the Latin *Analysis philologica Novi Testamenti graeci* has had great success during the past twenty years. Still, requests for an English edition became ever more frequent. A strict translation of this kind of work is hardly possible however. The needs and possibilities of English must be taken into consideration and the final result is, in many ways, a new work.

It is hoped that this English revised edition in its turn will mean that the Greek text of the New Testament will not remain exclusively a tool on the desks of a decreasing number of specialists but will become a living power in the hands of theologians, of preachers of the Word, of directors of Bible discussion-circles, and finally in the hands of those who pray in private from the Word of God. This is the purpose to be served. May God bless everyone helping it.

The student who has little knowledge of Greek should bear in mind while using this book that it is by no means necessary to understand immediately everything explained in it. The principle of one thing at a time will serve him well. Many of the linguistic subtleties go beyond the needs of the beginner and are intended for the more advanced student, interested perhaps in the characteristics of Hellenistic Greek as contrasted with classical Greek.

A helpful feature of this work (and a justification of its size) is the fact that a student can begin using it at whatever point he likes, each chapter being self-sufficient and not presupposing explanations given in the previous chapters. (In this connection the reader is referred to the details on the page facing p. 1.)

Whereas in the Latin edition the text of A. Merk was followed and variant readings were neglected, in the present English edition all variants mentioned in the *Revised Standard Version* are given and explained. The Greek text here

followed is that proposed for the forthcoming third edition
of *The Greek New Testament* edited by Kurt Aland, Matthew
Black, Bruce M. Metzger, and Carlo M. Martini.

Rome   M. ZERWICK
Pentecost, 1974

PREFACE TO VOL. II

The commentary on Galatians was not completed in
Oct. 1975 when the news broke that Father Zerwick had
died in Munich. "The Lord [hath taken] away thy master
from thy head today" were the first words that came to
mind on reading the notice and this sense of bereavement
was common to his colleagues and students far beyond the
sphere of the Institute to which he had devoted his life.

Some weeks later Father John Welch S. J. offered "to
be of any help he could" (to quote his own expression) —
an offer eagerly accepted and generously implemented to
the immense profit of this volume. In addition to Father
Welch's "help" which has involved reading critically every
word of the typescript and first proofs, suggesting and
correcting at innumerable points, Father Manuel Iglesias S.J.
and Father Klemens Stock S.J. have sacrificed time they
could ill afford to the correction of proofs and I should like
to thank them, not only for their valuable contribution but
also for the readiness with which they accepted this exact-
ing task. Nor can I fail to express my appreciation of
the skill and patience of the machine operator and the
compositor who achieved such a high degree of precision
in two languages of which they knew little or nothing.
To them also, sincere thanks are due.

MARY D. GROSVENOR

Rome
Feast of S. John the Evangelist, 1978

EXPLANATION OF SIGNS AND ABBREVIATIONS

Unless otherwise indicated it is to be assumed that nouns ending

a) in -ος are masc. and follow the paradigm :

sg	οἶκ-ος	pl.	-οι
	-ον		-ους
	-ου		-ων
	-ῳ		-οις

b) in -ον are neut. and follow the paradigm :

sg	τέκν-ον	pl.	-α
	-ον		-α
	-ου		-ων
	-ῳ		-οις

c) in -η are fem. and follow the paradigm :

sg	τιμ-ή	pl.	-αί
	-ήν		-άς
	-ῆς		-ῶν
	-ῇ		-αῖς

d) in -α preceded by ρ or a vowel* are fem. and follow the paradigm :

sg	καρδί-α	pl.	-αι
	-αν		-ας
	-ας		-ῶν
	-ᾳ		-αις

Adjectives, including participles, in -ος (fem. -η or -α, neut. -ον) are declined as *a*, *c* or *d*, and *b* above.

---

* All other fem. nouns in -α retain α in acc. sg only ; otherwise they are declined like those in -η.

A superior figure ² denotes strong or 2nd aorist (or future or perfect). Other superior figures indicate the paradigm for nouns not covered above.

³masc. nouns like προφήτης

	sg προφήτ-ης		pl.	-αι
	-ην			-ας
	-ου			-ῶν
	-η			-αις

⁴fem. nouns like πόλις

	sg	πόλ-ις		pl.	-εις
		-ιν			-εις
		-εως			-εων
		-ει			-εσι(ν)

⁵masc. nouns like βασιλεύς

	sg	βασιλ-εύς		pl.	-εῖς
		-έα			-εῖς
		-έως			-έων
		-εῖ			-εῦσι(ν)

⁶masc. & fem. nouns like ἐλπίς *

	sg	ἐλπίς		pl.	-ες
		ἐλπίδ-α			-ας
		-ος			-ων
		-ι			ἐλπίσι(ν)

---

* In this class the stem must be ascertained from gen. sg (supplied in the *Analysis*) thus :

σάρξ, σαρκός forms acc. σάρκ-α dat. σαρκ-ί dat. pl. σαρξί(ν)
αἰών, αἰῶνος forms acc. αἰῶν-α dat. αἰῶν-ι dat. pl. αἰῶσι(ν)

so the pronoun τίς; (and τις) and the masc. of the adjs εἷς and πᾶς:

τίς, τίνος   forms acc. τίν-α dat. τίν-ι dat. pl. τίσι(ν)
εἷς, ἑνός   forms acc. ἕν-α dat. ἑν-ί
πᾶς, παντός forms acc. πάντ-α dat. παντ-ί dat. pl. πᾶσι(ν)
thus also all the masc. participles not ending in -μενος.

⁷neut. nouns ending in -μα

	sg	πρᾶγ-μα	pl.	-ματα
		-μα		-ματα
		-ματος		-μάτων
		-ματι		-μασι(ν)

⁸neut. nouns ending in -ος

	sg	ὄρ-ος	pl.	-η
		-ος		-η
		-ους (= εος)		-ῶν (= -έων)
		-ει		-εσι(ν)

⁹adjectives masc. & fem. ending in -ης, neut. -ες

	sg	ἀληθ-ής	-ές	pl.	ἀληθ-εῖς	-ῆ
		-ῆ	-ές		-εῖς	-ῆ
		-οῦς			-ῶν	
		-εῖ			-έσι(ν)	

abs.	absolute, standing (syntactically) on its own
acc.	accusative
act.	active (voice)
adj.	adjective ; adjectival
adv.	adverb
advl	adverbial(ly)
aor.	aorist (tense)
appos.	in apposition (to)
Aram.	Aramaic ; Aramaism
art.	(definite) article
ass.	associate(d) ; association
aug.	augment
c.	*circa*, about
cf	Lat. *confer*, compare
class.	classics, classical Gk
cmpd	compound
cohort.	cohortative subjunctive (1st pers. only)
colloq.	colloquial, colloquialism
comp.	comparative ; comparison (in " gen. of comp.")
cond.	conditional
conj.	conjunction

consec.	consecutive
co-ord.	co-ordinate ; co-ordination
cstr	construction ; construe(d)
dat.	dative
delib.	deliberative
den.	denotes ; denoting
dep.	deponent
dim.	diminutive
dir.	direct
encl.	enclitic
Eng.	English
epexeg.	epexegetic
esp.	especially
etym.	etymology, etymologically
f., ff.	following verse(s), paragraph(s) etc.
fem.	feminine
foll.	followed ; following
Fr.	French
freq.	frequently
fut.	future (tense)
gen.	genitive
Ger.	German
Gk	Greek
HGk	Hellenistic Greek
Hebr.	Hebrew ; Hebraism
impers.	impersonal
impf	imperfect (tense)
impv	imperative (mood)
impvl	imperatival
incl.	including
indecl.	indeclinable
indef.	indefinite
indic.	indicative (mood)
indir.	indirect
inf.	infinitive
instr.	instrument(al)
interr.	interrogative

intr.	intransitive
irreg.	irregular
JB	Jerusalem Bible (in English)
κτλ.	καὶ τὰ λοιπά, and the rest, et cetera
Lat.	Latin, Latinism
lit.	literal(ly)
masc.	masculine
met.	metaphorical(ly)
mg	margin
mid.	middle (voice)
NEB	New English Bible
nec.	necessary, necessarily
neg.	negative ; negation
neut.	neuter
nom.	nominative
NT	New Testament
obj.	object ; objective
obs.	obsolete
occ.	occasionally
om.	omit(s) ; omitted
opp.	as opposed to, in contrast to
opt.	optative
orig.	original(ly)
OT	Old Testament
pass.	passive (voice)
perh.	perhaps
periphr.	periphrastic ; periphrasis
pers.	person ; personal
pf	perfect (tense)
pl.	plural
pleon.	pleonastic(ally) ; pleonasm
plpf	pluperfect (tense)
pred.	predicate
prep.	preposition ; prepositional
pres.	present (tense)
priv.	privative
prn	pronoun

prob.	probably
ptc	participle, participial
ref.	reference, referring to, with reference to
refl.	reflexive
rel.	relative ; relation (in the phrase " in rel. to ")
RSV	Revised Standard Version of the Bible
sc.	(scilicet), namely, one is to understand
Sem.	Semitic ; Semitism
sg	singular
sth	something
sts	sometimes
subj.	subjunctive (mood)
subord.	subordinate ; subordination
superl.	superlative
t.t.	technical term
trans.	transitive
transl.	translate(d)
transln	translation
usu.	usual(ly)
v.	verse
var.	variant, different form or reading
vb	verb
voc.	vocative
w.	with
Wm	Weymouth's translation
wt	without

GLOSSARY OF GRAMMATICAL TERMS

by Mary Grosvenor

Absolute (in the sense of "untrammelled, independent").
A verb is said to be absolute when it lacks its customary
object, and an adjective when it is used without a noun,
e.g. αἰτεῖτε, καὶ δοθήσεται ὑμῖν· ζητεῖτε, καὶ εὑρήσετε·
κρούετε, καὶ ἀνοιγήσεται ὑμῖν "ask, and it will be given you;
seek, and you will find; knock, and it will be opened to
you" Mt 7:7; μήτε ἐσθίων μήτε πίνων "neither eating nor
drinking" Mt 11:18 cf Lk 7:33; οἱ δίκαιοι "the just". —
A **genitive absolute** is a clause whose subject and verb (always
a participle) are in the genitive. It is called "absolute"
because it stands independently of the following clause and
can therefore be omitted without disturbing the syntax.
According to classical norms the gen. abs. should only be used
when its subject does not occur in the principal clause, otherwise the participle ought to be in the same case as its subject ;
that is to say, it ceases to be a gen. abs. and becomes a
"concordant" participle. To take first some examples in
translation : *"When the priest had given the blessing* the
congregation left the church". Here the italicized words
could well be expressed in Greek by a gen. abs. ; but "When
the priest had given the blessing he left the church" or
"When the priest left the church a crowd was waiting to
greet him" would not make a correct gen. abs. because the
same subject would appear in two different cases. In the
former example the participle should be nominative (to
agree with "he"), in the latter, accusative (to agree with
"him"). The two sentences should, strictly speaking, be
expressed thus : The priest εὐλογίαν ποιήσας (aor. ptc nom.)
left the church" and "a crowd was waiting to greet the
priest ἐξέρχοντα ἐκ τῆς ἐκκλησίας " (pres. ptc acc.). Similarly, instead of καθίσαντος αὐτοῦ (gen. abs.) προσῆλθον
αὐτῷ οἱ μαθηταί Mt 5:1 classical Greek would say καθίσαντι
αὐτῷ (concordant ptc) προσῆλθον οἱ μαθηταί; instead of μνη-
στευθείσης...Μαρίας τῷ Ἰωσήφ...εὑρέθη ἐν γαστρὶ ἔχουσα
Mt 1:18 : μνηστευθεῖσα...Μαρία τῷ Ἰωσήφ...εὑρέθη... But this

rule (never very strict) is frequently neglected in the po-
pular Greek of NT times §48-50.

Accusative : case of the direct object. — **Of place :** denoting
motion towards (answering the question "whither ?"), in
HGk usually accompanied by a preposition ; or denoting
extent (answering the question "how far ?") e.g. ἀπ' αὐτῶν...
λίθου βολήν "a stone's-throw from them" Lk 22:41 §66-
74. — **Of time :** denoting duration (answering "how long ?")
e.g. λατρεύουσα νύκτα καὶ ἡμέραν "worshipping night
and day" Lk 2:37, cf §54. — **Of respect :** with the force
of "in respect of", "as to", e.g. τὸν ἀριθμὸν ὡς πεντακισ-
χίλιοι "about 5000 in number" Jn 6:10 §74.

Anarthrous : without the article.

Aorist. A description may be thought of as enriching a concept, filling it out, but in grammatical terms it constitutes
a limitation ; thus, "an adjective *modifies* a noun" ('table'
is all-inclusive ; 'round table' excludes all other shapes,
'round, polished table' limits still further its application,
and so on). It is in this sense that the aorist bears the name
ἀ- (without) ὅρος (boundary, limit), i.e. "undetermined", in
so far as it implies nothing as to continuity or repetition
(= imperfect) or endurance into the present (= perfect)
§240f., 249 ; in short, if the aor. does not express duration,
neither does it preclude it *as a fact* but views the action,
of however long duration, as telescoped to a point. From
this basic character of the aor. emerges what is variously
known as the **constative, complexive,** or **global** use of the
aor. in which a "punctiliar" statement is made which, just
because it is a-orist, has the capacity to be all-embracing,
summarizing without detailing numerous instances. Perhaps
to continue the geometrical image it may be said that the
point here becomes the centre point of a circle which the
verb itself never describes but which is revealed by the context, either expressly or by logical inference. ὁ Χριστὸς οὐχ
ἑαυτῷ ἤρεσεν "Christ did not please himself" (Rom 15:3)
could, in isolation, just as well refer to one specific occasion ; that the aor. is constative must be inferred from the
context. In ἐκάθισεν ... ἐνιαυτὸν καὶ μῆνας ἕξ (Ac 18:11), the
idea that Paul's stay lasted a considerable time is imported
by the words following "he stayed" and must not be read

into the aor. which nevertheless is thereby shown to be constative §253-5. Other kinds of point action also denoted by the aorist are the point of entry into action (**ingressive** or **inceptive** aor.) whose force may sometimes be suggested by mentally prefixing such words as "come to..." before the verb in question (generally a verb signifying a state), e.g. ἐβασίλευε "was king, reigned", ἐβασίλευσε "became king, came to the throne"; ἔζη "lived", ἔζησε "came to life"; ἐπτώχευε "was poor", ἐπτώχευσε "became poor"; ἐσίγα "was silent", ἐσίγησε "fell silent" §250; and the point of completion (**effective** or **perfective** aor.) e.g. ἐγίνωσκε "knew", ἔγνω "realized"; ἐκώλυε "hindered", ἐκώλυσε "prevented"; ἔπειθε "urged", ἔπεισε "persuaded (effectively), convinced" §252*. The aor. indicative bears the augment of past time and usually the nearest English equivalent will be the past definite or perfect, for it is difficult to conceive of present or future events in the manner an aor. indicative presents them to the mind. The same factor operates in the use of the aor. participle (though to a lesser extent) for it takes the place of another indicative verb linked to the main one, sharing its past tense and very often its priority though not necessarily so, as the frequent ἀποκριθεὶς εἶπεν witnesses. The NT is full of examples where the aor. participle has been selected for its characteristic nuance and (as in the case of the indicative) it is precisely this which causes its temporal relation to the finite verb and not any intrinsic connection with past time §261-9. Its essential character becomes clearest in commands and prohibitions where, unencumbered by considerations of relative time, attention is free to concentrate on the nature of the action. Particularly revealing are parallel passages where aor. is found in one author and present in another : Lk 11:3 with Mt 6:11 ; also Lk 6:30 with Mt 5:42, and Lk 6:23 with Mt 5:12: in each case the present enunciates a general rule whereas the command in the aor. is linked by words in the context to a specific occasion. Though instances difficult to explain are not lacking, it may be assumed that the aor. impv is more

---

* It must not be supposed that these translations are appropriate to any and every instance of the aor., e.g. Rom 5:14 ἐβασίλευσεν ὁ θάνατος "death reigned" is clearly constative (global).

immediate and arresting, κρατήσατε αὐτόν "seize him" Mt
26:48, but κρατεῖτε τὰς παραδόσεις "hold to the traditions"
II Thess 2:15 ; ἆρον τὸν κράβαττόν σου καὶ περιπάτει "pick
up (now)...and walk" (for the rest of your days) Jn 5:8 ;
περιβάλου (aor. mid.) τὸ ἱμάτιόν σου καὶ ἀκολούθει μοι "throw
your cloak round you and keep following" me. Similarly
in the case of prohibitions, the negative μή with the present
imperative frequently means "stop doing" (interrupting something going on) whereas μή with the aor. subjunctive (the aor.
imperative is only used in positive injunctions) means "do
not do" (a prohibition containing no implication as to whether
or not the action has been committed) §242-8.

Apodosis. Associated with an "if"-clause (**protasis**) there is
usually another clause which expresses the consequence and
which could be mentally preceded by "then" ; this is the
apodosis. The two clauses together make up a complete
conditional sentence §299. The same terminology may be
used for other sentences with secondary clauses.

Apposition. When it is added to another noun (agreeing
in case) by way of explanation, a noun is said to be in
apposition, e.g. "a man of the Pharisees...a ruler of the Jews"
Jn 3:1 ; "Annas the high priest" Ac 4:6.

Article : in Greek stands for *the*, i.e. previously mentioned
or known. The indefinite article "a" is normally indicated
by the absence of the definite article since it has no Greek
equivalent except in the form of εἷς "one" or the pronoun
τις "a certain one, someone" §165-92.

Augment : a prefix (basically ἐ- but subject to modification) added to indicative tenses of Greek verbs indicating
past time. A verb compounded with a preposition is augmented (like its simple form) immediately before the stem :
βαίνω ἔ-βην: κατα-βαίνω κατ-έ-βην; οἰκοῦσι ᾤκουν: κατ-οικοῦσι
κατ-ᾤκουν. Note προφητεύει ἐ-προφήτευσε (there is no verb φη-
τεύω); ἀν-οίγω is found with one, two, and three augments :
ἤνοιξα, ἀν-έ-ῳξα, ἠν-έ-ῳξα.

Cognate = of the same derivation ; especially used of an
accusative or dative of the same root as the verb which
governs it e.g. ἐφοβήθησαν φόβον μέγαν "they were afraid

with great fear" Mk 4:41 ; ἐχάρησαν χαρὰν μεγάλην "they rejoiced with great joy" Mt 2:10 ; ἐξέστησαν ἐκστάσει μεγάλη "they were amazed with great amazement" Mk 5:42 ; and the Hebraic ἀκοῇ ἀκούσετε "with hearing you shall hear", i.e. "you shall indeed hear" Mt 13:14; ἐνυπνίοις ἐνυπνιασθήσονται "they shall dream (in) dreams" Ac 2:17, both from LXX §62.

Comparative : applied to adjectives and adverbs with the force of "to a greater degree", "more...", e.g. weaker, greater, more generous, more quickly. In Hellenistic Greek some- times stands for superlative §143-50.

Complexive, see Aorist.

Conative, see Imperfect.

Concomitant = accompanying, as in "the dative of conco- mitant circumstances" (or sociative dat.) and as " conco- mitant (or co-incident) action", i.e. taking place at the same time.

Concordant = agreeing, see Absolute (genitive abs.).

Conditional sentences propose a condition, "if..." (Greek εἰ or ἐάν) followed, when complete, by a clause expressing the result, "then..." ; but the latter is sometimes missing and in such cases the clause may express a wish, cf English "if only...". See Apodosis, Protasis. On the different kinds of conditional sentence §299-334.

Consecutive = following as a consequence or effect ; so, of all expressions of consequence such as *with the result that*, *so*, *so that*, in Greek ὥστε, and sometimes simply infinitive = *so as to* where no purpose is involved. It is important to distinguish "He leant so heavily against the door that it burst open" (consecutive) from "He leant with all his weight... so that it would burst open" which means "in order to" burst it open, a deliberate purpose ; see Final §350-3.

Constative, see Aorist.

Co-ordinate clauses are statements placed side by side with- out one being subordinated to (made to depend on) the

other ; in practice, clauses joined by *and, but, or, neither...nor,*
Greek καί, ἀλλά, ἤ, οὔτε...οὔτε, and other like conjunctions
which do not express temporal or logical connection. Where
the sense called for it, classical Greek preferred to highlight
the main proposition, subordinating other parts of the sentence by the use of participles and subordinate clauses (see
Subordinate), but the NT, while in large measure following
Greek tradition in this respect, yields to a colloquial tendency to co-ordination common to all languages ; so frequent are clauses joined by "and", that it seems the tendency
has in places been reinforced by Semitic influence, e.g. καὶ
ἦν...ὥρα ἕκτη καὶ σκότος ἐγένετο "And it was...the sixth hour
and darkness fell" Lk 23:44 §450-61.

Dative : the case of the indirect object ; its basic meaning
"to" or "for". Certain verbs which take a direct object in
English are followed in Greek by a dat., among the com-
moner are : verbs of command, παραγγέλλει τῷ ὄχλῳ "he com-
manded the crowd" Mk 8:6 (but not κελεύω τινά), also
"obey" = ὑπακούω, πειθάρχω; ἀκολουθέω "follow", and διακονέω and δουλεύω "serve". In the *Analysis* these verbs are
indicated by τινί. — **Of place** "where" (at rest ; for where
"whither" and "whence" see nn. on acc. and gen.). — **Of time**
"when", in Hellenistic Greek commonly with preposition.
Like the accusative the dative may convey the idea of "**in
respect of**", e.g. στερεοὶ τῇ πίστει "firm in your faith" I Pt
5:9 ; οἱ καθαροὶ τῇ καρδίᾳ "the pure in heart" Mt 5:8 §51-65.

Deliberative = involving deliberation ; especially of the subjunctive used in Greek to express this consideration of alternatives, e.g. τί ποιήσωμεν ; "what are we to do ?" Ac 4:16 ;
πῶς φύγητε ; "how are you to escape ?" Mt 23:33 ; πῶς πιστεύσωσιν; "how are they to believe ?" Rom 10:14 ; and indirect,
μὴ μεριμνᾶτε...τί φάγητε...τί ἐνδύσησθε "do not be anxious
what you are to eat...what you are to wear" Lk 12:22 §348.

Deponent : in the *Analysis* reserved for the passive aorist
(without passive force) of certain middle verbs, e.g. βούλομαι
aor. ἐβουλήθην; φοβέομαι aor. ἐφοβήθην; ἀποκρίνομαι, in con-
tradistinction to classical Greek, usually has aor. ἀπεκρίθην
§229-31.

Direct. The direct object is that which is directly affected by the action of the verb ; in cases of doubt it may be identified by turning the verb into the passive and asking "what ?" or "who ?" e.g. "He granted me an interview" ; by asking "What was granted ?" the direct object at once becomes evident ; and supposing one asks the "wrong" question first, "Who was granted ?" one is immediately aware that this is not a question that would be asked, but rather, "Who was granted the interview ?" or "Who was it granted to ?" thereby again revealing the true direct object. Note that some verbs take two direct objects : "they asked him a question" ; ἐδίδασκεν αὐτούς...πολλά "he taught them many things" Mk 4:2. Verbs which take a dir. object (accusative) in English are sometimes followed in Greek by genitive or dative and vice versa ; thus verbs in the *Analysis* will sometimes be followed by τινά or τι (denoting the dir. object) and τινί or τινός (denoting the indirect object) e.g. ἀφίημί τινί τι "forgive someone something".

— **Direct speech** means that in reporting the words of another the identical words spoken are repeated, λέγει...ἀφίενταί σου αἱ ἁμαρτίαι "he said [lit. says], 'Your sins are forgiven'"

— In the same way **direct questions** are questions in the words in which they were expressed. Contrast, "He asked her if she really wanted to go" with "He said to her : 'Do you really want to go ?'" The former is reported speech containing an indirect question, the latter a direct question finishing with a question mark. Note that the words need not be uttered : "I am wondering whether they will find the way" is an indirect form of the real question in my mind, "Will they find the way ?" So, in grammar, the term "direct speech" may equally refer to unspoken thoughts. Beside the interrogative τίς; (with acute accent) Greek has the direct interrogatives ποῖος; and ποταπός; "of what sort ?", πόσος; "how much/many ?", ποῦ; "where ?" (in NT also for "whither ?"), πόθεν; "whence ?" All these are also found as indirect interrogatives.

Effective, see Aorist.

Elative. A superlative is described as elative when it expresses a very high degree of some quality without the notion of comparison. "X. would be competent, Y. would be more competent, and Z. most competent of all", illustrates the true (or relative) superlative, but "Z., though no scholar, is a *most competent* administrator" is an elative superlative. It can also be expressed, of course, in other words, e.g. *very*, *extremely*, etc. as the relative superlative cannot.

Enclitic : a word that "leans on" the preceding word so as to shed its accent. Note however that successive syllables may not carry acute accents ; in such a case the accent of the enclitic disappears, e.g. ῥῆμά τι but λόγος τις.

Epexegetic = explanatory. An epexegetic genitive interprets or identifies the noun it follows, as if one were to insert between the two words, "which is", "viz.", "namely", or a simple comma, e.g. "a grain of mustard seed" Mk 4:31 ; τὸν στέφανον τ ῆ ς ζ ω ῆ ς "the crown, *namely life*" Apoc 2:10 ; τὸ σημεῖον Ἰ ω ν ᾶ "the sign *which is Jonah*", i.e. constituted by Jonah, Lk 11:29 ; θεμέλιον...μ ε τ α ν ο ί α ς... κ α ὶ π ί σ τ ε ω ς "a foundation, *repentance...and faith*" Heb 6:1. An infinitive is described as epexeg. when it explains a preceding demonstrative pronoun (= "this" or "that") §45, 410.

Final : with an end in view, denoting purpose ; especially of certain infinitives, and of subjunctives with similar force, "He travelled by night (*in order*) *to escape* notice", "He travelled slowly (*so*) *that* the others *might arrive* before him". (Contrast the absence of purpose in "He travelled by night so that he saw very little of the country" and, "He travelled so slowly that the others arrived before him", see Consecutive.) Final are μὴ καταβάτω ἆ ρ α ι τὰ ἐκ τῆς οἰκίας "Let him not come down *to take* what is in (lit. out of) his house" Mt 24:17 ; τί ποιήσω ἵ ν α ζωὴν αἰώνιον κ λ η ρ ο ν ο μ ή σ ω "what must I do (*in order*) *that I may inherit* eternal life ?" Mk 10:17.

Frequentative, see Imperfect.

Generic = typifying a whole class. Cf the different concepts in the following sentences : *a strong man* has nothing to fear (generic) ; *a strong man* has been put in charge (specific). As a rule in Greek a noun used in a generic sense is preceded by the article, e.g. οὐκ ἐπ' ἄρτῳ μόνῳ ζήσεται ὁ ἄ ν θ ρ ω π ο ς "man (= mankind) shall not live by bread

alone" Mt 4:4 ; ἡ ἀγάπη...συγχαίρει...τῇ ἀληθείᾳ love.,.rejoi-
ces in the truth I Cor 13:6. οἱ νεκροί when thinking
of the persons composing the dead Mt 8:22, I Cor 15:35
rather than the state of death as opposed to life : ἡ ἀνά-
στασις τῶν νεκρῶν Mt 22:31 but more often ἀνάστασις
νεκρῶν, ἐκ νεκρῶν — but here other factors intervene §180,
182f.

Genitive. (For gen. abs. see Absolute ; for epexeg. gen. see
Epexegetic.) Besides being the **possessive** case, of..., the
gen. may be used "**partitively**" to signify that of which
something forms a part, e.g. αὐτῶν τις or in NT τις ἐξ αὐτῶν or even εἷς ἐξ αὐτῶν "one of them", or it may express
the time "within which" (cf nn. on acc. and dat.) e.g. νυκτός
"at night" Jn 3:2, I Thess 5:7 ; χειμῶνος "in the winter"
Mt 24:20 — The gen. has another group of meanings arising
from a second basic signification : that of separation, "from...";
related to this is the gen. of **comparison** (gen. comp.), not
only = than, e.g. πολυτιμότερον χρυσίου "more precious
than gold" I Pt 1:7 ; μείζων Ἰωάννου " greater than John"
Mt 11:11, but also following verbs implying pre-eminence,
e.g. ὑμεῖς διαφέρετε τῶν πετεινῶν "you excel the
birds", "you are of more value than the birds" Lk 12:24 ; τὴν
ὑπερβαλλοῦσαν τῆς γνώσεως ἀγάπην "the love which
surpasses knowledge" Eph 3:19 ; βασιλεύει τῆς Ἰουδαίας
"he reigns over Judea" Mt 2:22 ; περισσεύονται ἄρτων
"they have an abundance of bread" Lk 15:17. — English
speaks of "full of..." but "fill with..." ; in Greek both are expressed by a gen., e.g. χορτάσαι ἄρτων "satisfy with bread"
Mk 8:4 ; ἐπληροῦντο χαρᾶς "they were filled with joy" Ac
13:52. — **Price** is expressed by the gen., ἐπράθη τριακοσίων
δηναρίων "it was sold for 300 denarii" cf Jn 12:5 ; τοσού-
του... ἀπέδοσθε; "did you sell (it) for so much?" Ac 5:8. —
Certain verbs which take direct objects in Eng. are followed
in Gk by the gen., e.g. ἅπτομαι "touch", δέομαι "beseech",
μιμνήσκομαι "remember", μετέχω "share" ; in the Analysis
these verbs will be indicated by τινός. — In exegesis it is important to realize the ambiguity sometimes latent in a gen.
In such phrases as "the love of God", "the hope of youth",
"the interest of children". Is the word in the gen. the "agent"
or the object ? Do the expressions mean "God's love for
man, God loving man", "youth hopes, is hopeful", "children's interest in..." or "the love man has for God", "one

is hoping for youth", "one's interest in children"? In the former case the gen. is described as **subjective,** in the latter, **objective** §36f. See also Epexegetic.

Hendiadys (one by means of two). Just as καί may co-ordinate two clauses one of which would normally be subordinated to the other, so καί may co-ordinate two individual words so as to express a complex idea involving the subordination of one word to the other. This is the figure called hendiadys ; e.g. Lk 2:47 τῇ συνέσει καὶ ταῖς ἀποκρίσεσιν αὐτοῦ "his understanding and his answers" = "the intelligence shown by his answers" ; Ac 23:6 περὶ ἐλπίδος καὶ ἀναστάσεως "about hope and the resurrection" = "about hope of the resurrection" §460.

Hortative or exhortative subjunctive takes the place of an imperative in the 1st person though, as its mood would suggest, it is less abrupt : διέλθωμεν "let us go over" Lk 2:15 ; ἄγωμεν "let us be going" Mk 14:42 ; περιπατήσωμεν "let us walk" Rom 13:13. Put in question form, the hort. becomes a deliberative subjunctive.

Imperative : the mood used to express a command, and in the present tense, a prohibition also, e.g. λέγω...π ο ρ ε ύ θ η τ ι, καὶ πορεύεται...ἔ ρ χ ο υ, καὶ ἔρχεται...π ο ί η σ ο ν τοῦτο, καὶ ποιεῖ "I say...'*Go*, and he goes...'*Come*', and he comes...'*Do* this', and he does it" Mt 8:9. Though there is no 1st pers. imperative (the hortative subjunctive taking its place) the impv applies to the 3rd person equally with the 2nd : ἐ ρ χ έ σ θ ω ...καὶ π ι ν έ τ ω "*let him come* and (*let him*) *drink*" Jn 7:37 ; μὴ γ ν ώ τ ω ἡ ἀριστερά σου "*Do not let* your left hand *know*" Mt 6:3. On the difference between present and aorist impv see Aorist §242-8.

Imperfect indicative is a past tense which represents an action as continued, repeated, or habitual. (Repeated action may be understood in two ways : as **frequentative,** of something which happened time and again, or as **iterative,** of something which the same person repeatedly performed.) The name "imperfect" is particularly evident in what is called the **conative** impf where the notion of trying ineffectively or "being on the point of" is present, e.g. ἐ κ ω λ ύ ο μ ε ν αὐτόν "*we tried to stop* him (Lk 9:49) to which Jesus replies μὴ κωλύετε "stop hindering him", showing that they had not been successful ; ἐ δ ί δ ο υ ν αὐτῷ … "*they offered* (tried to give) him…" Mk 15:23 ; ἐκάλουν αὐτό … Ζαχαρίαν "*they were going to call* him Z." Lk 1:59 ; ἐ β ο υ λ ό μ η ν … τοῦ ἀνθρώπου ἀκούειν not "I wished, or wish", but "*I should like* to listen to the man" Ac 25:22 ; ἤ θ ε λ ο ν … παρεῖναι "*I could wish* to be present" Gal 4:20. In other moods than the indicative the same connotations of continuity etc. are expressed by the present : ὁ σπείρων "he who sows, the sower" ; cf ὁ σπείρας (aor.) "the one who sowed" (on a particular occasion) Mt 13:37,39 ; οἱ σῳζόμενοι "those (in the course of) being saved" Ac 2:47 ; οἱ ἀπολλύμενοι "those on the road to perdition" I Cor 1:18 ; in Lk 5:6f. we find δ ι ε ρ ρ ή σ σ ε τ ο (impf) τὰ δίκτυα αὐτῶν "their nets *were (on the point of) breaking*" followed (v. 7) by the phrase ὥστε βυθίζεσθαι (pres. inf.) "so that *they began to sink*".

Impersonal. An impersonal verb has no expressed subject in Greek and as subject in English only an impersonal "it" which refers to no prior word and is irreplaceable. Compare. "it is raining" and "it is difficult". "What is difficult ?" may be answered in innumerable ways according to the context, but it is useless to ask "What is raining ?" because "to rain" (except in a metaphorical sense) is an impers. verb. So also in Greek : βρέχει "it is raining", δεῖ, ἔξεστι "it is right /permissible", μέλει "it is a care to", i.e. "one is concerned, one minds". — In addition to strictly impersonal verbs, other verbs are said to be used impersonally when the subject is a vague 3rd pers. pl. "they", referring to no persons in particular ; as "they" say (= it is said), so ταῦτα π ο ι ο ῦ σ ι ν "*they do* these things" Lk 23:31 (= these things are done) ; φ έ ρ ο υ σ ι ν αὐτῷ "*they bring* to him" Mk 7:32, all without antecedent.

Inceptive, see Aorist.

Indefinite, i.e. referring to no specific person or thing. Definite, "if he comes, tell him…" but indefinite, "*whoever* comes / if *anyone* comes, tell him…". The Greek indef. pronoun is τις (neut. τι), enclitic, meaning "anyone, something, a certain one", also as indef. adj. "any…at all, some, a (certain)".

Indirect object. The verb governs the indirect object but is not conceived as acting directly upon it as in the case of the direct object. When turned into the passive, for instance, it does not become the subject but remains unchanged. "They take the fruit to the market" becomes "The fruit is taken to the market by them." (It must be added that this rule is not inflexible : there exists an "indirect passive", e.g. in Eng., "has he been told ?" for "has it been told to him ?"; in Gk διακονέω τινί "serve (to) someone", but οὐκ ἦλθεν διακονηθῆναι "[the Son of Man] came not to be served" Mt 20:28 ; πιστεύομαί τινί τι "entrust something to one" but πεπίστευμαι τὸ εὐαγγέλιον "I have been entrusted with the Gospel" Gal 2:7 for "the G. has been entrusted to me".) Apart from such exceptional instances the indir. object is not difficult to identify in Greek as it is often preceded by a preposition and is always in the dative or genitive case. — **Indirect questions** are questions no longer in their original form (as if I should ask myself, "What was she like ?") but embodied in a statement, "I have forgotten what she was like", exactly like reported speech which is sometimes called "indirect". See Direct. In NT τίς is used as the indir. as well as the direct interrogative pronoun. For the indir. interrogative adj. ὁποῖος "of what sort" the direct ποῖος is often substituted ; for "where" the direct ποῦ may be found instead of ὅπου.

Ingressive, see Aorist.

Instrumental, i.e. of the means or instrument used by the agent. This "with" (in English) may be expressed by the dat. case in Gk : ἀνεῖλεν...Ἰάκωβον μαχαίρῃ "he killed James...*with the sword*" Ac 12:2, δικαιοῦσθαι πίστει to be justified *by faith* Rom 3:28, and in HGk by ἐν with the dative, βαπτίζω ἐν ὕδατι "I baptize *with water*" Mt 3:11.

Intransitive refers to verbs not taking a direct object, e.g. sleep, go, sit, die. It should be noted that very many verbs may be used transitively or intransitively, e.g. eat, hear, move. Other verbs which are transitive in English are intr. in Greek ; some common examples are given under Dative and Genitive. Not infrequently the passive voice of a transitive verb will carry out the functions of a corresponding intransitive, either instead of or in addition to its normal passive signification, e.g. φαίνω "show", φαίνομαι "appear" ; στρέφω "turn" (sth), στρέφομαι "turn" ; ἐγείρω "awaken /raise", ἐγείρομαι "wake up /rise". Intransitive also are particular tenses of ἵστημι and its compounds, viz. aor² (strong) and perfect ; in addition the perfect of ἵστημι has present meaning. Hence "I set up" (= cause to stand) is ἵστημι and "I stand" is ἔστηκα. ἀνίστημι makes use of the middle voice to express an intransitive meaning : ἀναστήσει "he will raise" but "he will rise" ἀναστήσεται.

Iterative, see Imperfect.

Koine. Greek as commonly written and spoken at the time the New Testament was composed.

Middle voice. The force of the middle voice is not always easy or even possible to ascertain with certainty, but it may be said to differ from the passive in that the subject of the verb is the agent and it can take a direct object ; it differs from the active in that the term of the action rests with the agent himself, either directly (reflexive) : ἐνιψάμην "I washed myself" Jn 9:15 ; βαπτίσαι "have yourself baptized, get baptized" Ac 22:16 ; or indirectly (to or for oneself) : προσκαλοῦμαι "call to oneself" ; ἐὰν μὴ νίψωνται τὰς χεῖρας "unless *they wash their* hands" Mk 7:3 ; οὗτοι...οὐκ ἐκομίσαντο τὴν ἐπαγγελίαν "these did not *receive* (lit. take to themselves) the promise" Heb 11:39 ; ὃν ... φυλάσσου "*against* whom *be on your guard, beware* of him" II Tim 4:15 ; τὸ χωρίον ἀπέδοσθε "*you sold* (lit. gave away, for yourself) the field" Ac 5:8. With the above cf the active ἐγὼ ἔνιψα ὑμῶν τοὺς πόδας "I have washed your feet" Jn 13:14 ; βαπτίζοντες αὐτούς "baptizing them" Mt 28:19 ; κομίσασα ἀλάβαστρον μύρου "bringing an alabaster flask of ointment" Lk 7:37 ; τῷ φυλάσσοντι αὐτὸν στρατιώτῃ "with the soldier that guarded him" Ac 28:16 ; ἀποδίδωμι τετραπλοῦν "I give back fourfold" Lk 19:8 §227-35.

The **optative** mood expresses a wish : "I only hope...", "I would that..." or, negative, "God forbid that..." e.g. μὴ γένοιτο "*May it* not *be!* Far be it !" §355. With following ἄν it may also indicate a theoretical possibility, the **potential optative,** εὐξαίμην ἄν not "I pray that" but "*I could pray* that..., *Would to God!*" Ac 26:29 ; at other

times ἄν is to be understood, διελογίζετο ποταπὸς εἴη "considered of what kind *it might be*" Lk 1:29; μήποτε αὐτὸς εἴη
ὁ Χριστός "whether *he might be* the Christ, whether *perhaps
he were* the Christ" Lk 3:15; "he made...every nation of
men...to seek God εἰ ἄρα γε...αὐτόν... εὕροιεν if *possibly
they might find* him, i.e. in the hope of finding him" Ac 17:27 ;
εἰ καὶ πάσχοιτε "even if *you should suffer*" I Pt 3:14 §356.
The optative (always without ἄν) **in reported speech** takes
the place of the subjunctive when the report is introduced
by a past tense, to preserve the sequence of tenses §346.
Since the examples cited above from Lk are indirect questions and lack ἄν, it is arguable whether they are potential
or to be classed in this third category.

Perfect. That the perfect tense in Greek is often perforce
translated by the English perfect (past indefinite) must not
be allowed to mislead one into supposing that they are
coterminous. "I have been in Greece but it was many
years ago" has little in common with the Greek perfect
whose peculiar character is that, while denoting an action
already accomplished, it also signifies that its results are
still present at the time of speaking. It is therefore as
much a present as a past tense. e.g. ἔγνω...ὅτι ἴαται "she
knew that *she was (finally) healed*" Mk 5:29; Μωϋσῆς εἰς ὃν
ὑμεῖς ἠλπίκατε "M. on whom *you have set (and continue
to set)* your hope" Jn 5:45. So in the sentence, "He has been
very ill but is completely cured" the Greek perfect could be
used to translate the English present but would not be at
all appropriate to the former verb, the Eng. pf. The perfect stem carries a reduplication (or its equivalent) as a
prefix, but this is not related to the augment of past time
§285-9.

Periphrasis (περί+φράζω declare) = a roundabout expression ; especially of a periphrastic tense composed of an auxi-
liary verb with a participle in place of a simple tense, e.g.,
instead of imperfect (ἐδίδασκε) ἦν διδάσκων "*he was teaching*" exactly as in English.

Pleonasm (πλέων more). The use of more words than are
necessary to convey an idea. Unlike tautology it is not
necessarily a fault of style but may be deliberately employed
for effect.

Pluperfect throws the perfect tense back into the past; therefore the result is conceived of as enduring, not to the time of speaking but to the *time about which* one is speaking; in other words, a plpf is a perfect in retrospect. The plpf is marked by the same reduplication at the beginning of the stem, itself prefixed by the augment of past time. However, the use or neglect of the augment is somewhat erratic in the plpf, note the example below. The Greek plpf is not used to mark relative past time (which in Gk has to be inferred). The Eng. plpf, on the other hand, must do duty not only for the Gk plpf but also for an aorist when it refers to time which is past in relation to the main verb, e.g. Mary Magdalene παρ' ἧς ἐκβεβλήκει ἑπτὰ δαιμόνια...πορευθεῖσα ἀπήγγειλεν τοῖς μετ' αὐτοῦ γενομένοις (aor.) Mk 16:9f. M. M. "from whom *he had cast out* (once for all) seven demons...went and told those who 'had been' (relative past time) with him". The former verb only is plpf in Greek §290.

The **positive** is the basic simple form of adjectives: good, bad, big, little, and of adverbs: well, badly, slowly, quickly, without implying comparison.

A **predicate** is whatever is asserted (or denied) of the subject: "what he is, what he does, or what he suffers". In grammar the verb which effects the link, known as the copula, is regarded as forming part of the predicate: All is not gold that glitters: All that glitters (subject) is not gold (pred.). Still waters (subject) run deep (pred.). Forewarned, forearmed, i.e. [To be] forewarned (subject) [is to be] forearmed (pred.). Many (subject) were wounded in the disaster (pred.) but none (subject) [were] killed (pred.). In English the order of words is often a guide to distinguishing subject and predicate but in Greek we have ἔρημός ἐστιν ὁ τόπος "the place *is lonely*" Mt 14:15 and ἐγώ εἰμι πρεσβύτης "I *am an old man*" Lk 1:18, again εἶχον...Ἰωάννην ὑπηρέτην "they had J. *as assistant*" Ac 13:5. A clue is sts afforded by the presence of the article which can often be trusted to identify the subject in doubtful cases. In the predicate, its presence or absence varies according to the sense: because the pred. is generally a qualitative concept the article is more commonly lacking, but where the concept is individual it has the article, thus: Peter is man but Peter is the rock; e.g. προφήτης εἶ σύ "you *are a pro-*

phet" Jn 4:19 but ὑμεῖς ἐστε τὸ ἄλας τῆς γῆς "you *are the salt of the earth*" Mt 5:13 §172ff.

Privative : term used of the ἀ- which denies the presence of the quality or substance denoted by the word following. ἀ priv. has been taken over into the English language in such words as a-moral, a-septic, a-theist. When prefixed to words beginning with a vowel (both in Gk and in Eng.) it becomes ἀν-, an-aemic, an-archist, an-onymous.

Prolepsis = anticipation ; in the *Analysis* applied to the **proleptic** use of a **pronoun** in anticipation of the noun to which it refers, e.g. ἄγουσιν αὐτὸν πρὸς τοὺς Φαρισαίους τόν ποτε τυφλόν "they brought (lit. bring) *him* to the Pharisees the man who had once been blind" Jn 9:13 ; and to the **proleptic** use of a **tense** such that it regards as having actually occurred what is still in the future, e.g. (proleptic perfect) "Anyone who is doubtful, ἐὰν φάγῃ (sc. food of uncertain provenance) κατακέκριται (lit. stands condemned) because he is not in good faith" Rom 14:23 meaning, "if he eats it, *will stand condemned*". More common is the proleptic aorist : "If a man comes into your assembly together with a poor man and you treat them differently οὐ διεκρίθητε...καὶ ἐγένεσθε κριταὶ διαλογισμῶν πονηρῶν; Jas 2:4, lit. "have you not ?" but meaning *"will you not have made distinctions...and (will you not have) become judges with evil reasonings* (= false standards) ? §257f.

Protasis of a conditional sentence is that part which states the condition. It is introduced by "if" (εἰ or ἐάν in Greek). See Apodosis.

Subordination of a clause serves to bring into prominence the principal statement and define the relationship to it of the other parts of the sentence. For this purpose Greek makes use of conjunctions such as ὡς or ὅτε "when" (temporal), ἵνα "in order that" (final), ὥστε "so that" = in such a way that (consecutive), ὅτι "because" (causal), καίτοι, καίπερ "although" (concessive) and the like, and of participles which, when not purely adjectival or used as nouns (e.g. οἱ ἑστηκότες "the bystanders" Mk 11:5, οἱ πιστεύοντες "the faithful" Rom 3:22), contain the force of one of these subordinating conjunctions. The temporal use is so common in comparison with others that it is easy to overlook the alternative possibilities, one of which might dispel an apparent difficulty. While English is in general closer to Greek idiom than to Hebrew, especially in the use of subordinate clauses and, to a lesser degree, of the present participle, the aorist participle (for which, of course, English has no direct equivalent) commonly defies literal translation. Where a corresponding subord. clause does not readily offer itself, one need not be afraid of using a co-ordinate clause — indeed, in the majority of cases this offers the most natural Eng. translation, e.g. πορευθέντες ἐξετάσατε not a stilted "having gone your way, find out" but *"go and find out"* Mt 2:8 ; or ἀποστείλας ἀνεῖλεν *"he sent and killed"* Mt 2:16. The subord. clause may precede the main statement, *"While he clung to Peter and John* all the people ran together" Ac 3:11 or follow it, "the Sadducees came upon them, annoyed *because they were teaching the people"* Ac 4:1f.

A **superlative** adjective or adverb raises a quality to its highest degree either absolutely (see Elative) or in comparison with others : "-est", "most...". See Comparative. §146-152.

Transitive describes a verb whose action "passes over" to the object so that it is directly affected. It may be readily turned into the passive, in which case the direct object which has undergone or "suffered" the action will appear as the subject. If this process presents difficulties a second look should be taken to confirm whether the verb is really transitive or not, e.g. "go your way" (= go on your way) ; "look sharp" (also adverbial) ; even "he looks his age" is not really transitive but = he looks like his age or as if he were... None of these is susceptible of a passive form. Every object of a transitive verb is in the accusative, but for beginners in the field of grammar it is perhaps worth pointing out that it is not safe to assume that every accusative following a verb is a direct object, e.g. in ἐμείναμεν ἡμέραν μίαν "we stayed one day" Ac 21:7 we have not to do with a direct object but with an accusative of duration = for one day (see Accusative). Here again this would be revealed if one were to attempt a passive version. Note that many transitive verbs may be used absolutely and therefore intransitively, see Intransitive.

LIST OF WORDS
OCCURRING OVER 60 TIMES IN THE NEW TESTAMENT

ἀγαθός	good
ἀγαπάω	love
ἀγάπη	love
ἄγγελος	messenger, angel
ἅγιος	holy
ἀδελφός	brother
αἷμα⁷	blood
αἴρω	take up, carry, take away
αἰτέω	ask (for)
αἰών⁶ -ῶνος ὁ	period, age
αἰώνιος -ον	eternal
ἀκολουθέω	follow
ἀκούω	hear
ἀλήθεια	truth
ἀλλά	but, (later) except
ἀλλήλων	each other
ἄλλος	other, another
ἁμαρτία	sin
ἀμήν	Hebr. amen, truly, indeed
ἄν	particle which serves to render a statement contingent
ἀναβαίνω	go or come up
ἀνήρ⁶	
ἀνδρός ὁ	man, husband
ἄνθρωπος	man, human being
ἀνίστημι	raise or set up ; (intr. in aor², pf, and mid.) rise
ἀνοίγω	open
ἀπέρχομαι	go away, depart
ἀπό	from
ἀποθνήσκω	die
ἀποκρίνομαι	answer
ἀποκτείνω	kill
ἀπόλλυμι	destroy ; lose ; (mid.) perish
ἀποστέλλω	commission, send
ἀπόστολος	messenger, apostle

ἄρτος	bread, loaf
ἀρχιερεύς⁵	high priest ; pl. chief priests
ἄρχω	rule (w. gen.) ; mid. begin
αὐτός, αὐτή, αὐτό	in nom. or with other personal prns -self ; in gen. he, she, it. ·
βάλλω	throw, put
βαπτίζω	dip, baptize
βασιλεία	kingdom
βασιλεύς⁵	king
βλέπω	see, look
γάρ	for (conj.)
γεννάω	beget, pass. be born
γῆ	earth
γίνομαι	become ; come about ; often, = be
γινώσκω	come to know, know
γραμματεύς⁵	scribe
γράφω	write
γυνή γυναικός ἡ	woman, wife
δαιμόνιον	demon
δέ	but, and
δεῖ w. acc. + inf.	(impers.) it is necessary, one must, δεῖ με I must
διά	(w. acc.) on account of, διὰ τί ; why ?
	(w. gen.) through
διδάσκω	teach
δίδωμι	give
δίκαιος	just, righteous, upright
δικαιοσύνη	justice, righteousness
δόξα	glory
δοῦλος	slave, servant
δύναμαι	be able
δύναμις⁴	power
δύο (dat. pl. δυσί(ν))	two
δώδεκα	twelve
ἐάν (= εἰ ἄν)	if
ἑαυτοῦ	himself, his own
ἐγείρω	rouse, raise up ; impv & sts pass. intr., rise
ἐγώ	I

ἔθνος[8]	race, people, nation ; pl. gentiles
εἰ	if
εἶδον	(aor² ὁράω) saw
εἰμί	be
εἶπον	(aor² λέγω) said
εἰρήνη	peace
εἰς	into, to
εἷς (gen. ἑνός)	
μία ἕν	one
εἰσέρχομαι	come or go in, enter
ἐκ, ἐξ	out of, from
ἕκαστος	each
ἐκβάλλω	throw or drive out
ἐκεῖ	there
ἐκεῖνος	that
ἐκκλησία	assembly, community, Church
ἐμός	mine, my
ἐν	in ; among (persons)
ἐντολή	commandment
ἐνώπιον	in the presence of
ἐξέρχομαι	come or go out, leave
ἐξουσία	authority, right
ἐπί	on
ἑπτά	seven
ἔργον	work
ἔρχομαι	come, go
ἐσθίω	eat
ἕτερος	other (of two) ; HGk another, different
ἔτι	(of time) still ; (of degree) even
εὐαγγέλιον	good news, gospel
εὐθύς, εὐθέως	immediately, straight away
εὑρίσκω	find
ἔχω	have
ἕως	(of time) until ; (of place) as far as
ζάω	live
ζητέω	seek
ζωή	life
ἤ	or, than, ἤ...ἤ either...or
ἦλθον	(aor² ἔρχομαι) came, so ἀπ- εἰσ- ἐξ- προσ-έρχομαι)
ἡμεῖς	we

ἡμέρα	day
θάλασσα	sea
θάνατος	death
θέλημα[7]	will
θέλω	will, wish, want
θεός	God
ἴδιος	one's own
ἰδού	lo and behold ! look ! here !
ἱερόν	temple
ἵνα	in order that
ἵστημι	make to stand, set up ; (intr. in aor², pf & mid.) stand
κάθημαι	be sitting
καθώς	just as
καί	and, also
καιρός	season, opportunity, (appointed) time
καλέω	call, invite
καλός	beautiful, noble, good
καρδία	heart
καρπός	fruit (lit. & met.)
κατά	(w. acc.) according to ; (w. gen.) down, against
καταβαίνω	go or come down
κεφαλή	head
κόσμος	world
κρίνω	judge
κύριος	a lord, master, Lord
λαλέω	speak
λαμβάνω	take, receive
λαός	a people
λέγω	say
λόγος	word, (the) Word
μαθητής[3]	disciple
μᾶλλον	more, rather
μαρτυρέω	testify, give evidence, be a witness
μέγας -άλη -α	great
μέλλω	w. inf. be about to, be destined to, intend to
μένω	remain, stay
μετά	(w. acc.) after ; (w. gen.) with
μή	not

μηδείς[6] (decl. as εἷς)	no one, nothing ; (after neg.) anyone, anything
μήτηρ -τρός ἡ	mother
μόνος	sole, only, alone ; (neut. as adv.) only
νεκρός	dead
νόμος	law, the Law
νῦν	now
νύξ[6] νυκτός ἡ	night
ὁ, ἡ, τό	the
ὁδός	way, road, journey
οἶδα	(pf w. force of pres.) know
οἶκος = οἰκία	house
ὅλος	whole, all
ὄνομα[7]	name
ὅπου	where
ὁράω	see
ὄρος[8]	mountain
ὅς, ἥ, ὅ	who, which
ὅσος	how great or much ; as much as ; pl. as many as, all who ; neut. pl. all that, everything
ὅστις	(indef.) whoever ; (def.) such as, who by his very nature, often just " who "
ὅταν	when(ever)
ὅτε	when
ὅτι	because ; that
οὐ	not
οὐδέ	not even ; (after a neg.) nor...either
οὐδείς[6] (decl. as εἷς)	no one, nothing ; (after a neg.) anyone, anything
οὖν	therefore, then, accordingly
οὐρανός	heaven
οὔτε...οὔτ	neither...nor
οὗτος, αὕτη, τοῦτο	this
οὕτως (οὕτω)	like this, thus, so
ὀφθαλμός	eye
ὄχλος	crowd
πάλιν	again
πάντες (pl. of πᾶς)	all ; τὰ πάντα all things

παρά	(w. acc.) along ; (w. gen.) from (persons) ; (w. dat.) with, beside
παραδίδωμι	hand over, hand down
παρακαλέω	appeal to, exhort ; encourage
πᾶς (gen. παντός) πᾶσα πᾶν	every, the whole, all
πατήρ -τρός ὁ	father
πέμπω	send
περί	(w. acc.) around ; (w. gen.) concerning
περιπατέω	walk
πίνω	drink
πίπτω	fall
πιστεύω (w. dat.)	believe
πίστις[4]	faith
πληρόω	fill, fulfil
πλοῖον	boat
πνεῦμα[7]	spirit
ποιέω	do, make
πόλις[4]	city
πολλοί (pl. of πολύς)	many
πολύς πολλή πολύ	much
πονηρός	bad, evil
πορεύομαι	travel, go
πούς[6] ποδός ὁ	foot
πρεσβύτερος (comp. of πρέσβυς)	elder
πρός	(w. acc.) to, towards
προσέρχομαι	approach, come up
προσεύχομαι	pray
πρόσωπον	face
προφήτης[3]	prophet
πρῶτος	first ; neut. as adv.
πῦρ πυρός τό	fire
πῶς ;	how ?
σάρξ[6] σαρκός ἡ	flesh
σημεῖον	sign
στόμα[7]	mouth

σύ	you (sg)
σύν	with
συναγωγή	synagogue
σῴζω	save, rescue
σῶμα⁷	body
τε	and (foll. the word it joins)
τέκνον	child
τηρέω	keep
τίθημι	put, lay
τίς; τί;	who ? what ?
τις τι (encl.)	someone, something
τόπος	place
τότε	then
τρεῖς (neut.	
τρία)	three
ὕδωρ ὕδατος τό	water
υἱός	son
ὑμεῖς	you (pl.)
ὑπάγω	(cf "with-draw") depart, go away
ὑπέρ	(w. acc.) above, beyond ; (w. gen.) for, on behalf of
ὑπό	(w. acc.) under ; (w. gen.) by (agent after pass. vb)
Φαρισαῖος	Pharisee
φοβέομαι	be afraid, fear
φωνή	voice
φῶς φωτός τό	light
χαίρω	rejoice, be glad
χάρις⁶ -ιτος ἡ	
(acc. χάριν)	grace
χείρ⁶ -ρός ἡ	hand
Χριστός	anointed, Christ
ψυχή	soul, life, self
ὧδε	here
ὥρα	hour
ὡς	(of time & manner) as, when
ὥστε	so that ; and so ; w. inf. so as to.

References preceded by paragraph sign § are to the author's *Biblical Greek*, English ed. Rome 1963.

Words in the select vocabulary will not appear in the *Analysis* unless the form requires explanation.

An explanation of the same word (or verb in the same tense) is not repeated in the two following verses, nor will it be given again after three occurrences in the same chapter.

To save unnecessary repetition (i) verbs in the present indicative are quoted only in the first person singular regardless of their person and number in the text ; (ii) in this vol. II the present inf. act. and pres. ptc (nom.) of uncontracted verbs in the vocabulary will not normally receive comment.

Unless otherwise specified, a verb is assumed to be in the active voice, the indicative mood, and the present tense. The weak (1st) aorist is to be presumed except where the strong (2nd) aorist is indicated thus : aor².

Verbs will sometimes be followed by τινά (of a person) or τι (of a thing) denoting the direct object, and/or τινός or τινί, a traditional and succinct method of showing the case(s) governed by the verb in question.

It will be evident that the position of the hyphen in abbreviating verbs is governed by purely practical considerations and carries no implications as to the stem.

ROMANS

δοῦλος wt art. a *slave/servant*. κλητός (< καλέω) *called*. **1**
ἀφ-ωρισμένος pf ptc pass. -ορίζω *separate* ; *set apart,
appoint*. εἰς purposive, *to* (sc. *proclaim*) *the gospel* ; εὐαγγέλιον wt art. owing prob. to foll. gen. ; further instances
in foll. vv. explainable as prep. phrases or as gens. governed
by anarthrous nouns §183. ‖ προ-επ-ηγγείλατο aor. mid. **2**
-αγγέλλω *promise beforehand/earlier*, constative aor. (looking back over the centuries the many occasions are telescoped) §253. γραφή a *writing*, pl. and sg, *scripture(s)*. ‖
γενομένου aor[2] ptc γίνομαι *come to be, be born*. σπέρμα[7] **3**
seed, hence *posterity, family*. Δαυίδ indecl. here gen. κατὰ
σάρκα *physically* ; here, *with regard to his human nature*. ‖
ὁρισθέντος aor. ptc pass. -ίζω *delimit* as a boundary (ὅρος), **4**
mark out. ἐν of concomitant circumstances (sociative),
with power, i.e. his power as Son ; ass. w. υἱοῦ rather than
w. the vb. ἁγιωσύνη *holiness*, a "Hebr." gen., "spirit of
holiness" meaning holy spirit §40 ; κατὰ πνεῦμα ἁγ. (opp.
κατὰ σάρκα) signifying the divine nature which Paul is
regarding from the standpoint of salvation : it is by means
of the Holy Spirit that Christ imparts his saving and
sanctifying power, and this in virtue of his glorification
by death and resurrection Jn 7:39. ἀνά-στασις[4] (< ἀν-
ίστημι) *resurrection*. ‖ ἐ-λάβομεν aor[2] λαμβάνω, if not epi- **5**
stolary pl. then ref. Paul and the other apostles. ἀπο-
στολή *commission, apostolate* ; χάρις καὶ ἀπ. hendiadys = *the
grace of an apostolic commission* §460. εἰς purposive, (to
work) *for*. ὑπ-ακοή (< ὑπ-ακούω) *obedience*, ὑπ. πίστεως
at one and the same time : subjective gen. "obedience
which springs from faith", obj. gen. "obedience to faith",
and epexeg. gen. "obedience which consists in faith"
§36-38. ὑπέρ *for the sake of*, i.e. to the glory of. ‖ ἐν **6**
among. κλητός v.1 ; κ. Ἰησοῦ *called by...* or pred. *called
to belong to Jesus*. ‖ οὖσιν dat. pl. ὤν ptc εἰμί. ἀγαπητός **7**
beloved. ἅγιος pred. *called to be dedicated/holy*. χάρις...

εἰρήνη combines and Christianizes Gk and Hebr. greetings, χαίρειν and šālôm. ‖

8 εὐ-χαριστέω τινί *give thanks, thank.* κατ-αγγέλλεται
9 pass. -αγγέλλω *proclaim, spread the knowledge of.* ‖ μάρτυς⁶ -υρος ὁ a *witness.* λατρεύω τινί *serve, worship* God. ἐν (2nd time) *by preaching* the gospel. εὐαγγέλιον τοῦ υἱοῦ gen. in a wide sense : the gospel which he brought, the gospel about him, and the gospel which is proclaimed at his commission and in his power, cf on ὑπακοὴ πίστεως v.5. μάρτυς...ὡς *witness...how.* ἀ-δια-λείπτως *without a break, ceaselessly.* μνεία *remembrance* ; μν. ποιοῦμαι (mid. ποιέω) *remember, make mention,* esp. before God; class. use of mid. where π. combines w. its obj. to express the same idea as the cognate vb (here μνημονεύω) Lk 5:33, Ac
10 23:13 §227. ὑμῶν *of you.* ‖ πάν-τοτε *always.* ἐπί w. gen. *at the time/on the occasion of.* προσ-ευχή *prayer.* δεόμενος ptc δέομαι *beg, beseech.* πώς encl. *somehow ; perhaps.* ἤδη *already.* ποτέ encl. *sometime ;* εἴ πως ἤδη ποτέ *if somehow sometime at last.* εὐ-οδωθήσομαι fut. pass. -οδόω *lead along a good route,* pass. *have a good journey ; succeed ;* in late Gk εἰ w. fut. may express uncertain hope §403. ἐν τ. θελήματι τ. θεοῦ *God willing.* ἐλθεῖν aor² inf. ἔρχομαι. ‖
11 ἐπι-ποθέω I *long.* ἰδεῖν aor² inf. ὁράω. μετα-δῶ aor² subj. -δίδωμι τινί τι *share* sth w. someone. χάρισμα⁷ (free) *gift.* πνευματικός *belonging to the Spirit, spiritual.* εἰς τό w. inf. = ἵνα w. subj. (*in order*) *that.* στηριχθῆναι aor. inf. pass. -ρίζω *strengthen, uphold.* ὑμᾶς acc. as subject of inf. ‖
12 τοῦτο δέ ἐστιν *that is, I mean.* συμ-παρα-κληθῆναι aor. inf. pass. -καλέω *encourage along with ;* σ. ἐν ὑμῖν *to be encouraged at the same time in you.* ἡ ἐν ἀλλήλοις πίστις *each other's*
13 *faith.* ‖ ἀ-γνοεῖν inf. -γνοέω *not to know, be ignorant ;* οὐ... ἀγνοεῖν I *should like you to know.* πολλάκις *often.* προ-ε-θέμην aor² προ-τίθεμαι (mid.) *propose, purpose, mean* to. ἐλθεῖν v.10. ἐ-κωλύθην aor. pass. -ύω *hinder,* aor. *often prevent.* ἄχρι *up to, until.* δεῦρο ref. time, *now.* σχῶ aor² subj. ἔχω, inceptive aor. *acquire ;* ἵνα...καρπόν σ. *that I might achieve some results.* ἐν v.6. οἱ λοιποί (< λείπω leave be-
14 hind) *the rest (of), the other.* ‖ Ἕλλην⁶ -ηνος ὁ a *Greek.* βάρβαρος a *non-Greek.* σοφός *wise.* ἀ-νόητος *un-learned,*
15 *simple.* ὀφειλέτης³ *one indebted, debtor.* ‖ οὕτως *so, hence.* τὸ κατ' ἐμέ *with respect to me, how I am faring* §130. πρό-θυμος *eager,* neut. as noun *eagerness, readiness* §140. εὐ-

ἀγγελίσασθαι aor. inf. -αγγελίζομαί τινι *evangelize, preach the gospel* to one. ‖

ἐπ-αισχύνομαί τι *be ashamed of* sth. εἰς (working) *for* v.5. σωτηρία *salvation.* πιστεύοντι ptc -εύω. πρῶτον for πρότερον §150. Ἕλλην here a *non-Jew, gentile.* ‖ δικαιοσύνη θεοῦ God's *mode of action in conformity w. his holiness and his plan of salvation promised to men* §38. αὐτῷ i.e. the gospel. ἀπο-καλύπτεται pass. -καλύπτω *un-veil, reveal.* ἐκ πίστεως εἰς π. *beginning and ending in faith* by which man appropriates the saving efficacy of the gospel. γέ-γραπται *it stands written,* pf pass. γράφω. ζήσεται fut. ζάω *live,* here *have life.* ‖

γάρ normally explanatory, here merely *continues what goes before* §473. ὀργή *wrath* of God. ἀ-σέβεια *im-piety, un-godliness,* πᾶσαν ἀσ. wt art. *every form of ungodliness* §188. ἀ-δικία *un-righteousness, wrongdoing.* ἀλήθεια in OT *less* sth *to be known than* sth *to be done.* ἐν instr. *by.* κατ-εχόντων ptc -έχω *hold down* or *back, obstruct.* ‖ δι-ότι = ὅτι causal, *for.* γνωστός (< γινώσκω) *known; knowable,* τό w. adj. *forming abstract noun, what may be known* §140. φανερός *evident.* ἐν of doubtful significance §120, cf foll. simple αὐτοῖς. ἐ-φανέρωσεν aor. -ρόω *make clear/evident.* ‖ ἀ-όρατος *in-visible,* τὰ ἀό. *invisible attributes.* κτίσις[4] *creation,* as in Eng. *both the act and the result* (v.25). ποίημα[7] *a thing made, creature;* instr. dat. *by means of the things* (he has) *made.* νοούμενα ptc pass. νοέω *understand.* καθ-ορᾶται pass. -οράω *perceive;* νοούμενα καθ. "being understood they are perceived", i.e. *by the mind, visible to the eye of reason* (NEB). ἥ τε here w. the force of *that is, I mean.* ἀΐδιος (< ἀεί *always*) masc. and fem. *eternal.* θειότης[6] -ότητος ἡ *deity.* εἰς τό w. acc.+inf. here consec. force, *so that they are...* §352. αὐτούς subject of εἶναι. ἀν-απο-λόγητος *without defence/excuse.* ‖ δι-ότι v.19. γνόντες aor[2] ptc γινώσκω. ἐ-δόξασαν aor. -άζω *glorify, praise.* ηὐχαρίστησαν aor. -χαριστέω v.8. ἐ-ματαιώθησαν aor. pass. -αιόω *make* μάταιος *vain/empty-headed, infatuate.* δια-λογισμός *reasoning, speculation.* ἐ-σκοτίσθη aor. pass. -ίζω (< σκότος[8] *darkness*) *darken.* ἀ-σύνετος *without understanding, undiscerning.* ‖ φάσκοντες ptc φάσκω *assert;* often *allege.* σοφοί pred., nom. because same subject as φάσκοντες §393. ἐ-μωράνθησαν aor. pass. μωραίνω *make* μωρός *foolish,* pass. intr. *become foolish.* ‖ ἤλλαξαν aor. ἀλλάσσω *make other* (ἄλλος) than it is, *change.* **ἄ-φθαρτος** *in-corrupt-ible*, hence *immortal.* **ὁμοίωμα**⁷ *likeness, copy.* **εἰκών**⁶ -κόνος ἡ *image,* epexeg. gen. §45. **φθαρτός** *corruptible, perishable.* **πετεινόν** *bird.* **τετρά-πους** (neut. -πουν) -ποδος *four-legged.*

24 *quadruped.* **ἑρπετόν** (< ἕρπω creep) *reptile.* ‖ **δι-ό** *there-fore, for this reason.* **παρ-έ-δωκεν** aor. παρα-δίδωμι *hand over/ leave* to. **ἐν** pleon. w. dat. §120. **ἐπι-θυμία** a *desire,* whether morally good or bad. **ἀ-καθαρσία** *impurity* ; esp. moral, *vice.* **τοῦ** + inf. consec. §383. **ἀ-τιμάζεσθαι** inf. pass. -άζω

25 *dis-honour* ; *degrade.* **ἐν** *among.* ‖ **οἵ-τινες** *such as.* **μετ-ήλλαξαν** aor. -αλλάσσω, w. ἐν or εἰς (v.26) *ex-change* sth *for* (cf ἀλλάσσω v.23). **ψεῦδος**⁸ *falsehood, lie.* **ἐ-σεβάσθησαν** aor. dep. -άζομαι *worship.* **ἐ-λάτρευσαν** aor. v.9. **κτίσις** v.20. **παρά** w. acc. in comp. sense *beyond,* hence "passing over", *to the exclusion of, instead of.* **κτίσαντα** aor. ptc -ίζω *create,* ὁ κτίσας *the one who created, the creator.* **εὐ-λογητός** *blessed* (in NT solely of God as worthy of all praise). **εἰς τοὺς αἰῶνας** esp. in doxologies, *to all eternity, for ever.* ‖

26 **πάθος**⁸ (< πάσχω suffer) *what is experienced or suffered* (hence freq. in Patristic writings of the *Passion* of Christ), in NT always *passion* in bad sense, here of unnatural lust. **ἀ-τιμία** *dis-grace* ; πάθη ἀτ. a "Hebr. gen." taking the place of an adj., *degrading passions* §40. **τε...τε** *both...and.* **θῆλυς** -λεια -λυ *female,* as noun, *woman.* **φυσικός** *natural,* i.e. in accordance w. nature. **χρῆσις**⁴ (< χράομαι use) *use, func-tion,* here of sexual relations. **φύσις**⁴ *nature,* παρὰ φ. *against*

27 *nature.* ‖ **ὁμοίως** *similarly.* **ἄρσην** (neut. -σεν) -σενος dat. pl. ἄρσεσι *male,* as noun, *man.* **ἀφ-έντες** aor² ptc -ίημι *leave, abandon.* **ἐξ-ε-καύθησαν** aor. pass. ἐκ-καίω (ἐκ- perfec-tive) lit. and met., *burn.* **ἐν** (1st time) causal, *with.* **ὄρεξις**⁴ *desire,* w. εἰς *for.* **ἀ-σχημοσύνη** (ἀ-σχήμων in-decent) *in-decency.* **κατ-εργαζόμενοι** ptc -εργάζομαι *do, perpetrate.* **ἀντι-μισθία** *corresponding reward.* **ἔ-δει** impf δεῖ : ἣν ἔδει which (sc. to receive) *was in the nature of things,* ἡ ἀντιμ. ἣν ἔδει *the inevitable recompense.* **ἀπο-λαμβάνοντες** ptc -λαμ-βάνω *receive* one's due. **πλάνη** (< πλανάομαι wander) a

28 *going astray, perversion.* ‖ **ἐ-δοκίμασαν** aor. -μάζω *put to the test,* hence *approve, think fit.* **ἐπί-γνωσις**⁴ *knowledge, recognition,* τὸν θεὸν ἔχειν ἐν ἐπ. *to recognize/acknowledge God.* **ἀ-δόκιμος** *not passing the test, discredited, unfit.* **νοῦς** νοός ὁ *mind, mentality.* **ποιεῖν** inf. ποιέω. **τὰ μὴ καθ-**

29 **ήκοντα** *what is not fitting,* ptc -ήκει *it is fitting.* ‖ **πεπληρω-**

μένους pf ptc pass. -ρόω. πᾶς wt art. *every kind of* §188.
ἀ-δικία v.18. πονηρία *wickedness*. πλεονεξία (πλέον ἔχειν)
selfish greed. κακία *malice*. μεστός *full*. φθόνος *envy*. φόνος
murder. ἔρις⁶ ἔριδος ἡ *rivalry*. δόλος properly a "bait";
deceit. κακο-ήθεια *malignity*. ψιθυριστής³ *whisperer* of slander, *insinuator*. ‖ κατά-λαλος *slanderer*. θεο-στυγής⁹ (< θεός 30
+ στυγέω hate) *inimical to God, God hater*. ὑβριστής³
insolent man. ὑπερ-ή-φανος *arrogant*. ἀλαζών⁶ -ζόνος *boastful*. ἐφ-ευρετής³ *inventor*, ἐφ. κακῶν *inventive scoundrel*.
κακός *bad*, τὰ κακά *evil deeds, crimes*. γονεύς⁵ *parent*. ἀ-
πειθής⁹ *dis-obedient*, γονεῦσιν ἀπειθεῖς *rebellious sons*. ‖
ἀ-σύνετος *without discernment*. ἀ-σύνθετος (< ἀ- priv. + 31
συν-τίθεμαι make an agreement) *treacherous*. ἄ-στοργος (ἀ-
priv. + στοργή family affection) *devoid of natural affection,
callous*. ἀν-ελεήμων⁶ -μονος neut. -μον *merciless*. ‖ οἵ-τινες 32
those who §215. δικαίωμα⁷ *pronouncement that sth is just,
decree*. ἐπι-γνόντες aor² ptc -γινώσκω *know exactly*, ptc
concessive, *though they know perfectly well*. τοιοῦτος *such*,
neut. pl. *such things*. πράσσοντες ptc πράσσω *practise, do*.
ἄξιος (< ἄγω draw down a scale, weigh) *worthy*. συν-
ευδοκέω τινί *be in agreement with, approve* one. ‖

δι-ό *therefore*. ἀν-απο-λόγητος 1:20. πᾶς ὁ κρίνων *who-   2
ever you are who judge* ; words appos. a voc. take the art.
ἐν (sc. τούτῳ ἐν) ᾧ *in the matter for which*. σε-αυτόν *your-
self*. κατα-κρίνω *condemn*. πράσσω *do*. ‖ κρίμα⁷ *judgement,   2
condemnation*. τοιοῦτος 1:32. πράσσοντας ptc. ‖ λογίζῃ   3
2nd sg -ζομαι *reckon, consider, think*. καί *adversative,
and at the same time, yet*. ποιῶν ptc ποιέω. ἐκ-φεύξῃ fut.
mid. -φεύγω (ἐκ- perfective) *escape altogether*. ‖ πλοῦτος   4
wealth. χρηστότης⁶ -ότητος ἡ *goodness, kindness*. ἀν-οχή
(< ἀν-έχομαι endure) *tolerance*. μακρο-θυμία (long-temper)
patience. κατα-φρονέω τινός *scorn, make light of*. ἀ-γνοῶν
un-aware, ptc -γνοέω *not to know*. χρηστός *good, kind* ;
neut. as noun, den. a concrete instance of χρηστότης 3:12
§140. μετά-νοια *change of mental attitude* (νοῦς), *repentance*.
ἄγω *lead, induce*. ‖ σκληρότης⁶ -ότητος ἡ *hardness, obduracy*.   5
ἀ-μετα-νόητος *un-repentant*. θησαυρίζω *store up*. σε-αυτόν
v.l. ὀργή *wrath* 1:18. ἐν *on the day or in pregnant cstr
§99 till, for* (θησαυρίζεις being understood as mental motion). ἀπο-κάλυψις⁴ *revelation*. δικαιο-κρισία *justice of judgement*. ‖ ἀπο-δώσει fut. -δίδωμί τινι *give one what is due,   6
reward* one. ‖ μέν...δέ, less common in NT than in class.   7

= Lat. *quidem...autem*, roughly "on the one hand...on
the other (hand)" or "...indeed...but" or "while...yet...".
ὑπομονή *steadfastness, perseverance*. ἔργου collective, obj.
gen. *in a work* of good. τιμή *honour*. ἀ-φθαρσία *incorrupti-
bility*, hence *immortality*. ζητοῦσιν dat. pl. ptc -τέω. ‖
8 οἱ ἐκ... may den. origin or close connection Jn 8:23 ; *those
belonging to* or *characterized by*... §134. ἐριθεία purchasing
favour and promotion by gifts, hence *ambition, self-seeking*. ἀ-πειθοῦσι ptc dat. pl. -θέω τινί *be dis-obedient* to
one. πειθομένοις ptc -ομαι (mid.) *let oneself be persuaded*.
ἀ-δικία *un-righteousness, wrong*. ὀργή v.5. θυμός *rage*. ‖
9 θλῖψις[4] (< θλίβω press) *pressure ; distress*. στενο-χωρία
(< στενός narrow + χῶρος space) *constraint ; anguish*. πᾶσα
ψυχὴ ἀνθρώπου *every human being*. κατ-εργαζομένου ptc
-εργάζομαι *do* evil ; the art. foll. an anarthrous noun is a
HGk idiom §192. κακός *bad*, τὸ κ. *evil*. πρῶτον for πρότερον
10 §151. Ἕλλην[6] 1:16. ‖ ἐργαζομένῳ ptc -ζομαι *work, do*. ‖
11 προσωπο-λημψία (< λαμβάνω) *partiality* based on social
12 standing, outward appearance, etc. ‖ ἀ-νόμως *outside the
law*. ἥμαρτον aor[2] ἁμαρτάνω *sin*. ἀπ-ολοῦνται fut. -όλλυμαι.
ἐν νόμῳ *under the law*. διὰ νόμου *by the law*. κριθήσονται
13 fut. pass. κρίνω. ‖ ἀκροατής[3] (< ἀκροάομαι listen) *hearer*.
δίκαιος pred. παρὰ τῷ θεῷ *with/before* God. ποιητής[3] *doer,
one who keeps* the law. δικαιωθήσονται fut. pass. -αιόω
in pagan literature, *justify, show to be in the right, pro-
14 nounce righteous* ; in Paul, a t.t. for a new creation. ‖ μή
in HGk negatives the ptc even when stating a matter of
fact §440. ἔχοντα ptc (concessive) neut. pl. ἔχω. φύσις[4]
nature ; φύσει *by nature*. τὰ τοῦ νόμου *the requirements of
the law*. ποιῶσιν subj. ποιέω. μὴ ἔχοντες ptc causal, *since
15 uhey have not*. ἑ-αυτοῖς *to themselves*. ‖ οἵ-τινες either = τί
or *who as suhc* §215. ἐν-δείκνυνται mid. -δείκνυμι *point
out* ; mid. *show* in oneself or by one's actions. τὸ ἔργον
τ. νόμου *the content of the taw*. γραπτός (< γράφω *written*.
συμ-μαρτυρούσης ptc -μαρτυρέω *bear witness also, join in
testifying*. συν-είδησις[4] (< σύν-οιδα be conscious) *moral
consciousness, conscience*. μεταξύ *between*, μ. ἀλλήλων *between themselves, with one another*. λολισμός *reasoning, in-
ward debate*. κατ-εγορούντων ptc -εγορέω *accuse*. ἀπο-
16 λογουμένων ptc -λογέομαι *defend oneself*. ‖ κρυπτός *hidden,
secret*. ‖

ἐπ-ονομάζῃ *you call yourself*, pass. -ονομάζω *name*. 17
ἐπ-ανα-παύομαι *repose/rely on*. καυχᾶσαι 2nd sg -χάομαι
boast. ‖ τὸ θέλημα *God's will*. δοκιμάζω *distinguish* by 18
testing or *approve* after testing. δια-φέροντα ptc -φέρω
differ ; *be superior, excel* ; τὰ δ. *things that differ* or *what
transcends the ordinary, what is best*. κατηχούμενος ptc
pass. -ηχέω *instruct, teach* by word of mouth. ‖ πέ-ποιθας 19
pf² πείθω *persuade*, pf² (w. pres. meaning) *be convinced,
believe*. σε-αυτόν v.1. ὁδηγός (< ὁδός + ἡγέομαι lead)
guide. τυφλός *blind*. σκότος⁸ *darkness*. ‖ παιδευτής⁹ *tutor*. 20
ἄ-φρων⁶ ἄφρονος *stupid*. διδάσκαλος *teacher*. νήπιος *infant,
child*. ἔχοντα (*just*) *because you have* ; ptc acc. sg, causal.
μόρφωσις⁴ *formulation*. γνῶσις⁴ *knowledge*. ἐν τῷ νόμῳ to
be ass. w. ἔχοντα. ‖ οὖν: instead of the expected apodosis 21
to vv.17ff. Paul fires a series of questions at his opponent. διδάσκων, κηρύσσων ptcs voc. -σκω, -ύσσω *preach* ;
transl. *you who...* κλέπτειν inf. -πτω *steal*. ‖ μοιχεύειν inf. 22
-εύω *commit adultery*. βδελυσσόμενος ptc -ομαι *detest,
abhor*. εἴδωλον *idol*. ἱερο-συλέω (< ἱερόν + συλάω rob) *rob
temples*. ‖ καυχᾶσαι v.17. παρά-βασις⁴ (< -βαίνω transgress) 23
trans-gression. ἀ-τιμάζω (< ἀ- priv. + τιμή honour) *dis-
honour*. ‖ βλασ-φημεῖται pass. -φημέω *blaspheme, speak evil
of*. γέ-γραπται 1:17. ‖ περι-τομή (< περι-τέμνω cut round) 24
circumcision. γάρ here, *of course* §473. ὠφελέω *do good, 25
be of use/benefit*. πράσσῃς subj. v.1. παρα-βάτης³ (< παρα-
+ βαίνω overstep) *transgressor*. ἧς subj. εἰμί. ἀκρο-βυστία
uncircumcision. γέ-γονεν pf² γίνομαι: ἀκρ. γ. *has become
ἀκρ*. i.e. *counts for nothing* (Wm), *is as if it had never been*
(NEB). ‖ ἀκροβυστία here stands for "uncircumcised", 26
abstract for concrete. δικαίωμα⁷ *pronouncement that sth is
just, ordinance, decree*. φυλάσσῃ subj. -άσσω *keep, observe*.
εἰς instead of pred. nom. §32. λογισθήσεται *he will count
as*, fut. pass. -ίζομαι *reckon* ; *consider* ; fut. if not simply
logical must ref. day of judgement. ‖ κρινεῖ fut. κρίνω. 27
φύσις v.14, ἡ ἐκ φ. ἀκροβυστία (art. generic) *uncircumcision
of the body*, i.e. *gentiles*. τελοῦσα ptc -λέω *accomplish, carry
out, observe* a law. σέ dir. obj. of κρινεῖ, sc. ὄντα *being*,
i.e. *who are*. διά w. gen. *with*, of mere circumstances and
implying "notwithstanding" : *you who with* (or *for*) *all
your written code and circumcision are...* §114. γράμμα⁷
letter of the alphabet ; *a writing*. ‖ φανερός *clear, visible* ; 28
ἐν τῷ φ. *publicly* ; *outwardly* ; elliptical : *not the one who is*

outwardly (sc. *a Jew*) *is the* (*real*) *Jew, nor that which is outwardly in the body the* (*true*) *circumcision.* 'Ιουδαῖός ἐστιν *who is the* (*real*) *Jew.* οὐδέ *nor is.* σαρκί dat. of σάρξ.

29 περιτομή *the* (*true*) *circumcision.* ‖ κρυπτός v.16, ἐν τῷ κ. *inwardly.* ἐν πνεύματι οὐ γράμματι *inspired by the spirit and not the letter of the law.* οὗ not ἧς (= περιτομῆς) because considering the person implied in the whole argu-

3 ment. ἔπ-αινος (< αἰνέω *praise*) *praise.* ‖ περισσός *more than usual, extra,* neut. as noun, *superiority, advantage.* τοῦ generic. ὠφέλεια *benefit,* the *good.* περιτομή *circumci-*

2 *sion.* ‖ τρόπος *manner, way,* κατὰ πάντα τ. *in every way.* ἐ-πιστεύθησαν aor. pass. -εύω τινί τι *entrust sth to one, entrust one with* sth, in pass. the person becomes subject, the thing an acc. of respect : πιστεύομαί τι *be entrusted with* sth §72. λόγιον *saying,* τὰ λ. *oracles,* God's *utterances* enshrined in OT, here esp. of messianic promises. ‖

3 τί γὰρ εἰ; *for what if?* ἠ-πίστησαν aor. ἀ-πιστέω *be unfaithful.* μή here introducing a rhetorical question expecting the answer "No". ἀ-πιστία *faithlessness.* πίστις *faithfulness.* κατ-αργήσει fut. -αργέω *render ineffectual, nullify.* ‖

4 γένοιτο aor² opt. γίνομαι : μὴ γ. lit. "let it not happen !", *far be it ! God forbid !* γινέσθω impv 3rd sg, *God must be.* ἀληθής[9] *true, truthful.* ψεύστης[3] *liar,* πᾶς δὲ ἄνθρωπος ψ. *and every man a liar.* γέ-γραπται *it stands written,* pf pass. γράφω. ὅπως ἄν (*in order*) *that.* δικαιωθῇς aor. subj. pass. -αιόω *pronounce righteous* ; pass. *be vindicated/recognized* as in the right. οἱ λόγοι are God's promises. νικήσεις fut. νικάω *be victorious.* ἐν τῷ in temporal sense w. acc. + inf. *when* §390. κρίνεσθαι inf. mid. or pass. κρίνω, mid. *when*

5 *you go to law* ; pass. *when you are tried.* ‖ ἀ-δικία *lack of righteousness/integrity/uprightness.* συν-ίστησι 3rd sg -ίστημι *recommend* ; *serve to show.* ἐροῦμεν fut. λέγω. μή v.3. ἄ-δικος *un-just.* ἐπι-φέρων ptc -φέρω *bring upon, loose on.* ὀργή *wrath* of God. μὴ ἄδ. ...λέγω *is God humanly speak-*

6 *ing unjust to loose on* (*us*) *his wrath?* ‖ ἐπεί *since* (sc. *if that were so*), *otherwise.* κρινεῖ fut. modal, *how can God / how is God to judge?* ‖ ἐν causal, *through.* ψεῦσμα[7] *a lie* ;

7 here, *refusal of the truth.* ἐ-περίσσευσεν aor. -εύω *abound* ; *redound.* τί ἔτι κἀγώ; (= καὶ ἐγώ) but ass. w. τί *why then* (καί) *am I still...?* on τί καί interr. §459. ἁμαρτωλός

8 *sinner.* κρίνομαι pass. ‖ καί as v.7. μή interr. καὶ μή... ποιήσωμεν κτλ. *then — as we are libelled and as some even*

affirm that we say — are we to do evil that good may come?
βλασ-φημούμεθα pass. -φημέω *defame, slander.* φασίν 3rd
pl. φημί w. acc. + inf. *affirm that.* ὅτι = "... ποιήσωμεν
subj. delib. ποιέω. κακός *bad,* τὸ κ. *evil.* ἔλθῃ aor² subj.
ἔρχομαι. τὰ ἀγαθά *good things, good.* ὧν *whose,* of the
accusers. κρίμα⁷ *judgement ; condemnation.* ἔνδικος *just,
deserved.* ‖

    προ-εχόμεθα mid. or pass. of -έχω *stand out ; be supe- 9
rior, excel.* Although mid. in the sense of act. would be
unique, it is generally so translated in this context, "are
we (sc. as Jews) superior ?" §234 ; another possibility is
pass. "are we (Jews) excelled ?" i.e. in a less good position. πάντως *altogether, in every way,* οὐ π. *not in any
way, not at all ;* or *not altogether* (cf I Cor 5:10). προ-
ητιασάμεθα *we have already accused,* aor. -αιτιάομαι (< αἰτία
a charge) *accuse beforehand of.* Ἕλλην 1:16. ὑπό w. acc.
under the power of, subject to. ‖ γέ-γραπται v.4. δίκαιος 10
a *just man.* οὐδὲ εἷς *not even one.* ‖ συν-ίων ptc -ίω, late 11
form of -ίημι, (put together, e.g. ideas) *understand.* ἐκ-
ζητῶν ptc -ζητέω *seek out, search for.* ‖ ἐξ-έ-κλιναν aor. 12
ἐκ-κλίνω *turn away.* ἅμα *together.* ἠ-χρεώθησαν aor. pass.
ἀ-χρε(ι)όω (ἀ- + χράομαι use) *make useless ;* pass. *become
useless.* ποιῶν ptc ποιέω. χρηστότης⁶ -ότητος ἡ *goodness,
kindness.* ἕως ἑνός *not so much as one.* ‖ τάφος *grave.* 13
ἀν-ε-ῳγμένος *open,* pf ptc pass. ἀν-οίγω. λάρυγξ⁶ -υγγος ὁ
throat. γλῶσσα *tongue.* ἐ-δολιοῦσαν for (-ίουν) impf -ιόω
deceivs. ἰός *poison, venom.* ἀσπίς -ίδος ἡ asp. χεῖλος⁸
lip. ‖ ἀρά *curse.* πικρία *bitterness.* γέμω τινός *be full of* sth. 14
‖ ὀξύς ὀξεῖα ὀξύ *sharp ; speedy* (cf Eng. "look sharp"). 15
ἐκ-χέαι (for -χεεῖν §489) aor² inf. -χέω *pour out ; shed* blood. ‖
σύν-τριμμα⁷ (< συν-τρίβω break, crush) *ruin.* ταλαιπωρία 16
misery. ‖ ἔ-γνωσαν aor² γινώσκω. ‖ φόβος *fear.* ἀπ-έν-αντι 17,18
before (local). ‖ ἐν τῷ νόμῳ *within the* jurisdiction *of the* 19
Law ; νόμος, like Torah, may sts den. the OT as a whole.
πᾶν στόμα *every mouth* §188. φραγῇ aor² subj. pass. φράσσω
stop (up). ὑπό-δικος *under the sentence of, accountable to.*
γένηται aor² subj. γίνομαι. ‖ δι-ότι = ὅτι *because.* ἐξ *by,* 20
on the ground of. ἔργα νόμου *deeds in fulfilment of law*
(wt art.) §177. οὐ...πᾶσα σάρξ Sem. for *not one, no man*
§446. σάρξ translating Hebr. *bāsār* den. *man in his frailty.*
δικαιωθήσεται fut. pass. -αιόω v.4, from LXX ; in this
context fut. perh. logical, *can (hope to) be justified,* other-

wise eschatological §284a Lat. ed⁵. ἐν-ώπιον w. gen. *in
the sight of.* διὰ νόμου... *through law (comes)...*, i.e. *law
brings...* ἐπί-γνωσις⁴ (sc. *merely*) *recognition, consciousness.* ‖

21 νυνὶ δέ *but now.* χωρίς *apart from, independently of.*
δικαιοσύνη Θεοῦ 1:17. πε-φανέρωται *is evident*, pf pass.
-ρόω *manifest, make clear.* μαρτυρουμένη "having testi-
22 mony borne to it", *attested*, ptc pass. -ρέω. ‖ δικ. δὲ
Θεοῦ: the repetition w. δέ introducing an amplification
and expressing only an implicit contrast, cf Eng. "...a
righteousness moreover..." §467. διά *through, by means of.*
Ἰησοῦ Χρ. obj. gen. πιστεύοντας ptc. δια-στολή (< δια-
23 στέλλω distinguish) *differentiation.* ‖ ἥμαρτον aor² ἁμαρτάνω *sin.* ὑστεροῦνται pass. -ρέω (< ὕστερος) *be late* ;
24 *lack* ; pass. w. gen. *fall short of.* ‖ δικαιούμενοι ptc pass.
-αιόω v.4. δωρεάν *freely, without charge.* τῆ...χάριτι dat.
of instr. *by grace.* ἀπο-λύτρωσις⁴ a *redeeming, liberation*
(ἀπο- either connoting "from" slavery or perfective,
"complete" redemption §132 n.). τῆς ἐν (*which has come
25 about*) *in.* ‖ προ-έ-θετο aor² -τίθεμαι (mid.) Lat. *pro-pono :
set before* one, *put forward publicly, propose* ; or "set before oneself", *intend, design.* ἱλαστήριον either *place of
propitiation*, i.e. mercyseat of OT conceived as the resting
place of God, or that which effects propitiation, a *means
of propitiation*, a *propitiatory sacrifice.* διά (sc. *apprehended* or *appropriated*) *through* faith. ἐν instr. §119.
αὐτοῦ in emphatic position, *his own.* εἰς final, *to be.*
ἔν-δειξις⁴ (< ἐν-δείκνυμι demonstrate) *proof.* πάρ-εσις⁴
(< πάρ-ειμι let pass) *overlooking*, not in the sense of "neg-
lecting" but allowing to go unpunished ; or perh. *partial
remission.* προ-γε-γονότων *previously committed*, pf² ptc
προ-γίνομαι *happen beforehand.* ἁμάρτημα⁷ a *sin* as sth
committed, as distinct from ἁμαρτία principle of sin. ‖
26 ἀν-οχή *tolerance.* πρὸς τὴν ἔν. art. ref. back to "the (aforesaid) proof" §165. δικαιοῦντα ptc. ὁ ἐκ πίστεως *the be-
27 liever* 2:8. Ἰησοῦ v.22. ‖ ποῦ; *where?* i.e. *what room is
there for?* καύχησις⁴ *boasting.* ἐξ-ε-κλείσθη aor. pass. ἐκ-
κλείω *preclude.* ποῖος; *what kind of? what?* νόμος in Gk
sense, *principle.* τῶν ἔργων (*that*) *of works*, i.e. *deeds.*
28 οὐχί emphatic *no.* ‖ λογίζομαι *reckon* ; *maintain, hold an
opinion.* δικαιοῦσθαι inf. pass. χωρίς v.21. ἔργα νόμου
29 v.20. ‖ ἤ...ὁ Θεός *or is God* (sc. *the God*)...? οὐχὶ καί;

(and) not also? ναί *yes, certainly.* ‖ εἴ-περ *if indeed, if* 30
it be true that. εἰς pred. δικαιώσει fut.; fut. perh. logical
rather than temporal, "who can be relied on to justify"
§284a Lat. ed⁵. περιτομή v.1, here standing for Jews.
ἀκρο-βυστία *uncircumcision,* here den. gentiles. τῆς πίστεως
art. referring back, cf πρὸς τὴν ἔνδειξιν v.26. ‖ κατ-αργέω 31
v.3. γένοιτο v.4. ἀλλά *on the contrary.* ἱστάνω late form
of ἵστημι *make to stand, establish, confirm.* ‖

 ἐροῦμεν fut. λέγω. εὑρηκέναι pf inf. εὑρίσκω *obtain,* 4
cf §227 [[var. om.]]. προ-πάτωρ⁶ -τορος ὁ *fore-father, ancestor.* κατὰ σάρκα *with regard to the flesh, by blood relationship / natural descent.* ‖ εἰ introducing a "real" condi- 2
tion, *if* as you maintain §306. ἐξ 3:20. ἐ-δικαιώθη aor.
pass. -αιόω *justify.* καύχημα⁷ *matter for boasting, something
to boast about.* πρὸς θεόν *before God.* ‖ γραφή *a writing,* 3
sg and pl. *scripture.* ἐ-πίστευσεν aor. -εύω. ἐ-λογίσθη
aor. pass. -ίζομαι *reckon, count.* εἰς *as,* w. pred. a Hebr.
§32. ‖ ἐργαζομένῳ ptc -ζομαι: ὁ ἐ. *the one who* habitually 4
works, the worker §371. μισθός *wage.* λογίζεται pass.
κατὰ χάριν *as a favour.* ὀφείλημα⁷ *a due, debt.* ‖ τῷ...μὴ 5
ἐργαζομένῳ *to one who does no work.* πιστεύοντι ptc -εύω.
ἐπί *in,* connoting confidence. δικαιοῦντα ptc -αιόω. ἀ-
σεβής⁹ *un-godly.* ‖ καθ-άπερ = καθ-ώς. λέγει *speaks of.* μα- 6
καρισμός *pronouncement of happiness, blessing.* χωρὶς *without, independently of.* ‖ μακάριος *blessed, happy.* ὧν *(those)* 7
whose. ἀφ-έθησαν aor. pass. -ίημι *let go; forgive.* ἀ-νομία
pl. *transgressions* of the law. ἐπ-ε-καλύφθησαν aor. pass.
-καλύπτω *cover.* ‖ οὗ...ἁμαρτίαν *whose sin.* οὐ μή w. aor. 8
subj. emphatic neg. ref. fut. §444. λογίσηται aor. subj.
v.3, οὐ μὴ λ. *will not reckon* (sc. *to his debit / against him*),
will not take into account. ‖ μακαρισμός v.6. ἐπί *on.* 9
περι-τομή *circumcision,* signifying "those who are circumcised". ἀκροβυστία *uncircumcision.* λέγομεν *we assert/
maintain.* It is tempting to ascribe to γάρ the force of
Eng. "Now," introducing the chain of argument in support of the Apostle's thesis, but there is no outside evidence for such a use, cf §473. ἐ-λογίσθη κτλ. v.3. ‖ ὄντι 10
ptc εἰμί representing impf, *when he was.* ἐν of concomitant circumstances (sociative ἐν) den. a state of being
§117. περιτομή *rite* or *state of circumcision.* ‖ ἔ-λαβεν 11
aor² λαμβάνω. σφραγίς -ῖδος ἡ *seal.* εἰς τό w. acc.+inf.
final or consec. §352. πιστεύων v.5, ὁ π. *the believer.*

διά w. gen. ref. manner (of action) or circumstances (of person) §114. λογισθῆναι aor. inf. pass. καὶ αὐτοῖς *to*

12 *them also.* δικαιοσύνην acc. as subject of inf. ‖ τοῖς... μόνον *those who do not rely only on their circumcision*; for ἐκ w. this sense §134. στοιχοῦσιν ptc dat. pl. -χέω *fall into line with* (lit. and met.), *assent, follow.* ἴχνος[8] *footprint*, met. *footstep.* ἡ ἐν ἀκροβυστίᾳ πίστις *faith (given to him) in a state of uncircumcision.* ‖

13   διά ref. the means. νόμος a (= any) *law.* ἐπ-αγγελία *promise.* σπέρμα[7] *seed*, hence *descendants.* τό...αὐτὸν εἶναι *that he should be*, τό w. acc. + inf. explaining in what the promise consists. κληρο-νόμος (< κλῆρος a lot + νέμω

14 assign) *heir.* ‖ οἱ ἐκ νόμου *whose who are adherents of the Law*, cf οἱ ἐκ περιτομῆς v.12. κληρονόμοι pred. *are inheritors.* κε-κένωται pf pass. κενόω *empty* (here) of meaning, *invalidate.* κατ-ήργηται pf pass. -αργέω (κατα- + α- +

15 ἔργος) *render inoperative/impotent, nullify.* ‖ ὀργή *wrath.* κατ-εργάζομαι *bring about, cause.* παρά-βασις[4] *trans-gres-*

16 *sion.* ‖ διὰ τοῦτο *for this reason, this is why* §112. ἐκ πίστεως *it is through faith.* ἵνα κατὰ χάριν *that it may be by grace*; supply from v.14, *that we become inheritors.* εἰς τό w. acc.+inf. final. βέβαιος *firm, reliable.* σπέρμα

17 v.13. τῷ sc. σπέρματι. Ἀβραάμ gen. ‖ γέ-γραπται pf ptc pass. γράφω. ὅτι = "... τέ-θεικα pf τίθημι *set, appoint.* κατ-έν-αντι *before, in the sight of.* οὗ ἐ-πίστευσεν (v.3) θεοῦ = κατέν. θεοῦ ᾧ ἐπ. where the antecedent θεοῦ is found in the rel. clause and the rel. attracted from dat. §18. ζῳο-ποιοῦντος ptc -ποιέω *make alive, give life.* καλοῦντος (ptc καλέω) ὡς ὄντα *not speaking of non-existent things as if they existed*, but *calling them into existence.* ‖

18 ἐλπίς[6] -ίδος ἡ *hope*; παρ' ἐλπίδα *against hope*; ἐπ' ἐλπίδι *in hope*, i.e. hoping in the apparently impossible. εἰς τό κτλ. v.12, *that he would become...* γενέσθαι aor[2] inf.

19 γίνομαι. εἰρημένον pf ptc pass. λέγω. ‖ ἀ-σθενήσας aor. ptc -νέω (ἀ- + σθένος[8] *strength*) *be weak/infirm*; inceptive aor. *weaken.* πίστει dat. for acc. of respect §53. κατ-ε-νόησεν aor. κατα-νοέω *take note of, consider.* ἤδη *by now.* νε-νεκρωμένον pf ptc pass. -ρόω *put to death*; ptc pass. *as good as dead*, here *impotent.* ἑκατοντα-ετής[9] *100 years old.* που w. numbers, *some, about.* ὑπ-άρχων ptc -άρχω *be.* νέκρωσις[4] *state of deadness.* μήτρα *womb.* This v. may illustrate a Gk practice of sts expressing the domi-

nant idea by a ptc and the subordinate one by a finite
vb, cf Heb 6:13 §376: *when A. considered* (aor.) *his own
body...his faith did not weaken* (ptc) *nor did he doubt* (aor.)... ||
εἰς *in view of* §98. δι-ε-κρίθη aor. dep. δια-κρίνομαι (δια- 20
to and fro + κρίνω) mid. "in oneself", *doubt, hesitate*.
ἀ-πιστία *dis-belief*, art. connoting "the" common, well-
known reaction to things seemingly incredible. ἐν-ε-
δυναμώθη aor. pass. -δυναμόω *strengthen*. τῇ πίστει either
by faith or dat. of respect, *in faith*. δούς aor² ptc δίδωμι. ||
πληρο-φορηθείς aor. ptc pass. -φορέω *carry out fully* ; *assure* 21
fully, convince. ἐπ-ήγγελται pf -αγγέλλομαι *promise* (sc.
God as subject). δυνατός *able*. ἐστίν tense of his actual
thought. καί *also*. ποιῆσαι aor. inf. ποιέω. || δι-ό *this is* 22
why. ἐ-λογίσθη, εἰς v.3. || ἐ-γράφη *it was set down in* 23
writing, aor² pass. γράφω. δι' αὐτόν *on his account, for
his sake*. || μέλλει λογίζεσθαι (inf. pass.) *is to be reckoned/* 24
counted. τοῖς πιστεύουσιν ptc dat. pl. *who believe*. ἐγεί-
ραντα aor. ptc -ρω: τὸν ἐγ. *him who raised*. || παρ-ε-δόθη 25
aor. pass. παρα-δίδωμι. παρά-πτωμα⁷ (< παρα- + πίπτω)
lapse, trespass. ἠγέρθη aor. pass. ἐγείρω. διά for §112.
δικαίωσις⁴ *justification*. ||

    δικαιωθέντες aor. ptc pass. -αιόω *declare just, justify*, 5
2:13. ἐκ πίστεως *through faith* in Christ. εἰρήνη *peace*.
ἔχομεν [[var. ἔχωμεν hort. subj. pres., *let us continue to
have, let us keep*]]. πρὸς τὸν θεόν *with God*. || καί (1st 2
time) foll. a rel. often wt special significance §463. προσ-
αγωγή *access*. ἐ-σχήκαμεν *we have gained*, pf ἔχω. τῇ
πίστει (if it is to be read) dat. of instr. *by faith* [[var. om.]].
ἑστήκαμεν *we stand*, pf (intr. w. pres. sense) ἵστημι. καυ-
χώμεθα indic. or subj. hort. καυχάομαι *boast*. ἐλπίς -ίδος ἡ
hope, ἐπ' ἐλπ. *in hope* (sc. of participating in). || ἐν *in* 3
not only "on the occasion of" but *because of* (Aram.)
§119. θλῖψις⁴ (< θλίβω *press*) *pressure* ; *distress, suffering*.
εἰδότες ptc οἶδα (pres.-pf). ὑπο-μονή (< μένω) *patience,
fortitude*. κατ-εργάζομαι *produce*. || δοκιμή *trial*, also of 4
what has come through tests, a *proven character*. || κατ- 5
αισχύνω *put to shame, disappoint, let one down*. ἡ ἀγάπη
τ. θεοῦ subjective gen. God's love for us §38. ἐκ-κέ-χυται
pf pass. ἐκ-χύν(ν)ω (= ἐκ-χέω) *pour out*. ἐν for εἰς "preg-
nant" cstr §99. δοθέντος aor. ptc pass. δίδωμι. || εἴ γε 6
if indeed as we believe. ὄντων ptc εἰμί, gen. abs. ἀ-
σθενής *without strength, weak*. κατὰ καιρόν *at the appointed*

time. ὑπέρ *on behalf of.* ἀ-σεβής⁹ *un-godly.* ἀπ-έ-θανεν

7 aor² ἀπο-θνήσκω. ‖ μόλις = μόγις *scarcely.* ἀπο-θανεῖται fut.

-θνήσκω. ὑπὲρ γὰρ τ. ἀγαθοῦ...ἀποθανεῖν a parenthesis, explaining the hesitation expressed in μόλις ("for, for the *good* man possibly someone might even have the courage to die"). τάχα *perhaps, possibly.* τολμάω ⸆*are.* ἀπο-

8 θανεῖν aor² inf. ‖ συν-ίστησιν 3rd sg -ίστημι *introduce ;* re-

9 commend. ἁμαρτωλός *sinner.* ὄντων v.6. ‖ πολλῷ...μᾶλλον *a fortiori, all the more.* δικαιωθέντες v.1. ἐν instr. §119. σωθησόμεθα fut. pass. σῴζω. ὀργή *just wrath* of God. ‖

10 ἐχθρός *enemy.* ὄντες 4:10. κατ-ηλλάγημεν aor² pass. -αλ-λάσσω *reconcile.* κατ-αλλαγέντες aor² ptc pass. ἐν τῇ ζωῇ

11 αὐτοῦ i.e. *by sharing in his risen life.* ‖ οὐ μόνον δέ, ἀλλὰ καὶ καυχώμενοι (ptc v.2) "and not only so but even exulting" ; more likely ptc stands for pres. indic. §374. κατ-αλλαγή *reconciliation.* ἐ-λάβομεν aor² λαμβάνω.

12 διὰ τοῦτο *so it is that.* ὥσ-περ *as.* ἑνός gen. of εἷς. δι-ῆλθεν aor² -έρχομαι *go through, pervade, spread to.* ἐφ' (= ἐπί) ᾧ: *inasmuch as, seeing that,* ἐπί causal §127.

13 ἥμαρτον aor² ἁμαρτάνω *sin.* ‖ ἄχρι w. gen. *up to, until,* here sc. *the advent of.* ἐλ-λογεῖται pass. -λογέω *reckon against, charge to one's account, take into account.* μὴ

14 ὄντος gen. abs. *when there is no law.* ‖ ἐ-βασίλευσεν aor. -εύω *reign.* μέχρι *until.* καί *even.* ἁμαρτήσαντας aor. ptc -τάνω (for aor² ἁμαρτόντας §491). ὁμοίωμα⁷ *likeness,* ἐπὶ τῷ ὁμ. *in the same way.* παρά-βασις⁴ *trans-gression.* τύπος *impression* of a die, *image, proto-type.* μέλλοντος

15 *of him who was to come,* ptc masc. μέλλω. ‖ Vv. 15f. con-trast type w. prototype : παρά-πτωμα⁷ (< πίπτω) *lapse, trespass.* οὐχ ὡς...οὕτως "not as (with)...so (with)", *it is not the same (with)...as it is (with),* i.e. one does not balance the other but far outweighs it. χάρισμα⁷ *act of grace.* ἀπ-έ-θανον aor² ἀπο-θνήσκω. πολλῷ μᾶλλον v.9. οἱ πολλοί not "many" but *all* (who are many), the fact of a great number being more prominent to the Sem. mind than the fact of totality, cf Mt 20:28. δωρεά *gift,* τῇ δ. ἐν χάριτι *his gift (given) in grace.* ἐ-περίσσευσεν *has overflowed, has been unbounded,* aor. -εύω *exceed the measure, abound.* ‖

16 δώρημα⁷ *gift.* δι' ἑνὸς ἁμαρτήσαντος "through one man having sinned", i.e. *the consequence of one...* τὸ μέν...τὸ δέ 2:7. κρίμα⁷ *judgement.* ἐξ ἑνός sc. παραπτώματος. εἰς (sc. *led*) *to.* κατά-κριμα⁷ *condemnation.* δικαίωμα⁷ here =

δικαίωσις *justification, acquittal.* ‖ ἐ-βασίλευσεν v.14, in- 17
ceptive, *established its reign* (NEB). οἱ...λαμβάνοντες (ptc)
those who receive. περισσεία *abundance.* βασιλεύσουσιν fut.
‖ ἄρα οὖν *so then.* εἰς (1st and 3rd time) *for*; (2nd and 18
4th time) (sc. *led*) *to.* δικαίωμα⁷ *act of justice, righteous
deed.* δικαίωσις ζωῆς epexeg. gen. *justification which is
life* §45. ‖ ὥσπερ v.12. παρ-ακοή *dis-obedience.* ἁμαρτωλός 19
v.8. κατ-ε-στάθησαν aor. pass. καθ-ίστημι *constitute, make.*
ὑπ-ακοή *obedience.* κατα-σταθήσονται fut. pass., fut. perh.
not temporal (den. what is yet to happen in the fut.)
so much as logical (what follows from the obedience of
the One). ‖ νόμος here, the element of law. παρ-εισ-ῆλθεν 20
aor² -έρχομαι *intrude, be introduced.* ἵνα consec. *with the
result that.* πλεονάσῃ aor. subj. -άζω *increase.* οὗ *where.*
ἐ-πλεόνασεν aor. ὑπερ-ε-περίσσευσεν aor. ὑπερ-περισσεύω
superabound. ‖ ἐ-βασίλευσεν aor. v.17, either inceptive or 21
constative, *reigned.* ἐν instr. *by* death. βασιλεύσῃ aor.
subj. ‖

ἐροῦμεν fut. λέγω. ἐπι-μένωμεν subj. delib. -μένω 6
stay on, w. dat. *remain/persist in.* πλεονάσῃ 5:20. ‖ γένοιτο 2
aor² opt. γίνομαι: μὴ γ. *far be it! God forbid!* οἵ-τινες *as
those who, seeing that we.* ἀπ-ε-θάνομεν aor² ἀπο-θνῄσκω
die. τῇ ἁμαρτίᾳ dat. of disadvantage, *died* (in relation)
to sin. ζήσομεν fut. ζάω, for subj. delib. *how can we
live...?* on the act. form of fut. §226. ‖ ἀ-γνοέω *not to 3
know, be unaware.* ὅσοι *all we who,* 1st pers. determined
by vb ἐ-βαπτίσθημεν aor. pass. -ίζω. εἰς τ. θάνατον αὐτοῦ
into his death, i.e. a baptism by which we participate in
his death. ‖ συν-ε-τάφημεν aor² pass. συν-θάπτω *bury* one 4
with another. βάπτισμα⁷ *baptism.* ὥσπερ...οὕτως *as...so...*
ἠγέρθη aor. pass. ἐγείρω. διά w. gen. instr., was raised
by §119. καινότης⁶ -ότητος ἡ *newness.* περι-πατήσωμεν
aor. subj. -πατέω *behave, live* in a certain way. ‖ σύμ- 5
φυτος *grown together,* hence *united.* γε-γόναμεν pf γίνομαι.
ὁμοίωμα⁷ *likeness.* Either *united with the likeness* (= *sharers*)
of his death or, sc. αὐτῷ *united to him in a death* (*like
his*). ἀλλά in apodosis, *then certainly.* καί *also.* ἀνά-
στασις⁴ *resurrection*; before the gen. it would seem necessary to understand ἐν ὁμοιώματι: either *sharers of his
resurrection* or *to a resurrection* (*like his*). ἐσόμεθα fut.
εἰμί, fut. connoting "now that we are baptized, we...",
logical rather than temporal (cf 5:19) §284a Lat. ed⁵. ‖

6 τοῦτο elucidated by ὅτι κτλ. γινώσκοντες ptc. παλαιός
old. συν-ε-σταυρώθη aor. pass. -σταυρόω *crucify together*;
sc. *with him.* κατ-αργηθῇ aor. subj. pass. -αργέω *render
inoperative, destroy.* τὸ σῶμα τ. ἀμαρτίας "Hebr." gen.,
equivalent to an adj. *the sinful body,* §40f. τοῦ w. inf.
final. μηκ-έτι *no longer.* δουλεύειν inf. -εύω *be a slave.*
ἀμαρτία regarded as ruling a kingdom (vv. 7,12,14) con-
7 scripting and paying his armies (vv. 13,23). ‖ ἀπο-θανών
aor² ptc -θνήσκω. δε-δικαίωται pf pass. -αιόω, pass. *be
8 acquitted/freed* from the claims of sin. ‖ ἀπ-ε-θάνομεν v.2.
9 συ-ζήσομεν fut. συ(ν)-ζάω *live with.* ‖ εἰδότες ptc οἶδα
(pres.-pf). ἐγερθείς aor. ptc pass. v.4. οὐκέτι = μηκέτι
v.6. αὐτοῦ object. κυριεύω τινός *hold sway over* one. ‖
10 ὅ *that which, that,* ὃ ἀπέθ. *in that he died* or *the death he
died.* τῇ ἀμαρτίᾳ v.2. ἐφ-άπαξ *once for all.* ζῇ 3rd sg ζάω.
11 τῷ θεῷ dat. of advantage. ‖ λογίζεσθε impv λογίζομαι
reckon ; consider. ἑ-αυτούς 3rd pl. for 2nd ὑμᾶς αὐτούς
§209. μέν...δέ 2:7. ζῶντας ptc. ἐν Χρ. Ἰησοῦ §117f. ‖
12 βασιλευέτω impv 3rd sg -εύω *reign,* pres. *continue to reign.*
θνητός *mortal.* εἰς τό w. inf. here consec. ὑπ-ακούειν inf.
-ακούω *obey.* ἐπι-θυμία *desire.* αὐτοῦ neut. ref. σῶμα. ‖
13 μή (v.12)...μηδέ *do not...and do not...* παρ-ιστάνετε *any
longer lend...to sin,* impv -ιστάνω τινί (late form of -ίστημι)
present, offer, put at one's *disposal.* μέλος⁸ *member* of
the body. ὅπλον *armour ; weapon ;* pl. *arms ;* pred. *as
instruments.* ἀ-δικία *un-righteousness, wrongdoing.* παραστήσατε aor. impv (once for all). ὡσ-εί (as if) *as.* ἐκ νεκρῶν
ζῶντας lit. "alive from the dead", Gk expression mean-
14 ing *brought from death to life.* ‖ κυριεύσει fut. v.9. ‖
15 ἀμαρτήσωμεν aor. (for aor²) subj. delib. *are we to
16 commit sin...?* §251. μὴ γένοιτο v.2. ‖ ᾧ *to whom.* δού-
λους pred. *as slaves.* εἰς *with a view to.* ὑπακοή *obedience.*
ὑπ-ακούω *obey.* ᾧ παριστάνετε κτλ. *when you offer yourselves in slavish obedience to anyone, you are slaves of the
one you obey.* ἤτοι...ἤ *whether...or.* εἰς θάνατον *resulting
17 in death.* ‖ χάρις w. dat. *thanks.* ὅτι *that* ref. ὑπηκούσατε.
ἦτε impf εἰμί: not co-ord. "thanks...that you were" but
subord. *...that though you were* §452. ὑπ-ηκούσατε *you
have become obedient,* aor. inceptive. ἐκ καρδίας *whole-
heartedly.* τύπος *impression* of a die, *type, pattern.* εἰς
ὅν...τύπον antecedent transferred to rel. clause, *to the pattern...to which.* παρ-ε-δόθητε aor. pass. παρα-δίδωμι *hand

over, commit. **διδαχή** (< διδάσκω) *doctrine, teaching.* ‖
ἐλευθερωθέντες aor. ptc pass. -ρόω (< ἐλεύθερος v.20) 18
free. **ἐ-δουλώθητε** aor. pass. -λόω *make* one *a slave.* ‖
ἀνθρώπινος *human*, neut. as adv. *in human terms*, or *with* 19
moderation. **ἀ-σθένεια** *weakness.* **σάρξ** for Hebr. *bāsār*
den. the frail nature of man. **ὥσπερ...οὕτως** v.4. **παρ-ε-**
στήσατε aor. v.13. **δοῦλος** adj. *enslaved, subject.* **ἀ-καθαρ-**
σία *im-purity, im-morality.* **ἀ-νομία** *lawless/wicked be-*
haviour ; (2nd time) *iniquity* as a principle diametrically
opp. δικαιοσύνη. **παραστήσατε** v.13. **ἁγιασμός** *holiness.* ‖
ἦτε v.17. **ἐλεύθερος** *free.* **δικαιοσύνη** dat. of respect 20
§53.ʹ ‖ **εἴχετε** impf ἔχω. **ἐφ'** (= ἐπί) *on the basis of, from*, 21
cf §126. **ἐπ-αισχύνομαι** *be ashamed*, ἐφ' οἷς νῦν ἐπαισχύ-
νεσθε *from* (*the things*) *of which you are now ashamed?*
a rhetorical question, sc. answer : None, *for...* **τέλος**[8]
end, result. **θάνατος** pred. ‖ **νυνὶ δέ** *but now.* **ἐλευθερω-**
θέντες v.18. **δουλωθέντες** aor. ptc pass. v.18. **εἰς** *for* ;
transl. *the fruit you get makes for holiness.* **ἁγιασμός** v.19. ‖
ὀψώνιον (< ὄψον a cooked relish to eat w. the basic ra- 23
tion + ὠνέομαι buy) hence the means to do so, *soldiers'*
pay ; in general, *wages.* **χάρισμα**[7] *act of grace, free gift.* ‖

ἀ-γνοέω ὅτι *not to know, be unaware that.* **γινώσκουσιν** 7
ptc dat. pl. *to those who know the meaning of law* / *under-*
stand what law is about. **κυριεύω** τινός *control, govern.*
ἐφ': ἐπί often added to acc. of measure §70, 125, ἐφ' ὅσον
χρόνον here, (*just*) *so long as.* **ζῇ** 3rd sg ζάω. ‖ **ὕπ-ανδρος** 2
subject to a husband, married. ἡ γυνή representing the
individual ; the husband, the Law. **ζῶντι** ptc, τῷ ζ. ἀνδρί
"her living husband", i.e. *her husband while he is alive.*
δέ-δεται pf pass. δέω *bind.* **ἀποθάνῃ** aor² subj. -θνήσκω.
κατ-ήργηται pf pass. -αργέω *annul* ; pf pass. (ἀπό τινος)
here and v.6, *be released.* ‖ **ἄρα οὖν** *so then.* **μοιχαλίς**[6] 3
-ίδος ἡ *adulteress.* **χρηματίσει** fut. -ίζω orig. "do business"
(χρῆμα) ; *be known as.* **γένηται** aor² subj. γίνομαι, γ. ἀνδρί
belong to a husband, become the wife of a man. **ἐλεύθερος**
free. **τοῦ μὴ εἶναι** consec. rather than final : *so that she*
is not. **γενομένην** aor² ptc, *by belonging.* ‖ **ἐ-θανατώθητε** 4
aor. pass. -τόω *put to death.* **τῷ νόμῳ** *to the Mosaic law,*
dat. of respect or of disadvantage, *you have died to the*
Law ; the idea that "the Law has become for you a dead
letter" would link v.4 w. the analogy of vv.1-3. **τοῦ**
σώματος τ. Χριστοῦ: through his crucifixion all who form

the body of Christ have died in him. **εἰς τό** w. acc.+inf. of purpose. **γενέσθαι** aor² inf. **ὑμᾶς** subject of inf. **ἐγερ-θέντι** *who rose*, aor. ptc pass. **ἐγείρω. καρπο-φορήσωμεν**

5 aor. subj. -**φορέω** *bear fruit*. || **ἦμεν** impf εἰμί. **ἐν τῇ σαρκί** *in a* (merely) *natural state*, subject to a nature corrupted and inclined towards evil. **πάθημα⁷** (< ἔπαθον aor² πάσχω) "what is suffered", *suffering*; pl. sts also *sinful passions*. **ἐν-ηργεῖτο** impf -εργέομαι *be at work*. **μέλος⁸** *member of* the body. **καρπο-φορῆσαι** aor. inf., subject παθήματα. ||

6 **νυνὶ δέ** *but now*. **κατ-ηργήθημεν** aor. pass. v.2. **ἀπο-θανόντες** aor² ptc v.2. **ἐν ᾧ** (sc. *to that*) *by which*. **κατ-ειχό-μεθα** impf -έχω *hold down, subjugate*. **δουλεύειν** inf. -εύω *serve* as a slave. **ἡμᾶς** subject of δουλεύειν. **καινότης⁶** -ότητος ἡ *newness*. **παλαιότης** -ότητος ἡ *age*; π. γράμματος *antiquated code*. **γράμμα⁷** "sth written", *letter*, here ref. the Law. ||

7 **ἐροῦμεν** fut. λέγω. **ἁμαρτία** pred. **μὴ γένοιτο** 6:2. **ἀλλά** *but, still*. **ἔγνων** aor² γινώσκω. **εἰ μή** *except*. **τε γάρ** *for indeed*. **ἐπι-θυμία** *desire*. **ᾔδειν** plpf (w. impf force) οἶδα, apodosis of an unreal condition (wt ἄν HGk), *I should not have known*. **εἰ μή...ἔ-λεγεν** *if...had not said*. **ἐπι-θυ-**

8 **μήσεις** fut. -θυμέω *desire*; categorical impv §280. || **ἀφ-ορμή** (< ἀπό + ὁρμή start, impulse) *starting point, oppor-tunity*. **λαβοῦσα** aor² ptc λαμβάνω. **κατ-ειργάσατο** aor. -εργάζομαι *achieve, produce, bring about*. **χωρίς** *without*.

9 **νεκρά** pred. || **ἔ-ζων** impf ζάω. **ποτέ** *once, formerly*. **ἐλ-θούσης** aor² ptc fem. ἔρχομαι, gen. abs. **ἀν-έ-ζησεν** *took*

10 *a new lease of life*, aor. ἀνα-ζάω *live anew*. || **ἀπ-έ-θανον** aor² v.2. **εὑρέθη** aor. pass. εὑρίσκω; pass. Fr. *se trouver, turn*

11 *out to be*. **εἰς** *for* (the purpose of). || **ἀφορμή, λαβοῦσα** v.8. **ἐξ-ηπάτησεν** aor. -απατάω *deceive*. **ἀπ-έ-κτεινεν** aor. ἀπο-

12 κτείνω *kill*. || **μέν** affirmative particle, here w. the force

13 of *indeed, in itself*. || **ἐ-γένετο** aor² γίνομαι. **μὴ γένοιτο** 6:2. **φανῇ** aor² subj. pass. φαίνω *show*; pass. here *reveal itself*. **ἁμαρτία** (2nd time) pred. *as sin*. **κατ-εργαζομένη** ptc v.8. **γένηται** v.3. **ὑπερ-βολή** (< ὑπερβάλλω exceed, surpass) *excess*, καθ' ὑπ. *to excess, exceedingly, in the ex-*

14 *treme*. **ἁμαρτωλός** *of sin, sinful*. || **πνευματικός** *spiritual*. **σαρκινός** *made of flesh, material*; here = σαρκικός *carnal, of flesh*; not nec. evil, but subject to the weaknesses of the flesh. **πε-πραμένος** pf ptc pass. πιπράσκω *sell*, metaphor from slavery. **ὑπό** w. acc. *under*, i.e. *in bondage to*. ||

γινώσκω here, *realize, understand.* πράσσω *practise, do.* 15
θέλω less deliberate and reasoned than βούλομαι: that
which I mean to do. μισέω *hate.* ‖ σύμ-φημι *agree.* ‖ νυνὶ 16,17
δέ v.6. οὐκ-έτι *no longer.* οἰκοῦσα ptc fem. οἰκέω *dwell.* ‖
τοῦτ' ἔστιν *i.e., that is (to say).* οὐκ οἰκεῖ...ἀγαθόν *nothing* 18
good dwells... σάρξ v.5. παρά-κειμαι (lie beside) *be at*
hand, lie ready. κατ-εργάζεσθαι inf. οὔ thus accented
and abs. *no, not so.* ‖ κακόν τό *evil.* πράσσω v.15. ‖ ἄρα 19,21
particle implying an inference, *so (it is)* (cf v.3). ὁ νόμος...ὅτι *this principle...that.* τῷ θέλοντι (ptc) ἐμοί *when*
I want. ‖ συν-ήδομαί τινι *rejoice/delight in* sth. κατά *with* 22
respect to. ἔσω *inside.* ὁ ἔσω ἄνθρωπος *my inner self,*
here = the mind (v.23). ‖ βλέπω here *I perceive.* μέλος 23
v.5. ἀντι-στρατευόμενον ptc -στρατεύομαι τινι *war against,*
be at war with. νοῦς νοός ὁ (dat. νοΐ) *mind.* αἰχμαλωτί-
ζοντα ptc -τίζω (< αἰχμή spear + ἁλίσκομαι be captured)
take prisoner ; αἰχ. με ἐν *making me captive to.* ὄντι ptc
εἰμί. ‖ ταλαί-πωρος *wretched, miserable,* τ. ἐγὼ ἄνθ. *wret-* 24
ched man that I am! ῥύσεται fut. ῥύομαι *deliver* from
death or disaster. τ. σῶμα τ. θαν. τούτου "the body of
this death", "Hebr." gen. = adj. *this mortal body* §41. ‖
χάρις w. dat. *thanks.* ἄρα οὖν v.3. αὐτός emphasiz- 25
ing ἐγώ, as if to say "It is I who...and no less I who..."
τῷ μὲν νοΐ...τῇ δὲ σαρκί *with my mind....while with my un-*
spiritual nature. δουλεύω v.6. ‖

    ἄρα 7:21. κατά-κριμα[7] *condemnation.* ἐν *sociative, in,* **8**
united with §117f. ‖ ἠλευθέρωσεν aor. ἐλευθερόω *free.* ‖ 2
ἀ-δύνατον *impossible* ; τὸ ἀ. τοῦ νόμου *what the Law was* 3
incapable of. ἐν ᾧ *causal, in that, because* §119. ἠσθένει
impf ἀ-σθενέω *be weak.* διά w. gen. here, *in consequence / as*
a result of. πέμψας aor. ptc πέμπω. ὁμοίωμα[7] *likeness* ;
not identity, because not prone to sin, not mere resem-
blance, as truly flesh. σάρξ ἁμαρτίας *sinful flesh* §40, cf 7:5.
περί ass. w. πέμψας: περὶ ἁμαρτίας in special sense of *to*
atone for sin. κατ-έ-κρινεν aor. κατα-κρίνω *condemn.* ἐν
τῇ σαρκί ass. w. κατέκρινεν. ‖ δικαίωμα[7] *decree, ordinance.* 4
πληρωθῇ aor. subj. pass. -ρόω. μή ref. to a matter of
fact (opp. class. usage) §441. περι-πατοῦσιν ptc dat. pl.
-πατέω *behave* 6:4. ‖ ὄντες ptc εἰμί: οἱ ὅ. *those who live.* 5
φρονέω *think, concentrate on, be devoted to* Mk 8:33. ‖
φρόνημα[7] *mentality, outlook* ; *aspiration.* θάνατος pred. 6
spells death. ‖ δι-ότι = ὅτι *for.* ἔχθρα *enmity.* ὑπο-τάσσεται 7

pass. -τάσσω *subject* ; pass. *be subjected/obedient.* οὐδὲ γὰρ
8 δύναται *nor can it be.* ‖ ὄντες v.5. ἀρέσαι aor. inf. ἀρέσκω
9 *be pleasing.* ‖ ἐν v.1. εἴ-περ *if indeed.* οἰκέω *dwell.* οὐκ
10 ἔστιν αὐτοῦ *is not his, does not belong to him.* ‖ τὸ μὲν
σῶμα beginning the apodosis. νεκρός here, *subject to
death,* virtually = θνητός v.11. διὰ ἁμαρτίαν *owing to sin.* ‖
11 ἐγείραντος aor. ptc ἐγείρω. ζωο-ποιήσει fut. -ποιέω *give
life.* θνητός (< θνήσκω be dying) *mortal.* ἐν-οικοῦντος
12 ptc -οικέω *dwell in.* ‖ ἄρα οὖν 7:3. ὀφειλέτης³ *debtor.* τοῦ
13 κατὰ σάρκα ζῆν (inf. ζάω) explaining ὀφ. τ. σαρκί. ‖ μέλλει
w. inf. *is destined to.* πρᾶξις⁴ (< πράσσω) *deed, act.* θανα-
14 τόω *put to death.* ζήσεσθε fut. ζάω. ‖ ἄγονται pass. ἄγω
lead ; pass. here *allow oneself to be led.* πνεῦμα being the
15 source of activity in the Christian life. ‖ ἐ-λάβετε aor²
λαμβάνω. δουλεία *servitude, slavery.* εἰς *resulting in* 6:16.
φόβος *fear.* υἱο-θεσία (< υἱός + τίθημι) *adoption* (both in
the sense of adopting and being adopted), πνεῦμα υἱοθ.
the gift which assures us of our status as his own sons by
adoption. ἐν ᾧ *whereby.* κράζω *call out, cry.* ὁ πατήρ
16 art. w. nom. for voc. §34. ‖ αὐτὸ τὸ πνεῦμα *the Spirit himself.* συμ-μαρτυρέω τινι *bear witness with* one. τέκνον not
fundamentally different from υἱός but w. a more intimate
17 sound as *child* compared w. "son". ‖ καί *also.* κληρο-
νόμος *heir* 4:13. συγ-κληρονόμος *fellow-heir.* εἴ-περ v.9.
συμ-πάσχω *suffer with, share* one's *suffering.* συν-δοξασθῶ-
μεν aor. subj. pass. -δοξάζω pass. *be glorified with, share in*
one's *glory.* ‖
18   λογίζομαι *reckon, consider, think.* ἄξιος *worthy,* οὐκ
ἄ. (sc. ἐστιν)...πρός *are not comparable to.* πάθημα⁷ *suffering.*
ὁ νῦν καιρός *the present time.* μέλλουσαν ptc fem. μέλλω.
ἀπο-καλυφθῆναι aor. inf. pass. -καλύπτω *unveil, reveal,* τὴν
μέλλουσαν...ἀποκ. *which is to be revealed.* εἰς *in its full*
19 sense of *unto* §106f. ‖ ἀπο-καρα-δοκία (the head (κάρα) out
(ἀπό) looking forward) *eager expectation.* κτίσις⁴ *creation.*
20 ἀπο-κάλυψις⁴ *revelation.* ἀπ-εκ-δέχομαι *await.* ‖ ματαιότης⁶
-ότητος ἡ *emptiness, futility.* ὑπ-ε-τάγη aor² pass. ὑπο-
τάσσω v.7. ἑκὼν ἑκοῦσα ἑκόν *willing(ly),* οὐχ ἑκών *not
willingly.* διά *because of.* ὑπο-τάξαντα aor. ptc (acc.)
-τάσσω either man by his sin or God punishing man's sin.
ἐλπίς⁶ -ίδος ἡ *hope,* ἐφ' ἐλπίδι (for ἐπ' ἐλπίδι) *in the hope.* ‖
21 ὅτι *that* ; [[unless the variant punctuation in v.20 is followed, omitting the comma after ὑποτάξαντα and adding

it after ἐλπίδι: in which case ὅτι would mean *because*.⟧
ἐλευθερωθήσεται fut. pass. -ρόω v.2. δουλεία v.15. φθορά
corruption, decay, (opp. immortality) δουλεία τ. φθ. because what is depraved knows no freedom and is often
bound to serve sin. ἐλευθερία *freedom* ; ἐλ. τῆς δόξης,
just as servitude is related to corruption, glory brings
with it liberty which is one of its elements ; alternatively
a "Hebr." gen., *glorious liberty* §40f. ‖ συ(ν)-στενάζω *groan* 22
together. συν-ωδίνω *be in travail together*. ἄχρι *till*. τὸ
νῦν noun, *now, the present*. ‖ οὐ μόνον δέ *and not only so*. 23
αὐτοί *ourselves*. ἀπ-αρχή *first-fruits* ; ἀπαρχὴ τ. πνεύματος
either the first of the Spirit's gifts or (epexeg. gen. §45)
the Spirit himself as the first-fruits of future glory. ἐν
ἑαυτοῖς for ἡμῖν αὐτοῖς §209. στενάζω *groan*. υἱο-θεσία
v.15. ἀπ-εκ-δεχόμενοι ptc v.19. ἀπο-λύτρωσις[4] (< ἀπο- +
λυτρόω ransom) *redemption*. ‖ ἐλπίς v.20, not dat. of 24
agent but of manner : *in hope* of a salvation yet to be
fully realized. ἐ-σώθημεν aor. pass. σώζω. βλεπομένη ptc
pass. βλέπω. ἐλπίζω *hope*. ‖ διά w. gen. of manner, *with*. 25
ὑπο-μονή *patience, steadfastness*. ἀπ-εκ-δέχομαι v.19. ‖ ὡσ- 26
αύτως *likewise*. συν-αντι-λαμβάνομαί τινι *help* one. ἀ-σθένεια *weakness*. τό making substantival the foll. words
which form the obj. of οἴδαμεν: "how we are to pray…
we know not". προσ-ευξώμεθα aor. subj. delib. -εύχομαι.
καθὸ δεῖ *as we ought*. αὐτὸ τὸ πνεῦμα v.16. ὑπερ-εν-τυγχάνω
intercede. στεναγμός *groan*. ἀ-λάλητος *un-utterable* or
word-less (Greg. Nyssa 4th cent.). ‖ ἐραυνῶν ptc -νάω 27
search, examine. φρόνημα v.6. ὅτι *that*, dependent on
οἶδεν. κατὰ θεόν *in God's way, according to God's will*.
ἐν-τυγχάνω ὑπέρ τινος *intercede for* one. ‖ ἀγαπῶσιν ptc dat. 28
pl. -πάω. συν-εργέω *co-operate in realizing* sth, *help to
bring about*. τοῖς ἀγαπῶσιν…εἰς ἀγαθόν *everything co-operates
with those who love God to achieve what is good* or *he* (God)
works in every way (πάντα) *with those…* ⟦var. after συνεργεῖ
add ὁ θεός *God works with those who love God…*⟧. Without
the var. the traditional (Vulgate) transln remains possible : *All things work together for good to those who love
God*. πρό-θεσις[4] (< προ-τίθημι set before) *purpose*, κατὰ π.
in accordance with his purpose. κλητός (< καλέω) *called*.
οὖσιν ptc dat. pl. εἰμί. ‖ ὅτι *for*. προ-έγνω aor[2] -γινώσκω 29
know beforehand, i.e. before they existed. προ-ώρισεν aor.
-ορίζω, of God, *pre-destine*, having in mind his πρόθεσις.

σύμ-μορφος *sharing the form*, pred. εἰκών⁶ εἰκόνος ἡ *image*, *likeness* ; "sharing the form of the likeness" i.e. *formed according to the likeness*. εἰς τό w. inf. final. πρωτό-τοκος

30 (< πρῶτος + τίκτω bear) *first-born.* ‖ ἐ-κάλεσεν aor. καλέω. ἐ-δικαίωσεν aor. -αιόω *justify*, 2:13. ἐ-δόξασεν aor. -άζω *bestow glory on* one. ‖

31,32   ἐροῦμεν fut. λέγω. ‖ γε particle emphasizing the foregoing word, ὅς γε *he who.* ἐ-φείσατο aor. φείδομαι τινος *spare* one (e.g. suffering). παρ-έ-δωκεν aor. παρα-δίδωμι. οὐχί = (an emphatic) οὐ. καί *also.* χαρίσεται fut. χαρί-

33 ζομαι *give* as a favour. ‖ ἐγ-καλέσει fut. -καλέω *accuse*, *bring a charge.* ἐκ-λεκτός *chosen.* δικαιῶν ptc v.30. ‖

34 κατα-κρινῶν fut. ptc -κρίνω *condemn* §282. ἀπο-θανών aor² ptc -θνήσκω. ἐγερθείς aor. ptc pass. ἐγείρω. δεξιός *right*, opp. left ; ἡ δεξιά (sc. χείρ) *right hand.* ἐντυγχάνω v.27. ‖

35 χωρίσει fut. -ίζω *separate.* θλῖψις⁴ *distress* ; *suffering.* στενο-χωρία *constraint*, *anguish.* διωγμός (< διώκω pursue) *persecution.* λιμός ὁ or ἡ *famine.* γυμνότης⁶ -ότητος ἡ *nakedness* ; met. *destitution.* κίνδυνος *danger.* μάχαιρα *sword*,

36 here perh. that of the executioner. ‖ γέ-γραπται *it stands written*, pf pass. γράφω. ὅτι = "... ἕνεκεν *for the sake of.* θανατούμεθα pass. v.13. ἡμέραν acc. of duration. ἐ-λο-γίσθημεν aor. pass. v.18, pass. *be regarded as.* πρόβατον a

37 *sheep.* σφαγή (< σφάζω slaughter, esp. animals for sacrifice) πρόβατα σφαγῆς *sheep for slaughter.* ‖ ἐν τούτοις πᾶσιν *in all these situations.* ὑπερ-νικάω *triumph gloriously.*

38 ἀγαπήσαντος aor. ptc v.28. ‖ πέ-πεισμαι *I am convinced*, pf pass. πείθω *persuade.* ἀρχή *ruler* ; pl. *angelic powers.* ἐν-εστῶτα *things present*, pf² (intr. w. pres. meaning) ptc ἐν-ίστημι in intr. tenses, *be present.* μέλλοντα *things to*

39 *come*, ptc μέλλω. ‖ ὕψωμα⁷ *height.* βάθος⁸ *depth.* κτίσις⁴ *creation* (act. or pass.), *creature.* ἕτερος for ἄλλος §153. δυνήσεται fut. δύναμαι. χωρίσαι aor. inf. v.35. ‖

9   ψεύδομαι *tell an untruth*, *lie.* συμ-μαρτυρούσης ptc -μαρτυρέω τινί *bear witness with* one, *join* one *in testifying.*

2 συν-είδησις⁴ *moral consciousness*, *conscience* 2:15. ‖ ὅτι *that.* λύπη *sorrow.* μοί ἐστιν *I have.* ἀ-διά-λειπτος *in-cessant*,

3 *continual.* ὀδύνη *pain*, *distress.* ‖ ηὐχόμην impf εὔχομαι = προσεύχομαι ; in HGk impf often takes the place of potential opt., *I could pray* Ac 25:22 ; Gal 4:20 §356. ἀνά-θεμα⁷ *something set aside*, *separated*, "*devoted*" *to the deity* ; *something accursed.* αὐτός nom. because same subject as

the finite vb governing εἶναι §393, αὐτὸς ἐγώ *I myself*.
συγ-γενής[9] *relative, kinsman*, here of all fellow countrymen.
κατὰ σάρκα *by blood relationship, by race*. ‖ οἵ-τινες = οἵ   4
or *seeing that they are* §215ff. υἱο-θεσία *adoption, sonship*
8:15. ἡ δόξα the *šekinah, the divine presence*. δια-θήκη
testament, will ; also for συν-θήκη *covenant*. νομο-θεσία
legislation, of the *Law* given at Sinai. λατρεία *service of
God, worship*. ἐπ-αγγελία *promise*. ‖ ὧν *of whom*, transl.   5
theirs (are). ἐξ ὧν transl. *from them*. ὁ Χριστός *the Messiah*. κατὰ σάρκα *physically* ; τὸ κ. σάρκα acc. of respect,
with regard to his human descent, cf 1:3. ὤν ptc εἰμί.
πάντων neut. pl. of πᾶς. After major punctuation ὁ ὤν
κτλ. will refer to God the Father : *May God who is over
all be blessed for ever ! Amen*. With a comma after σάρκα
ὁ ὤν would be in appos. to Christ, *the Messiah according
to the flesh who is over all, God blessed for ever, Amen* ;
others otherwise. ‖ οὐχ οἷον δὲ ὅτι "it is not so that",   6
emphatic, *not of course that*. ἐκ-πέ-πτωκεν pf ἐκ-πίπτω *fall
off* or *away, fail*. οἱ ἐξ *the descendants of*. ‖ οὐδ' ὅτι *nor   7
because*. σπέρμα[7] *seed*, hence *offspring, descendants*. ἐν
transl. *through*. κληθήσεται fut. pass. καλέω, in Hebr.
usage = *will be acknowledged as and will be*. σπέρμα[7]
(2nd time) subject of κληθήσεται. ‖ τοῦτ' ἔστιν *that is*,   8
this means. ἐπαγγελία v.4. λογίζεται *are regarded*, pass.
λογίζομαι (mid.) *reckon as*. εἰς for nom. pred. §32. ‖ οὗτος   9
pred. ref. what follows, instead of class. ὅδε §213. κατά
w. acc. ref. time, *at*. ἐλεύσομαι fut. ἔρχομαι. ἔσται fut.
εἰμί; "there will be to S.", *S. will have*... ‖ οὐ μόνον δέ   10
8:23. Ῥεβέκκα...ἔχουσα pendent nom. resumed by (ἐρ-
ρέθη) αὐτῇ v.12 §25. ἐξ ἑνός (masc.) *by one man*, meaning
that in this case the choice was between two full brothers.
κοίτη *marriage-bed*, κ. ἔχω *conceive*. Ἰσαάκ appos. ἑνός. ‖
μήπω *not yet*. γεννηθέντων aor. ptc pass. γεννάω *bear a*   11
child ; pass. *be born*, gen. abs. μηδέ *and not, nor*. πρα-
ξάντων aor. ptc πράσσω *do*. φαῦλος *worthless, bad*. Cstr is
ἵνα ἡ...πρόθεσις...μένη...ἐρρέθη (v.12). ἐκ-λογή *free choice*.
πρό-θεσις[4] *purpose* ; ἡ κατ' ἐκλογὴν πρ. "purpose according
to free choice", *freedom of choice in God's purpose* §130.
μένῃ subj. μένω, here, *be assured/preserved*. ‖ καλοῦντος ptc   12
καλέω: οὐκ...καλοῦντος *not on the ground of deeds but of
vocation*. ἐρρέθη aor. pass. λέγω: ἐρρ. αὐτῇ transl. *she
was told*. ὅτι = "... μείζων[6] -ζονος comp. of μέγας. δου-

λεύσει fut. -εύω τινί *serve* one. ἐλάσσων -σονος *younger*,
13 comp. of ὀλίγος. ‖ γέ-γραπται pf pass. γράφω. ἠγάπησα
aor. ἀγαπάω; aors. possibly representing Sem. pfs of vbs
den. a state and so may be transl. by Eng. pres. §256
Lat. ed[5]. ἐ-μίσησα aor. μισέω *hate*; in Sem. idiom an
opposition may sound absolute whereas it serves only to
14 heighten the comparison, Lk 14:26 §445. ‖ ἐροῦμεν fut.
λέγω. μή = Lat. *num*, interr. expecting the answer
"No". ἀ-δικία *in-justice*. γένοιτο aor[2] opt. γίνομαι: μὴ γ.
15 *far be it! God forbid!* ‖ ἐλεήσω fut. ἐλεέω τινά *show mercy
to* one. ὃν ἄν *whomsoever, anyone*. οἰκτιρήσω fut. -τίρω
16 *have pity on*. οἰκτίρω (after ἄν) subj. ‖ ἄρα οὖν *so then*.
θέλοντος ptc. τρέχοντος ptc τρέχω *run*; οὐ τ. θέλοντος...
τρέχοντος (understand as subject ἡ κατ᾿ ἐκλογὴν πρόθεσις
v.11) *is not a matter of man's will or effort*. ἐλεῶντος ptc
17 ἐλεάω late form of ἐλεέω. ‖ ἡ γραφή here means God in
scripture. ὅτι v.12. εἰς αὐτὸ τοῦτο *for this very purpose*.
ἐξήγειρα aor. -εγείρω *raise up*, ἐξή. σε *I brought you into
being*. ὅπως w. subj. final, *in order that*. ἐν-δείξωμαι aor.
subj. mid. -δείκνυμι *show*. δι-αγγελῇ aor[2] subj. pass.
18 -αγγέλλω *proclaim* (throughout). ‖ ὅν...ὅν... *one he..., another he...* σκληρύνω *harden*. ‖
19 ἐρεῖς v.14. μέμφομαι *blame*. βούλημα[7] *will*. ἀνθ-
έστηκεν pf (intr. w. pres. meaning) ἀνθ-ίστημι, in intr.
20 tenses *resist*. ‖ ὦ emphatic, *O (mere) man!* §35. μεν-
οῦν-γε *rather, more truly*. ἀντ-απο-κρινόμενος ptc perh. voc.
-κρίνομαι: σὺ τίς εἶ ὁ ἀντ.; *who are you to answer back?*
μή v.14. πλάσμα[7] (< πλάσσω) *creature*. πλάσαντι aor. ptc
πλάσσω (vb stem πλαθ-) *mould, form*; hence *create*. τί;
21 *why?* ἐ-ποίησας aor. ποιέω. ‖ κεραμεύς[5] *potter*. πηλός
clay. φύραμα[7] (< φυράω mix) *mass, lump*. ποιῆσαι aor.
inf. ποιέω. τιμή *honour*. σκεῦος[8] *receptacle, crock*. ἀ-
τιμία *dis-honour*; ὃ μὲν εἰς τιμὴν σκεῦος, ὃ δὲ εἰς ἀτ. *one a
22 special pot, another an ordinary one* (cf JB). ‖ εἰ δὲ θέλων
ὁ θεός *but what if God, although willing...* ptc concessive.
ἐν-δείξασθαι aor. inf. v.17. ὀργή *wrath*. γνωρίσαι aor.
inf. -ίζω *make known*. δυνατός *powerful*, neut. as noun,
power. ἤνεγκεν aor[2] φέρω *bear, carry*, here in sense of
bear with, endure. μακροθυμία (long-temper) *patience*.
σκεύη (acc. pl.) ὀργῆς *objects of his wrath*. κατ-ηρτισμένα
framed, pf ptc pass -αρτίζω (< ἄρτιος complete) *put to-
23 gether, prepare*. ἀπ-ώλεια *destruction*. ‖ γνωρίσῃ aor. subj.

πλοῦτος *wealth*. ἔλεος⁸ *mercy*, σκεύη ἐλ. *objects of his mercy*. προ-ητοίμασεν aor. -ετοιμάζω (< προ- + ἔτοιμος *ready*) *prepare beforehand*. ‖ καί foll. a rel. wt special 24 significance. ἐ-κάλεσεν aor. καλέω: οὕς...ἐκ. ἡμᾶς *we are those whom he thus called*. ἐξ *from among*. ‖ καλέσω fut. 25 κ. ...λαόν μου *I will call "my people"* one *not my people*. ἠγαπημένην pf ptc pass. ἀγαπάω: οὐκ ἠγ. like οὐ λαός μου serves as a proper name : *one not-my-people, one un-loved*, hence οὐ, not μή, w. ptc Hos 2:25. ‖ ἔσται v.9. οὗ *where*. 26 ἐρρέθη v.12. ὑμεῖς pred. κληθήσονται v.7. ζῶντος ptc gen. ζάω. ‖ κράζω *shout, cry*. ὑπέρ for περί §96. ᾗ subj. 27 εἰμί. ἀριθμός *number*. ἄμμος ἡ *sand*. ὑπό-λειμμα⁷ (< ὑπο-λείπω *leave behind) remnant*. σωθήσεται fut. pass. σῴζω. ‖ συν-τελῶν ptc -τελέω *accomplish, bring to pass*. συν-τέμνων 28 ptc -τέμνω *cut short* ; or *limit*. Meaning uncertain : perh. *the Lord will act, bringing to pass his word on the earth, "shortening the time"*, or *"restricting its application"* (sc. to the remnant). ‖ προ-είρηκεν pf -λέγω *foretell*. εἰ μή *if... not, unless*. ἐγ-κατ-έλιπεν aor² -κατα-λείπω *abandon, leave*, an unfulfilled condition w. ἄν in the apodosis §313. σπέρμα 29 v.7. ἐ-γενήθημεν *we should have become as S.*, aor. pass. γίνομαι. ὡμοιώθημεν lit. "we should have been made like", i.e. *we should be like G.*, aor. pass. ὁμοιόω *make like*. ‖

ἐροῦμεν v.14. ὅτι *that*. ἔθνη wt art. emphasizing 30 quality §171. διώκοντα ptc neut. pl. διώκω *pursue, go in search of*. κατ-έ-λαβεν aor² κατα-λαμβάνω *overtake, attain*. δικαιοσύνην δὲ τὴν ἐκ πίστεως *moreover the righteousness of faith* §467. ‖ εἰς νόμον *at/to the law*('s requirements). 31 ἔ-φθασεν aor. φθάνω class. *precede* ; HGk *arrive, attain*. ‖ ὅτι *because* (sc. they sought to attain it). ὡς ἐξ ἔργων 32 *as if (it could be attained) by works*. προσ-έ-κοψαν aor. -κόπτω *strike against* ; intr. *stumble over*. πρός-κομμα⁷ a *cause of stumbling, obstacle*, λίθος προσκόμματος "stone of stumbling", *occasion of falling*. ‖ γέ-γραπται v.13. πέτρα 33 *rock*. σκάνδαλον *trap* ; hence *stumbling block, temptation to sin*. καί *but* §455β. ἐπ' αὐτῷ ref. λίθος which stands for Christ. κατ-αισχυνθήσεται fut. pass. -αισχύνω *put to shame*, in Hebr. also *disappoint, let one down*. ‖ εὐ-δοκία **10** *goodwill* ; hence *wish, desire*. δέησις⁴ *petition*. σωτηρία *salvation*, εἰς σ. (sc. ἐστίν) *is for their salvation*. ‖ μαρτυρέω 2 τινί *testify in one's favour*. ζῆλος (< ζέω *boil) zeal, fer-*

vour. **ἐπί-γνωσις**[4] *knowledge*, οὐ κατ' ἐπ. *not directed by*
3 *knowledge*. ‖ **ἀ-γνοοῦντες** ptc ἀ-γνοέω τι *be ignorant, fail
to recognize* sth. **τοῦ θεοῦ δικαιοσύνη** 1:17. **ζητοῦντες**
ptc -τέω. **στῆσαι** aor. inf. ἵστημι *establish*. **ὑπ-ε-τάγησαν**
aor[2] pass. ὑπο-τάσσω *subject*; pass. sts refl. *subject oneself*
4 *or intr. submit, be obedient*. ‖ **τέλος**[8] *end* as both "termina-
tion" and "end in view, goal"; pred. **εἰς** *for*, i.e. *to
bring*. **πιστεύοντι** ptc -εύω. ‖
5   **τὴν δικ.** acc. of respect, γράφει τήν... *writes of...* **ἐκ**
having its origin in, springing from. **ποιήσας** aor. ptc
6 ποιέω. **ζήσεται** fut. ζάω. **ἐν** instr. *by* §119. ‖ **εἴπῃς** aor[2]
subj. λέγω. **ἀνα-βήσεται** fut. -βαίνω. **τοῦτ' ἔστιν** 9:8.
7 **κατ-αγαγεῖν** aor[2] inf. -άγω *bring down*. ‖ **κατα-βήσεται** fut.
-βαίνω. **ἄβυσσος** ἡ *abyss* (not in text of Deut), ref. Sheol.
8 **ἀν-αγαγεῖν** aor[2] inf. -άγω *bring up*. ‖ **ἐγγύς** w. gen. *near*.
9 **ῥῆμα**[7] *word*. **κηρύσσω** *preach*. ‖ **ὁμο-λογήσῃς** aor. subj.
-λογέω *confess, acknowledge*. **κύριον Ἰησοῦν** *Jesus is Lord*.
πιστεύσῃς aor. subj. -εύω. **ἤγειρεν** aor. ἐγείρω. **σωθήσῃ**
10 fut. pass. σῴζω. ‖ **καρδίᾳ** instr. *with (the) heart*. **πιστεύεται**
pass. "it is believed", i.e. *one believes, men believe*. **εἰς**
leading to. **ὁμο-λογεῖται** pass. *acknowledgement is made*.
11,12 **σωτηρία** v.1. ‖ For v.11 see 9:33. ‖ **δια-στολή** *distinction*.
Ἕλλην[6] -νος *a Greek*; *a gentile*. **ὁ...αὐτὸς κύριος** *the same
Lord*, (sc. as pred. κύριός ἐστιν). **πλουτῶν** *rich*, ptc -τέω
be rich. **ἐπι-καλουμένους** ptc mid. -καλέω *name*; mid.
13 *call upon, appeal to*. ‖ **ὃς ἂν** w. subj. *who-ever* ref. fut.
14 **ἐπι-καλέσηται** aor. subj. **σωθήσεται** fut. pass. v.9. ‖ **εἰς ὃν**
in whom, i.e. upon *one* they did not believe *in*. **ἐπικα-
λέσωνται, πιστεύσωσιν, ἀκούσωσιν, κηρύξωσιν** aor. subj.
delib. **οὗ** *of whom*, i.e. in *one* they have not heard *of*.
ἐ-πίστευσαν aor. -εύω. **ἤκουσαν** aor. ἀκούω. **χωρίς** w. gen.
15 *without*. **κηρύσσοντος** ptc gen. *preacher*, ptc v.8. ‖ **ἀπο-
σταλῶσιν** aor[2] subj. pass. -στέλλω. **γέ-γραπται** pf pass.
γράφω. **ὡς** *how!* **ὡραῖος** *beautiful*. **πόδες** pl. of πούς.
εὐ-αγγελιζομένων ptc -αγγελίζομαι *bring good news of*. ‖
16 **ὑπ-ήκουσαν** aor. -ακούω τινί *obey*, here *respond to*. **πιστεύω**
17 τινί *believe* sth (*to be true*). **ἀκοή** *report, message*. ‖ **ἄρα**
so (it is), you see then. **ἐξ** (*arises*) *from*. **ῥῆμα** v.8. **Χριστοῦ**
18 obj. gen., word *about Christ*. ‖ **μή** interr. expecting the
answer "No". **μεν-οῦν-γε** after a neg. sentence, *certainly
(they did)*. **φθόγγος** *sound*; *voice*. **πέρας** -ατος τό *limit*;
end. **οἰκουμένη** sc. γῆ (ptc pass. οἰκέω *dwell*) *inhabited*

world. ‖ ἔ-γνω aor² γινώσκω. **πρῶτος** adj. w. advl force, 19
first (of all). **παρα-ζηλώσω** fut. -ζηλόω τινὰ ἐπί τι *make*
one *jealous* of someone. **ἀ-σύνετος** *without understanding,*
un-discerning. **παρ-οργιῶ** fut. (class.) -οργίζω τινά *excite*
one's *anger.* ‖ **ἀπο-τολμάω** (ἀπο- perfective + τολμάω dare) 20
show great (here, *greater*) *daring.* **εὑρέθην** aor. pass.
εὑρίσκω. **ἐν** (if it is to be read) *among.* **ζητοῦσιν** v.3.
ἐμ-φανής⁹ *visible,* ἐμφ. γίνομαί τινι *become visible/show one-*
self to. **ἐ-γενόμην** aor² γίνομαι. **ἐπ-ερωτῶσιν** ptc dat. pl.
-ερωτάω *ask* a question, in OT in special sense : *inquire*
after God. ‖ **ἡμέραν** acc. of extent. **ἐξ-ε-πέτασα** aor. ἐκ- 21
πετάννυμι *stretch out.* **ἀ-πειθοῦντα** ptc -πειθέω *be disobe-*
dient. **ἀντι-λέγοντα** ptc -λέγω *contra-dict, be in opposition,*
resist. ‖

    μή interr. expecting the answer "No". **ἀπ-ώσατο** aor. 11
mid. -ωθέω *push away,* mid. from oneself, *repulse, reject.*
μὴ γένοιτο 9:14. **καὶ γὰρ ἐγώ** *for I also,* ἐγώ emphatic.
σπέρμα⁷ *seed,* ἐκ σ. a *descendant.* **φυλή** *tribe.* ‖ **προ-έγνω** 2
aor² -γινώσκω *know beforehand* 8:29. **ἐν 'Ηλίᾳ** *in the pas-*
sage about Elijah, cf Mk 12:26. **ἐν-τυγχάνω** τινί *chance*
upon one ; also *call upon,* ἐντ. τινὶ κατά τινος *plead with*
one *against another.* ‖ **ἀπ-έ-κτειναν** aor. ἀπο-κτείνω. **θυ-**
σιαστήριον (< θυσιάζω from θύω sacrifice) *altar.* **κατ-έ-**
σκαψαν aor. κατα-σκάπτω (σκάπτω dig) *destroy by digging*
up. **κἀγώ** = καὶ ἐγώ. **ὑπ-ε-λείφθην** aor. pass. ὑπο-λείπω
leave over/remaining. **ζητέω** τὴν **ψυχήν** *seek one's life.* ‖
χρηματισμός *oracle,* God's *reply.* **κατ-έ-λιπον** 1st sg aor² 4
κατα-λείπω *leave behind.* **ἐμ-αυτῷ** *for myself/me.* **ἐπτ-ακισ-**
χίλιοι 7 times 1000 = 7000. **οἵ-τινες** *such as* §215. **ἔ-**
καμψαν aor. κάμπτω *bend.* **γόνυ** γόνατος τό *knee.* **Βάαλ**
occ. fem., through custom of reading the execrable name
as *bošeth,* LXX αἰσχύνη (shame) both of which are fem. ‖
λεῖμμα⁷ (< λείπω) *remainder, remnant.* **ἐκ-λογή** (< ἐκ-λέ- 5
γομαι choose) *free choice,* κατ' ἐκλ. χάριτος "according to a
free choice of grace", i.e. *freely chosen by grace.* **γέγονεν**
pf² γίνομαι (subject λεῖμμα). ‖ **χάριτι** *by grace* 3:24. **οὐκ-** 6
έτι *no longer.* **ἐξ** *by, on the ground of* 3:20. **ἐπεί** *since*
(sc. *in that case*). **γίνεται** *for* ἐστί (influenced perh. by
preceding γέγονεν) *grace is no longer, ceases to be grace.* ‖
ἐπι-ζητέω *seek, pursue.* **ἐπ-έ-τυχεν** aor² ἐπι-τυγχάνω *attain,* 7
reach. **ἐκ-λογή** here in pass. sense like ἐκ-λεκτός (God's)
chosen. **οἱ λοιποί** *the rest, the others.* **ἐ-πωρώθησαν** aor.

pass. -ρόω *harden*, esp. in pass. *become insensible* to God's
8 revelation and promptings. ‖ γέ-γραπται pf pass. γράφω.
ἔ-δωκεν aor. δίδωμι. κατά-νυξις⁴ *torpor*. τοῦ w. inf. final
or consec. §384. ὦτα pl. of οὖς ὠτός τό *ear*. σήμερον *pre-*
9 *sent (day), today*. ‖ γενηθήτω aor. impv dep. γίνομαι §229 ;
γ. εἴς τι for pred. nom., a Sem. (LXX quotation). τράπεζα
table. παγίς⁶ -ίδος ἡ *trap, snare*. θήρα (< θήρ wild animal) *net, trap*. σκάνδαλον *stumbling-block*. ἀντ-από-δομα⁷
10 (a gift in return) *requital ; quid pro quo*. ‖ σκοτισθήτωσαν
aor. impv pass. -τίζω (< σκότος darkness) *darken*. νῶτος
the *back* of man or animal. σύγ-καμψον aor. impv -κάμπτω
bend ; make one bend/bow. διὰ παντός *always, for ever*. ‖
11   μή v.l. ἔ-πταισαν aor. πταίω *stumble*. ἵνα *that*, final
or consec. §353. πέσωσιν aor² subj. πίπτω ; *if* ἵνα is consec.
their fall would be decisive (and the aor. effective §252).
μὴ γένοιτο 9:14. παρά-πτωμα⁷ *false step, lapse* ; in moral
sense, *trespass*, dat. of instrument. σωτηρία *salvation*,
understand "comes". παρα-ζηλῶσαι aor. inf. -ζηλόω *make*
12 *one jealous*. ‖ πλοῦτος *riches, wealth*. ἥττημα⁷ (< ἧσσα defeat) *defeat*, i.e. *failure*. πόσος ; *how great?* πόσῳ μᾶλλον
(by) how much more. πλήρωμα⁷ *fulness, full number*, i.e.
13 when all come to believe. ‖ ἐφ' (= ἐπί) ὅσον *in so far as*.
14 διακονία *ministry*. δοξάζω *honour*. ‖ εἰ indir. interr. w.
the force of *to see if* or *in the hope that perhaps* §403. πῶς
somehow. παρα-ζηλώσω aor. subj. or fut. v.11. μοῦ τὴν
σάρκα *my fellow-countrymen*, cf συγγενὴς κατὰ σ. 9:3. σώσω
15 aor. subj. σῴζω. τινὰς ἐξ αὐτῶν §80. ‖ ἀπο-βολή (< ἀπο-βάλλω
throw away) *rejection*. κατ-αλλαγή (< καταλλάσσω reconcile) *reconciliation*, pred., supply "means", "spells". πρόσ-
λημψις⁴ (< προσλαμβάνω accept a person) *acceptance*, τίς
ἡ πρ. εἰ μή *what does their acceptance mean if not...?* ‖
16 ἀπ-αρχή *first-fruit*. ἅγιος *consecrated*. καί *also*. φύραμα⁷
17 *mass, lump*. ῥίζα *root*. κλάδος *branch*. ‖ ἐξ-ε-κλάσθησαν
aor. pass. ἐκ-κλάω *break off*. ἀγρι-έλαιος (< ἄγριος wild +
ἐλαία) *wild olive*. ὤν ptc εἰμί. ἐν-ε-κεντρίσθης aor. pass.
ἐγ-κεντρίζω *spur on* ; *graft on* (to). συγ-κοινωνός τινος
sharer in. πιότης⁶ -τητος ἡ *fatness*, here of *sap* ⟦var. τῆς
ῥίζης τῆς πιότητος⟧. ἐλαία *olive(-tree)*. ἐ-γένου aor² γίνο-
18 μαι. ‖ κατα-καυχῶ (ά + ου) impv 2nd sg -καυχάομαί τινος
(κατά *against* + καυχάομαι boast) *exult over* sth. κατα-
καυχᾶσαι 2nd sg for -καυχᾷ §488. Before οὐ σύ understand
e.g. "bear in mind that", "do not forget that." βαστάζω

carry. ‖ ἐρεῖς fut. λέγω. ἐγ-κεντρισθῶ aor. subj. pass. ‖ 19
καλῶς exclamatory, *that is true, very well.* ἀ-πιστία *un-* 20
belief, dat. of cause, *...cut off for their unbelief* §58. ἔστηκας
pf (intr. w. pres. meaning) ἵστημι, *you stand/remain* because of faith. ὑψηλός *high,* neut. pl. here, *thoughts of*
pride, cf Lk 16:15. φρόνει impv -νέω *preoccupy oneself*
with. φοβοῦ impv φοβέομαι. ‖ φύσις⁴ *nature,* κατὰ φύσιν 21
natural. ἐ-φείσατο aor. φείδομαί τινος *spare* one. μή πως
before οὐδέ (if it is to be read) *lest in some way or other,*
here understanding some prior expression of fear or
caution, transl. μ. οὐδέ freely, *is it likely that...?* φείσεται
fut. ‖ ἴδε aor² impv ὁράω. χρηστότης⁶ -ότητος ἡ ⌈goodness, 22
kindness. ἀπο-τομία *severity.* ἐπί *towards, to.* μέν...δέ
2:7. πεσόντας aor² ptc πίπτω. ἐπι-μένῃς subj. -μένω *stay*
on; *persevere.* ἐπεί sts *otherwise,* (i.e. if you do not).
ἐκ-κοπήσῃ fut² pass. (-κοπήσομαι) -κόπτω *cut out or off.* ‖
κἀκεῖνοι = καὶ ἐκεῖνοι. ἀ-πιστία v.20. ἐγ-κεντρισθήσονται 23
fut. pass. v.17. δυνατός *able.* ἐγ-κεντρίσαι aor. inf. ‖
κατὰ φύσιν v.21. ἐξ-ε-κόπης aor² pass. ἐκ-κόπτω. ἀγρι- 24
έλαιος v.17. παρὰ φύσιν *against nature.* ἐν-ε-κεντρίσθης
v.17. καλλι-έλαιος *cultivated olive.* πόσῳ μᾶλλον v.12. ‖

    ἀ-γνοεῖν inf. ἀ-γνοέω *not to know* ; οὐ...ἀγνοεῖν *I should* 25
like you to understand. μυστήριον (< μυέω initiate) *secret*
rites ; in NT *secret* of God's plan. τοῦτο ref. forward to
ὅτι κτλ. ἦτε subj. εἰμί. παρ' ἑαυτοῖς 3rd pers. pl. for
2nd, *in yourselves,* i.e. *in your own estimation.* φρόνιμος
wise. πώρωσις⁴ process of *hardening/becoming insensible.*
μέρος⁸ *part,* ἀπὸ μ. *in part, partly.* γέ-γονεν v.5, *has hap-*
pened. ἄχρι w. gen. *until,* ἄχρι(ς) οὗ (= ἄχρι τοῦ χρόνου ᾧ)
w. aor. subj. ref. fut. πλήρωμα⁷ *full number.* εἰσ-έλθῃ
aor² subj. -έρχομαι. ‖ οὕτως (*only*) *so.* πᾶς Ἰσραήλ al- 26
though wt art. *all* (= the whole of) Israel §190. σωθήσεται fut. pass. σώζω. γέ-γραπται v.8. ἥξει *will come,*
fut. ἥκω pres. w. pf sense, *has come.* ῥυόμενος ptc ῥύομαι
deliver, ὁ ῥ. *the deliverer.* ἀπο-στρέψει fut. -στρέφω *turn*
away (trans.). ἀ-σέβεια *ungodliness,* pl. considering acts
of impiety rather than a state of mind. ‖ αὕτη (sc. ἐστίν). 27
αὐτοῖς dat. of advantage. δια-θήκη *testament, will* ; also
for συν-θήκη *covenant.* ἀφ-έλωμαι aor² subj. mid. -αιρέω,
act. and mid. *take away.* ‖ κατὰ μὲν τὸ εὐαγγέλιον *from* 28
the aspect of (*spreading*) *the gospel.* ἐχθρός *enemy.* δι' ὑμᾶς
on your account §112. ἐκ-λογή v.5. ἀγαπητός *beloved.*

29 **πατέρες** here, the *patriarchs*. ‖ **ἀ-μετα-μέλητος** (< μετα-μέλομαι change one's mind, repent) *irrevocable*. **χάρισμα**[7] *act of grace, free gift*. **κλῆσις**[4] (< καλέω) *call, vocation*. ‖

30 **ὥσ-περ...οὕτως** (v.31) *in the same way as...so...* **ποτέ** *at some time* ; *once* (indef.). **ἠπειθήσατε** aor. **ἀ-πειθέω** τινί *be disobedient* to one. **ἠλεήθητε** aor. pass. **ἐλεέω** τινά *show mercy* to one ; pass. *find mercy*. **τούτων** ref. Israel. **ἀ-πείθεια** *dis-obedience* ; dat. of cause, *through/because of*

31 *their disobedience* §58. ‖ **ὑμέτερος** *your*, obj., the mercy *shown to you*. **ἔλεος**[8] *mercy*, dat. parallel to foregoing **ἀπειθείᾳ**. **νῦν** (2nd time) has considerable MS support but is difficult to explain [[var. om.]]. **ἐλεηθῶσιν** aor.

32 subj. pass. ‖ **συν-έ-κλεισεν** aor. **συγ-κλείω** *shut up*, σ. εἰς **ἀπειθείαν** *consign to disobedience*. **ἐλεήσῃ** aor. subj. ‖

33 **βάθος**[8] *depth*. **πλοῦτος** v.12. **σοφία** *wisdom*. **γνῶσις**[4] *knowledge*. **ἀν-εξ-εραύνητος** (< ἐραυναω examine) *inscrutable*. **κρίμα**[7] *judgement, decision*. **ἀν-εξ-ιχνίαστος** (< ἴχνος[8] *foot-*

34 *print*) *untraceable*. ‖ **ἔ-γνω** aor[2] γινώσκω. **νοῦς** νοός ὁ *mind*. **σύμ-βουλος** *adviser, counsellor*. **ἐ-γένετο** aor[2] γίνο-

35 μαι. ‖ **προ-έ-δωκεν** aor. προ-δίδωμι, here *give beforehand*. **καί** *so that* §455γ. **ἀντ-απο-δοθήσεται** fut. pass. -δίδωμι *repay* ; ...καὶ ἀντα. αὐτῷ ; "who has first given him (any-

36 thing) so as to have it repaid to him?" ‖ **ἐκ** indicating source. **διά** indicating agent §113. **εἰς** indicating goal. ‖

12   **διά** of manner, *by* §114. **οἰκτιρμός** *compassion*, pl. Hebr. **παρα-στῆσαι** aor. inf. παρ-ίστημι *present* ; *offer*. **θυσία** *sacrifice*. **ζῶσαν** ptc fem. ζάω. **εὐ-άρεστος** (< εὖ well + ἀρέσκω please) *pleasing, acceptable*. **λογικός** *of the reason* (opp. mechanical) ; *spiritual*. **λατρεία** *service*, λ. **λογικήν** *worship of the mind and spirit* opp. external rites ;

2 appos. **θυσίαν**. ‖ **συ-σχηματίζεσθε** impv συ(ν)-σχηματίζομαι pass. or mid. *be conformed to, model oneself on*. ὁ **αἰὼν οὗτος** *the present age*, this world opp. the world to come. **μετα-μορφοῦσθε** impv pass. -μορφόω, pass. *be transformed* (μορφή, as opp. σχῆμα, being the outward expression of what springs from within) ; pres. continuous. **ἀνα-καί-νωσις**[4] *renewal*. **νοῦς** νοός ὁ *mind*. **εἰς τό** w. acc.+inf. = **ἵνα** (*in order*) *that*. **δοκιμάζειν** inf. -άζω *test in order to prove* ; *determine* by searching and testing. **τὸ ἀγαθόν**

3 *what is good*. **τὸ τέλειον** *what is perfect*. ‖ **δοθείσης** aor. ptc pass. fem. δίδωμι. **ὄντι** ptc εἰμί: παντὶ τῷ ὄντι ἐν ὑμῖν *to each one among you* §188. **ὑπερ-φρονεῖν** inf. -φρονέω

esteem oneself too highly, be superior (= lofty) ; introducing a play of words on φρονεῖν. **παρ' ὅ** *beyond, more than*. **φρονεῖν** inf. *-νέω think* ; (2nd time) perh. *give one's mind to.* **εἰς τό** here consec. rather than final, " but so to think *as* to be reasonable" ; alternatively, "but to make it your concern to be reasonable". **σω-φρονεῖν** inf. *-νέω be of sound* (σῶς) *mind* ; *be sober-minded/reasonable/ sensible*. **ἐ-μέρισεν** aor. *-ίζω divide into parts* (μέρος[8]) ; *ap-portion*. **μέτρον** *measure*. ‖ **καθ-άπερ** = καθώς. **ἑνί** dat.   4 of εἷς. **μέλος**[8] *member*. **ὁ αὐτός** *the same*. **πρᾶξις**[4] *function, activity*. ‖ **τὸ καθ' εἷς** *singly, individually*, treated as   5 a stereotyped phrase and so indeclinable §10. ‖ **ἔχοντες**   6 ptc **ἔχω**. **χάρισμα**[7] a *gift* of God's grace, for the benefit of the community. **δοθεῖσαν** v.3. **διά-φορος** *different, differing*, ref. χαρίσματα. **εἴτε...εἴτε** *whether...or.* **προφητεία** *prophetic gift, prophecy*, the gift of speaking as divinely inspired. Supply "let it be done" ; likewise in the case of all seven gifts a vb must be supplied. **ἀνα-λογία** *pro-portion*, κατὰ τὴν ἀν. τ. πίστεως *in proportion to our faith*. ‖ **διακονία** *service*, (1st time perh. *office of a deacon*). **ὁ δι-**   7 **δάσκων** *the teacher*, here *the one with the gift of teaching*. Here and in following supply "let him use it" in... **δι-δασκαλία** *teaching*. ‖ **παρα-καλῶν** ptc *-καλέω*. **παρά-κλησις**[4]   8 *exhortation* ; *encouragement*. **μετα-διδούς** ptc *-δίδωμι give a share*. **ἐν** of manner, *with* §117. **ἁπλότης**[6] *-τητος ἡ simplicity*, i.e. single-minded generosity. **προ-ϊστάμενος** ptc *-ίστημι* (stand in front) *take the lead, rule*. **σπουδή** *diligence, earnestness*. **ἐλεῶν** ptc ἐλεέω *show mercy*. **ἱλα-ρότης**[6] *-τητος ἡ gladness*. ‖

     ἀγάπη sc. ἔστω *let your love be*. **ἀν-υπό-κριτος** *without*   9 *pretence, sincere*. All the foll. ptcs, adjs, and infs have impvl force §373. **ἀπο-στυγοῦντες** ptc *-στυγέω ab-hor.* **κολλώμενοι** ptc pass. κολλάω *stick*, pass. intr. *adhere, cling.* ‖ **φιλ-αδελφία** *brotherly love, love of the brethren.* **φιλό-στοργος** *warm in affection, tenderly affectionate* ; supply "show yourselves"... **τιμή** *honour, respect*, dat. of respect. **προ-ηγούμενοι** ptc *-ηγέομαι giving a lead to* each   10 other in (mutual) respect or (in sense of ἡγέομαι) *consider-ing* each other *more highly* (than oneself) — a meaning unknown elsewhere. ‖ **σπουδή** v.8. **ὀκνηρός** *timid* ; *inert*.   11 **ζέοντες** ptc ζέω *boil* ; met. *be fervent*. **δουλεύοντες** ptc *-εύω τινί serve* one. ‖ **ἐλπίς**[6] *-ίδος ἡ hope*, dat. of cause, *in*   12

hope §58. **θλῖψις**[4] *distress, trouble.* **ὑπο-μένοντες** ptc -μένω *bear up.* **προσ-ευχή** *prayer.* **προσ-καρτεροῦντες** ptc -καρτερέω (< προς- + καρτερός staunch) *remain constant, con-*
13 *tinue faithfully.* ‖ **χρεία** *need.* **ἅγιος** ὁ as one dedicated to God, a baptized believer. **κοινωνοῦντες** ptc -νέω *con-tribute.* **φιλο-ξενία** (ξένος strange(r)) *hospitality.* **διώκον-τες** ptc -κω, in v.14 *persecute* ; here *pursue, i.e. aim at,*
14 *seek to practise.* ‖ **εὐ-λογεῖτε** impv -λογέω *bless.* **κατ-**
15 **αρᾶσθε** impv -αράομαι *curse.* ‖ **χαίρειν,** impvl inf. **χαι-ρόντων** ptc, *those who are joyful.* **κλαίειν, κλαιόντων** inf.,
16 ptc, **κλαίω** *weep.* ‖ **τὸ αὐτό** *the same (way).* **φρονοῦντες** ptc, v.3, *thinking along the same lines, having the same outlook,* colloq. "speaking the same language". **ὑψηλός** *high,* hence *exalted, proud.* **ταπεινός** *humble.* **συν-απ-αγό-μενοι** ptc pass. -άγω *lead away together* ; pass. *be led...,* but also *accommodate oneself to, associate with.* **γίνεσθε** impv γίνομαι, supplying impv for εἰμί. **φρόνιμοι παρ'**
17 **ἑαυτοῖς** 11:25. ‖ **κακός** *evil,* τὸ κ. prob. *injury.* **ἀντί** w. gen. *(in return) for.* **ἀπο-διδόντες** ptc -δίδωμι *render, repay.* **προ-νοούμενοι** ptc mid. -νοέω act. and mid. *think before-hand, have a regard for.* **καλά** neut. pl. *what is honour-*
18 *able.* **ἐν-ώπιον** *in the eyes of.* ‖ **δυνατόν** *possible.* **τὸ ἐξ ὑμῶν** *for your part.* **εἰρηνεύοντες** ptc -εύω *live at peace.* ‖
19 **ἐκ-δικοῦντες** ptc -δικέω *vindicate.* **ἀγαπητός** *beloved.* **δότε** aor[2] impv δίδωμι: δ. τόπον *leave a place for, allow to take its course.* **ἡ ὀργή** the just *wrath* of God. **γέ-γραπται** pf pass. γράφω. **ἐμοί** *for me, i.e. mine,* sc. ἐστί. **ἐκ-δίκησις**[4] *vindication, justice.* **ἐγώ** emphatic. **ἀντ-απο-δώσω** fut.
20 -δίδωμι *repay.* ‖ **πεινάω** *be hungry.* **ἐχθρός** *enemy.* **ψώμιζε** impv -ίζω *feed* (cf ψωμίον Jn 13:26). **διψάω** *be thirsty.* **πότιζε** impv -ίζω *give* one (something) *to drink.* **ποιῶν** ptc, *by doing.* **ἄνθραξ**[6] -ακος ὁ *coal.* **πυρός** "Hebr." gen. (commonly taking the place of an adj.), ἄνθρακας π. *live coals* §40 ; a proverbial expression. **σωρεύσεις** fut. -εύω
21 (< σωρός a pile) *heap.* ‖ **νικῶ** (ά + ου) impv pass. νικάω *conquer,* μὴ ν. *be not / do not let yourselves be conquered* ; for the form cf κατακαυχῶ 11:18. **νίκα** impv. **ἐν** instr. §119. τὸ ἀγαθόν *good,* art. generic. τὸ κακόν v.17. ‖

13 **ψυχή** in Hebr. sense of *man.* **ἐξουσίαι** *authorities.* **ὑπερ-εχούσαις** ptc fem. pl. -έχω *be above/superior,* hence *be in authority,* ἐξουσίαι ὑπ. *supreme authorities.* **ὑπο-τασσέσθω** impv pass. -τάσσω *subordinate,* pass. *be sub-*

ject, submit. **εἰ μή** *except.* **οὖσαι** ptc fem. pl. **εἰμί**: αἱ δὲ οὖσαι *the existing* (authorities), *those in existence* cf Ac 5:17. **τεταγμέναι εἰσίν** *are appointed/put there* by God, periphrastic pf pass. **τάσσω** *order, assign.* ‖ **ἀντι-τασσό-** 2 **μενος** ptc **-τάσσομαι** (range oneself against) *oppose.* **δια-ταγή** (< **δια-τάσσω** command) *order, direction.* **ἀνϑ-έστηκεν** pf-pres. (intr.) **-ίστημί τινι** *withstand, resist.* **ἀνϑ-εστη-κότες** pf-pres. ptc. **κρίμα**[7] *judgement, condemnation.* **λήμ-ψονται** fut. **λαμβάνω.** ‖ **ἄρχων**[6] ἄρχοντος ὁ *ruler.* τῷ ἀγαϑῷ 3 **ἔργῳ** collective, *good conduct/behaviour.* **φόβος** in act. sense, a *terror.* **κακός** *bad.* **φοβεῖσϑαι** inf. φοβέομαι. τὸ ἀγαϑόν *what is good.* **ποίει** impv ποιέω; pres. den. a general rule. **ἔξεις** fut. ἔχω. **ἔπαινος** *praise, commendation.* ‖ **διάκονος** *servant,* here *an instrument.* **εἰς** final, *for,* σοὶ εἰς τὸ ἀγαϑόν *for your good.* **ποιῇς** subj. ποιέω. **φοβοῦ** impv. **εἰκῇ** *in vain, for nothing.* **μάχαιρα** *sword.* **φορέω** *wear.* **ἔκ-δικος** *executor of justice.* **εἰς ὀργήν** (12:19) lit. "for wrath", i.e. *to visit with divine wrath* (in the form of punishment). **πράσσοντι** ptc πράσσω *do,* ὁ τὸ κακὸν πράσ-σων *wrongdoer.* ‖ **διό** *therefore.* **ἀνάγκη** *need, necessity* ; 5 sc. ἐστί *it is necessary.* **ὑπο-τάσσεσϑαι** inf. pass. v.l. **συν-είδησις**[4] *conscience.* ‖ **φόρος** *tribute, tax.* **τελέ ω** φόρους 6 *pay* taxes. **λειτουργός** *minister* whether in civil or divine service. **αὐτὸ τοῦτο** *this very thing* ; ass. w. **προσκαρτε-ροῦντες** ptc **-καρτερέω** *attend constantly to, occupy oneself* with. ‖ **ἀπό-δοτε** aor[2] impv **-δίδωμι** *pay* what is due. **πᾶσιν** 7 *to each one.* **ὀφειλή** *a due, debt.* τῷ τ. **φόρον** τ. φ. *to whom the tax* (is due), *the tax.* **τέλος** *customs due, toll.* **φόβος** *fear,* here chiefly in the form of *respect.* **τιμή** *honour.* ‖

ὀφείλετε impv **-λω** *owe.* **εἰ μή** v.l. **ἀγαπᾶν** inf. **-πάω** ; 8 *in mutual love there can be no balancing of accounts.* **πε-πλήρωκεν** pf **-ρόω.** ‖ **τό** indicating a quotation = "...*, or* 9 it may signify *the* (*well-known*) commandments... **μοι-χεύσεις** fut. **-εύω** *commit adultery* ; this and the three futs. following having the force of categorical impvs, *you shall* (not), *you are* (not) *to* §280. **φονεύσεις** fut **-εύω** *murder.* **κλέψεις** fut. κλέπτω *steal.* **ἐπι-ϑυμήσεις** fut. **-ϑυμέω** *covet.* **ἕτερος** for ἄλλος §153. **ἀνα-κεφαλαιοῦται** pass. **-κεφαλαιόω** *sum up.* **πλησίον** adv. *near,* ὁ π. *neighbour.* **σε-αυτόν** *your-self.* ‖ **κακὸν οὐκ ἐργάζεται** (2:10) *does no* 10 *harm.* **πλήρωμα**[7] *fulfilment.* ‖

11 καὶ τοῦτο transl. *and especially*. εἰδότες ptc pf-pres. οἶδα. ἤδη *already*. ὑμᾶς subject of ἐγερθῆναι. ὕπνος *sleep*. ἐγερθῆναι aor. inf. pass. ἐγείρω, pass. intr. *awake*. ἐγγύτερον comp. of ἐγγύς *near*. σωτηρία *salvation*. ἐ-πιστεύ-

12 σαμεν aor. -εύω, inceptive, *we first believed* §250. ‖ προ-έ-κοψεν *is far advanced*, aor. προ-κόπτω *advance, make progress*. ἡ ἡμέρα the *day* of the Lord. ἤγγικεν *is at hand*, pf ἐγγίζω (< ἐγγύς) *approach, draw near*. ἀπο-θώμεθα aor² subj. -τίθεμαι (mid.) *put off* or *away, rid one-self of*, subj. hort. (as also foll. subjs). σκότος⁸ *darkness*. ἐν-δυσώμεθα aor. subj. -δύομαι (mid.) *clothe oneself with*,

13 *put on*. ὅπλον *weapon*, pl. *armour*. ‖ εὐ-σχημόνως *properly*. περι-πατήσωμεν aor. subj. hort. -πατέω *let us walk*, in ethical sense of "conduct ourselves, live". κῶμος *orgy*, dat. of manner §60. μέθη *drunkenness*. κοίτη *bed* ; euphemism for sexual intercourse. ἀ-σέλγεια *debauchery*. ἔρις⁶ ἔριδος ἡ *rivalry*. ζῆλος *zeal* ; in bad sense, *jealousy*. ‖

14 ἐν-δύσασθε aor. impv. τῆς σαρκός position of emphasis opp. new life in Christ. πρό-νοια *forethought*. ποιεῖσθε impv mid. ποιέω: ποιοῦμαι πρόνοιαν = προνοέω ; when π. thus combines w. a noun to give the same meaning as the cognate vb, mid. is customary in class. usage 1:9 §227. εἰς either final, *to (satisfy) its appetites*, or consec., *so as to (create) desires*. ἐπι-θυμία *a desire*. ‖

14 ἀσθενοῦντα ptc -νέω *be weak*. πίστει dat. of respect §53. προσ-λαμβάνεσθε impv -λαμβάνομαι *receive, welcome*. διά-κρισις⁴ *distinguishing*, hence *deciding*. δια-λογισμός

2 *argument, dispute*. ‖ φαγεῖν aor² inf. ἐσθίω: πιστεύει φ. πάντα has the assurance to eat everything, *believes in eating*

3 *everything*. λάχανον *vegetable*. ‖ ἐξ-ουθενείτω impv 3rd sg -ουθενέω *think nothing of, despise*. κρινέτω impv κρίνω *judge, sit in judgement upon*. προσ-ε-λάβετο aor² v.l. ‖

4 σὺ τίς εἶ ὁ κ.; *who are you to judge?* ἀλλότριος *another's*. οἰκέτης³ *servant*. στήκω (late form developed from ἕστηκα pf (intr. w. pres. meaning) ἵστημι *stand* §493. σταθήσεται fut. pass. ἵστημι class. *he will be made to stand/upheld*, but in HGk often w. middle force, *he will stand* §231. δυνατεῖ 3rd sg -τέω *have the power* to. στῆσαι aor. inf.

5 ἵστημι. ‖ ὃς μέν...ὃς δέ *the one...the other*. κρίνω sts *heed, regard*. ἡμέραν παρ᾽ ἡμέραν *one day in comparison with another* cf 12:3 §145. νοΐ dat. of νοῦς νοός ὁ *mind*. πληρο-φορείσθω impv 3rd sg mid. -φορέω *assure fully, convince*,

mid. *feel quite sure, be absolutely convinced.* || φρονῶν ptc 6
-νέω *consider* (and so *give attention to, observe*). κυρίῳ
to/in honour of the Lord ; in each case ass. dat. w. the
finite vb and not w. ptc. εὐχαριστέω *give thanks.* ||
ἑαυτῷ ζῇ *lives / is accountable to himself alone.* || ζῶμεν (1st 7,8
time) after ἐάν, subj. (form same as indic.). ἀπο-θνήσκωμεν
subj. τοῦ κυρίου ἐσμέν *we belong to the Lord.* || τοῦτο 9
elucidated by ἵνα... ἀπ-έ-θανεν aor² ἀπο-θνήσκω. ἔ-ζησεν
aor. ζάω, aor. inceptive, *came to life.* κυριεύσῃ aor. subj.
-εύω w. gen. (foll. vb of pre-eminence), aor. inceptive,
establish his lordship. || τί; = διὰ τί; *why?* ἢ καί *or* 10
again you (other). ἐξ-ουθενέω v.3. παρα-στησόμεθα fut.
παρ-ίσταμαι (mid.) *come and stand before.* βῆμα⁷ *judgement
seat.* || γέ-γραπται pf pass. γράφω. ζῶ ἐγώ formula for an 11
oath, hence ὅτι, *As I live...* κάμψει fut. bow. γόνυ γόνατος τό *knee,* πᾶν γ. wt art. *every knee* §188. γλῶσσα *tongue.*
ἐξ-ομο-λογήσεται fut. -λογέομαι *confess publicly, acknow-
ledge* ; addressed to God, *praise, give thanks.* || ἄρα οὖν 12
so then. λόγος *reckoning, account.* δώσει fut. δίδωμι. ||

μηκ-έτι *no longer.* κρίνωμεν subj. hort. κρίνω. τοῦτο 13
ref. what follows (= τόδε) §213. κρίνατε aor. impv v.5.
τι-θέναι inf. τίθημι. πρόσ-κομμα⁷ *obstacle.* σκάνδαλον *temp-
tation.* || πέπεισμαι *I am convinced,* pf pass. πείθω *per-* 14
suade. κοινός *common* to all ; *ordinary* ; *profane* ; ceremonially *unclean* ; 3 times pred. (sc. ἐστί). δι' ἑαυτοῦ *in
itself.* εἰ μή for ἀλλά §469f. λογιζομένῳ ptc -ζομαι *reckon,
consider.* || βρῶμα⁷ (< βιβρώσκω eat) *food.* λυπεῖται pass. 15
λυπέω *grieve.* οὐκέτι = μηκέτι v.13. περι-πατέω 13:13.
ἀπ-όλλυε impv -όλλυμι: μή w. pres. impv connoting *cease
to destroy...* ἀπ-έ-θανεν v.9. || βλασ-φημείσθω impv pass. 16
3rd sg -φημέω *defame, slander* ; *let not your good* (behaviour, right and justifiable in your estimation) *be miscon-
strued so as to give you a bad name,* i.e. *do not invite mis-
understanding by doing just what to you seems good.* ||
βρῶσις⁴ *eating.* πόσις⁴ *drinking.* χαρά *joy.* || ἐν τούτῳ *on* 17,18
this principle. δουλεύων ptc -εύω *serve,* ὁ...δ. *he who
serves.* εὐ-άρεστος *pleasing.* δόκιμος (< δέχομαι receive) *ac-
ceptable, approved.* || ἄρα οὖν v.12. διώκωμεν *let us pursue/* 19
aim at, hort. subj. διώκω. τὰ τῆς εἰρήνης...εἰς ἀλλήλους
what makes for each other's peace and edification. || ἔνεκεν 20
w. gen. *for the sake of.* βρῶμα v.15. κατά-λυε impv -λύω
overthrow, destroy. καθαρός *clean, pure.* κακόν *evil,* sc.

ἐστὶν βρῶμα. **διά** w. gen. ref. manner of action §114. **πρόσ-κομμα** v.13, διὰ πρ. lit. "with scandal/offence": objective, ref. the strong brother creating an occasion of sin

21 to the weak. **ἐσθίοντι** ptc -ίω. ‖ **φαγεῖν** v.2. **κρέας** -έως τό *meat*, pl. κρέα. **πιεῖν** aor² inf. πίνω. **οἶνος** *wine*. **μηδέ** nor. **ἐν ᾧ** (sc. to do anything) *at which* ; ἐν of occasion and cause §119. **προσ-κόπτω** *stumble*, i.e. *is led to sin* ⟦[var. add ἢ σκανδαλίζεται ἢ ἀσθενεῖ *or is upset or is weakened* (σκανδαλίζεται pass. -ίζω cause to stumble or sin)]⟧. ‖

22 **κατὰ σεαυτόν** advl, to be referred to ἔχεις §130. **ἔχε** impv ἔχω, pres. continuous. **σύ...θεοῦ** *as for you* (whether strong or weak) *keep to yourself before God* (i.e. *between yourself and God) the faith which is yours*. **μακάριος** *happy, blessed*, sc. ἐστίν. **κρίνων ἑαυτόν** in weaker sense, *reproach*

23 *himself*. **δοκιμάζω** *approve*. ‖ **δια-κρινόμενος** *beginning to doubt*, ptc -κρίνομαι *doubt, be in two minds*. **φάγῃ** aor² subj. ἐσθίω. **κατα-κέ-κριται** *will stand condemned*, proleptic pf pass. -κρίνω *condemn* §257. **ὅτι οὐκ ἐκ πίστεως** *because (his action) does not spring from faith* (= assurance). ‖

15 **ὀφείλω** *owe* ; w. inf. *ought*. **δυνατός** ⌈*strong, capable* (because of a firm and enlightened faith). **ἀ-σθένημα**⁷ *weakness*. **ἀ-δύνατος** *weak, in-capable* (because lacking in steady conviction). **βαστάζειν** inf. -άζω *carry*. **ἑαυτοῖς** for ἡμῖν αὐτοῖς §209. **ἀρέσκειν** inf. -σκω τινί *please one*. ‖

2 **πλησίον** adv. *near*, ὁ πλ. *neighbour*. **ἀρεσκέτω** impv 3rd sg. **εἰς** *with a view to, for*. **τὸ ἀγαθόν** *his good*. **οἰκο-δομή**

3 *edification, building up* in the faith. ‖ **ἤρεσεν** aor. ἀρέσκω, constative aor. §253. **γέ-γραπται** pf pass. γράφω. **ὀνει-δισμός** *reproach*. **ὀνειδιζόντων** ptc -δίζω *reproach, insult*.

4 **ἐπ-έ-πεσαν** aor² ἐπι-πίπτω *fall on*, (-αν for -ον §489). ‖ **προ-ε-γράφη** aor² pass. προ-γράφω *write beforehand*. **ἡμέτερος** *our*. **διδασκαλία** *instruction*. **ἐ-γράφη** aor² pass. **ὑπο-μονή** *endurance, constancy*. **παρά-κλησις**⁴ *exhortation* ; *encouragement* ; *consolation*. **τῶν γραφῶν** gen. of origin, *derived from*

5 *scripture*. **ἐλπίς** -ίδος ἡ *hope*. **ἔχωμεν** subj. ἔχω. ‖ **δῴη** aor² opt. 3rd sg δίδωμι, opt. expressing a wish §355. **τὸ αὐτὸ φρονεῖν** *to think in the same way / along the same lines* 12:16. **κατὰ Χριστόν** *according to the mind of Christ*. ‖

6 **ὁμο-θυμαδόν** *with one mind/intent*. **δοξάζητε** subj. -άζω *glorify*, w. God as obj., *praise*. ‖

δι-ό *therefore*. προσλαμβάνεσθε impv -λαμβάνομαι *re-* 7
ceive, welcome. προσ-ε-λάβετο aor². εἰς v.2. ‖ λέγω γάρ 8
I mean to say (cf Jo 6:71). διάκονος *servant.* γε-γενῆσθαι
pf inf. γίνομαι, pf connoting lasting effect. περιτομή
circumcision, den. the Jews. ὑπέρ *on behalf of, for.* ἀλήθεια *truthfulness, fidelity.* εἰς τὸ βεβαιῶσαι...τὰ δὲ ἔθνη...
δοξάσαι...*that he might realize / give substance to...and that
the gentiles might praise...* βεβαιῶσαι aor. inf. -αιόω *confirm.* ἐπ-αγγελία *promise.* τῶν πατέρων obj. gen. *(made)
to the Fathers.* ‖ ἔλεος⁸ *mercy.* γέγραπται v.3. ἐξομο- 9
λογήσομαι 14:11. ψαλῶ fut. ψάλλω τινί *sing praises* to
one. ‖ εὐ-φράνθητε aor. impv pass. -φραίνω *make someone* 10
glad ; pass. intr. *be glad/joyful.* ‖ αἰνεῖτε impv αἰνόω 11
praise. ἐπ-αινεσάτωσαν aor. impv 3rd pl. -αινέω = simplex. ‖ ἔσται *there shall be,* fut. εἰμί. ῥίζα *root.* καί 12
epexeg. *that is to say, namely.* ἀν-ιστάμενος ptc -ίσταμαι
arise (here = *appear*) pres. ptc for fut. §283. ἄρχειν τινός
rule. ἐλπιοῦσιν fut. -ίζω *hope,* ἐλπ. ἐπί τινι *hope in* one. ‖
ἐλπίς v.4. πληρώσαι aor. opt. -ρόω. χαρά *joy,* gen. after 13
a vb of filling, *with joy.* ἐν τῷ πιστεύειν here not temporal
but causal, *by reason of believing, in your life of faith,*
connoting the source. εἰς τό final v.8. περισσεύειν inf.
-εύω *abound, overflow.* ἐν δυνάμει *by the power* §119. ‖
πέ-πεισμαι *I am convinced,* pf pass. πείθω *persuade.* 14
αὐτὸς ἐγώ *I myself, for my part, personally.* περὶ ὑμῶν
concerning you. αὐτοί *you yourselves.* μεστός *full.* ἀγαθωσύνη *goodness.* πε-πληρωμένοι pf ptc pass. γνῶσις⁴ *knowledge.* δυνάμενοι (well) *able,* ptc δύναμαι. νου-θετεῖν inf.
-θετέω (< νοῦς *mind* + τίθημι) *admonish, advise.* ‖ τολμη- 15
ρότερον *rather boldly,* comp. of τολμηρῶς *boldly.* ἔ-γραψα
aor. γράφω. μέρος⁸ *part,* ἀπὸ μ. *in part,* here *on occasion.*
ἐπ-ανα-μιμνήσκων ptc -μιμνήσκω *remind.* δοθεῖσαν aor. ptc
pass. fem. δίδωμι. ‖ δοθεῖσαν μοι...εἰς τὸ εἶναί με *given to* 16
me...to be. λειτουργός *minister,* cf v.27 (λειτουργῆσαι).
ἱερουργοῦντα ptc -γέω τι *sacrifice* ; *serve sth in the capacity
of a priest,* λειτουργόν...ἱερ. τὸ εὐαγγέλιον *a minister...a
priest serving the gospel.* γένηται aor² subj. γίνομαι. προσ-
φορά (< προσ-φέρω *offer*) *offering, sacrifice.* εὐ-πρόσ-δεκτος
(εὖ *well* + προσδέχομαι *receive*) *well received, acceptable.*
ἡγιασμένη *consecrated,* pf ptc pass. ἁγιάζω *make holy,
consecrate.* ‖ καύχησις⁴ *matter for boasting.* τὰ πρὸς τ. θεόν 17
advl acc. *in my work for God.* ‖ τολμήσω fut. -μάω *dare,* 18

venture. τι after a neg. *any.* λαλεῖν inf. λαλέω τι *speak of* sth. κατ-ειργάσατο aor. -εργάζομαι *accomplish* ; τι...ῶν οὐ κ. Χρ. "any of the things which Christ did not...", i.e. *anything other than what Christ accomplished.* εἰς v.2.

19 ὑπ-ακοή *obedience.* ‖ τέρας -ατος τό a *wonder, prodigy.* κύκλος a *circle,* κύκλῳ an adv. *round about, making a circuit* Mk 6:6. πε-πληρωκέναι pf inf. -ρόω sts *complete,* πεπλ. τὸ εὐαγγέλιον ...*have completed* (*the task of preaching*)

20 *the gospel.* ‖ φιλο-τιμούμενον ptc -τιμέομαι *make a point of, be particular to.* εὐ-αγγελίζεσθαι inf. -ίζομαι *preach the gospel.* ὠνομάσθη aor. pass. ὀνομάζω *name* ; οὐχ ὅπου ὠνομ. Χριστός lit. "not where Christ was named", meaning *where the name of Christ was not known.* ἀλλότριος *another's.* θεμέλιος (< τίθημι) *foundation.* οἰκο-

21 δομῶ subj. -δομέω *build.* ‖ γέγραπται v.3. ἀν-ηγγέλη aor[2] pass. -αγγέλλω *announce* ; *make known,* οἷς...αὐτοῦ *those to whom nothing was told about him.* ὄψονται fut. ὁράω. ἀκηκόασιν pf ἀκούω, sc. *of him.* συν-ήσουσιν fut. -ίημι *understand.* ‖

22   δι-ό *for this reason.* ἐν-ε-κοπτόμην impf pass. ἐγ-κόπτω *block, hinder.* τὰ πολλά advl acc. *so many times.* ἐλθεῖν aor[2] inf. ἔρχομαι: τοῦ ἐλ. *from coming,* gen. of sepa-

23 ration §386. ‖ νυνί = νῦν. μηκ-έτι *no longer.* τόπος *place, room, opportunity* (cf Ac 25:16) i.e. *for apostolic work.* ἔχων (both times) causal, *as/seeing that I have,* whereas Fr. (like Gk) *ayant...depuis...* : Eng. idiom requires...*have had...for many years.* κλῖμα[7] *region.* ἐπι-ποθία a *desire, longing.* τοῦ ἐλθεῖν *to come* (= "of coming", contrast v.22 where τοῦ ἐλ. follows a vb of hindering). ἔτος[8] *year,* ἀπὸ πολλῶν ἐ. *for many years,* ἀπό instead of acc. of dura-

24 tion §70c. ‖ ὡς ἄν w. subj. *when.* πορεύωμαι subj. pres. durative. ἐλπίζω v.12. δια-πορευόμενος ptc -πορεύομαι *pass through.* θεάσασθαι aor. inf. θεάομαι *see* (= come to see). προ-πεμφθῆναι aor. inf. pass. -πέμπω *send on* one's *way* w. funds and supplies. ἐκεῖ *there* (= thither, class. ἐκεῖσε). ὑμῶν obj. of ἐμπλησθῶ. πρῶτον adv. *first* (as in Eng. for comp. §153). ἀπὸ μέρους v.15, *for a while.* ἐμ-πλησθῶ aor. subj. (after ἐάν) pass. -πί(μ)πλημι *satisfy* ; pass. w.

25 gen. of person, *enjoy* one's *company.* ‖ διακονῶν ptc -νέω *serve* ; *care for, support* (cf Lk 8:3). ἅγιος ὁ *saint,* title

26 of all believers 12:13. ‖ εὐ-δόκησαν aor. (freq. wt aug.) -δοκέω *consider good,* hence w. inf. *resolve/decide to.* κοι-

νωνία *communion, fellowship* ; in tangible form, *contribution.* ποιήσασθαι aor. inf. mid. ποιέω (κοινωνίαν π. =
κοινωνέω and so mid. 1:9, 13:14 §227). πτωχός *poor.*
ἀγίων partitive, *among the* ἀ. ‖ καί *and indeed.* ὀφειλέτης³ 27
debtor. πνευματικός *spiritual.* ἐ-κοινώνησαν aor. -νωνέω *have
a share.* ὀφείλω v.1, here, *owe it to them to.* σαρκικός
fleshly, material. λειτουργῆσαι aor. inf. -γέω τινί (< λαός
public + ἔργον) *render public service* whether civic or
religious, more generally *minister to, serve.* ‖ ἐπι-τελέσας 28
aor. ptc -τελέω *complete, accomplish.* σφραγισάμενος aor.
ptc mid. -ίζω *seal,* in transferred sense perh. *having
personally ensured to them.* καρπός *benefit, proceeds.*
ἀπ-ελεύσομαι fut. -έρχομαι. δι᾽ ὑμῶν *by way of you.* ‖ ἐρχό- 29
μενος *in coming.* ἐν of concomitant circumstances (sociative), *with* §117. πλήρωμα⁷ *fullness.* εὐ-λογία *blessing* [[var.
add τοῦ εὐαγγελίου]]. ἐλεύσομαι fut. ἔρχομαι. ‖ ἀγάπη τοῦ 30
πνεύματος *love inspired by the Spirit.* συν-αγωνίσασθαι
aor. inf. -αγωνίζομαί τινι *strive in company with* one.
προσ-ευχή *prayer.* ὑπὲρ ἐμοῦ *on my behalf, for me.* ‖ ῥυσθῶ 31
aor. subj. pass. ῥύομαι *deliver.* ἀ-πειθούντων *unbelieving,*
ptc ἀ-πειθέω *be disobedient,* in early Christian literature
sts implying disobedience to God's revelation in Christ.
διακονία *aid* (cf v.25). εὐ-πρόσ-δεκτος v.16. ἅγιος v.25.
γένηται v.16. ‖ χαρά v.13. ἐλθών aor² ptc ἔρχομαι. συν- 32
ανα-παύσωμαι aor. subj. -παύομαι *refresh* oneself *together
with.* ‖ A prayer : *May the God...be...* 33

συν-ίστημι (cause to stand together) *introduce, recom-* **16**
mend. ἀδελφή *sister.* οὖσαν ptc εἰμί. διάκονος here fem.
deaconess. ‖ προσ-δέξησθε aor. subj. -δέχομαι *receive, wel-* 2
come. ἀξίως (adj. ἄξιος *worthy*) *fittingly,* w. gen. *in a
way worthy of.* ἀγίων meaning "of Christians" 15:25.
παρα-στῆτε aor² (intr.) subj. παρ-ίστημι *present, offer,* in
intr. tenses *stand by to help.* ὃ ἄν indef. *whatever,* ass. w.
πρᾶγμα. χρήζῃ subj. χρήζω τινός *stand in need of, need*
sth. πρᾶγμα⁷ *matter, thing.* καὶ γάρ *for indeed.* προ-
στάτις⁶ -ιδος ἡ *patroness, benefactress,* fem. of -στάτης³
patron, protector. ἐ-γενήθη aor. dep. γίνομαι; for ἐγένετο
§229. ‖ ἀσπάσασθε aor. impv ἀσπάζομαι *greet.* συν-εργός 3
fellow-worker. ‖ οἵτινες *who are such that* ¦or simply = οἵ 4
§215 f. ψυχή in Hebr. sense of *life.* τράχηλος *neck.* ὑπ-
έ-θηκαν aor. ὑπο-τίθημι *sub-ject to danger, risk.* εὐχαριστέω
offer thanks, express gratitude. ‖ ‖ κατ᾽ οἶκον *in the house.* 5

6   ἀγαπητός *beloved.* ἀπ-αρχή *first-fruit.* ‖ ἥ-τις *the one who*
§215. πολλά acc. pl. as adv. intensifying the vb, here
hard. ἐ-κοπίασεν aor. -ιάω *labour.* εἰς sts used as a
7   dat. of advantage, *for* §51. ‖ συγγενής⁹ *akin* ; hence, as
noun, *relation* ; *fellow-countryman* (9:3). συν-αιχμάλωτος
fellow-prisoner, cf 7:23. ἐπί-σημος *notable, outstanding.* ἀπόστολος also *missionary, evangelist.* πρὸ ἐμοῦ *before me* if
γέ-γοναν (pf² γίνομαι) transl. by Eng. past, *were,* but perh.
8,9   better, *have been longer than* I. ‖ ἀγαπητός v.5. ‖ συνεργός
10   v.3. ‖ δόκιμος *proven, tried.* οἱ ἐκ τῶν τινος *who are of*
11,12 *the household of...* ‖ συγγενής v.7. ὄντας ptc εἰμί. ‖ κο-
13   πιώσας ptc fem. v.6. πολλά v.6. ‖ ἐκ-λεκτός *chosen* ; here
15-17 *eminent.* ‖ ἀδελφή v.1. ‖ ἐν *with.* φίλημα⁷ *kiss.* ‖ σκοπεῖν
inf. *watch, look out for.* διχο-στασία *dissension.* σκάνδαλον
obstacle, difficulty. παρά w. acc. *along,* here w. idea of
by-passing, hence *against,* cf π. φύσιν 11:24. διδαχή *teaching.* ἐ-μάθετε aor² μανθάνω *learn.* ποιοῦντας ptc ποιέω
make, create. ἐκ-κλίνετε impv -κλίνω (bend away) *hold
18   aloof.* ‖ τοι-οῦτοι (who are) *such people.* δουλεύω τινί
serve one. κοιλία a *hollow* ; *belly.* χρηστο-λογία *fair speech,
plausibility.* εὐ-λογία *fine words, flattery.* ἐξ-απατάω *be-
19   guile.* ἄ-κακος *guile-less, simple.* ‖ γάρ confirms the previous γάρ: steer clear of them *for* they are deceivers, *for*
(= and) you are faithful. ὑπ-ακοή *obedience,* i.e. to the
gospel, cf on ἀπειθέω 15:31. ἀφ-ίκετο aor² -ικνέομαι *reach* ;
transl. (*the report of*) *your obedience has come to everyone's
ears.* ἐφ᾽ ὑμῖν...χαίρω *I rejoice over you.* σοφός *wise.* εἰς
in the sphere of, with regard to. ἀ-κέραιος *un-mixed* ;
20   *guile-less, innocent.* κακόν τό *evil.* ‖ συν-τρίψει fut. -τρίβω
(rub together) ; *shatter, crush.* Σατανᾶς -νᾶ Hebr. *enemy,
Satan.* τάχος⁸ *speed,* ἐν τ. *with speed, quickly, soon* ⟦var.
21   om. ἡ χάρις to end of v. and reinsert as v.24⟧. ‖ συνεργός
22   v.3. συγγενής v.7. ‖ γράψας aor. ptc γράφω: *I, T.,* who
23   *have committed to writing.* ἐπι-στολή *epistle, letter.* ‖ ξένος
stranger ; hence *guest* but also *host,* cf Fr. *hôte.* ὅλης τ.
ἐκκλησίας *all the church* (here), cf v.5. ‖ οἰκο-νόμος *steward* ;
οἰκ. τῆς πόλεως *city treasurer.* ὁ ἀδελφός *our brother.* ‖
25   δυναμένῳ ptc δύναμαι. στηρίξαι aor. inf. -ίζω *strengthen, uphold.* κήρυγμα⁷ (< κηρύσσω preach) *preaching,
proclamation.* Ἰησοῦ *about Jesus,* obj. gen. ἀπο-κάλυψις⁴
revelation. μυστήριον *mystery,* truth which may only be
apprehended through revelation. χρόνος *time,* χρ. αἰω-

νίοις *from eternity* ; in HGk dat. sts connotes duration like acc. Lk 8:29 §54. σε-σιγημένου *preserved in silence, kept secret,* pf ptc pass. σιγάω *be silent.* ‖ φανερωθέντος 26 aor. ptc pass. -ρόω *reveal.* γραφή a *writing, scripture.* προ-φητικός *prophetic,* ref. OT as a whole. ἐπι-ταγή (< ἐπι-τάσσω order) *command,* κατ' ἐπιταγήν τινος *by the command of.* εἰς (1st time) *for* the furtherance of, *to promote.* ὑπακοή v.19, ὑπ. πίστεως 1:5. γνωρισθέντος aor. ptc. pass. -ίζω *make known.* ‖ σοφός v.19. Without ᾧ vv.25-27 27 would form one long sentence, τῷ δυναμένῳ ὑμᾶς στηρί-ξαι...(sc. ἔστω) ἡ δόξα; reading ᾧ creates a break in the cstr. It is easy to account for its omission, difficult to see why it should have been inserted and MS evidence for its inclusion is strong. ‖

I CORINTHIANS

1   κλητός (< καλέω) *called.* ὁ ἀδελφός *our brother.* ‖
2 οὔσῃ ptc εἰμί. ἡγιασμένοις *made and kept holy,* pf ptc
pass. ἁγιάζω *consecrate,* pl. according to the meaning.
ἐν Χρ. 'Ιησοῦ, i.e. through union with him §117f. κλητοῖς
ἁγίοις *called to be saints.* ἐπι-καλουμένοις ptc -καλέομαι
call upon ; οἱ ἐπικ. τὸ ὄνομα τ. κυρίου representing a Hebr.
expression often applied to Israel in rel. to Jahweh, here
in rel. to Jesus, the complete phrase meaning "with all
those who worship our Lord Jesus Christ as God". αὐτῶν
κ. ἡμῶν ref. τόπος or κύριος, *their (Lord) as well as ours.* ‖
3 χάρις significantly replacing the usual Gk salutation χαί-
4 ρειν: on χ. καὶ εἰρήνη Rom 1:7. ‖ εὐχαριστέω τινί *thank* one,
give thanks. μου [[var. om.]]. πάν-τοτε *at all times.* ἐπί
for, w. dat. indicating the ground for thanksgiving §126.
5 δοθείσῃ aor. ptc pass. δίδωμι. ‖ παντί neut. *everything.*
ἐ-πλουτίσθητε aor. pass. -τίζω *enrich.* ἐν παντὶ λόγῳ *in
all* (= every kind of) *speech* (see chaps 12 - 14) or λόγος
den. *the word* of God, *revelation,* in which case λ. καὶ γνῶσις
might mean "knowledge of revealed truth". γνῶσις[4]
6 *knowledge.* ‖ καθώς causal, *for.* μαρτύριον *testimony,* here
that borne to Christ in Christian preaching. ἐ-βεβαιώθη
7 aor. pass. -αιόω *make firm* (βέβαιος), *confirm.* ‖ ὑστερεῖσθαι
inf. pass. -ρέω *lack,* ὑστ. ἐν be *lacking in.* χάρισμα[7] *gift
of grace* for the benefit of the community. ἀπ-εκ-δε-
χομένους ptc -δέχομαι *await.* ἀπο-κάλυψις[4] (< ἀπο-καλύπτω
8 un-cover) *revelation.* ‖ βεβαιώσει fut. τέλος[8] *end.* ἀν-έγκλητος (ἀν- priv. + ἐγκαλέω accuse) *irreproachable.* ἐν on.
ἡ ἡμέρα τ. κυρίου...'Ιησοῦ *the parousia,* the second coming. ‖
9 πιστός *faithful, to be relied on.* διά here of principal cause
§113. ἐ-κλήθητε aor. pass. καλέω. κοινωνία τινός *com-
munion/fellowship with* one. ‖
10   παρακαλῶ...διὰ τ. ὀνόματος *I appeal to you in the name
of...,* i.e. with the authority of...Jesus Christ. ἵνα for inf.
§407. τὸ αὐτό *the same* ; here, *with one voice,* i.e. in harmony. λέγητε subj. λέγω. ᾖ, ἦτε subj. εἰμί. σχίσμα[7]

(< σχίζω split, tear apart) *division*. κατ-ηρτισμένοι pf ptc pass. -αρτίζω *fit together* ; *put in order* ; *complete*. κατηρ. ἐν τῷ αὐτῷ...αὐτῇ *consolidated in identity of...and of...* νοῦς νοός ὁ *mind*. γνώμη *opinion* ; *purpose* ; *resolve*. ‖ ἐ-δηλώθη aor. pass. -λόω *make clear* (δῆλος), 11 *reveal*. οἱ Χλόης *those of Chloe's household*. ἔρις[6] -ιδος ἡ *rivalry*. ‖ μέν...δέ Lat. *quidem...autem* (Rom 2:7), here best 12 rended into Eng. by emphasizing the prn, *I am for* P., *I am for* A. etc. ‖ με-μέρισται pf pass. -ίζω (< μέρος[8] a 13 part) *divide* ; a question ; others understand as a statement (*thus*) *Christ is divided*. μή interr. expecting the answer "No". ἐ-σταυρώθη aor. pass. -ρόω *crucify*. ἐ-βαπτίσθητε aor. pass. -τίζω. εἰς τὸ ὄνομά τινος *into union with, so as to belong to* someone. ‖ εὐχαριστῶ v.4. ἐ-βάπτισα 14 aor. εἰ μή *with the exception of*. ‖ ἵνα consec. §352. εἴπῃ 15 aor[2] subj. λέγω: ἵνα μή τις εἴπῃ *so that no one can say*. ‖ λοιπόν adv. *for the rest, apart from that*. ‖ ἀπ-έ-στειλεν 16,17 aor. ἀπο-στέλλω. The contrast contained in οὐ...ἀλλά εὐαγγελίζεσθαι is not nec. absolute but may be the Sem. idiom meaning *not so much to...as to preach* §445. εὐαγγελίζεσθαι inf. -ίζομαι *spread the good news, preach the gospel*. ἐν *with* §117. σοφία here (as in v.19) *wisdom* acquired by study opp. that inspired by God, σ. λόγου *choice phrase, eloquence*. ἵνα μή *lest, so that...not*. κενωθῇ aor. pass. κενόω (< κενός empty) *empty* sth *of meaning, nullify*. σταυρός *cross*. ‖

     μέν...δέ v.12. ἀπ-ολλυμένοις ptc mid. -όλλυμι: οἱ ἀπ. 18 *those on the road* (pres.) *to perdition*. μωρία *foolishness*. σωζομένοις ptc pass. σώζω: τοῖς σῳ. ἡμῖν *to us who are being saved*. ‖ ‖ γέ-γραπται *it stands written*, pf ptc pass. 19 γράφω. ἀπ-ολῶ (= ἀπ-ολέσω) fut. σοφός *wise*. σύν-εσις[4] (< συν-ίημι understand) *understanding, discernment*. συν-ετός *intelligent, discerning* §142. ἀ-θετήσω fut. -θετέω *render invalid* (ἄ-θετος), *annul, disregard*. ‖ ποῦ ; *where?* 20 συ(ν)-ζητητής[3] *debater*. ὁ αἰὼν οὗτος *the present age*, in contrast to the "age to come". οὐχί Lat. *nonne*, interr. expecting the answer "Yes". ἐ-μώρανεν aor. μωραίνω *render foolish*. ‖ ἐπει-δή *since*. σοφία τ. θεοῦ *wisdom of* 21 *God* manifested in the world, cf Rom 1:20. ἔ-γνω aor[2] 3rd sg γινώσκω in Hebr. sense of acknowledging and obeying, obj. τὸν θεόν. εὐ-δόκησεν aor. -δοκέω *think good to*, so *elect* to. μωρία v.18. κήρυγμα[7] *Christian preaching*,

the *gospel*. σῶσαι aor. inf. σώζω. πιστεύοντας ptc -εύω. ‖
22,23 'Ιουδαῖος *Jew*. ῞Ελλην⁶ -ηνος ὁ a *Greek*. ‖ κηρύσσω *pro-claim, preach*. ἐ-σταυρωμένον *crucified*, pf ptc pass. -ρόω
24 *crucify*. μέν...δέ v.12. σκάνδαλον *cause of offence*. ‖ κλητός
25 v.1. ‖ μωρός *foolish*, τὸ μ. *what is* (in the case of God =
"seems") *foolish*. σοφώτερον comp. of σοφός. ἀ-σθενής⁹
26 *weak*. ἰσχυρότερον comp. of ἰσχυρός *strong*. ‖ βλέπετε impv
-πω, or possibly indic. interr. κλῆσις⁴ *vocation, call*. κατὰ
σάρκα *humanly speaking, in man's estimation*. δυνατός
27 *powerful*. εὐ-γενής⁹ *well-born, of noble birth*. ‖ ἐξ-ε-λέξατο
aor. ἐκ-λέγομαι *choose for oneself*. κατ-αισχύνῃ subj., pres.
28 or aor. -αισχύνω *put to shame*. ‖ ἀ-γενής⁹ (*without lineage*)
of low birth, ignoble. ἐξ-ουθενημένα pf ptc pass. -ουθενέω
think nothing (οὐδέν) *of, despise*. τὰ μὴ ὄντα *the non-existent, shadows*. τὰ ὄντα *things in existence, realities*.
κατ-αργήσῃ aor. subj. -αργέω (< κατ- + α- + ἔργος put
29 out of action) *render inoperative, bring to nothing*. ‖ ὅπως
final, (*in order*) *that*. καυχήσηται aor. subj. -χάομαι *boast*.
μή...πᾶσα Hebr. for *none, no*. σάρξ den. man in his unaided
30 human nature. ‖ ἐξ αὐτοῦ *it is due to him that*... ἐ-γενήθη
dep. *who became* or pass. *who was made*, aor. pass. γίνο-μαι §230. ἁγιασμός *holiness*. ἀπο-λύτρωσις⁴ *redemption*,
31 *liberation, freedom*. ‖ γέ-γραπται v. 19. καυχώμενος ptc.
ἐν κυρίῳ ass. w. the impv καυχάσθω 3rd sg. ‖
2   κἀγώ = καὶ ἐγώ. ἐλθών aor² ptc ἔρχομαι. ὑπερ-οχή
(< ὑπερ-έχω be superior) *excellence*, καθ' ὑπεροχὴν λόγου
with sublime words (lit. "sublimity of word"). κατ-αγ-γέλλων ptc -αγγέλλω *announce*. μυστήριον τ. θεοῦ *God's
mystery* or *secret plan of salvation*, the gospel ⟦var. μαρ-
2 τύριον *testimony*⟧. ‖ ἔ-κρινα aor. κρίνω *distinguish* ; hence
choose, decide, οὐ...ἔκρ. τι εἰδέναι *I determined not to
know anything*... or *I deliberately knew nothing*... εἰδέναι
inf. οἶδα pf pres. εἰ μή *except* ἐ-σταυρωμένον 1:23. ‖
3 ἀ-σθένεια *weakness*. φόβος *fear*. τρόμος *trembling*. ἐ-γε-
4 νόμην aor² γίνομαι: ἐγ. πρός *came to*. ‖ κήρυγμα⁷ *preaching
about* Christ, *gospel message*. οὐκ ἐν *was not* (couched)
in. πειθοῖς (if so to be read) dat. pl. of πειθός *persuasive*,
a word unknown elsewhere ⟦var. πειθοῖ σοφίας (omitting
λόγοις) *persuasiveness* of wisdom (πειθώ -θοῦς ἡ persuasive-ness)⟧. ἀπό-δειξις⁴ *demonstration, proof*. πνεύματος κ. δυ-νάμεως obj. gen. *of spirit and power* (perh. = *spiritual*

power (JB)), or gen. epexeg. *consisting in spirit and power*. ‖
ἤ (subj. εἰμί)...ἐν here, *be based on*. ‖　　　　　　　　　　　　　5

ἐν *among*. τέλειος *perfect* ; *complete* ; *mature*. δέ (2nd　6
time) amplifying rather than adversative, *and* a wisdom...,
a wisdom *moreover*... §467. ἄρχων ἄρχοντος ὁ *ruler*, either
of human authorities or angelic powers. κατ-αργουμένων
who pass away or *are doomed to destruction*, or for fut.,
who will be brought to nothing §283, ptc pass. -αργέω 1:28. ‖
μυστήριον v.1, ἐν μ. *as a mystery*. ἀπο-κε-κρυμμένην pf　7
ptc pass. -κρύπτω *hide* (*away*). προ-ώρισεν aor. -ορίζω
fore-ordain. πρὸ τῶν αἰώνων *before the ages, from eternity*. ‖
ἔ-γνωκεν pf γινώσκω. ἔ-γνωσαν aor², εἰ...ἔγ. *if they had
known*, protasis of an unreal (unfulfilled) condition w. ἄν
in the apodosis §313. οὐκ ἄν...ἐ-σταύρωσαν (aor. v.2) *they
would not have crucified*. ‖ γέ-γραπται pf ptc pass. γράφω.　9
ἅ *the things that*. οὖς ὡτός τό *ear*. ἤκουσεν aor. ἀκούω.
ἀν-έ-βη aor² ἀνα-βαίνω: ἐπὶ τ. καρδίαν ἀνεβ. a Hebr. for
an idea *arising in/occurring to* one's mind. ἡτοίμασεν
aor. ἐτοιμάζω (< ἕτοιμος ready) *prepare*. ἀγαπῶσιν ptc
dat. pl. -πάω. ‖ ἀπ-ε-κάλυψεν aor. -καλύπτω *un-cover*,　10
reveal ; as dir. obj. understand "these things". ἐραυνάω
examine, explore. βάθος⁸ a *depth*. ‖ τίς...ἀνθρώπων; *who*　11
among men? τὰ τ. ἀνθρώπου *a man's state*, here it would
seem, of mind. εἰ μή v.2. ἔ-γνωκεν v.8. ‖ πνεῦμα τ.　12
κόσμου = σοφία τ. αἰῶνος τούτου v.6. ἐ-λάβομεν aor² λαμβάνω. εἰδῶμεν subj. of pf-pres. οἶδα. χαρισθέντα aor.
ptc pass. -ίζω *bestow/give freely*. ‖ διδακτός *taught*, δ. ...　13
λόγοις *terms taught by human wisdom*. ἀνθρώπινος *human*.
ἀλλ' ἐν διδακτοῖς πνεύματος *but in what is* (if neut.) *taught*...
or (if masc.) *but in terms taught by the Spirit*. πνευματικός
spiritual. συγ-κρίνοντες ptc -κρίνω *combine*. The ambiguity of the vb together w. the uncertainty whether
πνευματικοῖς is masc. or neut. results in various interpretations : *examine and compare* ; "examining together/
comparing the spiritual with the spiritual" (i.e. the prophetic scriptures w. the spiritual fulfilment in Christ) ;
or w. the sense *explain, interpret*, either "explaining
spiritual things in spiritual terms" (Wm) or (recommended
by what follows) "interpreting spiritual things to spiritual
people" (RSV, JB, NEB). ‖ ψυχικός *natural*, guided by　14
human reason alone. δέχομαι *receive*. μωρία *foolishness*. γνῶναι aor² inf. γινώσκω. πνευματικῶς *spiritually*,

with the aid of the Spirit. ἀνα-κρίνομαι pass. -κρίνω *exa-*
15 *mine,* and so *judge.* ‖ ὁ πνευματικός *the man aided by*
16 *the Spirit.* ‖ ἔ-γνω v.8. νοῦς νοός ὁ *mind.* συμ-βιβάσει
fut. -βιβάζω *bring together* : *to unite/to compare/to conclude,*
in LXX and NT *advise, teach.* ‖

3 κἀγώ = καὶ ἐγώ. ἠδυνήθην aor. dep. δύναμαι. λαλῆσαι aor. inf. λαλέω. πνευματικός 2:13. σάρκινος properly,
made of flesh ; often for σαρκικός (v. 3) *carnal; materially-*
2 *minded.* νήπιος *infant.* ‖ γάλα γάλακτος τό *milk.* ἐ-πότισα
aor. -ίζω τινά τι *give* one sth *to drink.* βρῶμα[7] (< βιβρώσκω
eat) *food,* esp. *solid food.* οὔ-πω *not yet.* ἐ-δύνασθε impf,
transl. *you were not yet able* (*to take it*), *you were not yet*
ready. ἀλλά = ἀλλ' οὐδέ *nor indeed are you.* ἔτι *still,*
3 ἔτι νῦν *even now.* ‖ ὅπου *where* ; causal, *in so far as.* ἐν
among. ζῆλος *fervour* ; *jealousy.* ἔρις[6] ἔριδος ἡ *rivalry.*
οὐχί = Lat. *nonne,* interr. expecting the answer "Yes".
καί perh. *in other words, that is* §455ζ. κατὰ ἄνθρωπον *on*
a (*purely*) *human level.* περιπατέω in ethical sense of
4 *behave, live.* ‖ λέγῃ subj. λέγω. μέν...δέ 1:12. οὐκ ἄνθρω-
5 ποί ἐστε; *are you not* (*all too*) *human?* (NEB). ‖ διάκονος *servant, helper.* ἐ-πιστεύσατε *you came to believe,*
aor. inceptive -εύω §250. ἑκάστῳ i.e. of the "helpers".
6 ἔ-δωκεν aor. δίδωμι. ‖ ἐ-φύτευσα aor. -εύω *plant.* ἐ-πότισεν
v.2. ηὔξανεν impf αὐξάνω *increase, cause to grow,* impf
7,8 durative. ‖ φυτεύων, ποτίζων, αὐξάνων ptcs. ‖ ἕν neut.
they do not work against each other, but as one. μισθός
9 *reward.* λήμψεται fut. λαμβάνω. κόπος *labour, toil.* ‖ σύν-
εργος *fellow-worker.* γεώργιον (cultivated) *field.* οἰκο-δομή
10 a *building.* ‖ δοθεῖσαν aor. ptc pass. δίδωμι. σοφός *wise.*
ἀρχι-τέκτων[6] -τέκτονος ὁ (< τέκτων) craftsman) *master-*
builder. θεμέλιος (< τίθημι) *foundation.* ἔ-θηκα aor. τίθημι *lay.* ἐπ-οικοδομέω *build upon.* βλεπέτω 3rd sg
11 βλέπω *look* in the sense of "look to", *watch.* ‖ θεῖναι aor[2]
inf. τίθημι. ἄλλον...παρά τι *another...besides, a...other than.*
κείμενον ptc pass. κεῖμαι, used as pf pass. of τίθημι. ‖
12 χρυσός *gold.* ἄργυρος *silver.* λίθος *stone.* τίμιος *precious.*
ξύλον *wood,* pl. *wood* as building material. χόρτος *hay.*
13 καλάμη *straw.* ‖ φανερός *clear, evident, visible* (opp. hidden or secret). γενήσεται fut. γίνομαι. ἡ ἡμέρα *the day*
(of judgement). δηλώσει fut. δηλόω *make clear, show.*
ἐν *by.* ἀπο-καλύπτεται (sc. *that day*) *is to be revealed,* pass.
-καλύπτω *reveal.* ὁποῖος *of what kind.* δοκιμάσει fut. -άζω

prove by testing. || μενεῖ fut. μένω. ἐπ-οικοδόμησεν aor. 14
v.10. μισθός, λήμψεται v.8. || κατα-καήσεται fut² pass. 15
-καίω *burn up.* ζημιωθήσεται fut. -ιόομαι (pass.) (< ζημία
loss) *be damaged, suffer loss.* αὐτός emphatic, *he himself.*
σωθήσεται fut. pass. σώζω. ὡς διὰ πυρός *but as (by going)
through fire.* || ναός *temple.* οἰκέω *dwell.* || φθείρω *cor-* 16,17
rupt ; a building, *destroy.* φθερεῖ fut. οἵτινες = οἵ §216. ||
ἐξ-απατάτω impv 3rd sg -απατάω *deceive.* δοκέω *seem.* 18
σοφός v.10. μωρός *foolish.* γενέσθω aor² impv 3rd sg
pass. γίνομαι. γένηται aor² subj. || μωρία *foolishness.* 19
παρὰ θεῷ *in God's eyes, to God.* γέ-γραπται pf pass. γράφω.
δρασσόμενος ptc -ομαι *catch, trap.* ἐν instr. §119 ; God
causes their cunning to defeat their own ends and serve
his. παν-ουργία (< παν-οῦργος *ready for (to do) anything)*
cunning. || δια-λογισμός *a thought.* μάταιος (< μάτη *folly)* 20
vain, futile. || καυχάσθω impv -χάομαι: κ. ἐν ἀνθρώποις 21
make human beings his boast, take pride in (mere) *men.* ||
ἐν-εστῶτα *things present,* pf² ptc neut. pl. ἐν-ίστημι; pf 22
ἐνέστηκα intr. w. pres. meaning *be at hand, be present.*
πάντα ὑμῶν *all things (are) yours.* ||

λογιζέσθω impv 3rd sg -ζομαι *calculate, reckon, con-* 4
sider. ὑπ-ηρέτης³ (< ὑπό *under* + ἐρέτης *rower) assis-*
tant, servant. οἰκο-νόμος *steward.* μυστήριον 2:1. || ὧδε 2
in this connection. λοιπόν *moreover.* ζητεῖται *is sought,*
pass. -τέω: ζ. ...ἵνα *what one looks for in stewards* (art.
generic) *is...* πιστός *faithful.* ἵνα for subject inf. §408.
εὑρεθῇ... *that one be found,* aor. subj. pass. εὑρίσκω. || εἰς 3
for pred. nom. §32. ἐλάχιστος *least* (superl. of μικρός
small), ἐμοί...εἰς ἐλ. ἐστιν *it does not matter in the least
to me.* ἀνα-κριθῶ aor. subj. pass. -κρίνω *examine* and so
judge. ἀνθρώπινος *human.* ἡμέρα of a special day, e.g.
day fixed for a court hearing, hence *tribunal,* cf 1:8.
ἀλλ' οὐδέ *nor indeed.* || σύν-οιδά τι *be conscious of* sth. 4
ἐμ-αυτῷ dat. of disadvantage, *to my disadvantage, against
myself.* ἐν causal, ἐν τούτῳ *for that.* δε-δικαίωμαι *stand
acquitted,* pf pass. -αιόω *justify.* || πρό w. gen. *before.* 5
κρίνετε impv, pres. do not *(continue to) judge* §246. ἕως
ἄν w. aor. subj. *until* ref. fut. ἔλθῃ aor² subj. ἔρχομαι.
φωτίσει fut. -ίζω τι *shed light on* sth.; *bring* sth *to light.*
κρυπτός *hidden.* σκότος³ *darkness,* τὰ κρυπτὰ τ. σκ. *things
hidden in darkness.* φανερώσει fut. -ρόω *reveal.* βουλή
purpose, here *motive.* ἔπ-αινος (< αἰνέω *praise) praise.*

γενήσεται   fut. γίνομαι: γεν. ἑκάστῳ "there will be to
6 each", *each will have.* ‖ μετ-ε-σχημάτισα aor. μετα-σχημα-
τίζω *transform,* also *change the metaphor,* transl. *I have
applied.* μάθητε aor² subj. μανθάνω *learn.*   τό introducing
what appears to be a proverbial saying = "..." or a gloss.
μὴ ὑπὲρ ἅ (acc.) γέγραπται (3:19) *do not (go) beyond what
is written.* εἰς ὑπὲρ τοῦ ἑνός...κατὰ τ. ἑτέρου ...*one for
the sake of the other* (? the other's favour) *at the expense
of the third.* φυσιοῦσθε for -ιῶσθε (ο + η), subj. pass.
-ιόω τινά *make* one *conceited* ; pass. *be inflated with pride,*
7 *exaggerate one's own importance.* ‖ δια-κρίνω *differentiate,*
τί σε διακρίνει; *what distinguishes you* (from the rest)?
ἔ-λαβες aor² λαμβάνω. εἰ δὲ καί *even if (in fact).* καυχᾶσαι
2nd sg -χάομαι *boast.* λαβών aor² ptc λαμβάνω: ὡς μὴ λ.
8 *as if you had not received it.* ‖ ἤδη *already.* κε-κορεσμένοι
pf ptc pass., w. ἐστέ forming pf pass. periphr. κορέννυμι *satisfy,* pass. *eat one's fill.* ἐ-πλουτήσατε aor. -τέω
be rich, aor. inceptive, *you have become rich.* χωρίς w.
gen. *without.* ἐ-βασιλεύσατε *have gained a kingdom,* aor.
-εύω *reign.* ὄφελον *would that!* particle foll. by indic.
introducing a wish unlikely to be realized, impf ref. pres.
time, aor. ref. past, here "would that you had (indeed)
gained..." §355 and n. συμ-βασιλεύσωμεν aor. subj. -εύω
9 *reign together* or *with.* ‖ δοκέω *I think, it seems to me.*
ἔσχατος *last,* pred. ἀπ-έ-δειξεν aor. ἀπο-δείκνυμι *show,*
whether in sense of *demonstrate* a point or *exhibit* ; also
appoint, make. ἐπι-θανάτιος *under sentence of death.* θέατρον *theatre,* hence *spectacle.* ἐ-γενήθημεν aor. dep. γίνο-
10 μαι. ‖ μωρός *foolish,* pred. φρόνιμος *wise.* ἀ-σθενής *weak.*
ἰσχυρός *strong.* ἔν-δοξος *esteemed, eminent.* ἄ-τιμος *with-
11 out honour, obscure* ; or actually *dishonoured.* ‖ ἄχρι *until,
up to.* ἄρτι *now, the present.* καί...καί *both...and.* πεινάω
be hungry. διψάω *be thirsty.* γυμνιτεύω *go half-naked/ill
clad.* κολαφιζόμεθα *we are roughly treated / knocked about,*
pass. -ίζω *give* one *a blow with the fist* (κόλαφος). ἀ-στατέω
12 *never to stand still, be always on the move.* ‖ κοπιάω *toil.*
ἐργαζόμενοι ptc -ζομαι *work.* χερσίν dat. pl. χείρ. λοι-
δορούμενοι ptc pass. -ρέω *swear at, abuse.* εὐ-λογέω *bless.*
διωκόμενοι ptc pass. διώκω *persecute.* ἀν-έχομαι (mid.)
13 *endure.* ‖ δυσ-φημούμενοι ptc pass. -φημέω *slander, vilify.*
παρα-καλέω *speak gently* (*Apol.* of Aristides (2nd cent.) in
this sense). περι-κάθαρμα⁷ *refuse, dregs.* ἐ-γενήθημεν v.9.

περί-ψημα⁷ *off-scouring, scrapings,* removed in the process of cleaning, sts in transferred sense of *scapegoat,* or *expiatory sacrifice,* all of which meanings are possible here. ‖ ἐν-τρέπων ptc -τρέπω τινί *put* one *to shame.* ἀγαπητός 14 *beloved.* νου-θετῶν ptc -τέω (< νοῦς mind + τίθημι) *put* one *in mind, exhort, warn.* ‖ μύριοι = 10,000. παιδ-αγωγός 15 *tutor.* ἔχητε subj. ἔχω: ἐὰν ἔ. *if you were to have.* ἀλλά *yet* ; understand "you would not have". ἐ-γέννησα aor. γεννάω *beget, become* one's *father.* ‖ μιμητής³ *imitator.* 16 γίνεσθε impv γίνομαι (= εἰμί whose impv 2nd pl. almost obs.). ‖ ἔ-πεμψα aor. πέμπω *send.* ἀγαπητός v.14. πιστός 17 *faithful* ; *trustworthy* ; π. ἐν κυρίῳ (act. sense) *who in the Lord is a believer* or *is faithful.* ἀνα-μνήσει fut. -μιμνήσκω τινά τι *remind* one of sth. ὁδός *way of life.* πᾰντα-χοῦ *everywhere.* ‖ ἐρχομένου ptc ἔρχομαι, gen. abs., ὡς μὴ ἐρχ. 18 μου *as though I was not coming.* ἐ-φυσιώθησαν aor. pass. -ιόω v.6. ‖ ἐλεύσομαι fut. ἔρχομαι. ταχέως adv. (adj. 19 ταχύς) *quickly, soon.* θελήσῃ aor. subj. θέλω. γνώσομαι fut. γινώσκω. πε-φυσιωμένων pf ptc pass. masc. ‖ οὐ...ἐν 20 λόγῳ supply ἐστί: *is not a matter of...but of...* or *does not lie in...but in...* ‖ τί θέλετε; *what would you? which do* 21 *you want?* ἐν of concomitant circumstances (sociative), *with* §116. ῥάβδος ἡ *rod.* ἔλθω aor² subj. ἔρχομαι, subj. delib. *am I to come?* πραΰτης⁶ -τητος ἡ *meekness,* ἐν... πνεύματι...πραΰτητος *in a spirit of gentleness,* "Hebr." gen. §40.

ὅλως *actually.* ἀκούεται pass. ἀκούω, *is reported.* ἐν 5 *among.* πορνεία *fornication,* any form of *sexual immorality.* τοιοῦτος *of such a kind, such.* ἥ-τις = οἷα §219. καὶ τοιαύτη πορνεία ἥτις οὐδέ... *and such immorality as* (*does*) *not* (*exist*) *even...* γυνή κτλ. *wife of one's father* = *stepmother.* τινά (masc.) subject of ἔχειν (acc.+inf. after ὥστε). ‖ ὑμεῖς emphatic. πε-φυσιωμένοι ἐστέ pf pass. 2 -ιόω *make one conceited* ; pass. *be full of one's own importance,* here perh. *be* (pf *remain*) *self-satisfied/smug.* οὐχί emphatic form of οὐ. ἐ-πενθήσατε aor. -θέω *mourn.* ἵνα consec. §352 ; or final (JB Fr.) or, which seems to make better sense, understood as impv, RSV, cf NEB, JB (Eng.) §415. ἀρθῇ aor. subj. pass. αἴρω. μέσος *middle,* ἐκ μ. ὑμῶν *from your midst/among you.* πράξας aor. ptc πράσσω *do.* ‖ ἐγώ opp. ὑμεῖς v.2. ἀπ-ών ptc -ειμι (ἀπο- + 3 εἰμί be) *be absent/away.* παρ-ών ptc -ειμι *be present.* κέκρικα (pf) w. text as punctuated, *I have reached the decision that...* (v.4) *we should deliver* (inf. v.5). κατ-εργα-σάμενον aor. ptc -εργάζομαι *accomplish*, in pejorative sense, *perpetrate*, τὸν κατεργ. obj. of παραδοῦναι v.5. ‖

4 V.4 describing the circumstances of the decision. συν-αχθέντων aor. ptc pass. -άγω *bring together* ; pass. *be assembled*, gen. abs. σ. ὑμῶν καὶ τοῦ ἐμοῦ πνεύματος κτλ. *you being assembled and I (too) in spirit, with the power of our*

5 *Lord Jesus.* ‖ παρα-δοῦναι aor² inf. -δίδωμι. τοι-οῦτος v.1, here noun, *such a man.* Σατανᾶς -νᾶ *adversary, Satan.* ὄλεθρος *destruction.* σωθῇ aor. subj. pass. σώζω. κυρίου

6 ⟦var. add 'Ιησοῦ⟧. ‖ καύχημα⁷ a *boast.* μικρός *small*, here *a small amount of*, *a little.* ζύμη *leaven, yeast.* φύραμα⁷

7 *lump, mass.* ζυμόω *leaven.* ‖ ἐκ-καθάρατε aor. impv -κα-θαίρω *purge away, get rid of*, aor. ref. to a specific act. παλαιός *old.* ἦτε subj. εἰμί. νέος *new, fresh.* καθώς causal, *since.* ἄ-ζυμος *un-leavened.* καὶ γάρ *for indeed.* πάσχα (indecl.) τό (Aram. "pass over") *passover* ; here *paschal*

8 *lamb.* ἐ-τύθη aor. pass. θύω *slay* for sacrifice. ‖ ἑορτά-ζωμεν *let us keep the feast*, subj. hort. -άζω (< ἑορτή) *celebrate a feast.* μηδέ *nor.* κακία *malice*, gen. epexeg. "leaven which is malice and..." §45. πονηρία *wickedness.* ἄ-ζυμοι pl. *un-leavened bread.* εἰλικρίνεια (adj. εἰλικρινής

9 *sincere ;* etym. uncertain) *sincerity.* ‖ ἔ-γραψα aor. γράφω. ἐπι-στολή *letter.* συν-ανα-μίγνυσθαι inf. pass. -μίγνυμι *mix up together* ; pass. *mix/associate with.* πόρνος *fornicator ;*

10 sts more generally, *one leading an immoral life.* ‖ οὐ πάντως *not at all* ; here, *not altogether.* τοῦ κόσμου τούτου *of this world* (opp. the "brother Christian" of v.11 ; neglect of this distinction has caused the Corinthians to misunderstand what Paul said.) πλεον-έκτης³ a *greedy*/"*having*" *person* (cf πλεονεξία Mk 7:22, Rom 1:29). ἄρπαξ⁶ ἅρπαγος ὁ (< ἁρπάζω *seize and carry off*) a *grasping person.* εἰδωλο-λάτρης³ (< εἴδωλον *idol* + λάτρις *servant*) *idolater.* ἐπεί *since.* ὠφείλετε *you would have to*, impf ὀφείλω *owe* ; w. inf. *ought, be obliged* ; impf representing sth which is not the case (cf Eng. past tense "ought") ; w. vbs den. fitness and obligation ἄν is om. from the apodosis of unfulfilled conditions §319. ἄρα *in that case.* ἐξ-ελθεῖν

11 aor² inf. -έρχομαι. ‖ νῦν δέ either *but now*, in which case ἔγραψα *I write* (epistolary aor. = "I have written" this letter, i.e. by the time they read it), so NEB ; or νῦν δέ

expresses a contrast, *but in fact/rather I wrote...* (Wm, RSV, JB). ὀνομαζόμενος ptc pass. -μάζω *call* by a name, τις ἀδελφὸς ὄν. *anyone called a brother.* ᾖ subj. εἰμί. λοίδορος *one who uses abusive language.* μέθυσος *drunkard.* τοιοῦτος v.5. μηδέ = οὐδέ *not even.* συν-εσθίειν inf. -εσθίω τινί *eat with* one. ‖ τί γάρ μοι; (sc. ἐστίν) *what business is it of mine?* οἱ ἔξω *those outside* the Christian community, non-Christians. οὐχί v.2. ἔσω *inside,* οὐχί...ὑμεῖς κρίνετε: *is it not those inside that you judge?* ‖ κρινεῖ fut. ἐξ-άρατε aor. impv -αίρω *take away, drive out.* ἐξ ὑμῶν αὐτῶν (from LXX, class. form of refl.) *from (among) you.* ‖ 12 13

τολμᾷ 3rd sg -μάω *dare.* πρᾶγμα⁷ *matter,* ἔχω πρ. πρός τινα *have a suit against* one. ὁ ἕτερος *the other, his fellow.* κρίνεσθαι mid. *go to law, take a case to the courts.* ἐπί w. gen. in legal context, *before* Ac 24:19. ἄ-δικος *un-just,* i.e. not ἅγιος, *gentile.* οὐχί an emphatic οὐ. οἱ ἅγιοι Rom 12:13. ‖ κρινοῦσιν fut. ἐν instr. *by* you. κρίνεται pass. ἀν-άξιος *un-worthy.* κριτήριον *law-court : unworthy of / unfit for the smallest tribunals.* But many scholars prefer the meaning *lawsuit,* supplying "to judge" or "to try" i.e. *unworthy/unfit to try petty disputes.* ἐλάχιστος superl. (elative) of μικρός *small.* ‖ κρινοῦμεν v.2. μήτιγε *not to speak of, let alone.* βιωτικός *belonging to everyday life, everyday* (adj.), neut. pl. *commonplace matters.* ‖ βιωτικά...κριτήρια *courts dealing with secular business* ; or (see v.2) *ordinary lawsuits/cases.* ἔχητε subj. ἔχω, a general condition §325. ἐξ-ουθενημένους pf ptc pass. -ουθενέω *think nothing* (οὐδέν) *of, despise* ; pass. *be of no account.* καθίζω *make* one *sit* ; as punctuated in text : *do you appoint to sit* (as judges) *those who are despised in the church?* (i.e. the pagans) or καθίζετε may be impv : (ironically) *Appoint (as judges) those in the church who are of no account.* ‖ ἐν-τροπή *shame* (< ἐντρέπω 4:14), πρὸς ἐντ. ...λέγω *I say (this) to your shame / to shame you.* ἔνι = ἐν, w. ἐστίν equivalent to ἔνεστιν *there is.* σοφός *wise man.* ὅς in sense of ὅστις (consec.) δυνήσεται fut. δύναμαι, *is there not one wise man among you able to...?* δια-κρῖναι aor. inf. -κρίνω *distinguish* ; *take a decision* ; *judge.* μέσος *middle,* neut. as noun, ἀνὰ μέσον *between,* ἀνὰ μ. τ. ἀδελφοῦ *understand and another.* ‖ κρίνεται, ἐπί v.1. καὶ τοῦτο *and that* before... ἄ-πιστος *un-believer.* ‖ ἤδη *already.* ὅλως *actually.* ἥττημα⁷ *defeat, failure,* here 6 2 3 4 5 6 7

moral. ὅτι the fact *that*. κρίμα⁷ here, *lawsuit*. μεθ᾽ ἑαυτῶν = μετ᾽ ἀλλήλων *with each other*. οὐχί v.1. ἀ-δικεῖσθε
pass. ἀ-δικέω *harm/wrong* one ; pass. *suffer an injustice / a*
8 *wrong*. ἀπο-στερεῖσθε pass. -στερέω *defraud*. ‖ καὶ τοῦτο
9 ἀδελφούς *and brothers* (Christians) *at that*. ‖ ἄ-δικος *wrong-
doer*. κληρο-νομήσουσιν fut. -νομέω (< κλῆρος a lot + νέμω
assign) *inherit*. πλανᾶσθε impv pass. -νάω *mislead*, μὴ πλ.
make no mistake! the pres. supposing that they are §246.
πόρνος 5:9. εἰδωλο-λάτρης³ 5:10. μοιχός *adulterer*. μαλα-
κός *soft, effeminate* ; *catamite, homosexual*. ἀρσενο-κοίτης³
10 (ἄρσην male + κοίτη bed) *sodomite, homosexual*. ‖ κλέπτης³
thief. πλεον-έκτης³...ἄρπαξ⁶ ἅρπαγος 5:10. μέθυσος, λοί-
11 δορος 5:11. ‖ ἦτε impf εἰμί: ταῦτά τινες ἦτε *such were
some of you*. ἀπ-ε-λούσασθε *you have had yourselves washed*
i.e. in baptism aor. ἀπο-λούομαι *wash (oneself)*. ἡγιάσθητε
aor. pass. ἁγιάζω *dedicate, consecrate, make holy*. ἐδι-
καιώθητε aor. pass. -αιόω *justify*, Rom 2:13. ἐν causal,
through §119. τῷ ὀνόματι τ. κυρίου meaning τῷ κυρίῳ. ‖
12 ἔξ-εστιν *it is allowed*, πάντα μοι ἔξ. *I am free to do
anything* : seems to be the Pauline utterance wrenched
from its context by his enemies to show him as a libertine. συμ-φέρει impers. *it is useful/good* for one. ἐξ-
ουσιασθήσομαι fut. pass. -ουσιάζω τινός *have authority* over
one ; pass. *be dominated/enslaved* (a play on ἔξεστιν,
13 ἐξουσ.). ‖ βρῶμα⁷ *food*. κοιλία a *hollow* ; *belly*. κατ-αργήσει
fut. -αργέω *bring to nothing, do away with* 1:28. δέ *but*
(implying "it is otherwise with the body"). πορνεία
14 *fornication, immorality*. ‖ καί...καί *both...and*. ἤγειρεν aor.
15 ἐγείρω. ἐξ-εγερεῖ fut. -εγείρω *raise*. ‖ μέλος⁸ *member*.
ἄρας aor. ptc αἴρω *shall I take...and...*? ποιήσω fut. ποιέω.
πόρνη *prostitute, whore*. γένοιτο aor² opt. γίνομαι: μὴ γ.
16 *let it not be! God forbid!* ‖ κολλώμενος ptc pass. κολλάω
stick, join, unite. ἔσονται fut. εἰμί. φησίν 3rd sg φημί
say, i.e. God in scripture. εἰς σάρκα in place of pred.
18 nom. σάρξ §32. ‖ φεύγετε impv -γω *flee*, in moral sense,
shun. ἁμάρτημα⁷ a *sin* as sth committed, as distinct
from ἁμαρτία as principle of sin. ὃ ἐάν (= ἄν) *whatever*.
ποιήσῃ aor. subj. ποιέω transl. *commit*. ἐκτός w. gen.
outside. πορνεύων ptc -εύω *practise fornication*. ἁμαρ-
19 τάνω *sin*. ‖ ναός *temple*. οὗ attracted from ὅ (ref. σῶμα)
§16. ἔχετε *you hold/possess*. ἑαυτῶν *your own*, 3rd pl.
20 for 2nd §209. ‖ ἠγοράσθητε aor. pass. ἀγοράζω *buy*. τιμή

price, gen. of price, transl. *you were bought* (made his) *at a price.* **δοξάσατε** aor. impv -άζω *glorify.* **δή** *therefore.* **ἐν** instr. *with* §119. ‖

περὶ ὧν for **περὶ τούτων ἅ** by attraction of the rel. 7 §16. **ἐ-γράψατε** aor. γράφω. **καλόν** sc. **ἐστίν** *it is a good thing*, κ. ἀνθρώπῳ *it is good for a man.* **ἅπτεσθαι** inf. **ἅπτομαί τινος** *touch* one. ‖ **πορνεία** 6:13. **ἐχέτω** impv 3rd 2 sg ἔχω. ‖ **ὀφειλή** *due*, here ref. conjugal rights. **ἀπο-διδότω** 3 impv 3rd sg -δίδωμι *give* what is due, *fulfil* a duty. **ὁμοίως** *likewise.* ‖ **ἐξ-ουσιάζω** τινός *have authority/power* over sth. ‖ 4 **ἀπο-στερεῖτε** impv -στερέω *deprive.* **εἰ μήτι ἄν** *unless* 5 *perhaps* (μήτι = μή). **σύμ-φωνος** *harmonious*, neut. as noun, *agreement.* **πρὸς καιρόν** *for the time being, temporarily.* **σχολάσητε** aor. subj. -άζω *be unoccupied*, and so w. τινί *free to devote oneself* to sth. **προσ-ευχή** *prayer.* **ἐπὶ τὸ αὐτό** *together.* **ἦτε** subj. εἰμί. **πειράζῃ** subj. -άζω *tempt.* **ἀ-κρασία** *want of control.* ‖ **συγ-γνώμη** *fellow-feeling*, hence 6 *forbearance*, κατὰ σ. *by way of concession.* **ἐπι-ταγή** *command.* ‖ **χάρισμα**⁷ *gift* 1:7. **ὁ μὲν οὕτως, ὁ δὲ οὕτως** *one of* 7 *one kind and the other another.* ‖ **ἄ-γαμος** *un-married.* 8 **χήρα** *widow.* **καλόν** v.1. **μείνωσιν** aor. subj. μένω *consta-* tive aor. connoting "to the end" §253. **κἀγώ** = **καὶ ἐγώ.** ‖ **εἰ...οὐκ** *if...not* ; distinguish **εἰ μή** *unless.* **ἐγ-κρατεύομαι** 9 *control oneself.* **γαμησάτωσαν** aor. impv 3rd pl. γαμέω *marry.* **κρείττων** -ονος neut. κρεῖττον, comp. of ἀγαθός. **πυροῦσθαι** inf. pass. πυρόω *burn* sth ; pass. *burn* (intr.), *be inflamed*, here with desire. ‖ **γε-γαμηκόσιν** pf ptc dat. pl. γαμέω. 10 **παρ-αγγέλλω** *charge, command.* **χωρισθῆναι** aor. inf. pass. -ίζω *separate.* ‖ **ἐὰν δὲ καί** *but if.* **χωρισθῇ** aor. subj. pass. 11 **μενέτω** impv 3rd sg μένω. **ἄ-γαμος** v.8. **κατ-αλλαγήτω** aor² impv pass. 3rd sg -αλλάσσω *reconcile.* **ἀφ-ιέναι** inf. -ίημι *send away, divorce* ; inf. depending on παραγγέλλω v.10. ‖ **λοιπός** *left* behind ; οἱ λ. *the rest.* **ἄ-πιστος** masc. 12 and fem. *un-believing*, i.e. a non-Christian. **συν-ευ-δοκέω** (seem good to one and the other) *consent, agree.* **οἰκεῖν** inf. οἰκέω *live*, pres. continuous. **ἀφ-ιέτω** impv 3rd sg. ‖ **ἡγίασται** pf pass. ἁγιάζω τινά *make* one ἅγιος, *consecrate.* 14 **ἐν** *by union with.* **ἐπεὶ ἄρα** *since in that case* (viz. if it were not so). **ἀ-κάθαρτος** *unclean.* **ἐστίν** transl. *would be* (sg w. neut. pl. subject). **νῦν δέ** *whereas.* ‖ **χωρίζεται** 15 uncompleted action, *wants a separation*, pass. v.10. **χωρι-ζέσθω** *let him be separated*, impv pass. **δε-δούλωται** *is*

not *under compulsion*, pf pass. -λόω *en-slave*. ἐν τοῖς τοιούτοις *in such cases*. ἐν...εἰρήνη transl. w. NEB, (*to live*) *in peace*. κέ-κληκεν pf καλέω, here in Pauline sense
16 of calling to faith. ὑμᾶς [[var. ἡμᾶς]]. ‖ γύναι voc. of γυνή. εἰ indir. interr. *whether*. σώσεις fut. σῴζω: τί οἶδας...εἰ...σώσεις; is neutral, *how do you know whether you may save...or not?* ἄνερ voc. of ἀνήρ. ‖
17   εἰ μή for ἀλλά §470. ἐ-μέρισεν aor. -ίζω *divide, distribute*. περι-πατείτω impv 3rd sg -πατέω 3:3. δια-τάσσομαι
18 *give instructions, ordain*. ‖ περι-τε-τμημένος *circumcised*, pf ptc pass. -τέμνω *cut round*; *circumcise*. ἐ-κλήθη aor. pass. καλέω. ἐπι-σπάσθω impv pass. 3rd sg -σπάω *draw over*, hence mid. *obliterate the effect of circumcision*. ἀκρο-βυστία *uncircumcision*, ἐν...ἀκρ. *when* (*he is*) *uncircumcised*. κέ-κληται pf pass. περι-τεμνέσθω impv pass. 3rd sg. ‖
19 περι-τομή *circumcision*. ἀλλά, understand "what counts is...". τήρησις[4] (< τηρέω hold, keep) *observance, keeping*. ‖
20 κλῆσις[4] *calling, vocation* from God (not occupation). ᾗ
21 instr. dat. *whereby*. μενέτω v.11. ‖ μελέτω impv μέλει τινί impers. *it is a care* to one, μή σοι μελέτω *don't let it pre-occupy/worry you*. εἰ καί *even though; if actually*. δύνασαι 2nd sg. ἐλεύθερος *free*. γενέσθαι aor[2] inf. γίνομαι. χρῆσαι aor. impv χράομαί τινι *make use of* sth; *suffer/live under certain circumstances*. Does the (understood) obj. refer to slavery or to liberation? i.e. which are we to understand? *but even though you have the possibility of becoming free, suffer it* (slavery) *rather*, or (linking καί w. the vb) *but if you actually have the possibility of becoming free, make use of it* (the chance) *rather*. In either case the passage is concerned to stress the indifference of external conditions and the primary importance of inner
22 freedom. ‖ ἐν κυρίῳ *in the Lord* §116, 118. κληθείς aor.
23 ptc pass. ἀπ-ελεύθερος *freedman*. ὁμοίως v.3. ‖ τιμῆς ἠγο-ράσθητε 6:20. γίνεσθε impv, either *do not become* (Wm, RSV, NEB), or γίνεσθε is supplying an impv 2nd pl. (virtually obs.) for εἰμί, *do not remain* (= continue to be). ‖
24 ἐν ᾧ...ἐν τούτῳ *in what* (*state*)...*in that*. μενέτω v.11. ‖
25   παρθένος ἡ *virgin*. ἐπιταγή v.6. γνώμη *opinion*. ἠλεη-μένος *having found mercy*, pf ptc pass. ἐλεέω τινά *show mercy* to one, ὡς ἠλ. ...εἶναι *as one who by the Lord's mercy*
26 *is trustworthy*. πιστός *trustworthy*. ‖ νομίζω *think*, w. acc. + inf. *think that...* ὑπ-άρχειν inf. -άρχω *be from the*

beginning ; *exist* ; often simply *be*. **ἐν-εστῶσαν** *present*, pf²
(intr. w. pres. sense) ptc -ίστημι in intr. tenses, *be at hand/
present*. **ἀνάγκη** *necessity* ; *stress*. **καλὸν ἀνθρώπῳ** v.1. ‖
δέ-δεσαι pf pass. 2nd sg δέω *bind* ; pf den. a lasting state 27
§285. **ζήτει** (ε + ε) impv ζητέω. **λύσις**⁴ *release* ; of marriage, *dissolution*. **λέ-λυσαι** *are you free?* pf pass. λύω. ‖
ἐὰν δὲ καί *but even though*. **γαμήσῃς** aor. subj. v.9. **ἥμαρτες** 28
aor² ἁμαρτάνω, proleptic aor. for *you will not have sinned*
§257. **γήμῃ** aor. subj. (class. form). **παρθένος** v.25.
θλῖψις⁴ (< θλίβω press) *stress* ; *trouble*. **τῇ σαρκί** *in their
earthly life*, dat. of respect §53. **τοιοῦτος** *such a person*.
φείδομαι *spare* ; transl. w. Wm, *I am for sparing* you. ‖
τοῦτο (opp. class. use §213) ref. what follows. **φημί** *I say*. 29
συν-ε-σταλμένος w. εἰμί forming pf pass. of συ(ν)-στέλλω
contract, shorten. **τὸ λοιπόν** neut. of λοιπός (v.12) *and so*,
or as adv. of time, *from now on*. **ἵνα** impvl §415. **ἔχοντες**
ptc ἔχω. **ὡς** *as if*. **ὦσιν** subj. εἰμί: *ἵνα...ὦσιν let those
with wives be...* ‖ **κλαίοντες** ptc κλαίω *weep*. **χαίροντες** 30
ptc χαίρω *rejoice*. **ἀγοράζοντες** ptc -άζω *buy*. **κατ-έχοντες** ptc
-έχω *hold fast, keep* in one's possession. ‖ **χρώμενοι** ptc 31
χράομαί τινι *use* ; cstr w. acc. late and very rare. **κατα-
χρώμενοι** ptc -χράομαι *use* (*to the full*). **παρ-άγω** *pass by* ;
be transitory/passing. **σχῆμα**⁷ the *external* (*changeable*)
form, i.e. the world as we know it. ‖ **ἀ-μέριμνος** (μέριμνα 32
worry) *care-free*. **ἄ-γαμος** v.8. **μεριμνάω** *concern oneself
with, be solicitous about*. **τὰ τοῦ κυρίου** *the Lord's business*.
ἀρέσῃ aor. subj. ἀρέσκω τινί *please* one, subj. delib. §348. ‖
γαμήσας aor. ptc γαμέω v.9. ‖ **με-μέρισται** *is divided/torn*, 33-4
pf pass. -ίζω v.17. **παρθένος** v.25. **ᾗ** subj. εἰμί. **σώματι**
dat. of respect. ‖ **σύμ-φορον** *benefit*, one's *good*. **βρόχος** 35
noose, i.e. *restraint*. **ἐπι-βάλω** aor² subj. -βάλλω *throw
upon* or *over*, i.e. catch you in the noose of an imposed
celibacy which contains its own pitfalls. **εὐ-σχήμων**⁶
-μονος masc. and fem. -μον neut. *seemly, dignified* ; τὸ
εὔσχ. *what is seemly* etc. §140. **εὐ-πάρ-εδρος** *faithful*, *devoted*. **ἀ-περι-σπάστως** (ἀ- + περι-σπάω dis-tract) *without
distraction*, cf περισπάομαι Lk 10:40. ‖ Paul gives answers 36
to three cases none of which are clear to us. Note the
uncertainty of subjects and the ambiguity of terms.
ἀ-σχημονέω *behave dishonourably*. **ἐπί** *towards*. **τὴν παρ-
θένον αὐτοῦ** *his un-married daughter* ; or *his betrothed*, or
his spiritual "sister" in celibacy, (see γαμέω below). **νο-**

μίζω *think of, have in mind.* ᾖ, subject is the virgin or (possibly) the man. ὑπέρ-ακμος (< ἀκμή *maturity*) *past* (ὑπέρ) *maturity* or *over/uncontrollably passionate* ; for ὑπέρ *beyond* 4:6 ; 2 Cor 1:8). καὶ οὕτως κτλ. continues the condition εἴ τις νομίζει. ὀφείλω w. inf. *must.* γίνεσθαι inf. *happen, come about.* ποιείτω impv 3rd sg ποιέω. γαμείτωσαν *let them marry,* impv 3rd pl. ; the vb γαμέω (rather than γαμίζω but see v.38) and esp. the pl. number would seem to exclude a father/daughter relationship ; on the other hand, what was later to become a serious problem of church discipline, that of "spiritual companions", is not elsewhere mentioned before 2nd cent. ||

37 ὅς the man *who.* ἔστηκεν *stands,* pf (intr. w. pres. meaning) ἵστημι. ἑδραῖος (< ἕδρα *seat*) *firm.* καρδία as seat of thought sts = *mind.* ἀνάγκη v.26, ἔχων ἀ. *being under compulsion.* ἐξουσίαν ἔχει περί *has control over.* κέκρικεν pf κρίνω *judge, decide.* τηρεῖν τ. ἑαυτοῦ παρθένον i.e. to keep her a virgin. καλῶς *well.* ποιήσει fut. ||

38 ὥστε *so, therefore.* καί...καί *both...and.* γαμίζων ptc -ίζω orig. *give in marriage* (which would demand a father/daughter relationship in v.36) but in HGk possibly used for γαμέω. κρεῖσσον neut. of κρείσσων (or κρείττων v.9)

39 as adv. || δέ-δεται v.27. χρόνος *time,* ἐφ' ὅσον χρ. for simple acc. of duration, *for as long as* §80. ζῇ 3rd sg ζάω. κοιμηθῇ *fall asleep* (for *die*), aor. subj. dep. κοιμάομαι *sleep.* ἐλεύθερος v.21. γαμηθῆναι aor. inf. pass., the pass. appropriate to a woman, *be married.* ᾧ θέλει

40 *to the one she wants.* || μακαριώτερος -ρα -ρον comp. of μακάριος *happy.* μείνῃ v.8. γνώμη v.25. δοκέω *think, believe.* κἀγώ = καὶ ἐγώ *I too.* ἔχειν inf.

8   εἰδωλό-θυτος *sacrificed to an idol,* esp. τὰ εἰδ. *meat (which has been) sacrificed to idols, sacrificial meat.* γνῶσις[4] *knowledge,* here an *informed conscience.* φυσιόω *inflate* (φυσάω) *with self-complacency, make conceited.* οἰκο-δομέω

2 *edify, build (up).* || δοκέω *think, suppose.* ἐ-γνωκέναι pf inf. γινώσκω. Understand e.g. "it means that" he has not yet... οὔπω *not yet.* ἔ-γνω aor² 3rd sg. γνῶναι aor²

3 inf. || ἔ-γνωσται pf pass., in OT sense of *is acknowledged/*

4 *loved.* || βρῶσις[4] *eating.* οὐδὲν εἴδωλον ἐν κόσμῳ must mean *there is no (such thing as an) idol...* in view of the

5 parallel οὐδεὶς θεὸς εἰ μὴ εἷς *there is no God save one.* || καὶ γὰρ εἴπερ *for granted that, for although.* λεγόμενοι *called,*

ptc pass. λέγω. **εἴτε...εἴτε** *whether...or.* **ὥσπερ εἰσίν** *as (indeed) there are.* ‖ **ἐξ** *from,* ref. source. **εἰς** *for.* ‖ **γνῶσις** 6,7 v.1. **συν-ήθεια** (< σύν + ἦθος *custom*) *custom,* τῇ σ. *from habit, following their habit.* **ἕως ἄρτι** *up to now.* **εἴδωλον** v.4, τ. εἰδώλου art. generic, *of/to idols.* **εἰδωλόθυτον** v.1, **ἐσθίουσιν** *they eat* (supply : *this food*) *as sacrificed to idols.* **συν-είδησις⁴** *con-science.* **ἀ-σθενής⁹** *weak.* **οὖσα** ptc fem. **εἰμί.** **μολύνεται** pass. -ύνω *defile.* ‖ **βρῶμα⁷** *food.* **παρα-** 8 **στήσει** fut. παρ-ίστημι *present* ; *commend.* **φάγωμεν** aor² subj. ἐσθίω. **ὑστερούμεθα** *are we worse off, do we lose anything,* pass. of -ρέω *be late* ; hence *be short of, lack* ; pass. in same sense. **περισσεύω** *have* sth *over and above /extra,* here, *gain anything.* ‖ **βλέπετε** impv, β. μή πως 9 *take care that...not.* **ἐξουσία** *right,* so *freedom.* **πρόσ-** **κομμα⁷** *stumbling-block, occasion of sin.* **γένηται** aor² subj. γίνομαι. ‖ **ἴδη** aor² subj. ὁράω. **ἔχοντα** ptc ἔχω. **γνῶσις** 10 v.7. **εἰδωλεῖον** *temple for an idol.* **κατα-κείμενον** *reclin-ing/sitting* at table. **οὐχί** = Lat. *nonne,* interr. expecting the answer "Yes". **συνείδησις, ἀσθενής** v.7. **ὄντος** ptc εἰμί. **οἰκο-δομηθήσεται** fut. pass. v.1, here in sense of *embolden, encourage.* **εἰδωλόθυτον** v.1. ‖ **γάρ** would seem 11 to refer back to v.9. **βλέπετε κτλ.** rather than to the intervening explanation §478 Lat. ed⁵. **ἀ-σθενῶν** ptc -νέω *be without strength, be weak,* ὁ ἀσ. *the weak man.* **σός** *your* (sg). **ἀπ-έ-θανεν** aor² -θνήσκω. ‖ **ἁμαρτάνοντες** 12 ptc -άνω. **εἰς** *against.* **τύπτοντες** ptc τύπτω *beat,* met. *wound.* **ἀσθενοῦσαν** ptc fem. ‖ **δι-ό-περ** *that is why.* **βρῶμα** 13 v.8. **σκανδαλίζω** *cause to stumble* or *sin.* **φάγω** v.8 ; οὐ μὴ φ. *I will never eat* (strong neg.) §444. **κρέας,** gen. κρέως (= κρέαος) pl. κρέα, τό *meat.* **εἰς τὸν αἰῶνα** *for ever.* **σκαν-δαλίσω** aor. subj. ‖

ἐλεύθερος *free.* **οὐχί** interr. expecting the answer **9** "Yes". **ἑώρακα** pf ὁράω. ‖ **εἰ...οὐκ...ἀλλά γε...** *if...not...at* 2 *least...* ; γε a particle stressing the preceding word. **σφρα-γίς⁶** -ῖδος ἡ *seal,* as sign or confirmation of authenticity. **ἀπο-στολή** *apostleship.* ‖ **ἀπο-λογία** *defence.* **ἀνα-κρίνουσιν** 3 ptc -κρίνω *interrogate, examine.* **αὕτη** *as follows* (HGk idiom), in class. always ref. foregoing matter §213. ‖ **μή** 4 here forming a tentative question, cf Jn 4:29 ; μὴ οὐκ ἔχομεν ; *have we no...?* (= "are we without ?" (ans. "No")). **φαγεῖν** aor² inf. ἐσθίω. **πεῖν** aor² inf. πίνω. ‖ **ἀδελφή** *sister,* 5 i.e. a Christian (fem.). **περι-άγειν** inf. -άγω *take about.*

λοιπός *remaining*, οἱ λ. ἀπόστολοι *the rest of the apostles.* ‖
6 ἐργάζεσθαι inf. -ζομαι *work*, dependent on ἐξουσία. ‖
7 τίς...ποτέ; *who ever...?* στρατεύομαι *serve as a soldier.*
ὀψώνιον (< ὄψον cooked relish to eat w. the basic ration
+ ὠνέομαι buy) hence *provision money* and so *soldiers'
pay*, ἰδίοις ὀψ. *at his own expense.* φυτεύω *plant.* ἀμπελών[6] -ῶνος ὁ *vineyard.* ποιμαίνω *shepherd, tend.* ποίμνη
8 *flock.* γάλα γάλακτος τό *milk.* ‖ μή v.4. κατὰ ἄνθρωπον
in the manner of/as a man, on a human level, esp. in con-
9 trast to God. καί *also.* ‖ γέ-γραπται pf γράφω. κημώσεις
fut. κημόω *muzzle*, impvl fut. §280. βοῦς βοός ὁ *ox.* ἀλοῶντα
ptc ἀλοάω *thresh*, here *by trampling out*, Deut 25:4. μέλει
τινί *it is a care/concern to one*, μή...θεῷ; *is it really for the
10 oxen that God is concerned?* ‖ δι' ἡμᾶς *on our account.*
πάντως *altogether.* γάρ *in a reply*, *certainly*, *to be sure.*
ἐ-γράφη aor² pass. γράφω. ὀφείλω w. inf. *ought.* ἐλπίς[6]
-ίδος ἡ *hope*, ἐπ' ἐλ. *in hope.* ἀροτριῶν ptc -ιάω *plough.*
ἀροτριᾶν inf. μετ-έχειν inf. -έχω τινός *partake (of), share
(in)* sth, τοῦ μ. dependent on ἐλπίς, *of sharing* (sc. the
11 produce). ‖ πνευματικός *spiritual*, neut. pl. *spiritual things.*
ἐ-σπείραμεν aor. σπείρω *sow.* μέγα neut. of μέγας, here
something extraordinary, *a great thing.* σαρκικός opp.
12 πνευματικός *material.* θερίσομεν fut. -ίζω *harvest.* ‖ ὑμῶν
ἐξουσία obj. gen. *claim upon you.* ἐ-χρησάμεθα aor. χράομαί τινι *use, make use of, exercise* a right. στέγω *endure,
bear.* ἐγ-κοπή (ἐν + κόπτω cut) *hindrance*, ἐγκ. δίδωμι
13 *hamper.* δῶμεν aor² subj. δίδωμι. ‖ ἱερός *holy, sacred.*
ἐργαζόμενοι ptc -ζομαι *work, do*, οἱ τὰ ἱερὰ ἐρ. *those who
perform the Temple services.* θυσιαστήριον (< θυσιάζω
from θύω sacrifice) *altar.* παρ-εδρεύοντες ptc -εδρεύω *sit
beside* sth ; hence *occupy oneself with, serve.* συμ-μερί-
ζονται mid. -ίζω *share out* ; mid. w. dat. *have a share in.* ‖
14 δι-έ-ταξεν aor. δια-τάσσω τινί *command* one. κατ-αγγέλλουσιν
15 ptc -αγγέλλω *proclaim.* ζῆν inf. ζάω. ‖ κέ-χρημαι pf χράομαι v.12. ἔ-γραψα aor. γράφω, prob. epistolary aor., cf
5:11. γένηται aor² subj. γίνομαι. ἐν ἐμοί *in my case.*
καλόν μοι μᾶλλον *it is better for me, I would rather.*
ἀπο-θανεῖν aor² inf. -θνήσκω. καύχημα[7] *boast.* κενώσει
16 fut. κενόω *empty, make empty.* ‖ εὐ-αγγελίζωμαι subj.
-αγγελίζομαι *preach the gospel.* ἀνάγκη *necessity.* ἐπί-
κειμαί τινι *lie/be laid upon* one. οὐαί *woe (to)!* here,
17 *(it would be) misery to.* εὐ-αγγελίσωμαι aor. subj. ‖ ἑκών

adj. used as adv. *willing(ly)*, *voluntary(-arily)*, *of my own choice*. πράσσω *do*. μισθός *reward*, i.e. what I receive is a payment. ἄκων *unwilling(ly)*; here, *involuntarily*. οἰκο-νομία *administration* ; *commission*. πε-πίστευμαι pf pass. -εύω τί τινι *entrust* one *with* sth, in pass. the person becomes subject πιστεύομαί τι *be entrusted with* sth §72. || ἵνα for 18 subject inf. §408. εὐ-αγγελιζόμενος ptc, *in my preaching*. ἀ-δάπανος *free of charge*. θήσω fut. τίθημι in sense of *present, offer*, for aor. subj. §340. εἰς τὸ μή *so as not to* (whether final or consec. is debatable) §352 ; when following ἵνα, εἰς τό usu. refers to an ultimate aim or result, ἵνα to the immediate objective. κατα-χρήσασθαι aor. inf. -χράομαί τινι *use to the full* his right to a reward. || ἐλεύ- 19 θερος v.l. ὤν ptc εἰμί, concessive. ἐκ for ἀπό §87. ἐμ-αυτόν *myself*. ἐ-δούλωσα aor. δουλόω *make* one *a slave*. πλείονες comp. pl. πολύς: οἱ π. *the greater part*. κερδήσω aor. subj. κερδαίνω *gain, win over*. || ἐ-γενόμην aor² 20 γίνομαι. αὐτός (*my-*)*self*. || ἄ-νομος *without law* ; *out-* 21 *side the Law*. ἔν-νομος *subject to the Law*. κερδάνω (= κερδήσω v.19) from var. aor. ἐκέρδανα, formed in analogy to σημαίνω ἐσήμανα §492. || ἀσθενής *weak*. γέ-γονα pf² 22 γίνομαι. πάντως *by every means*, others transl. *at any rate*. σώσω aor. subj. σώζω. || συγκοινωνός τινος *participant, sharer* in sth. αὐτοῦ i.e. of the gospel, συγκοινωνὸς 23 αὐ. meaning participation in its furtherance or, more likely, in its blessings. γένωμαι aor² subj. γίνομαι. || στάδιον *stadium*. τρέχοντες ptc τρέχω *run*. βραβεῖον 24 *prize* awarded for a contest by the adjudicator (βραβεύς). οὕτως...ἵνα *so...that*, either ref. foregoing : *in the same way* as the winning athlete *in order that*...(final) or ref. what follows : *in such a way that*... (consec.) §352. τρέχετε impv. κατα-λάβητε aor² subj. -λαμβάνω *make one's own, win* (supply "the prize"). || ἀγωνιζόμενος ptc -ζομαι *take* 25 *part in a contest*, ὁ ἀγ. *athlete*. πάντα acc. of respect, *in everything*. ἐγ-κρατεύομαι *practise self-control*, of athletes, *train*. ἐκεῖνοι μὲν οὖν...ἡμεῖς δέ *they...but we...* φθαρτός *perishable, that will wither*. στέφανος *crown, wreath*. λά-βωσιν aor² subj. λαμβάνω. ἄ-φθαρτον *imperishable, lasting*. || τοίνυν = οὖν *so, then*. ἀ-δήλως *falteringly* as if the objec- 26 tive is unclear (ἄδηλος). πυκτεύω *fight*. ἀήρ ἀέρος ὁ *air*. δέρων ptc δέρω *beat*, ἀέρα δ. of a blow that misses. || ὑπ- 27 ωπιάζω (< ὤψ part of the face under the eye) *give one a black eye*, hence *deal severely with, wear down* (cf Lk 18:5). δουλ-αγωγέω *lead into slavery, subjugate*, or possibly *bear my body about* like the winner parading those he has beaten in the arena. μή πως *lest*. κηρύξας aor. ptc -ύσσω *preach*. αὐτός v.20. ἀ-δόκιμος lit. "not passing the test", *rejected, discredited*. γένωμαι v.23. ||

10   ἀ-γνοεῖν inf. ἀγνοέω *not to know*, οὐ...ἀγνοεῖν *I would not have you fail to consider*. νεφέλη *cloud*. ἦσαν impf

2 εἰμί. δι-ῆλθον aor² -έρχομαι *go through*. || εἰς τὸν Μωϋσῆν *unto Moses*, phrase chosen to parallel εἰς Χριστόν and meaning "pledged to Moses" in baptism. ἐ-βαπτίσθησαν aor.

3 pass. -ίζω. || πνευματικός *spiritual*, here viewed as miraculous and as typifying the eucharist. βρῶμα⁷ *food*. ἔ-

4 φαγον aor² ἐσθίω. || ἔ-πιον aor² πίνω. πόμα⁷ *drink*. ἔ-πινον impf (repeatedly). ἀκολουθούσης ptc fem. -θέω. πέτρα

5 *rock*. || ἐν in sense of *pleased with* is causal cf 4:4. πλείο-νες 9:19. εὐ-δόκησεν aor. -δοκέω *consider good, take pleasure in*. κατ-ε-στρώθησαν aor. pass. κατα-στρώννυμι *spread about*; pass. *be strewn*, sts of place, *be strewn with* sth, here of corpses, *were strewn around*. γάρ here supplying the evidence rather than the reason. ἔρημος ἡ

6 (sc. χώρα) *desert*. || τύπος (< τύπτω beat) *image, type ; symbol*. ἐ-γενήθησαν aor. dep. γίνομαι = ἐγένοντο §174. εἰς τὸ μή w. inf. final, *so that...not*. ἐπι-θυμητής³ *one who desires, coveter*. κακός *evil*, τὰ κ. *evil things*. κἀκεῖνοι = καὶ ἐκεῖνοι. ἐπ-ε-θύμησαν aor. ἐπι-θυμέω *desire, covet*.

7 μηδέ *and not*. εἰδωλο-λάτρης³ (εἴδωλον idol + λάτρις servant) *idolater*. γίνεσθε impv for obs. 2nd pl. impv εἰμί. γέ-γραπται pf pass. γράφω. ἐ-κάθισεν aor. -ίζω *make to sit* ; also intr. *sit down*. φαγεῖν...πεῖν (contracted form of πιεῖν) aor² inf. vv.3,4. ἀν-έ-στησαν *stood up*, aor² (intr.)

8 ἀν-ίστημι. παίζειν inf. παίζω *amuse oneself*. || πορνεύωμεν subj. -εύω *commit fornication*, μηδὲ π. subj. hort. *and let us not commit f*. ἐ-πόρνευσαν aor. ἔ-πεσαν (for -ον §489) aor² πίπτω. εἴκοσι τρεῖς = 23. χιλιάς⁶ -άδος ἡ = 1000. ||

9 ἐκ-πειράζωμεν subj. hort. -πειράζω *try, provoke* by their lack of faith in difficult situations. Χριστόν [[var. κύριον]]. ἐ-πείρασαν aor. ; when a simplex resumes a compound vb it may retain the same force (class.). ὑπό of agent with an intrans. vb may stand for Eng. *from, by reason of*. ὄφις⁴ ὁ *serpent*. ἀπ-ώλυντο impf mid. -όλλυμι, impf

10 *perished* one after the other. || γογγύζετε impv -ύζω *grum-*

ble. **καθ-ά-περ** = καθώς. **ἐ-γόγγυσαν** aor. **ἀπ-ώλοντο** aor²
mid. -όλλυμι. **ὀλοθρευτής**³ *destroyer.* || **τυπικῶς** *typologi-*   11
cally, as a foreshadowing. **συν-έ-βαινεν** impf συμ-βαίνω *hap-*
pen. **ἐ-γράφη** aor² pass. γράφω. **πρός** w. acc. *for (the*
purpose of). **νου-θεσία** (< νοῦς mind + τίθημι) *warning,*
πρὸς ν. ἡμῶν *for a warning to us.* **τέλος**⁸ *end,* τ. τῶν αἰώνων
the completion of the ages. **κατ-ήντηκεν** pf -αντάω *come*
down, come upon. || **ὥστε** *so that.* **δοκῶν** ptc δοκέω *think,*   12
suppose. **ἑστάναι** *stand,* pf² (intr. w. pres. meaning)
ἵστημι. **βλεπέτω** impv 3rd sg βλέπω w. subj. *see (to it)* /
take care that. **πέσῃ** aor² subj. v.8. || **πειρασμός** *tempta-*   13
tion. **εἴληφεν** pf² λαμβάνω *seize* (pf : seize and hold §285).
εἰ μή *except.* **ἀνθρώπινος** *human, belonging/suited to man* ;
here meaning "limited to man's power to resist". **πιστός**
faithful, to be trusted, i.e. to give them what he has promised. **ἐάσει** fut. ἐάω *allow.* **πειρασθῆναι** aor. inf. pass.
-άζω v.9, here *tempt.* **ὑπὲρ ὃ δύνασθε** *beyond what you are*
able (sc. to resist). **ποιήσει** fut. ποιέω. **ἔκ-βασις**⁴ (< ἐκ-
βαίνω) *a way out.* **τοῦ δύνασθαι** gen. of quality describing
ἔκβασις, *such that you are able,* or consec. inf. *so that...*
ὑπ-ενεγκεῖν aor² inf. ὑπο-φέρω *bear (up under), endure.* ||
δι-ό-περ *therefore.* **ἀγαπητός** *beloved.* **φεύγετε** impv φεύγω   14
flee, keep away. **εἰδωλο-λατρία** *idolatry.* || **φρόνιμος** *thoughtful,*   15
wise. **κρίνατε** aor. impv κρίνω: κ. ὑμεῖς *judge for your-*
selves. **φημί** *I say.* || **ποτήριον** *wine-cup.* **εὐ-λογία** (< εὐ-   16
λογέω) *blessing.* **εὐ-λογέω** *bless, consecrate.* **οὐχί** interr.
expecting the answer "Yes". **κοινωνία** *communion,* κ.
τινός *participation in* sth. **ὁ ἄρτος** (subject of ἐστίν) has
become acc. by "inverse rel. attraction" into the case
of the rel. ὅν §19. **κλάω** *break.* || **ἐκ** for partitive gen. §80.   17
μετ-έχω *partake, share.* || **βλέπετε** impv, *look at!* **κατὰ σάρκα**   18
according to the flesh, historic Israel. **οὐχ** = οὐχί. **ἐσθίον-**
τες ptc -ίω. **θυσία** (< θύω v.20) *sacrifice.* **κοινωνός** *par-*
ticipant. **θυσιαστήριον** *altar* ; i.e. by eating the sacrificial
meat from the altar they make profession of the same
religion. || **τί οὖν φημί**; *what do I mean?* **εἰδωλό-θυτον**   19
8:1. **τί** encl. *something, anything* (the accent being re-
ceived from ἐστιν). **εἴδωλον** *idol.* || **ἀλλά** strong adver-   20
sative ; after a question may = *not at all, but...* **θύω**
sacrifice. **γίνεσθαι** inf. || **ποτήριον** v.16. **τράπεζα** *table.* **μετ-**   21
έχειν inf. v.17. || **παρα-ζηλόω** *provoke to jealousy and anger.*   22

μή interr. expecting the answer "No". ἰσχυρότερος comp. of ἰσχυρός strong. αὐτοῦ gen. of comp. ‖

23   ἔξ-εστιν is allowed. συμ-φέρει it is profitable/useful/a
24   good thing. οἰκο-δομέω edify, build up. ‖ τὸ ἑαυτοῦ "what is his own", i.e. his own interests. ζητείτω impv 3rd sg
25   ζητέω. τοῦ ἑτέρου of the other. ‖ μάκελλον meat/food market. πωλούμενον ptc pass. πωλέω sell. ἐσθίετε impv. ἀνα-κρίνοντες ptc -κρίνω examine, inquire, μηδὲν ἀνακ. διὰ τ. σ. for the sake of conscience asking no questions, without
26   heart-searchings. συν-είδησις[4] con-science. ‖ πλήρωμα[7] full-ness ; full complement ; ἡ γῆ καὶ τὸ π. the earth and all it
27   holds. ‖ καλέω invite. ἄ-πιστος un-believing, as noun un-believer, τῶν ἀπ. depending on τις. πορεύεσθαι to go, inf. παρα-τιθέμενον ptc pass. -τίθημί τινι set food before one. ‖
28   εἴπῃ aor[2] subj. λέγω. ἱερό-θυτος sacrificial. ἐσθίετε impv. διά w. acc. for the sake of. μηνύσαντα aor. ptc μηνύω make known, point out, inform. καὶ τ. συνείδησιν and for con-
29   science sake. ‖ λέγω I mean. οὐχί a strong neg. ἑ-αυτοῦ your own, 3rd for 2nd pers. §209, or indef. one's own, the meaning being that the exercise of one's freedom must be limited by considering its effect on others, cf Rom 14:16. ἱνατί; why? γάρ ref. οὐχὶ τὴν ἑαυτοῦ for (granted the inalienable freedom of the Christian con-science) why...? ἐλευθερία freedom. κρίνεται pass., here be determined. ἄλλης σ. lit. "another conscience", but transl.
30   another's conscience. ‖ χάριτι with gratitude, dat. of attendant circumstances. ‖ μετ-έχω v.17. βλασ-φημοῦμαι pass. -φημέω vilify, here blame. ὑπὲρ οὗ = ὑπὲρ τούτου ὑπὲρ οὗ
31   for that for which. εὐ-χαριστέω give thanks. ‖ εἴτε...εἴτε... εἴτε whether...or...or. τι anything (at all). ποιεῖτε (2nd
32   time) impv. ‖ ἀ-πρόσ-κοπος (ἀ- priv. + προσκόπτω stumble against) without offence, either "blameless" (Ac 24:16) or (here) causing/giving no offence. καί...καί both...and. γί-νεσθε impv, be! generally replaces impv 3rd pl. of εἰμί
33   (7:23). Ἕλλην[6] -ηνος ὁ a Greek. ‖ κἀγώ = καὶ ἐγώ. πάντα acc. of respect, in all things. ἀρέσκω try to give pleasure to / to fit in with. ζητῶν ptc -τέω. ἐμ-αυτοῦ my own. σύμ-φορον benefit, advantage. σωθῶσιν aor. subj. pass. σῴζω. ‖

11   μιμητής[3] imitator. γίνεσθε impv. ‖
2   ἐπ-αινέω praise. πάντα acc. of respect, in all things. μέ-μνησθε you keep me in mind, pf μιμνήσκομαί τινος remember one. παρ-έ-δωκα aor. παρα-δίδωμι. παρά-δοσις[4]

tradition. κατ-έχω *hold fast/firmly.* ‖ εἰδέναι inf. οἶδα (pf- 3
pres.). ‖ προσ-ευχόμενος ptc -εύχομαι. προφητεύ ων ptc 4
-εύω *prophesy.* κατὰ κεφαλῆς ἔχω *have something on one's
head, have one's head covered.* κατ-αισχύνω *dishonour.* ‖
ἀ-κατα-κάλυπτος masc. and fem. *uncovered*; ἀκ. τῇ κεφαλῇ 5
dat. of manner, *with her head uncovered.* ἕν καὶ τὸ αὐτό
(she is) *one and the same* (thing). ἐ-ξυρημένη pf ptc
pass. ξυράω *shave.* τῇ is generic, τῇ ἐξ. *as a woman that
has been shorn,* i.e. *had her hair cut off.* ‖ κατα-καλύπτεται 6
pass. or mid. -καλύπτω *veil.* καί *also.* κειράσθ ω aor.
impv mid. 3rd sg κείρω *shave*; mid. *have one's hair cut off.*
αἰσχρός *shameful, disgraceful.* κείρασθαι aor. inf. mid.
ξυρᾶσθαι inf. mid. or pass. ξυράω *shear, shave.* κατα-
καλυπτέσθ ω impv mid. 3rd sg. ‖ μὲν γάρ...δέ *for indeed...
but.* ὀφείλω w. inf. *ought.* κατα-καλύπτεσθαι inf. mid.
εἰκών[6] εἰκόνος ἡ *image, likeness.* ὑπ-άρχ ων ptc -άρχω *be
from the beginning*; *exist*; often synonymous w. εἰμί,
but here perh. in its proper sense, *since he is* in origin,
being so constituted. ‖ καὶ γάρ Lat. *etenim, for in fact.*
ἐ-κτίσθη aor. pass. κτίζω *create.* διά w. acc. *for the sake
of.* ‖ ἐξουσία here? *a sign of power/authority* or *dignity* 10
depending on exegesis of the v. διὰ τ. ἀγγέλους ?because
they too (according to rabb. tradition) veil themselves
before God (Is 6:2) and are present at public worship
(cf 4:9, Ps 137:1 (LXX)). ‖ πλήν *nevertheless.* χωρίς w. 11
gen. *without.* οὔτε γυνὴ χωρὶς ἀνδρὸς οὔτε... *woman cannot dispense with man nor...* ‖ ὥσπερ *just as.* ἐκ (was 12
formed) *from.* καί *too.* διά (comes into being) *through,* (is
born) *of.* ‖ ἐν ὑμῖν αὐτοῖς judge *for yourselves* (class. form 13
of refl. prn). κρίνατε aor. impv. πρέπον ptc neut. πρέπω,
usu. impers. π. ἐστίν *it is fitting/seemly.* ἀ-κατα-κάλυπτος
v.5. προσ-εύχεσθαι inf. ‖ οὐδέ...διδάσκει *does not even...*
teach. φύσις[4] *nature,* φ. αὐτή *nature itself.* κομᾷ subj. 14
κομάω *wear one's hair long.* ἀ-τιμία *dis-grace.* ‖ ἀντί 15
w. gen. *instead/in place of.* περι-βόλαιος (< περι-βάλλω
put around) *cloak.* δέ-δοται pf pass. δίδωμι. ‖ δοκέω 16
think, suppose, δοκεῖ...εἶναι *has a mind to be, is inclined
to be.* φιλό-νεικος (φιλέω *love* + νεῖκος *strife*) *captious,
argumentative,* εἰ...φ. εἶναι *if anyone is inclined to dispute*
(the fact). Before ἡμεῖς understand "Let me say that..."
τοιοῦτος *such* (as this). συν-ήθεια *custom.* ‖

17   παρ-αγγέλλων ptc -αγγέλλω *command, give instructions*;
in giving you this direction. ἐπαινέω v.2. κρείσσων masc.
and fem. κρεῖσσον neut. (comp. of ἀγαθός) *better,* εἰς τὸ κρ.
for the better. ἥσσων, ἧσσον neut. (comp. of κακός) *worse.*

18 συνέρχομαι *come together, meet.* || συν-ερχομένων ptc gen.
abs. ἐκκλησία *company* or *congregation of the faithful.*
ἀκούω *I hear* in the sense of "have heard" (as in Eng.).
σχίσμα[7] (< σχίζω tear) *division,* pl. *separate groups, fac-*
tions. ὑπάρχειν *exist,* inf. v.7. μέρος[8] *part,* μ. τι πιστεύω

19 *I half believe it.* || αἵρεσις[4] (< αἱρέομαι choose) *choice ;*
school of thought ; party. δόκιμος (< δέχομαι receive) *ap-*
proved. φανερός *evident, known.* γένωνται aor[2] subj.

20 γίνομαι. || ἐπὶ τὸ αὐτό *together in one place.* οὐκ ἔστιν
there is no (question of) *eating, it cannot be to eat.* κυριακός *of the Lord.* δεῖπνον *principal meal, dinner ;* here

21 of the Lord's *supper.* φαγεῖν aor[2] inf. ἐσθίω. || προ-λαμ-
βάνω *forestall ; anticipate, be beforehand.* ὃς μέν...ὃς δέ...

22 *one...another...* πεινάω *be hungry.* μεθύω *be drunk.* || μή...
οὐκ ἔχετε; *have you really no...?* εἰς τὸ ἐσθίειν lit. "for
eating", *to eat in.* κατα-φρονέω τινός *despise* sth, *have no
respect for.* κατ-αισχύνω *humiliate, put to shame.* τοὺς μὴ
ἔχοντας *those who have nothing,* i.e. *the poor.* εἴπω aor[2]
subj. λέγω, subj. delib. ἐπ-αινέσω; aor. subj. delib. v.2,
am I to praise you? ἐν τούτῳ *in this matter,* ref. fore-
going. ||

23   παρ-έ-λαβον aor[2] παρα-λαμβάνω *receive from,* παρέλ. ὁ
κ. παρέδ. here most prob. of oral tradition : *I received*
(as handed down) *from the Lord what* (in turn) *I passed
on to you;* contrast Gal 1:12. ἀπό perh. for this reason
instead of the usu. παρά. παρ-έ-δωκα aor. παρα-δίδωμι
deliver, hand on. νυκτί dat. of νύξ. παρ-ε-δίδετο (for
-οτο, cf Ac 4:35) impf pass. *deliver up, hand over.* ἔ-λαβεν

24 aor[2] λαμβάνω. || εὐ-χαριστήσας aor. ptc -χαριστέω *give
thanks.* ἔ-κλασεν aor. κλάω *break.* τὸ ὑπὲρ ὑμῶν *which is
for you* [[var. ὑμῶν κλώμενον *broken for you* (κλώμενον ptc
pass. κλάω)]] ; if not expressed, κλώμενον must be understood. ποιεῖτε impv. εἰς *for, as.* ἀνά-μνησις[4] *memorial,*
εἰς τὴν ἐμὴν ἀν. generally understood of the disciples re-
membering Christ ; but in Palestinian usage ἀνάμνησις
is referred to God, with a view to his intervention (Joa-
chim Jeremias) and the rendering would be : *do this that*

25 *God may remember me.* || ποτήριον (wine-)*cup.* δειπνῆσαι

aor. inf. -νέω *dine*, μετὰ τὸ δ. *after dining, when he had finished supper.* καινός *fresh, new.* δια-θήκη *testament, will,* in scripture for συν-θήκη *covenant.* ὁσάκις ἐάν (= ἄν) w. subj. *as often as.* πίνητε subj. πίνω. ‖ ἐσθίητε subj. 26 κατ-αγγέλλω *proclaim.* ἄχρις οὗ w. subj. *until* (= ἄ. τοῦ χρόνου ᾧ) §16f. ἔλθῃ aor² subj. ἔρχομαι. ‖

ἀν-αξίως *un-worthily.* ἔν-οχος (< ἐν-έχομαι be held ; 27 be liable) w. gen. *be liable to* or *guilty of.* ἔσται fut. εἰμί. ‖ δοκιμαζέτω impv 3rd sg -άζω *test, examine.* ἐσθιέτω, 28 πινέτω impv 3rd sg. ἐκ τοῦ for simple partitive gen. §67f. ‖ ἐσθίων, πίνων ptcs. κρίμα⁷ *judgement,* obj. of ἐσθίει... 29 πίνει. δια-κρίνων ptc -κρίνω *differentiate, distinguish,* i.e. from ordinary bread, ptc signifying *when* or *if he does not distinguish.* ‖ ἀ-σθενής⁹ *without strength, ailing.* ἄρ-ρωστος 30 (< ἀ- priv. + ῥώννυμι be strong) *weak, sickly.* κοιμάο-μαι *sleep, fall asleep, die.* ἱκανός *enough* ; pl. *not a few.* ‖ ἑ-αυτούς 3rd for 1st pl. §209. δι-ε-κρίνομεν here, *examine,* 31 impf ; εἰ w. past tense introducing an unfulfilled (unreal) condition. οὐκ ἂν ἐ-κρινόμεθα (impf pass.) *we should not be judged* §313f. ‖ κρινόμενοι ptc pass., *when we are judged/ 32 punished.* παιδευόμεθα -εύομαι *educate ; discipline.* κατα-κριθῶμεν aor. subj. pass. -κρίνω *condemn.* ‖ συν-ερχόμενοι 33 v.18. εἰς τό of purpose. φαγεῖν v.20. ἐκ-δέχεσθε impv -δέχομαι *wait for.* ‖ πεινάω *be hungry.* ἐν οἴκῳ *at home.* 34 ἐσθιέτω impv 3rd sg. κρίμα v.29. συν-έρχησθε subj. τὰ λοιπά *the remaining things, the rest.* ὡς ἄν w. subj. = ὅταν *when* ref. fut. ἔλθω aor² subj. ἔρχομαι. δια-τάξομαι fut. -τάσσομαι (= διατάσσω) *give directions about, settle.* ‖

πνευματικός *spiritual,* τὰ πν. special gifts of the Holy **12** Spirit in which the church of Corinth more than others abounded. ἀ-γνοεῖν inf. -γνοέω *not to know, be ignorant.* ‖ ὅτι *that* explained by ὡς ἄν. ἔθνη (pl.) *pagans.* ἦτε impf 2 εἰμί. εἴδωλον *idol.* ἄ-φωνος *voice-less, dumb.* ἄν w. impf iterative (for class. opt. §358) den. repeated action in the past. ἤγεσθε impf pass. ἄγω *lead.* ἀπ-αγόμενοι ptc pass. -άγω *lead away,* ὡς ἂν ἤγεσθε ἀπαγ. *how you were ir-resistibly drawn* (ἤγεσθε ἀπαγ. translating a very emphatic Hebr. idiom cf §61), so JB. Others (mentally supplying a first ἦτε after ὅτε) cstr ἦτε w. ἀπαγόμενοι to form a periphr. impf constituting a temporal clause, *...when still pagans you used to be led astray to dumb idols...* ; ὡς ἂν ἤγεσθε would then mean *as you were for ever being*

3   led (cf Wm, RSV, NEB). ‖ διό = δι' ὅ *this is why.* γνωρίζω *make known, point out.* ὅτι *that,* understand *just as*
no one... (see καί below). ἐν (sociative) of close personal
relationship §116ff. λαλῶν ptc λαλέω. ἀνά-θεμα[7] (< ἀνα-
+ τίθημι) *something set aside, "devoted"* to the deity ;
esp. *something accursed,* pred. καί *so* §451. εἰπεῖν aor[2] inf.

4   λέγω. κύριος pred. εἰ μή *except.* ‖ δι-αίρεσις[4] (< δι-αιρέω
distinguish) *division ; difference, variety.* χάρισμα[7] *gift* from
God for the service of the community, the variety of
gifts not effacing their unity which is grounded in the
one God : τὸ πνεῦμα (v.4), ὁ κύριος (v.5), ὁ θεός (v.6).

5   εἰσίν *there are.* ὁ αὐτός *the same.* ‖ διακονία *ministry,*
6   *service.* ‖ ἐν-έργημα[7] (< ἐνεργέω) a *working, activity.* ἐν-
7   εργῶν ptc -εργέω *work.* ‖ δίδοται pass. δίδωμι. φανέρωσις[4]
manifestation. συμ-φέρον ptc neut. -φέρει *it is advanta-*
8   *geous/useful,* τὸ σ. *benefit.* ‖ ᾧ μέν...ἄλλῳ δέ *to one...to an-*
other. διά *through,* not invariably limited to an intermediary cause §113. λόγος σοφίας *expression of wisdom.*
λόγος γνώσεως *presentation of knowledge.* σοφία is the
wider term and generally understood to refer to the
profound and fundamental Christian verities, γνῶσις to
Christian principles ; in both cases the χάρισμα is the
9   capacity to impart to others : λόγος. ‖ ἕτερος = ἄλλος
10   §153. χάρισμα v.4. ἴαμα[7] (< ἰάομαι cure) *cure.* ‖ ἐνέργημα
v.6. προφητεία *prophecy.* διά-κρισις[4] *power of dis-crimi-*
nation. γένος[8] a *kind.* γλῶσσα *tongue ; language ;* γένη γ.
ref. speaking ecstatically in unknown tongues. ἑρμηνεία
11   *interpretation.* ‖ ἐν-εργέω v.6. δι-αιροῦν ptc neut. -αιρέω
divide ; apportion. ἰδίᾳ advl, *individually.* βούλομαι *will.* ‖
12   καθ-ά-περ = καθώς. μέλος[8] *member.* ὄντα ptc εἰμί,
concessive. οὕτως καὶ ὁ Χριστός *so it is with Christ.* ‖
13   καὶ γάρ *for indeed.* ἐ-βαπτίσθημεν aor. pass. -τίζω. εἴτε...
εἴτε *whether...or.* Ἕλλην[6] -ηνος ὁ a *Greek.* ἐλεύθερος
free. ἐ-ποτίσθημεν aor. pass. -ίζω τί τινα *give* one some-
14   thing *to drink.* ‖ γάρ emphasizing the multiplicity in unity
refers logically to v.12 (rather than v.13) §478 Lat. ed[5]. ‖
15   εἴπῃ aor[2] subj. λέγω. ὅτι *because.* οὐκ...σώματος *I do not*
belong to the body. παρὰ τοῦτο *because of this, for this*
reason ; οὐ παρά...σώματος lit. "not for this (reason) does
it not belong to the body", i.e. *it does not follow that it*
does not belong... or *it belongs to the body all the same.* ‖
16,17   οὖς ὠτός τό *ear.* ‖ ποῦ; *where?* ἀκοή *hearing,* ποῦ ἡ ἀκ. ;

where would its hearing be? ὄσφρησις⁴ *sense of smell.* ||
νυνὶ δέ *but as it is.* ἔ-θετο aor² mid. τίθημι, mid. connot- 18
ing "for his own purposes". μέλος v.12. εἰς ἕκαστος
each one. ἠθέλησεν aor. θέλω. || εἰ...ἦν *if...were,* εἰ w. 19
past tense of indic. forming protasis of an unfulfilled
(unreal) condition §313. τὰ πάντα *they all.* || πολλὰ μέν...ἓν 20
δέ *while...are many, yet...is one.* || εἰπεῖν aor² inf. λέγω. 21
χρεία *need.* || ἀλλὰ πολλῷ μᾶλλον...ἀναγκαῖα *but rather/on* 22
the contrary...much more necessary. δοκοῦντα ptc δοκέω
intr. *seem.* ἀ-σθενέστερος (comp. of ἀ-σθενής⁹) *weaker.*
ὑπ-άρχειν here simply *be* (cf 11:7). ἀναγκαῖος *necessary,*
vital. || δοκέω *think, suppose.* ἀ-τιμότερα (comp. of ἄ- 23
τιμος) *less honourable.* τιμή *honour.* περισσότερος (comp.
of -ισσός abundant) *even more, even greater.* περι-τίθημι
put around, esp. *put on* clothing; *invest with.* ἀ-σχήμων⁶
-μονος, neut. ἄσχημον *in-decent, un-presentable,* τὰ ἀσχ.
ἡμῶν *our private parts.* εὐ-σχημοσύνη *presentability,* here
in the form of clothing. || εὐ-σχήμων⁶ -μονος *decent, pre-* 24
sentable. χρεία v.21. συν-ε-κέρασεν aor. συγ-κεράννυμι
blend; compose, compound. ὑστερουμένῳ ptc pass. -ρέω
act. and pass. *lack, be without.* δούς aor² ptc δίδωμι. || ἦ 25
subj. εἰμί. σχίσμα⁷ *division.* τὸ αὐτό *the same.* μεριμνῶ-
σιν subj. -μνάω *have concern,* pl. because τὰ μέλη (neut.
pl. subject) are considered as separate entities. || καί 26
and so. εἴτε...εἴτε v.13. πάσχω *suffer.* συμ-πάσχω *suf-*
fer with or *together.* δοξάζεται pass. -άζω *honour,* pass.
have honour shown to one. συγ-χαίρω *rejoice with* or *to-*
gether. || μέρος⁸ *part,* ἐκ μ. *in part; individually.* || οὕς 27,28
μέν (lacking οὕς δέ) *some.* ἔ-θετο v.18. δεύτερος *second,*
neut. as adv. τρίτος *third.* διδάσκαλος *teacher.* ἔπειτα
then. δυνάμεις v.10, normally den. the activity, in v.29
seems to denote the persons endowed w. the gift. χάρισμα
v.4. ἴαμα v.9. ἀντί-λημψις⁴ *helping (others),* den. the cor-
poral works of mercy. κυβέρνησις⁴ *guidance, administra-*
tion. γένη γλωσσῶν v.10. || μή = Lat. *num,* interr. expect- 29
ing a neg. answer, *not* all are apostles, *are they?* ||
διερμηνεύω *interpret.* || ζηλοῦτε impv ζηλόω τι *be zealous/* 30,31
eager for sth. μείζων⁶ -ζονος, neut. μεῖζον comp. of μέγας.

ἔτι *yet, still.* ὑπερ-βολή (< ὑπερ-βάλλω go beyond,
surpass) *pre-eminence,* καθ᾽ ὑπερβολήν Fr. *par excellence,*
an *incomparable* way, a way *better than any* (cf NEB,
JB). || γλῶσσα 12:10, γλ. τῶν ἀγγέλων the way in which **13**

angels are thought to express their adoration. ἐάν...
λαλῶ (pres. subj.) a possible condition §323. ἔχω pres.
subj. γέ-γονα pf² γίνομαι, in pf *be*. χαλκός *brass*; *copper*. ἠχῶν ptc ἠχέω *make a sound* or *noise*. κύμβαλον
cymbal. ἀλαλάζον ptc -άζω *wail loudly* (Mk 5:38); of a
2 cymbal, *clang*. ‖ προφητεία (*gift of*) *prophecy*. εἰδῶ subj.
οἶδα (pf-pres.). μυστήριον (< μυέω initiate) *secret rites*;
in NT the *secret mystery* of the divine plan. γνῶσις *knowledge*. μεθ-ιστάναι inf. -ίστημί τι *move, remove* sth else-
3 where. οὐ-θέν = οὐδέν. ‖ ψωμίσω aor. subj. -ίζω (cf ψωμίον
Jn 13:26) *dole out* so as to feed. ὑπ-άρχοντα ptc ὑπ-άρχω
7:26, ὑπ. τινί *belong* to one, τὰ ὑπ. *possessions*. παρα-δῶ
aor² subj. -δίδωμι. καυχήσωμαι aor. subj. -χάομαι *boast*
〚var. ἵνα καυθήσομαι *that I may be burnt* (καυθήσομαι fut.
pass. καίω burn §340)〛. οὐδέν *in no way*. ὠφελοῦμαι
pass. -λέω *help, be profitable* or *good*; pass. *be helped/bene-
4 fited*. ‖ μακρο-θυμέω (adj. μακρό-θυμος long-tempered) *be
slow to get angry, be patient*. χρηστεύομαι *be kind* (χρηστός).
ζηλόω 12:31; also *be jealous* or *envious*. περπερεύομαι
put oneself forward, colloq. "show off". φυσιοῦμαι pass.
5 -ιόω *inflate*; pass. *be full of one's own importance*. ‖ ἀ-
σχημονέω *behave dis-honourably* or *in-decently*. τὰ ἑαυτῆς
"what are its own", i.e. *its own interests*. παρ-οξύνομαι
(< ὀξύς sharp) *be hot-tempered*. λογίζομαι *put down to*
one's *account*; *reason*; *consider*; *brood over*. κακόν *evil*;
6 *injury*. ‖ ἀ-δικία *unrighteousness, wrongdoing*. συγ-χαίρω
7 τινί *rejoice with*. ‖ στέγω *bear*. ἐλπίζω *hope*. ὑπο-μένω
8 *endure*. ‖ οὐδέ-ποτε *never*. πίπτω met. *fail*. εἴτε...εἴτε...
whether (*it be*)...*or*... προφητεία *prophecy*. κατ-αργηθήσεται
(1st time) fut. pass. -αργέω *bring to nothing* (ἄ-εργος idle,
inoperative). γλῶσσα 12:10. παύσονται fut. mid. παύω
restrain; mid. *cease*. γνῶσις *knowledge*. κατ-αργηθήσεται
9 transl. *will be superseded*. ‖ μέρος⁸ part, ἐκ μ. *partially, in
10 part*. προφητεύω *prophesy*. ‖ ἔλθῃ aor² subj. ἔρχομαι. τέλειος *complete*; *perfect*. τὸ ἐκ μέρους *what is partial/in-
11 complete*; *what is imperfect*. ‖ ἤμην impf εἰμί. νήπιος
infant; *child*. ἐ-λάλουν impf λαλέω. ἐ-φρόνουν impf -νέω
think. ἐ-λογιζόμην impf -ζομαι v.5. γέ-γονα v.1, ὅτε γέγ.
since I became or preferably *now I am*. κατ-ήργηκα pf
-αργέω here, *have finished/done with*. τὰ τ. νηπίου *childish
12 things*. ‖ ἄρτι *now*. ἐλπίς 9:10. ἔσ-οπτρον *mirror*, of
polished metal, usu. bronze, δι' ἐσ. *in a mirror*. αἴνιγμα⁷

riddle, so ἐν αἰν. "in a puzzling way", *obscurely, indistinctly*. ἐκ μέρους v.9. ἐπι-γνώσομαι *I shall really know*, fut. -γινώσκω *know thoroughly/perfectly*. ἐπ-ε-γνώσθην aor. pass. *I am known* (by God). ‖ νυνὶ δέ *and now*. τρία neut. 13 of τρεῖς. μείζων 12:31, comp. for superl. *greatest* §148. ἡ ref. ἀγάπη as previously mentioned (anaphoric). ‖

διώκετε impv διώκω *pursue*, δ. τ. ἀγάπην *be eager in* 14 *pursuit of love* (cf Wm). ζηλοῦτε impv ζηλόω τι *be zealous for* sth. πνευματικός *spiritual* ; τὰ πν. *spiritual matters* (9:11), esp. *spiritual gifts*. μᾶλλον *preferably*. ἵνα w. subj. = obj. inf., see v.5 (θέλω). προφητεύητε subj. -εύω *prophesy*. ‖ λαλῶν ptc λαλέω. γλῶσσα *tongue* ; *language* ; 2 here throughout of ecstatic utterance. ἀκούω sts *understand*. πνεύματι dat. of instr. μυστήριον orig. place of initiation, hence *secret things* ; *mystery*. ‖ προφητεύων ptc. 3 οἰκο-δομή *edi-fication*. παρά-κλησις[4] (invitation) *exhortation* ; *encouragement*. παρα-μυθία *encouragement, consolation*. ‖ οἰκο-δομέω *edify, build up*, ἑαυτὸν οἱ. *benefits himself (only)*. ἐκκλησία wt art. *a community?* or *(the)* 4 *church?* ‖ μᾶλλον *even more*. θέλω ἵνα προφητεύητε grammatically equivalent to θέλω ὑμᾶς λαλεῖν: *I want you all* 5 *to speak with tongues but even more that you may prophesy* (= to prophesy). μείζων comp. of μέγας. ἐκτός *unless* ; pleon. w. εἰ μή (*except*). εἰ μή here w. subj, prob. because standing for ἐὰν μή §332. δι-ερμηνεύῃ subj. -ερμηνεύω *interpret*. ἵνα consec. *in such a way/so that*. λάβῃ aor² subj. λαμβάνω. ‖ νῦν δέ Fr. *or* ; *now then...* (atemporal). 6 ἔλθω aor² subj. ἔρχομαι. ὠφελήσω fut. -λέω *help/benefit/do good* to one, τί ὑμᾶς ὠ. *what good will I do you?* λαλήσω aor. subj. ἐν *in* (*the form of*). ἀπο-κάλυψις[4] *revelation*. γνῶσις[4] *knowledge*, sc. of the Christian gospel. προφητεία *prophecy*. διδαχή *instruction*. ‖ ὅμως usu. *nevertheless* ; un- 7 explained ; perh. in the sense of ὁμῶς (= ὁμοίως). ἄ-ψυχος *inanimate*. διδόντα ptc neut. pl. δίδωμι. αὐλός *flute*. κιθάρα *harp*. δια-στολή *distinction, difference*. φθόγγος *tone, note*. δῷ aor² subj. δίδωμι: διαστολὴν δ. *make some distinction*. γνωσθήσεται fut. pass. γινώσκω. αὐλούμενον ptc pass. αὐλέω *play the flute*. κιθαρίζω *play the harp*. ‖ καὶ γάρ *for again*. ἄ-δηλος *in-distinct, vague*. σάλπιγξ 8 -ιγγος ἡ *trumpet*. παρα-σκευάσεται fut. mid. -σκευάζω τι *prepare* sth ; mid. *make preparations*. πόλεμος *war*, here *battle*. ‖ διά *by means of, with*. εὔ-σημος *clearly defined*, 9

whose meaning is clear. **λαλούμενον** ptc pass. v.2. **ἔσεσθε**
fut. εἰμί: ἔ. λαλοῦντες periphr. fut. *you will be speaking.*

10 **ἀήρ**[6] ἀέρος ὁ *air.* ‖ **τοσοῦτοι** pl. *so many.* **τύχοι** aor[2] opt.
τυγχάνω *happen*, εἰ τ. *if it should so happen, it could be,
perhaps*, ref. τοσαῦτα (rather than εἰσίν) *who knows how
many.* **γένος**[8] *kind.* **φωνή** sts *language.* **ἄ-φωνος** *dumb*

11 (12:2) ; *without meaning* or *un-intelligible.* ‖ **εἰδῶ** subj.
οἶδα (pf-pres). **δύναμις**[4] *force, meaning.* **βάρβαρος** *not
knowing Greek, foreign.* **ἐν ἐμοί** *to me* (= "in my estimation"); **ἐν** sts pleon., parallel to simple dat. (τῷ λαλοῦντι)

12 §120. ‖ **ἐπεί** *since* (causal). **ζηλωτής**[3] w. foll. gen. *one
ardent/eager for.* **πνεύματα** here, *spiritual gifts.* **πρός** *for.*
οἰκοδομή v.3. **ζητεῖτε** impv ζητέω, foll. by ἵνα w. subj.
seek/try to. **περισσεύητε** (sc. in them) subj. -εύω *excel.* ‖

13 **διό** *this is why.* **προσ-ευχέσθω** (he) *must pray*, impv 3rd

14 sg -εύχομαι. **δι-ερμηνεύῃ** v.5. ‖ **προσ-εύχωμαι** subj. **νοῦς**
νοός ὁ *mind.* **ἄ-καρπος** *fruit-less, without effect, idle.* ‖

15 **τί οὖν ἐστιν;** *how do matters stand then?* **προσ-εύξομαι** fut.
νοΐ dat. of νοῦς: τῷ νοΐ *intelligently.* **ψαλῶ** fut. ψάλλω

16 *sing praise.* ‖ **ἐπεί** *since* (sc. *if that were so*), *otherwise*
(Rom 3:6). **εὐ-λογῇς** subj. -λογέω "speak well of", *praise.*
ἀνα-πληρῶν ptc -πληρόω *fill up* ; so *occupy a place.* **ἰδιώτης**[3] *unlearned ; uninitiated* in the faith who does not speak
w. tongues, *outsider.* **ἐρεῖ** fut. λέγω. **σός** *your* (sg).
εὐ-χαριστία *thanksgiving.* **ἐπειδή** *since* (causal). **τί** indir.

17 interr. **οἶδεν** *know* in sense of "understand". ‖ **μὲν γάρ**...
ἀλλά *for*...*no doubt, but.* **καλῶς** *well, properly.* **εὐ-χαριστέω**

18 *give thanks.* **οἰκο-δομεῖται** pass. v.4. ‖ **ὑμῶν** gen. of comp.

19 **μᾶλλον** *more.* ‖ **ἐκκλησία** Christian *congregation, assembly*
of the faithful. **θέλω**...**ἤ:** supply μᾶλλον *I would rather...
than.* **πέντε** = 5. **νοΐ** v.15, w. aid of ordinary graces. **λαλῆσαι** aor. inf. **κατ-ηχήσω** aor. subj. -ηχέω *instruct* orally.

20 **μύριοι** = 10,000. ‖ **παιδίον** (dim. of παῖς) *child.* **γίνεσθε**
be !, show yourselves ! impv γίνομαι (supplying for impv
2nd pl. εἰμί). **φρήν** φρενός ἡ *mind*, pl. *mentality, outlook.*
κακία *evil*, dat. of respect §53. **νηπιάζετε** impv -άζω *be*

21 *like a child.* **τέλειος** *mature, adult.* ‖ **γέ-γραπται** *it stands
written*, pf pass. γράφω. **ὅτι** = "... **ἑτερό-γλωσσος** ὁ *one
speaking another language.* **χεῖλος**[8] *lip* ; pl. Hebr., ἐν χ.
ἑτέρων *by the lips of foreigners.* **λαλήσω** fut. λαλέω.

22 **εἰσ-ακούσονται** fut. -ακούω τινός *listen to, obey* one. ‖ **εἰς**
for pred. nom. *as* §32. **πιστεύουσιν** ptc dat. pl. -εύω: οἱ

πιστεύοντες *the believers.* ἄ-πιστος *un-believing.* προφητεία v.6. ‖ συν-έλθῃ‖ aor² subj. -έρχομαι *come together,* 23
gather, meet. ἐπὶ τὸ αὐτό *in one place, together.* λαλῶσιν
subj. εἰσ-έλθωσιν aor² subj. -έρχομαι. ἰδιώτης, ἐροῦσιν
v.16. μαίνομαι *be mad* or *raving.* ‖ προφητεύωσιν v.1. 24
ἐλέγχεται pass. ἐλέγχω *point out ; convince, convict.*
ἀνα-κρίνεται pass. -κρίνω *inquire into ; challenge.* ‖ κρυπτός 25
hidden, secret. φανερός *clear, evident.* πεσών aor² ptc
πίπτω. προσ-κυνήσει fut. -κυνέω τινί *worship one.* ἀπ-
αγγέλλων ptc -αγγέλλω *declare.* ὅτι v.21. ὄντως *in reality, really, truly.* ‖

τί οὖν ἐστιν ; v.15. συν-έρχησθε subj. v.23. ψαλμός 26
hymn. διδαχή, ἀποκάλυψις v.6. ἑρμηνεία *interpretation.*
πρός v.12. γινέσθω *let...be done ! ...is to be done,* impv 3rd
sg γίνομαι. ‖ εἴτε wt a second εἴτε, *if.* κατὰ δύο ἤ...τρεῖς 27
two or...three at one time, i.e. during one meeting. πλεῖστος
superl. of πολύς, neut. used advl, *at most.* μέρος⁸ *part,*
ἀνὰ μέρος *in turn.* δι-ερμηνευέτω impv -εύω *interpret.* ‖
ᾗ subj. εἰμί. δι-ερμηνευτής³ *interpreter.* σιγάτω impv 28
3rd sg σιγάω *keep silent.* λαλείτω impv. ‖ λαλείτωσαν 29
impv 3rd pl. δια-κρινέτωσαν impv -κρίνω *distinguish ;
use one's discernment/judgement.* ‖ ἀπο-καλυφθῇ *a revela-* 30
tion is made, aor. subj. pass. -καλύπτω *reveal.* καθημένῳ
ptc -ημαι *sit,* ἄλλῳ κ. *to another sitting by.* ‖ καθ᾽ ἕνα *one* 31
by one. προφητεύειν inf. μανθάνωσιν subj. -άνω *learn.*
παρα-καλῶνται subj. pass. -καλέω *encourage.* ‖ πνεύματα 32
v.12. ὑπο-τάσσεται pass. -τάσσω *subject ;* pass. *be under
the control of* (dat.). ‖ ἀ-κατα-στασία *dis-order.* ‖ σιγάτωσαν 33,34
3rd pl. v.28. ἐπι-τρέπεται pass. -τρέπω τινί w. inf. *allow*
one to... λαλεῖν inf. ὑπο-τασσέσθωσαν impv pass. ‖ μα- 35
θεῖν aor² inf. v.31. ἐν οἴκῳ *at home.* ἴδιος in HGk often
= *his, her, their.* ἐπ-ερωτάτωσαν impv -ερωτάω *ask* one a
question. αἰσχρός *disgraceful.* ‖ ἀφ᾽ ὑμῶν... emphatic po- 36
sition, *was it from you that...?* κατ-ήντησεν aor. -αντάω
come down or *to.* ‖ πνευματικός v.1. ἐπι-γινωσκέτω impv 37
-γινώσκω *recognize.* ‖ ἀ-γνοέω *not to know,* here *not to* 38
acknowledge God's precepts ; pass. *he is not...* ‖ ζηλοῦτε 39
v. 1. κωλύετε impv κωλύω *hinder, discourage ;* sts a pres.
impv in a prohibition retains the durative character of
the pres., not "stop..." but *never...* Lk 10:7, I Tim
4:14. ‖ εὐ-σχημόνως *properly.* τάξις⁴ *right order,* κατὰ τ. 40
with order. γινέσθω v.26. ‖

15   γνωρίζω *make known*; *remind.* εὐ-ηγγελισάμην aor.
-αγγελίζομαί τί τινι *announce* some good news / *preach*
to one. παρ-ε-λάβετε aor² παρα-λαμβάνω *take over, receive.*
ἑστήκατε *you stand*, pf (intr. w. pres. meaning) ἵστημι. ‖

2   σῴζεσθε *you are being saved*, pass. σῴζω. τίνι as indir.
interr., τίνι λόγῳ *in what words.* κατ-έχω τι *hold* sth
back or *down*; *hold firmly, retain* sth. ἐκτός *unless*, w.
εἰ μή pleon. 14:5. εἰκῇ *frivolously, heedlessly.* ἐ-πιστεύσατε
you made the act of faith / *became believers*, aor. inceptive

3   -εύω. ‖ παρ-έ-δωκα, aor. παρα-δίδωμι, w. παραλαμβάνω t.t.
for reception and transmission of church doctrine. ἐν
πρώτοις *in the first place.* ἀπ-έ-θανεν aor² ἀπο-θνῄσκω.
ὑπέρ (*to atone*) *for.* γραφῇ a *writing*; pl. *the scriptures.* ‖

4   ἐ-τάφη aor² pass. θάπτω *bury.* ἐ-γήγερται pf pass. ἐγείρω;
pf connoting "he has been raised and lives" §287, though
here the definite time indication imposes the transln

5   *was raised.* τρίτος *third.* ‖ ὤφθη aor. pass. ὁράω; pass.

6   intr. w. dat. *appear to* one. εἶτα *then, next.* ‖ ἔπειτα *then,
thereafter.* ἐπ-άνω *above, over.* πεντα-κόσιοι = 500. ἐφ-
άπαξ *at one time.* πλείων⁶ πλείονος neut. πλεῖον (comp. of
πολύς) *more,* οἱ πλ. *the greater number.* ἄρτι *now, the present time.* ἐ-κοιμήθησαν aor. dep. -μάομαι *be/fall asleep,*

8   also in sense of *die.* ‖ ἔσχατος *last,* neut. used advl.
ὡσ-περ-εί *as it were,* (colloq.) *sort of.* ἔκ-τρωμα⁷ an *abor-
tion,* preferably an *untimely birth* sc. into the apostolic

9   family. κἀμοί = καὶ ἐμοί *to me also.* ‖ ἐλάχιστος (superl.
of μικρός small) *least.* ἱκανός *enough, adequate* ; so, *worthy.*
καλεῖσθαι inf. pass. καλέω. δι-ότι *because.* ἐ-δίωξα aor.

10   *pursue* ; *persecute.* ‖ ἡ εἰς ἐμέ (*given*) *to me.* κενός *empty,
ineffectual.* ἐ-γενήθη aor. dep. γίνομαι (= ἐγένετο) supplying constative (global) aor. (§253) for εἰμί. περισσότερος (comp. of περισσός excessive) neut. advl, *yet more.*

11   αὐτῶν gen. of comp. ἐ-κοπίασα aor. -ιάω *toil.* ‖ εἴτε...εἴτε
whether...or. κηρύσσω *preach.* ἐ-πιστεύσατε v.2. ‖

12   κηρύσσεται pass. ὅτι *to the effect that.* ἐγήγερται v.4.
ἐν ὑμῖν τινες *some of you.* ἀνά-στασις⁴ *resurrection.* οὐκ

14   ἔστιν (not encl.) *does not exist, there is no.* ‖ κενός v.10.
ἄρα *then, in that case.* κήρυγμα⁷ *theme of our preaching,*

15   *what we preach.* ‖ εὑρισκόμεθα pass. εὑρίσκω, pass. *find
oneself, be.* ψευδο-μάρτυς⁶ -μάρτυρος ὁ *false witness.* τοῦ
θεοῦ gen. obj. *about God.* ἐ-μαρτυρήσαμεν aor. -ρέω *testify.*
κατὰ τ. θεοῦ in HGk possibly wt hostile connotation :

about God. ἤγειρεν aor. ἐγείρω. εἴπερ ἄρα *if in fact,*
"real" condition notwithstanding its denial of what is
reality §306. ‖ ματαία fem. of μάταιος masc. (and sts fem.) 17
pointless, futile. ἔτι *still.* ‖ ἄρα v.14. κοιμηθέντες aor. 18
ptc dep. v.7. ἀπ-ώλοντο *are lost,* aor² mid. -όλλυμι. ‖
ἠλπικότες pf ptc ἐλπίζω *hope,* ἠλπ. ἐσμέν periphr. cstr, 19
we have hope. μόνον: word order would indicate "only
hope" but the argument requires "only in this life".
ἐλεεινότερος comp. of ἐλεεινός *pitiable* ; comp. for superl.
§147. ‖ νυνὶ δέ *but as it is, but the fact is.* ἀπ-αρχή *first* 20
fruits consecrated to God in token of the entire harvest
which they represent and for which they are substituted ;
each element having its application to the resurrection
of Christ. κε-κοιμημένων pf v.6. ‖ ἐπειδή *since, here* ἐ. 21
γάρ *for.* ἀνάστασις v.12. ‖ ὥσ-περ *as.* ζῳο-ποιηθήσονται 22
fut. pass. -ποιέω *bring to life.* ‖ τάγμα⁷ military *rank;* 23
more generally, *order.* ἀπαρχή v.20. ἔπειτα v.6. οἱ τ.
Χριστοῦ *those (who are) Christ's,* = ἐν Χριστῷ transcending
obj. and subjective categories and den. mystical union
of Christians w. Christ their Head §39. παρ-ουσία (< πάρ-
ειμι be present ; to have come) *advent* of Christ. ‖ εἶτα 24
v.5. τέλος⁸ *end ; consummation.* παρα-διδῷ subj. 3rd sg
-δίδωμι *surrender, deliver up.* ὁ Θεὸς κ. πατήρ *God the
Father.* κατ-αργήσῃ aor. subj. -αργέω *bring to nothing.*
ἀρχή *rule* ; ἀρχή, ἐξουσία, δύναμις hierarchies of spiritual
powers. ‖ βασιλεύειν inf. -εύω *reign.* ἄχρι οὗ *until* 11:26. 25
Θῇ aor² subj. τίθημι. ἐχθρός *enemy.* ‖ ἔσχατος v.8. κατ- 26
αργεῖται pass. transl. the last enemy *to be brought to noth-
ing/destroyed.* ‖ ὑπ-έ-ταξεν aor. ὑπο-τάσσω *put under.* ὅταν 27
εἴπῃ *when he has (shall have) said,* aor² subj. ref. fut.
ὑπο-τέ-τακται pf pass. *is in subjection.* δῆλος *clear, evident,*
δῆλον ὅτι *it is clear that (he means).* ἐκτός w. gen. *except,
excluding.* ὑπο-τάξαντος aor. ptc gen. *him who has subjected,* i.e. God. αὐτῷ i.e. Christ. ‖ ὑπο-ταγῇ aor² pass. 28
[καὶ] αὐτὸς ὁ υἱός [even] *the Son himself.* ὑπο-ταγήσεται
fut. pass. intr. *submit* or refl. *subject oneself,* cf Rom 10:3.
ᾖ subj. εἰμί. ‖ ἐπεί *for (otherwise).* ποιήσουσιν fut. ποιέω. 29
οἱ βαπτιζόμενοι ptc pass. or mid. *those who are baptized*
or *who have / get themselves baptized.* ὑπέρ *for =* "in
favour of"; or "in place of" §91. ὅλως...οὐκ *definitely not,
not...at all.* ἐγείρονται v.15. βαπτίζονται pass. ‖ τί καὶ 30
ἡμεῖς; *why ever are we?* ⌐or *why are we still?* (v.30

do we still?) §459. κινδυνεύω *run risks.* πᾶσαν ὥραν
31 *all the time.* ‖ καθ' ἡμέραν *every day,* κατά distributive.
ἀπο-θνήσκω *I die.* νή w. acc. (*I swear*) *by.* ὑμέτερος *your,*
gen. obj. *in you.* καύχησις[4] *boasting,* also *ground for boast-*
32 *ing, pride.* ‖ κατὰ ἄνθρωπον variously interpreted : *as a*
(mere) *man* (opp. a Christian) ; or *with all my strength* ;
or, most likely, *as we say,* introducing a familiar expression. ἐ-θηριο-μάχησα (< θηρίον wild beast + μάχομαι
fight) *fight with wild beasts,* presumably met. ?of struggles
with determined and unscrupulous men. ὄφελος[8] (< ὀφέλλω increase) *advantage, use.* φάγωμεν, πίωμεν aor² subj.
hort. ἐσθίω, πίνω. αὔριον *tomorrow.* ἀπο-θνήσκομεν pres.
33 for fut. §278. ‖ πλανᾶσθε 6:9. φθείρω *destroy* ; *corrupt.*
ἦθος[8] *habit, way.* χρηστός (< χράομαι use) *good.* ὁμιλία
(< ὁμιλέω associate with) *companionship, company.* κακός
34 *bad.* ‖ ἐκ-νήψατε aor. impv -νήφω *come out of your stupor* ;
become sober. δικαίως *justly, like upright men.* ἁμαρτάνετε
impv -τάνω *sin,* μὴ ἁμ. *sin no more* §246. ἀ-γνωσία *ignorance,*
failure to recognize. θεοῦ obj. gen. ἐν-τροπή *shame,* 6:5,
πρὸς ἐ. ὑμῖν *to shame you.* ‖
35   ἐρεῖ fut. λέγω, fut. for class. opt. §356. ποῖος ; *of*
what sort? instr. dat. ἔρχονται as often in fut. sense
36 §278. ‖ ἄ-φρων[6] ἄφρονος neut. ἄφρον *sense-less, foolish.*
σπείρω *sow.* ζῳο-ποιεῖται pass. v.23. ἀπο-θάνῃ aor² subj.
37 -θνήσκω. ‖ γενησόμενον fut. ptc, οὐ τὸ σῶμα τὸ γ. *not the*
body to be. γυμνός *bare.* κόκκος *grain, seed.* εἰ τύχοι *it*
could be 14:10. σῖτος *wheat.* λοιπός (< λείπω leave) *left*
38 *behind,* οἱ λ. *the rest.* ἠ-θέλησεν aor. θέλω, aor. (he has
willed already before giving). καί epexegetic, *that is, i.e.*
39 §455ζ. σπέρμα[7] *seed.* ‖ ὁ αὐτός *the same.* ἄλλος μέν...
ἄλλος δέ... *there is one...another...* κτῆνος[8] (< κτάομαι
acquire ; possess) *farm animal.* πτηνός *winged* ; as noun,
40 *bird.* ἰχθύς -ύος ὁ *fish.* ‖ ἐπ-ουράνιος *heavenly.* ἐπί-γειος
41 *earthly.* ‖ ἥλιος *sun.* σελήνη *moon.* ἀστήρ[6] ἀστέρος ὁ *star.*
δια-φέρω τινός *differ from sth,* ἀστήρ...ἀστέρος διαφ. *one*
42 *star differs...from another.* ‖ ἀνάστασις v.12. σπείρεται
pass. v.36. ἐν of manner §116. φθορά *liability to perish/*
43 *decay.* ἀ-φθαρσία *im-perishability.* ‖ ἀ-τιμία *dishonour* ; as
44 opp. δόξα, *humiliation.* ἀ-σθένεια *weakness.* ‖ ψυχικός endowed with ψυχή principle of life, *animal, living* ; (as opp.
πνευματικός) *physical.* πνευματικός *spiritual.* ἔστιν (non-
45 encl.) *there exists.* ‖ γέ-γραπται pf pass. γράφω. ἐ-γένετο

aor² γίνομαι. εἰς for pred. nom. §32, *Adam became a living being*. ψυχή = Lat. *anima*. ζῶσαν ptc fem. acc. ζάω. ἔσχατος v.8, superl. for comp. (ὕστερος) §151. ζῳο-ποιοῦν *life-giving*, ptc neut. v.23. ‖ πρῶτον for πρότερον §151 ; 46 pred., *was not first*. ἔπειτα v.6. ‖ χοϊκός (< χοῦς earth, 47 dust) *made from dust, earthy*. δεύτερος *second*. ‖ οἷος... 48 τοιοῦτος = Lat. *qualis...talis, as...so*, men of dust are of a piece with the man made from dust. ἐπ-ουράνιος v.40. ‖ ἐ-φορέσαμεν aor. φορέω *wear* (as clothes). εἰκών⁶ -κόνος ἡ 49 *likeness*. φορέσομεν fut. ⟦var. φορέσωμεν *let us wear* (aor. subj. hort.)⟧. ‖ τοῦτο in HGk may refer to what follows 50 §213. φημί *I say*, often approximating to *I mean*. κληρο-νομῆσαι aor. inf. -νομέω *inherit* (the Kingdom may be said to be "inherited" in as much as God assigns (νέμει) it). φθορά, ἀ-φθαρσία v.42, abstract for concrete : *the perishable, the imperishable*. ‖ μυστήριον *mystery* 13:2. κοιμηθησόμεθα 51 fut. dep. -μάομαι v.6. ἀλλαγησόμεθα fut² pass. ἀλλάσσω *change*. ‖ ἄ-τομος (< ἀ- + τέμνω cut) *in-divisible, instant* 52 of time so short as to preclude division, a *flash*. ῥιπή (< ῥίπτω throw) a rapid movement such as a *twinkling* of an eye. σάλπιγξ⁶ -ιγγος ἡ *trumpet* ; *blast* on the trumpet, *trumpet-call*. σαλπίσει fut. -ίζω *play the trumpet* ; of a trumpet, *sound*. ἐγερθήσονται fut. pass. v.15. ἄ-φθαρτος *imperishable, immortal*. ‖ φθαρτός *perishable*, τὸ φ. *what is* 53 *perishable, this perishable nature*. ἐν-δύσασθαι aor. inf. -δύομαι (mid.) *wear*, aor. *put on* oneself as a garment. ἀ-φθαρσία *incorruption, integrity* v.42. θνητός *mortal*, τὸ θ. *mortality, mortal nature*. ἀ-θανασία *immortality*. ‖ ἐν-δύ- 54 σηται aor. subj. mid. γενήσεται fut. γίνομαι : γεν. ὁ λόγος *the word...will come to pass / be accomplished*. γε-γραμμένος *written* (sc. in scripture), pf ptc pass. γράφω. κατ-ε-πόθη aor. pass. κατα-πίνω *drink down*, hence *swallow up, engulf*, lit. and met. νῖκος⁸ *victory*, εἰς ν. swallowed up *in victory*. ‖ ποῦ ; *where?* θάνατε voc. of θάνατος. κέντρον *sting*. ‖ ἡ 55,56 ἁμαρτία...ὁ νόμος both pred. ‖ χάρις w. dat. *thanks*. διδόντι 57 ptc dat. δίδωμι, in agreement w. θεός : *to God who gives us...* ‖ ὥστε *so then*. ἀγαπητός *beloved*. ἑδραῖος (< ἕδρα 58 seat) *firm*. γίνεσθε impv γίνομαι *prove yourselves* or for impv of εἰμί *be !* ἀ-μετα-κίνητος *unshakeable, immovable*. περισσεύοντες here = *doing all in your power for*, ptc -εύω *have in abundance, be rich in*. πάντοτε *always*. εἰδότες ptc of pf-pres. οἶδα. κόπος *toil, labour*. κενός *empty, vain*. ‖

16   λογεία *collection*. εἰς *for*, instead of dat. of advantage. οἱ ἅγιοι wt qualification, *the Christians* / *the church* at Jerusalem. ὥσπερ *as*. δι-έ-ταξα aor. δια-τάσσω *direct*,

2 *order*. ποιήσατε aor. impv ποιέω. ‖ μία σαββάτου ordinal number prob. a Hebr., *first day of the week* ; earliest mention of Sunday observance. κατά distributive, *every*. παρ' ἑαυτῷ *at home*. τιϑέτω impv τίϑημι *set aside*. ϑησαυρίζων ptc -ίζω *treasure, save up*. ὅ τι ἐάν (= ἄν) *whatever*. εὐοδῶται subj. -οδόομαι "be well led", *do well, prosper* ; so, *whatever he can afford*. ἔλϑω aor² subj. ἔρχομαι. γίνωνται subj. γίνομαι here *be taking place* : *so that the collection will*

3 *not be going on when I come*. ‖ παρα-γένωμαι aor² subj. -γίνομαι *come on the scene, arrive*. ἐάν = ἄν. δοκιμάσητε aor. subj. -άζω *approve* (after testing) ; cstr thus : "*any whom you have approved...these I will send...*" ἐπι-στολή *letter*, here of recommendation. διά of attendant circumstances, *with* letters §114 ; or (ass. w. δοκιμάσητε foll. the var. punctuation reading a comma only after ἐπιστολῶν) instr., *by means of* letters. πέμψω fut. πέμπω. ἀπ-ενεγκεῖν aor² inf. ἀπο-φέρω *take* (away), ἀπο- perfective §132. χάρις

4 *gift*. ‖ ἄξιος of things, *worthy, appropriate*, ἐάν...πορεύεσθαι *if it is worth while for me to go*. ᾗ subj. εἰμί. κἀμέ = καὶ ἐμέ. πορεύεσθαι, πορεύσονται inf. and fut. -εύομαι. ‖

5   ἐλεύσομαι fut. ἔρχομαι. ὅταν M. δι-έλϑω (aor² subj. -έρχομαι) *when I have* (fut.) *passed through* M. M. γὰρ διέρχομαι *for I pass through* M. (that is my route). ‖

6 τυχόν (aor² neut. ptc τυγχάνω) *perhaps* ; *possibly*. παρα-μενῶ fut. -μένω stay, π. πρός τινα *stay with* one. καί *even*. παρα-χειμάσω fut. -χειμάζω *spend the winter*. ὑμεῖς in emphatic position. προ-πέμψητε aor. subj. -πέμπω *see* one *off, send on one's way*, implying provision for the journey. οὗ ἐάν (= ἄν) w. subj. *from wherever*. πορεύωμαι subj.

7 *I leave/set out on a journey*. ‖ ἄρτι *now*. πάρ-οδος ἡ *passage*, ἐν π. *in passing*. ἰδεῖν aor² inf. ὁράω. ἐλπίζω *hope*. χρόνος *time*, χρόνον τινά *for some time*, acc. of extent. ἐπι-μεῖναι aor. inf. -μένω *stay on*. ἐπι-τρέψῃ aor. subj.

8 -τρέπω *allow*. ‖ ἐπι-μενῶ fut. πεντηκοστή (fem. of -κοστός fiftieth) *Feast of Weeks*, celebrated on the fiftieth day after

9 Passover. ‖ ϑύρα *door*. ἀν-έ-ῳγεν pf² ἀν-οίγω, pf² intr., *is/ stands open*. μεγάλη fem. of μέγας. ἐν-εργής *effective*, here, *more than promising*. ἀντι-κείμενοι ptc -κειμαι *oppose* ; ptc *opponent*. ‖ ἔλϑῃ v.2, an eventual condition

§320, 322. **βλέπετε** impv βλέπω: β. **ἵνα** *see* (to it) *that*, *make sure that*. **ἀ-φόβως** *without fear* or *diffidence*. **γένηται** aor² subj. γίνομαι: **ἵνα ἀφόβως γ.** *that he begins to feel at home, that he loses his diffidence with you*. **ἐργάζομαι** *work, do work*. **κἀγώ** = καὶ ἐγώ. || **ἐξ-ουθενήσῃ** aor. subj. 11 **-ουθενέω** (< οὐδέν) *disdain*. **προ-πέμψατε** aor. impv v.6. **ἐν εἰρήνῃ** *in peace*, Hebr. expression. **ἐκ-δέχομαι** *expect*. || **πολλά** acc. pl. used advl (= *much*) to strengthen the ver- 12 bal idea, here *strongly*. **παρ-ε-κάλεσα** aor. παρα-καλέω *urge*. **ἵνα** for inf. §407. **καί** but §455β. **πάντως** *altogether*, π. οὐ *not at all*. **θέλημα**? *his will*, ? *God's will*. **ἐλεύσεται** v.5. **εὐ-καιρήσῃ** *when he gets a good opportunity*, aor. subj. *-καιρέω* *have a good opportunity*. ||

γρηγορεῖτε impv -ορέω (vb formed from pf ἐγρήγορα 13 of ἐγείρω) *be watchful/alert*. **στήκετε** impv στήκω (late form derived from pf intr. of ἵστημι) *stand* firm. **ἀνδρί-ζεσθε** impv -ίζομαι mid. (< ἀνήρ) *show oneself a man*. **κραταιοῦσθε** impv -αιόομαι *hold out strongly*. || **γινέσθω** *let* 14 (*it*) *be done*, impv 3rd sg γίνομαι. **πάντα ὑμῶν** *your every* act. || **οἰκία** *household*. **ἀπ-αρχή** *first-fruits*, i.e. earliest con- 15 verts. **διακονία** *service*. **ἔ-ταξαν** aor. τάσσω *place, sta-tion* ; τ. ἑαυτόν *devote oneself*. || **ἵνα** abs. w. impv force 16 §415. **ὑπο-τάσσησθε** subj. -τάσσω *put under, make subject* ; pass. intr. *submit*. **τοιοῦτος** *such a one*. **συν-εργοῦντι** ptc -εργέω *co-operate*, ptc *fellow-worker*. **κοπιῶντι** ptc -ιάω *labour*. || **παρ-ουσία** *coming, arrival*. **ὑμέτερος** obj. *of you*. 17 **ὑστέρημα**⁷ a *lack, want*, ὑ. ὑμέτερον *lack of you, your ab-sence*. **ἀν-ε-πλήρωσαν** aor. ἀνα-πληρόω *fill up, make up for*. || **ἀν-έ-παυσαν** aor. ἀνα-παύω *give rest, refresh*. **ἐπι-γινώσκετε** 18 impv -γινώσκω *recognize* for what they are, *appreciate*. || **ἀσπάζομαι** *greet*. **Ἀσία** Apoc 1:4. **πολλά** v.12, here, *warmly*. 19 **ἡ κατ' οἶκον αὐτῶν ἐκκλησία** *the congregation which meets in their house*. || **ἀσπάσασθε** aor. impv. **φίλημα**⁷ *kiss*. || **ἀσπα-** 20,21 **σμός** *greeting*. **ἐν τ. ἐμῇ χειρί** *in my own hand(writing)*. || **φιλέω** *love*. **ἤτω** impv 3rd sg εἰμί. **ἀνά-θεμα** *accursed* 12:3. 22 **Μαρανα θα** transliterated from Aramaic, *our Lord, come!* Others read as **Μαραν αθα** *our Lord has come*. ||

II CORINTHIANS

1 οὔσῃ ptc fem. εἰμί. οἱ ἅγιοι because dedicated to God ; title of all believers. 'Αχαΐα Roman province of
2 (the southern half of) Greece. ‖ χάρις...καὶ εἰρήνη I Cor 1:3. ‖
3 εὐ-λογητός blessed (be). οἰκτιρμός compassion, pl. being Hebr. παρά-κλησις⁴ consolation, encouragement ; πᾶσα π.
4 every consolation §188. ‖ παρα-καλῶν ptc -καλέω. πᾶς w. art. all our distress. θλῖψις⁴ (< θλίβω press) distress. εἰς τό w. acc. + inf. so that, hovering between final and consec. sense. δύνασθαι inf. δύναμαι. παρα-καλεῖν inf. ἐν πάσῃ θλίψει wt art. in every/any distress §188. ἧς for ᾗ by attraction of rel. §16. παρα-καλούμεθα pass. αὐτοί
5 (we our)selves. ‖ περισσεύω exceed the measure, be without measure. πάθημα⁷ (< πάσχω v.6) what is felt or suffered,
6 suffering. καί also. ‖ εἴτε...εἴτε if...if. θλιβόμεθα pass. θλίβω press, pass. be hard pressed/in straits or distress. ὑπέρ κτλ. understand ἐστίν (it is) for. σωτηρία salvation. ἐν-εργουμένης ptc mid. -εργέω be at work, be effective, mid. w. non-personal subject. ὑπο-μονή endurance. ὁ αὐτός the same. ὧν for ἅ by attraction, ὧν...πάσχομεν
7 which we also endure. πάσχω suffer. ‖ ἐλπίς⁶ -ίδος ἡ hope. βέβαιος firm. ὑπέρ for (= περί concerning) §96. εἰδότες ptc pf-pres. οἶδα. κοινωνός sharer. τῶν παθημάτων (from
8 context) our sufferings. ‖ ἀγνοεῖν inf. ἀ-γνοέω not to know, οὐ γάρ...ἀγνοεῖν we should like you to realize. ὑπέρ v.7. θλῖψις v.4. γενομένης aor² ptc γίνομαι. ὅτι that explains θλίψεως. ὑπερ-βολή (< ὑπερ-βάλλω exceed, surpass) excess, καθ' ὑπ. exceedingly, utterly. ὑπέρ w. acc. beyond. ἐ-βαρήθημεν aor. pass. -ρέω weigh down. ἐξ-α-πορηθῆναι aor. inf. dep. -α-πορέω or -α-πορέομαι be utterly (ἐξ-) without (ἀ-) a way (πόρος), w. gen. (of separation), be at one's wit's end about, despair of or for ἐξαπ. ἡμᾶς καὶ τοῦ ζῆν (inf.) we despaired even of living / for our lives. ‖
9 αὐτοὶ ἐν ἑαυτοῖς shown by 1st pl. vb (ἐσχήκαμεν) to signify

we (ἑαυτοῖς for 1st pl. ἡμῖν αὐτοῖς) *within/inside ourselves.*
ἀπό-κριμα⁷ *answer* ; in law, *sentence.* **ἐσχήκαμεν** pf ἔχω
perh. w. aoristic force (avoiding aor. as almost exclusively = "acquired" v.15 §289) ; or perh. pf must be
understood to include the intended effect ἵνα...ἐπὶ τῷ θεῷ.
πε-ποιθότες pf² (w. pres. meaning) ptc πείθω *persuade,* in
pf² and pass. w. ἐπί and dat., *trust in, rely on* one. **ὧμεν**
subj. εἰμί, w. πεπ. forming periphr. cstr. **ἐγείρων** ptc :
ὁ ἐγ. (*he*) *who raises.* ‖ **τηλικοῦτος** *so great,* τ. θανάτου
so great a (*danger of*) *death.* **ἐρ-ρύσατο** aor. ῥύομαι *rescue.*
ῥύσεται fut. **ἠλπίκαμεν** *we have fixed our hope,* pf ἐλπίζω
hope. **[ὅτι] καὶ ἔτι** *that yet again.* ‖ **συν-υπ-ουργούντων** ptc
-ουργέω *join in serving, co-operate,* gen. abs. **δέησις**⁴ *supplication, prayer,* dat. of instr. **πρόσ-ωπον** *face* ; *person,
individual.* **χάρισμα**⁷ *gift, favour,* esp. from God. **εὐ-
χαριστηθῇ** aor. subj. pass. -χαριστέω, *give thanks* : "while
you will help by your prayer for us, in order that thanks
may be offered on our behalf by (ἐκ) many persons for
the favour (χάρισμα) granted us through (διά ?in answer
to their prayers) many". ‖

    γάρ introduces the ground for his confidence that he
may count on their help. **καύχησις**⁴ *boasting,* here, *reason
for boasting.* **μαρτύριον** *testimony.* **συν-είδησις**⁴ (< σύν-οιδα
be conscious of) *moral consciousness, con-science.* **ἁπλότης**⁶
-ότητος ἡ *simplicity.* **εἰλι-κρινεία** *sincerity* (I Cor 5:8), εἰ.
τ. θεοῦ *a godly sincerity.* **σοφία** *wisdom.* **σαρκικός,** opp.
πνευματικός, *worldly.* **ἀν-ε-στράφημεν** aor² pass. ἀνα-στρέφω
over-turn ; pass. refl., *behave oneself, live* in a certain way ;
aor. constative (global) §253. **περισσοτέρ ως** (comp. of
περισσῶς) *even more, above all.* **πρός** w. acc. of person
with. ‖ **οὐ...ἄλλα...ἀλλ᾽ ἤ** *nothing other than.* **ἀνα-γινώσκω**
read, ἃ ἀν. ἢ καὶ ἐπιγινώσκετε (*just*) *what you read and
what is familiar to you* (= you recognize) ; a play on
ἀνα- ἐπι- γινώσκω. **ἐλπίζων** ptc v.10. **τέλος**⁸ *end,* ἕως τ. *to
the end* (sc. of the age), *to the last,* meaning the day of
our Lord (v.14) ; alternatively, *fully, thoroughly* in contrast to ἀπὸ μέρους (v.14). **ἐπι-γνώσεσθε** fut. ‖ **ἐπ-έ-γνωτε**
aor². **μέρος**⁸ *part* ; ἀπὸ μ. *in part.* **ὅτι** *that,* cstr w. ἐπιγνώ-
σεσθε. **καύχημα**⁷ *object of* one's *boast,* (*cause for*) *pride,*
κ. ὑμῶν ἐσμεν *we are your pride.* **καθάπερ καί** *as you also*
(*are*) *ours.* ‖ **πεποίθησις**⁴ (cf πεποιθότες v.9) *confidence.* **ἐ-
βουλόμην** impf βούλομαι *will* ; *want* ; *intend.* **πρότερος** *for-*

mer, neut. as adv. *formerly*. ἐλθεῖν aor² inf. ἔρχομαι. δεύτερος *second*. χάρις here *benefit* (i.e. a visit) 〚var. χαράν a double *pleasure* (χαρά joy)〛. σχῆτε aor² subj.

16 ἔχω, aor. inceptive *get* §250. ‖ δι' ὑμῶν *via/by way of you*. δι-ελθεῖν aor² inf. -έρχομαι *pass through*, aor. effective *reach*. προ-πεμφθῆναι aor. inf. pass. -πέμπω *see one off*,

17 *send on* one's *way* (with funds and supplies). ‖ βουλόμενος ptc, *in planning*. μήτι interr. expecting the answer "No". ἄρα *then* not always translatable in questions. ἐλαφρία (< ἔλαφρος light (weight)) *levity*, τῇ ἐλ. *with that irresponsibility* (art. implying "of which you accuse me"). ἐ-χρησάμην aor. χράομαι *use* ; w. adv. or advl phrase, *act* (cf Ac 27:3 = *act towards / treat* a person). βουλεύομαι *deliberate* ; *resolve*. κατὰ σάρκα *according to the flesh, from a merely human standpoint*. ἵνα consec. *with the result that with me it is yes, yes, and no, no at the same time* — *shilly-*

18 *shallying*. ῇ subj. εἰμί. ναί *yes*. ‖ πιστός *to be trusted, faithful*, a formula for swearing : *As God is true...* ὁ λόγος

19 ἡμῶν *our language* (= *way*) with you. ‖ κηρυχθείς aor. ptc pass. κηρύσσω *proclaim, preach*, lit. "Christ proclaimed among you through us". ἐ-γένετο aor², γέ-γονεν pf²

20 γίνομαι, pf connoting an abiding "Yes" §285. ‖ ἐπ-αγγελία *promise*, ὅσαι ἐπ. *however many or all the promises*. τὸ Ναί (sc. ἐστίν) *in him is their Yes* (i.e. fulfilment). διὸ καὶ κτλ. *therefore through him also the Amen from us to*

21 *God for his glory*. ‖ βεβαιῶν ptc -αιόω *make firm, establish*. εἰς Χριστόν i.e. ptc χρίω *anoint*. θεός pred. *it is God who gives us together with you security in Christ and has*

22 *anointed us*. ‖ σφραγισάμενος aor. ptc mid. -ίζω *seal* : χρίσας...σφρ. indicating baptism (cf the later custom of chrismation and consignation). δούς aor² ptc δίδωμι. ἀρραβών⁶ -ῶνος ὁ *deposit of money, instalment, pledge*, lit.

23 and met. ‖ μάρτυς⁶ -τυρος ὁ *a witness*, pred. *I call upon God as witness*. ἐπι-καλοῦμαι *call upon, invoke*. ἐπὶ τ. ἐμὴν ψυχήν *over my life*, i.e. *I stake my life on it*. φειδόμενος ptc -δομαί τινος *spare* one, φ. ὑμῶν *it was to spare*

24 *you that...* οὐκ-έτι *not yet*. ‖ κυριεύω τινός *domineer* over one. συν-εργός *fellow-worker*, σ. τῆς χαρᾶς ὑμῶν *as companions we work for your happiness*. τῇ...πίστει *by your faith*. ἑστήκατε *you stand firm*, pf (intr. w. pres. meaning)

2 ἵστημι. ‖ ἔ-κρινα aor. κρίνω *judge, deem* and so ἔκ. ἐμαυτῷ *I made up my mind, decided*. ἐμ-αυτῷ "dat. of advantage"

often wt equivalent in Eng. τοῦτο ref. what follows §213.
τὸ μή...ἐλθεῖν (aor[2] inf. ἔρχομαι) *not to come.* ἐν *with* of
concomitant circumstances (§116) admits of the connotation "bringing sorrow" (to you) as well as (coming)
"in sorrow". λύπη *sorrow.* ‖ ἐγώ emphatic. λυπέω τινά 2
sadden, cause sadness to one. καί in interr. §459. εὐ-
φραίνων ptc -νω *gladden, cheer.* εἰ μή *if not, except.* λυπού-
μενος *made sad,* ptc pass. ἐξ = ἀπό = ὑπό §87,90. ‖ ἔ- 3
γραψα aor. γράφω possibly an "epistolary aor." *I write*
(i.e. by the time they read it Paul will "have written")
but more likely Paul refers to an earlier letter no longer
extant. τοῦτο αὐτό *this very thing.* ἐλθών aor[2] ptc ἔρχομαι.
σχῶ aor[2] subj. ἔχω, in aor. *acquire, get.* ἀφ᾽ ὧν (for ἀπὸ
τούτων ἀφ᾽ ὧν) *from those from whom.* ἔδει impf δεῖ
I ought to have... ; since Eng. "ought" is already strictly
a past tense, the past must be made evident in the com-
plementary inf. χαίρειν inf. χαίρω *rejoice, be happy,*
ἀφ᾽...χ. lit. "from those from whom I ought to have
derived joy". πε-ποιθώς pf[2] (w. pres. meaning) ptc πείθω
persuade ; πεπ. ἐπί...ἐστιν *relying on, trusting in you all
that my joy is* (that) *of all of you.* χαρά *joy.* ‖ θλῖψις[4] 4
distress. συν-οχή *tension, anxiety.* διά w. gen. ref. attendant circumstances §114. δάκρυον a *tear.* λυπηθῆτε aor.
subj. pass. λυπέω. γνῶτε aor[2] subj. γινώσκω. εἰς the love
I have *for* or I bear *to.* περισσοτέρως (comp. of περισσῶς)
adv. "more than abundantly", *beyond measure.*

λε-λύπηκεν *has caused sadness,* pf v.2. μέρος[8] *part,* 5
ἀπὸ μ. *in part, in a way.* ἐπι-βαρέω *weigh heavily on, bear
hardly on* ; here *exaggerate.* ‖ ἱκανός *enough* ; neut. as noun, 6
cf Lat. *satis.* τοιοῦτος *such a one.* ἐπι-τιμία *punishment.*
πλείων[6] πλείονος (comp. of πολύς) *more,* ὁ πλ. *the majority.* ‖
τοὐναντίον (= τὸ ἐναντίον) *on the contrary.* χαρίσασθαι 7
aor. inf. χαρίζομαι *give freely,* hence *grant pardon, forgive,*
ὥστε...ὑμᾶς χ. *so...you should forgive.* παρα-καλέσαι aor. inf.
-καλέω *encourage.* μή πως w. subj. final, *so that...not* ; *lest
perhaps.* περισσότερος cf v.4 *excessive.* λύπη v.1. κατα-
ποθῇ aor. subj. pass. -πίνω *drink down,* hence *overwhelm,*
lit. and met. ‖ δι-ό *for this reason.* κυρῶσαι aor. inf. κυρόω 8
confirm, authenticate, κυρῶσαι...ἀγάπην *give him an assurance of love.* ‖ εἰς τοῦτο *to this end.* ἔ-γραψα v.3. γνῶ 9
v.4. δοκιμή *trial,* so of what has passed the test, *proven
character* (v.13 ; Rom 5:4), γινώσκω τὴν δ. ὑμῶν *know* (*the*

result of) *your testing,* i.e. *your true character.* ὑπ-ήκοος
10 (< ὑπ-ακούω obey) *obedient.* ‖ χαρίζομαι v.7. κἀγώ = καὶ
ἐγώ *I too* (*forgive*). καὶ γάρ *for indeed.* εἴ τι κε-χάρισμαι
(pf) a parenthesis, meaning *if I have had anything to for-*
give. πρόσωπον *person* 1:11, ἐν π. X. *in the person of Christ,*
i.e. as his representative ; or *in the presence of Christ.* ‖
11 πλεον-εκτηθῶμεν aor. subj. pass. -εκτέω (< πλέον *more* +
ἔχω) *take advantage of, cheat* (to deny love and forgiveness
to the sinner would provide Satan with a handle) ; often
ass. w. thieving and robbery (I Cor 5:10, 6:10) so some
would transl. *be robbed* (i.e. of one our brothers). νόημα[7]
what one has in mind (νοέω) : *thought ; intention.* ἀ-γνοέω
be ignorant of : οὐ...ἀγν. *we do not need to be told of.* ‖
12   ἐλθών v.3. εἰς τὸ εὐαγγέλιον *to preach the gospel.*
θύρα *door,* met. *opening.* ἀν-ε-ῳγμένης pf ptc pass. ἀν-
13 οίγω, gen. abs. ‖ ἔ-σχηκα pf (? aoristic pf) ἔχω 1:9 §289.
ἄν-εσις[4] (< ἀν-ίημι relax) *relaxation, relief,* οὐκ ἔσχ. ἄν. *I re-*
mained ill at ease. εὑρεῖν aor[2] inf. εὑρίσκω : τῷ μὴ εὑρ. με
at (my) *not finding, because I did not find.* ἀπο-ταξάμενος
aor. ptc -τάσσομαί τινι *take one's leave of,* say *farewell*
14 to one. ‖ θεῷ χάρις *thanks be to God.* πάν-τοτε *always.*
θριαμβεύοντι ptc -εύω *lead around* (as, e.g., prisoners) *in*
a triumphal procession, hence usu. *make a spectacle of* ;
here ref. the apostles as Christ's willing captives : *who*
leads us about in his triumph in Christ. ὀσμή *smell, fra-*
grance. γνῶσις[4] *knowledge,* epexeg. gen. "fragrance which
is the knowledge" §45. αὐτοῦ obj. gen. *of him.* φανε-
ροῦντι ptc -ρόω *reveal, make known.* τῷ πάντοτε...ἐν παντὶ
τόπῳ lit. "who is ever leading us around in his triumph
in Christ and everywhere making known through us that
15 fragrance which is the knowledge of himself". ‖ εὐωδία
sweet smell, aroma, by ass. became t.t. for a sacrifice accepted by God. σῳζομένοις...ἀπ-ολλυμένοις ptc pass. σῴζω,
ἀπ-όλλυμι: τοῖς σῳζ. ...τοῖς ἀπολ. *those on the road to salva-*
16 *tion...to perdition* (cf I Cor 1:18). ‖ οἷς μέν...οἷς δέ *to one...to*
the other. ἱκανός *equal* to a task or calling, *worthy.* ‖
17 ὡς οἱ πολλοί *like so many.* καπηλεύοντες ptc -εύω *trade in,*
i.e. make money out of and may (like Eng. "huckster")
imply *adulterate.* εἰλι-κρινεία *sincerity* (1 Cor 5:8). ἀλλά
nay,... ἐκ θεοῦ *from/sent by God.* κατ-έν-αντι *before God,*
in God's presence. ‖

ἑ-αυτούς 3rd for 1st pl. refl. prn §209. συν-ιστάνειν **3**
inf. -ιστάνω (late form of συν-ίστημι) *commend*. μή interr.
expecting the answer "No". χρήζω τινός *need*. συ-στατι-
κός *introducing*, σ. ἐπιστολή *letter of recommendation/intro-
duction*. ‖ ἐγ-γεγραμμένη pf ptc pass. ἐγ-γράφω *in-scribe*. **2**
ἡμῶν (2nd time) [[var. ὑμῶν]]. γινωσκομένη ptc pass. -σκω.
ἀνα-γινωσκομένη ptc pass. -γινώσκω. ‖ φανερούμενοι ptc pass. **3**
-ρόω *reveal*, *make known*, φ. ὅτι ἐστέ *you are shown to be*.
διακονηθεῖσα aor. ptc pass. -νέω *serve*, *minister*, indicating
an intermediary role (ultimately, of course, the conversion of the Corinthians) : *delivered* (RSV, NEB) ; better,
JB's *drawn up*. μέλαν -ανος τό *ink*. ζῶντος ptc ζάω:
θεοῦ ζ. anarthrous stressing his nature. πλάξ[6] πλακός ἡ
tablet. λίθινος *of stone*, a ref. to those of the Old Law.
σαρκινός *made of flesh*, καρδίαις σ. appos. πλάξιν, *ta-
blets which are hearts...* ‖ πε-ποίθησις[4] *confidence*, *trust*. **4**
τοιοῦτος *such*. ‖ ἀφ' ἑαυτῶν (v.1) *of ourselves*. ἱκανός *here* **5**
adequate, *qualified* 2:6. λογίσασθαι aor. inf. -ίζομαι *reckon* ; *put down to one's account*, λ. τι ὡς ἐξ ἑαυτῶν *credit
ourselves with anything as coming from ourselves/originat-
ing with ourselves*. ἀλλά *on the contrary*. ἱκανότης[6] -τητος ἡ
adequacy, *qualification*. ‖ ὃς καί: *who has also* made, but **6**
cf §464. ἱκάνωσεν aor. -νόω *make fit/equal to* (*being*).
διάκονος *servant*, *minister*. καινός *new*. δια-θήκη (< δια-
+ τίθημι) *will*, *testament*, often for συν-θήκη *covenant*.
γράμμα *letter*, also in sense opp. "spirit". ἀπο-κτέννω =
-κτείνω. ζῳο-ποιέω *give life*. ‖ διακονία *administration*. ἐν-
τε-τυπωμένη pf ptc pass. ἐν-τυπόω *en-grave*. λίθος *stone*. ἐ- **7**
γενήθη *was instituted*, aor. pass. or dep. (= ἐ-γένετο) γίνομαι
come to be. ἐν of concomitant circumstances §116. ὥστε
consec. *so that* ; *such that*. δύνασθαι inf. δύναμαι. ἀτενίσαι
aor. inf. -ίζω *look intently*, *gaze*. κατ-αργουμένην *destined
to fade away*, *transient*, ptc pass. -αργέω (< κατ- + α- +
ἔργος put out of action) *render ineffectual*, *bring to nothing*. ‖
οὐχί emphatic form of οὐ. πῶς οὐχὶ μᾶλλον *a fortiori*, *how* **8**
much more/greater. διακονία τ. πνεύματος opp. διακ. τ.
θανάτου v.7, τοῦ πνεύμ. gen. may connote of his inspiration, of his institution, in him and for him, cf §38. ἔσται
fut. εἰμί, ref. the present, a "logical fut." §284a ed.[5] Lat. ‖
τῇ διακονίᾳ *in the administration*. κατάκρισις[4] *condemna-* **9**
tion, i.e. of law which condemns. περισσεύω τινί *exceed
in*. ‖ καὶ γάρ *for in fact*. δε-δόξασται pf pass. δοξάζω **10**

glorify, οὐ δεδ. *is now not endowed with splendour* (being outshone). **δε-δοξασμένον** pf ptc pass. *what has been endowed with splendour* (i.e. in the former dispensation) ; subject of δεδόξασται. **μέρος**[8] *part*, ἐν τούτῳ τῷ μ. *in this case*. **εἴνεκεν** (= ἕνεκεν) *because of*. **ὑπερ-βαλλούσης** *exceeding*, ptc fem. -βάλλω *go beyond, surpass*. ‖

11 **κατ-αργούμενον** v.7. **διά** w. gen. ref. attendant circumstances, δ. δόξης *with/in splendour* 2:4 §114. **μένον** ptc

12 neut. μένω. ‖ **ἔχοντες** ptc ἔχω. **τοιοῦτος** v.4. **ἐλπίς**[6] -ίδος ἡ *hope*. **παρρησία** (< πᾶς + ῥῆσις full liberty of speech) *boldness*. **χράομαί** τινι *use sth*, χρ. παρρησίᾳ *behave with*

13 *boldness*. ‖ **καθ-ά-περ** = καθώς. **ἐ-τίθει** impf τίθημι. **κάλυμμα**[7] (< καλύπτω cover, hide) *veil*. **ἀτενίσαι** v.7. **τέλος**[8]

14 *end*, εἰς τὸ τέλος *up to the end*, i.e. the parousia. ‖ **ἀλλά** perh. understanding "notwithstanding our plain speaking" v.12. **ἐ-πωρώθη** aor. pass. -ρόω *harden* ; hence render *insensible, dull, obtuse*. **νόημα**[7] *mind, thought*. **ἄχρι** *until*. **σήμερον** adv. *today*. ὁ **αὐτός** *the same*. **ἀνά-γνωσις**[4] *reading*. **παλαιός** *old*. **δια-θήκη** v.6. **ἀνα-καλυπτόμενον** ptc pass. -καλύπτω *uncover* ; perh. "the veil remains unlifted", but others would divide the sentence after μένει, treating ἀνακαλυπτόμενον as nom. abs. μὴ ἀνακ. ὅτι ἐν Χριστῷ καταργεῖται "(the fact) not having been revealed that in Christ it (the old dispensation) is done away". **καταργεῖται** pass.

15 v.7. ‖ **ἡνίκα** (*at the time*) *when*, ἤν. ἄν *when-ever* (particle cited from the quotation in v.16). **ἀνα-γινώσκηται** subj. pass. v.2, pres. frequentative. **καρδία** considered as the seat of intellect as well as emotion and will. **κεῖμαι**

16 used as pf pass. of τίθημι, a veil *lies* (= is laid). ‖ **ἐάν** = ἄν. **ἐπι-στρέψῃ** (sc. τις) aor. subj. -στρέφω *turn sth to*, also intr. in refl. sense ; in Ex 34:34 ref. Moses, but here the text is referred to the people of Israel as a whole ; in Paul's mind Moses is a type prefiguring what is to come. **περι-αιρεῖται** pass. -αιρέω *take away* what is around sth. ‖

17 In S. Paul **κύριος** den. *the Lord God* and ὁ **κύριος** den. *Christ*. It seems that ὁ here refers back to κύριον in the passage just quoted, ἐστίν being used in the sense of *means* (Mt 9:13, Mk 9:10) : *Now this "Lord" is the Spirit*. **οὗ** *where*. **ἐλευθερία** (sc. *there is*) *freedom*. ‖ **ἀνα-κε-καλυμμένῳ** pf ptc pass. v.14 ; dat. of manner, *with unveiled face* §60. **κατ-οπτριζόμενοι** ptc mid. -οπτρίζω *produce a reflection*, mid. *look in a mirror* at oneself, hence   *gaze*

on, contemplate ; or, as (in the view of J. Dupont) Paul's argument demands, here *reflect as in a mirror* : the former giving *we all, contemplating with unveiled face the splendour of the Lord, are being transformed from one degree of splendour to another into the same image...* ; the latter, *we all with unveiled face, reflecting as a mirror the splendour of the Lord, are being transformed...* ὁ αὐτός v.14. εἰκών εἰκόνος ἡ *image, likeness.* μετα-μορφούμεθα pass. -μορφόω *trans-form* ; here τινά τι someone *into* sth, in pass. retaining acc. of the thing : *we are transformed... into the same image.* καθ-ά-περ v.13. ἀπὸ κυρίου πνεύματος *from the Lord* (*who is*) *the Spirit* §47, also possible, *from the Spirit of the Lord.* ||

διὰ τοῦτο *therefore.* ἔχοντες ptc ἔχω. διακονία *minis-* 4 *try.* ἠλεήθημεν aor. pass. ἐλεέω τινά *show mercy / be merciful to,* pass. *receive mercy, have mercy shown to* one. ἐγ-κακέω *be weary ; lose heart.* || ἀπ-ειπάμεθα (for -όμεθα) 2 mid. of ἀπ-εῖπον (aor²) *have renounced.* κρυπτός *hidden, secret.* αἰσχύνη *shame,* τὰ κρυπτὰ τῆς αἰσ. *the deeds one hides for shame.* περι-πατοῦντες ptc -πατέω, in ethical sense of *behave, live* in a certain way. παν-ουργία (< πανοῦργος *ready for* (to do) *anything*) *craft, cunning.* μηδέ *and not.* δολοῦντες ptc δολόω *falsify, cheapen.* φανέρωσις[4] *manifestation,* here, *open declaration,* w. obj. gen. συνιστάνοντες ptc -ιστάνω (late form of -ίστημι) *commend.* ἑαυτούς for ἡμᾶς αὐτούς 3:1. συν-είδησις[4] *conscience* 1:12, πᾶσαν σ. ἀνθρώπων *every man's conscience.* || εἰ...καί *and if.* 3 ἔστιν *it is.* κε-καλυμμένον pf ptc pass. καλύπτω *cover, veil.* ἐν sts added pleon. to simple dat. §120. ἀπ-ολλυμένοις ptc mid. -όλλυμι: ἐν τοῖς ἀπ. prob. w. force of *just to those on the road to perdition.* || ἐν οἷς *in whose case.* ὁ αἰών 4 οὗτος *the present age,* to be succeeded by ὁ αἰὼν ὁ μέλλων / ἐρχόμενος the Messianic age. ὁ θεός... cf ὁ ἄρχων τ. κόσμου τούτου Jn 12:31 etc. = Satan. Others regard αἰῶνος as an epexeg. gen., *in whose case their god who is this world...* cf Phil 3:19. ἐ-τύφλωσεν aor. -λόω *blind.* νόημα[7] *thought ; understanding, mind.* ἄ-πιστος *unbelieving.* αὐγάσαι aor. inf. -άζω *dawn* ; trans. *see.* φωτισμός *light ; illumination.* τοῦ εὐαγγελίου *of* (i.e. from) *the gospel.* εἰκών[6] εἰκόνος ἡ *image, likeness.* || ἑαυτούς v.2. κηρύσσω 5 *preach, proclaim.* κύριος pred. *as Lord* (opp. the Apostle as δοῦλος). || εἰπών aor² ptc λέγω. σκότος[8] *darkness.* 6

λάμψει fut. λάμπω *shine* ; *cause to shine.* ἔ-λαμψεν aor. γνῶσις[4] *knowledge.* ἐν προσώπῳ *on the face* or *in the person.* ||

7 θησαυρός *treasure.* ὀστράκινος (made of) *earthenware*, connoting fragility. σκεῦος[8] *vessel*, *jar*, of the body. ὑπερβολή *excess, immensity* ; ὑ. τῆς δυνάμεως den. the immense power (efficacy) of the apostolic charisma. ᾖ subj. εἰμί, here, *may be seen to be* God's and not (to come) from us. ||

8 θλιβόμενοι *hard-pressed,* ptc pass. θλίβω *press, constrict.* οὐ w. ptc may lend emphasis, "by no means", but is liable to replace μή when it negatives a single word. στενοχωρούμενοι *reduced to straits, at the end of our tether,* ptc pass. -χωρέω (< στενός narrow + χῶρος space) *confine, restrict.* ἀ-πορούμενοι ptc mid. ἀ-πορέω act. and mid. *be at a loss.* ἐξ-απορούμενοι ptc mid. ἐξ-α-πορέω (ἐξ- perfective + ἀπορέω) 1:8, *be utterly at a loss, be at one's wit's*

9 *end.* || διωκόμενοι ptc pass. διώκω *track* ; *persecute.* ἐγκατα-λειπόμενοι ptc pass. -λείπω *desert, abandon.* καταβαλλόμενοι ptc pass. -βάλλω *throw/strike down.* ἀπ-ολλύμενοι

10 ptc pass. -όλλυμι. || πάν-τοτε *always.* νέκρωσις[4] *putting to death, dying.* περι-φέροντες ptc -φέρω *carry round* with one. φανερωθῇ aor. subj. pass. -ρόω *manifest, show clearly.*

11 || ἀεί *ever.* ζῶντες ptc ζάω. παρα-διδόμεθα pass. -δίδωμι.

12 θνητός *mortal.* || ἐν-εργεῖται mid. -εργέω *be at work,* act.

13 of persons, mid. of things in same sense. || ἔχοντες v.1. ὁ αὐτός *the same* (sc. as the Psalmist). γε-γραμμένον pf ptc pass. γράφω: τὸ γεγ. *what stands written* (in scripture). ἐ-πίστευσα, ἐλάλησα aor. πιστεύω, λαλέω. δι-ό *therefore.* εἰδότες ptc (pf-pres.) οἶδα. ἐγείρας aor. ptc -ρω.

14 ἐγερεῖ fut. παρα-στήσει fut. -ίστημι *cause to come and stand by* ; *will bring us together with you to stand before him.* ||

15 δι' ὑμᾶς *for your sake.* πλεονάσασα aor. ptc fem. -άζω *increase.* πλείων, comp. of πολύς, τῶν πλ. *the greater number* ; *the many.* εὐ-χαριστία *thanksgiving.* περισσεύσῃ aor. subj. -εύω *abound, overflow* ; in late Gk occasionally trans. *cause to abound.* This proposition allows of various translns : "that grace, diffused among the many, may cause thanksgiving to overflow to the glory..." ; or "that grace may increase and, by thanksgiving of the many, overflow to the glory...".

16 ἐγ-κακοῦμεν v.1. εἰ καί v.3. ἔξω *outside* ; ὁ ἔξω as adj. *outer.* δια-φθείρεται pass. -φθείρω *destroy* ; *corrupt* ; pass. of the body, *waste* (away). ἀλλά in apodosis of a

condition, *yet*. ἔσω *inside* ; as adj. *inner*. ἀνα-καινοῦται
pass. -καινόω *re-new*. ‖ παρ-αυτίκα *present, immediate*. ἐλα- 17
φρός *light* (weight). θλῖψις⁴ *distress, trouble*. ὑπερβολή v.7 ;
καθ' ὑπ. *exceeding, incomparable* ; καθ' ὑπερβολὴν εἰς ὑ. *incomparable, indeed immeasurable*. βάρος⁸ *weight* ; a word
perh. suggested by Hebr. where "weight" and "glory"
share the same root. κατ-εργάζομαι (cf Eng. "work out")
effect, achieve. ‖ σκοπούντων ptc -πέω *watch, keep one's* 18
eye on. τὰ βλεπόμενα *the things that are seen*, ptc pass.
βλέπω. πρόσ-καιρος *lasting only for time, transient*. ‖ ἐπί- 5
γειος (< γῆ) masc. and fem. *earthly*. σκῆνος⁸ *tent* ; cur-
rent in secular authors to den. the body as inhabited by
the soul ; gen. epexeg., *our earthly house or tent* §47. κατα-
λυθῇ aor. subj. pass. -λύω *destroy* ; ἐάν w. aor. subj. an
eventual condition §320ff. οἰκο-δομή *building*. οἰκία a
house, appos. οἰκοδομή, both of the spiritual body. ἀ-χειρο-
ποίητος *not made by hands*. ‖ καὶ γάρ *and indeed*. στενάζω 2
groan. οἰκητήριον *dwelling*. ἐπ-εν-δύσασθαι aor. inf. -δύομαι
put on something else (as a garment), *put sth on* over.
ἐπι-ποθοῦντες ptc -ποθέω *long (for)*. ‖ γε particle strengthen- 3
ing the foregoing (or attached) word, εἴ γε καί *if, that is*.
ἐκ-δυσάμενοι *having stripped off* this body, aor. ptc -δύομαι
take off one's clothes, strip. γυμνός *naked*. εὑρεθησόμεθα
fut. pass. εὑρίσκω, pass. Fr. *se trouver, find oneself* = be. ‖
ὄντες ptc εἰμί. σκῆνος v.1. βαρούμενοι ptc pass. βαρέω 4
weigh down, burden. ἐφ' ᾧ *because*, ἐπί w. dat. giving the
grounds for an action §127. ἐκ-δύσασθαι (aor. inf.) *not...*
to strip ourselves but *to put on* sth else. κατα-ποθῇ aor.
subj. pass. -πίνω *drink down* ; *swallow up, absorb*. θνητός
mortal, τὸ θν. *mortality, mortal nature*. ‖ κατ-εργασάμενος 5
aor. ptc -εργάζομαί τινα εἴς τι *prepare* one *for* sth. αὐτὸ
τοῦτο *precisely/just this*. θεός pred., *the one who...is God*.
δούς aor² ptc δίδωμι. ἀρραβών⁶ -ῶνος ὁ *deposit* of money,
instalment, pledge. τοῦ πνεύματος *of the Spirit*, epexeg. =
namely, *the Spirit* §47. ‖ θαρροῦντες ptc θαρρέω (= θαρσέω) 6
be courageous, be of good heart. πάν-τοτε *always*. εἰδότες
ptc pf-pres. οἶδα. ἐν-δημοῦντες ptc -δημέω (be among
one's own people δῆμος) *be at home*, opp. ἀπο-δημέω (Mk
12:1) and ἐκ-δημέω *be away* (from home). ‖ διά of conco- 7
mitant circumstances, *by* faith §114. εἶδος⁸ *visible form* ;
sight as opp. faith (cf Jn 20:29). ‖ εὐ-δοκέω *think good* ; 8
εὐδ. μᾶλλον + inf. *we would rather*. ἐκ-δημῆσαι aor. inf.,

aor. inceptive *go away from, leave.* ἐν-δημῆσαι aor. (inceptive) inf. *go home.* πρός w. acc. *to* the Lord and so
9 to be *with* him. ‖ διὸ καί *and so.* φιλο-τιμέομαι *have as one's ambition, aspire to.* ἐν-δημοῦντες, ἐκ-δημοῦντες (ptcs)
10 v.6. εὐ-άρεστος *pleasing.* ‖ φανερωθῆναι aor. inf. pass. -ρόω 4:10, pass. *be made clear/evident,* so here, *we shall all be seen for what we are* (as in v.11), or intr. *appear.* ἔμ-προσθεν *before.* βῆμα⁷ (< βαίνω) *step* ; *tribunal.* κομίσηται aor. subj. mid. κομίζω *bring,* mid. *receive* what one owns or deserves. τά obj. of κομίσηται. διὰ τοῦ σώματος *in the body* (i.e. during his time on earth) though *through* (*the instrumentality of*) *the body* is also possible. πρὸς ἅ *corresponding to what.* ἔ-πραξεν aor. πράσσω *do* : i.e. each will get his deserts for what he did διὰ τ. σώματος. φαῦλος *worthless.* ‖
11 εἰδότες v.6. φόβος *fear* which God inspires. πείθω *persuade,* pres. conative, *try to persuade/convince.* πε-φανερώμεθα pf pass. v.10. ἐλπίζω *hope.* συν-είδησις⁴ *conscience.* πε-φανερῶσθαι *?to be seen for what I am,* pf inf.
12 pass. ‖ ἑ-αυτοὺς συνιστάνομεν *we are* not *commending ourselves* 4:2. ἀφ-ορμή (point "whence" comes "an impulse"), *incentive; occasion.* διδόντες ptc δίδωμι, continuing cstr. begun w. συνιστάνομεν §374. καύχημα⁷ *matter for boasting,* a *boast,* a *pride.* ὑπὲρ ἡμῶν *about/in us* §96. ἔχητε subj. ἔχω. πρόσωπον orig. a *mask,* so ἐν πρ. *in appearances.*
13 καυχωμένους ptc -χάομαι *boast.* ‖ ἐξ-έ-στημεν aor² (intr.) -ίστημι *put out of place,* met. *send out of* one's *mind* ; aor² (intr.) *be beside oneself.* θεῷ dat. of advantage, *it is for God.* σω-φρονέω *be of sound* (σῶς) *mind* ; *be sober-minded/ reasonable.* ‖ Χριστοῦ embracing obj. and subjective gen. §36. συν-έχω *hold* sth *fast* or *together, hold in one's grip* ; here, *constrain, compel.* κρίναντας aor. ptc κρίνω *judge, deem, consider* ; κρ. τοῦτο aor. effective, *having once reached the conclusion.* ὑπέρ *for* = ἀντί *instead of* §91. ἀπ-έ-θανεν
15 aor² ἀπο-θνήσκω. ἄρα *so.* ‖ ζῶντες ptc ζάω. μηκ-έτι *no longer.* ζῶσιν subj. ἀπο-θανόντι aor² ptc. ἐγερθέντι aor.
16 ptc pass. ἐγείρω. ‖ ἀπὸ τοῦ νῦν *henceforth.* οἴδαμεν here used (like its Hebr. counterpart) in the sense of *consider, regard.* κατὰ σάρκα *according to the flesh, from a worldly standpoint* wt the revaluation introduced by life in the Spirit. εἰ καί *even if.* ἐ-γνώκαμεν *we did once regard,* aor. γινώσκω. ἀλλά in apodosis after εἰ has the force of

yet ; sts best left untranslated. **οὐκ-έτι = μηκέτι**. **γιν-ώσκο-μεν** *we no longer know* (*him so*). ‖ **ἐν Χριστῷ** *in* (*union with*) 17 *Christ* §117f. **καινός** *fresh, new*. **κτίσις**[4] *creation, creature*. **ἀρχαῖος** *old*, τὰ ἀρχ. *things of the past, the old order*. **παρ-ῆλθεν** aor[2] -έρχομαι *pass by*. **γέ-γονεν** pf[2] γίνομαι. ‖ **κατ-** 18 **αλλάξαντος** aor. ptc -αλλάσσω *reconcile*. **δόντος** v.5. **δια-κονία** *ministry*. **κατ-αλλαγή** *reconciliation*. ‖ **ὡς ὅτι** *that is, that...* **κατ-αλλάσσων** ptc, some regard as periphrastic 19 §360. **λογίζομαι** *reckon, count* ; *put down to* one's *account*. **αὐτοῖς** pl. according to the sense of κόσμος as the world of men. **παρά-πτωμα**[7] (< παρα-πίπτω *fall away*) in moral sense, *trespass*. **θέμενος** aor[2] ptc mid. τίθημι, mid. connoting "for his own purpose" cf I Cor 12:18. ‖ **ὑπέρ** *on* 20 *Christ's behalf, for* Christ. **πρεσβεύω** *be an ambassador*. **ὡς** *as if*. **παρα-καλοῦντος** ptc -καλέω, gen. abs. **δέομαι** *beseech, beg*. **κατ-αλλάγητε** aor[2] impv pass. -αλλάσσω. ‖ **γνόντα** aor[2] ptc γινώσκω: τόν...γν. *him who knew no sin*, 21 obj. of ἐποίησεν. **ἐ-ποίησεν** aor. ποιέω τινά τι (pred.) *make one* (into) sth. **ἁμαρτίαν** (2nd time) pred., ἁμ. ἐποίησεν meaning that God treated him as if he had been sin's embodiment ; others think of the Hebr. use of "sin" as "sin-offering". **γενώμεθα** aor[2] subj. γίνομαι, Christ is identified w. man's sin and man is identified w. God's righteousness ; a desperate attempt to put into words the inexpressible mystery whose inner principle transcends all human understanding. ‖ **συν-εργοῦντες** *as those engaged* 6 *together in* God's *work*, ptc -εργέω *co-operate*. **κενός** *empty*, εἰς κ. *in vain*. **δέξασθαι** aor. inf. δέχομαι: μή... δέξασθαι *not to have received the grace...in vain* (by proceeding to squander it). ‖ **λέγει** *he says* (i.e. the Lord). **δεκτός** 2 (< δέχομαι) *acceptable*. **ἐπ-ήκουσα** aor. -ακούω τινός *listen to, heed* one. **σωτηρία** *salvation*. **ἐ-βοήθησα** aor. βοηθέω τινί *come to* one's *help*. **εὐ-πρόσ-δεκτος = δεκτός**. ‖ **ἐν** 3 **μηδενί** neut., w. a neg. *in anything*. **διδόντες** ptc δίδωμι. **προσ-κοπή** *obstacle* against which one stumbles (προσκόπτει), *occasion of offence*, διδόντες μηδεμίαν πρ. *provide* (i.e. constitute in oneself) *no obstacle, give no offence*. Vv. 3-10: Paul is fond of continuing a finite vb w. co-ordinate ptcs, adjs, prep. expressions etc., equivalent to as many independent sentences. **μωμηθῇ** aor. subj. pass. μωμάομαι *find fault with, blame* ; pass. *be faulted, have fault found with* sth. **διακονία** *ministry*, ἡ δ. (from context) *our ministry*. ‖ **συν-** 4

ἱστάντες ptc (-ιστάς) -ίστημι *commend.* ἑ-αυτούς 5:12.
διάκονος *servant.* ὑπο-μονή *endurance.* θλῖψις[4] *distress, suffering.* ἀνάγκη *necessity.* στενο-χωρία *constraint ; anguish.*
5 ‖ πληγή (< πλήσσω strike) *blow,* esp. *stripe* of the lash.
φυλακή (< φυλάσσω guard) *prison.* ἀ-κατα-στασία (< ἀ- + καθ-ίστημι establish) *disturbance, riot.* κόπος *toil.* ἀγρ-υπνία (< ἀγρός + ὕπνος sleep out of doors) *wakeful or sleepless night.* νηστεία *fasting* whether enforced or absti-
6 nence from food. ‖ ἁγνότης[6] -ότητος ἡ *purity* (of mind), *sanctity.* γνῶσις *knowledge.* μακρο-θυμία (long-temper) *patience.* χρηστότης[6] -ότητος ἡ *goodness, kindness.* ἀν-υπό-
7 κριτος *without pretence, sincere.* ‖ ὅπλα (pl. only) *armour,* ὅ. δικαιοσύνης perh. meaning, "which the God of righteousness supplies"; more likely, "wherewith to fight for righteousness". δεξιός *right* (opp. left), ἡ δεξιά (sc. χείρ)
8 *right hand.* ἀρίστερος *left.* ‖ διά w. gen. of manner §114.
δόξα *honour.* ἀ-τιμία *disgrace ;* as opp. δόξα, *humiliation.*
δυσ-φημία *ill-repute.* εὐ-φημία *good repute.* ὡς...καί... w. the force of "we are called (or, we seem)...and we are...".
9 πλάνος *misleading,* as noun, *deceiver.* ‖ ἀ-γνοούμενοι *unknown,* ptc pass. ἀ-γνοέω *not to know.* ἐπι-γινωσκόμενοι *known,* ptc pass. -γινώσκω *know, recognize.* ἀπο-θνήσκοντες *dying,* ptc -θνήσκω here (only) replacing simplex (durative) *be dying.* καὶ ζῶμεν *we are alive* interrupts the series of ptcs (cf v.4). παιδευόμενοι ptc pass. -εύω *chastise.* θανα-
10 τούμενοι ptc pass. -τόω *put to death.* ‖ λυπούμενοι ptc pass.
λυπέω *make sad.* ἀεί *ever, always.* πτωχός (< πτώσσω cower) *poor.* πλουτίζοντες ptc -ίζω *make rich.* κατ-έχοντες
11 ptc -έχω *hold fast ; possess.* ‖ ἀν-έ-ῳγεν pf[2] ἀν-οίγω intr. in pf[2], *stand/remain open,* τὸ στόμα ἀνέ. πρὸς ὑμᾶς *we* (= I) *speak frankly to | we are completely open with you.*
πε-πλάτυνται pf pass. -ύνω *make wide, enlarge ;* pf pass.
12 *stands wide open.* ‖ στενο-χωρέω *confine, cramp, restrict, you are not cramped | short of space in us, you are cramped in your own affections,* i.e. any constraint in our relations is on your side, not on mine. σπλάγχνα τά *bowels ; emo-*
13 *tions, feelings.* ‖ ἀντι-μισθία *recompense,* τὴν δὲ αὐτὴν ἀντιμ. appos. πλατύνθητε *as recompense in kind.* πλατύνθητε aor. impv pass. *show yourselves expansive.* καὶ ὑμεῖς *you also, in your turn.* ‖
14 γίνεσθε impv γίνομαι: μὴ γ. pres. *do not be* (for ἔστε, obs. impv 2nd pl.). ἑτερο-ζυγοῦντες ptc -ζυγέω *be yoked*

to an animal of another kind, be yoked unevenly. ἄ-πιστος *un-believing,* as noun, *un-believer.* μετ-οχή (< μετ-έχω *share*) *partnership.* ἀ-νομία *lawlessness, iniquity,* lit. "what partnership is there to δ. and to ἀν. ?" i.e. *what has r. to do with i.?* Rom 6:19. κοινωνία (< κοινός *common*) a *sharing, association.* σκότος⁸ *darkness,* τίς κοινωνία φωτὶ καὶ σκ.; *what have light and darkness in common?* ‖ συμ- 15 φώνησις⁴ *agreement, concord.* μερίς⁶ -ίδος ἡ *part, share* ; τίς μ. *what part or lot* has a believer with... ? ‖ συγ-κατά- 16 θεσις⁴ (< συγ-κατα-τίθεμαι *agree* Lk 23:51) *agreement.* ναός *temple.* εἴδωλον *idol.* ἡμεῖς *emphatic* §198. ζῶντος ptc ζάω 3:3. ὅτι = "... ἐν-οικήσω fut. -οικέω *dwell in.* ἐμ-περι- πατήσω fut. -πατέω *move about among.* ἔσομαι fut. εἰμί. ‖ δι-ό *therefore.* ἐξ-έλθατε aor² impv (for -έλθετε §489) 17 -έρχομαι *come out.* μέσος *middle,* neut. as noun ἐκ μέσου *from* their *midst.* ἀφ-ορίσθητε aor. impv pass. in refl. sense -ορίζω *separate.* ἀ-κάθαρτος *un-clean.* ἅπτεσθε impv ἅπτομαί τινος *touch* sth. κἀγώ = καὶ ἐγώ. εἰσ-δέξομαι fut. -δέχομαι *receive* as into one's house. ‖ εἰς a Hebr., instead 18 of nom. pred. §32. θυγάτηρ -τρός ἡ *daughter.* παντο- κράτωρ⁶ -κράτορος *al-mighty.* ‖ ἔχοντες ptc ἔχω. ἐπ-αγγελία **7** *promise.* ἀγαπητός *beloved.* καθαρίσωμεν aor. subj. (hort.) -ίζω *cleanse.* ἑ-αυτούς 3rd for 1st pl. §209. πᾶς wt art. *every.* μολυσμός *stain, defilement.* ἐπι-τελοῦντες ptc -τελέω *perfect, complete.* ἁγιωσύνη *sanctification, holiness.* φόβος *fear.* ‖

χωρήσατε aor. impv χωρέω intr. *go, proceed* ; trans. 2 *have room for, hold,* aor. *make room for* (met.) sc. in your hearts. ἠδικήσαμεν aor. ἀ-δικέω τινά *treat unjustly, do wrong to* one. ἐ-φθείραμεν aor. φθείρω *corrupt, ruin.* ἐ- πλεον-εκτήσαμεν aor. πλεον-εκτέω *take advantage of, de- fraud.* ‖ κατά-κρισις⁴ *condemnation,* κ. λέγω *accuse.* προ- 3 είρηκα *I have already said,* pf -λέγω *say beforehand.* εἰς τό *in suchwise that.* συν-απο-θανεῖν aor² inf. -θνήσκω *die to- gether.* συ(ν)-ζῆν inf. -ζάω *live together.* ‖ πολλή μοι *I have* 4 *much,* (transl.) *great.* παρρησία *confidence.* καύχησις⁴ *boast- ing.* ὑπέρ (= περί §96) *about.* πε-πλήρωμαι pf pass. -ρόω. παρά-κλησις⁴ *comfort,* τῇ connoting known to the readers. ὑπερ-περισσεύομαι τινι *I overflow* with sth, pass. -εύω *superabound.* χαρά *joy.* ἐπί w. dat. *over, at* ref. the ground of an emotion §126. θλῖψις⁴ *distress, troubles.* ‖ ἐλθόντων 5 aor² ptc ἔρχομαι gen. abs. ἔσχηκεν ἄνεσιν 2:13. σάρξ in

Hebr. sense stressing human frailness and weakness. ϑλιβόμενοι *hard-pressed*, ptc ϑλίβω *constrict, press*, abs. ptc w. force of impf indic. (cf 5:12 §374). ἔξω-ϑεν *from outside* ; *outside*. μάχη *strife*. ἔσω-ϑεν *from within*. φόβος

6 v.1. ‖ παρα-καλῶν ptc -καλέω, appos. ὁ ϑεός: *God who consoles*. ταπεινός *humble*, here of the *downcast*. παρ-ε-

7 κάλεσεν aor. ἐν instr. §119. παρ-ουσία *arrival*. ‖ παρά-κλησις v.4. παρ-ε-κλήϑη aor. pass. *he had been consoled about you*, rel. past disregarded in Gk §290. ἐπί w. dat. *about* v.4. ἀν-αγγέλλων ptc -αγγέλλω *announce, tell*. ἐπι-πόϑησις⁴ *longing*. ὀδυρμός *grieving*. ζῆλος *zeal, ardour*. μᾶλλον *even more*. χαρῆναι aor² inf. dep. χαίρω. ‖

8 εἰ καί *even if*. ἐ-λύπησα aor. *cause sadness to, sadden*. μετα-μέλομαι lit. "change what one has at heart (μέλει)", *change one's mind* ; hence, *regret, be sorry*. μετ-ε-μελόμην impf. βλέπω *see, perceive*. πρὸς ὥραν *only for a time*. ‖

9 ἐ-λυπήϑητε aor. pass. εἰς (*leading*) *to*. μετά-νοια *repentance*. κατὰ ϑεόν *as God would wish, in God's way* (cf κατὰ σάρκα / πνεῦμα). ἵνα consec. §352. μηδενί neut. ζημιωϑῆτε aor. -ιόομαι pass. (< ζημία *loss*) *suffer damage/loss*. ἐξ ἡμῶν

10 *through us* (our act). ‖ λύπη *sorrow*, ἡ κατὰ ϑεὸν λ. *godly sorrow*. σωτηρία *salvation*, μετάνοιαν εἰς σ. may stand for *salutary repentance*. ἀ-μετα-μέλητος *without regrets, admitting no second thoughts*. κατ-εργάζομαι *work out, ef-*

11 *fect, produce*. ‖ αὐτὸ τοῦτο τό...λυπηϑῆναι (aor. inf. pass.) *this very experience of godly sorrow*, τοῦτο connoting "well known to you". πόσος *how much, what*. κατ-ειργάσατο aor. (more often κατηργ-). σπουδή *eagerness, earnestness*. ἀλλά = ἀλλὰ καί *and not only so but...* ἀπο-λογία *a defence ; explanation*. ἀγανάκτησις⁴ *indignation*. φόβος *respect, fear*. ἐπι-πόϑησις, ζῆλος v.7. ἐκ-δίκησις⁴ *vindication*. ἐν παντί *in every regard*. συν-ε-στήσατε aor. -ίστημι *commend* ; w. refl. prn *prove/show oneself*. ἑ-αυτούς for 2nd pers. ἁγνός *pure, innocent*. πρᾶγμα⁷ (< πράσσω do) *matter, af-*

12 *fair*, τῷ π. *in this affair*, dat. of respect §53. ‖ ἄρα *so then*. εἰ καί *even though*. ἔ-γραψα aor. γράφω. ἕνεκεν *for the sake of*, οὐχ ἕ. *it was not for...* ἀ-δικήσαντος aor. ptc -δικέω *do wrong*, ὁ ἀδ. *the wrong-doer, offender*. ἀ-δικη-ϑέντος aor. ptc pass., ὁ ἀδ. *the one who suffered the wrong, the injured party*. φανερωϑῆναι aor. inf. pass. -ρόω *make*

13 *evident*. πρὸς ὑμᾶς *to you*. ‖ διὰ τοῦτο *what is why*. παρα-κε-κλήμεϑα pf pass. -καλέω. ἐπί (1st time) *in addition to*,

besides. **παράκλησις** v.4. **περισσοτέρως**, comp. of περισσῶς, *superabundantly*, π. μᾶλλον *more than ever.* **ἐ-χάρημεν** aor² dep. χαίρω. **ἐπί** v.4. **χαρά** *joy, happiness.* **ἀνα-πέπαυται** *is set at rest*, pf pass. -παύω *give rest.* **ἀπό** = ὑπό §90. ‖ **ὑπέρ** (= περί) *about* §96. **κε-καύχημαι** pf καυχάομαί τι 14 *boast of* sth εἴ τι...κεκ. *if I have boasted to him about anything to do with you.* **κατ-ῃσχύνθην** aor. pass. -αισχύνω *put to shame, shame.* **ἐ-λαλήσαμεν** aor. λαλέω: ὡς...ὑμῖν *as all we said to you proved true* (lit. "in truth"). **καύχησις**[4] *boasting.* **ἐπὶ Τίτου** *before T.* (as if a judge). **ἐ-γενήθη** aor. dep. γίνομαι (= ἐγένετο aor² §230). ‖ **σπλάγχνων** pl. 15 *bowels ; emotions, affection,* σπλ. εἰς ὑμᾶς ἐστιν *his heart goes out to you.* **ἀνα-μιμνησκομένου** *as he recalls*, ptc -μιμνήσκομαι *recall.* **ὑπ-ακοή** *obedience.* **φόβος** *fear.* **τρόμος** *trembling.* **ἐ-δέξασθε** aor. δέχομαι *receive, welcome.* ‖ **θαρρέω** 16 (= θαρσέω) *have courage/confidence,* ἐν παντὶ θ. ὑμῶν modal, *I can be sure of you.* ‖

     γνωρίζω τι *make* sth *known*, transl. *we must let you* **8** *know about.* **δε-δομένην** pf ptc pass. δίδωμι. ‖ **δοκιμή** *trial,* 2 *test.* **θλῖψις**[4] *distress, trouble,* gen. epexeg. "consisting of θλ." §45. **περισσεία** *abundance.* **χαρά** *joy.* **βάθος**[8] *depth,* ἡ κατὰ β. πτωχεία lit. "their poverty in depth", i.e. the *depth of their poverty.* **πτωχεία** *great poverty.* **ἐ-περίσσευσεν** aor. -εύω *be* or *have in excess, overflow.* **πλοῦτος** *wealth,* met. **ἁπλότης**[6] -ότητος ἡ *simplicity, sincerity* ; of single-minded *generosity* (as Rom 12:8). ‖ **κατὰ δύναμιν** *according to their ability/means.* **παρὰ δύναμιν** *beyond their means.* **αὐθαίρετος** (< αὐτός + αἱρέω choose) adj. w. advl force (cf αὐτόματος Ac 12:10) *of* one's *own accord, freely.* ‖ **παρά-κλησις**[4] *appeal, entreaty,* μετὰ πολλῆς π. *most earnestly.* 4 **δέομαί** τί τινος *beseech, beg* one for sth. **χάρις** *favour.* **κοινωνία** *sharing,* χάρις καὶ κοινωνία τινός a hendiadys : *favour of sharing in* sth. **διακονία** *ministry, service.* **εἰς** for dat. of advantage. **οἱ ἅγιοι** *the saints* 1:1, here of the church in Jerusalem. ‖ **οὐ καθώς** *not just as.* **ἠλπίσαμεν** 5 aor. ἐλπίζω *hope*, here rather *expect.* **ἔ-δωκαν** aor. δίδωμι. **πρῶτον** *primarily, in the first place.* ‖ **εἰς τό** consec. *with the* 6 *result that we...* **παρα-καλέσαι** aor. inf. -καλέω *ask* one to do sth. **ἡμᾶς** subject of παρακαλέσαι. **ἵνα...ἐπιτελέσῃ** standing for obj. inf. §408. **προ-εν-ήρξατο** *he had already begun* §290, aor. -άρχομαι *begin earlier* ; word unknown outside this v. and comments on it. **ἐπι-τελέσῃ** aor. subj. -τελέω

complete. εἰς ὑμᾶς *among you.* τὴν χάριν *this work of*
7 *generosity.* ‖ περισσεύω v.2. γνῶσις *knowledge.* σπουδή
zest, eagerness. ἵνα abs. introducing a wish, *may you...*
8 §415. περισσεύητε subj. ‖ ἐπι-ταγή (< ἐπιτάσσω give orders) a *command.* διά *by.* ἕτερος for ἄλλος §153. καί
also. ὑμέτερος *your* (pl.). γνήσιος *genuine,* τὸ γν. *genuineness,* obj. of δοκιμάζων *as testing,* ptc -άζω *put to the*
9 *proof, try.* ‖ ἐ-πτώχευσεν aor. -εύω be poor, aor. inceptive,
became poor §250f. πλούσιος *rich.* ὤν ptc εἰμί, concessive, *though (he was).* πτωχεία *poverty.* πλουτήσητε aor.
subj. -τέω be rich, ἵνα...πλ. *that you might become rich.* ‖
10 γνώμη *opinion.* συμ-φέρει τινί *it is to one's interest/good*
for one. οἵτινες *you who, seeing that you* §217. τὸ ποιῆσαι
the doing, aor. inf. ποιέω. τὸ θέλειν *the having the will/
purpose,* inf. θέλω. προ-εν-ήρξασθε v.6. πέρυσι adv. *last
year; seeing that last year you led the way not only
in taking action but in having the intention/desire* (to
11 do so). ‖ νυνὶ δέ *and now.* ἐπι-τελέσατε aor. impv -τελέω
complete. ὅπως *so that,* no vb follows, understand ᾖ (after
οὕτως). καθ-ά-περ *just as.* προ-θυμία w. gen. *eagerness/
enthusiasm* for. ἐπι-τελέσαι aor. inf., καθάπερ...οὕτως καὶ
τὸ ἐπιτ. lit. "as...so...", *your enthusiasm for the project may
be matched by its completion.* ἐκ τοῦ ἔχειν *from what you*
12 *can afford, according to your means.* ‖ πρό-κειται *lie before ; be present.* καθό = καθ' ὅ *in proportion to what.*
ἐάν = ἄν. ἔχῃ subj. ἔχω, supply τις as subject. εὐ-πρόσ-
13 δεκτος *it* (the gift) *is acceptable.* ‖ οὐ γάρ *not that.* ἄλλοις
"to others", i.e. *others may have.* ἄν-εσις⁴ *relaxation, ease*
2:13. θλῖψις⁴ *hardship.* ἰσότης⁶ -ότητος ἡ *equality,* ἐξ ἰ.
14 *by equality.* ‖ περίσσευμα⁷ *surplus.* ὑστέρημα⁷ (< ὑστερέω
come late ; go short) *lack, shortage.* ὅπως (v.11) *parallels*
15 ἵνα. γένηται aor² subj. γίνομαι. ‖ γέ-γραπται pf pass.
γράφω. ὁ τὸ πολύ (ref. the manna) *he who (gathered) much.*
ἐ-πλεόνασεν aor. -άζω *have a surplus/something over.* ὀλίγος
little, neut. as noun, *a little.* ἠλαττόνησεν aor. ἐλαττονέω
(< ἐλάσσων less) *have less ; go short.* ‖
16 χάρις *thanks.* δόντι aor² ptc δίδωμι. ὁ αὐτός *the same.*
17 σπουδὴ ὑπέρ τινος *lively concern for someone.* ‖ παρά-κλησις
v.4. ἐ-δέξατο aor. δέχομαι *accept.* σπουδαιότερος (comp.
of σπουδαῖος *full of concern*) *more eager than ever in his
concern.* ὑπ-άρχων ptc -άρχω *be from the beginning ;
exist ; often simply be.* αὐθ-αίρετος v.3. ἐξ-ῆλθεν *if T.*

had not left already the aor. is epistolary 2:3 (ἔγραψα). ||
συν-ε-πέμψαμεν aor. συμ-πέμπω *send* one *with* another, or   18
epistolary aor. *I am sending.* **ἔπ-αινος** *praise* ; οὗ ὁ ἔπ. ἐν
τῷ εὐαγγελίῳ *who is well known for (his service to) the*
gospel I Thess 3:2. **διά** *throughout.* || **χειρο-τονηθείς** aor.   19
ptc pass. -τονέω (< χείρ + τείνω stretch out) *elect* ; *ap-*
point ; ptc instead of finite vb §374. **συν-έκ-δημος** *travel-*
ling companion. **σύν** (understand : *to help*) *with.* **χάρις**
v.6. **διακονουμένη** ptc pass. -νεω *serve, administer.* **προ-**
θυμία v.11, strangely under one art. w. τοῦ κυρίου δόξαν,
to serve the glory of the Lord [*himself*] *and (as an outlet*
for) our eagerness. || **στελλόμενοι** (*the intention being*) *to*   20
avoid, ptc στέλλομαι (mid.) *shrink from, avoid.* **μωμήσηται**
aor. subj. μωμάομαί τινα *find fault with, blame* one. **ἀδρό-**
της[6] -ότητος ἡ *vigour; abundance; munificence* : *lest any-*
one should find fault with our administration of this lavish
gift, lit. "over this...gift administered by us". || **προ-νοέω**   21
think beforehand; be solicitous, have a care for. **καλά** neut.
pl. *what is honourable.* **ἐν-ώπιον** *in the eyes of.* || **συνεπέμ-**   22
ψαμεν v.18. **ἐ-δοκιμάσαμεν** whom *we have tested* (and
found), i.e. *proved* to be, aor. -μάζω v.8. **πολλοῖς** *in many*
directions/ways. **πολλάκις** *often, many times.* **σπουδαῖος**
v.17. **ὄντα** ptc εἰμί. **νυνὶ δέ** v.11. **πολύ** neut. as adv.
much, transl. *even* more eager. **πε-ποίθησις**[4] *confidence,*
dat. of cause, *because of* his great confidence in you. ||
εἴτε...εἴτε *whether...or* ; εἴτε ὑπέρ *whether* (on the subject)   23
of Titus. **ὑπέρ** = περί §96. **κοινωνός** *sharer, partner,* sc.
ἐστιν. **συν-εργός** *fellow-worker.* **εἰς ὑμᾶς** *for you.* **εἴτε οἱ**
ἀδελφοί *or whether our brethren* (are in question). **ἀπόστολοι**
messengers, sc. εἰσίν. || **ἔν-δειξις**[4] *proof.* **καύχησις**[4] *boasting* ;   24
ἡμῶν κ. ὑπέρ ὑμῶν εἰς αὐτούς *our boasting to them about you.*
ἐν-δεικνύμενοι ptc -δείκνυμαι *demonstrate, show* (*proof*), ptc
w. impv force §373. **εἰς πρόσωπον** *in front of, before.* ||

   διακονία *ministration, service,* ἡ δ. ἡ εἰς τ. ἁγίους *the*   **9**
charitable contribution destined for the church in Jerusalem 8:4. **περισσός** *superfluous,* π. μοί ἐστιν + inf. *there*
is no need for me to... || **προ-θυμία** *readiness, eagerness.*   2
ὑπέρ = περί §96. **καυχάομαί τι** *boast of* sth. **Μακεδών**[6]
-δόνος *a Macedonian.* **παρ-ε-σκεύασται** *has been ready,* pf
mid. παρα-σκευάζω *prepare* ; mid. oneself ; pf mid. *be ready.*
ἀπό *since.* **πέρυσι** *last year.* **ζῆλος**[8] (sts neut.) *zeal, fer-*
vour. **ἠρέθισεν** aor. ἐρεθίζω *stimulate, rouse* (here, to emu-

lation). **πλείων**, comp. of πολύς: οἱ πλεί. *the greater part,*
3 *most* of them. ‖ **ἔ-πεμψα** aor. πέμπω. **καύχημα**[7] *boast.* **κενωθῇ**
may not *prove hollow,* aor. subj. pass. κενόω *empty* sth.
μέρος[8] *part,* ἐν τ. μέρει τούτῳ *in this affair.* **ἵνα** (2nd time)
parallel to ἵνα μή. **ἔ-λεγον** impf 1st sg λέγω. **παρ-ε-σκευα-**
4 **σμένοι** pf ptc mid. **ἦτε** subj. εἰμί. ‖ **μή πως** *lest.* **ἔλθωσιν** aor[2]
subj. ἔρχομαι. **εὕρωσιν** aor[2] subj. εὑρίσκω. **ἀ-παρα-σκεύαστος**
un-prepared. **κατ-αισχυνθῶμεν** aor. subj. pass. -αισχύνω *put*
to shame. **ἵνα μή λέγω** subj., transl. *not to say "you"* Phm
19. **ὑπό-στασις**[4] *that which underlies,* e.g. *foundation,* so
5 *ground of hope,* then *hope, confidence* itself. ‖ **ἀναγκαῖος**
necessary. **ἡγησάμην** aor. ἡγέομαι *think, consider.* **παρα-**
καλέσαι aor. inf. -καλέω *urge.* **ἵνα** for obj. inf. §407. **προ-**
έλθωσιν aor[2] subj. -έρχομαι *come first* / *in advance, go ahead.*
προ-κατ-αρτίσωσιν aor. subj. -αρτίζω *put in order before-*
hand. **προ-επ-ηγγελμένην** *already promised,* pf ptc pass.
-αγγέλλω *promise beforehand.* **εὐ-λογία** *blessing ;* in tangible
form, *generous gift.* **ταύτην** acc. as subject of inf. **ἕτοιμος**
ready. **εἶναι** inf. final, *that in this way* (οὕτως) *it may be*
ready as a generous gift and not... **πλεον-εξία** *extortion ;*
or *stinginess :* the former opp. a free gift, the latter opp.
6 a generous one. ‖ **τοῦτο δέ** (sc. φημί) ref. what follows
§213. **σπείρων** ptc -ρω *sow ;* pres. ptc habitual = *sower.*
φειδομένως (adv. formed from φειδόμενος ptc -δομαι *spare*)
sparingly. **θερίσει** fut. -ίζω *reap.* **ἐπί** (w. dat.) = *with*
7 + εὐλογίᾳ forming adv., *liberally.* ‖ **ἕκαστος** understand
"let each one give". **προ-ῄρηται** pf -αιρέομαι *pre-fer ;*
choose ; decide. **λύπη** *grief,* ἐκ λ. *reluctantly.* **ἀνάγκη** *ne-*
cessity, ἐξ ἀν. *under constraint, against his will.* **ἱλαρός**
8 *cheerful, glad.* **δότης**[3] (< δίδωμι) *giver.* ‖ **δυνατέω** *have the*
power to. **περισσεῦσαι** aor. inf. -εύω when trans. *cause* sth
to abound to one, *make one rich in* sth. **πάν-τοτε** *at all*
times. **αὐτ-άρκεια** *self-sufficiency, independence.* **περισσεύη-**
τε subj. -εύω intr. of persons, *have an abundance of, be*
9 *rich in.* ‖ **γέ-γραπται** pf pass. γράφω. **ἐ-σκόρπισεν** aor. -ίζω
scatter, lavish. **ἔ-δωκεν** aor. δίδωμι. **πένης**[6] -ητος ὁ *poor*
man (obliged to labour (πένεσθαι) but not destitute like
10 πτωχός). **εἰς τὸν αἰῶνα** *for ever.* ‖ **ἐπι-χορ-ηγῶν** ptc -χορ-ηγέω
(provide the expenses for a χόρος) in general, *supply,*
provide for. **σπέρμα**[7] *seed.* **σπείροντι** v.6. **βρῶσις**[4] *eating.*
χορηγήσει fut. -γέω *supply.* **πληθυνεῖ** fut. -ύνω *multiply.*
σπόρος *seed.* **αὐξήσει** fut. αὐξάνω *make* sth *grow.* **γένημα**[7]

crop, fruit (cf γέννημα[7] offspring). || **πλουτιζόμενοι** ptc 11
pass. -ίζω *make rich*, ptc w. impvl sense. **ἁπλότης**[6] -ότητος
ἡ *generosity* (cf 8:2, Rom 12:8). **ἥ-τις** *such that* §215. **κατ-
εργάζομαι** *produce, create.* **εὐ-χαριστία** *thanksgiving.* || **ὅτι** 12
for. **διακονία** *service ; administration/doing* of a service.
λειτουργία (< λαός public + ἔργον) any *public service*, religious or secular, in NT always w. religious connotation.
προσ-ανα-πληροῦσα ptc fem. -πληρόω *fill up, supply* sth
lacking. **ὑστέρημα**[7] *shortage, need* 8:14. **ἀλλὰ καί** *but also.*
περισσεύουσα ptc fem. intr. of things, *be in excess, overflow.* **διά** *through,* instr. or of manner ; *in the form of
widespread thanksgiving to God.* || **διά τ. δοκιμῆς** gen. 13
epexeg. §45f, continues the argument of v.11. **δοκιμή**
test ; evidence, proof. **δοξάζοντες** ptc -άζω *glorify, praise,
through the evidence of this service praising God...* **ἐπί** w.
dat. *on the ground of, for.* **ὑπο-ταγή** (< ὑποτάσσω subject)
subjection, obedience. **ὁμο-λογία** (act.) *confession.* **κοιν ωνία**
communion, sharing in material things, *contribution* Rom
15:26, ἐπὶ τ. ὑποταγῇ κτλ. *for the obedience in your profession of the gospel and for the generosity of your contribution
to them and to all* (i.e. through the mother church). ||
δέησις[4], *supplication, prayer,* suspended dat. **ἐπι-ποθούν-** 14
των ptc -ποθέω τινά *long for* one. **ὑπερ-βάλλουσαν** *exceed-
ing,* ptc fem. -βάλλω *go beyond, surpass.* || **χάρις** w. dat. 15
thanks. **ἀν-εκ-δι-ήγητος** (< ἀν- + εκ- + δι-ηγέομαι describe)
inexpressible. **δ ωρεά** *gift.* ||

αὐτός *myself.* **διά** *by.* **πραΰτης**[6] -τητος ἡ *meekness,* **10**
gentleness. **ἐπι-είκεια** *consideration, kindness.* **κατὰ πρόσωπον** *face to face.* **ταπεινός** *humble.* **ἐν** *with* you. **ἀπ-ών**
ptc -ειμι *be absent.* **θαρρέω** (= θαρσέω) *be courageous/con-
fident.* || **δέομαί** τί τινος *beg* sth *of* one, obj. being τὸ μή... 2
θαρρῆσαι: *I beg of you that when I come* (παρών) *I be not*
(i.e. do not have to be) *"courageous" with the self-assurance with which I count on standing up to certain* (people)
who regard us as living a worldly life. **παρ-ών** (opp. ἀπών)
ptc -ειμι *be present* ; nom. because the subject is that of
δέομαι as well as of θαρρῆσαι §393. **θαρρῆσαι** aor. inf. **πε-
ποίθησις**[4] *confidence, assurance.* **λογίζομαι** *reckon ; consider
as ; think ; intend.* **τολμῆσαι** aor. inf. -μάω *dare ; show
boldness.* **ἐπί** w. acc. sts *against.* **κατὰ σάρκα** *in accordance with* (purely) *human standards.* **περι-πατοῦντας** ptc
-πατέω 4:2. || **ἐν σαρκί** *in* (the) *flesh* (a body). **περιπα-** 3

τοῦντες concessive, *though we are living.* στρατεύομαι *wage war,* κατὰ σάρκα στρ. *wage a secular war, a war of this*
4 *world.* || ὅπλα (pl. only) *arms.* στρατεία *campaign.* σαρκικός *human* opp. divine. δυνατός *powerful.* τῷ θεῷ either *because of God,* (NEB) *divinely potent,* or dat. of advantage, *for God.* καθ-αίρεσις[4] *destruction.* ὀχύρωμα[7] *stronghold,* met. λογισμός *reasoning ;* here *sophistries* devised against the gospel. καθ-αιροῦντες ptc -αιρέω *throw down, des-*
5 *troy,* ptc continuing cstr begun w. στρατευόμεθα. || ὕψωμα[7] a *height* (lit. of enemy defences) meaning their *arrogance.* ἐπ-αιρόμενον *setting itself up,* ptc pass. -αίρω *lift up.* γνῶσις *knowledge.* αἰχμ-αλωτίζοντες ptc -ίζω *take captive,* lit. and met. (Rom 7:23). νόημα[7] *thought.* ὑπ-ακοή *obedience.* ||
6 ἕτοιμος *ready,* ἐν ἕτ. ἔχω *be ready ;* ἔχω w. adv. or advl phrase often = *be* (Mk 1:32 ; Ac 15:36 etc.). ἐκ-δικῆσαι aor. inf. -δικέω *vindicate ;* so *punish ;* subject still that of στρατευόμεθα (v.3). παρ-ακοή *dis-obedience.* πληρωθῇ aor. subj. pass. -ρόω: w. aor. subj. ὅταν introduces a temporal
7 clause ref. future. || κατὰ πρόσωπον v.1 ; τὰ κ. πρ. *what is before your eyes/staring you in the face.* βλέπετε impv, or perh indic. *you (only) see.* πέ-ποιθεν *is convinced,* pf[2] (w. pres. meaning) πείθω *persuade.* τοῦτο 9:6. λογιζέσθω impv 3rd sg -ίζομαι v.2, τοῦτο λ. πάλιν *let him go on to consider this fact.* ἐφ᾽ ἑαυτοῦ *for himself.* καθ ὡς...οὕτως...
8 *as...so... ;* i.e. *if he is...so equally are we.* || ἐάν τε *and if.* περισσότερον comp. of περισσῶς *abundantly* for positive §150, π. τι *rather much.* καυχήσωμαι aor. subj. -χάομαι *boast.* ἧς attracted from ἥν §16. ἔ-δωκεν aor. δίδωμι. οἰκο-δομή *building up.* καθαίρεσις v.4. αἰσχυνθήσομαι *I shall not be shamed,* (i.e. because his boast can be sub-
9 stantiated) fut. pass. -ύνω *put one to shame.* || ἵνα remains wt apodosis. δόξω aor. subj. δοκέω *seem.* ὡς ἄν *as it*
10 *were.* ἐκ-φοβεῖν inf. -φοβέω *frighten.* || ὅτι (*I write thus*) *because.* αἱ ἐπιστολαί begins a quotation : "His letters..." μέν...δέ Lat. *quidem...autem, on the one hand...on the other hand, ...indeed...but, while...yet...* φημί *say,* 3rd sg φησί(ν) w. the force of Eng. impers. *someone is saying.* βαρύς -ρεῖα -ρύ *heavy ;* met. *weighty.* ἰσχυρός *strong ;* met. *for-cible.* παρ-ουσία (< πάρειμι v.2) *presence.* ἀ-σθενής[9] *with-out strength, weak ;* met. *unimpressive.* ὁ λόγος *his preach-ing.* ἐξ-ουθενημένος *nothing to speak of, ineffective,* pf
11 ptc pass. -ουθενέω *ignore, despise.* || τοῦτο λογιζέσθω v.7.

τοι-οῦτος *such a person,* ὁ τ. *this individual.* οἱοι...τοιοῦτοι Lat. *quales...tales, what* we are...when absent, *that (we are)...when present.* τῷ λόγῳ δι' ἐπιστολῶν *in our written word* §114. ἀπ-όντες v.1. παρ-όντες v.2. ‖ γάρ purely 12 transitional §473. τολμάω *dare.* ἐγ-κρῖναι aor. inf. -κρίνω *put in the same class, rate* one *with* another. συγ-κρῖναι aor. inf. -κρίνω *compare (to).* ἑ-αυτούς (1st time) 3rd for 1st pl. *our-selves* §209. τισίν *to some* (masc). ἑ-αυτούς (2nd time) *themselves.* συν-ιστανόντων ptc -ιστάνω (late form of -ίστημι) *recommend.* αὐτοί *they.* ἐν ἑαυτοῖς *by their own standards.* μετροῦντες ptc μετρέω *measure.* συγ-κρίνοντες ptc, here rather *comparing (with).* ἑαυτοῖς for ἀλλήλοις, i.e. *with one another.* συνιᾶσιν 3rd pl. -ίημι *understand* ; i.e. in measuring themselves by their own standards and comparing themselves with each other they are not showing themselves very intelligent. ‖ ἄ-μετρος *without* 13 *or beyond measure,* εἰς τὰ ἄμ. advl, *beyond proper limits,* i.e. *excessively* or *outside our proper sphere* as v.15. καυχησόμεθα fut. v.8. κανών⁶ κανόνος ὁ *rule, norm* ; also a *field/sphere* of action, κατὰ τ. μέτρον τ. κανόνος *within the limits of the field.* οὗ seemingly attracted into the case of κανόνος (which is *not* its antecedent) and μέτρου then added to make this clear. ἐ-μέρισεν aor. -ίζω *divide ; distribute ; which God has apportioned us.* ἐφ-ικέσθαι aor² inf. -ικνέομαι *arrive at, reach,* inf. epexeg. (It formed part of God's plan that Paul should be first to bring the gospel to Corinth but he has no ambition to exceed the limits of his commission which would be to build on another man's foundation, Rom 15:20). ἄχρι w. gen. of place, *as far as, all the way to.* καί *even.* ‖ ἐφ-ικνούμενοι ptc. 14 ὑπερ-εκ-τείνω (stretch beyond) *over-reach; for we are not over-stretching ourselves, as if we did not reach as far as you.* ἐ-φθάσαμεν perh. w. class. connotation, *we were the first to come,* aor. φθάνω *arrive, come to.* ἐν *with,* of concomitant circumstances (sociative) §116. ‖ καυχώμενοι... 15 ἔχοντες ptcs taking the place of finite vbs, cf v.4f. ἀλ-λότριος *belonging to another, others'.* κόπος *labour.* ἐλπίς -ίδος ἡ *hope.* αὐξανομένης ptc pass. -άνω *make sth grow* ; pass. *grow* (intr.), gen. abs. ἐν ὑμῖν *in among you.* μεγα-λυνθῆναι aor. inf. pass. -ύνω *magnify,* pass. *increase* (intr.). κατὰ τ. κανόνα (v.13) *within our proper field.* περισσεία *abundance,* εἰς π. *to a vast extent.* ‖ ὑπερ-έκεινα adv. *beyond* ; 16

used as a prep. w. gen. τὰ ὑπ. ὑμῶν *the places beyond you.*
εὐ-αγγελίσασθαι aor. inf. -ίζομαι abs. *preach the gospel,*
ref. ἐλπίδα. ἕτοιμος v.6, τὰ ἔτ. *places already evangelized.*
Vv. 15,16 may be fairly lit. transl. *We do not boast outside
our limits about work done by others but we have the hope
that as your faith increases we may be enlarged among you
— (always) within our proper field — to a vast extent,
even to (the point of) spreading the gospel to places beyond
you, (though) not so as to boast about another's sphere of*
17 *places already evangelized.* ‖ καυχώμενος v.15. καυχάσθω
18 aor. impv 3rd sg, κ. ἐν κυρίῳ *boast about the Lord.* ‖ συν-
ιστάνων v.12. δόκιμος *approved.* συν-ίστησιν 3rd sg -ίστημι
v.12. ‖

11   ὄφελον particle, *would that! if only!* w. past tense of
indic. introducing an unrealized (or improbable) wish,
w. impf ref. pres. time, "if only you would put up with..."
§355 and n. ἀν-είχεσθε impf -έχομαί τί τινος lit. "bear/
put up with one over/with regard to sth", *put up with
sth from someone.* μικρός *small,* μικρόν τι *a little,* w. partitive gen. *a little (bit of).* ἀ-φροσύνη *foolishness.* ἀλλὰ
καί w. indic. *but in fact you do,* or impv 2nd pl. *nay, you*
2 *must...* ἀν-έχεσθε indic. or impv. ‖ ζηλόω τινά *be eagerly
concerned/jealous for one.* ζῆλος *ardour, jealousy,* θεοῦ ζ.
God's own ardour/jealousy. ἡρμοσάμην aor. mid. ἁρμόζω
betroth. ἑνὶ ἀνδρί *to a single husband.* παρθένος ἡ *virgin.*
ἁγνός *pure, chaste.* παρα-στῆσαι aor. inf. παρ-ίστημι *present,* inf. final : I betrothed you... *to present you as a chaste*
3 *virgin.* ‖ μή πως I am afraid *that.* ὄφις[4] ὁ *serpent.* ἐξ-
ηπάτησεν aor. -απατάω (ἐξ- perfective + ἀπατάω *deceive)
deceive.* παν-ουργία *cunning* 4:2. φθαρῇ aor[2] subj. pass.
φθείρω *corrupt, seduce.* νόημα[7] *thought, mind.* ἁπλότης[6]
4 -ότητος ἡ *simplicity, sincerity.* ἁγνότης[6] *purity.* ‖ εἰ w.
indic. a real condition §311. ὁ ἐρχόμενος *the (new-)
comer.* κηρύσσω *preach, announce.* ἐ-κηρύξαμεν aor. ἕτερος for ἄλλος §153, ἔτ. ὃ οὐκ ἐλάβετε "which you did not
receive", i.e. *different from the one you received.* ἐ-λάβετε
aor[2] λαμβάνω. ἐ-δέξασθε aor. δέχομαι *accept.* καλῶς *well,*
5 here ironic, *with ease.* ἀνέχομαι v.1. ‖ λογίζομαι *count,
consider.* γάρ would imply an ellipse, e.g. "you accept
them, why not me?" but γάρ seems on occasion to = δέ
§473. μηδέν acc. of respect. ὑστερηκέναι pf inf. -ρέω *fall
short.* ὑπερ-λίαν *superlatively,* ὑπ. ἀπόστολοι *super-apostles* ;

I reckon myself in no way inferior to these super-apostles. ||
εἰ...καί *even if.* ἰδιώτης³ an *amateur* (in Eng. sense), *not* 6
a specialist, not proficient. λόγος *speech,* dat. of respect
§53. εἰ... (sc. εἰμί) ἀλλά *even if* (*I am*)...*yet.* οὐ τῇ γν.
not so in knowledge. ἐν παντί...ἐν πᾶσιν *in every respect.*
φανερώσαντες aor. ptc -ρόω *make clear* or *evident,* again
ptc for finite vb, *we have made* (*that*) *plain to you.* || ἤ 7
introducing a question. ἁμαρτία *mistake.* ἐ-ποίησα aor.
ποιέω. ταπεινῶν *in lowering,* ptc -νόω *humiliate, degrade.*
ὑψωθῆτε aor. subj. pass. ὑψόω *exalt.* ὅτι *in that.* δωρεάν
adv. *gratis, freely, without payment.* εὐ-ηγγελισάμην aor.
-αγγελίζομαι *preach the gospel.* || ἐ-σύλησα aor. συλάω *rob.* 8
λαβών *by taking,* aor² ptc λαμβάνω. ὀψώνιον a *wage* I Cor
9:7. πρός *with a view to.* διακονία *service,* τὴν ὑμῶν δ.
gen obj., i.e. *to serving you.* || παρ-ών ptc -ειμι *be present,* 9
π. πρὸς ὑμᾶς *while I was with you.* ὑστερηθείς aor. ptc
pass. -ρέω v.5, pass. abs. *be in need, go short* aor. inceptive,
ran short. κατ-ε-νάρκησα aor. κατα-ναρκάω (orig. stupefy,
numb) w. gen. *be a burden to* one. οὐθενός for οὐδενός.
ὑστέρημα⁷ *need.* προσ-αν-ε-πλήρωσαν aor. -ανα-πληρόω *sup-*
ply what is lacking. ἐλθόντες aor² ptc ἔρχομαι. ἐν παντί
v.6. ἀ-βαρής⁹ (ἀ- + βαρύς heavy) *not burdensome.* ἐ-τή-
ρησα aor. τηρέω *keep.* τηρήσω fut. || ἔστιν...ὅτι form of 10
asseveration, *by the truth of Christ in me* (*I assure you*)
that. καύχησις⁴ *boasting.* φραγήσεται fut² pass. φράσσω *stop*
up, pass. met. *be stifled.* εἰς ἐμέ *against me* ; not directly
translatable into Eng. (Fr. *ne me sera ravi*) ; *I will not*
be stopped from boasting, this boasting will never be stifled
in me. κλίμα⁷ *district, territory* (smaller than a χώρα). ||
οἶδεν *knows,* sc. *that I do.* || ποιήσω fut. ἐκ-κόψω aor. 11,12
subj. -κόπτω *cut out* or *off.* ἀφ-ορμή (point "whence"
comes "an impulse") *pretext, opportunity* ἐκκόψω τὴν ἀφ.
of Eng. *I will cut the ground from under the feet...* θελόντων ptc gen. pl. θέλω. εὑρεθῶσιν aor² subj. pass. εὑρίσκω:
τῶν θελόντων ἵνα...εὑρεθῶσιν καθὼς καὶ ἡμεῖς *of those who*
want to be found/regarded as our equals. καυχῶνται 3rd
pl. -χάομαι *boast,* ἐν ᾧ κ. *in what they boast about.* || τοι- 13
οῦτοι pl. *such people.* ψευδ-απόστολος *false apostle,* pred.
sc. εἰσίν. ἐργάτης³ *workman.* δόλιος *deceitful, dishonest.*
μετα-σχηματιζόμενοι εἰς *disguising themselves as,* ptc -σχη-
ματίζω *change the appearance* (σχῆμα) *of.* || θαῦμα⁷ a *wonder,* 14
καὶ οὐ θ. *and no wonder.* αὐτός...ὁ Σ. *Satan himself.* ||

15 μέγα neut. of μέγας: οὐ μέγα οὖν *it is no great thing then.*
καί *also.* διάκονος *servant.* ὧν *whose.* τέλος[8] *end.* ἔσται
fut. εἰμί. ‖

16   γε particle emphasizing the foregoing word. δόξῃ
aor. subj. δοκέω *think, suppose,* μή γε τίς με δόξῃ *let no one
suppose that I...* ἄ-φρων[6] ἄφρονος neut. ἄφρον *sense-less,
foolish.* εἰ δὲ μή γε *otherwise.* κἄν = καὶ ἐάν an incomplete
condition, *if (so), if (you must).* δέξασθε aor. impv δέχομαι *accept.* κἀγώ = καὶ ἐγώ *I too.* μικρόν τι v.l. καυ-

17 χήσωμαι aor. subj. v.12. ‖ κατὰ κύριον *in the spirit of the
Lord.* ἀ-φροσύνη *folly.* ὑπό-στασις[4] *assurance, confidence*
9:4, sts also *a matter.* καύχησις v.10, transl. *in this matter
of boasting,* or understanding κ. as "Hebr." gen. *in this*

18 *boastful self-assurance.* ‖ ἐπεί *since.* καυχῶνται v.12. κατὰ

19 σάρκα *in a wordly spirit.* καυχήσομαι fut. ‖ ἡδέως *gladly.*
ἀν-έχομαι v.l. φρόνιμος *wise.* ὄντες ptc εἰμί, (ironically)

20 causal, *seeing that you are...* ‖ κατα-δουλόω *enslave, domineer over* one. κατ-εσθίω *eat up, devour;* a person, *exploit.* λαμβάνω *catch,* ref. hunting or fishing, hence perh.
catch one unawares so as to *take advantage of.* ἐπ-αίρεται
pass. -αίρω *lift* or *hold up;* pass. met. *be supercilious,*

21 *lofty* towards one. δέρω *beat; slap.* ‖ ἀ-τιμία *dis-grace,
shame;* κατ' ἀτιμίαν λέγω *to my shame I confess.* ὡς ὅτι =
ὅτι *that.* ἠ-σθενήκαμεν pf ἀ-σθενέω *be weak.* τολμάω *be
bold/presumptuous, assert oneself,* ἐν ᾧ δ' ἄν τις τολμᾷ *on
whatever score one may...* ἐν ἀφροσύνῃ λέγω a parenthesis.

22 κἀγώ = καὶ ἐγώ. ‖ 'Εβραῖος in NT era preponderantly ref.
language, here in an earlier sense connoting Hebrew by
descent, residence, and tradition. 'Ισραηλίτης i.e. one
of the people of God. σπέρμα[7] *seed, descendant,* σ. 'Αβραάμ
so inheritor of the promises and of the Covenant. ‖

23 διάκονος v.15. παρα-φρον ῶν ptc -φρονέω *be beside oneself,* π.
λέγω *I speak like a madman.* ὑπέρ retaining its orig. advl
force, ὑπὲρ ἐγώ "I (go) beyond", *I surpass them, I more
so* §78. κόπος *hard work.* περισσοτέρως *yet more often,*
comp. of περισσῶς *abundantly.* φυλακή *prison.* πληγή
(< πλήσσω *strike) stroke* of the lash, any *blow.* ὑπερ-
βαλλόντως (adv. from ptc -βάλλων *surpassing) exceedingly,
even more.* θάνατος *danger of death.* πολλ-άκις *many*

24 *times.* ‖ πεντ-άκις *five times.* τεσσεράκοντα = 40, τ. παρὰ
μίαν (sc. πληγάς) 40 *minus* 1 *(strokes).* ἔ-λαβον v.4, consta-

25 tive (global) aor. §253. ‖ τρίς *three times.* ἐ-ραβδίσθην

aor. pass. -ίζω *beat* with rods. ἅπαξ *once.* ἐ-λιθάσθην aor.
pass. -άζω *stone.* ἐ-ναυ-άγησα aor. ναυ-αγέω (< ναῦς ship
+ ἄγνυμι break) *be shipwrecked.* νυχθ-ήμερον (νυκτ- stem
of νύξ: τ before ἡ becomes θ and κ must assimilate to
the same order) *a day (and) a night, 24 hours* (the Jews'
day began w. the evening). βυθός *the deep,* i.e. *the open
sea.* πε-ποίηκα pf ποιέω sts *pass/spend* time, perh. aor.-pf,
but may indicate a horror vividly present in recollection. ‖ ὁδοι-πορία *journey,* this and foll. datives = dat.   26
w. ἐν. πολλάκις v.23. κίνδυνος *danger.* ποταμός *river.*
λῃστής[3] *robber.* γένος[8] *family,* a *people,* here *fellow-countrymen.* ἐρημία *deserted/lonely place.* ψευδ-άδελφος *false brother.* ‖ κόπος v.23. μόχθος *heavy labour.* ἀγρυπνία *wake-*   27
fulness, sleeplessness 6:5. λιμός ὁ and ἡ, *hunger.* δίψος[8]
thirst. νηστεία *fasting.* ψῦχος[8] *cold.* γυμνότης[6] -ότητος ἡ
nakedness. ‖ χωρίς w. gen. *without, apart from.* τὰ παρ-   28
εκτός *all else.* ἐπί-στασις[4] (< ἐφ-ίστημι come upon) cf Ac
24:12, here prob. a *pressure* or *weight* upon one, *preoccu-
pation.* καθ' ἡμέραν *daily,* κατά distributive. μέριμνα *care,*
w. gen. *concern for.* ‖ ἀ-σθενέω v.21, καὶ οὐκ ἀσθ. *without*   29
my sharing his weakness. σκανδαλίζομαι *be made to stumble,
be led into sin.* πυρόομαι *burn,* met. *blaze* with indignation. ‖ καυχᾶσθαι inf. -άομαι. ἀ-σθένεια *weakness,* τὰ τῆς   30
ἀ. μου *the occasions of my weakness.* καυχήσομαι v.18. ‖
ὤν v.19 (ὄντες). εὐ-λογητός *blessed.* εἰς τ. αἰῶνας *for*   31
ever. ψεύδομαι *tell an untruth, lie.* ‖ ἐθν-άρχης[3] *ethnarch,*   32
a *governor.* Ἀρέτα gen. of Ἀρέτας. ἐ-φρούρει impf φρου-
ρέω *guard.* Δαμασκηνός a *Damascene, inhabitant of Dama-
scus.* πιάσαι aor. inf. πιάζω *apprehend, arrest*; inf. final. ‖
θυρίς[6] -ίδος ἡ *window.* σαργάνη flexible *basket.* ἐ-χαλά-   33
σθην aor. pass. χαλάω *lower.* τεῖχος[8] *wall,* διὰ θυρίδος...διὰ
τοῦ τ. *through a window in the wall.* ἐξ-έ-φυγον aor[2] ἐκ-
φεύγω *escape.* ‖

    καυχᾶσθαι inf. -χάομαι *boast.* συμ-φέρον ptc neut. -φέρει   **12**
impers. *it is an advantage/good/useful,* οὐ συμφέρον μέν...
δέ while *it serves no good purpose, it is no use...yet.*
ἐλεύσομαι fut. ἔρχομαι. εἰς = πρός *to* §97. ὀπτασία a
vision. ἀπο-κάλυψις[4] *revelation.* ‖ ἄνθρωπον ἐν Χρ. *a Chris-*   2
tian man. πρό *before,* ago, to be ass. w. ἁρπαγέντα; the
position of πρό a HGk idiom, §71. ἔτος[8] *year.* δεκα-
τέσσαρες = 14. εἴτε...εἴτε *whether...or.* ἐκτός w. gen. *out
of.* ἁρπαγέντα (*who*) *was caught up,* aor[2] ptc pass. ἁρπάζω

3 *seize and carry off.* τρίτος *third.* ‖ τοι-οῦτος *such a man,*
4 *this man.* χωρίς w. gen. *without.* ‖ ἡρπάγη aor² pass.
ἁρπάζω. **παράδεισος** Persian word, *garden* ; *paradise, home
of the blessed.* ἤκουσεν aor. ἀκούω. ἄρ-ρητος *in-effable,*
either as in-expressible or (as here) not to be expressed.
ῥῆμα⁷ *word.* ἐξ-όν ptc neut. ἔξ-εστιν impers. *it is permit-
ted,* οὐκ ἐξὸν ἀνθρώπῳ *a man may not.* λαλῆσαι aor. inf.
5 λαλέω here, *utter.* ‖ ὑπέρ for περί *about* §96. **καυχήσομαι**
fut. v.1, κ. ὑπέρ or ἐν *boast about* or *of.* ἐμ-αυτοῦ *my-self.*
6 εἰ μή *except.* ἀ-σθένεια *weakness.* ‖ ἐάν...θελήσω (aor. subj.
θέλω) *if I should want,* an eventual condition §320. **καυ-
χήσασθαι** aor. inf. ἔσομαι fut. εἰμί. ἄ-φρων *foolish,* ἔσομαι
ἄ. (in this context) *I shall not be making a fool of myself.*
ἐρῶ fut. λέγω. **φείδομαι** *spare* ; *restrain* oneself. **λογίσηται** aor. subj. -ίζομαι 11:5 ; λ. εἰς ἐμέ *should think of
me/regard me as.* ὑπέρ *above, better than.* ὃ βλέπει...ἐξ
ἐμοῦ *what he sees me (to be) or anything he hears from me.* ‖
7 **ὑπερ-βολή** *excess* ; *exceptional nature* ; pendent dat. of
cause. **ἀποκάλυψις** v.1. δι-ό *for this reason.* **ὑπερ-αίρωμαι**
subj. -αίρομαι *be elated.* ἐ-δόθη aor. pass. δίδωμι. **σκόλοψ**⁶
-λοπος ὁ *thorn.* Σατανᾶς -ᾶ *Satan.* **κολαφίζη** subj. -ίζω
rain blows on, batter, knock one *about* (I Cor 4:11). ‖
8 ὑπέρ v.5. τρίς *three times.* **παρ-ε-κάλεσα** aor. παρα-καλέω
entreat, beg. ἀπο-στῇ *that it would go away,* aor² (intr.)
9 subj. ἀφ-ίστημι *cause to stand away.* ‖ **εἴρηκεν** pf λέγω, pf
connoting *he has said and it stands,* the reply was final.
ἀρκέω *be enough.* ἀσθένεια v.5. **τελεῖται** *comes to its
fulness,* pass. τελέω *complete.* **ἥδιστα** (superl. of ἡδέως)
most gladly. καυχήσομαι v.5. **ἐπι-σκηνώσῃ** aor. subj. -σκη-
10 νόω *make one's home* ; aor. *come to rest.* ‖ διό v.7. **εὐ-
δοκέω** *be content.* **ὕβρις** *insolence,* pl. *acts of insolence.*
ἀνάγκη *hardship.* **διωγμός** *persecution.* **στενο-χωρία** *constraint* ; *distress.* ἀσθενῶ subj. -νέω *be weak.* **δυνατός**
strong. ‖
11 **γέ-γονα** pf² γίνομαι. ἄφρων v.6. **ἠναγκάσατε** *you drove
me (to it),* aor. ἀναγκάζω *force.* ὤφειλον impf ὀφείλω *owe,*
w. inf. *ought to,* cf II Cor 2:3 (ἔδει). **συν-ίστασθαι** inf.
pass. -ίστημι *recommend.* οὐδέν *in nothing,* acc. of respect. **ὑστέρησα** aor. -ρέω *fall short of.* ὑπερ-λίαν 11:5 ; a
reply to an attack on his apostleship. εἰ καί *even though.* ‖
12 **κατειργάσθη** aor. pass. -εργάζομαι *work, do.* ἐν *among.* ὑπο-
μονή *endurance.* **τέρας** τέρατος τό a *wonder.* **δύναμις** pl. *mi-*

racles. ‖ **ὅ** acc. of respect. **ἡσσώθητε** aor. ἐσσόομαι = ἡττάο-   13
μαι *be defeated* (< ἥσσων v.15) ἐσσ. ὑπέρ *be inferior to.*
λοιπός (< λείπω leave) *remaining,* the *other* churches. **εἰ**
μή v.5. **κατ-ε-νάρκησα** aor. κατα-ναρκέω (orig. stupefy,
numb), w. gen. *be a burden to* one. **χαρίσασθε** aor. impv
-ίζω τινί τι *bestow* sth *on* one ; *forgive* one sth. **ἀ-δικία**
injury, wrong (ironical). ‖ **τρίτον** adv. *a third time,* τρ.   14
τοῦτο *this is the third time.* **ἑτοίμως ἔχω** *be ready,* cf 10:6.
ἐλθεῖν aor² inf. ἔρχομαι. **κατα-ναρκήσω** fut. **τὰ ὑμῶν** *what*
is yours. **ὀφείλω** v.11, οὐ...ὀφείλει τὰ τέκνα w. inf. *chil-*
dren are not obliged to. **γονεῖς** οἱ dat. pl. γονεῦσιν *pa-*
rents. **θησαυρίζειν** inf. -ίζω *treasure, save up.* ‖ **ἥδιστα** v.9.   15
δαπανήσω fut. -νάω *spend.* **ἐκ-δαπανηθήσομαι** fut. pass.
-δαπανάω *spend ; I will spend and be spent.* **περισσοτέρως**
more intensely or *far more* 7:13. **ἀγαπῶν** ptc. **ἥσσων** *less,*
neut. ἧσσον as adv. **ἀγαπῶμαι** pass. *am I to be loved?* ‖
ἔστω *so be it,* impv 3rd sg εἰμί. **κατ-ε-βάρησα** aor. κατα-   16
βαρέω *weigh down.* **ὑπ-άρχων** ptc -άρχω *be* 8:17 ptc causal.
παν-οῦργος *cunning, unscrupulous,* cf 4:2 (πανουργία). **δόλος**
properly "a bait" ; *deceit,* δόλῳ *by subterfuge.* **ἔ-λαβον**
aor² λαμβάνω here *take* one *in* (= *deceive*). ‖ **μή** interr.   17
expecting the answer "No". **τινα** pendent acc. under
the influence of **ἀπ-έ-σταλκα** pf ἀπο-στέλλω. **ὧν** by attraction for ἐκείνων οὕς §17. **ἐ-πλεον-έκτησα** aor. -εκτέω τινα
take advantage of, defraud one, lit. "any of those I sent
to you, have I defrauded you through him?" **αὐτοῦ**
resumes the pendent acc. ‖ **παρ-ε-κάλεσα** v.8, sc. to come   18
to you. **συν-απ-έ-στειλα** aor. -απο-στέλλω *send* one *with*
another. **μήτι** a strengthened form of μή, *surely T. did*
not...did he? **οὐ** as interr. expecting "Yes" as answer.
ὁ αὐτός *the same.* **περι-ε-πατήσαμεν** aor. περι-πατέω in
ethical sense, *live.* **ἴχνος**⁸ *footprint, track : Have we not*
lived by the same Spirit? followed the same trail? ‖ **πάλαι**   19
formerly ; so far, up to now. **δοκέω** *think, suppose.* **ἀπο-**
λογέομαι *make a defence, defend* oneself. **κατ-έν-αντι** adv.
used as prep. w. gen. *before* §83. **ἀγαπητός** *beloved.* **οἰκο-**
δομή *edification, building up.* ‖ **μή πως** I fear *that.* **ἐλθών**   20
when I come, aor² ptc ἔρχομαι. **οἷος** *such as.* **εὕρω** *I may*
find, aor² subj. εὑρίσκω. **κἀγώ** = καὶ ἐγώ. **εὑρεθῶ** aor²
subj. pass. **μή πως** still understanding φοβοῦμαι. **ἔρις**⁶
-ιδος ἡ *rivalry.* **ζῆλος** (here in bad sense) *jealousy.* **θυμός**
anger, pl. e.g. *outbursts of anger.* **ἐριθεία** *selfish ambition,*

esp. as pursued by unworthy means Rom 2:8. If deemed
necessary, the pls of these abstract nouns may be rendered
by "occasions of..., acts of...". **κατα-λαλιά** *evil-speaking,
backbiting.* **ψιθυρισμός** *whispering,* hence *gossip.* **φυσίωσις⁴**
inflation, hence *self-importance, conceit.* **ἀ-κατα-στασία** pl.

21 *disturbance(s).* || **ἐλθόντος** gen. abs. instead of ἐλθόντα
agreeing w. με. **ταπεινώσῃ** aor. subj. -νόω *humiliate.*
πρὸς ὑμᾶς *before you.* **πενθήσω** fut. -θέω *mourn.* **προ-
ημαρτηκότων** pf ptc -αμαρτάνω *sin earlier/in time past* ; pf
continue in their former sins. **μετα-νοησάντων** aor. ptc
-νοέω *repent* : μεταν. ἐπί τινι *repent of* sth. **ἀ-καθαρσία** *im-
purity, im-morality.* **πορνεία** *fornication.* **ἀ-σέλγεια** *debauchery,* three under one art. §184. **ᾗ** attracted from
ἥν §17. **ἔ-πραξαν** aor. πράσσω *practise.* ||

13   **τρίτον τοῦτο** 12:14. **στόμα⁷** *mouth* ; ἐπὶ στόματος Hebr.
idiom, *on the evidence.* **μάρτυς⁶** -τυρος ὁ *witness.* **τριῶν**
gen. of τρεῖς. **σταθήσεται** fut. pass. ἵστημι *establish, sub-
2 stantiate.* **ῥῆμα⁷** *word, thing.* || **προ-είρηκα** pf -λέγω *say
beforehand.* **ὡς...καί** *as...so.* **παρ-ών** ptc -ειμι *be present.*
τὸ δεύτερον *the second time,* i.e. on his second visit. **ἀπ-ών**
ptc -ειμι *be away/absent.* **προ-ημαρτηκόσιν** pf ptc dat. pl.
-αμαρτάνω 12:21. **λοιπός** (λείπω *leave) left,* οἱ λ. *the rest.*
προείρ. ...πᾶσιν *I already told those who continue in their
former sins and all the rest of you when I was with you
on my second visit, and I repeat it now in (my) absence*
(i.e. *before I come).* **ἐάν...ἔλθω** (aor² subj.) *if I come* ;
eventual condition §320ff. **εἰς τὸ πάλιν** *another time* ; to
be referred to ἔλθω ? or φείσομαι ? **φείσομαι** fut. φείδομαι
3 *spare,* abs. *be lenient.* || **ἐπεί** *since* (causal). **δοκιμή** *proof.*
ζητεῖτε *you seek/require* (Mk 8:11). **λαλοῦντος** ptc λαλέω,
proof "of Christ speaking", i.e. *that Christ speaks.* **ὅς**
(sc. Christ) *who.* **εἰς ὑμᾶς** *towards/with you.* **ἀ-σθενέω** *be
weak.* **δυνατέω** *have power, be powerful.* **ἐν** *among.* ||
4 **καὶ γάρ** *for in fact.* **ἐ-σταυρώθη** aor. pass. -ρόω *crucify.*
ἀ-σθενεία *weakness,* ἐξ ἀ. *through weakness.* **ζῇ** 3rd sg ζάω.
ζήσομεν fut. w. intensive force, *we shall show ourselves very
5 much alive.* || **ἐ-αυτούς** emphatic, 3rd for 2nd pers. **πει-
ράζετε** impv -άζω *examine.* **δοκιμάζετε** impv -άζω *test.*
ἐπι-γινώσκω *realize.* **ἑαυτούς** (2nd time) *with regard to
yourselves.* **μητί** a strengthened μή: εἰ μ. *unless, that is,...*
ἀ-δόκιμος lit. "not passing the test", *not up to standard,*
6 a *failure.* || **ἐλπίζω** *hope.* **γνώσεσθε** *you will come to*

know, fut. γινώσκω. ‖ **εὔχομαι** *pray,* εὐχ. τι *pray for* sth ; 7
w. acc. + inf. *pray...that.* **ποιῆσαι** aor. inf. ποιέω. **κακός**
wrong, μὴ π. ...μηδέν *that you may do nothing wrong* or
that I may have to do you no hurt. **φανῶμεν** *be shown,*
appear, aor² subj. pass. φαίνω *show.* **δόκιμος** *successful*
in the test, approved ; not so that we may be shown
(thereby) to be δ., meaning "not because we want to make
use of you in order to be seen to be 'approved', but simply
that you may do..." **τὸ καλόν** *what is noble, right.* **ποιῆτε**
subj. **ὡς ἀδόκιμοι** *as it were not approved / failures* (ὡς
because wt opportunity to prove himself). **ἡμεῖς...ὦμεν**
(subj. εἰμί) *and we remain...* ‖ **κατά** w. gen. *against.* ‖ 8
ἀ-σθενῶμεν subj. -νέω *be weak.* **δέ** and you *(on the other* 9
hand). **δυνατός** *strong.* **ἦτε** v.7 (ὦμεν). **κατ-άρτισις⁴** (κατ-
αρτίζω put in order, complete) *restoration to perfection.* ‖
διὰ τοῦτο *this is why.* **ἀπ-ών** *while (still) absent.* **παρ-ών** 10
v.2. **ἀπο-τόμως** (< ἀπο- + τέμνω *cut) severely.* **χρήσωμαι**
aor. subj. χράομαί τινι *use sth ; treat / deal with* a person,
I shall not have to deal... **κατά** w. acc. *in virtue of.* **ἔ-δωκεν**
aor. δίδωμι. **οἰκο-δομή** *building up.* **καθ-αίρεσις⁴** *pulling*
down. ‖ **λοιπόν** adv. *finally.* **χαίρετε** impv (as the 4 fol- 11
lowing vbs are). **κατ-αρτίζεσθε** mid. *amend your ways.*
παρα-καλεῖσθε mid. *encourage each other* or pass. *be en-*
couraged. **τὸ αὐτό** *the same.* **φρονεῖτε** *think,* τὸ αὐτὸ φ. *be of*
one mind. **εἰρηνεύετε** *live at peace.* ‖ **ἀσπάσασθε** aor. impv 12
-άζομαι *greet.* **φίλημα⁷** *kiss.* ‖ **κυρίου...** note the Trinitarian 13
nature of the prayer ; all 3 gens. are subjective, of the
source. **κοινωνία** *communion, fellowship,* or *communica-*
tion, imparting (sc. of grace).

GALATIANS

1 θεὸς πατήρ I Thess 1:1. ἐγείραντος aor. ptc ἐγείρω
2,3 rouse ; raise. || οἱ...πάντες all wt exception §188. || χάρις
Christian version of Gk salutation χαίρειν + Hebr.
4 "Peace !" || δόντος aor² ptc δίδωμι. ὑπὲρ τῶν ἁμαρτιῶν ἡμῶν
for (= in expiation of) our sins. ὅπως w. subj. final, so
that. ἐξ-έληται aor² subj. mid. -αιρέω take out ; mid. rescue, deliver. ἐν-εστῶτος present, pf (intr. w. pres. meaning)
5 ptc -ίστημι be present. || ᾧ to whom, understand (may
there) be. εἰς τ. αἰῶνας τ. αἰώνων for ever and ever. ||
6 θαυμάζω I am astonished. ταχέως (adj. ταχύς) quickly,
soon. μετα-τίθεσθε mid. -τίθημι trans-fer sth ; mid. transfer
oneself, μ. ἀπό...εἰς desert...for..., i.e. (and go over) to. καλέσαντος aor. ptc καλέω. ἐν χάριτι in grace or by grace
7 (instr. §119). ἕτερος different. || ἄλλο another — there
exists no alternative gospel, but the gospel may be dis-
torted and so "different". εἰ μή for ἀλλά §470. ταράσ-
σοντες ptc -άσσω disturb, trouble. θέλοντες ptc θέλω.
μετα-στρέψαι aor. inf. -στρέφω over-turn ; misrepresent, dis-
8 tort. || ἀλλὰ καὶ ἐάν but though, w. subj. eventual condi-
tion §320. εὐ-αγγελίζηται subj. -ίζομαι preach the (here,
a) gospel. παρ' ὅ contrary to that which I Cor 3:11, cf
Rom 1:26. εὐ-ηγγελισάμεθα aor. ἀνά-θεμα⁷ (< ἀνα- + τίθημι) something set aside, "devoted" to the deity ; esp.
9 something accursed. ἔστω impv εἰμί. || ὡς...καί as...so.
προ-ειρήκαμεν pf -λέγω say beforehand/already. ἄρτι now.
εἰ...εὐαγγελίζεται a real condition "if indeed..." §303ff.
παρ-ε-λάβετε aor² παρα-λαμβάνω receive (esp. as handed down
10 (παρα-δοθέν) by tradition). || πείθω persuade ; curry favour
with. ἀρέσκειν inf. ἀρέσκω try to please. ἔτι still. ἤρεσκον
impf ἀρέσκω ; unfulfilled condition w. ἄν in apodosis §313.
ἤμην impf εἰμί: οὐκ ἂν ἤμην I would not be. ||
11 γάρ perh. = δέ §473. γνωρίζω make known, γν. ...
ὑμῖν...ὅτι I want you to realize that. εὐ-αγγελισθέν aor. ptc
pass. neut. κατὰ ἄνθρωπον man-devised, of human origin. ||
12 παρ-έ-λαβον v.9. ἐ-διδάχθην aor. pass. διδάσκω. ἀπο-κάλυ-

ψις⁴ *revelation.* ‖ ἠκούσατε aor. ἀκούω. ἀνα- 13
στρέφομαι live, behave) *manner of life.* ποτέ *at one time.*
'Ιουδαϊσμός *the Jewish faith.* ὑπερ-βολή (ὑπερ-βάλλω exceed, surpass) *excess,* καθ' ὑπ. *exceedingly* ; w. διώκω, *violently.* ἐ-δίωκον impf διώκω *pursue* ; *persecute.* ἐ-πόρθουν
impf -θέω *lay waste,* impf conative, *tried to destroy/make
havoc of.* ‖ προ-έ-κοπτον impf -κόπτω *progress,* so, *go fur-* 14
ther. συν-ηλικιώτης³ (συν- + ἡλικία age) *of my age.* ἐν
among. γένος⁸ *family, a people,* τὸ γ. μου *my own people.*
περισσοτέρως (comp. of περισσῶς) *even more* i.e. *than they*
were. ζηλωτής³ *fanatic* ; *activist.* ὑπ-άρχων ptc -άρχω *be
from the beginning* ; *exist* ; often simply *be.* πατρικός *of
our fathers/forebears.* παρά-δοσις⁴ (< παρα-δίδωμι) *tradition.* ‖ εὐ-δόκησεν aor. -δοκέω *be pleased* ; εὐδόκησεν ὁ θεός 15
...ἀποκαλύψαι *God...was pleased to reveal.* ἀφ-ορίσας aor.
ptc -ίζω *separate, set apart.* κοιλία a *hollow* ; *womb.* καλέσας
v.6. ‖ ἀπο-καλύψαι aor. inf. -καλύπτω *un-cover, reveal.* ἐν 16
ἐμοί possibly simple dat. (I Cor 14:11) but here rather
in me connoting interior revelation. εὐ-αγγελίζωμαι v.8.
ἐν (τοῖς ἔθνεσιν) *among.* προσ-αν-ε-θέμην aor² -ανα-τίθεμαί
τινι mid. *lay before* ; *consult with.* σὰρξ κ. αἷμα i.e. (*any*)
man. ‖ ἀν-ῆλθον aor² -έρχομαι *go up.* πρό w. gen. *before.* 17
ὑπ-έ-στρεψα aor. ὑπο-στρέφω *turn sth back,* also w. refl.
sense, *go back.* ‖ ἔπ-ειτα *thereafter.* ἔτος⁸ *year.* τρία neut. 18
of τρεῖς. ἱστορῆσαι aor. inf. -ρέω *visit* places and persons, hence *meet and get to know.* ἐπ-έ-μεινα aor. ἐπι-μένω
stay (on). πρός w. acc. of person, *with* him I Cor 16:6,
II Cor 5:8, 11:9. δεκα-πέντε = 15. ‖ ἔτερος for ἄλλος, 19
ἔτ....οὐκ *not...any other.* εἰ μή v.7. ‖ ἅ acc. of respect, 20
in what I am writing. ἐνώπιον τ. θεοῦ lit. "in the sight
of God", i.e. *I swear to God.* ψεύδομαι *tell an untruth, lie.* ‖
ἔπειτα v.18. κλίμα⁷ *district, territory* (smaller than χώρα). ‖ 21
ἤμην v.10. ἀ-γνοούμενος *un-known,* ptc pass. -γνοέω *not* 22
to know. τῷ προσώπῳ *by sight,* dat. of respect §53. ‖ ἀκούον- 23
τες ἦσαν periphrastic impf, *they were* only *hearing it said.*
ὅτι = "... διώκων ptc v.13, ὁ δ. ἡμᾶς ποτε (v.13) *our one-
time persecutor.* ἐ-πόρθει v.13. ‖ ἐ-δόξαζον impf -άζω 24
glorify, give praise to God. ἐν ἐμοί *because of me,* ἐν
causal §119. ‖

ἔπειτα *then, afterwards.* διά w. gen. temporal, in 2
class. sense, *after.* δεκα-τέσσαρες = 14. ἔτος⁸ *year.* ἀν-
έβην aor² ἀνα-βαίνω. συμ-παρα-λαβών aor² ptc -λαμβάνω

2 *take along with* one. ‖ **κατά** *by,* i.e. *as a result of and in accordance with.* **ἀπο-κάλυψις⁴** *revelation.* **ἀν-ε-θέμην** aor² **ἀνα-τίθεμαί τινι** (mid.) *lay before, put it to* one so as to consult. **κηρύσσω** *preach.* **ἐν** *among.* **ἴδιος** *proper to, one's own* ; **κατ' ἰδίαν** *apart.* **δοκοῦσιν** ptc dat. pl. **δοκέω** *seem, be thought*..., abs. *be well thought of | held in regard.* **μή πως** *so that...not* : when ref. fut. w. subj., w. indic. ref. sth past (about which there can no longer be doubt), *so that I might not run or have run* §344. **κενός** *empty* ; **εἰς κ.**

3 *in vain.* **τρέχω** subj. *run.* **ἔ-δραμον** aor² **τρέχω.** ‖ **ἀλλά** *moreover.* **Ἕλλην -ηνος** a *Greek.* **ὤν** ptc **εἰμί** concessive, *although he was* a Greek (and therefore uncircumcised.) **ἠναγκάσθη** aor. pass. **ἀναγκάζω** *compel.* **περι-τμηθῆναι** aor.

4 inf. pass. **-τέμνω** *cut round, circumcise.* ‖ **διά** *because of* ; vv.4f. break the cstr and stand on their own wt principal vb. **παρ-είσ-ακτος** *brought in surreptitiously.* **ψευδ-άδελφος** *false brother.* **ὅστις** *for* **οἵ** §216 *or who, being what they are* §218. **παρ-εισ-ῆλθον** aor² **-έρχομαι** *intrude, slip/ steal in.* **κατα-σκοπῆσαι** aor. inf. final **-σκοπέω** *spy out.* **ἐλευθερία** *freedom.* **κατα-δουλώσουσιν** fut. (HGk) for aor.

5 subj. **-δουλόω** *enslave* §340. ‖ **πρὸς ὥραν** *for a moment.* **εἴξαμεν** aor. **εἴκω** *yield, give way.* **ὑπο-ταγή** *subjection, submission,* dat. of manner, *in submission,* i.e. *meekly* §60. **δια-μείνη** aor. subj. **-μένω** *endure, continue unchanged.* **πρός**

6 1:18. ‖ **δοκούντων** v.2, τῶν δ. εἶναί τι *those considered to be something | held in regard.* **ὁ-ποῖος** indir. interr. *of what sort,* ὅπ. ποτε ἦσαν *whatever they were.* **δια-φέρει τινί** impers. *it makes a difference to* one, *it matters.* **πρόσωπον** (orig. an actor's mask) *face,* hence the face one presents to the world, outward circumstances or position, π. λαμβάνω Hebr. *show favour/partiality* in accordance w. such considerations, *be a respecter of persons.* **προσ-αν-έ-θεντο** aor² **-ανα-τίθεμαί τινι** (mid.) *make an addition,* here *add any*

7 *provisos.* ‖ **τοὐναντίον** = **τὸ ἐναντίον** *on the contrary.* **ἰδόν-τες** aor² ptc **ὁράω.** **πε-πίστευμαι** of pass. **-εύω τινί τι** *entrust* sth to one ; in pass. the person becomes subject, the thing an acc. of respect, *be entrusted with* sth §72. **ἀκροβυστία** *uncircumcision,* i.e. gentiles ; gen. obj. *to.* **περι-**

8 **τομή** *circumcision.* ‖ **ἐν-εργήσας** aor. ptc **-εργέω** *work* or *effect* sth ; abs. *be active.* **Πέτρῳ** dat. of advantage. **ἀπο-**

9 **στολή** *apostleship.* **ἐν-έργησεν** aor. ‖ **γνόντες** *recognizing,* aor² ptc **γινώσκω.** **δοθεῖσαν** aor. ptc pass. **δίδωμι.** **δο-**

κοῦντες v.2, *considered*. στῦλος *pillar*. δεξιός *right* (opp.
left), ἡ δεξιά (sc. χείρ) *right hand*. ἔ-δωκαν aor. δίδωμι.
κοινωνία *association, partnership*; also an *agreement*, δεξιάς
...κοινωνίας *shook hands with me and B. in token of our
partnership*, sc. in spreading the gospel. ἵνα *namely, to
the effect that* we (go) to the gentiles and they to the Jews. ||
πτωχός *poor*, τῶν πτ. *their poor*, preponderantly of Jerusa-   10
lem. ἵνα impvl §415. μνημονεύωμεν *we were to bear in
mind*, subj. -εύω *have in mind*. ἐ-σπούδασα aor. -άζω
hurry; be eager. αὐτὸ τοῦτο *that very thing, just that*.
ποιῆσαι aor. inf. ποιέω. ||

     κατὰ πρόσωπον *to his face*. ἀντ-έ-στην *resisted*, aor[2]   11
(intr.) ἀνθ-ίστημι *set against, oppose*. κατ-ε-γνωσμένος *stood
condemned*, or better, *blameworthy, in fault*. pf ptc pass.
κατα-γινώσκω *condemn*. || πρὸ τοῦ w. acc. + inf. *before*.   12
ἐλθεῖν aor[2] inf. ἔρχομαι. ἀπό for παρά *from* a person. συν-
ήσθιεν impf -εσθίω *eat with*. ὑπ-έ-στελλεν impf ὑπο-στέλλω
draw back, impf inceptive, *he made a move to draw back
and...* ἀφ-ώριζεν impf -ορίζω (< ἀπο- + ὅρος boundary)
separate; ἀφορ. ἑαυτόν *hold aloof*. φοβούμενος ptc (causal)
φοβέομαι. περι-τομή v.7, here ref. Christians of Jewish
origin. || συν-υπ-ε-κρίθησαν aor. -υπο-κρίνομαί τινι dep. *join*   13
one *in a* (hypocritical) *pretence*. λοιπός *left behind, remaining*; οἱ λ. *the others*. ὥστε *to the point that*. συν-απ-
ήχθη aor. pass. -απ-άγω *lead/carry away*; force of indic.
(opp. inf.) *was actually...* §350. ὑπό-κρισις[4] *hypocrisy*, dat.
by or (*to join*) *in* their hypocrisy. || ὀρθο-ποδέω: At one   14
time believed to be a hapax, the meaning had to be inferred from this context, and from commentaries on it,
as *walk straight* or *uprightly* (in ethical sense, so Origen)
in which case πρός must stand for κατά *in accordance with*.
Two recent discoveries indicate an alternative meaning,
go straight forward, progress, be on the right road; πρός will
then bear its normal sense, *towards*. ἔμ-προσθεν *in front
of*. ὑπ-άρχων ptc -άρχω be 1:14. ἐθνικῶς *like a gentile*.
οὐχί emphatic form of οὐ. Ἰουδαϊκῶς *like a Jew*. ζῆς
2nd sg ζάω. ἀναγκάζω v.3. Ἰουδαΐζειν inf. -ίζω *live as
a Jew* (i.e. by the Law). ||

     φύσις[4] *nature*, dat. of respect, *by nature*. ἁμαρτωλός   15
sinner, i.e. lacking the knowledge and guidance of the
Law. || εἰδότες pf-pres. ptc οἶδα. δικαιοῦται pass. -αιόω   16
in pagan literature, *justify, show to be in the right, pronounce*

righteous ; in Paul, a t.t. for a new creation. **ἐὰν μή** for **ἀλλά** 1:7. **ἐ-πιστεύσαμεν** aor. -εύω, inceptive aor. *took the step of believing* §250. **δικαιωθῶμεν** aor. subj. pass. **δικαιωθήσεται** fut. pass. **οὐ...πᾶς** Hebr. *none, no,* οὐ...πᾶσα

17 **σάρξ** *no man* §446. ‖ **ζητοῦντες** ptc ζητέω. **δικαιωθῆναι** aor. inf. pass. **εὑρέθημεν** aor² pass. εὑρίσκω: εὑρ. αὐτοί *we were found to be.* **ἁμαρτωλοί** i.e. like the gentiles, wt the Law (having rejected it as a means to salvation). **ἆρα** interr. particle, implying impatience, *do you mean to say that?* (NEB). Christ would be "the servant of sin" by being responsible for our turning from the Law to faith

18 in him. **γένοιτο** aor² opt. γίνομαι: μὴ γ. *God forbid!* ‖ **κατ-έ-λυσα** aor. κατα-λύω *destroy.* **οἰκο-δομέω** *build up.* **παρα-βάτης³** *trans-gressor.* **συρ-ιστάνω** *present* one. *For if I re-construct what I have demolished* (viz. a legalistic sys-tem) *I show myself a transgressor.* The 1st pers. is used to typify "anyone".

19 ‖ **ἐγώ** indicates Paul himself. **διὰ νόμου** *through the Law* (given to lead us to Christ 3:24, Rom 10:4). **ἀπ-έ-θανον** aor² ἀπο-θνήσκω: νόμῳ ἀπέθ. *I died to law,* dat. of disadvantage. **ζήσω** aor. subj. ζάω. **συν-ε-σταύρωμαι** pf ptc pass. συ(ν)-σταυρόω *crucify* one *with* another. Through the Law I was led to have nothing more to do with legalism and to live for God. For me being cruci-

20 fied with Christ means dying to the Law. ‖ **οὐκ-έτι** *no longer.* **ζῇ** 3rd sg. **ὅ** obj. *(the life) that,* neut. because ref. to the general sense of what follows. **ἀγαπήσαντος**

21 aor. ptc -πάω. **παρα-δόντος** aor² ptc (-δώς) -δίδωμι. ‖ **ἀ-θετέω** *render* ἄ-θετος (invalid) ; *render sth null and void, cancel.* **διὰ νόμου** (comes) *through/by way of law.* **ἄρα** *then.* **δωρεάν** acc. of δωρεά as adv., *gratis* ; here *in vain.* ‖

3 **ὦ** w. voc. in HGk betraying emotion §35. **ἀ-νόητος** *ignorant* ; *foolish.* **ἐ-βάσκανεν** aor² βασκαίνω *fascinate, be-witch.* **κατ' ὀφθαλμούς** *before (your) eyes.* **προ-ε-γράφη** aor² pass. προ-γράφω *put up* as a public notice, *exhibit* ; pass. *be on view.* **ἐ-σταυρωμένος** pf ptc pass. -ρόω *crucify.* ‖

2 **μαθεῖν** aor² inf. μανθάνω *learn,* aor. *ascertain.* **ἐξ** (twice) *by.* **ἐ-λάβετε** aor² λαμβάνω. **ἀκοή** *hearing* ; *obedience* ;

3 **ἀκ.** πίστεως *heeding the faith preached.* ‖ **ἐν-αρξάμενοι** aor. ptc -άρχομαι *begin / make a beginning in* or *with.* **σάρξ** ref. the observances demanded by the Judaizers. **ἐπι-**

4 **τελέομαι** mid. *finish* ; or pass. *be completed.* ‖ **τοσ-οῦτος**

so great, so much. ἐ-πάθετε aor² πάσχω *suffer, experience.* εἰκῇ *in vain, for nothing,* εἴ γε καὶ εἰκῇ *if indeed it was for nothing,* γε emphasizing the foregoing word. ‖ ἐπι-χορηγῶν 5 ptc -χορηγέω *supply,* II Cor 9:10, i.e. "the one who granted ...sc. did he do it *by...?*" ἐν-εργῶν ptc -εργέω *work* (trans.). ἀκοὴ πίστεως v.2. ‖ ἐ-πίστευσεν aor. -εύω. ἐ-λογίσθη aor. 6 pass. λογίζομαι *reckon, count.* εἰς *as,* w. pred. a Hebr. §32. ‖ γινώσκετε impv. ἄρα *then, so.* οἱ ἐκ πίστεως *the* 7 *faithful,* i.e. those whose life is determined by faith §134. ‖ προ-ϊδοῦσα aor² ptc -οράω *fore-see.* γραφή *scripture.* ἐκ 8 πίστεως *by means of faith.* δικαιοῖ 3rd sg δικαιόω *justify* 2:17. προ-ευ-ηγγελίσατο aor. -αγγελίζομαι *give the good news beforehand.* ὅτι = "... ἐν-ευ-λογηθήσονται fut. pass. -λογέω *bless one in/through.* ‖ εὐ-λογοῦνται pass. -λογέω 9 *bless.* πιστός *faithful,* here esp. *believing.* ‖ ὅσοι...νόμου 10 *who rely on observance of the Law* §134. κατ-άρα a *curse.* γέ-γραπται pf pass. γράφω. ἐπι-κατ-άρατος *accursed.* ἐμ-μένω τινί *remain in/abide by,* here *persevere in* doing sth §191. γε-γραμμένοις pf ptc pass. neut. pl. βιβλίον orig. dim., came to = βίβλος ἡ *papyrus* (βῦβλος) *roll, book.* ποιῆσαι aor. inf. ποιέω: τοῦ π. i.e. putting into practice §392. ‖ ὅτι *that.* ἐν instr. *by.* δικαιοῦται pass. v.8. δῆλος 11 *clear, evident* (sc. *is*). ὅτι (2nd time) *because,* introducing arguments from Scripture. ζήσεται fut. ζάω. ‖ οὐκ ἔστιν ἐκ 12 πίστεως *is not grounded in faith* v.7. αὐτά, the precepts of the Law. ‖ ἐξ-ηγόρασεν aor. -αγοράζω (buy out) *ran-* 13 *som, deliver.* κατάρα v.10. γενόμενος aor² ptc γίνομαι. ὑπὲρ ἡμῶν *for our sake,* prob. also (= ἀντί) *in our stead* §91. γέ-γραπται v.10. ἐπι-κατ-άρατος *cursed.* κρεμάμενος ptc pass. κρεμάννυμι *hang.* ξύλον *wood,* of various wooden implements ; *gallows* ; in NT *cross.* ‖ εὐ-λογία *blessing.* 14 γένηται aor² subj. γίνομαι, w. εἰς *come to/be extended to.* ἐπ-αγγελία *promise,* ἐπαγ. τ. πνεύματος gen. obj., promise of the gift of the Spirit, hardly differing from "the pro-mised Spirit". λάβωμεν aor² subj. v.2. ‖

κατὰ ἄνθρωπον λέγω "I speak as a man", *I will take* 15 *an example from human/everyday life.* ὅμως *nevertheless,* does not fit this context (cf I Cor 14:7), perh. *in the same way as.* κε-κυρωμένην pf ptc pass. κυρόω *confirm legally, ratify* a will. δια-θήκη *testament, will.* ἀ-θετέω *annul.* ἐπι-δια-τάσσομαι *add a codicil* to a will. ‖ ἐρρέθησαν aor. 16 pass. λέγω here, *make* a promise. λέγει (*Scripture*) *says.*

σπέρμα⁷ seed ; descendant. ἐπί w. gen. (on the subject)
17 of. ‖ τοῦτο δέ λέγω this is what I mean. προ-κε-κυρωμένην
pf ptc pass. προ-κυρόω ratify earlier/beforehand. ὁ...γεγονώς
(pf² ptc γίνομαι) νόμος the law which has come into force
(lit. "being"). τετρα-κόσιοι = 400. τριάκοντα = 30. ἔτος⁸
year. ἀ-κυρόω annul. εἰς τό in such a way as to, consec.
κατ-αργῆσαι aor. inf. -αργέω (< κατ- + α + ἔργον put out
18 of action) render ineffectual, cancel. ‖ ἐκ νόμου based on
law. κληρο-νομία (< κλῆρος lot + νέμω assign) inheritance. οὐκ-έτι no longer, here w. logical, not temporal
ref., then (it is) not. κε-χάρισται pf χαρίζομαι mid. grant
a favour or bestow sth (as a favour) ; pf den. an inheritance
19 for all time. ‖ τί; = διὰ τί; why? παρά-βασις⁴ (< παρα- +
βαίνω go beyond) trans-gression. χάριν w. gen. because
of, on account of. παράβασις differs from ἁμαρτία in that
it implies breaking a law, thus law formalized sin and
increased it, revealing it for what it is and demonstrating
the necessity for redemption,..cf Rom 5:20, 7:7ff. προσ-ε-
τέθη aor. pass. -τίθημι add. ἄχρις οὗ until (the time) when
— a form of ἄχρι sts used before a vowel. ἔλθῃ aor² subj.
ἔρχομαι. σπέρμα v.16. ᾧ to whom. ἐπ-ήγγελται pf pass.
-αγγέλλω promise ; transl. the promise was made. δια-
ταγείς aor² ptc pass. -τάσσω ordain. διά by means of.
ἐν χειρί Hebr. signifying through the agency of. μεσίτης⁹
20 mediator (Ac 7:53). ‖ ἑνὸς οὐκ ἔστιν κτλ. is not of (needed
for) one. But God is one : prob. implying "to make a promise one is enough".
21   κατά w. gen. against. μὴ γένοιτο 2:17. ἐ-δόθη aor.
pass. δίδωμι: εἰ...ἐδ. ...ἂν ἦν if...had been given an unfulfilled condition §313. ὁ δυνάμενος (ptc δύναμαι) w. inf.
able to, on art. §192. ζωο-ποιῆσαι aor. inf. -ποιέω make
alive, give life. ὄντως actually, in fact. ἂν ἦν would have
22 been (= resulted). ‖ συν-έ-κλεισεν aor. συγ-κλείω shut up,
confine, cf Rom 11:32. δοθῇ aor. subj. pass. πιστεύουσιν
23 ptc dat. pl. -εύω. ‖ πρὸ τοῦ...ἐλθεῖν 2:12. πίστιν acc. as
subject of inf. ἐ-φρουρούμεθα we were held, impf pass.
-ρέω guard. συγ-κλειόμενοι ptc pass. μέλλουσαν ptc μέλλω.
ἀπο-καλυφθῆναι aor. inf. pass. -καλύπτω reveal, τ. μέλλουσαν
24 ...ἀποκ. destined to be revealed. ‖ παιδ-αγωγός (παῖς + ἄγω
lead) tutor. γέ-γονεν pf γίνομαι. δικαιωθῶμεν aor. subj.
25 pass. v.8. ‖ ἐλθούσης aor² ptc fem., gen. abs. οὐκέτι v.18. ‖
27 ἐ-βαπτίσθητε aor. pass. -ίζω. ἐν-ε-δύσασθε aor. mid. ἐν-

δύω *clothe* one ; mid. *clothe oneself in, put on.* ‖ ἔνι = ἐν   28
w. ἐστίν understood (= ἔνεστιν) *there is.* Ἕλλην 2:3.
ἐλεύθερος *free,* as noun *freeman.* ἄρσην -σενος neut. ἄρσεν
male. θῆλυς -λεως θήλεια neut. θῆλυ *female.* εἷς masc.
one. ‖ ἄρα v.7. σπέρμα v.16. ‖ κληρο-νόμος (< κλῆρος   29 4
lot + νέμω assign) *inheritor.* χρόνος *time,* ἐφ' ὅσον χρ.
for as long as. νήπιος *infant* ; a *minor* (in law). οὐδέν
in no way, neut. as adv. δια-φέρω w. gen. *differ from.*
ὤν ptc εἰμί concessive, *although he is.* ‖ ἐπί-τροπος *fore-*   2
man ; *guardian.* οἰκο-νόμος *steward* ; *custodian.* ἄχρι *until.*
προ-θεσμία (sc. ἡμέρα) *appointed term, date.* τοῦ πατρός i.e.
set by his father. ‖ ἦμεν impf εἰμί. στοιχεῖον τ. κόσμου   3
possible meanings in this context are, in pl. (a) *elements
of matter,* standing for material things which constituted
the horizon of their former life ; (b) *elements of knowledge,*
here ref. pre-Christian religions incl. Judaism as prepara-
tory to the full revelation in Christ. (c) *heavenly bodies,*
perhaps already thought of as spiritual beings : these
governed "times and seasons" and so 'legalistic' religious
observances ; (d) *elemental spirits* inhabiting the physical
world and ass. w. the phenomena of nature : these also
supernatural and affecting closely the everyday life of
man. It would be normal for Paul to share the beliefs
of his time ; in any case he is not here concerned to deny
their existence but to show that faith in Jesus Christ
lifts men out of a life dominated by uncertainty and fear
into the peace and assurance of sons of God. δε-δουλω-
μένοι pf pass. -λόω *enslave.* ‖ πλήρωμα[7] *full complement,*   4
fullness, ὅτε...χρόνου *when the time* set by God *had reached
its full term.* ἐξ-απ-έ-στειλεν aor. -απο-στέλλω *send (out).*
γενόμενον aor[2] ptc γίνομαι *be born.* ‖ ἐξ-αγοράσῃ aor. subj.   5
-αγοράζω *ransom, redeem.* υἱο-θεσία (υἱὸν τίθεμαι adopt)
adoption as a son. ἀπο-λάβωμεν aor[2] subj. -λαμβάνω *receive.* ‖ ὅτι is best understood as *that* you are sons (is   6
evident seeing that) God sent... ; "because" is difficult
since sonship would follow the bestowal of the Spirit.
κρᾶζον ptc κράζω *cry out.* ὁ πατήρ, nom. w. art. serving
as voc. §34. ‖ οὐκέτι 3:18. κληρονόμος v.1. διὰ θεοῦ *by*   7
the will of God. ‖

μέν...δέ Rom 2:7. οὐ w. ptc, class. use for matters   8
of fact §440. εἰδότες ptc οἶδα pf-pres. ἐ-δουλεύσατε aor.
-εύω τινί *serve* as a slave ; abs. *be in bondage.* φύσις[4]

9 *nature*, φύσει *by nature*. οὖσιν dat. pl. of ὤν v.1. ‖ γνόντες
aor² ptc γινώσκω. γνωσθέντες aor² ptc pass. πῶς; *how
is it?* ἐπι-στρέφω *turn to* (trans. and intr.). ἀ-σθενής⁹
weak. πτωχός *poor*. στοιχεῖον v.3. ἄνω-θεν *from above*;

10 *from the beginning, all over again*. δουλεύειν inf. ‖ παρα-
τηρεῖσθε mid. -τηρέω *watch closely*; mid. *observe* whether
ref. observation or, as here, observance. μήν⁶ μηνός ὁ

11 *month*. ἐνιαυτός Fr. *année*, *year* of 12 months. ‖ φοβοῦμαι μή πως ὑμᾶς w. indic. *I am afraid* on your account
that perhaps. εἰκῆ *in vain, to no purpose*. κε-κοπίακα pf
-ιάω *toil* ; indic. after μή πως ref. past time 2:2 §344. εἰς
ὑμᾶς *for you*, εἰς for dat. of advantage II Cor 8:4 cf §51. ‖

12 γίνεσθε replacing obs. ἔστε (impv εἰμί). ὡς ἐγώ i.e. in
freedom from bondage to the Law. κἀγώ = καὶ ἐγώ.
ὡς ὑμεῖς presumably *as you were* when I first came, not
seeking salvation through observance of the Law. δέομαί
τινος *beseech, beg* one. ἠ-δικήσατε aor. ἀ-δικέω *do wrong*

13 or *harm to* one, οὐδέν με ἠδ. *you did me no wrong*. ‖ ἀ-
σθένεια *weakness*, δι᾽ ἀσθένειαν τῆς σαρκός *because of an
illness* (which prolonged my stay?). εὐ-ηγγελισάμην aor.
-αγγελίζομαί τινι *preach the gospel* to one. πρότερον
former, τὸ π. *the first time* (strictly of two, but not neces-

14 sarily in HGk §147ff. esp. §151 ed⁵ Lat.). ‖ πειρασμός
trial. ἐν τῇ σαρκί μου *over my state of health*, or *caused by
my state of health*. ἐξ-ουθενήσατε aor. -ουθενέω *think
nothing of, despise*. ἐξ-ε-πτύσατε aor. ἐκ-πτύω *spit* (*out*)
lit. as a prophylactic against the disease or met. *disdain*.

15 ἐ-δέξασθε aor. δέχομαι *receive, welcome*. ‖ ποῦ; *where?*
μακαρισμός *happiness* (?with which you greeted my presence). μαρτυρέω ὑμῖν *I can bear you witness*. εἰ (sc. ἦν)
introducing an unfulfilled condition, *if it had been...* in
HGk ἄν omitted after δυνατόν *possible* §319. ἐξ-ορύξαντες
aor. ptc -ορύσσω *dig out*, transl. *you would have torn out

16 your eyes and given...* ἐ-δώκατε aor. δίδωμι. ‖ ὥστε *so
now*. ἐχθρός *enemy*. γέ-γονα *have I become?* pf² γίνομαι.
ἀληθεύων *by speaking the truth*, ptc -εύω *tell the truth*. ‖

17 ζηλόω *envy ; be enthusiastic about* sth, *cultivate* a person,
(colloq.) *run after* someone. καλῶς *well, in a good way*.
ἐκ-κλεῖσαι aor. inf. -κλείω *exclude, shut out* (sc. from the
gospel) or *shut away* (from me). ζηλοῦτε standing for

18 ζηλῶτε subj. §341, *that you may cultivate* them. ‖ καλόν
neut. *a good thing*, pred. ζηλοῦσθαι inf. pass., subject.

ἐν καλῷ *about/over something good.* ἐν τῷ w. inf. *while.*
πάν-τοτε *at all times.* παρ-εῖναι inf. -ειμι *be present.* πρός
w. acc. *of person, with* 1:18. ‖ ὠδίνω *suffer birth pangs,* 19
w. acc. *be in travail with.* μέχρις οὗ (= μέχρι τοῦ χρόνου ᾧ)
μορφωϑῇ *until such time as* Christ *be formed...* μορφωϑῇ
aor. subj. pass. -φόω *form, shape.* ‖ ἤ-ϑελον impf ϑέλω 20
replacing potential opt. *I could wish, I would fain* §356.
ἄρτι *now.* ἀλλάξαι aor. inf. ἀλλάσσω *make other* (ἄλλος)
than it is, change, ἀλλ. φωνήν *change one's tone.* ἀ-πορέο-
μαι *I do not know what to make of you,* mid. ἀ-πορέω act.
and mid. *be at a loss.* ἐν ὑμῖν *about you.* ‖

　λέγετε (impv) *tell me!* ϑέλοντες ptc, οἱ ϑ. *you who* 21
want. ‖ γέγραπται pf pass. γράφω. ἔσχεν aor² ἔχω. ἕνα... 22
καὶ ἕνα for ἕνα...ἕτερος §156. παιδίσκη *maid-servant,* woman
slave. ἐλευϑέρα *free-woman.* ‖ ὁ μέν...ὁ δέ *the one...the* 23
other. κατὰ σάρκα *in the normal way.* γε-γέννηται pf pass.
γεννάω *beget ;* also *bear ;* pass. *be born.* ἐπ-αγγελία *promise.*
‖ ἅ-τινα = ἅ §216. ἀλληγορούμενα *an allegory,* lit. "things 24
being expressed in..." ptc pass. -ρέω *express in an allegory.*
δια-ϑήκη *covenant* II Cor 3:6. δουλεία *slavery.* γεννῶσα
ptc fem. γεννάω. ἥ-τις = ἥ §216. ‖ ἐστίν *means, stands* 25
for 〚var. τὸ γὰρ Σινᾶ *for Sinai is a mountain...*〛. συ(ν)-
στοιχέω *keep/be in line ;* hence, *correspond to.* νῦν *present.*
δουλεύω v.8. ‖ ἄνω *above,* ἡ ἄνω Ἰερουσαλήμ i.e. *the Chris-* 26
tian community living the life of the new heavenly J.
ἐλεύϑερος adj. *free.* ἥ-τις v.24. ἡμῶν emphatic, *who is*
our mother. ‖ γέ-γραπται v.22. εὐ-φράνϑητι aor. impv pass. 27
-φραίνω *make glad ;* pass. *be glad/joyful.* στεῖρα *barren*
woman. τίκτουσα ptc τίκτω *give birth.* ῥῆξον aor. impv
ῥήγνυμι *break ; break out/forth.* βόησον aor. impv βοάω
call aloud, cry out. ὠδίνουσα ptc v.19. πολλά pred., positive for comp. §145. ἔρημος masc. and fem. *solitary,*
deserted, ἡ ἐ. *solitary woman.* ἐχούσης ptc ἔχω. τὸν ἄνδρα
her husband. ‖ ἐπ-αγγελία v.23. ‖ ὥσπερ *just as.* κατὰ σάρκα 28,29
v.23 ; γεννηϑείς aor. ptc pass. v.23 ; ὁ κ. σάρκα γ. ...τὸν κ.
πνεῦμα *the child of the flesh...the child of the spirit* (= διὰ
τ. ἐπαγγελίας v.23). ἐ-δίωκεν impf διώκω *pursue ; perse-*
cute. ‖ ἡ γραφή *the words of* Sarah *endorsed by God.* 30
ἔκ-βαλε aor² impv -βάλλω *throw out ; drive out.* οὐ...μή
w. subj. (or fut.) emphatic neg. ref. fut. w. impv! connotation, *shall not, shall never.* κληρο-νομήσει fut. -νομέω
ᵢnherit. ἐλευϑέρα v.22. ‖ παιδίσκη wt art. *a slave,* v.22. ‖ 31

5 τῇ referring back, *this* freedom. **ἐλευθερία** *freedom.* **ἠλευ-θέρωσεν** aor. **ἐλευθερόω** *set free.* **στήκετε** impv στήκω (late form developed from ἔστηκα pf (intr. w. pres. sense) ἵστημι) *stand firm.* **ζυγός** *yoke.* **δουλεία** 4:24. **ἐν-έχεσθε** impv pass. -έχω *hold fast in* ; *have a grudge against* ; pass. *be entangled/involved in.*

2   **ἴδε** aor[2] impv ὁράω. **περι-τέμνησθε** *you have yourselves* or *allow yourselves to be circumcised,* subj. pass. -τέμνω *circumcise* ; pass. *undergo circumcision.* **ὠφελήσει** fut.

3 ὠφελέω τινά (or τινί) *be of use/benefit/advantage.* ‖ **μαρτύ-ρομαι** *affirm solemnly, declare.* **πάλιν** ref. v.2 ? or to what he has said in the past ? cf 1:9a. **παντὶ ἀνθρώπῳ** wt art. *every man.* **περι-τεμνομένῳ** ptc pass. **ὀφειλέτης**[3] *debtor,* so one under obligation. **ποιῆσαι** aor. inf. ποιέω : π. τὸν

4 νόμον *to keep the law.* ‖ **κατ-ηργήθητε** aor. pass. -αργέω *annul* ; pass. w. ἀπό *be cut off* ; proleptic aor. (cf Jn 15:6,8) §257. **οἵ-τινες** *all (you) who.* **δικαιοῦσθε** pass. δικαιόω *justify* ; pres. here conative, *are seeking to be justified.* **ἐξ-ε-πέσατε** (for -σετε §489) aor[2] ἐκ-πίπτω *fall off* or *away* ;

5 met. w. gen. *lose.* ‖ **πνεύματι** *by the power of the Spirit, through the work of the Spirit.* **ἐκ πίστεως** *by faith.* **ἐλπίς**[6] -ίδος ἡ *hope,* ἐ. **δικαιοσύνης** *hope of righteousness,* meaning either (abstract for concrete) *the hope of the righteous,* or (gen. epexeg.) *the hope which is* that perfected *righteousness,* i.e. eschatological and only partially realized in

6 this world. **ἀπ-εκ-δεχόμεθα** *await eagerly.* ‖ **περι-τομή** *circumcision.* **ἰσχύω** *be strong* or *able* ; hence *be valid/effective, count for* something. **ἀκροβυστία** *uncircumcision.* **ἐν-**

7 **εργουμένη** *active,* ptc -εργέομαι *be at work.* ‖ **ἐ-τρέχετε** impf τρέχω *run.* **καλῶς** *well.* **ἐν-έ-κοψεν** aor. ἐγ-κόπτω *block, hinder,* w. μή + inf. *from...* **πείθεσθαι** inf. pass. πείθω

8 *persuade* ; pass. w. dat. *obey.* ‖ **πεισμονή** *persuasion,* ἡ π.

9 transl. *that persuasion.* **καλοῦντος** ptc καλέω. ‖ **μικρός** *small, a little* (piece of). **ζύμη** *leaven, yeast.* **φύραμα**[7]

10 *lump, mass.* **ζυμόω** *leaven.* ‖ **πέ-ποιθα** pf[2] (w. pres. meaning) *be convinced* ; *have confidence, believe in.* **φρονήσετε** fut. -νέω *think.* **ταράσσων** ptc -άσσω *disturb, trouble.* **βαστάσει** fut. -τάζω *carry, bear.* **τὸ κρίμα**[7] *his condemnation.* **ὅσ-τις ἐάν** (= ἄν) ᾖ *who-ever he may be,* subj. εἰμί. ‖

11 **περιτομή** v.6. **κηρύσσω** *preach,* εἰ...κ. *if indeed* (as my enemies maintain) *I preach...,* a real condition §303, 306. **τί** *why?* **διώκομαι** pass. διώκω *pursue* ; *persecute.* **ἄρα**

then. **κατ-ήργηται** *is abolished,* pf pass. v.4. **σκάνδαλον** *stumbling-block, occasion of sin.* **σταυρός** *cross.* || **ὄφελον** 12 *would that!* particle introducing a wish not likely to be realized, here ref. fut. **καί** *even.* **ἀπο-κόψονται** fut. mid. **-κόπτω** *castrate,* transl. *Would that they would go on and have themselves castrated!* **ἀνα-στατοῦντες** ptc -τόω *upset.* || **ἐπί** w. dat. may den. purpose, *to* §129. **ἐλευθερία** 13 v.1. **ἐ-κλήθητε** aor. pass. **καλέω.** **ἀφ-ορμή** *pretext* II Cor 11:12, **μή...ἀφ.** elliptical, *do not* turn *your freedom into a pretext,* or better, *do not let your freedom become.* **δου-λεύετε** impv -εύω τινί *serve* one. || **ὁ...πᾶς νόμος** *the law* 14 *in its entirety* §188. **λόγος** here, *commandment.* **πε-πλή-ρωται** pf pass. **πληρόω** *fulfil.* **τό** introduces a quotation by treating the whole as a noun. **ἀγαπήσεις** impv fut. *you shall/must love.* **πλησίον** adv. *near* ; **ὁ πλ.** *neighbour.* **σε-αυτόν** *your-self.* || **δάκνω** *bite.* **κατ-εσθίω** *eat up, devour* ; 15 a person, *exploit.* **βλέπετε** impv, **β.** **μή** *watch/take care that...you are not.* **ἀν-αλωθῆτε** aor. subj. pass. -αλίσκω *annihilate, destroy.* ||

λέγω δέ *I mean this.* **πνεύματι** v.5. **περι-πατεῖτε** impv 16 -πατέω in ethical sense, *live.* **ἐπι-θυμία** *desire.* **οὐ μή** w. aor. subj. emphatic neg. ref. fut. *there is no likelihood that/of* §444. **τελέσητε** aor. subj. τελέω *complete,* hence *satisfy* a desire, here rather *yield to.* || **ἐπι-θυμέω** *desire,* 17 *have desires.* **ἀντί-κειμαί** τινι *oppose, be in opposition to.* **ἵνα** consec. §351f. **ἐάν** = **ἄν.** **θέλητε, ποιῆτε** subj. θέλω, ποιέω. || **ἄγεσθε** pass. ἄγω *lead.* || **φανερός** *clear, obvious.* 18,19 **ἅ-τινα** = **ἅ** §216. **πορνεία** *fornication.* **ἀ-καθαρσία** *impu-rity.* **ἀ-σέλγεια** *in-decency.* || **εἰδωλο-λατρία** *idolatry.* **φαρμα-** 20 **κεία** *sorcery.* **ἔχθρα** *enmity,* pl. *quarrels.* **ἔρις**⁶ **ἔριδος ἡ** *rivalry.* **ζῆλος** *jealousy.* **θυμός** *rage,* pl. *fits of rage.* **ἐρι-θεία** *selfish ambition* involving corruption Rom 2:8. **διχο-στασία** *dissension.* **αἵρεσις**⁴ *faction.* || **φθόνος** *envy.* **μέθη** 21 *drunkenness,* pl. *drinking bouts.* **κῶμος** *orgy.* **ὅμοιος** *like.* **προ-λέγω** *say before/earlier,* hence *give notice, forewarn.* **προ-εῖπον** aor². **τοι-οῦτος** *such,* neut. pl. *such things.* **πράσσοντες** ptc **πράσσω** do. **κληρο-νομήσουσιν** fut. -νομέω *inherit.* || **καρπός** *fruit.* **χαρά** *joy.* **μακρο-θυμία** (long tem-per) 22 *patience.* **χρηστότης**⁶ -τότητος **ἡ** *kindness.* **ἀγαθω-σύνη** *goodness.* || **πραΰτης**⁶ -ΰτητος **ἡ** *gentleness.* **ἐγ-κράτεια** 23 *self-control.* || **οἱ...τοῦ Χριστοῦ** *those who belong to Christ.* 24 **ἐ-σταύρωσαν** aor. -ρόω *crucify.* **πάθημα**⁷ *passion.* **ἐπι-θυμία**

25 v.16. ‖ πνεύματι v.5. στοιχῶμεν hort. subj. -χέω *keep in*
26 *line*, met. *follow* his guidance. ‖ γινώμεθα *let us not be*,
hort. subj. γίνομαι. κενό-δοξος *vainglorious, inordinately
conceited*. προ-καλούμενοι ptc mid. -καλέω act. and mid.
provoke. φθονοῦντες ptc -νέω τινί *envy* one. ‖

6   προ-λημφθῇ aor. subj. pass. -λαμβάνω *overtake, surprise*
one doing sth. ἄνθρωπος virtually = τις. παρά-πτωμα[7]
(< παρα- + πίπτω) *transgression*. πνευματικός *spiritual*, as
masc. noun *one who lives by the Spirit*. κατ-αρτίζετε impv
-αρτίζω (< κατα- + ἄρτιος perfect) *restore to proper con-
dition/ta a right mind*. τοι-οῦτος *such*, ὁ τ. *such a person*.
πραΰτης 5:23. σκοπῶν ptc -πέω τι or τινά *be on the look
out for* sth or someone, σκ. ἑαυτὸν μή *look to oneself in case...*
σε-αυτόν *your-self*. καί *also*. πειρασθῇς aor. subj. pass.
2 -άζω *tempt*. ‖ βάρος[8] *weight, burden*. βαστάζετε impv -άζω
3 *carry, bear*. ἀνα-πληρώσετε fut. -πληρόω *fulfil*. ‖ δοκέω
think, suppose, δ. εἶναί τι in Eng. idiom, *thinks himself
somebody*. ὤν ptc εἰμί, *when* (= whereas) *he is*. φρεν-
απατᾷ 3rd sg -απατάω (φρήν mind + ἀπατάω deceive) *de-
4 lude*. ‖ δοκιμαζέτω impv 3rd sg -άζω *put to the test*. καύχημα[7] *matter for boasting, reason for pride*, εἰς ἑαυτὸν κ. ἔχω
have pride in oneself / on one's own account. ἕξει fut.
5,6 ἔχω. ‖ φορτίον *burden*. βαστάσει fut. v.2. ‖ κοινωνείτω
impv 3rd sg -νέω here τινὶ ἔν τινι *communicate/share* sth
with another, here in giving. κατ-ηχούμενος ptc pass.
-ηχέω w. double acc., *teach* one sth *by word of mouth* ; in
pass. the thing taught remains in acc. §72. κατ-ηχοῦντι
7 ptc. ἀγαθοῖς neut. pl. ‖ πλανᾶσθε impv pass. -νάω *mislead*, μὴ πλ. *make no mistake !* the pres. supposing that
they are §246. μυκτηρίζεται pass. -ίζω τινά *turn up the
nose* (μυκτήρ) at one ; pass. *be mocked*. ὅ...ἐάν (for ἄν)
what-ever. σπείρῃ subj. or aor. subj. σπείρω *sow*. ἄνθρωπος
8 v.1. θερίσει fut. -ίζω *reap*. ‖ σπείρων ptc. εἰς *in* the
field of. σάρξ *unredeemed nature*. φθορά *corruption*. ‖
9 ποιοῦντες ptc ποιέω. ἐγ-κακῶμεν hort. subj. -κακέω *be
weary, lose heart*, ποιῶν ἐγκακέω *to be tired of doing*. καιρῷ
ἰδίῳ *in due time*. ἐκ-λυόμενοι ptc pass. -λύω *slacken*, pass.
grow faint, flag ; μὴ ἐ. ptc conditional, *provided we do not...* ;
10 also poss. in HGk *without flagging, tirelessly* §441. ‖ ἄρα
οὖν *so then*. ὡς temporal, *while*. ἐργαζώμεθα subj. hort.
-ζομαι *work, do*. μάλιστα *most* (of all), *especially*, superl.,
comp. μᾶλλον. οἰκεῖος *one of the family or household*. ‖

ἴδετε aor² impv ὁράω. πηλίκος *how big!* in HGk the 11
interr. used in exclamations (for class. rel. ἡλίκος, cf πῶς
for ὡς e.g. Mk 10:23 etc.) §221. γράμμα⁷ *letter* of the alphabet. ἔ-γραψα aor. γράφω. ‖ εὐ-προσωπῆσαι aor. inf. 12
-προσωπέω *make a good showing, cut a good figure.* ἐν
σαρκί here prob. in external matters such as observances.
ἀναγκάζω w. acc. + inf. *compel,* here conative, *they try
to force* you *to...* cf 5:4. περι-τέμνεσθαι inf. pass. -τέμνω
circumcise. σταυρός *cross,* dat. of cause, *for/because of
the cross* §58. διώκωνται subj. pass. διώκω *pursue ; persecute,* μόνον ἵνα...μὴ δ. *with the sole purpose of avoiding persecution.* ‖ οὐδέ...οἱ περιτεμνόμενοι (ptc pass.) *for not even* 13
those who are circumcised. αὐτοί nom. emphatic, *themselves.* φυλάσσω *keep, observe.* ὑμέτερος *your.* καυχήσων-
ται aor. subj. -χάομαι ἐν *boast of.* ‖ γένοιτο aor² opt. γίνο- 14
μαι: ἐμοί...μὴ γ. *far be it from me to...,* God forbid that I...
καυχᾶσθαι inf. εἰ μή *except.* οὗ *through whom* or *which*
(den. Christ or the cross). κόσμος wt art. perh. signifying
what characterizes the world, all that is purely mundane
and in opposition to God. ἐ-σταύρωται pf pass. -ρόω *crucify ;* pf, once for all, a metaphor for complete separation.
Having (in baptism) been made a partaker in Christ's
death, Paul is separated from the world as the dead are
from the living, and to him the world is "crucified" (i.e.
accursed 3:13) and conversely he to the world. κἀγώ = καὶ
ἐγώ. ‖ περι-τομή *circumcision.* τι w. neg. *anything.* ἀκρο- 15
βυστία *uncircumcision.* καινός *new.* κτίσις⁴ *creation.* ‖ ὅσοι 16
w. fut. = ὅσοι ἄν w. subj. §335. κανών⁶ κανόνος ὁ a *rule.*
στοιχήσουσιν fut. -χέω τινί *keep in line with* sth. εἰρήνη
ἐπ᾽ αὐτούς *peace* (be) *upon them.* ἔλεος⁸ *mercy.* καί (3rd
time) may stand for *that is* §455 ζ. ‖ λοιπός *left, remain-* 17
ing (< λείπω *leave*), λοιπόν or τοῦ λοιποῦ (sc. χρόνου) *from
now on.* κόπος *trouble.* παρ-εχέτω impv 3rd sg -έχω
provide ; cause/give, e.g. trouble. στίγμα⁷ *brand* or *mark*
used to identify a slave esp. those in temple service ;
here of scars left by flogging and stoning which Paul had
undergone as the slave of Jesus. βαστάζω v.2. ‖

EPHESIANS

1 οἱ ἅγιοι because dedicated to God ; title of all believers. οὖσιν ptc εἰμί [[var. om. ἐν Ἐφέσῳ]]. πιστός *faith-*
2 *ful.* || χάρις καὶ εἰρήνη Rom 1:7. ||
3 εὐ-λογητός *blessed* (*be*). εὐ-λογήσας aor. ptc -λογέω
τινά τινι *bless* one *with* sth. ἐν instr. §119. εὐ-λογία
blessing. πνευματικός *spiritual.* ἐπ-ουράνιος *heavenly,* (whether existing in heaven or coming from heaven or leading to heaven), here, it would seem as v.20 and 2:6,
4 *in heaven.* || καθ-ώς here perh. causal, *for.* ἐξ-ε-λέξατο
aor. ἐκ-λέγομαι *choose.* πρό *before.* κατα-βολή (< κατα-
βάλλω lay a foundation) *foundation.* εἶναι inf., so w.
subject and pred. in acc. ἅγιος v.l. ἄ-μωμος *unblemished.*
5 κατ-εν-ώπιον *in the sight of, before* §83. || προ-ορίσας aor. ptc
-ορίζω (< ὅρος boundary) of God, *pre-destine* (having in
mind his πρόθεσις v.11). υἱο-θεσία *adoption* as a son,
εἰς υἱ. διὰ Ἰησοῦ Χρ. εἰς αὐτόν *to* (*receive*) *through Jesus
Christ sonship to himself.* αὐτόν for ἑαυτόν §208. εὐ-δοκία
6 *goodwill,* κατά...αὐτοῦ transl. *as it pleased his will.* || εἰς
den. purpose, *to, for.* ἔπ-αινος *praise.* ἧς *by which,* attracted from ᾗ instr. §17. ἐ-χαρίτωσεν aor. -τόω *favour*
one *with* sth, *bestow* sth *freely on* one. ἠγαπημένῳ *beloved,*
7 pf ptc pass. ἀγαπάω. || ἐν ᾧ masc. *in whom*; a key thought
in this chapter. ἀπο-λύτρωσις[4] *redemption, liberation* Rom
3:24. ἄφ-εσις[4] (< ἀφ-ίημι forgive) *forgiveness.* παρά-πτωμα[7]
8 (< παρα- + πίπτω) *transgression.* πλοῦτος[8] *wealth.* || ἧς
attracted from ἥν. ἐ-περίσσευσεν aor. -εύω lit. "cause sth
to overflow" to one, i.e. *cause* one *to overflow with* sth,
lavish/shower sth *upon* one. The words ἐν...φρονήσει may
be ass. w. the preceding words or w. those which follow.
9 σοφία *wisdom.* φρόνησις[4] *understanding.* || γνωρίσας aor.
ptc -ίζω *make known.* μυστήριον (< μυέω initiate) in
Paul, *mystery, secret,* of truths only apprehended through
revelation, esp. ref. God's plan. εὐ-δοκία v.5. προ-έ-θετο
aor[2] mid. προ-τίθημι set before, mid. *propose, purpose.* ἐν
10 αὐτῷ i.e. to be realized in Christ. || εἰς v.6. οἰκο-νομία

administration, esp. God's *plan* of salvation. πλήρωμα⁷
fullness, πλ. τ. καιρῶν cf Gal 4:4, but here embracing the
messianic era in its entirety w. special ref. to its consummation. ἀνα-κεφαλαιώσασθαι (< κεφαλή) aor. inf. mid.
-κεφαλαιόω *sum up under one head* (either sums or e.g. a
discussion) ; also *recapitulate* ; the context favours *to sum
up/comprehend* all things in Christ *as head*. ἐπὶ τ. οὐρανοῖς *in heaven* ; the gen. after ἐπὶ (τ. γῆς) bears no percepti-
ble difference in meaning. ‖ ἐ-κληρώθημεν aor. pass. -ρόω   11
appoint or *choose by lot* (κλῆρος) ; possible translns : "in
whom we were chosen" ; "in whom we were allotted
(sc. an inheritance)" ; or "in whom we have been made
his heritage, i.e. claimed as God's own" (JB). προ-ορι-
σθέντες aor. ptc pass. -ορίζω v.5. πρό-θεσις⁴ (< προ-τίθημι
set before) *purpose*, κατὰ π. *in accordance with the purpose*.
ἐν-εργοῦντος ptc -εργέω *work, effect, carry out*. βουλή of
God, *intention*. ‖ εἰς τό w. acc. + inf. final, den. the   12
purpose, here of the choice. εἰμὶ εἰς *exist for*. ἔπαινος
v.6. προ-ηλπικότας pf ptc -ελπίζω *hope before ; be the first
to hope*. ‖ καί *also, too*. ἀκούσαντες aor. ptc ἀκούω.   13
σωτηρία *salvation*. πιστεύσαντες aor. ptc -εύω ; ἐν ᾧ...π.
resumes the former ἐν ᾧ ref. Christ. ἐ-σφραγίσθητε aor.
pass. -ίζω *affix a seal* (σφραγίς) sts in order to close, at
others to identify, ref. the gift of the Spirit ; many exe-
gétes see here a specific ref. to baptism which was called
ἡ σφραγίς from the earliest extra-canonical writings onwards, as marking Christians as children of God and heirs
of heaven. ἐπ-αγγελία *promise*, τ. πνεῦμα τ. ἐπ. *the Spirit
promised* by the prophets. ‖ ἀρραβών⁶ -ῶνος ὁ *earnest*   14
(*-money*), *pledge*. κληρο-νομία (< κλῆρος *lot* + νέμω assign) *inheritance*. εἰς temporal, *until*. ἀπο-λύτρωσις⁴ v.7.
περι-ποίησις⁴ (περι-ποιέω acquire) *acquisition* ; as in Eng.
may mean the act of acquiring, *redemption which is our
acquisition* by God (gen. epexeg.) I Thess 5:9, II Thess
2:14 or in pass. sense of the thing acquired, a concrete
possession, signifying his people (obj. gen.), so, w. λαός
in I Pt 2:9. εἰς ἔπαινον v.6. ‖

　　διὰ τοῦτο *for this reason*. κἀγώ = καὶ ἐγώ. κατά w.   15
acc. often standing (in HGk) for possessive gen., καθ᾽ ὑμᾶς
your §130. τὴν ἀγάπην *your love* [[var. om.]]. ἅγιος v.1. ‖
παύομαι *cease*. εὐ-χαριστῶν ptc -χαριστέω *give thanks*. ὑπὲρ   16
ὑμῶν ref. to ποιούμενος ptc mid. ποιέω. μνεία *remembrance*,

μ. ποιοῦμαι *mention, remember* esp. before God ; class. use of mid. where π. combines w. a noun to express the same idea as the cognate vb (here = μνημονεύων) Rom 1:9

17 §227. ἐπί *on the occasion of, in.* προσ-ευχή *prayer.* ‖ ἵνα den. content, *that.* δώῃ aor² subj. δίδωμι. σοφία v.8. ἀπο-κάλυψις⁴ *revelation* as an "uncovering" of the truth. ἐπί-γνωσις⁴ *knowledge,* the knowledge of God involving personal commitment, ἐπιγ. αὐτοῦ *knowledge of him* (obj.

18 gen.). ‖ πε-φωτισμένους pf ptc pass. -ίζω *shed light on ;* met. *enlighten,* either attributive, "grant to you...enlightened inner eyes" or predicative, "grant to you that the eyes of your heart be enlightened" §186. καρδία as seat of thought and will as well as emotion. εἰς τό v.12. εἰδέναι inf. οἶδα pf-pres. τίς as indir. interr. ἐλπίς⁶ -ίδος ἡ *hope.* κλῆσις⁴ *calling, vocation.* πλοῦτος v.7. κληρο-

19 νομία v.14. ‖ ὑπερ-βάλλον ptc neut. -βάλλω *exceed, surpass.* μέγεθος⁸ *greatness.* πιστεύοντας ptc -εύω. ἐν-έργεια *working, activity.* κράτος⁸ *might.* ἰσχύς⁶ -ύος ἡ *strength, power.*

20 ‖ ἐν-ήργησεν *exerted,* aor. -εργέω v.11. ἐγείρας aor. ptc ἐγείρω. καθίσας aor. ptc -ίζω *make one sit.* ἐν δεξιᾷ (sc.

21 χειρί) *at his right hand.* ἐπ-ουράνιος v.3. ‖ ὑπερ-άνω w. gen. *far above.* ἀρχή *rule, sovereignty.* κυριότης⁶ -τητος ἡ *dominion ;* ἀρχή...κ. hierarchies of spiritual powers. ὄνομα here, title. ὀνομαζομένου *that is* (to be) *named,* ptc pass.

22 -άζω *name.* ὁ αἰών...ὁ μέλλων *the age to come.* ‖ ὑπ-έ-ταξεν aor. ὑπο-τάσσω *make subject, put under.* ἔ-δωκεν aor. δίδωμι,

23 Hebr. *he made him...* κεφαλήν pred. ‖ ἥτις = ἥ §216. πλήρωμα v.10, in act. sense, *completion, complement ;* or pass. *fullness, plenitude.* πληρουμένου ptc pass. -ρόω, or ?ptc mid. in act. sense (the latter wt known parallel). Interpretations include : "the fullness (pass.) of him who fills (mid. act.) all things in every respect (or with all good)" or "his body...the complement (act.) of him who is being filled (pass.) completely in all his members" and Origen (3rd cent.) who explains that Christ fills all things and those who in every generation come to him do but bring to his body the fullness with which he as πλήρωμα has filled them until such time as their number is complete, i.e. πλήρωμα (pass.) as appos. to αὐτόν (v.22) "him...the plenitude of what is being filled (pass. i. e. his body) completely in every respect". ‖

ὄντας ptc εἰμί. παρά-πτωμα⁷ (< παρα- + πίπτω) *trans-* 2 *gression*. || ποτέ (encl.) *once, at one time*. περι-ε-πατήσατε 2 aor. -πατέω, in ethical sense, *live*. ἄρχων⁶ ἄρχοντος ὁ *ruler*. ἐξουσία here, *domain* (Lk 22:53). ἀήρ⁶ ἀέρος ὁ *air*; ὁ ἄρχων τῆς ἐξουσίας τ. ἀέρος being Satan. ἐν-εργοῦν-τος ptc -εργέω *be at work/active*. ἀ-πείθεια (ἀπειθέω be disobedient) *dis-obedience*, υἱοὶ τῆς ἀπ. Hebr. *those given to disobedience* §43. || ἀν-ε-στράφημεν aor² pass. ἀνα-στρέφω 3 *overturn*; pass. refl. *conduct oneself, live* in a certain way, constative (global) aor. ἐπι-θυμία *desire*. ποιοῦντες ptc ποιέω. διά-νοια *thought*. ἤμεθα = ἦμεν impf εἰμί. φύσις⁴ *nature*; φύσει *by nature*, ? = unaided by grace. ὀργή *wrath*; like υἱός, τέκνον w. a foll. gen. den. a dominant characteristic or the end to which one is tending, τ. ὀργῆς *destined for* or *objects of wrath*. λοιπός *left, remaining*; οἱ λ. *the rest*. || πλούσιος *rich*. ὤν v.1. ἔλεος⁸ *mercy*. 4 ἥν internal cognate acc.: the love (*with*) *which* he loved. ἠγάπησεν aor. ἀγαπάω. || παράπτωμα v.1. συν-ε-ζωο-ποίησεν 5 aor. συ(ν)-ζωο-ποιέω τινά τινι *make one alive with* another. χάριτι instr. dat., wt art. emphasizes the manner in which salvation is given, i.e. freely, cf v.8 §176. σε-σωσμένοι pf ptc pass. σώζω, w. εἰμί forming periphr. pf pass. || συν- 6 ήγειρεν aor. -εγείρω τινά τινι *raise together* (one *with* another). συν-ε-κάθισεν aor. συγ-καθίζω *make one sit with* another. ἐπ-ουράνιος 1:3. || ἐν-δείξηται aor. subj. mid. 7 -δείκνυμι (in NT mid. only) *show, prove*. ἐπ-ερχόμενος ptc -έρχομαι *come upon*; *come on*, ἐν τ. αἰῶσιν τοῖς ἐπερ. *in the ages to come*. ὑπερ-βάλλον 1:19. πλοῦτος⁸ *wealth*. χρηστότης⁶ -οτητος ἡ *goodness* in sense of kindness. || τῇ 8 χάριτι art. den. the work of redemption (done freely), cf v.5. ἐστε σεσωσμένοι v.5. δῶρον *gift*. || καυχήσηται aor. 9 subj. -χάομαι *boast*. || αὐτοῦ in emphatic position. ποίημα⁷ 10 *something made*, a piece of *handiwork*, a *creature*. κτι-σθέντες aor. ptc pass. κτίζω *create*. ἐπί w. dat. sts den. purpose, *for* §129. οἷς attracted from ἅ §16. προ-ητοί-μασεν aor. -ητοιμάζω *prepare beforehand*. περι-πατήσωμεν aor. subj. v.2. ||

δι-ό *therefore*. μνημονεύετε impv -εύω *remember*. ποτέ 11 v.2. τὰ ἔθνη appos. ὑμεῖς. ἐν σαρκί *physically*. λεγόμενοι ptc pass. λέγω *call* (Mk 10:18). ἀκροβυστία *uncircumcision*. περι-τομή *circumcision*; both terms concrete, standing for persons in that state, cf Gal 2:7. χειρο-ποίητος *wrought/*

12 *made by the hands of men* ; ref. περιτομή. ‖ ἦτε impf εἰμί. χωρίς w. gen. *without, apart from.* ἀπ-ηλλοτριωμένοι pf ptc pass. -αλλοτριόω τινά τινος *estrange/alienate* one from sth. πολιτεία *polity, a society,* gen. of separation. ξένος *foreign, strange,* ξ. τινός *a stranger to.* δια-θήκη *covenant* II Cor 3:6. ἐπ-αγγελία *promise,* αἱ διαθῆκαι τῆς ἐπ. signifying the covenants with their promise. ἐλπίς⁶ -ίδος ἡ

13 *hope.* ἔχοντες ptc ἔχω. ἄ-θεος *without God.* ‖ νυνὶ δέ *but now.* ὄντες v.1. μακράν (sc. ὁδόν) adv. *far away* sc. *from God,* οἱ μ. *the gentiles.* ἐ-γενήθητε aor. pass. γίνομαι. ἐγγύς

14 *near.* ἐν instr. §119. ‖ αὐτός emphatic. ποιήσας aor. ptc ποιέω. τὰ ἀμφότερα *both.* ἕν neut. *one thing.* μεσό-τοιχον (μέσον middle + τοῖχος wall) *dividing-wall,* prob. ref. the wall dividing Jews from gentiles in the Temple. φραγμός *hedge* ; *partition.* λύσας aor. ptc λύω *loosen* ;

15 *destroy.* ἔχθρα *enmity.* ‖ δόγμα⁷ *decree,* ἐν δ. expressed in/ consisting of decrees, cf I Cor 4:20 (ἐν λόγῳ). κατ-αργήσας aor. ptc -αργέω *annul* Gal 3:17. κτίσῃ aor. subj. v.10.

16 αὐτῷ for refl. §208. καινός *fresh, new.* ποιῶν ptc. ‖ ἀπο-κατ-αλλάξῃ aor. subj. -αλλάσσω *reconcile.* σταυρός *cross.* ἀπο-κτείνας aor. ptc -κτείνω. ἐν αὐτῷ ?for refl. *by himself* or ?*by it* (the cross), grammatically either transln possible §211. ‖ ἐλθών aor² ptc ἔρχομαι. εὐ-ηγγελίσατο aor.

17 -αγγελίζομαι *bring good news, preach.* μακράν v.13. ἐγγύς

18 v.13. ‖ προσ-αγωγή *access.* ἔχομεν...οἱ ἀμφότεροι *we both*

19 *have.* ἄρα οὖν *so then.* οὐκ-έτι *no longer.* ξένος v.12. πάρ-οικος orig. a *neighbour* ; later *one from elsewhere, stranger.* συμ-πολίτης³ *fellow citizen.* ἅγιος 1:1. οἰκεῖος

20 *member of the household.* ‖ ἐπ-οικο-δομηθέντες aor. ptc pass. -δομέω *build on.* θεμέλιος (< τίθημι) *foundation.* τ. ἀπο-στόλων gen. epexeg. §45 ; τῶν ἀπ. καὶ προφητῶν under one art. and thereby closely ass., so perh. of prophets in the church as 3:5. ὄντος gen. abs. ἀκρο-γωνιαῖος adj. *corner-,* sc. λίθος *corner-stone* which ensures stability to a building ; others would transl. *keystone* symbolizing the completion of the building begun with θεμέλιος, thus introduc-

21 ing an eschatological element. ‖ οἰκο-δομή *building,* πᾶσα οἱ. *the whole building* despite absence of art. §190. συν-αρμο-λογουμένη (< ἁρμός a joint) *fit together* parts of a building.

22 αὔξω form of αὐξάνω *grow.* ναός *temple, sanctuary.* ‖ συν-οικο-δομεῖσθε pass. -δομέω *build* one thing *with* another;

build together, understand "with us Jews". **κατ-οικητή-ριον** *dwelling*. ‖

χάριν w. gen. *because of* ; or *for the sake of*. **δέσμιος** 3
(< δέω bind) *prisoner*. ‖ **εἴ γε** *if, as I suppose* ; *surely*. 2
ἠκούσατε aor. ἀκούω *hear of*. **οἰκο-νομία** *administration*.
δοθείσης aor. ptc pass. δίδωμι. **εἰς** indicating aim or end,
for you. ‖ **ὅτι** (if it is to be read) *namely that*. **ἀπο-κάλυ-** 3
ψις⁴ *revelation*, κατὰ ἀ. *by revelation*. **ἐ-γνωρίσθη** aor. pass.
-ίζω *make known*. **μυστήριον** (< μυέω initiate) *secret
mystery* of the divine plan. **προ-έ-γραψα** *I mentioned above*,
aor. προ-γράφω *write earlier* (*on*). **ὀλίγος** *small*, ἐν ὀ.
briefly. ‖ **πρὸς ὅ** *in accordance with which, in the light of* 4
which. **ἀνα-γινώσκοντες** *as you read*, ptc -γινώσκω *read*.
νοῆσαι aor. inf. νοέω *understand*, aor. *perceive, appreciate*. **σύν-εσις⁴** (< συν-ίημι understand) *understanding, insight*. ‖ **ἕτερος** for ἄλλος §153. **γενεά** *generation*, dat. of 5
time. **ἀπ-ε-καλύφθη** aor. pass. ἀπο-καλύπτω *reveal*. **προφή-
ταις** in the church 2:20. ‖ **εἶναι τὰ ἔθνη** κτλ. "that the 6
gentiles are co-heirs" etc. being the content of the revelation. **συγ-κληρο-νόμος** *inheriting with*, usu. as noun,
co-heir. **σύσ-σωμος** *one body with*. **συμ-μέτοχος** *fellow-
sharer*. **ἐπ-αγγελία** *promise*. ‖ **ἐ-γενήθην** either aor. pass. 7
γίνομαι *I was made* or aor. dep. (= ἐγενόμην §230) *I became*. **διάκονος** *minister*. **κατά** v.3 (κ. ἀποκάλυψιν). **δωρεά**
free gift. **δοθείσης** aor. ptc pass. δίδωμι. **ἐνέργεια** *working, activity*. ‖ **ἐλαχιστότερος** comp. of the superl. ἐλά- 8
χιστος ! designed to express *less than the least*, cf I Cor
15:9. **ἐ-δόθη** aor. pass. **εὐ-αγγελίσασθαι** aor. inf. 2:17.
ἀν-εξ-ιχνίαστος (ἀν- + ἐξ- out + ἴχνος⁸ footprint, trace)
untraceable, fathomless. **πλοῦτος** *riches*. ‖ **καί** epexeg. 9
that is to say. **φωτίσαι** aor. inf. *bring to light, elucidate* ;
reading πάντας, *enlighten*. **τίς** as indir. interr. **οἰκο-
νομία** v.2. **μυστήριον** v.3. **ἀπο-κε-κρυμμένον** pf ptc pass.
-κρύπτω *hide* (*away*). **κτίσαντι** aor. ptc κτίζω *create*. ‖
γνωρισθῇ aor. subj. pass. v.3. **ἀρχαὶ καὶ ἐξουσίαι** of cos- 10
mic spiritual powers, *rulers and authorities*. **ἐπ-ουράνιος**
1:3. **πολυ-ποίκιλος** *variegated* ; *with many aspects, mani-
fold*. ‖ **πρό-θεσις⁴** *purpose* 1:11, πρ. τ. αἰώνων *eternal pur-* 11
pose "Hebr. gen." §40. **ἐ-ποίησεν** here, *realized, accomplished*, aor. ποιέω. ‖ **παρ-ρησία** (< πᾶς + ῥῆσις⁴ full liberty 12
of speech) *boldness, complete assurance*. **προσ-αγωγή** *free
access*. **πε-ποίθησις⁴** (πέ-ποιθα trust) *confidence, assurance*.

13 **αὐτοῦ** obj. gen. *in him*. || **δι-ό** *therefore*. **αἰτοῦμαι** *I pray that (you)* do not...or *I beg (you)* not to... or (for himself) *I pray* not to... **ἐγ-κακεῖν** inf. -κακέω *lose heart*. **ἐν** *over*. **θλῖψις**[4] (< θλίβω press) *tribulation, suffering*. **ἥ-τις** agreeing w. pred. but transl. *inasmuch as they* §215. **δόξα** here reason for glorying, *source of pride*. ||

14 V.14 introduces the prayer which Paul was on the point of beginning in v.1. **τούτου χάριν** v.1. **κάμπτω**

15 *bend*. **γόνυ** γόνατος τό *knee*. || **πατριά** *family* in widest sense, w. stress on its ultimate common paternity, ?incl. the hierarchies of spiritual beings, πᾶσα π. wt art. *every*

16 *family*. **ὀνομάζεται** pass. -άζω *name*. || **ἵνα** indicating content of his prayer, *that*. **δῷ** aor[2] subj. δίδωμι. **πλοῦτος** v.8. **δυνάμει** instr. dat., *with power*. **κραταιωθῆναι** aor. inf. pass. -αιόω *strengthen*. **εἰς** may be the solitary instance where Paul uses it for ἐν but εἰς may well be (as in v.3) : *with a view to, for* the renewal of the inner man (cf II

17 Cor 4:16) §110. **ἔσω** *inside, interior*. || **κατ-οικῆσαι** aor. inf. -οικέω *dwell*, this inf. and κραταιωθῆναι (both dependent on δῷ) are effective aor. §252 ed. Lat.[5] **ἐρ-ριζωμένοι** *rooted*, pf ptc pass. ῥιζόω *cause to root*. **τε-θεμελιωμένοι** pf ptc pass. -λιόω *found*, met. *bas?* ; the noms., detached from the syntax, must be understood as according w. the

18 sense. || **ἐξ-ισχύσητε** aor. subj. -ισχύω (ἐξ- perfective) *be strong enough/equal to*. **κατα-λαβέσθαι** aor[2] inf. mid. -λαμβάνω *seize, apprehend* ; also mentally, *grasp*. **τί** indir.; supply ἐστί. **πλάτος**[8] *width*. **μῆκος**[8] *length*. **ὕψος**[8] *height*.

19 **βάθος**[8] *depth*. || **γνῶναι** aor[2] inf. γινώσκω. **ὑπερ-βάλλουσαν** ptc -βάλλω τινός *exceed, surpass* sth. **γνῶσις** *knowledge*. **πληρωθῆτε** aor. subj. pass. -ρόω. **εἰς** *to the extent of*.

20 **πλήρωμα**[8] *fullness*. || **ὁ δυνάμενος** (ptc) *he who is able*. **ποιῆσαι** aor. inf. ποιέω. **ὑπερ-εκ-περισσοῦ** adv. *beyond all measure* ; w. gen. *far more than*. **νοέω** *think, conceive* in

21 the mind. **ἐν-εργουμένην** ptc mid. -εργέω *be at work*. || **αὐτῷ** *to him* (be). **γενεά** v.5. **εἰς...αἰώνων** *from generation to generation for evermore*. ||

4 **δέσμιος** *prisoner*. **ἀξίως** w. gen. *worthily* of. **περι-πατῆσαι** aor. inf. -πατέω, in ethical sense of *behave, live*. **κλῆσις**[4] *call, vocation*. **ἧς** attracted from ᾗ §17. **ἐ-κλήθητε**

2 aor. pass. καλέω. || **ταπεινο-φροσύνη** *humility*, πᾶσα τ. wt art. *all humility* §188. **πραΰτης**[6] -τητος ἡ *gentleness*. **μακρο-θυμία** (long temper) *patience*. **ἀν-εχόμενοι** ptc -έχομαί τινος

bear/put up with one ; ptc agreeing w. the *logical* subject of περιπατῆσαι, cf 3:17. ‖ σπουδάζοντες ptc -άζω *be eager*, 3 *do everything* to. τηρεῖν inf. τηρέω *keep, preserve.* ἑνότης⁶ -τητος ἡ *unity,* i.e. of all members in the Spirit. σύν- δεσμος *bond,* both as fettering (Ac 8:23) and as cementing (here). ‖ ἐκλήθητε v.l. ἐλπίς *hope.* κλῆσις v.l. ‖ βάπτι- 4,5 σμα⁷ *baptism.* ‖ εἷς ἕκαστος *each one.* ἐ-δόθη aor. pass. 7 δίδωμι. μέτρον *measure.* δωρεά *gift,* κατά τ. μέτρον τῆς δ. τ. Χριστοῦ i.e., *the measure with which Christ confers his gifts.* ‖ δι-ό *therefore.* λέγει sc. *scripture.* ἀνα-βάς 8 aor² ptc -βαίνω. ὕψος⁸ *height,* εἰς ὕ. *on high,* i.e. to heaven. ᾐχμαλώτευσεν aor. αἰχμαλωτεύω (< αἰχμή lance + ἁλίσκομαι capture) *lead captive.* αἰχμαλωσία *captivity* ; abstract for concrete, *prisoners.* ἔ-δωκεν aor. δίδωμι. δόμα⁷ *gift.* ‖ τό 9 introducing a quotation : *the* (*word*) "ἀνέβη". ἀν-έ-βη aor² ἀνα-βαίνω. τί ἐστιν; *what does it mean?* "mean" having no equivalent in Hebr.-Aram. ὅτι *that.* κατ-έ-βη aor² κατα-βαίνω. κατώτερος (comp. of κάτω below) *lower.* μέρος⁸ *part.* τ. γῆς perh. epexeg. *that is, the earth* §45, others otherwise. ‖ κατα-βάς aor² ptc -βαίνω: ὁ κ. *he who descended.* 10 αὐτός ἐστιν *is he* (not ὁ αὐτός "the same"). ὑπερ-άνω w. gen. *far above.* πληρώσῃ aor. subj. -ρόω *fill.* τὰ πάντα *the universe.* ‖ ἔ-δωκεν v.8. τοὺς μέν...τοὺς δέ *some...others...* 11 εὐ-αγγελιστής³ *evangelist.* ποιμήν⁶ -μένος ὁ *shepherd, pastor.* διδάσκαλος *teacher.* ‖ πρός w. acc. *for.* κατ-αρτισμός *mak-* 12 *ing ready, equipping.* εἰς *for.* διακονία *service.* οἰκο-δομή *building up.* ‖ μέχρι w. subj. *until.* κατ-αντήσωμεν aor. 13 subj. -αντάω *attain, arrive at.* ἑνότης v.3, so here, of all in faith and knowledge. ἐπί-γνωσις⁴ *knowledge.* τέλειος *perfect,* ἀνὴρ τ. *mature manhood.* μέτρον v.7. ἡλικία *stature.* πλήρωμα⁷ *fullness* ; εἰς μέτρον ...Χρ. meaning *to the stage at which we* (as a body) *may possess in full the gifts of Christ.* ‖ μηκ-έτι *no longer, no more.* ὦμεν subj. 14 εἰμί. νήπιος *infant,* also in legal sense *minor.* κλυδωνι- ζόμενοι ptc -ίζομαι (< κλύδων⁶ wave) *be tossed about* by waves. περι-φερόμενοι ptc -φέρομαι *be carried hither and thither.* ἄνεμος *wind.* διδασκαλία *teaching.* κυβεία (< κύ- βος dice) *trickery.* παν-ουργία (παν-οῦργος ready for any- thing) *cunning.* πρός *in the interests of.* μεθ-οδεία *me- thod, device* ; *scheming, wiliness.* πλάνη *error, deception.* ‖ ἀληθεύοντες ptc -εύω *speak the truth.* αὐξήσωμεν aor. subj. 15 hort. αὐξάνω trans. and intr. *grow.* τὰ πάντα acc. of

16 respect, *in every way.* ‖ **ἐξ οὗ** i.e. from Christ. **συν-αρμο-λογούμενον** ptc pass. *-λογέω fit together* 2:21. **συμ-βιβαζό-μενον** ptc pass. *-βιβάζω put together, join.* **ἀφή** *band, ligament.* **ἐπι-χορηγία** (< ἐπι-χορ-ηγέω provide the expenses for a chorus ; in general, provide for) *supply, support.* **ἐν-έργεια** *working, activity.* **μέτρον** v.7. **εἰς ἕκαστος** *each individual.* **μέρος**[8] v.9. **αὔξησις**[4] *growth.* **ποιεῖται** mid. ποιέω (αὔξησιν π. = αὐξάνει and so ποιεῖται mid. 1:16 §227). **τοῦ σώματος** repeating τὸ σῶμα of the subject instead of ἑαυτοῦ which is required in the next clause. **οἰκοδομή** v.12. The imagery of v.16 is obscure to us and its exact meaning uncertain : lit. "from whom the whole body, being fitted together and joined by means of every ligament of supply (?bringing sustenance) corresponding to the activity in the measure of (?grace possessed by) each and every part, makes for the body's growth for the building up of itself in love". ‖

17 **μαρτύρομαι** *testify,* also *conjure, implore.* **μηκ-έτι** v.14. **περι-πατεῖν** v.1. **ματαιότης**[6] *-τητος ἡ futility.* **νοῦς** νόος ὁ

18 *mind.* ‖ **ἐ-σκοτωμένοι** pf ptc pass. σκοτόω *darken.* **διά-νοια** *mind, thought,* dat. of respect §53. **ὄντες** ptc εἰμί. **ἀπ-ηλλοτριωμένοι** pf ptc pass. *-αλλοτριόω τινά τινος estrange/alienate* one *from* sth. **ἄ-γνοια** *ignorance,* here wilful. **οὖσαν** ptc fem. εἰμί. **πώρωσις**[4] *hardening.* ‖ **ἀπ-ηλγηκότες**

19 *beyond feeling* (i.e. morally insensible) pf ptc *-αλγέω become devoid of feeling,* here in the sphere of morals. **παρ-έ-δωκαν** aor. (for aor² παρέδοσαν) παρα-δίδωμι. **ἀσέλγεια** *debauchery.* **ἐργασία** *work ; practice.* **ἀ-καθαρσία** *im-purity.* **πᾶς** wt art. *every kind of* §188. **ἐν πλεον-εξίᾳ** (πλέον ἔχειν)

20 *to excess* ‖. **ἐ-μάθετε** aor² μανθάνω *learn ;* the use of μανθάνω and ἀκούω (v.21) w. dir. obj. of a person is unknown ; perh. Paul thus emphasizes that what the Christian learns

21 is the living Christ. ‖ **εἴ γε** surely *if* (implying "as you surely have"). **ἠκούσατε** aor. ἀκούω, possibly "heard his call". **ἐν αὐτῷ** i.e. as Christians. **ἐ-διδάχθητε** aor.

22 pass. διδάσκω. ‖ **ἀπο-θέσθαι** aor² inf. mid. *-τίθημι,* in mid. *put away from oneself, cast off ;* prob. inf. epexeg. **ὑμᾶς** acc. as subject of inf. **πρότερος** *former.* **ἀνα-στροφή** (< ἀνα-στρέφομαι live, behave) *way of life.* **παλαιός** *old,* κατά... ἄνθρωπον virtually, *the old man of your former ways* §130. **φθειρόμενον** *destroying himself* or *decaying,* ptc mid. or pass. φθείρω *destroy ; corrupt.* **κατά** (2nd time) *by virtue*

of, in. **ἐπι-θυμία** *desire.* **ἀπάτη** *deceit* ; also (in HGk) *sinful pleasure* ; here prob. *desires* "of deceit" ("Hebr." gen.) *which deceive* §40. ‖ **ἀνα-νεοῦσθαι** inf., prob. pass. 23 rather than mid. **-νεόω** *renew* ; pres. connoting constant renewal. **νοῦς** v.17. ‖ **ἐν-δύσασθαι** aor. inf. mid. **-δύω** 24 *clothe* one ; mid. *put on oneself,* cf **ἀνανεοῦσθαι** pres. **καινός** *new.* **τὸν κατὰ θεόν** *in God's way,* possibly, *in God's image.* **κτισθέντα** aor. ptc pass. **κτίζω** *create.* **ὁσιότης**[6] **-τητος ἡ** *holiness.* **ἀληθείας** "Hebr." gen. = *true righteousness* etc. §40. ‖

δι-ό v.8. **ἀπο-θέμενοι** aor² ptc mid. v.22. **ψεῦδος**[8] 25 *falsehood, lie.* **λαλεῖτε** impv **λαλέω.** **πλησίον** adv. *near* ; **ὁ π.** *neighbour.* **μέλος**[8] *member.* ‖ **ὀργίζεσθε** perh. conces- 26 sive impv, *be angry* (if you must) *but...* **μὴ ἁμαρτάνετε** *do not sin.* **ἥλιος** *sun.* **ἐπι-δυέτω** impv 3rd sg **-δύω,** of the sun, *set/go down.* **παρ-οργισμός** *incitement/provocation to anger* ; in pass. sense *anger.* ‖ **μηδέ** *and...not, neither.* 27 **δίδοτε** impv **δίδωμι.** **τόπον** meaning *opening, loophole.* **διά-βολος** (< **δια-βάλλω** *slander*) *accuser,* the *devil.* ‖ **κλέπτων** 28 ptc **-πτω** *steal,* **ὁ κ.** (pres.) *he who is* or *was in the habit of stealing, the thief* ; art. generic. **μηκ-έτι** v.14. **κλεπτέτω** impv 3rd sg. **κοπιάτω** impv **-ιάω** *labour.* **ἐργαζόμενος** ptc **-ζομαι** *work.* **τὸ ἀγαθόν** "what is good", i.e. some honest work. **ἔχῃ** subj. **ἔχω,** w. inf. *be in a position to, be able to.* **μετα-διδόναι** inf. **-δίδωμί τινι** *impart to / share with* another. **χρεία** need, **χ. ἔχων** (ptc) *one in need.* ‖ **πᾶς...μή** 29 Sem. *not one, no* §446. **σαπρός** *rotten,* **λόγος σ.** *bad/foul language.* **ἐκ-πορευέσθω** impv **-πορεύομαι** *go out,* **ἐκπ. ἐκ τ. στόματος ὑμῶν** *escape your lips.* **ἀλλὰ εἰ** *but* (only) *if.* **τις ἀγαθὸς πρός** *one good for.* **οἰκοδομή** v.12, **οἰ. τῆς χρείας** perh. a hendiadys "needed edification", transl. *edification in case of need.* **δῷ** aor² subj. **δίδωμι.** **ἀκούουσιν** ptc dat. pl., **ὁ ἀκούων** *the hearer.* ‖ **λυπεῖτε** impv **λυπέω** 30 *grieve.* **ἐ-σφραγίσθητε** aor. pass. **-ίζω** *seal* 1:13. **εἰς** *for.* **ἀπο-λύτρωσις**[4] *redemption.* ‖ **πικρία** *bitterness.* **θυμός** 31 *rage.* **ὀργή** *anger.* **κραυγή** (< **κράζω** shout) *shouting.* **βλασ-φημία** *cursing* or *slander* depending on whether directed against God or man. **ἀρθήτω** aor. impv pass. 3rd sg **αἴρω.** **κακία** *malice.* ‖ **γίνεσθε** impv **γίνομαι,** supplying ob- 32 solete 2nd pl. impv for **εἰμί.** **χρηστός** *kind.* **εὔ-σπλαγχνος** *compassionate.* **χαριζόμενοι** ptc **-ίζομαί τινι** *give freely* ; also *forgive.* **ἐ-αυτοῖς** for **ἀλλήλοις.** **ἐ-χαρίσατο** aor. ‖

5 1 γίνεσθε 4:32. μιμητής³ *imitator*. ἀγαπητός *beloved*. ‖ περι-
πατεῖτε impv 4:1. ἠγάπησεν aor. ἀγαπάω. παρ-έ-δωκεν aor.
παρα-δίδωμι. προσ-φορά (< προσ-φέρω offer) *offering*. θυσία
(< θύω) *sacrifice*. ὀσμή (< ὄζω smell) a *smell*. εὐ-ωδία
fragrance, ὀσμή εὐ. Hebr. *sweet odour/fragrance* of sacrifice. ‖
3 πορνεία *fornication*. ἀ-καθαρσία *im-purity*. πλεον-εξία 4:19.
ὀνομαζέσθω impv pass. -άζω *name*. ἐν *among*. πρέπει
4 τινί *it is fitting* for one. ‖ αἰσχρότης⁶ -τητος ἡ moral *filth*.
μωρο-λογία *foolish chatter*. εὐ-τραπελία (< εὖ + τρέπω turn)
ready wit ; here as turned to bad use, *double entendre*,
allusive joke depending on a play on words. ἀν-ῆκεν
impf -ήκει impers. *it is seemly/proper* ; impf representing
what ought to be and is not (note the corresponding Eng.
past "should, ought" Ac 22:22). εὐ-χαριστία *thanksgiv-*
5 *ing*. ‖ ἴστε impv (or pf-pres. indic.) οἶδα. γινώσκοντες ptc
-σκω : ἴστε γ. ὅτι... may reflect the emphasis of the Hebr.
cstr w. inf. absolute §61, *you may be sure that*... πᾶς...οὐ
4:29. πόρνος *fornicator*. ἀ-κάθαρτος *vicious*, *immoral*.
πλεον-έκτης *rapacious*. ὅ ἐστιν *that is to say*, i.e. εἰδωλο-
λάτρης³ *idolater* because letting his appetites usurp the
place of God. κληρο-νομία *inheritance* 1:14. The joining
of Χριστοῦ and θεοῦ under one art. is to be noted §185. ‖
6 ἀπατάτω impv 3rd sg -τάω *deceive*. κενός *empty* lit.
and met. ὀργή *wrath*. ἀ-πείθεια *disobedience* ; υἱοί τῆς ἀπ.
7 2:2. ‖ γίνεσθε 4:32. συμ-μέτοχος *fellow-sharer* in sth (3:6) ;
8 here rather *associate, partner* in some action. ‖ ἦτε impf
εἰμί. ποτέ *at some time, once*. σκότος⁸ *darkness*. τέκνα
9 φωτός 2:3. περι-πατεῖτε v.2. ‖ ἐν sc. *consists in*. ἀγαθωσύνη *goodness*. ἀλήθεια meaning truth in word and ac-
10 tion. ‖ δοκιμάζοντες ptc -άζω *put to the test, examine*
and so here *decide* ; ptc ref. back to περιπατεῖτε. εὐ-άρεστος
11 *pleasing*. ‖ συγ-κοινωνεῖτε impv -κοινωνέω τινί *share* or
take part in sth. ἄ-καρπος *barren*. ἐλέγχετε impv -χω
12 *expose*. ‖ κρυφῇ adv. *in secret*. γινόμενα *done*, ptc γίνομαι.
αἰσχρός *shameful, disgraceful*, neut. as ref. inf. καί
13 *even*. ‖ ἐλεγχόμενα ptc pass. φανεροῦται pass. -ρόω *re-*
14 *veal, show*. ‖ φανερούμενον ptc pass. ἔγειρε impv -ρω.
καθεύδων ptc *sleeping*, impvs indicate 2nd pers. sg *you*
who sleep. ἀνά-στα (= ἀνά-στηθι) *rise !* aor² (intr.) impv
ἀν-ίστημι *raise up*. ἐπι-φαύσει fut. -φαύσκω τινί *arise/*
15 *shine* upon one. ‖ βλέπετε impv. ἀκριβῶς (adj. ἀκριβής⁹
exact, accurate) *carefully*. ἄ-σοφος *foolish*. σοφός *wise*. ‖

ἐξ-αγοραζόμενοι ptc mid. -αγοράζω (ἐξ- from + ἀγοράζω 16 buy) *redeem* ; the meaning of mid. is doubtful, perh. *exploiting* the opportunity. ‖ γίνεσθε 4:32. ἄ-φρων⁶ (< ἀ- 17 priv. + φρήν mind) -φρονος neut. ἄφρων *senseless, foolish*. συν-ίετε impv -ίημι *understand*. ‖ μεθύσκεσθε impv pass. 18 -σκω *intoxicate*, pass. *get drunk*. οἶνος *wine*. ἀ-σωτία (ἀ- + σώζω save, keep) *dissipation*. πληροῦσθε *let yourselves be filled*, impv pass. -ρόω. ἐν w. dat. fill *with* instead of usual gen. ‖ λαλοῦντες ptc. ἑ-αυτοῖς for ἀλλήλοις. ψαλ- 19 μός *song of praise* accompanied on the harp. ὕμνος *hymn*. ᾠδή *song*. πνευματικός *spiritual*. ᾄδοντες ptc ᾄδω *sing*. ψάλλοντες ptc ψάλλω *pluck/play* esp. the harp ; *sing to harp accompaniment*. ‖ εὐ-χαριστοῦντες ptc -τέω *give* 20 *thanks*. πάν-τοτε *at all times*. πάντων masc. *all men* or neut. *everything*. τῷ θεῷ κ. πατρί *God the Father*. ‖ ὑπο- 21 τασσόμενοι *subordinating yourselves, submitting*, ptc pass. -τάσσω *subjugate*. φόβος *fear*. ‖

σωτήρ⁶ -ῆρος ὁ *saviour*. ‖ ὑπο-τάσσεται pass. ‖ ἀγαπᾶτε 23-5 impv -πάω. ἠγάπησεν aor. παρ-έ-δωκεν v.2. ‖ ἁγιάσῃ aor. 26 subj. -άζω *make holy*. καθαρίσας aor. ptc -ίζω *cleanse, purify* ; later a term for baptism. λουτρόν (λούω wash) a *washing*, λ. τοῦ ὕδατος *a washing in water*. ἐν *accompanied by, with*, sociative ἐν §116. ῥῆμα⁷ *word*, sts comprehensive, e.g. of "teaching", here as summed up in "a form of words" ; ὕδατος ἐν ῥ. the matter and form of the sacrament. ‖ παρα-στήσῃ aor. subj. παρ-ίστημι *present*. ἔν-δοξος 27 *resplendent*. ἔχουσαν ptc fem. ἔχω. σπίλος *spot*. ῥυτίς⁶ -ίδος ἡ *wrinkle*. τοιοῦτος *such*, τι τῶν τοιούτων after a neg. *anything of the kind*. ᾖ subj. εἰμί. ἄ-μωμος *without blemish*. ‖ ὀφείλω *owe* ; w. inf. *ought*. ἀγαπᾶν inf. -πάω. 28 ἀγαπῶν ptc, ὁ ἀγ. *one who loves*. ‖ ποτέ w. neg. *ever*. ἐ- 29 μίσησεν aor. μισέω *hate*. ἐκ-τρέφω *bring up, provide for*. θάλπω *cherish, care for*. ‖ μέλος⁸ *member*. ‖ ἀντὶ τούτου = 30-1 τούτου ἕνεκεν Mk 10:7 *for this reason*. κατα-λείψει fut. -λείπω *leave behind*. προσ-κολληθήσεται fut. pass. -κολλάω (< κόλλα glue) *join sth to*, pass. *join oneself to, adhere to* (cf colloq. "stick to"). ἔσονται fut. εἰμί. εἰς for nom. pred., Sem. §32. ‖ μυστήριον *mystery* ref. to matters made 32 known through revelation. εἰς *with reference to*, ἐγώ...λέγω εἰς *I refer it to / am speaking of*. ‖ πλήν *but still* §479 Lat. 33 ed⁵. εἷς ἕκαστος 4:7, ὑμεῖς οἱ καθ' ἕνα ἕκαστον *each of you individually*. ἀγαπάτω impv 3rd sg -πάω. ἵνα w. subj. sts standing for impv §415. φοβῆται subj. φοβέομαι. ‖

6 τὰ τέκνα nom. w. art. for voc., so vv. 4,5,9 §34. ὑπ-
2 ακούετε impv -ακούω *obey.* γονεύς⁵ *parent.* ‖ τίμα impv
τιμάω *honour.* ἥ-τις = ἥ §216, ref. pred. ἐντολή. ἐπ-
αγγελία *promise* ; ἥτις...ἐπ. *which is* (the) *first commandment
with a promise.* ἐν *of* concomitant circumstances (socia-
3 tive) §116. ‖ εὖ *well.* γένηται aor² subj. γίνομαι. ἔσῃ
fut. εἰμί; fut. after ἵνα is HGk usage §340 ; the meaning
"and so you will be" is also possible. μακρο-χρόνιος
4 *long-lived.* ‖ παρ-οργίζετε impv -οργίζω *exasperate.* ἐκ-
τρέφετε impv -τρέφω *provide for* ; *bring up.* παιδεία
discipline, training. νου-θεσία (< νοῦς mind + τίθημι)
exhortation ; *warning* ; *instruction.* ‖
5 ὑπακούετε v.l. κατὰ σάρκα *earthly.* κύριος *master.*
φόβος *fear.* τρόμος *trembling,* μετὰ φόβου κ. τρ. *conscien-
tiously in the fear of God.* ἁπλότης⁶ -τητος ἡ *singleness* ;
6 *sincerity.* ‖ κατά w. acc. *in the manner of.* ὀφθαλμο-δουλία
"eye-service", i.e. service under the eye of the master.
ἀνθρωπ-άρεσκος *one currying favour* (with men). ποιοῦντες
7 ptc ποιέω. ἐκ ψυχῆς *from the heart.* ‖ εὔ-νοια *goodwill.*
8 δουλεύοντες ptc -εύω *serve.* ‖ εἰδότες ptc pf-pres. οἶδα.
ποιήσῃ aor. subj. ποιέω. κομίσεται fut. mid. -ίζω *bring* ;
mid. *receive* back. εἴτε...εἴτε *whether...or.* ἐλεύθερος *free*
9 (*man*). ‖ κύριος v.5. τὰ αὐτά *the same things* ; τά...αὐτούς
act in the same way to them. ποιεῖτε impv. ἀν-ιέντες ptc
-ίημι *loosen, relax* ; *stop, give up.* ἀπειλή *threat.* καί...καί
both...and. προσωπο-λημψία (< λαμβάνω) *partiality* based on
social standing, outward appearance, etc. ‖
10 τοῦ λοιποῦ (sc. χρόνου) *from now on* (Gal 6:17), here
finally. ἐν-δυναμοῦσθε impv pass. -δυναμόω *strengthen* ;
pass. *be strong.* κράτος⁸ *might.* ἰσχύς -ύος ἡ *strength,*
11 *power.* ‖ ἐν-δύσασθε aor. impv mid. -δύω *put on* another ;
mid. *have on, wear,* aor. *put on* oneself. παν-οπλία (πᾶς +
ὅπλα (τά) arms) *suit of armour, armour.* τ. θεοῦ i.e. which
God supplies. πρὸς τό w. acc. + inf. final. δύνασθαι inf.
δύναμαι. στῆναι *to stand firm,* aor² (intr.) inf. ἵστημι.
πρός w. acc. sts *against.* μεθ-οδεία *scheming* 4:14. διά-
12 βολος *devil* 4:27. ‖ πάλη *wrestling,* more generally a *fight,
struggle.* αἷμα κ. σάρξ Hebr., *mortal*(s). ἀρχή, ἐξουσία
3:10. κοσμο-κράτωρ⁶ -τορος ὁ *world-ruler.* σκότος⁸ *darkness.* τὰ πνευματικά *spirit-forces.* πονηρία *evil.* ἐπ-ουράνιος *heavenly* ; neut. pl. *the heavenly places, heaven.*
13 ἀνα-λάβετε aor² impv -λαμβάνω *take up.* δυνηθῆτε aor.

dep. δύναμαι. ἀντι-στῆναι *to resist* v.11 (στῆναι). ἅπαντα = πάντα. κατ-εργασάμενοι here perh. *having won through*, aor. ptc -εργάζομαι *work out* ; *accomplish*. ‖ στῆτε aor² 14 impv. περι-ζωσάμενοι aor. ptc mid. -ζώννυμι *gird* another ; mid. oneself. ὀσφύς -ύος ἡ *loins*. ἐν instr. *with*. ἐνδυσάμενοι aor. ptc mid. v.11. θώραξ⁶ -ακος ὁ *breast-plate*, w. gen. epexeg. §45. ‖ ὑπο-δησάμενοι aor. ptc mid. -δέω 15 "bind under", mid. *put* (e.g. sandals) *on* the feet. ἑτοιμασία (ἕτοιμος ready) *readiness* ; καὶ ὑποδησάμενοι κτλ. transl. *and being well shod, (ever) in readiness (to spread) the good news of peace*. ‖ ἀνα-λαβόντες aor² ptc v.13. 16 θυρεός *shield*. δυνήσεσθε fut. δύναμαι. βέλος⁸ *dart*. πεπυρωμένα *flaming*, pf ptc pass. πυρόω *set fire to*, pass. *burn* (intr.). σβέσαι aor. inf. σβέννυμι *quench*. ‖ περι-κεφαλαία 17 *helmet*. σωτήριον = σωτηρία *salvation*. δέξασθε aor. impv δέχομαι *take*. μάχαιρα *sword*. ὅ ἐστιν 5:5. ῥῆμα⁷ *word*. ‖ διά w. gen. *with*. προσ-ευχή *prayer*. δέησις⁴ *petition*. προσ- 18 ευχόμενοι ptc -εύχομαι. ἐν παντὶ καιρῷ *on every occasion*. εἰς αὐτό *to this end*. ἀγρ-υπνοῦντες ptc -υπνέω (< ἀγρός + ὕπνος sleep in the open) *be watchful/alert*. προσ-καρτέρησις⁴ *assiduity, perseverance*. περί for ὑπέρ, cf ὑπέρ v.19 §96. ‖ δοθῇ aor. subj. pass. δίδωμι. ἅν-οιξις⁴ act of *opening*, ἐν 19 ἀν. τ. στόματος *when I begin to speak*. παρρησία the *freedom of complete confidence* 3:12. γνωρίσαι aor. inf. -ίζω *make known*. ‖ πρεσβεύω *be an ambassador, envoy*. ἅλυσις⁴ 20 *chain*, ἐν ἅ. "in a chain" = *a prisoner*. παρ-ρησιάσωμαι aor. subj. -άζομαι *speak out freely and confidently*. λαλῆσαι aor. inf. λαλέω. ‖

εἰδῆτε subj. of pf-pres. οἶδα. τὰ κατ᾽ ἐμέ *my circum-* 21 *stances, how I am faring* 1:15 §130. πράσσω *do*. γνωρίσει *will let you know*, fut. -ίζω v.19. ἀγαπητός *beloved*. πιστός *faithful*. διάκονος *minister, helper*. ‖ ἔ-πεμψα aor. πέμπω, 22 "epistolary" aor., transl. *I am sending* (when T. brings them the letter Paul will "have sent" him). γνῶτε aor² subj. γινώσκω. τὰ περὶ ἡμῶν *our news*. παρα-καλέσῃ aor. subj. -καλέω *encourage*, π. τ. καρδίας ὑμῶν *put fresh heart into you* (NEB). ‖ ἡ χάρις (may) *grace* (be). ἀγαπώντων 24 ptc -πάω. ἀ-φθαρσία *in-corruption* ; *im-mortality* ; ἐν ἀφθ. may ref. to all who love the Lord (who already possess eternal life) ; or to the Lord (as reigning immortal in heaven) or again, ass. w. χάρις, it could form part of Paul's wish as if "grace...and immortality". ‖

PHILIPPIANS

1 ἅγιοι because dedicated to God ; title of all believers.
οὖσιν ptc εἰμί. ἐπί-σκοπος (ἐπι- + σκοπέω look out) *over-*
seer, superintendent, pl. indicating that no distinction
was yet made between ἐπ. and πρεσβύτερος: σύν, that
their office deserved special mention. διάκονος *minister,*
2 *helper.* ‖ χάρις καὶ εἰρήνη I Cor 1:3. ‖
3 εὐχαριστέω *give thanks.* ἐπί on the occasion of.
μνεία *recollection, remembrance.* ὑμῶν *of you,* gen. obj. ‖
4 πάν-τοτε *always.* δέησις⁴ *petition.* χαρά *joy.* ποιούμενος
ptc mid. ποιέω: δέησιν π. class. use of mid. when π. combines w. its obj. to express the same idea as the cognate
5 vb (here = δεόμενος). ‖ ἐπί w. dat. giving the grounds
for his joy §126. κοινωνία *contribution, co-operation.* εἰς
to the furtherance/spread of the gospel. ἄχρι w. gen.
6 *until.* ‖ πε-ποιϑώς *confident,* pf² (w. pres. sense) ptc πείθο-
μαι *persuade* ; pf² πέποιθά τι *be convinced/confident* of sth.
αὐτὸ τοῦτο *precisely this,* ref. what follows. ἐν-αρξάμενος
aor. ptc -άρχομαι *begin.* ἐπι-τελέσει fut. -τελέω *complete.*
ἄχρι (v.5) here *by* a certain time. ἡμέρα Χρ. 'Ι. i.e. the
parousia ; a set phrase, moreover in Sem. cstr would be
7 wt art. §182. ‖ φρονεῖν inf. -νέω *think.* ὑπέρ perh. for
περί §96. διὰ τό w. acc. + inf. *because.* με subject, ὑμᾶς
obj. of ἔχειν. δεσμός (< δέω bind) pl. *bonds,* i.e. *imprisonment.* ἀπο-λογία *defence.* βεβαίωσις⁴ (βεβαιόω confirm) *confirmation.* συγ-κοινωνός *fellow-sharer, partner.* ὄντας v.1
8 (οὖσιν). ‖ μάρτυς⁶ -υρος ὁ *witness.* ὡς *how.* ἐπι-ποθέω τινά
long for one. σπλάγχνα τά *entrails* as source of feelings,
9 = Eng. *heart, affection.* ‖ ἵνα for obj. inf. §407. περισ-
σεύῃ subj. -εύω *abound, be rich in,* here *increase* (Ac 16:5).
ἐπί-γνωσις⁴ *knowledge.* αἴσθησις⁴ (αἰσθάνομαι perceive) *per-
10 ception, insight.* ‖ εἰς τό w. acc. + inf. final, *that you may...*
δοκιμάζειν inf. -άζω *distinguish* by testing or approve
after testing. δια-φέροντα ptc -φέρω *differ* ; *be superior,
excel* ; τὰ δ. *things that differ* or *what transcends the ordinary,
what is best.* ἦτε subj. εἰμί. εἰλικρινής *pure, sincere.*

ἀ-πρόσ-κοπος (ἀ- priv. + προσ-κόπτω stumble against) *not giving offence* (I Cor 10:32) also (as here) "not stumbling", *blameless.* εἰς τὴν ἡμέραν *for the day.* ‖ πε-πληρωμένοι pf 11 ptc pass. -ρόω usu. τινά τινος, sts w. double acc. *fill* one *with* sth. καρπός met. (the acc. of the thing with vbs taking a double acc. remains acc. in pass.) cf Gal 2:7, 6:6 §73. τὸν διά *that comes by/through.* εἰς to. ἔπ-αινος (< αἰνέω praise) *praise.* ‖

γινώσκειν inf. βούλομαι w. acc. + inf. *want* you *to.* 12 τὰ κατ' ἐμέ *my circumstances* Eph 6:21. προ-κοπή (< προ-κόπτω advance) *progress.* ἐ-λήλυθεν pf² ἔρχομαι: εἰς...ἐλ. *have led rather to progress of the gospel* (than otherwise). ‖ δεσμός v.7 ; pl. δεσμοί or δεσμά Ac 20:23. φανερός *clear,* 13 *evident.* ἐν causal. γενέσθαι aor² inf. γίνομαι: τοῖς...γενέσθαι *that my imprisonment on account of Christ has become well known* ; less credibly : (*the fact*) *that my imprisonment is on Christ's account has become evident* to... πραιτώριον = Lat. praetorium, by extension *praetorian guard* ; in the provinces, *the governor's official residence* and so perh. *government officers.* λοιπός *left behind,* οἱ λ. *the rest.* ‖ πλείων (comp. of πολύς) *more,* οἱ πλείονες *the majority.* 14 πε-ποιθότας v.6, to be ass. w. ἐν κυρίῳ: τούς...πεπ. acc. as subject of τολμᾶν. τοῖς δεσμοῖς causal dat. *because of my bonds* §58. περισσοτέρως *more than ever,* comp. of -ισσῶς *exceedingly.* τολμᾶν inf. -μάω *dare,* inf. dependent on ὥστε. ἀ-φόβως *fearlessly.* ὁ λόγος almost t.t. for *the Christian message, the gospel.* λαλεῖν inf. λαλέω. ‖ τινὲς μέν...τινὲς δέ 15 *some...others.* φθόνος *envy.* ἔρις⁶ ἔριδος ἡ *rivalry.* εὐδοκία *good-will.* κηρύσσω *preach.* ‖ εἰδότες ptc pf-pres. 16 οἶδα, ptc causal, "because they know". ἀπο-λογία v.7. κεῖμαι *I am put* (here), used as pf pass. of τίθημι *be placed/ put/appointed.* ‖ ἐριθεία *purchasing favour and promotion* 17 *by gifts, self-seeking* ; also *party-spirit.* κατ-αγγέλλω *proclaim.* ἁγνῶς (< ἁγνός pure) *with pure motives,* οὐχ ἁ. *with mixed motives.* οἰόμενοι ptc οἴ(ο)μαι *think.* θλῖψις² (< θλίβω press) *distress, trouble.* ἐγείρειν inf. -ρω. ‖ τί 18 γάρ ; *what matter?* πλήν *save that, provided only that.* τρόπος *manner, way,* dat. of manner, παντὶ τρ. *in one way or another* §60. εἴτε...εἴτε *either...or.* πρό-φασις⁴ *pretext* ; προφάσει *under pretence* §60. κατ-αγγέλλεται pass. ἀλλὰ καί *not only so, but.* χαρήσομαι fut. χαίρω. ‖ ἀπο- 19 βήσομαι fut. -βαίνω *go out* ; *issue, result in.* σωτηρία *deli-*

verance. δέησις v.4. ἐπι-χορηγία *provision, supply, support* ; the one art. perh. showing the close relation in
20 which the two stand in Paul's mind. ‖ ἀπο-καρα-δοκία *eager expectation*, Rom 8:19. ἐλπίς⁶ -ίδος ἡ *hope*. αἰσχυν-θήσομαι fut. pass. -ύνω *put to shame* ; pass. *be disgraced* (here by failure in one's charge or, as Paul regards it, by forfeiting a grace (v.7)). παρ-ρησία (< πᾶς + ῥῆσις full liberty of speech) *frankness, openness*, ἐν π. *openly*. ὡς... καί *as...so*. πάντοτε v.4. καὶ νῦν *so now*. μεγαλυνθήσε-
21 ται fut. pass. -ύνω *make great, so glorify*. ‖ ζῆν inf. ζάω. Χριστός pred. ἀπο-θανεῖν aor² inf. -θνήσκω. κέρδος⁸ *gain*. ‖
22 εἰ δέ *if then*. τὸ ζῆν *living*. ἐν σαρκί *in the body*. Given the punctuation in the text, καί must introduce the apodosis. Vv. 20b-22a ...*that now as always Christ will be glorified...for, for me, living* (supply "is", "means", or more freely "has no meaning apart from") *Christ and* (so) *to die would be a gain, but if living* (on) *in the body, this means that my work will bear fruit* (lit. there will be to me fruit of work), *in that case...* αἱρήσομαι fut. αἱρέομαι *choose*. γνωρίζω *make known* ; transl. (w. Wm and NEB)
23 *I cannot tell*. ‖ συν-έχομαι pass. -έχω *hold fast, restrain* ; pass. *be in the grip of, be caught*. δέ explanatory, *indeed* §467. ἐπι-θυμία *desire*. ἔχων ptc ἔχω. εἰς wt sense of purpose. ἀνα-λῦσαι aor. inf. -λύω *depart*, as in Eng. euphemism for "die". κρείσσων⁶ -ονος neut. κρεῖσσον, used as comp. of ἀγαθός: πολλῷ μᾶλλον κρ. *infinitely better*. ‖
24 ἐπι-μένειν *stay on, remain*. ἀναγκαιότερον comp. of -καῖος *necessary*, the *more necessary* of the two alternatives or
25 comp. for superl. §146f. ‖ πε-ποιθώς *convinced*, v.6, trans. *I am convinced and...* μενῶ fut. μένω ; as echoing ἐπιμένω in v.24 has perh. the same connotation. παρα-μενῶ fut. -μένω *stay beside/with*. εἰς final, *for*. προ-κοπή v.12 ; sharing one art., πρ. καὶ χαράν form a hendiadys = *your joyful*
26 *progress in the faith* §184. χαρά v.4. ‖ καύχημα⁷ *boast, ground for boasting*. περισσεύη subj. -εύω v.9, *exceed the measure, know no bounds*. ἐν ἐμοί *because of me*. παρ-
27 ουσία *coming*, π. πάλιν *coming back*. ‖ ἀξίως w. gen. *in a way worthy of*. πολιτεύεσθε impv -εύομαι *live as a citizen* ; in general, live according to certain norms. εἴτε... εἴτε v.18. ἐλθών aor² ptc ἔρχομαι. ἰδών aor² ptc ὁράω. ἀπ-ών ptc -ειμι *be absent/away*. τὰ περὶ ὑμῶν *news of you*. στήκω *stand firm*, late form developed from ἕστηκα pf

(intr. w. pres. sense) ἵστημι. ψυχή *mind.* συν-αθλοῦντες ptc -αθλέω met. *fight/struggle together/side by side.* τῇ πίστει *for the faith.* ‖ πτυρόμενοι ptc -ρομαι *be scared/alarmed.* 28 ἀντι-κειμένων ptc -κειμαι *oppose,* ptc *adversary.* ἥ-τις (i.e. "your intrepidity") = ᾗ §216, agreeing w. pred. (ἔνδειξις). ἔν-δειξις⁴ *indication, pointer.* ἀπ-ώλεια *destruction.* σωτηρία v.19. ‖ ἐ-χαρίσθη aor. pass. -ίζω *grant as a grace or privi-* 29 lege. τό (1st time) introducing a noun clause specifying what was granted. πάσχειν inf. πάσχω *suffer.* ‖ ἀγών⁶ 30 -ῶνος ὁ *contest* in the arena, hence any *struggle.* οἷος *such as.* ἔχοντες ptc ἔχω, nom. agreeing w. the logical subject of the clause (ὑμεῖς) §394 Lat. ed⁵. ‖

εἴ τις sc. ἐστίν. παρά-κλησις⁴ *encouragement.* παρα- **2** μύθιον *consolation.* ἀγάπης *from love.* κοινωνία *communion.* σπλάγχνα τά *affection* 1:8 ; a lack of concord in number and gender of τις is not found elsewhere, though freq. in the case of τι §9. οἰκτιρμός *compassion.* ‖ πληρώσατε aor. 2 impv -ρόω *complete.* χαρά *joy.* φρονῆτε subj. -νέω *think* ; πληρ. implies an exhortation "that" : ἵνα τὸ αὐτὸ φρον. *by thinking along the same lines, by having the same outlook* Rom 12:16. σύμ-ψυχος *in harmony of mind.* τὸ ἕν φρο-νοῦντες (ptc) *being concerned for unity* or, giving the art. its full force, *being concerned for the one thing.* ‖ μηδέν 3 (supply *do*) *nothing.* ἐριθεία 1:17, κατ᾽ ἐ. *for personal ad-vantage.* μηδέ *nor.* κενο-δοξία *vainglory, pride.* ταπεινο-φροσύνη *humility.* ἡγούμενοι ptc ἡγέομαι *consider, think.* ὑπερ-έχοντας ptc -έχω *be above/better.* ἐ-αυτῶν gen. of comp. ‖ τὰ ἑαυτῶν *your own interests* (ἑαυτῶν for ὑμῶν 4 αὐτῶν §209). ἕκαστος *each (of you).* σκοποῦντες ptc -πέω *look out, watch.* ἀλλὰ καί *but also.* ἕκαστοι pl. rare, transl. *everyone.* ‖ φρονεῖτε impv ; τοῦτο φρ. ...Ἰησοῦ *have* 5 *this frame of mind in you which was also in Christ Jesus.* ‖ μορφή *form;* like "form", μ. can den. anything from "out- 6 ward appearance" to "substance", in vv. 6-7 perh. transl. *nature.* ὑπ-άρχων ptc -άρχω though often simply *be,* the exact sense is *be* from the beginning, w. ref. to God would mean *being from all eternity.* ἁρπαγμός *robbery* ; hence *booty* ; also *prize, privilege* to be retained or to be grasped at ; prob. a tacit allusion to Adam who tried to usurp equality w. God. ἡγήσατο aor. v.3. ἴσος *equal,* neut. pl. advl ; pred. ‖ ἐ-κένωσεν transl. *he stripped himself,* aor. 7 -νόω *empty.* λαβών *by taking,* aor² ptc λαμβάνω *take.*

ὁμοίωμα⁷ *likeness* (Rom 8:3) denies nothing of the content of μορφή but of itself indicates simply that in every respect he was like a man. γενόμενος aor² ptc γίνομαι *be born* ; (v.8) *become*. σχῆμα⁷ refers to his outward *appearance*, dat. of respect §53. εὑρεθείς aor. ptc pass. εὑρίσκω, pass. *be found to be*. With μορφῇ, ὁμοίωμα, σχῆμα note the different vbs : ὑπάρχων (divine nature), λαβών (human nature), γενόμενος (likeness of man), εὑρεθείς (appearance). ‖

8 ἐ-ταπείνωσεν aor. -νόω *abase, humble*. ὑπ-ήκοος (< ὑπ-ακούω obey) *obedient*. μέχρι w. gen. *to the point of*. δέ

9 intensive, *and...at that* §467. σταυρός *cross*. ‖ δι-ό *that is why*, διὸ καί a stereotyped expression sts indistinguishable from simple διό §462. ὑπερ-ύψωσεν aor. -υψόω *raise/exalt to a great height*. ἐ-χαρίσατο aor. -ίζομαι *bestow, give*. τὸ ὄνομα τὸ ὑπὲρ πᾶν ὄνομα i.e. his own name : the LORD

10 of OT (Jahweh), κύριος. ‖ ἐν *at* the name..., ἐν of concomitant circumstances (sociative) §116. γόνυ γόνατος τό *knee*. κάμψῃ aor. subj. κάμπτω *bend*. ἐπ-ουράνιος *heavenly*.

11 ἐπί-γειος *on earth*. κατα-χθόνιος *under the earth*. ‖ γλῶσσα *tongue*. ἐξ-ομο-λογήσηται aor. subj. -λογέω *confess publicly, acknowledge*. κύριος pred. εἰς *to*. ‖

12   ἀγαπητός *beloved*. πάν-τοτε *always*. ὑπ-ηκούσατε aor. -ακούω *obey*, aor. constative §253. μή (instead of οὐ) is grammatically explained by the foll. impv κατεργάζεσθε, the key word of vv. 12,13. In fact the sense precludes a dir. ass. "do not...bring about..." for two ideas are interwoven : (1) "just as you have always obeyed me — not when in my presence only but much more now in my absence — (2) do your best to bring about your own salvation in fear and trembling for it is God who is at work in you...", i.e. with or without Paul's guidance every believer's salvation is ultimately achieved through dependence on and response to God who inspires and empowers him. παρ-ουσία *presence*. πολλῷ μᾶλλον *even more*. ἀπ-ουσία *absence*. φόβος *fear*. τρόμος *trembling* Eph 6:5. ἐ-αυτῶν v.4. σωτηρία *salvation*. κατ-εργάζεσθε *do your best to bring about*, impv -εργάζομαι *achieve, bring*

13 *about*, pres. conative. ‖ ἐν-εργῶν ptc -εργέω *be at work/ active* ; in HGk also trans. *activate, arouse*. καί...καί *both...and*. θέλειν, ἐνεργεῖν (inf.) *to will, to act*. ὑπέρ *for* the sake of. εὐ-δοκία *good will/purpose*, cf Rom 10:1. ‖

14 ποιεῖτε impv ποιέω. χωρίς w. gen. *without*. γογγυσμός

muttering, grumbling. **δια-λογισμός** *argument.* ‖ **γένησθε** 15
become, also *live* (= conduct oneself) aor² subj. **ἄ-μεμπτος**
(< μέμφομαι blame) *blame-less.* **ἀ-κέραιος** (< κεράννυμι
mix) *un-mixed; in-nocent, guile-less, simple.* **ἄ-μωμος** *un-blemished.* **μέσον** w. gen. = ἐν μέσῳ *in the midst of.*
γενεά *generation.* **σκολιός** *crooked.* **δι-ε-στραμμένης** *per-verse,* pf ptc pass. **δια-στρέφω** *per-vert.* **ἐν οἷς** pl. *according
to* the sense, *among whom.* **φαίνεσθε** pass. φαίνω trans.
show ; intr. *shine* ; pass. *appear,* also *shine.* **φωστήρ**⁶ -ῆρος ὁ
luminary ; met. *star.* **ἐν κόσμῳ** ass. w. φαίνεσθε ; art.
commonly omitted in prep. phrases §183. ‖ **λόγος ζωῆς** i.e. 16
the gospel. **ἐπ-έχοντες** ptc -έχω *hold fast* ; also *hold out,*
hence *present.* **εἰς** to serve *as.* **καύχημα** 1:26. **εἰς** τ.
ἡμέραν 1:10. **ὅτι** *in that,* explaining καύχημα. **κενός** *empty* ;
εἰς κ. *in vain.* **ἔ-δραμον** aor² τρέχω *run,* constative (glo-bal) aor. **ἐ-κοπίασα** aor. κοπιάω *labour.* ‖ **εἰ καί** *and if.* 17
σπένδομαι pass. σπένδω *pour out* a libation, transl. here,
my (*blood*) *is to be poured out,* ref. martyrdom. **ἐπί** *as,
in.* **θυσία** *sacrifice.* **λειτ-ουργία** II Cor 9:12 *service* to
God, w. θυσία under one art. *sacrificial offering* §184.
τ. **πίστεως ὑμῶν** (consisting) *of your faith,* or possibly *for
your faith.* **συγ-χαίρω** *rejoice together* with. ‖ **τό...αὐτό** *in* 18
the same way. **χαίρετε, συγχαίρετε** impv. ‖
     ἐλπίζω *hope.* **ταχέως** *quickly, soon.* **πέμψαι** aor. inf. 19
πέμπω. **κἀγώ** = καὶ ἐγώ. **εὐ-ψυχῶ** subj. -ψυχέω *be of good
heart.* **γνούς** aor² ptc γινώσκω aor. *come to know, learn.*
τὰ περὶ ὑμῶν 1:27. ‖ **ἰσό-ψυχος** (ἴσος equal + ψυχή) *like-* 20
minded. **ὅσ-τις** *such as, of the kind who.* **γνησίως** *genuinely.*
μεριμνήσει fut. -μνάω *care about* sth. ‖ **τὰ ἑαυτῶν** *their* 21
own affairs/concerns. **ζητέω** *be intent on* Lk 12:29. ‖
δοκιμή *trial* ; *proof,* also a *proven character.* **ἐ-δούλευσεν** 22
aor. -εύω *serve as a slave.* **εἰς τὸ εὐαγγέλιον** *for the spread
of the gospel* II Cor 2:12. ‖ **μὲν οὖν** *resuming, so then.* 23
ἐλπίζω πέμψαι v.19. **ὡς ἄν** *when-ever.* **ἀφ-ίδω** (the anoma-lous aspirate carried over from ὁράω) aor² subj. -οράω
look away from (the present) *to* (the future), *see ahead.*
ἐξ-αυτῆς (sc. τῆς ὥρας) *immediately,* ὡς ἄν...ἐξαυτῆς *as soon
as ever.* τὰ περὶ ἐμέ here = τὰ περί w. gen. *my circumstan-ces,* transl. *what is going to happen to me.* ‖ **πέ-ποιθα** pf² 24
(w. pres. sense) ptc πείθω *persuade,* pf² *be convinced/con-fident.* **καὶ αὐτός** *I too* will come *myself* (1st pers. indi-cated by ἐλεύσομαι). **ταχέως** v.19. **ἐλεύσομαι** fut. ἔρχο-

25 μαι. ‖ ἀναγκαῖος *necessary*. ἡγησάμην v.6. συν-εργός *fellow-worker*. συ(ν)-στρατιώτης³ *fellow-soldier, comrade in arms*. λειτ-ουργός (cf II Cor 9:12) one holding an official appointment, religious or secular, *public servant* (in the sense of civil "servant"), *delegated assistant*. χρεία *need*.

26 πέμψαι v.19. ‖ ἐπει-δή *since*. ἐπι-ποθῶν *longing*, ptc -ποθέω *long (for)*. ἀδημονῶν *much distressed*, ptc -νέω *be in great distress*. δι-ότι *because*. ἠκούσατε aor. ἀκούω. ἠ-σθένησεν *he had been ill* (§290) cf v.27, aor. ἀ-σθενέω "*be without*

27 *strength*", *be ill*. ‖ καὶ γάρ *and indeed*. ἠσθένησεν *he did fall ill*. παρα-πλήσιος *near*, neut. as adv. used here as prep. §83, ἠσθένησεν π. θανάτῳ *he became so ill that he nearly died*. ἠλέησεν aor. ἐλεέω τινά *have mercy on* one. λύπη

28 *sorrow*. σχῶ aor² subj. ἔχω. ‖ σπουδαιοτέρως comp. of -δαίως (σπουδή haste ; eagerness) *the more urgently*, or *with greater eagerness*. ἔ-πεμψα aor. πέμπω, "*epistolary*" aor. (Eph 6:22). ἰδόντες aor² ptc ὁράω. χαρῆτε aor² subj. dep. χαίρω. κἀγώ v.19. ἀ-λυπότερος (comp. of ἄ-λυπος *free from sorrow*) *to a certain extent relieved*. ὦ subj. εἰμί. ‖

29 προσ-δέχεσθε impv -δέχομαι *welcome, receive*. χαρά v.2. τοιοῦτος *such* ; οἱ τ. *people like him*. ἔν-τιμος *honoured*. ἔχετε impv ἔχω w. double acc. *hold/regard* one *as* sth. ‖

30 μέχρι (*almost*) *to*, cf v.8. ἤγγισεν aor. ἐγγίζω *come near* (ἐγγύς). παρα-βολευσάμενος aor. ptc -βολεύομαί τι (< παρά-βολος *daring*) *risk* sth. ψυχή *life*. ἀνα-πληρώση aor. subj. -πληρόω *fill up, complete*. ὑμῶν subjective gen. ὑστέρημα⁷ a *lack* ; here, ref. the fact that they could not all come personally. λειτ-ουργία v.17 ; i.e. in the form of support for the Apostle. ‖

3   τὸ λοιπόν *finally*. χαίρετε (impv χαίρω) lit. *rejoice*, or (in sense of customary greeting) *farewell*. γράφειν inf. γράφω: γ. τὰ αὐτά *repeat oneself*. ὀκνηρός of a variety of dissuasive factors, here poss. *trouble*. ἀ-σφαλής⁹ (ἀ- priv.

2 + σφάλλω trip up) *safe* ; τὸ ἀ. *safeguard*. ‖ βλέπετε *look out for !* impv βλέπω. κύ ων⁶ κυνός ὁ *dog*. κακός *bad, evil*. ἐργάτης³ *worker, doer*, κ. ἐργ. *dishonest/deceitful worker*. κατα-τομή (< τέμνω cut) *con-cision (mutilation)*, play on

3 the word περιτομή. ‖ περι-τομή *circumcision*, ἡμεῖς...π. οἵ... *we constitute the* (true) *circumcision, we who*... πνεύματι dat. of instr. *by the Spirit of God*. λατρεύοντες ptc -εύω *worship* (esp. public worship by priest or by laity alike) ⟦var. θεῷ who worship *God* in spirit⟧. καυχώμενοι ptc

-χάομαι *glory*. πε-ποιθότες pf² (w. pres. sense) ptc πείθω *persuade* ; pf² *have confidence, trust*. ‖ καίπερ *although*. ἐγώ emphatic. ἔχων ptc ἔχω, transl. by indic. *have (grounds for)*. πε-ποίθησις⁴ *trust, confidence* here = καύχησις *pride*. δοκέω *think, suppose*. πε-ποιθέναι pf² inf., εἴ τις δοκεῖ ἄλλος πεπ. *if any other man thinks himself (entitled) to trust*... μᾶλλον *more so*. ‖ περιτομῇ dat. of respect §53. ὀκτα-ήμερος *on my eighth day*. γένος⁸ *race*. φυλή *tribe*. Ἑβραῖος ἐξ Ἑβρ. *a Hebrew, the son of Hebrews*, i.e. of Hebrew traditions and language. κατὰ νόμον *with regard to / as to the Law*. ‖ ζῆλος⁸ (< ζέω boil) *zeal*. διώκων ptc διώκω *pursue* ; *persecute*, "pres." ptc w. iterative (not temporal) force §371. ἐν νόμῳ *in the sphere of law*. γενόμενος aor² ptc γίνομαι. ἄ-μεμπτος *blame-less*. ‖ ἅ-τινα *what-ever*. κέρδος⁸ *gain*. ἥγημαι pf ἡγέομαι *consider, think* ; pf : a settled frame of mind since his conversion. ζημία *loss*. ‖ μεν-οῦν-γε intensive, *nay rather, indeed* ; note pres. for pf and πάντα for ἅτινα. διά *by reason of*. ὑπερ-έχον ptc neut. of -έχω (2:3) as abstract noun, *supreme good*. γνῶσις⁴ *know-ledge*. ἐ-ζημιώθην aor. pass. -ιόω *inflict loss* ; pass. *suffer loss*. σκύβαλον *rubbish, dung*. κερδήσω aor. subj. -δαίνω *gain*. ‖ εὑρεθῶ aor. subj. pass. εὑρίσκω. ἐμὴ δικαιοσύνη wt art. concentrating on quality, *a righteousness of my own* §180. ἐπί w. dat. *based on*. ‖ τοῦ w. inf. final §383. γνῶναι aor² inf. γινώσκω. ἀνά-στασις⁴ (< ἀν-ίστημι) *resur-rection*. κοινωνία *participation, sharing*. πάθημα⁷ (< ἔ-παθον aor² πάσχω) *what is felt or suffered, suffering*. συμ-μορφιζόμενος ptc pass. -μορφίζω τινί pass. *be conformed to sth*, transl. *in growing conformity with his death* (NEB), pres. ptc connoting a continuous process. ‖ εἴ πως indir. interr. w. force of *if somehow, if only* §403. κατ-αντήσω aor. subj. -αντάω *reach*. ἐξ-ανά-στασις *resurrection from*. ‖

ἤδη *already*. ἔ-λαβον aor² λαμβάνω *receive* ; abs. may bear the meaning "receive money" so perh. *receive the prize* or poss. = κατα-λαμβάνω abs. *arrive*. τε-τελείωμαι *I have already reached perfection*, pf pass. -ειόω *perfect*. διώκω *I continue my pursuit*, v.6. εἰ here, *in the hope of*. κατα-λάβω aor² subj. -λαμβάνω abs. *arrive; take / gain pos-session* ; on subj. §349. ἐφ' ᾧ *seeing that* §127 ; or final, *(that) for which* §129. κατ-ε-λήμφθην aor. pass. ‖ ἐγώ opp. some other people. ἐμ-αυτόν *myself*. λογίζομαι *reckon, consider*. κατ-ει-ληφέναι pf inf. ἓν δέ supply : *I do*. τὰ μέν...τοῖς δέ Rom 2:7. ὀπίσω *behind.* ἐπι-λανθανόμενος ptc -λανθάνομαι *forget.* ἔμ-προσθεν *before, ahead.* ἐπ-εκ-τεινό-

14 μενος ptc -τείνομαι *forge eagerly ahead.* ‖ σκοπός (< σκοπέω v.17) *mark* to be aimed at, *aim, goal,* κατὰ σ. *towards the goal.* βραβεῖον *prize* awarded for contest by the adjudicator (βραβεύς). ἄνω *above,* ἡ ἄνω = *the heavenly.* κλῆσις⁴ *calling,* the condition to which God calls man, in this sense gen. epexeg. : *the prize which is God's heavenly cal-*

15 *ling in Christ Jesus.* ‖ τέλειος *perfect,* not perh. wt a glance at those who would claim the name, v.12a. φρονῶμεν subj. hort. -νέω *think,* τοῦτο φρ. pres. continuous. *let us remain in this frame of mind.* ἑτέρως *differently, otherwise,* εἴ τι ἑτ. φρονεῖτε *if you view anything differently.*

16 ἀπο-καλύψει fut. -καλύπτω *reveal.* ‖ πλήν *only.* ἐ-φθάσαμεν aor. φθάνω (HGk) *arrive, reach,* εἰς ὃ ἐφθ. *whatever the stage we have reached.* στοιχεῖν inf. -χέω *keep in line,* inf. impvl, here hort., *let us continue to hold to the same course.* ‖

17 συμ-μιμητής³ *imitator along with others* ; συμμ. μου γίνεσθε *together be imitators of me.* σκοπεῖτε impv σκοπέω *watch, keep an eye on.* οὕτω = οὕτως. περι-πατοῦντας ptc -πατέω *live* Eph 2:2. καθώς *in the way that.* τύπος *example,* pred. *you have us as an example* ; σκοπεῖτε...ἡμᾶς *look to those*

18 *who are living the way we showed you.* ‖ πολλάκις *many times,* often. ἔ-λεγον impf 1st sg λέγω τινά *mention, speak about* one. κλαίων *in tears,* ptc κλαίω *weep.* ἐχθρός *enemy,*

19 acc. agreeing w. οὕς. σταυρός *cross.* ‖ τέλος⁸ *end.* ἀπ-ώλεια *destruction,* pred. κοιλία (a hollow) *belly.* αἰσχύνη *shame.* ἐπί-γειος *earthly.* φρονοῦντες ptc -νέω v.15, οἱ...φρ.

20 *whose thoughts are earth-bound.* ‖ ἡμῶν emphatic. γάρ here, *on the other hand* §472. πολίτευμα⁷ *citizenship* ; *commonwealth* ; *colony.* ὑπ-άρχω 2:6. σωτήρ⁶ -ῆρος ὁ *saviour, deliverer.* ἀπ-εκ-δέχομαί τινα *expect, wait eagerly for* one. ‖

21 μετα-σχηματίσει fut. -σχηματίζω *trans-form.* ταπείνωσις⁴ *humble state,* σῶμα τ. ταπ. ἡμῶν "Hebr." gen. = *our humble body* §41. σύμμορφός τινι *conformed to, sharing the form* of sth. τ. σώματι τ. δόξης αὐτοῦ = *his glorious body.* ἐν-έργεια *working, power.* δύνασθαι inf. δύναμαι: τὴν ἐνέργειαν τοῦ δ. *his power enabling him* §392 or epexeg. *his power,* viz. *his ability to...* ὑπο-τάξαι aor. inf. -τάσσω *put*

4 *under* ; *subjugate.* ‖ ἀγαπητός *beloved.* ἐπι-πόθητος *longed for.* χαρά *joy.* στέφανος *crown.* στήκετε impv -κω *stand firm* 1:27. ‖

φρονεῖν inf. -νέω *think*, τὸ αὐτὸ φρ. *agree together, live* 2
in harmony. ‖ ναί *yes.* ἐρωτάω *ask.* καί *also.* γνήσιος 3
genuine, true. σύ(ν)-ζυγος *yoke-fellow, companion*, or perh.
a proper name. συλ-λαμβάνου impv -λαμβάνομαί τινι *help*
one. αἵ-τινες *those who, seeing they.* συν-ήθλησαν aor.
-αθλέω τινί *struggle together with* one. ἐν τ. εὐαγγελίῳ
in (the field of) *the gospel.* λοιπός *left* (behind), οἱ λ. *the
rest.* συν-εργός *fellow-worker.* βίβλος ἡ (= βύβλος papyrus) *book.* ‖ χαίρετε impv -ρω. πάν-τοτε *always.* ἐρῶ fut. 4
λέγω, fut. for hort. subj. §341. ‖ ἐπι-εικής⁹ *considerate*, neut. 5
as noun, *forbearance.* γνωσθήτω aor. impv pass. γινώσκω. ἐγγύς *near* (possibly "to you to help you") but more
likely *at hand* (about to return I Cor 16:22). ‖ μεριμνᾶτε 6
impv -μνάω *be anxious.* προσ-ευχή *prayer*, δέησις⁴ *petition* ; both dat. instr. εὐ-χαριστία *thanksgiving.* αἴτημα⁷
request. γνωριζέσθω impv pass. -ίζω *make known.* ‖ ὑπερ- 7
έχουσα ptc -έχω *surpass.* νοῦς νοός ὁ *mind, understanding*,
ὑπερέχουσα π. ν. *beyond all imagination.* φρουρήσει fut.
-ρέω *guard.* νόημα⁷ *thought.* ‖ τὸ λοιπόν 3:1. ἀληθής⁹ *true.* 8
σεμνός (< σέβομαι worship ; revere) *inspiring reverence ;
honourable.* ἁγνός *pure.* προσ-φιλής⁹ *lovable ; admirable.*
εὔ-φημος *praiseworthy ; noble.* εἴ τις sc. ἐστίν. ἀρετή *virtue.* ἔπ-αινος (< αἰνέω praise) *praise.* λογίζεσθε impv
-ίζω *consider, think about.* ‖ ἐ-μάθετε aor² μανθάνω *learn.* 9
παρ-ε-λάβετε aor² παρα-λαμβάνω *receive* (as a tradition).
ἠκούσατε aor. ἀκούω. πράσσετε impv πράσσω *practise, do.*
ἔσται fut. εἰμί.

ἐ-χάρην aor² dep. χαίρω. μεγάλως *greatly.* ἤδη ποτέ 10
at last. ἀν-ε-θάλετε aor² ἀνα-θάλλω *bloom afresh*, met.
revive. φρονεῖν v.2, τὸ ὑπὲρ ἐμοῦ φρ. *your thought on behalf
of/for me.* ἐφ᾽ ᾧ final (cf 3:12) *for* (to) *which end* §129.
ἐ-φρονεῖτε impf *you continued to give thought.* ἠ-καιρεῖσθε
(< ἄ-καιρος un-timely) impf ἀ-καιρέομαι *have no time, lack
opportunity.* ‖ οὐχ ὅτι *not that.* ὑστέρησις⁴ a *lack, want* ; 11
οὐχ...λέγω lit. "not that I speak as a result of want",
i.e. *not that I am prompted to speak by any lack.* ἔ-μαθον
1st sg v.9, ἔμαθον...εἶναι *I have learnt how to be.* ἐν οἷς
εἰμί *in the circumstances in which I am/find myself.* αὐτ-
άρκης⁹ "self-sufficient" wt modern pejorative sense, *independent, content.* ‖ ταπεινοῦσθαι inf. pass. -νόω *humble* ; 12
pass. sts *be chastened.* περισσεύειν inf. -εύω *overflow* w.
sth ; abs. *have enough and to spare.* ἐν παντὶ καὶ ἐν πᾶσιν

(neut.) *in all and every circumstance.* με-μύημαι *I have
learnt the secret,* pf pass. μυέω *initiate.* χορτάζεσθαι *to
have* (*eaten*) *enough,* inf. pass. -άζω *satisfy,* orig. of feeding
animals with, e.g. hay (χόρτος), in HGk it superseded
κορέννυμι (Act 27:38) §493. πεινᾶν inf. -νάω *be hungry.*
ὑστερεῖσθαι *to go without,* inf. pass. -ρέω *come too late,*
13 hence *lack.* ‖ ἰσχύω *have strength* (ἰσχύς) *for.* ἐν instr.
through. ἐν-δυναμοῦντι ptc -δυναμόω τινά *strengthen* one,
14 *give* one *power.* ‖ πλήν *only* (adversative), *but still.* καλῶς
well, nobly ; κ. ἐ-ποιήσατε (aor. ποιέω) w. ptc, *it was good
of you* (Ac 10:33). συγ-κοινωνήσαντες aor. ptc -κοινωνέω
15 τινί *share* (*in*) sth. θλῖψις⁴ *distress.* ‖ ἀρχή *beginning.* ἐ-
κοινώνησεν aor. κοινωνέω *contribute.* λόγος *settlement of
an account.* δόσις⁴ *payment.* λῆμψις⁴ *receipt,* δόσις κ. λ.
16 *debit and credit.* εἰ μή *except.* ‖ ὅτι *for* (explaining v.15).
ἅπαξ *once.* δίς *twice,* ἅπ. καὶ δίς *more than once.* χρεία *need.*
ἐ-πέμψατε aor. πέμπω: εἰς τ. χρείαν μοι ἐπ. *you sent me*
(μοι) *something towards my* (τήν) *needs* ⟦var. μου *you sent*
17 *something towards my* needs⟧. ‖ ἐπι-ζητέω *be in search
of, be looking for.* δόμα⁷ (< δίδωμι) *gift.* ἀλλά *after a*
neg. sts *rather.* καρπός *here profit, benefit.* πλεονάζοντα
18 *accruing,* ptc -άζω *increase.* λόγος v.15. ‖ ἀπ-έχω *receive/
have in full,* t.t. for "received payment in full"; ἀπο-
perfective (cf Eng. "pay off" etc.) §132. περισσεύω *have
in abundance.* πε-πλήρωμαι pf pass. -ρόω Fr. *combler,
supply fully.* δεξάμενος aor. ptc δέχομαι *receive.* τὰ παρ'
ὑμῶν "the things from you", i.e. *the offering you sent.*
ὀσμὴ εὐωδίας Eph 5:2. θυσία *sacrifice.* δεκτός (δέχομαι)
19 *acceptable.* εὐ-άρεστος *pleasing.* ‖ πληρώσει fut. v.18.
χρεία v.16. πλοῦτος⁸ *riches.* ἐν δόξῃ, cstr ⌜w. πληρώσει,
? *with glory in* (union with) *Christ Jesus* ⌝or *his riches
20 in glory in Christ Jesus.* ‖ Understand εἴη ἡ δόξα. ‖
21   ἀσπάσασθε aor. impv -άζομαι *greet.* πᾶς ἅγιος distri-
22 butive, *every saint* (= Christian 1:1). ‖ μάλιστα (superl.
of comp. μᾶλλον) *most of all.* ‖

COLOSSIANS

οἱ ἅγιοι because dedicated to God ; title of all belie- **1** 2
vers. πιστός *faithful, full of faith*, under one art. w. ἅγιοι
§184. χάρις...καὶ εἰρήνη combines and Christianizes Gk
and Hebr. greetings : χαίρειν and *šālôm*. ‖

εὐ-χαριστέω *give thanks.* πάν-τοτε *always*, uncertain **3**
whether to be ass. w. εὐχαριστοῦμεν or προσ-ευχόμενοι ptc
-εύχομαι. ‖ ἀκούσαντες aor. ptc ἀκούω *hear of/about.* ‖ **4**
ἐλπίς -ίδος ἡ *hope*, i.e. what is hoped for. ἀπο-κειμένην **5**
ptc -κειμαι *put away/on one side*, w. dat. *reserve for.* προ-
ηκούσατε aor. *hear beforehand/already.* λόγος τ. ἀληθείας
possibly "Hebr." gen. *true word* §41. ‖ παρ-όντος ptc -ειμι **6**
be present, have come, in latter sense sts w. πρός or εἰς.
καρπο-φορούμενον ptc mid. -φορέω *bear fruit* ; mid. same
?of itself. αὐξανόμενον ptc pass. αὐξάνω *cause to grow,
increase* ; pass. intr. *grow.* ἀφ' ἧς ἡμέρας = ἀπὸ τῆς ἡμέρας ᾗ.
ἠκούσατε aor. ἐπ-έ-γνωτε aor² ἐπι-γινώσκω *know* ; aor.
came to know of. ‖ ἐ-μάθετε aor² μανθάνω *learn.* ἀγαπητός **7**
beloved. σύν-δουλος *fellow-servant.* πιστός v.2, here prob.
trustworthy. ὑπὲρ ὑμῶν *on your behalf* [[var. ὑπὲρ ἡμῶν *in
our stead* §91]]. διάκονος *assistant, minister.* ‖ δηλώσας **8**
here, *told us of*, aor. ptc δηλόω *show.* ‖

ἀφ' ἧς ἡμέρας ἠκούσαμεν v.6. παυόμεθα pass. παύω **9**
check, stop; pass. *cease.* προσ-ευχόμενοι v.3. αἰτούμενοι *be-
seeching*, ptc mid. αἰτέω: προσευχ. αἰτ. perh. a hendiadys,
asking in my prayers for you, cf Mk 11:24 §460. πληρωθῆτε
aor. subj. pass. -ρόω. ἐπί-γνωσις⁴ *knowledge* (If a vb in
the act. takes a double acc., in the pass. one acc. may
remain, Gal. 2:7 §72). ἐν instr. §119. σοφία *wisdom.*
σύν-εσις⁴ (< συν-ίημι) *understanding, insight.* πνευματικός
spiritual. ‖ περι-πατῆσαι aor. inf. -πατέω in ethical sense, **10**
behave, live. ἀξίως w. gen. *in a manner worthy of.* ἀρε-
σκεία *desire to please*, εἰς πᾶσαν ἀρ. *seeking to please him
in all things.* καρπο-φοροῦντες (ptc), αὐξανόμενοι v.6. ‖
πᾶσα δύναμις wt art. *power of every kind.* δυναμούμενοι **11**
ptc pass. -μόω *strengthen.* κράτος⁸ *might, power.* τῆς

δόξης *of his glory* (i.e. divinity) or *his glorious might* ("Hebr." gen. §41). εἰς *with a view to.* ὑπο-μονή *fortitude.* μακρο-θυμία (long temper) *patience.* χαρά *joy*; μετὰ

12 χαρᾶς *joyfully,* as punctuated in our text ass. w. ‖ εὐ-χαριστοῦντες (ptc v.3). ἱκανώσαντι aor. ptc -νόω (< ἱκανός sufficient) *make fit.* ὑμᾶς ⟦var. ἡμᾶς⟧. εἰς *for,* i.e. to receive. μερίς⁶ -ίδος ἡ (< μέρος⁸ part) *portion.* κλῆρος

13 apportioned *lot.* ‖ ἐρρύσατο aor. ῥύομαι *deliver.* σκότος⁸ *darkness.* μετ-έ-στησεν aor. μεθ-ίστημι *remove, trans-fer.*

14 τῆς ἀγάπης "Hebr." gen. = *beloved* §41. ‖ ἀπο-λύτρωσις⁴ *redemption, liberation.* ἄφ-εσις⁴ (< ἀφ-ίημι) *forgiveness.* ‖

15 εἰκών⁶ εἰκόνος ἡ *image.* ἀ-όρατος *un-seen; invisible.* πρωτό-τοκος (< πρῶτος + τίκτω give birth) *first-born* w. the primacy due to such, cf Rom 8:29. κτίσις⁴ *creation* ; as

16 gen. of comp. perh. *over all creation.* ‖ ἐν possibly of a personal agent, *by* (Mt 9:34). ἐ-κτίσθη aor. pass. κτίζω *create.* ὁρατός *visible.* εἴτε...εἴτε *whether...or.* θρόνος *throne,* θρ. ...ἐξουσίαι hierarchies of spiritual powers. κυριό-της⁶ -ότητος ἡ *dominion.* διά may include, along with instr. cause, also principal cause. ἀρχή *sovereignty,* cf

17 v.18. εἰς αὐτόν *for him.* ἔ-κτισται pf pass. ‖ πρό *before* (temporal). συν-έ-στηκεν pf (intr.) συν-ίστημι Lat. con-sto, *cohere, be established* ; on the tenses in vv. 16-17 §287. ‖

18 ἐκκλησίας appos. to σώματος. ἀρχή *source, beginning.* πρωτό-τοκος v.15. γένηται aor² subj. γίνομαι. πρωτεύων ptc

19 -εύω *take precedence, be pre-eminent.* ‖ εὐ-δόκησεν aor. -δοκέω w. acc. + inf. *be pleased to..., will to.* πλήρωμα⁷ (πληρόω fill) *fullness, plenitude,* of divine perfection 2:9. κατ-οικῆσαι aor. inf. -οικέω *dwell* ; aor. inceptive, *take up* his abode. ‖

20 ἀπο-κατ-αλλάξαι aor. inf. -αλλάσσω *reconcile.* εἰς αὐτόν *to himself* §211. εἰρηνο-ποιήσας aor. ptc -ποιέω *make peace.*

21 σταυρός *cross.* εἴτε...εἴτε *whether...or...* ‖ ὑμᾶς obj. of ἀπο-κατήλλαξεν (v.22), *and you...has he now reconciled.* ποτέ *sometime, once.* ὄντας ptc εἰμί. ἀπ-ηλλοτριωμένους pf ptc pass. -αλλοτριόω *alienate, estrange.* ἐχθρός *enemy.* διάνοια

22 *mind.* ‖ ἀπο-κατ-ήλλαξεν aor. σῶμα τ. σαρκὸς αὐτοῦ "Hebr." gen. *his mortal body.* παρα-στῆσαι aor. inf. παρ-ίστημι *present.* ἄ-μωμος *un-blemished.* ἀν-έγκλητος (ἀν- priv. + ἐγκαλέω accuse) *ir-reproachable.* κατ-εν-ώπιον αὐτοῦ *in his*

23 *sight* §208, 211. ‖ εἴ γε *if, that is,...* ἐπι-μένω τινί *remain in* sth. τε-θεμελιωμένοι *established, settled,* pf ptc pass. -λιόω (θεμέλιος foundation) *found* ; pass. *be grounded.*

ἑδραῖος (< ἕδρα seat) *stable*. μετα-κινούμενοι ptc -κινέομαι *remove* from one place to another, *shift about*; μὴ μ. *not to be moved from, immovable in*. ἐλπίς v.5. ἠκούσατε aor. ἀκούω τινός. κηρυχθέντος aor. ptc pass. κηρύσσω *preach*. κτίσις v.15, wt art. normally "every creature" but here almost certainly *the whole creation* §190. οὗ *of which*. ἐ-γενόμην aor² γίνομαι. διάκονος v.7. ||

πάθημα⁷ (< πάσχω suffer) *what is felt or suffered*, *suffering*. ἀντ-ανα-πληρόω *fill up/complete* in place of another, *contribute* one's *share to*. ὑστέρημα⁷ *what is wanting/lacking*. Man can add nothing to Christ's work of atonement but as a member of Christ his road to life likewise leads through sacrifice in the measure of his capacity. θλῖψις⁴ *suffering*. || οἰκο-νομία *administration*; *dispensation*, *arrangement*. δοθεῖσαν aor. ptc pass. δίδωμι. εἰς *for*. πληρῶσαι aor. inf. -ρόω: πλ. τὸν λόγον *complete* God's *work of evangelization*. || μυστήριον *mystery*, *secret* of God's plan of salvation. ἀπο-κε-κρυμμένον pf ptc pass. -κρύπτω *hide (away)*. γενεά *generation*; the repetition of ἀπό and art. distinguishing eternity from the beginnings of human history §184. ἐ-φανερώθη (aor. pass. -ρόω *reveal*) begins a new cstr after the break at τῶν γενεῶν. || ἠθέλησεν aor. θέλω. γνωρίσαι aor. inf. -ίζω *make known*. τί indir. interr. sc. ἐστίν. πλοῦτος⁸ *wealth*. ἐν (1st time) *among*. ὅ ἐστιν *which* (the mystery) *is*. ἐν (2nd time) *in*. ἐλπίς v.5. || κατ-αγγέλλω *proclaim*. νου-θετοῦντες (< νοῦς + τίθημι) ptc -τέω *admonish, advise*. διδάσκοντες ptc. πᾶς ἄνθρωπος wt art. *everyone*. σοφία v.9. παρα-στήσωμεν aor. subj. -ίστημι v.22. τέλειος *perfect*. || εἰς ὅ *to which end, for this*. καί after a rel. sts wt special significance §463. κοπιάω *labour*. ἀγωνιζόμενος *striving*, ptc -ίζομαι *take part in a contest* (ἀγών). ἐνέργεια *working, power*. ἐνεργουμένην ptc mid. -γέω w. impers. subject, *be at work/effective*. ἐν δυνάμει *with power, powerfully*. || εἰδέναι inf. οἶδα pf-pres. ἡλίκος *how great*. ἀγών⁶ ἀγῶνος ὁ *contest* in the arena, any *struggle*. ὅσοι = ποσῶν ὅσοι *all who, all the others who* (καί being inclusive of foregoing). ἑ-όρακαν (for -κασι) pf ὁράω: οὐχ ἑόρ. ...σαρκί *have not seen me in person*. || παρα-κληθῶσιν aor. subj. pass. -καλέω *encourage*. συμ-βιβασθέντες aor. ptc pass. -βιβάζω *bring together, unite*. πλοῦτος⁸ *wealth*. πληρο-φορία *conviction*. σύν-εσις⁴ *understanding*. ἐπί-γνωσις⁴ *knowledge*. μυστήριον 1:26. || θησαυ-

24

25

26

27

28

29

2

2

3

ρός *treasure.* σοφία 1:28. γνῶσις[4] *knowledge.* ἀπό-κρυφος
4 *hidden (away),* pred. ‖ παρα-λογίζηται subj. pass. -λογίζομαι
mis-construe, so *delude.* πιθανο-λογία *plausible argument(s).*
5 ‖ εἰ...καί *if, though.* τῇ σαρκί *in body, physically,* dat. of
manner §60. ἄπ-ειμι *be absent.* ἀλλά *yet* introducing the
apodosis. χαίρων ptc -ρω. βλέπων ptc -πω. τάξις[4] *military formation,* hence *order, discipline.* στερέωμα[7] a solid
body, so of army presenting a *solid front* ; met. *firmness,
steadfastness.* ‖

6   παρ-ε-λάβετε aor[2] παρα-λαμβάνω *receive* (as a tradition).
περι-πατεῖτε impv, pres. (continue to) *walk,* i.e. *live* 1:10. ‖
7 ἐρ-ριζ ωμένοι *rooted,* pf ptc pass. ῥιζόω *cause to root.* ἐπ-
οικο-δομούμενοι ptc pass. -δομέω *build on* (pres. ref. a
progressive building). βεβαιούμενοι ptc pass. βεβαιόω *make
firm* (βέβαιος), *establish.* τῇ πίστει *in the faith.* ἐ-διδάχθητε
aor. pass. διδάσκω. περισσεύοντες ptc -εύω *be* or *have
8 abundantly, be rich* in. εὐχαριστία *thanksgiving.* ‖ βλέπετε
(impv) μή *take care lest/that...not* §344. ἔσται fut. εἰμί.
συλ-αγ αγῶν ptc -αγωγέω (< σύλη *booty* + ἄγω) *take captive ;
despoil* ; met. *carry away* by e.g. specious argument,
βλέπετε μή...σ. *take care that someone does not come and
carry you away* with his theorizing. φιλο-σοφία *philosophy,*
here in unfavourable sense. κενός *empty, vain.* ἀπάτη
deceit. παρά-δοσις[4] *tradition.* στοιχεῖα τ. κόσμου Gal 4:3,
9 κατὰ τὰ στ. *based on the elements* of the world. ‖ κατ-οικέω
dwell. πλήρωμα[7] *fullness, plenitude.* θεότης[6] -τητος ἡ *deity,
Godhead* (distinguish from θειότης "divinity" which den.
a quality). σωματικῶς *embodied* ; or perh. *in reality* v.17
10 (σῶμα). ‖ πε-πληρ ωμένοι pf ptc pass. -ρόω. ἀρχή *sovereignty*
11 1:16. ‖ ἐν (1st time) *in.* περι-ε-τμήθητε aor. pass. -τέμνω
circumcise. περι-τομή *circumcision.* ἀ-χειρο-ποίητος *made
without the hand (of man).* ἐν (2nd time) *by.* ἀπ-έκ-δυσις[4]
divesting, taking off. σῶμα τ. σαρκός "Hebr." gen. *fleshly
body,* here not the physical but that which serves sin
§41. ἐν (3rd time) *with.* ἡ περιτομὴ τ. Χριστοῦ not only
that willed by Christ but that undergone "in Christ"
12 §38. ‖ συν-ταφέντες aor. ptc pass. -θάπτω τινί *bury together with.* βαπτισμός *baptism.* συν-ηγέρθητε aor. pass.
-εγείρω *raise together with.* ἐν-έργεια *working, power.* ἐγεί-
13 ραντος aor. ptc -ρω. ‖ ὄντας ptc εἰμί. παρά-πτωμα[7] (< παρα-
+ πίπτω) *lapse, trespass.* ἀκροβυστία *uncircumcision,* i.e.
unregenerate state. συν-ε-ζ ωο-ποίησεν aor. συν-ζωο-ποιέω

make one *alive with* another. **χαρισάμενος** aor. ptc -ίζομαι
bestow freely, hence *forgive.* ‖ **ἐξ-αλείψας** aor. ptc -αλείφω **14**
wipe away/out. **κατά** w. gen. *against.* **χειρό-γραφον** sth
hand-written, *manuscript, signature,* esp. a (signed) *certi-
ficate of indebtedness, bond,* χ. τ. δόγμασιν J. A. Robinson
suggests *subscription to the ordinances,* usu. transl. *the
bond expressed in decrees* or *the bond with its claims* (on
us). **δόγμα**[7] *decree.* **ὑπ-εν-αντίον** *against.* **καὶ αὐτό** introducing an additional statement. **ἦρκεν** pf αἴρω, *has once
for all removed,* pf. **μέσον** *middle,* ἐκ τοῦ μ. *from our midst.*
προσ-ηλώσας aor. ptc -ηλόω τί τινι (< ἧλος nail) *nail* sth
to sth. **σταυρός** *cross.* ‖ **ἀπ-εκ-δυσάμενος** aor. ptc -δύομαι **15**
take off a garment ; aor. ptc *having divested himself of /
shed* or *having disarmed* (mid. for himself) the supernatural
powers. **ἀρχή** v.10. **ἐ-δειγμάτισεν** aor. -τίζω *make an
example* (δεῖγμα[7]) *of, expose.* **παρ-ρησία** *frankness, openness,*
ἐν π. *openly, in public.* **θριαμβεύσας** aor. ptc -εύω *lead
around* (as, e.g., prisoners) *in a triumphal procession.*
ἐν αὐτῷ *by it* (the cross). ‖ **κρινέτω** impv 3rd sg κρίνω : **16**
μή...τις...κρ. *let no one judge.* **ἐν** *about, over* a matter of
βρῶσις[4] *eating.* **πόσις**[4] *drinking.* **μέρος**[8] *part ;* also in sense
of "category", ἐν μέρει *on the subject* of. **ἑορτή** *festival.*
νεο-μηνία *new month, new moon.* **σάββατον** *seventh day of
Jewish week, sabbath.* ‖ **σκιά** *shadow.* **μελλόντων** ptc μέλλω : **17**
τὰ μέλλοντα *things to come.* **σῶμα** here opp. σκιά, *substance,
reality.* **τοῦ Χριστοῦ** pred. "is of Christ", *belongs to Christ.* ‖
Inadequate knowledge about the nature of the heresy **18**
challenged by Paul renders the significance and therefore the transln of this v. uncertain. **κατα-βραβευέτω**
impv 3rd sg -βραβεύω (the act of a judge or umpire, βραβεύς) *give judgement against, disqualify.* **θέλων** (ptc) perh.
advl *willingly ;* but θέλω sts signifies *order, require,* so
θέλων ἐν *by insisting on ;* alternatively, in LXX esp., θ.
often transl. a Hebr. word = *take pleasure* in (Mk 12:38).
ταπεινο-φροσύνη *humility* is enjoined on Christians by the
Apostle in 3:12, here it clearly refers to some practice
of his opponents ; in view of the intimate connection
between the two in OT and contemporary literature,
others transl. *fasting,* cf βρῶσις, πόσις v.16. **θρησκεία**
cult ; θ. τ. ἀγγέλων usu. understood as obj. gen. = worship offered to angels, but subjective gen. cannot be ruled
out = worship (of God) by angels, participation in which

would supposedly be attained through mystical experience.
ἃ obj. of ἑόρακεν may be cstr w. ἐμβατεύων (as indicated
in our text by the foll. comma), or w. φυσιούμενος, and
may refer to ταπ. and θρ. or less specifically "that which"
he has seen. ἑ-όρακεν pf ὁράω. ἐμβατεύων ptc -εύω enter
into a place or possession ; search into, examine a matter ;
as t.t. in mystery religions, be initiated, as such may be
trans. or abs. Possible translns : entering into possession
of or searching into what he has seen ; or, being initiated
into what he saw ; or, if abs., which things (or, the things
which) he saw when he was being initiated. See below
(φυσιούμενος). εἰκῇ vainly, without reason. φυσιούμενος
ptc pass. -ιόω make one conceited ; pass. be inflated with
pride ; wt the comma after ἐμβατεύων, ἃ could well be
cstr w. φ. as acc. of respect : unreasonably inflated about
what he saw when he was being initiated. νοῦς νοός ὁ
mind, ν. τῆς σαρκός a mind dominated by the senses, his
sensuous mind. Whatever be the precise significance of
the above practices, the Apostle warns the Colossian Christians about those who were urging as the way to heaven
"traditions (v.11), injunctions, and teachings (v.22) de-
vised by men" to such a point that they were in danger
of relying on their own efforts and losing touch with the
19 Head. ‖ κρατῶν ptc -τέω seize, hold fast in various senses,
here hold on/fast to. σῶμα of the church as Christ's body
1:14, 24. ἀφή band, ligament. σύν-δεσμος bond ; in the
body perh. sinew. ἐπι-χορηγούμενον ptc pass. -χορηγέω
provide for, supply Eph 4:16 (ἐπιχορηγία). συμ-βιβαζόμενον
ptc pass. v.2. αὔξω var. of αὐξάνω cause to grow ; in HGk
grow (intr.), here w. cognate acc. αὔξησις⁴ growth, αὐ. τ.
θεοῦ growth derived from or willed by God. ‖
20   ἀπ-ε-θάνετε aor² ἀπο-θνήσκω: ἀ. ἀπό (instead of usu.
dat.) die to. στοιχεῖα τ. κόσμου v.8. τί; why? ζῶντες
ptc ζάω. δογματίζεσθε pass. -ίζω decree ; τί δογματίζεσθε;
21 why do you let yourselves be dictated to? ‖ ἅψῃ aor. subj.
ἅπτομαι touch, handle, hold. μηδέ and...not, nor. γεύσῃ
aor. subj. γεύομαι taste. θίγῃς aor² subj. θιγγάνω touch
22 (lightly). ‖ ἅ ἐστιν πάντα εἰς things which are all (destined)
for (Ac 8:20). φθορά decay. ἀπό-χρησις⁴ using up, wear
and tear. ἔν-ταλμα⁷ (< ἐν-πέλλομαι command) order,
instruction. διδασκαλία doctrine, under one art. w. ἐντάλ-
23 ματα. ‖ ἅ-τινα = ἅ §216. ἐστίν...ἔχοντα periphr. tense =

ἔχει. λόγος...σοφίας (v.3) the *name/reputation of wisdom.*
ἐθελο-θρησκία *self-chosen worship.* ταπεινο-φροσύνη v.18.
ἀ-φειδία (< ἀ- + φείδομαι spare) *rigour,* ἀφ. τ. σώματος
asceticism. τιμή *value* ; *honour* οὐκ ἐν τ. τινι *not of any
value.* πρός w. acc. prob. *against.* πλησμονή *satiety* ; *gra-
tification, indulgence.* ‖ συν-ηγέρθητε aor. pass. -εγείρω 3
raise one with another ; pass. *be raised with.* ἄνω *above,*
τὰ ἄνω *what is above.* ζητεῖτε impv ζητέω *aim at* (Lk
17:33). οὗ *where.* ἐν δεξιᾷ (sc. χειρί) *at the right hand.*
καθήμενος ptc -ημαι *be sitting, sit.* ‖ φρονεῖτε impv -νέω 2
think, pres. *give your minds to.* ‖ ἀπ-ε-θάνετε *you have* 3
died, aor² ἀπο-θνῄσκω. κέ-κρυπται pf pass. κρύπτω *hide.* ‖
φανερωθῇ aor. subj. pass. -ρόω *reveal,* pass. *appear.* ἡ ζωή 4
ὑμῶν appos. Χριστός. φανερωθήσεσθε fut. pass., φ. ἐν δόξῃ
will appear with him *in glory.* ‖ νεκρώσατε aor. impv -ρόω 5
put to death. μέλος³ *member.* πορνεία *fornication.* ἀ-καθαρσία *im-purity.* πάθος³ here (sensual) *passion.* ἐπι-θυμία
desire. κακός *evil.* πλεον-εξία (πλέον ἔχειν) *graspingness,
selfish greed* ; πλ. alone has the art. as if "that πλ. known
to all". εἰδωλο-λατρία *idolatry* Eph 5:5 (εἰδωλολάτρης). ‖
ὀργή just *wrath* of God. ἀ-πείθεια *dis-obedience,* υἱοὶ τῆς ἀπ. 6
those given to disobedience §43 [[var. om. ἐπί...ἀπειθείας]]. ‖
περι-ε-πατήσατε aor. constative περι-πατέω 1:10. ποτέ *some-* 7
time, once. ἐ-ζῆτε impf ζάω. ἐν τούτοις i.e. *in that way.* ‖
νυνί = νῦν. ἀπό-θεσθε aor² impv mid. -τίθημι mid. *put* 8
off or *away, rid oneself of.* τὰ πάντα *all* (these) *things.*
ὀργή *anger.* θυμός *rage.* κακία *malice.* βλασ-φημία *slander;*
rather than "blasphemy" here. αἰσχρο-λογία *obscenity,
foul language.* ‖ ψεύδεσθε impv -δομαι *tell an untruth, lie* 9
pres. *tell no more untruths !* ἀπ-εκ-δυσάμενοι aor. ptc -δύομαι
take/strip off as a garment, ptc causal, *for you have stripped
off.* παλαιός *old* Eph 4:22. πρᾶξις⁴ *deed,* pl. *behaviour.* ‖
ἐν-δυσάμενοι aor. ptc -δύομαι *have on, wear* ; aor. *put on* 10
oneself. νέος *new* (temporal ; καινός ref. quality). ἀνα-
καινούμενον *being renewed,* ptc pass. -καινόω *renew.* εἰς
leading to. ἐπί-γνωσις⁴ *knowledge.* εἰκών⁶ εἰκόνος ἡ *image,*
κατ᾽ εἰκ. κτλ. *in the image...,* a knowledge resulting in
likeness to its object. κτίσας aor. ptc κτίζω *create,* τοῦ κτ.
of the one who created. ‖ ὅπου *where* (i.e. in the new state). 11
ἔνι = ἐν w. ἐστίν understood (= ἔνεστιν), *there is.* Ἕλλην⁶
-νος ὁ *Greek.* περι-τομή *circumcision* 2:11. ἀκροβυστία *uncircumcision* 2:13. βάρβαρος *non-Greek,* esp. not speaking

Greek and so illiterate. **Σκύθης**[3] *Scythian* as typifying
12 barbarism. **ἐλεύθερος** *free.* ‖ **ἐν-δύσασθε** aor. impv. **ἐκ-λεκτός** *elect, chosen.* **ἠγαπημένος** pf ptc pass. ἀγαπάω. **σπλάγχνα** τά *entrails* as seat of feelings, cf Eng. "heart", σ. οἰκτιρμοῦ Phil. 2:1, "Hebr." gen. *feelings of compassion, compassion* §40. **χρηστότης**[6] -ότητος ἡ *goodness, kindness.* **ταπεινο-φροσύνη** *humility.* **πραΰτης**[6] -ύτητος ἡ *gentleness.*
13 **μακρο-θυμία** (long-temper) *patience.* ‖ **ἀν-εχόμενοι** ptc -έχομαί τινος *bear/put up with* one. **χαριζόμενοι** ptc -ζομαί τινι *give freely ; forgive.* ἑ-αυτοῖς for ὑμῖν αὐτοῖς §209 or ἀλλήλοις. **ἔχῃ** subj. ἔχω. **μομφή** *cause for blaming* (μέμφομαι),
14 *complaint.* **ἐ-χαρίσατο** aor. ‖ **ἐπὶ πᾶσιν** *above all.* **ὅ ἐστιν** *that is to say,* i.e. **σύν-δεσμος** *bond.* **τελειότης** -τητος ἡ *perfection ;* love ensures the presence of all the virtues
15 that go to make up perfection. ‖ **βραβευέτω** impv 3rd sg -εύω *preside* as a judge/umpire (βραβεύς). **ἐ-κλήθητε** aor. pass. καλέω. **εὐ-χάριστος** *thankful.* **γίνεσθε** impv γίνομαι
16 in sense of *show/prove yourselves ! be !* I Cor 14:20. ‖ **ἐν-οικείτω** impv 3rd sg -οικέω *dwell in.* **πλουσίως** *richly.* **διδάσκοντες** ptc -σκω; ptc wt subject, prob. standing for impv, cf Rom 12:9ff. §373. **νου-θετοῦντες** ptc -θετέω (< νοῦς + τίθημι) *admonish, advise.* ἑ-αυτούς for ἀλλήλους. **ψαλμός** *song of praise* accompanied on the harp. **ὕμνος** *hymn.* **ᾠδή** *song.* **πνευματικός** *spiritual.* **ἐν [τῇ] χάριτι** *by grace ;* if read wt τῇ perh. *with thankfulness.* **ᾄδοντες**
17 ptc **ᾄδω** *sing.* ‖ **ὅ τι ἐάν** (= ἄν) *what-ever.* **ποιῆτε** subj. ποιέω. **πάντα** neut. pl. *everything,* understand an impv = "do". **εὐχαριστοῦντες** ptc -τέω *give thanks.* ‖
18 αἱ **γυναῖκες** nom. w. art. for voc. §33. **ὑπο-τάσσεσθε** impv pass. -τάσσω *put under ; subject ;* pass. w. dat. *subordinate oneself/be submissive* to. **ἀν-ῆκεν** impf -ήκει impers., *it is proper, one should,* Eph 5:4 §319. ‖ **ἀγαπᾶτε**
19 impv -πάω. **πικραίνεσθε** impv pass. -αίνω *embitter ;* pass.
20 *be bitter,* π. πρός τινα *be sharp with* one. ‖ **τὰ τέκνα** voc. v.18 (αἱ γυναῖκες). **ὑπ-ακούετε** impv -ακούω τινί *obey* one. **γονεύς**[5] *parent.* **κατὰ πάντα** *in everything.* **εὐ-άρεστος** *pleasing.* **ἐν κυρίῳ** *in the Lord,* i.e. among Christians. ‖
21 **ἐρεθίζετε** impv -ίζω *rouse, provoke.* **ἀ-θυμῶσιν** subj. -θυμέω
22 *be despondent, lack spirit.* ‖ **κατὰ σάρκα** *earthly.* **κύριος** *master.* **ὀφθαλμο-δουλία** "eye-service", i.e. service under the eye of the master. **ἀνθρωπ-άρεσκος** *one currying favour.* **ἁπλότης**[6] -τητος ἡ *single-mindedness.* **φοβούμενοι**

ptc φοβέομαι. ‖ ὃ ἐὰν ποιῆτε v.17. ἐκ ψυχῆς *with your* 23
(whole) heart. ἐργάζεσθε *work* (at it), impv -ζομαι. ‖
εἰδότες ptc pf-pres. οἶδα. ἀπο-λήμψεσθε fut. -λαμβάνω *re-* 24
ceive from. ἀντ-από-δοσις⁴ (ἀντ-απο-δίδωμι repay) *reward.*
κληρο-νομία *inheritance,* w. art. den. eternal life, gen.
epexeg. "consisting in". δουλεύετε impv -εύω τινί *serve*
one. ‖ ἀ-δικῶν ptc -δικέω *do wrong,* ὁ ἀδ. *wrongdoer.* 25
κομίσεται *will be requited for,* fut. mid. -ίζω *bring*; mid.
receive; *get back.* ἠδίκησεν aor. ἀδικέω: ὁ ἠδ. "that
which he did wrong", *the wrong he did.* προσωπο-λημψία
partiality, favouritism (Eph 6:9). ‖ τὸ δίκαιον *justice.* 4
ἰσότης⁶ -τητος ἡ *equity*; *fairness.* παρ-έχεσθε impv -έχομαι
provide; π. τινι δίκαιον *show justice* to one. εἰδότες *in*
the knowledge that 3:24. κύριος 3:22. ‖

     προσ-ευχή *prayer.* προσ-καρτερεῖτε impv -καρτερέω 2
(< προσ- + καρτερός staunch) *remain constant, continue*
faithful. γρηγοροῦντες ptc -γορέω (vb formed from pf
(ἐγρήγορα) of ἐγείρω) *be watchful/alert.* ἐν (2nd time) of
concomitant circumstances (sociative) *with.* εὐ-χαριστία
thanksgiving. ‖ προσ-ευχόμενοι ptc -εύχομαι. ἅμα *at the* 3
same time. ἀν-οίξη aor. subj. -οίγω. θύρα *door,* met. an
opening. ὁ λόγος t.t. for *the Christian message, the gospel.*
λαλῆσαι aor. inf. λαλέω. μυστήριον *mystery, secret.* δέ-δεμαι
pf pass. δέω *bind.* ‖ ἵνα renewing the previous ἵνα, "pray- 4
ing that...(and) that...". φανερώσω aor. subj. -ρόω *make*
clear or *plain.* ‖ ἐν v.2. σοφία *wisdom,* ἐν σ. *wisely.* περι- 5
πατεῖτε impv. ἔξω *outside,* οἱ ἔξω *outsiders, non-Christians.*
ἐξ-αγοραζόμενοι *buy back* ?to make better use of, *exploit*
Eph 5:16. ‖ λόγος *speech,* understand *may/let your speech* 6
be. πάν-τοτε *always.* ἐν v.2, ἐν χάριτι *courteous, amiable.*
ἅλας ἅλατος τό *salt.* ἠρτυμένος pf ptc pass. ἀρτύω *season.*
εἰδέναι inf. pf-pres. οἶδα, inf. final or consec. εἷς ἕκαστος
each individual/person. ἀπο-κρίνεσθαι inf. -κρίνομαι. ‖

     τὰ κατ' ἐμέ *my circumstances, how I am faring* Eph 7
1:15 §130. γνωρίσει *will let you know,* fut. -ίζω *make*
known. ἀγαπητός *beloved.* πιστός *faithful.* σύν-δουλος *fel-*
low-servant. ‖ ἔ-πεμψα aor. πέμπω, epistolary aor. Eph 8
6:22. εἰς αὐτὸ τοῦτο *precisely for this*:... (τοῦτο ref. what
follows §213). γνῶτε aor² subj. γινώσκω, inceptive aor.
come to know, learn. τὰ περὶ ἡμῶν *all about us.* παρα-
καλέσῃ aor. subj. -καλέω Eph 6:22. ‖ ἐξ ὑμῶν who is *one* 9
of you. τὰ ὧδε *the news from here.* ‖ ἀσπάζομαι *greet.* 10

συν-αιχμ-άλωτος (< συν- + αἰχμή spear + ἁλίσκομαι be captured) *fellow-prisoner*. ἀνεψιός *cousin*. ἐ-λάβετε aor² λαμβάνω. ἐάν here approximating in meaning to ὅταν §322n.
ἔλθῃ aor² subj. ἔρχομαι. δέξασθε *you must welcome*, aor.
11 impv δέχομαι *receive*. ‖ λεγόμενος *called*, ptc pass. λέγω.
ὄντες ptc εἰμί. περι-τομή *circum-cision*. συν-εργός *fellow-
worker*, pred. εἰς *for*. οἵ-τινες *who are such that, who are
the kind* to be. ἐ-γενήθησαν aor. dep. (= ἐγένοντο) γίνομαι
12 §229. παρ-ηγορία *consolation*. ‖ ὁ ἐξ ὑμῶν v.9. πάντοτε v.6.
ἀγωνιζόμενος ptc -ζομαι *take part in a contest* (ἀγών), *strive*,
here as it were w. God. προσευχή v.2. σταθῆτε aor.
subj. pass. ἵστημι class. *that you may be made to stand/
upheld*, but in HGk often w. mid. (intr.) force, *that you
may stand* §231. τέλειος *perfect*. πε-πληρο-φορημένοι pf
ptc pass. -φορέω *assure fully, convince*, mid. *be absolutely
convinced, feel certain*. ἐν παντὶ θελήματι *as to every (aspect
13 of) God's will*. ‖ μαρτυρέω τινί *bear witness* in favour of
14 one. πόνος *labour, hard work*. ‖ ἰατρός *doctor*. ἀγαπητός
15 v.7. ‖ ἀσπάσασθε aor. impv ἀσπάζομαι. κατ' οἶκον αὐτῆς *at
16 her house*. ‖ ἀνα-γνωσθῇ aor. subj. pass. -γινώσκω *read*.
παρ' ὑμῖν *among you*. ποιήσατε ἵνα (aor. impv ποιέω) "make
it that", i.e. *see that* it is read, *arrange for* it to be read.
τὴν ἐκ Λ. *that from L.*, i.e. P's epistle to the Laodiceans
which was to be sent on "from L." to Colossae. ἀνα-
17 γνῶτε aor² subj. ‖ εἴπατε aor² impv λέγω. βλέπε...ἵνα impv
βλέπω *see to...that...* διακονία *ministry*. παρ-έ-λαβες aor²
18 παρα-λαμβάνω *receive*. πληροῖς subj. -ρόω. ‖ ἀσπασμός
greeting. μνημονεύετε impv -εύω τινός *remember* sth. δεσμός
chain, bond. ‖

I THESSALONIANS

ἐν θεῷ...Χριστῷ serves to distinguish the Christian **1**
from civil assemblies and those of the Jews ; ἐν of personal relationship, here ref. the local Christian community as a whole. θεὸς πατήρ wt art., already a fixed phrase
Gal 1:1. χάρις καὶ εἰρήνη Rom 1:7. ‖

εὐχαριστέω *give thanks.* πάν-τοτε *always.* περί = **2**
ὑπέρ Eph 1:16, Phil 1:8 §96 ; ass. w. εὐχαριστοῦμεν. μνεία
remembrance. ποιούμενοι ptc mid. ποιέω: μν. ποιοῦμαι *remember, mention,* esp. before God ; class. use of mid. where
π. combines w. its obj. to express the same idea as the
cognate vb (here = μνημονεύοντες) Rom 1:9 ; Eph 1:16
§227. προσ-ευχή *prayer.* ἀ-δια-λείπτως *continually.* ‖ μνη- **3**
μονεύοντες ptc -εύω *remember* ; *mention* μν. τινός...ἔμπρο-
σθεν τ. θεοῦ *remember* someone or sth *before God.* ὑμῶν
your, subjective gen. ἔργον τῆς πίστεως action inspired
by faith and carried out in faith. κόπος *labour.* ὑπο-
μονὴ τῆς ἐλπίδος *constancy* in hope or the *patience* involved
in the practice of hope. ἐλπίς⁶ -ίδος ἡ *hope.* τοῦ κυρίου
gen. not exclusively obj. or subjective : the hope Christ
gives and which looks to his coming. Published translations reveal a variety of interpretations of the gens.
in this v. ἔμπροσθεν *before, in the presence of.* ‖ εἰδότες **4**
ptc pf-pres. οἶδα. ἠγαπημένοι pf ptc pass. ἀγαπάω. ἐκ-
λογή t.t. for *election* by God. ‖ ἐ-γενήθη aor. dep. (for **5**
mid. ἐγένετο §229), ἐγ. εἰς came to. ἐν instr. *by* or sociative *with/in.* λόγῳ μόνον *in bare words.* ἐν πνεύματι ἁγίῳ
wt art. stressing not the Person so much as his activity
in inspiring his preachers §181. πληρο-φορία *conviction.*
οἷος *such (as),* οἷοι ἐγενήθημεν aor. dep. *the kind of men
we were.* δι' ὑμᾶς final, *on your account, for your own sake*
§112. ‖ μιμητής³ *imitator.* δεξάμενοι aor. ptc δέχομαι *re-* **6**
ceive, welcome. θλῖψις⁴ (< θλίβω press) *distress, suffering,*
imposed by persecution from without and so not incom-
patible w. interior joy ; ἐν of concomitant circumstances,
ἐν θ. πολλῇ *with all its attendant suffering.* χαρά *joy,* ass. w.

7 δεξάμενοι. ‖ γενέσθαι aor² inf. τύπος *example*. πιστεύουσιν
ptc dat. pl. -εύω. τῇ Μ. καί...τ. 'Α. signifies two different
provinces, cf v.8 τῇ Μ. καὶ 'Α. which (if ἐν τῇ is to be om.)
brackets the two provinces opp. παντὶ τόπῳ *everywhere*
8 *else* §184. ‖ ἐξ-ήχηται *resounds*, pf pass. -ηχέω *sound forth*
(trans.) ; pass. *be caused to sound forth*, and intr. *sound
forth*. ἐξ-ελήλυθεν pf² -έρχομαι: ἡ πίστις ὑμῶν...ἐξε. (*the
report of) your faith has spread*. χρεία *need*. ἡμᾶς subject
9 of λαλεῖν (inf. λαλέω). τι after a neg., *anything*. ‖ ἀπ-
αγγέλλω *report, declare*. ὁποῖος Lat. *qualis, what sort of*.
εἴσ-οδος ἡ *entrance* and, by extension, *reception* given on
entrance. ἔσχομεν aor² ἔχω, aor. inceptive, *get*. πρός w.
acc. *at your hands, among*. ἐπ-ε-στρέψατε aor. -στρέφω *turn,
convert*; also intr. *be converted*. εἴδωλον *idol*. δουλεύειν
inf. -εύω τινί *serve one*. Anarthrous θεῷ foll. τὸν θεόν
highlights a contrast in nature §171. ζῶντι ptc ζάω.
10 ἀληθινός *true, real*. ‖ ἀνα-μένειν τι *wait for* sth. ἤγειρεν aor.
ἐγείρω. ῥυόμενον ptc ῥύομαι *deliver, rescue*, τὸν ῥ. ἡμᾶς
prob. *who rescues us* ; or, standing for obsolescent fut.
ptc, *who will rescue us*. ὀργή just *wrath* of God. ἐρχομένης
coming, ptc ἔρχομαι, pres. replacing fut. ptc and (as in
Eng.) ref. fut. equally w. the present §282. ‖

2 εἴσοδος, πρός 1:9. κενός *empty, vain, fruitless*. γέ-
2 γονεν pf² γίνομαι. ‖ προ-παθόντες aor² ptc -πάσχω *suffer
before*. ὑβρισθέντες aor. ptc pass. -ίζω *treat with insolence*
(ὕβρις), *insult*. ἐ-παρ-ρησιασάμεθα aor. παρ-ρησιάζομαι *speak
freely, openly, boldly* ; w. inf. *have the courage to...* ἐν τῷ
θεῷ ass. w. λαλῆσαι aor. inf. λαλέω. ἀγών⁶ -ῶνος ὁ *contest*,
3 ἐν πολλῷ ἀ. *amid strong opposition/contestation*. ‖ παρά-
κλησις⁴ (< παρακαλέω) *appeal*. πλάνη *error*. ἀ-καθαρσία
im-purity, here *mixed motives, in-sincerity*. δόλος pro-
4 perly a "bait" ; *deceit*, ἐν δ. *by subterfuge* §117. ‖ δε-δοκι-
μάσμεθα *we have been adjudged fit*, pf pass. -άζω *put to
the test*, hence *approve*. πιστευθῆναι *to be entrusted*, aor.
inf. pass. -εύω τί τινι *entrust* sth to one ; in pass. the person
becomes subject, the thing acc. of respect : πιστεύομαί τι
I am entrusted with sth §72. οὕτως *accordingly*. ἀρέσκον-
5 τες ptc -σκω τινί *try to please one*. δοκιμάζοντι ptc. ‖ ποτέ
sometime, once ; w. neg. *ever*. κολακεία *flattery*, λόγῳ
κολακείας "Hebr." gen. *flattering speech, verbal flattery*
§40. ἐ-γενήθημεν aor. dep. πρό-φασις⁴ *pretext*. πλεον-εξία
6 *rapacity*, Col 3:5. μάρτυς⁶ -υρος ὁ *witness*, pred. ‖ ζητοῦν-

τες *looking for, with an eye on,* ptc ζητέω. ἐκ for ἀπό §87. δόξα *honour.* ‖ δυνάμενοι ptc -μαι, ptc concessive, *although we are capable of.* βάρος[8] *weight ;* ἐν β. εἰμί *impose* one's *weight* or *authority.* ὡς *as, qua.* νήπιος *infant* ⟦var. ἤπιοι *gentle*⟧. ὡς ἐάν (= ἄν). τροφός ἡ (< τρέφω feed) *nursing mother.* θάλπη subj. -πω *cherish.* ‖ ὁμειρόμενοι ptc -ρομαί τινος *long for* one. εὐ-δοκέω *consider good,* w. inf. *be determined to.* μετα-δοῦναι aor[2] inf. -δίδωμι *share.* ψυχή the *vital principle ;* the *self.* δι-ότι = ὅτι *because, for.* ἀγαπητός *very dear.* ἐ-γενήθητε *had become,* rel. past §290. ‖ μνημονεύω τινός (also τι) *remember* sth. κόπος *labour.* μόχθος *toil.* νυκτὸς καὶ ἡμέρας (by) *day* and (by) *night,* gen. of time "within which". ἐργαζόμενοι ptc -ζομαι *work.* πρὸς τὸ μή w. inf. *in order not to.* ἐπιβαρῆσαι aor. inf. -βαρέω τινά *be a burden* (βάρος[8]) *to* one. τις after a neg. *any, anyone.* ἐ-κηρύξαμεν aor. -ρύσσω *preach.* ‖ μάρτυς v.5. ὁσίως *devoutly.* δικαίως *uprightly.* ἀ-μέμπτως *blamelessly.* πιστεύουσιν 1:7. ἐ-γενήθημεν *we behaved.* ‖ καθ-ά-περ = καθώς. εἰς ἕκαστος *each one.* ‖ παρα-καλοῦντες ptc -καλέω. παρα-μυθούμενοι ptc -μυθέομαι *console, cheer.* μαρτυρόμενοι ptc -ρομαι *affirm,* also *conjure, implore.* The ptcs are prob. to be understood as indics, *you know how we encouraged...each one of you like a father his children ;* otherwise ἐγενήθημεν must be understood. εἰς τό w. inf. *that...* indicating the content of the exhortation. περι-πατεῖν inf. -πατέω in ethical sense, *behave, live.* ἀξίως (adj. ἄξιος) w. gen. *in a way worthy of.* καλοῦντος ptc καλέω, pres. atemporal, because God's will is unchangeable and eternal §372. βασιλεία and δόξα under one art. suggesting an eschatological interpretation for βασιλεία as well §184. ‖ In the expression διὰ τοῦτο καί, the καί seems stereotyped in this position though referring to the vb εὐχαριστοῦμεν *and for this reason we thank* §462. εὐχαριστέω, ἀδιαλείπτως 1:2. παρα-λαβόντες aor[2] ptc -λαμβάνω *receive* (esp. as sth handed down (παρα-δοθέν) by tradition). ἀκοή *hearing ;* also a *report, message* Jn 12:38 = Is 53:1. τοῦ θεοῦ sc. λόγον, pred. *as* (the *word*) *of God.* ἐ-δέξασθε aor. δέχομαι *receive.* ἀληθῶς *truly, really.* ὅς ref. λόγος. καί foll. a rel. prn often wt special significance §463. ἐν-εργεῖται mid. -εργέω act. and mid. (w. non-personal subject) *be at work, be active.* πιστεύουσιν 1:7. ‖ μιμηταὶ ἐγενήθητε *you became copies.* οὐσῶν ptc εἰμί. τὰ

7

8

9

10

11,12

13

14

αὐτά *the same things*; i.e. *in the same way*. ἐ-πάθετε aor²
πάσχω *suffer*. συμ-φυλέτης³ (< συν- + φυλή tribe) *fellow-*
15 *countryman*. ‖ ἀπο-κτεινάντων aor. ptc -κτείνω. ἐκ-διω-
ξάντων aor. ptc -διώκω *drive out*. ἀρεσκόντων v.4. ἐν-αν-
16 τίος *contrary*; *hostile*. ‖ κωλυόντων ptc -ύω *hinder*, w.
inf. *hinder from*. λαλῆσαι aor. inf. λαλέω. σωθῶσιν aor.
subj. pass. σῴζω. εἰς τό w. inf. in sense between final
and consec. ἀνα-πληρῶσαι aor. inf. -πληρόω *fill up*, *complete*
the measure of. πάν-τοτε *at all times*. ἔ-φθασεν aor. φθάνω
(HGk) *have come*. ὀργή 1:10. τέλος⁸ *end*; εἰς τ. *to the
full*, *to the utmost*. ‖
17   ἀπ-ορφανισθέντες aor. pass. -ορφανίζω *make an orphan*;
pass. *be bereft*. πρὸς καιρὸν ὥρας *for the time being*. προσώπῳ οὐ καρδίᾳ *to sight*, *not to mind*. περισσοτέρως *more
than ever*. ἐ-σπουδάσαμεν aor. -άζω *be eager*. ἰδεῖν aor²
18 inf. ὁράω. ἐπι-θυμία *desire*, *longing*. ‖ δι-ότι v.8. ἠθελή-
σαμεν aor. θέλω. ἐλθεῖν aor² inf. ἔρχομαι. ἅπαξ *once*.
δίς *twice*, καὶ ἅπαξ κ. δίς *more than once*. ἐν-έ-κοψεν aor.
19 ἐγ-κόπτω *block*, *hinder*. Σατανᾶς *adversary*, *Satan*. ‖ ἐλπίς⁶
-ίδος ἡ *hope*. χαρά *joy*. στέφανος *crown*. καύχησις⁴ *boasting*, (matter for) *pride*, στέφανος καυχήσεως *crown in which
we glory*. οὐχί interr. expecting the answer "Yes", οὐχὶ
καὶ ὑμεῖς; *is it not you?* ἔμ-προσθεν *before*, *in the presence
of*. παρ-ουσία *coming*; *presence*; t.t. for the *advent* of
3 Christ. ‖ δι-ό *so* (*it was*). μηκ-έτι *no longer*. στέγοντες
ptc στέγω *endure*, *bear*. εὐ-δοκήσαμεν aor. -δοκέω *consider
good*; *resolve*, *determine*. κατα-λειφθῆναι aor. inf. pass.
2 -λείπω *leave behind*. ‖ ἐ-πέμψαμεν aor. πέμπω. συν-εργός
fellow-worker, *helper*. ἐν τῷ εὐαγγελίῳ *in* (*spreading*) *the
gospel*, Rom 1:9, cf Phil 2:22. εἰς τό w. inf. final giving
the purpose of the mission. στηρίξαι aor. inf. -ίζω *strengthen*, *make resolute*. παρα-καλέσαι aor. inf. -καλέω. ὑπέρ =
3 περί *concerning*, *in* (the matter of) *your faith* §96. ‖ τό
w. acc. + inf. indicating scope of the exhortation, cf 4:1.
σαίνεσθαι inf. pass. σαίνω, orig. of a dog, *wag the tail*;
hence pass. *be agitated/disturbed*. ἐν instr. *by*. θλῖψις⁴
trouble, *suffering*, esp. of persecution. αὐτοί (*you*) *yourselves*. κεῖμαι *be placed/set*, hence *be destined*, cf Ac 14:22. ‖
4 πρὸς ὑμᾶς 1:9. προ-ε-λέγομεν impf iterative προλέγω *fore-
warn*, *tell beforehand*. θλίβεσθαι inf. pass. θλίβω *press*;
pass. *have pressure brought to bear on one*, *be persecuted*. ‖
5 κἀγώ = καὶ ἐγώ. διὰ τοῦτο κἀγώ...ἔπεμψα (v. 2) *and for this*

reason I...sent 2:13. μηκέτι στέγων v.l. ἔ-πεμψα v.2.
εἰς τό w. inf. final. γνῶναι aor² inf. γινώσκω, aor. inceptive
come to know, find out. μή πως *whether perhaps.* ἐ-πείρασεν
had tempted, aor. -άζω *tempt*; indic. ref. past fact
§344. ὁ πειράζων ptc as noun, *the tempter* §371. κενός
2:1, εἰς κ. *in vain, for nothing.* γένηται *might be,* future
and still avoidable, aor² subj. γίνομαι. κόπος *labour.* ‖
ἄρτι *now.* ἐλθόντος aor² ptc ἔρχομαι, gen. abs. *now that* 6
T. has come...and... εὐ-αγγελισαμένου aor. ptc -αγγελίζομαί
τί τινι *bring good news of* sth to one. μνεία *recollection,*
remembrance. πάν-τοτε *always.* ἐπι-ποθοῦντες ptc -ποθέω
long, have a longing. ἰδεῖν aor² inf. ὁράω. καθ-ά-περ =
καθώς. καί ἡμεῖς ὑμᾶς *as we too (have to see) you.* ‖ παρ-ε- 7
κλήθημεν *we have been consoled,* aor. pass. παρα-καλέω.
ἐφ' ὑμῖν *about you*; ἐπί w. dat. den. obj. (and cause) of
the emotion §126. ἐπί (2nd time) *on the occasion of, in.*
ἀνάγκη *distress.* θλῖψις v.3, a certain unity may be implied by the one art. §184. διά *through, by.* ‖ ζῶμεν cf 8
Eng. idiom "it is life to us". ἐάν w. indic. instead of εἰ,
a simple condition §330f. στήκω *stand firm,* Phil 1:27. ‖
εὐ-χαριστία *thanks(giving).* ἀντ-απο-δοῦναι aor² inf. -δίδωμι 9
give in exchange, εὐχαριστίαν ἀνταποδ. ἐπί *return thanks for.*
ἐπί w. dat. giving grounds for an action or emotion §126.
χαρά *joy,* cognate dat. §62. ἔμπροσθεν 2:19. ‖ νυκτός καί 10
ἡμέρας 2:9. ὑπερ-εκ-περισσοῦ adv. *exceedingly*; ref. prayer,
most earnestly. δεόμενοι ptc δέομαι *beseech, beg.* εἰς ...
w. inf. *that...* here den. the content of the prayer 2:12.
ἰδεῖν v.6. κατ-αρτίσαι aor. inf. -αρτίζω (< κατα- + ἄρτιος
complete) *restore to proper condition, mend*; *make good,*
complete. ὑστέρημα⁷ (< ὑστερέω come late and so lack)
what is lacking, a *want.* ‖ κατ-ευθύναι aor. opt. 3rd sg 11
-ευθύνω (< εὐθύς straight) *straighten out*; so *prosper* a
journey; opt. expressing a wish, *may God...prosper our*
way. αὐτός...ὁ θεός...Ἰησοῦς *God our Father himself and*
our Lord Jesus; too much must not be read into the sg
vb which has many parallels, but undoubtedly Jesus is
presented as in intimate association with God the Father,
in unity of action, and as one to whom prayer may be
addressed. ‖ πλεονάσαι aor. opt. -άζω *increase*; trans. τινά 12
τινι *cause* one *to increase in* sth. περισσεύσαι aor. opt.
-εύω *have more than enough*; trans. π. τινά τι *make* one *rich*
in sth. καθάπερ (v.6)...ὑμᾶς *as we (do) to you.* ‖ εἰς τό w. 13

inf. final. **στηρίξαι** v.2. **ἄ-μεμπτος** *blame-less.* **ἁγιωσύνη** *holiness.* **ἔμπροσθεν, παρουσία** 2:19. **οἱ ἅγιοι** Eph 1:1. ||

4 **λοιπόν** adv. *for the rest* ; *finally.* **ἐρωτάω** *ask* ; later sense, *appeal to.* **ἵνα** *that,* for obj. inf. §407. **παρ-ε-λάβετε** aor² -**λαμβάνω** *receive* (as a tradition). **τό** comprises the whole indir. question. **περι-πατεῖν** inf. 2:12. **ἀρέσκειν** inf. 2:4. **ἵνα** takes up the previous **ἵνα**, (*and*) *that.* **περισσεύητε** subj. -**εύω** *excel* I Cor 14:12, π. μᾶλλον *do still bet-*

2 *ter.* || **τίς** as indir. interr. **παρ-αγγελία** *precept, rule.* **ἐ-δώκαμεν** aor. δίδωμι. **διά** here approximating to ἐν, *in the*

3 *name of/on the authority of.* || **τοῦτο** ref. what follows §213. **ἁγιασμός** *sanctification.* **ἀπ-έχεσθαι** inf. -ἔχομαι (mid.) *abstain/keep away from.* **ὑμᾶς** subject of ἀπέχ. **πορνεία** *for-*

4 *nication.* || **εἰδέναι** inf. pf-pres. οἶδα, w. inf. *know how to.* **σκεῦος**⁸ *utensil,* often met., Rom 9:22f. and II Cor 4:7 of the *body* ; in rabbinic use, *wife,* which best suits the normal meaning of κτᾶσθαι. **κτᾶσθαι** inf. κτάομαι *acquire* ; if σκεῦος is not to be equated w. "wife" κτ. must be understood as *gain possession* (= control) *of.* **τιμή** *honour.* ||

5 **πάθος**⁸ what is experienced or suffered ; *passion,* Rom 1:26. **ἐπι-θυμία** *desire.* **καθ-ά-περ** 3:6. **εἰδότα** ptc neut.

6 pl. pf-pres. οἶδα. || **ὑπερ-βαίνειν** inf. -βαίνω *go beyond* ; *transgress* ; like ἀπέχεσθαι and εἰδέναι appos. to ἁγιασμός. **πλεον-εκτεῖν** inf. -εκτέω (πλέον + ἔχω) *take advantage of, defraud.* **πρᾶγμα**⁷ *matter, affair, business* ; the art. indicates sth already mentioned and points to sexual irregularities (as ἀκαθαρσία does in v.7) ; apart from these factors πλεονεκτεῖν ἐν πρ. could well refer to dishonesty in business dealings. **δι-ότι** *for.* **ἔκ-δικος** *executor of justice.* **τούτων** neut. **προ-είπαμεν** aor² (for -ομεν §489) -λέγω *fore-warn, tell already.* **δι-ε-μαρτυράμεθα** aor. δια-μαρτύρομαι *testify*

7 *solemnly.* || **ἐ-κάλεσεν** aor. καλέω. **ἐπί** w. dat. *to,* den. purpose, "with a view to, for", cf Gal 5:13, Eph 2:10 §129. **ἀ-καθαρσία** *im-purity.* **ἐν** ?abridged expression for (*to live*) *in* or ? "pregnant" cstr after καλέω understood

8 to imply motion to §99. **ἁγιασμός** v.3. || **τοι-γαρ-οῦν** *consequently.* **ἀ-θετῶν** ptc -θετέω (ἄθετος (not established)) *disregard.* **διδόντα** ptc δίδωμι: ὁ δ. *who gives,* pres. atemporal

9 (it is God's nature to give) §372. || **φιλ-αδελφία** *love of the brethren, brotherly love.* **χρεία** *need,* οὐ χ. ἔχετε γράφειν "you have not need of...", i.e. *you do not need* (*us*) *to write...* **αὐτοί...ὑμεῖς** *you yourselves.* **θεο-δίδακτος** *taught*

by God, i.e. his inspiration in hearts united to him by love.
εἰς τὸ ἀγαπᾶν (inf. -πάω) taught...*to love.* ‖ καὶ γάρ *for actually.* 10
ποιεῖτε *you practise.* περισσεύειν μᾶλλον v.1. ‖ φιλο-τιμεῖ- 11
σθαι inf. -τιμέομαι *have as* one's *ambition, make a point of.*
ἡσυχάζειν inf. -άζω *be quiet/silent* ; *live in tranquillity.*
πράσσειν inf. πράσσω *practise,* esp. *carry on, attend to a*
business. τὰ ἴδια *one's own affairs/business.* ἐργάζεσθαι
inf. -ζομαι. χερσίν dat. pl. χείρ. παρ-ηγγείλαμεν aor. -αγ-
γέλλω τινί *charge, command.* ‖ περι-πατῆτε subj. 2:12. 12
εὐ-σχημόνως *properly.* ἔξω *outside,* οἱ ἔξω *outsiders, non-*
Christians. ἔχητε subj. ἔχω: μηδενὸς χρείαν ἔχ. *that you*
may not have need of/depend on anybody or, *if* μηδενός is
neut. *that you may not lack for anything.* ‖

ἀ-γνοεῖν inf. ἀγνοέω *not to know, be in ignorance.* 13
κοιμωμένων ptc (inceptive) -μάομαι *go to sleep,* οἱ κ. *those*
who have fallen asleep (= died). λυπῆσθε aor. subj. pass.
λυπέω *cause grief* ; pass. intr. *be sad.* λοιπός *left behind,*
οἱ λ. *the rest.* ἐλπίς[6] -ίδος ἡ *hope.* ‖ εἰ w. indic. simple 14
condition §303. ἀπ-έ-θανεν aor[2] ἀπο-θνήσκω. ἀν-έστη *rose,*
aor[2] (intr.) -ίστημι. οἱ κοιμηθέντες i.e. *who died,* aor.
ptc dep. -μάομαι. διὰ τ. Ἰησοῦ in ambiguous position,
preferably w. κοιμηθ. in sense close to that of ἐν in I Cor
15:18 (cf διὰ τ. πνεύματος Ac 11:28). ἄξει fut. ἄγω *bring.* ‖
ἐν λόγῳ κυρίου *on the word of the Lord,* i.e. as taught by 15
the Lord. ζῶντες ptc ζάω. περι-λειπόμενοι ptc pass. -λείπω
leave behind ; of π. here *those who survive.* εἰς temporal,
until. παρ-ουσία 2:19. οὐ μή w. subj. emphatic neg. ref.
fut. §444. φθάσωμεν aor. subj. φθάνω *arrive, come*; φ. τινά
here, *forestall.* ‖ αὐτὸς ὁ κύριος *the Lord himself.* ἐν of 16
concomitant circumstances (sociative) *with* §116. κέλευ-
σμα[7] (< κελεύω command) *summons.* ἀρχ-άγγελος *arch-*
angel. σάλπιγξ[6] -ιγγος ἡ *trumpet.* κατα-βήσεται fut. -βαίνω.
ἀνα-στήσονται fut. ἀν-ίσταμαι (mid. intr.) *rise.* ‖ ἔπ-ειτα 17
thereupon, then. ἅμα *at the same time, together.* ἁρπαγησό-
μεθα *shall be caught up,* fut[2] pass. -άζω *seize and carry off.*
νεφέλη *cloud.* ἀπ-άντησις[4] (ἀπαντάω meet) the act of *meet-*
ing, εἰς ἀπ. *to meet,* esp. of public welcome of an official
Mt 8:34 (ὑπάντησις). ἀήρ[6] ἀέρος ὁ *air.* πάν-τοτε *always.*
ἐσόμεθα fut. εἰμί. ‖ παρα-καλεῖτε *console !* impv -καλέω. 18
ἐν instr. §119. ‖ χρόνος *time* in general (opp. καιρός a specific 5
time or occasion). χρεία *need.* γράφεσθαι inf. pass. γράφω:
οὐ χρείαν ἔχετε ὑμῖν γρ. *you do not need* (*anything*) *to be*

2 *written to you*, i.e. *to have anything written*... ‖ αὐτοί (*you*) *yourselves.* ἀκριβῶς *accurately* ; ἀ. οἴδατε *you know perfectly well.* κλέπτης³ *thief.* ‖ λέγωσιν subj. λέγω pres. durative. ἀ-σφάλεια (< ἀ- priv. + σφάλλω trip up) *security.* αἰφνίδιος *sudden* ; pred. "as some one sudden", i.e. *suddenly.* ἐφ-ίσταται mid. -ίστημι, mid. intr. *come upon and stand by.* ὄλεθρος *destruction, disaster.* ὠδίν -ῖνος ἡ *birth-pang.* γαστήρ⁶ -τρός ἡ *belly* ; *womb,* ἐν γ. ἔχουσα (ptc fem. ἔχω) a *woman with child.* οὐ μή 4:15. ἐκ-φύγωσιν aor² subj.

4 -φεύγω *escape.* ‖ σκότος⁸ *darkness.* ἵνα = ὥστε §352. κατα-

5 λάβῃ aor² subj. -λαμβάνω *seize, overtake.* ‖ υἱός *son, child,* see Eph 2:3 (ὀργή), υἱοὶ φωτός i.e. *partakers of light or who live for Christ the Light* Lk 16:8 (φῶς) ; light and day being equated with the good as darkness and night are

6 w. evil §43. ‖ ἄρα *consequently, so,* ἄρα οὖν *so then.* καθεύ-δωμεν subj. hort. -εύδω *sleep.* οἱ λοιποί 4:13. γρηγορῶμεν subj. hort. -ρέω *be watchful/alert,* vb formed from pf (ἐγρήγορα) of ἐγείρω. νήφωμεν subj. hort. νήφω *be sober.* ‖

7 καθεύδοντες ptc. νυκτός *at night,* gen. of time "within which". μεθυσκόμενοι ptc pass. -σκω *make one drunk* ;

8 pass. *be drunk.* μεθύω *be drunk.* ‖ ὄντες ptc εἰμί causal, ἡμεῖς δὲ ἡμέρας ὄ. *as we* (emphatic) *belong to the day.* ἐν-δυσάμενοι aor. ptc mid. -δύω *put on* another ; aor. mid. *put on* oneself. θώραξ⁶ -ακος ὁ *breast-plate,* w. gen. epexeg. §45. περι-κεφαλαία pred. *as a helmet.* ἐλπίς 4:13. σωτηρία

9 *salvation, deliverance.* ‖ ἔ-θετο aor² mid. τίθημι, mid. signifying for one's purposes : *arrange* ; *appoint* ; *destine.* ὀργή

10 *wrath.* περι-ποίησις⁴ *acquisition* Eph 1:14. ‖ ἀπο-θανόντος aor² ptc -θνήσκω. εἴτε...εἴτε *whether ...or* ; on εἰ w. subj. §332. γρηγορῶμεν, καθεύδωμεν v.6. ἅμα *together.* ζήσωμεν

11 aor. subj. ζάω, aor. inceptive, *enter into life* §250. ‖ δι-ό *therefore, so.* παρα-καλεῖτε impv -καλέω. οἰκο-δομεῖτε impv -δομέω *build up, strengthen.* εἰς τὸν ἕνα Sem. = ἀλλήλους. ‖

12 ἐρωτάω 4:1. εἰδέναι here, *acknowledge* the true value of, *appreciate,* inf. pf-pres. οἶδα. κοπιῶντας ptc κοπιάω *labour.* ἐν *among.* προ-ϊσταμένους ptc mid. (intr.) -ίσταμαί τινος *be a leader, be in authority over* one. νου-θετοῦντας

13 ptc -θετέω (< νοῦς + τίθημι) *admonish, advise.* ‖ ἡγεῖσθαι aor. inf. ἡγέομαι *lead* ; *consider, regard,* hence *have regard for* one. ὑπερ-εκ-περισσοῦ *beyond measure,* ἡγεῖσθαί τινα ὑπ. *esteem* one *most highly, have an immense regard for* one. εἰρηνεύετε impv -εύω *live at peace.* ἐν ἑαυτοῖς prob.

for ἐν ἀλλήλοις *with one another.* ‖ νου-θετεῖτε impv. ἄ- 14
τακτος *un-disciplined, dis-orderly.* παρα-μυθεῖσθε impv -μυ-
θέομαι *console, cheer.* ὀλιγό-ψυχος *faint-hearted.* ἀντ-έχεσθε
impv -έχομαί τινος *be attached/faithful to, stand by* (ready
to help). ἀ-σθενής⁹ (ἀ- + σθένος⁸ strength) *weak.* μακρο-
θυμεῖτε impv -θυμέω *be patient* with one. ‖ ὁρᾶτε (impv) 15
μή τις *see/take care that no one.* κακόν τό *wrong, injury.*
ἀντί w. gen. (*in return*) *for.* ἀπο-δῷ aor² subj. -δίδωμι
render, repay. πάν-τοτε *always.* διώκετε impv, pres. *continue to pursue.* εἰς *for.* ‖ χαίρετε impv as are all the vbs 16
in vv. 16-22. ‖ ἀ-δια-λείπτως *constantly.* ‖ εὐ-χαριστέω *give* 17,18
thanks. ‖ σβέννυμι *quench.* ‖ προφητεία ref. the gift or the 19,20
content of charismatically inspired *prophecy.* ἐξ-ουθενέω
ignore, despise. ‖ δοκιμάζω *test, examine.* κατ-έχω *hold* 21
fast. ‖ παντός wt art. *every* §188. εἶδος⁸ *form.* πονηροῦ 22
neut. ἀπ-έχομαι *keep away, avoid.* ‖ ἁγιάσαι aor. opt. -άζω 23
make holy. ὁλο-τελής⁹ *complete, perfect,* αὐτός...ὁλοτελεῖς
may the God of peace himself make you perfect in holiness.
ὁλό-κληρος *entire, complete, whole,* ὁλοκλ. ὑμῶν *your entirety, the whole of you;* subject of τηρηθείη. ἀ-μέμπτως
irreproachable. παρουσία 2:19. τηρηθείη *may...be kept/
preserved,* aor. opt. pass. 3rd sg τηρέω. ‖ πιστός pred. *to* 24
be trusted. ὁ καλῶν (ptc καλέω) pres. ptc timeless, God is
he who calls §372. ποιήσει fut. *he will effect* (*it*), i.e. sub-
stantiate his promise. ‖ προσ-εύχεσθε impv, πρ. περί *pray* 25
for...! ‖ ἀσπάσασθε aor. impv -άζομαι *greet.* ἐν *with.* 26
φίλημα⁷ *kiss.* ‖ ἐν-ορκίζω τινά τι (or τινα) *adjure one by* 27
sth or someone. ἀνα-γνωσθῆναι aor. inf. pass. -γινώσκω
read, transl. *to have* this letter *read.* ἐπιστολή *letter.* ‖

II THESSALONIANS

1 2   ἐν θεῷ πατρί... I Thess 1:1. ‖ χάρις...καὶ εἰρήνη Rom 1:7. ‖
  3   εὐχαριστεῖν inf. -τέω *give thanks*. ὀφείλω *owe*, w. inf.
ought, must, lit. "we owe (it) to God to give thanks", i.e.
our thanks are at all times *due to God*. πάν-τοτε *always*.
περί = ὑπέρ §96, I Thess 1:2. ἄξιος *worthy* ; impers.
ἄξιόν ἐστιν *it is fitting/proper*. ὑπερ-αυξάνω (αὐξάνω grow)
flourish. πλεονάζω *increase*. εἷς ἕκαστος *every one*. εἰς
  4   ἀλλήλους *for each other*. ‖ αὐτοὶ ἡμεῖς *we ourselves*. ἐγ-
καυχᾶσθαι ἐν inf. -καυχάομαι ἐν (ὑμῖν) *make a boast of, take
pride in* (2nd ἐν is local). ὑπέρ for περί. ὑπο-μονή *fortitude*. διωγμός (< διώκω persecute) *persecution*. θλῖψις[4]
pressure, suffering. αἷς attracted from ἅς (or ὧν). ἀν-
  5   έχομαί τι or τινος *endure, put up with* sth. ‖ ἔν-δειγμα[7]
evidence, acc. appos. or nom. understanding ὅ ἐστιν (ἔνδ.).
κρίσις[4] *judgement*. εἰς τό w. acc. + inf. final. κατ-αξιω-
θῆναι aor. inf. pass. -αξιόω *consider worthy*. πάσχω *suffer*. ‖
  6   εἴ-περ *if indeed* ; sts *since*. παρὰ θεῷ *in God's estimation,
in the eyes of God*. ἀντ-απο-δοῦναι aor[2] inf. -δίδωμί τινί τι
re-pay, requite one *with* sth. θλίβουσιν ptc dat. pl. θλίβω
press, put pressure on, afflict. ὑμᾶς obj. of θλίβουσιν. ‖
  7   θλιβομένοις *suffering affliction*, ptc pass. ἄν-εσις[4] (< ἀν-
  8   ίημι relax) *relief, rest*. ἀπο-κάλυψις[4] *revelation*. ‖ φλόξ[6]
φλογός ἡ *flame*, "Hebr." gen. πῦρ φλογός *a flaming fire*
§40. διδόντος ptc δίδωμι: δ. ἐκδίκησιν *inflict punishment*.
ἐκ-δίκησις[4] *punishment*. εἰδόσιν ptc dat. pl. pf-pres. οἶδα.
  9   ὑπ-ακούσουσιν ptc -ακούω τινί *obey* one or sth. ‖ οἵ-τινες
men who, such as, or just = *who* §218. δίκη *justice* (absolute) hence *punishment*. τίσουσιν fut. τίνω *pay* ; δίκην τ. τι
pay sth *as a penalty, pay the penalty of* sth. ὄλεθρος
destruction, doom. πρόσωπον here, *presence*, ἀπὸ π. possibly
ref. the source of punishment but more likely den. the
exclusion which constitutes the punishment, Is 2:10,
  10   19, 21. ἰσχύς -ύος ἡ *strength, power*. ‖ ὅταν w. subj.
when ref. fut. ἔλθῃ aor[2] subj. ἔρχομαι. ἐν-δοξασθῆναι aor.
inf. pass. -δοξάζω *be glorified, have one's glory acknowledged*,

inf. final. **ἐν τοῖς ἁγίοις αὐτοῦ** *in those dedicated to him.*
θαυμασθῆναι aor. inf. pass. -άζω *wonder,* pass. *be the object
of wonder, be marvelled at.* **πιστεύσασιν** aor. ptc -εύω,
those who have embraced the faith/become believers. (ὅτι...
ὑμᾶς a parenthesis : **ἐ-πιστεύθη** aor. pass. **μαρτύριον** *testimony.* **ἐπί** w. acc. *to.*) **ἐν τ. ἡμέρᾳ ἐκείνῃ** ass. w. ὅταν
ἔλθῃ κτλ. ‖ **ἀξιώσῃ** aor. subj. -ιόω τινά τινος *make* one 11
worthy of sth. **κλῆσις**[4] *calling.* **πληρώσῃ** aor. subj. -ρόω.
εὐ-δοκία *good will, favour,* hence *desire.* **ἀγαθωσύνη** *goodness,* obj. gen., *of/for goodness.* **ἔργον πίστεως** I Thess
1:3. **ἐν δυνάμει** *by his power.* ‖ **ὅπως** w. subj. final, *in order* 12
that. **ἐν-δοξασθῇ** aor. subj. pass. ‖

    ἐρωτάω *ask ;* later, *appeal to, beg.* **ὑπέρ** = περί *in* 2
connection with. **παρ-ουσία** I Thess. 2:19. **ἐπι-συν-αγωγή**
foregathering, coming together. **ἐπί** w. acc. *to.* ‖ **εἰς τό** w. 2
acc. + inf., obj. of ἐρωτῶμεν. **ταχέως** (adj. ταχύς quick)
hastily. **σαλευθῆναι** aor. inf. pass. -εύω *shake, agitate.*
νοῦς νοός ὁ *mind, good sense.* **μηδέ** *and not,* nor. **θροεῖσθαι**
inf. pass. -έω, pass. *be inwardly disturbed, alarmed,* θρ. ...
ὡς ὅτι *be disturbed...as if.* **μήτε...μήτε** after a neg. = *either...
or.* **πνεῦμα**[7] here, *charismatic predictions.* **λόγος** *spoken
word.* **ἐπι-στολή** I Thess. 5:27. **ὡς** *supposedly.* **ἐν-έ-στη-
κεν** pf (intr. w. pres. meaning) ἐν-ίστημι in intr. tenses,
to have come. ‖ **ἐξ-απατήσῃ** aor. subj. -απατάω *deceive,* μή 3
τις ἐξα. *let nobody deceive.* **τρόπος** *way.* **ἔλθῃ** 1:10. **ἀπο-
στασία** *apostasy,* ἐάν...πρῶτον *unless the apostasy comes first...,*
the art. indicating that the readers know about this.
ἀπο-καλυφθῇ aor. subj. pass. -καλύπτω *reveal,* here implying
"in his true light". **ἀ-νομία** *lawlessness, iniquity, wickedness,* here w. eschatological overtones Mt 24:12. [var.
ἁμαρτίας]]. **ἀπ-ώλεια** (< ἀπ-όλλυμι) *destruction ; perdition,*
ὁ ἄνθρωπος τ. ἀνομίας, ὁ υἱός τῆς ἀπ. *the embodiment of lawlessness, doomed to perdition.* ‖ **ἀντι-κείμενος** *adversary ;* 4
also appos. to ἄνθρωπος. **ὑπερ-αιρόμενος** ptc -αίρομαι *ἐπί*
(w. acc.) *exalt oneself over* sth. **λεγόμενον** *called,* ptc pass.
λέγω. **πάντα** masc. *every being* given the name of "god."
σέβασμα[7] (< σεβάζομαι worship) *object of worship.* **εἰς** for
ἐν §99. **ναός** *temple.* **καθίσαι** aor. inf. -ίζω intr. *sit* (down),
ὥστε...κ. *to the point of taking his seat...* **ἀπο-δεικνύντα**
ptc -δείκνυμι *claim.* **ἔστιν** tense of dir. speech §347. ‖
μνημονεύω *remember ;* interrog. **ὤν** ptc εἰμί. **ἔ-λεγον** impf 5
I used to tell you. ‖ **κατ-έχον** *what is restraining* (him), ptc 6

neut. -έχω *restrain, hold back.* εἰς τό v.2. ἀπο-καλυφθῆναι aor. inf. pass. v.3. αὐτόν the Enemy. ἐν understand *"only" at...* τῷ ἑαυτῷ καιρῷ *his proper time,* meaning the

7 time appointed for him. ‖ μυστήριον...τῆς ἀνομίας *the secret (workings) of iniquity.* ἤδη *already.* ἐν-εργεῖται mid. -γέω, mid. w. impers. subject, *be active/at work.* μόνον... ἕως *only until* ; ἕως w. subj. often wt ἄν §336. ὁ κατέχων ἄρτι *he who is now doing the restraining/holding (him) back.* μέσος *middle,* ἐκ μέσου (neut.) *from the scene* (lit. "midst").

8 γένηται aor² subj. γίνομαι. ‖ ἀπο-καλυφθήσεται fut. pass. ἄ-νομος *law-less;* ὁ ἄ. *this iniquity in person.* ἀν-ελεῖ fut. -αιρέω *destroy, kill.* πνεῦμα⁷ *breath.* κατ-αργήσει fut. -αργέω *annihilate.* ἐπι-φάνεια *manifestation,* by act or appearance, of a divinity ; hence also *splendour, radiance,* ἐπιφ. τ. παρουσίας αὐτοῦ *manifestation* or *splendour of his*

9 *presence.* παρουσία I Thess 2:19. ‖ οὗ *whose,* i.e. of the "lawless" one. ἐν-έργεια *action, activity* ; κατ᾽ ἐν. Σατανᾶ *according to S.'s way of working.* τέρας -ατος τό *prodigy, wonder.* ψεῦδος⁸ *falsehood,* "Hebr." gen. = *spurious* §40. ‖

10 ἀπάτη *deception* ; in HGk also *allurement.* ἀ-δικία *wickedness* ; "Hebr." gen., *wicked deception* (or, *?allurement to wickedness).* ἀπ-ολλυμένοις ptc mid. -όλλυμι *those on the road to* (pres.) *perdition.* ἀνθ᾽ (= ἀντί) ὧν lit. "in return for which", *because* §17. ἐ-δέξαντο aor. δέχομαι *receive, accept.* εἰς τό w. acc. + inf. *so that* (consec.). σωθῆναι

11 aor. inf. pass. σῴζω. ‖ πλάνη (< πλανάω *lead astray, delude*) *error, delusion,* ἐνέργεια π. *a force of delusion, a deceiving power,* "Hebr." gen. §40. πιστεῦσαι aor. inf. -εύω τινί

12 *believe* sth. ‖ κριθῶσιν aor. subj. pass. κρίνω. πιστεύσαντες aor. ptc. εὐ-δοκήσαντες aor. ptc -δοκέω τινί *take pleasure in* sth. ‖

13 ὀφείλομεν...ὑμῶν 1:3. ἠγαπημένοι *beloved,* pf ptc pass. ἀγαπάω. εἵλατο aor² αἱρέομαι *choose.* ἀπ-αρχή pred. *as firstfruits* [[var. ἀπ᾽ ἀρχῆς *from the beginning*]]. σωτηρία *salvation,* εἰς σ. ἐν *for salvation through.* ἁγιασμός *sanctification.* πνεύματος gen. of author, (the work) *of the Spirit, in the Spirit* ; or (like ἀληθείας) obj. gen. ref. the highest part of man's nature, *sanctification of your spirit.* πίστις ἀλη-

14 θείας *faith in truth.* ‖ ἐ-κάλεσεν aor. καλέω. περι-ποίησις⁴

15 *acquisition* ; *gaining possession* w. obj. gen. ‖ ἄρα οὖν *so then.* στήκετε impv στήκω *stand firm,* Phil 1:27. κρατεῖτε impv -τέω *keep, observe.* παρά-δοσις⁴ *tradition* ; acc. of

the thing retained in pass. of vbs taking a double acc.
§72. ἐ-διδάχθητε aor. pass. διδάσκω τινά τι. εἴτε...εἴτε
either...or. λόγος...ἐπιστολή v.2. ‖ αὐτός...ὁ κύριος I Thess　16
3:11. ἀγαπήσας aor. ptc sg -πάω. δούς aor² ptc δίδωμι.
παρά-κλησις⁴ encouragement. αἰωνία unfailing, fem. of αἰώνιος (which freq. serves also for fem.). ἐλπίς -ίδος ἡ hope. ‖
παρα-καλέσαι aor. opt. 3rd sg -καλέω, opt. expressing a　17
wish, may...Jesus Christ and God our Father...encourage.
στηρίξαι aor. opt. -ίζω confirm, strengthen. παντὶ ἔργῳ κ.
λόγῳ ἀγαθῷ every good deed and word. ‖

　　τὸ λοιπόν finally. προσ-εύχεσθε impv. περί for ὑπέρ　3
§96. τρέχῃ subj. τρέχω run, met. make rapid strides.
δοξάζηται subj. pass. -άζω honour. καθ ὡς καὶ πρὸς ὑμᾶς
as has been the case with you. ‖ ρυσθῶμεν aor. subj. pass.　2
ρύομαι deliver, rescue. ἄ-τοπος (out of place) perverse.
οὐ...πάντων ἡ πίστις "faith is not of all", i.e. all do not
have faith. ‖ πιστός faithful, to be trusted. στηρίξει fut.　3
2:17. φυλάξει fut. -άσσω guard, keep safe. ‖ πονηροῦ neut.　4
or masc. ? πε-ποίθαμεν pf² πείθω persuade ; pf² be confident.
ἐφ' ὑμᾶς concerning you. παρ-αγγέλλω charge, command.
ποιήσετε will continue to do, fut. ποιέω. ‖ κατ-ευθύναι aor.　5
opt. 3rd sg -ευθύνω straighten out ; direct. ὑπο-μονή constancy. ‖

　　στέλλεσθαι inf. mid. στέλλω send ; mid. shun, avoid.　6
ὑμᾶς subject of inf. ἀ-τάκτως in a disorderly/undisciplined
way. περι-πατοῦντος living, ptc -πατέω. παρά-δοσις⁴ tradition. παρ-ε-λάβοσαν aor² (for -λαβον) παρα-λαμβάνω receive. ‖ μιμεῖσθαι inf. μιμέομαι imitate, copy. ἠ-τακτήσαμεν　7
aor. ἀ-τακτέω be undisciplined/slack. ἐν among, with,
understand "when we were". ‖ δωρεάν (acc. of δωρεά free　8
gift) gratis, without payment. ἐ-φάγομεν aor² ἐσθίω. παρά
w. gen. Fr. chez, at one's house. κόπος...ὑμῶν I Thess. 2:9. ‖
ἐξουσία a right. ἑαυτούς for ἡμᾶς αὐτούς §209. τύπος　9
(< τύπτω beat) type, symbol, example. δῶμεν aor² subj.
δίδωμι here, offer ourselves as an example. ‖ καὶ γάρ indeed.　10
παρ-ηγγέλλομεν impf v.4. ἐργάζεσθαι inf. -ζομαι work. μηδέ
not...either. ἐσθιέτω impv ἐσθίω. ‖ περι-πατοῦντας, ἀ-　11
τάκτως v.6. ἐργαζομένους ptc. περι-εργαζομένους ptc
-εργάζομαι meddle, fuss : a play on ἐργαζομένους, περι-εργ.:
Eng. versions usu. contrasting "busy" and "busybody". ‖
τοιοῦτος such a person. ἵνα for obj. inf. ἡσυχία quiet,　12
μετὰ ἡσ. quietly. ἐσθίωσιν subj. ἐσθίω. ‖ ἐγ-κακήσητε aor.　13

subj. -κακέω *be weary, lose heart,* w. ptc *be tired of* doing
14 sth.   **καλο-ποιοῦντες** ptc -ποιέω *do what is right.* ‖ ὑπ-ακούω
τινί *obey* one or sth.   **διὰ τῆς ἐπιστολῆς** *by this letter.* ση-
μειοῦσθε impv mid. -όω *mark* ; mid. *for oneself, take note
of.*   συν-ανα-μίγνυσθαι inf. pass. -μίγνυμι *mix up together* ;
pass. *mix/associate with.*   ἐν-τραπῇ aor² subj. pass. -τρέπω
15 *put to shame* ; pass. intr. *be/feel ashamed.* ‖ **καί** *at the same
time, still* §455α.   ἐχθρός *enemy.*   ἡγεῖσθε impv ἡγέομαι
consider, regard as.   νουθετεῖτε impv -θετέω τινά *admonish,
give advice to* one. ‖
16   **αὐτός...ὁ κύριος** *the Lord himself.*   δῴη aor² opt. δίδωμι.
διὰ παντός (sc. χρόνου) *at all times.*   τρόπος *manner, way,*
ἐν παντὶ τρ. *in every way.*   ὁ κύριος, understand *be.* ‖
17 ἀσπασμός *greeting.*   ὅ, his signature.   σημεῖον *here, iden-
tifying mark, sign of authenticity.* ‖

I TIMOTHY

ἐπι-ταγή (< ἐπι-τάσσω order) command. σωτήρ⁶ -ῆρος ὁ **1**
saviour. ἐλπίς⁶ -ίδος ἡ hope. ‖ γνήσιος genuine, true. ἔλεος⁸ **2**
mercy. θεὸς πατήρ I Thess 1:1.

καθώς introduces a cstr which is unfinished when v.5 **3**
begins a new sentence. παρ-ε-κάλεσα aor. παρα-καλέω.
προσ-μεῖναι aor. inf. -μένω stay on. πορευόμενος when I
was going, ptc -εύομαι. παρ-αγγείλῃς aor. subj. -αγγέλλω
τινί command, impress on one. ἑτερο-διδασκαλεῖν inf.
-διδασκαλέω teach other doctrines. ‖ μηδέ and not. προσ- **4**
έχειν inf. -έχω (sc. τὸν νοῦν) τινί give one's mind/pay attention to sth. μῦθος myth. γενεαλογία genealogy, perh. early
Gnostic speculations about aeons ? ἀ-πέραντος (< περαίνω
bring to an end) in-terminable. ἐκ-ζήτησις⁴ speculation.
παρ-έχω provide ; here, lead to, encourage. οἰκο-νομία
management as the duty of a steward (οἰκονόμος) ; esp.
divine order, dispensation. τὴν ἐν πίστει which is (realized) in
faith ; others understand οἰκ. ...ἐν π. as training in faith. ‖
τέλος⁸ aim, purpose. παρ-αγγελία command. καθαρός clean, **5**
pure. συν-είδησις⁴ (< σύν-οιδα be conscious) moral consciousness, conscience. ἀν-υπό-κριτος without pretence, sincere. ‖ ὧν from which. ἀ-στοχήσαντες aor. ptc -στοχέω **6**
(< ἀ- + στόχος target) be wide of the mark. ἐξ-ε-τράπησαν
aor² pass. ἐκ-τρέπω turn sth aside ; pass. in refl. sense,
turn away from, also turn aside to (εἰς or ἐπί) sth. ματαιο-
λογία senseless talk. ‖ θέλοντες ptc θέλω. νομο-διδάσκαλος **7**
teacher of the law. νοοῦντες ptc (concessive) νοέω understand. μήτε...μήτε after a neg. either...or. ἅ ?for τίνα
§221. δια-βεβαιόομαι assert. ‖ νομίμως (< νόμος) legitimate- **8**
ly. χρῆται subj. χράομαί τινι use sth. ‖ εἰδώς ptc pf-pres. **9**
οἶδα. τοῦτο ref. what follows §213. δικαίῳ masc. κεῖμαι
(used as pf pass. τίθημι) be put, lie ; of law, be instituted/
given. ἄ-νομος law-less. ἀν-υπό-τακτος (< ὑποτάσσω subjugate) in-subordinate, un-ruly. ἀ-σεβής⁹ (σέβομαι worship) im-pious, ir-reverent. ἁμαρτωλός sinner. ἀν-όσιος
(to whom nothing is holy) ir-religious. βέβηλος (< βαίνω

where all and sundry can go, profane) *godless.* **πατρο-**
λῴης[3] (< πατήρ + ἀλοάω strike down) *parricide.* **μητρο-**
10 **λῴης**[3] *matricide.* **ἀνδρο-φόνος** *murderer.* || **πόρνος** *fornicator.*
ἀρσενο-κοίτης[3] *sodomite, homosexual.* **ἀνδρα-ποδιστής**[3] *kid-*
napper. **ψεύστης**[3] *liar.* **ἐπί-ορκος** (ἐπί against + ὅρκος
oath) *perjurer.* **ὑγιαινούσῃ** ptc fem. ὑγιαίνω *be sound.*
ἕτερος (of two) for ἄλλος. **διδασκαλία** *instruction.* **ἀντί-κειμαι**
11 *be opposed* to. || **μακάριος** *blessed.* **ἐ-πιστεύθην** aor. pass.
-εύω τί τινι *entrust* sth to one ; in pass. the person becomes
subject, the thing acc. of respect : πιστεύομαί τι *be en-*
trusted with sth §72. |
12 **χάρις** *thanks,* χ. ἔχω...ὅτι *be thankful...that.* **ἐν-δυναμ**-
ώσαντι aor. ptc -δυναμόω τινά *give strength to* one. **πιστός**
trustworthy. **ἡγήσατο** aor. ἡγέομαι *deem, consider.* **θέμενος**
aor[2] ptc pass. τίθημι, mid. *appoint* ; the transposition of
ptc and finite vb being an idiom of Gk style §263, =
"having considered me trustworthy he appointed me"
but transl. *he deemed me trustworthy enough to appoint me...*
13 **διακονία** *ministry.* || **τὸ πρότερον** comp. adv. *formerly,*
before. **ὄντα** ptc εἰμί, ref. με: *who was.* **βλάσ-φημος** *blas-*
phemer. **διώκτης**[3] *persecutor.* **ὑβριστής**[3] *an insolent, ag-*
gressive man. **ἠλεήθην** aor. pass. ἐλεέω *show mercy* ; pass.
be treated mercifully, find mercy. **ἀ-γνοῶν** *in ignorance,*
ptc -γνοέω *be ignorant.* **ἐ-ποίησα** *I acted,* aor. ποιέω.
14 **ἀ-πιστία** *un-belief.* || **ὑπερ-ε-πλεόνασεν** aor. -πλεονάζω *in-*
crease to overflowing, know no bounds. **δέ** w. progressive
force, *and moreover* §467. **μετὰ πίστεως** κ. **ἀγάπης**, faith
15 and love being effects of grace. || **πιστὸς ὁ λόγος** *trust-*
worthy is the saying (5 times in the Pastoral Epistles).
ἀπο-δοχή (ἀπο-δέχομαι welcome) *acceptance ; approval.* **ἄξιος**
(< ἄγω draw down a scale, weigh) *worthy.* **ἁμαρτωλός** v.9.
16 **σῶσαι** aor. inf. σῴζω. **πρῶτος** *foremost.* || **διὰ τοῦτο** *for this*
reason, this was why §112. **ἠλεήθην** v.13. **ἐν ἐμοὶ πρώτῳ**
in me as foremost. **ἐν-δείξηται** aor. subj. mid. -δείκνυμι
(in NT mid. only) *prove, show.* **ἅπας** = πᾶς. **μακρο-θυμία**
(long temper) *forbearance, patience.* **πρός** w. acc. for. **ὑπο-**
τύπωσις[4] a *type, first instance.* **μελλόντων** ptc μέλλω.
17 **πιστεύειν** inf. **εἰς** for. || **αἰών** *world,* incl. subterranean and
superterrestrial. **ἄ-φθαρτος** *in-corruptible, im-mortal.* **ἀ-**
18 **όρατος** *in-visible.* **μόνος** *only.* **τιμή** *honour.* || **παρ-αγγελία**
v.5. **παρα-τίθεμαι** mid. *entrust.* **προ-αγούσας** ptc fem. -άγω
go ahead, precede, πρ. ἐπί σε προφ. *prophecies leading (point-*

ing) *to you* or *former proph. about you.*   προφητεία *prophecy.*
στρατεύῃ subj. -εύομαι *serve* as a soldier, *fight.*   ἐν αὐταῖς
by their means, in their strength.   στρατεία *campaign.* ‖
συν-είδησις v.5.   ἀπ-ωσάμενοι aor. ptc -ωθέομαι mid. *thrust*   19
away from oneself, turn one's back on.   περί *in respect of,*
as to.   ἐ-ναυ-άγησαν aor. ναυ-αγέω (< ναῦς ship + ἄγνυμι
break) *be shipwrecked.*   τὴν πίστιν acc. of respect, *over their*
faith : in Eng. idiom, *have made shipwreck of their faith.* ‖
παρ-έ-δωκα aor. παρα-δίδωμι.   Σατανᾶς -νᾶ *adversary, Satan.*   20
παιδευθῶσιν aor. subj. pass. -εύω *chastise* ; also *teach* ; pass.
learn.   βλασ-φημεῖν inf. -φημέω *blaspheme.* ‖

ποιεῖσθαι δεήσεις Phil 1:4.   προσ-ευχή *prayer.*   ἔν-   2
τευξις⁴ (< ἐντυγχάνω appeal) *petition.*   εὐχαριστία *thanks-*
giving. ‖   ὑπερ-οχή *superiority* (ὑπερ-έχω be superior), ἐν ὑπ.   2
in high places, in authority.   ὄντων ptc εἰμί.   ἤρεμος *tran-*
quil, undisturbed.   ἡσύχιος *quiet.*   βίος *life, existence,* ref.
the means, duration, or manner of life whereas ζωή den.
life absolutely, life in its essence.   δι-άγωμεν subj. -άγω
spend time, *lead* a life.   εὐ-σέβεια *piety, godliness.*   σεμνό-
της⁶ -τητος ἡ *seriousness, dignity.* ‖   ἀπόδεκτος (< ἀπο-   3
δέχομαι welcome) *welcome, pleasing.*   σωτήρ 1:1 ‖ σωθῆναι   4
aor. inf. pass. σῴζω.   ἐπί-γνωσις⁴ *knowledge.*   ἐλθεῖν aor² inf.
ἔρχομαι.   ‖ εἷς...θεός *there is one God.*   μεσίτης³ *mediator.* ‖   5
δούς aor² ptc δίδωμι.   ἀντί-λυτρον *ransom.*   μαρτύριον *evi-*   6
dence, testimony, i.e. to what has just been stated (v.4).
καιροῖς ἰδίοις *at the proper time* (time ordained by God). ‖
εἰς ὅ *to/for which.*   ἐ-τέθην *I was made,* aor. pass. τίθημι   7
appoint.   κήρυξ⁶ -υκος ὁ *herald, preacher.*   ψεύδομαι *lie,*
tell an untruth.   διδάσκαλος *teacher.* ‖ βούλομαι w. acc. +   8
inf. *will, wish, want.*   προσ-εύχεσθαι inf.   ἐπ-αίροντας ptc
-αίρω *lift up.*   ὅσιος *holy.*   χωρίς w. gen. *without.*   ὀργή
anger.   δια-λογισμός *argument.* ‖ ὡσ-αύτως *likewise.*   γυναῖ-   9
κας subject of κοσμεῖν (acc. + inf. after βούλομαι).   κατα-
στολή Fr. *tenue, dress* (in general), possibly also *bearing,*
behaviour.   κόσμιος (for class. fem. κόσμια) *in good taste.*
αἰδώς -δοῦς ἡ *modesty.*   σωφροσύνη *sobriety.*   κοσμεῖν inf.
-μέω *adorn* ; in a comprehensive sense, *attire, dress* (oneself).   πλέγμα⁷ a *wave* or *plait* (of hair) meaning *elaborate*
hair style (NEB).   χρυσίον *gold.*   μαργαρίτης³ *pearl.*   ἱμα-
τισμός *clothes.*   πολυ-τελής⁹ *expensive.* ‖ πρέπει τινί *is fit-*   10
ting for one.   ἐπ-αγγελλομέναις ptc -αγγέλλομαι *promise* ;
profess.   θεο-σέβεια *worship of God.*   διά *with* rather than

11 "by", cf v.15. ‖ ἡσυχία *silence, quiet.* μανθανέτω impv 3rd
12 sg -θάνω *learn.* ὑπο-ταγῇ *submission.* ‖ διδάσκειν inf. -άσκω.
ἐπι-τρέπω τινί *allow* one. αὐθεντεῖν inf. -τέω τινός *domi-*
neer over one. ἀνδρός *her husband,* though anarthrous.
13 εἶναι impvl inf. ‖ πρῶτος superl. (as Eng.) for comp. §147.
14 ἐ-πλάσθη aor. pass. πλάσσω *form.* εἶτα (*only*) *then.* ‖ ἠπα-
τήθη aor. pass. ἀπατάω *deceive.* ἐξ-απατηθεῖσα aor. ptc
pass. fem. -απατάω (ἐξ- intensive). παρά-βασις[4] *trans-gres-*
sion, sin. γέ-γονεν pf[2] γίνομαι: γεγ. ἐν (?aoristic pf)
15 *fell into.* ‖ σωθήσεται fut. pass. σῴζω. διά *through, by means*
of or *throughout* the process of. τεκνο-γονία *child-bearing.*
μείνωσιν aor. subj. μένω. ἁγιασμός *holiness.* σωφροσύνη
v.9. ‖

3   πιστὸς ὁ λόγος 1:15. ἐπι-σκοπή *over-sight, super-inten-*
dency, so the *office of bishop* ; but the distinction between
bishop and presbyters (5:17, Tit 1:5) is far from clear, and
little is known of their precise functions. ὀρέγομαί τινος
2 *aspire* to sth. ἐπι-θυμέω τινός *desire* sth. ‖ ἐπί-σκοπος
bishop. ἀν-επί-λημπτος (ἀν- priv. + ἐπι-λαμβάνομαι catch
(out)) *un-impeachable.* νηφάλιος *sober.* σώφρων σώφρονος
neut. σῶφρον *temperate.* κόσμιος *well - behaved.* φιλό-ξενος
(< φιλέω + ξένος stranger) *hospitable.* διδακτικός *with*
3 *a gift for teaching.* ‖ πάρ-οινος *over-fond of wine.* πλήκτης[3]
(< πλήσσω strike) *pugnacious man.* ἐπι-εικής[9] *considerate.*
ἄ-μαχος *not quarrelsome, peaceable.* ἀ-φιλ-άργυρος *no lover*
4 *of money.* ‖ καλῶς *well.* προ-ϊστάμενον ptc -ίσταμαί τινος
preside over, supervise sth. ἔχοντα ptc ἔχω. ὑπο-ταγῇ
5 2:11. σεμνότης 2:2. ‖ προ-στῆναι aor[2] (intr.) inf. -ίστημι.
6 ἐπι-μελήσεται fut. -μελέομαί τινος *look after.* ‖ νεό-φυτος
(newly planted) *novice.* τυφωθείς aor. ptc τυφόομαι (pass.)
be conceited. κρίμα[7] *condemnation.* ἐμ-πέσῃ aor[2] subj.
-πίπτω *fall into.* τοῦ διαβόλου *of* (same as) *the devil* or
7 subjective gen. (as in v.7) *engineered by the devil* (Satan
the accuser). ‖ μαρτυρία *testimony,* hence *reputation.* οἱ
ἔξωθεν *those outside* (sc. the Church). ὀνειδισμός *disgrace.*
καί epexeg. *which is.* παγίς[6] -ίδος ἡ a *snare.* ‖

8   διάκονος *deacon.* ὡσ-αύτως *likewise.* σεμνός *inspiring*
respect, high-principled, honourable. δί-λογος *double-faced,*
insincere. οἶνος *wine.* προσ-έχοντας ptc -έχω *be addicted*
to. αἰσχρο-κερδής[9] (αἰσχρός base + κέρδος[8] gain) *greedy*
9 *for* dishonest *gain.* ‖ ἔχοντας v.4. μυστήριον τῆς πίστεως
collective, of *mysteries of the faith* (Christian revelation).

καθαρός *clean.* συν-είδησις[4] *conscience* 1:5. ‖ δοκιμαζέσθωσαν 10
impv pass. 3rd pl. -άζω *test.* εἶτα *then.* διακονείτωσαν
impv -νέω *serve as deacon.* ἀν-έγκλητος (ἀν- + ἐγκαλέω
accuse) *ir-reproachable.* ὄντες ptc εἰμί, *conditional, if
they prove/are found to be.* γυναῖκας (*their) wives*; or, 11
deaconesses. σεμνός v.8. διάβολος masc. and fem. *accuser, slanderer.* νηφάλιος masc. and fem. v.2. πιστός
trustworthy. ‖ ἔστωσαν impv 3rd pl. εἰμί. καλῶς, προ- 12
ϊστάμενοι v.4. ‖ διακονήσαντες aor. ptc. βαθμός (< βαίνω 13
step, grade, standing. περι-ποιέομαί τι (mid.) *acquire* sth.
παρρησία *assurance* Eph 3:12. ἐν πίστει *in (the life of)
faith.* ‖

ἐλπίζων ptc -ίζω *hope,* ?concessive, *though hoping.* 14
ἐλθεῖν aor[2] inf. ἔρχομαι. τάχος[8] *speed,* ἐν τάχει *in a short
while, soon.* ‖ βραδύνω *delay,* subj. (pres. and aor. subj. 15
same in form as pres. indic.) ἐὰν δὲ β. κτλ. *in case I am
delayed, so that you may know...* or, *if I am delayed
you should know...* (ἵνα impvl §415). εἰδῇς subj. οἶδα.
οἶκος *household.* ἀνα-στρέφεσθαι inf. -στρέφομαι *behave.*
ἥ-τις = ἥ or *such as*; gender agreeing w. foll. noun. ζῶντος
ptc ζάω: θεοῦ ζ. wt art. thus underlining nature of
God §171ff. στῦλος *pillar.* ἐδραίωμα[7] *firm base, support*;
appos. to ἐκκλησία. ‖ ὁμο-λογουμένως *undeniably, certainly.* 16
εὐ-σέβεια *piety, godliness,* εὐ. μυστήριον being the revelation of
Christ himself, note ὅς masc. [[var. θεός]]. ἐ-φανερώθη aor.
pass. -ρόω *manifest.* The rest of the vbs in this v. are
also aor. pass., aor. being the characteristic tense of hymns
and prayers §155. ἐ-δικαιώθη -αιόω *justify, vindicate.* ἐν
in the sphere of *the Spirit.* ὤφθη aor. pass ὁράω, in
pass. esp. ref. God or his messengers, *appear.* ἐ-κηρύχθη
-ύσσω *proclaim, preach.* ἐν *among.* ἐ-πιστεύθη *he was
believed in,* -εύω §72. ἀν-ε-λήμφθη ἀναλαμβάνω *take up.* ‖

ῥητῶς *expressly, in so many words.* ὕστερος *later,* 4
comp. for superl. §149. ἀπο-στήσονται fut. ἀφ-ίσταμαι
(stand off from) *fall away, defect.* προσ-έχοντες ptc -έχω
τινί *pay attention to, heed* sth. πλάνος (< πλανάω *cause
to err) misleading, erroneous, wrong.* διδασκαλία *instruction.*
‖ ὑπό-κρισις[4] *hypocrisy.* ψευδο-λόγος *liar.* κε-καυστηριασμέ- 2
νων pf ptc pass. καυ(σ)τηριάζω *cauterize; sear.* συν-είδησις 3:9. ‖ κωλυόντων ptc -ύω *discourage* or *forbid.* γαμεῖν 3
inf. γαμέω *marry.* ἀπ-έχεσθαι inf. (mid.) -έχομαί τινος
avoid, abstain from (the inf. requires a vb of command;

understand "ordering them"). βρῶμα⁷ (< βιβρώσκω eat)
food. ἔ-κτισεν aor. κτίζω *create*. μετά-λημψις⁴ (< μετα-
λαμβάνω receive/take a share, esp. food) *partaking*. εὐχαριστία *thanksgiving*. πιστός *faithful*. ἐπ-ε-γνωκόσι pf ptc

4 ἐπι-γινώσκω *know* ; under one art. §184. || κτίσμα⁷ *creature*,
πᾶν κτ. θεοῦ *everything created by God*. καλόν pred. ἀπό-
βλητος (ἀπο-βάλλω) *to be rejected*. λαμβανόμενον ptc pass.

5 -βάνω, *when it is received* with thanksgiving. || ἁγιάζεται
pass. -άζω *sanctify, make holy*. ἔν-τευξις 2:1, in general
sense of *prayer*. ||

6   ὑπο-τιθέμενος ptc mid. -τίθημί τινι *sub-ject* one e.g.
to danger ; mid. *pro-pose ; advise ; enjoin ; instruct*. καλός
pred. ἔσῃ fut. εἰμί. διάκονος 3:8. ἐν-τρεφόμενος ptc
pass. -τρέφω *nourish*. διδασκαλία v.l. παρ-ηκολούθηκας
pf -ακολουθέω τινί *follow* sth *closely*, ᾗ π. *which you con-*

7 *tinue to* (pf) *follow closely*. || βέβηλος *godless* 1:9. γραώδης⁹
old women's (γραῦς old woman + εἶδος⁸ sort). μῦθος 1:4.
παρ-αιτοῦ impv -αιτέομαι (mid.) *excuse oneself ; refuse,
avoid*. γύμναζε impv -άζω *exercise, train*. εὐ-σέβεια *piety*,

8 *godliness*. || σωματικός *physical*. γυμνασία *training*. ὀλίγος
little. ὠφέλιμος *useful*, πρὸς ὀλίγον...ὠφ. *of little use*. ἐπ-
αγγελία a *promise*. ἔχουσα *holding* as it does, ptc ἔχω.
τῆς νῦν *for the present time*. τῆς μελλούσης *for the time to
come*, ptc fem. μέλλω: τῆς νῦν καὶ τ. μ. *here and hereafter*. ||

9,10 πιστός κτλ. 1:15. || εἰς τοῦτο *with this in view*, i.e. promise
of life. κοπιάω *labour*. ἀγωνίζομαι *struggle, strive* [[var.
ὀνειδιζόμεθα *we suffer reproach*]]. ἠλπίκαμεν *we have set our
hope*, pf ἐλπίζω *hope*. ζῶντι ptc ζάω 3:15. σωτήρ⁶ -ῆρος ὁ
saviour. μάλιστα (superl. of μᾶλλον) *most (of all), above all*. ||

11,12 παρ-άγγελλε impv -αγγέλλω *command ; inculcate*. || νεότης⁶
-τητος ἡ *youth*. κατα-φρονείτω impv -φρονέω *despise*.
τύπος (< τύπτω beat) *type ; symbol ; example*. γίνου *become!* impv γίνομαι. τῶν πιστῶν *to the faithful*. ἀνα-
στροφή (< ἀναστρέφομαι 3:15) *behaviour*. ἁγνεία *purity*. ||

13 ἕως w. indic. *while* I am on my way / ?preparing to come.
πρόσ-εχε impv v.l. ἀνά-γνωσις⁴ *reading* (public or private),
art. generic. παρά-κλησις⁴ *exhortation*. διδασκαλία v.l. ||

14 ἀ-μέλει impv -μελέω τινός *overlook, neglect* sth; μὴ ἀμ. *never
neglect/forget* ; sts a pres. impv in a prohibition retains
the usual iterative force of pres. ("continue not to...")
5:19, I Cor 14:39. χάρισμα⁷ *gift*, esp. of grace, here of the
abiding (ἐν σοί) gift of ordination. ἐ-δόθη aor. pass.

δίδωμι. **προφητεία** *prophecy*, which seems to have preceded T.'s calling and ordination 1:18. **ἐπί-θεσις**[4] (ἐπιτίθημι 5:22) τῶν χειρῶν *imposition/laying* on of hands. **πρεσβυτέριον** *college of presbyters*. ‖ **μελέτα** impv -τάω *put into practice, cultivate*. **ἴσθι** impv 2nd sg εἰμί: **ἴσθι ἐν** *be (absorbed) in, immerse yourself in*. **προ-κοπή** *progress*. **φανερός** *evident*. ᾖ subj. εἰμί. ‖ **ἔπ-εχε** impv -έχω τινί *be attentive* to. **ἐπί-μενε** impv -μένω τινί *remain steadfast, persevere* in sth. **ποιῶν** ptc ποιέω: τοῦτο π. *in so doing*. **καί...καί** *both...and*. **σε-αυτόν** *your-self*. **σώσεις** fut. σῴζω. **τοὺς ἀκούοντάς** (ptc ἀκούω) **σου** *your hearers*. ‖

15

16

πρεσβύτερος (comp. of πρεσβύς) fem. -τέρα *older*; as noun, *older/elderly man*. **ἐπι-πλήξῃς** aor. subj. -πλήσσω τινί *attack* one physically or verbally; *reprimand*. **παρα-κάλει** impv -καλέω. **νεώτερος** fem. -τέρα (comp. of νέος) *younger*. ‖ **ἀδελφή** *sister*. **ἁγνεία** *purity*. ‖ **χήρα** *widow*. **τίμα** impv τιμάω *honour* (like 4th commandment incl. practical help and support). **ὄντως** *really, veritably*. ‖ **ἔκ-γονος** *born of*; as noun, *descendant*, esp. *grandchild*. **μανθανέτωσαν** *they must* first *learn*, impv 3rd pl. -θάνω *learn*. **οἶκος** *household, family*. **εὐ-σεβεῖν** τινα inf. -σεβέω *reverence*; *be dutiful to, do one's duty by* one. **ἀμοιβή** a *recompense, return*. **ἀπο-διδόναι** inf. -δίδωμι *give back, give* what is due. **πρό-γονος** *forebear*, incl. parents. **ἀπό-δεκτος** *pleasing*. ‖ **με-μονωμένη** pf ptc pass. μονόω *leave solitary/ alone*. **ἤλπικεν** 4:10. **προσ-μένω** τινί *continue/be constant* in sth. **δέησις**[4] *supplication*. **προσ-ευχή** *prayer*. **νυκτὸς κ. ἡμέρας** I Thess 2:9. ‖ **σπαταλῶσα** ptc fem. -λάω *be self-indulgent/pleasure-loving*. **ζῶσα** ptc fem. ζάω: σπαταλῶσα ζ. *live a life of self-indulgence*. **τέ-θνηκεν** *is dead*, pf of obs. θνήσκω *be dying*. ‖ **παρ-άγγελλε** impv -αγγέλλω *command*; *inculcate, insist on*. **ἀν-επί-λημπτος** *irreproachable*. **ὦσιν** subj. εἰμί. ‖ **οἱ ἴδιοι** *one's relatives*. **μάλιστα** superl. of comp. **μᾶλλον** *most, above all*. **οἰκεῖος** *member of one's household*. **προ-νοέω** τινός *provide for* one. **ἤρνηται** pf ἀρνέομαι *deny*, here by actions. **ἄ-πιστος** *un-believer*. **χείρων**[6] -ονος neut. χεῖρον comp. of κακός. ‖ **χήρα** v.3. **κατα-λεγέσθω** impv pass. 3rd sg -λέγω *enroll*. **ἐλάσσων** (= ἐλάττων) *less*, comp. of ὀλίγος; neut. ἔλασσον as adv. **ἔτος**[8] *year*. **ἑξήκοντα** = 60. **γε-γονυῖα** pf ptc fem. γίνομαι. **ἀνήρ, γυνή** *husband, wife*. ‖ **μαρτυρουμένη** *bearing a character/reputation for*, ptc pass. fem. -ρέω *witness, testify*; pass. *attested*. **ἐ-τεκνο-τρόφησεν**

5

2,3

4

5

6

7

8

9

10

aor. -τροφέω (τέκνον + τρέφω feed) *rear/bring up children.*
ἐ-ξενο-δόχησεν aor. -δοχέω (ξένος stranger + δέχομαι receive) *show hospitality.* ἔ-νιψεν aor. νίπτω *wash.* θλιβομένοις *those in distress,* ptc pass. θλίβω *press, oppress.*
ἐπ-ήρκεσεν aor. -αρκέω τινί *help* one. ἐπ-ηκολούθησεν aor.

11 -ακολουθέω *follow,* hence *devote oneself* to. ‖ νεώτερος v.1.
παρ-αιτοῦ impv -αιτέομαι *reject.* ὅταν w. subj. *when* in
fut. κατα-στρηνιάσωσιν aor. subj. -νιάω τινός word apparently coined by Paul to express at one and the same
time *sensuality* and rebellion *against,* ὅταν κ. *when sensuality turns them against Christ.* γαμεῖν inf. γαμέω *marry.* ‖

12 ἔχουσαι ptc fem. ἔχω. κρίμα⁷ *judgement,* ἔχ. κ. *earning
condemnation.* πρῶτος 2:13. πίστις of solemn *promise/
pledge* such as that made at marriage. ἠθέτησαν aor.
ἀ-θετέω *render* ἄ-θετος *(ineffective)* ; *set aside, disregard.* ‖

13 ἅμα *at the same time.* ἀργός (ἀ-εργός) *idle,* supply εἶναι.
μανθάνω v.4. περι-ερχόμεναι ptc -έρχομαι *go around,*
π. τ. οἰκίας *go from house to house.* φλύαρος *chattering.*
περί-εργος *interfering, busy-body.* λαλοῦσαι ptc fem. λαλέω.
δέοντα ptc (neut. pl.) δεῖ: τὰ μὴ δέοντα *of what must not*
(be mentioned), i.e. *of things about which they ought not.* ‖

14 βούλομαι *will, wish, want.* νεώτερος v.1. γαμεῖν v.11.
τεκνο-γονεῖν inf. -γονέω *bear children, have a family.*
οἰκο-δεσποτεῖν inf. -τέω *be mistress of a house, keep house.*
ἀφ-ορμή (ἀπό + ὁρμή start, impulse) *occasion, pretext.* διδό-
ναι inf. δίδωμι. ἀντι-κείμενος *opponent,* ptc -κειμαι *oppose.*
λοιδορία *reproach.* χάριν *for, because of* ; μηδεμίαν ἀφ.

15 λοιδορίας χ. *no pretext for reproach.* ‖ ἤδη *already.* ἐξ-ε-
τράπησαν aor² pass. ἐκ-τρέπω *turn* sth *aside* ; pass. refl.
turn aside from the right path. ὀπίσω w. gen. *after, in the*

16 *wake* of. ‖ πιστή fem. of πιστός meaning *?a woman believer*
or (in context) *?a faithful widow.* [[varr. πιστός: πιστὸς
ἢ πιστή]]. ἐπ-αρκείτω *she* (var. *he*) *must help them,* impv
-αρκέω v.10. βαρείσθω impv pass. 3rd sg βαρέω *burden,*
μὴ β. *let not the church be burdened.* ὄντως v.3. ἐπ-αρκέσῃ

17 aor. subj., subject ἡ ἐκκλησία. ‖ καλῶς *well.* προ-εστῶτες
pf (w. pres. sense) ptc -ίστημι *govern,* καλῶς πρ. *show
themselves good leaders,* cf 3:4. πρεσβύτεροι *presbyters.*
διπλοῦς -πλῆ -πλοῦν *double.* τιμή *honour,* prob. incl.
an honorarium, v.18. ἀξιούσθωσαν impv pass. 3rd pl.
ἀξιόω *regard* or *treat as worthy.* μάλιστα v.8. κοπιῶντες
ptc -ιάω *labour.* λόγος *the word,* t.t. for the gospel, i.e.

preaching. **διδασκαλία** *teaching.* || **γραφή** *scripture.* **βοῦς** 18
βοός ὁ *ox.* **ἀλοῶντα** ptc ἀλοάω *thresh,* i.e. by trampling out.
φιμώεις fut. φιμόω *muzzle,* fut. impvl (Dt 25:4 cited
I Cor 9:9). **ἄξιος** *worthy* ; ἁ. ...αὐτοῦ words ascribed to Jesus
Lk 10:7, whether as original or as making use of a common expression (and in this way familiar to the author
of this epistle) is not known. **ἐργάτης**[3] *worker.* **μισθός**
wages, recompense. || **κατ-ηγορία** *accusation, charge.* **παρα-** 19
δέχου impv -δέχομαι *accept,* μὴ π. "continue not to...",
never accept 4:14. **ἐκτὸς εἰ μή** pleon. *unless.* **ἐπί** *on the
basis of.* **τριῶν** gen. of τρεῖς. **μάρτυς**[6] -τυρος ὁ *witness.* ||
τ. ἁμαρτάνοντας *those who do sin,* ptc -τάνω *sin.* **ἔλεγχε** 20
impv ἐλέγχω *reprimand.* **ἐνώπιον πάντων** *publicly.* **λοιπός**
left (behind), οἱ λ. *the rest.* **φόβος** *fear.* **ἔχωσιν** subj. ἔχω. ||
δια-μαρτύρομαι *affirm solemnly.* **ἐκ-λεκτός** *elect.* **φυλάξῃς** 21
aor. subj. φυλάσσω *keep, observe.* **χωρίς** *without.* **πρό-**
κριμα[7] *pre-judice,* i.e. in favour of one or another. **ποιῶν**
ptc ποιέω. **πρόσ-κλισις**[4] *leaning, inclination,* i.e. to par-
tiality. || **ταχέως** *hastily.* **ἐπι-τίθει** impv -τίθημι *lay on.* 22
μηδέ *and...not.* **κοινώνει** impv -νέω τινί *take part in.*
ἀλλότριος *another's.* **σε-αυτόν** *your-self.* **ἁγνός** *pure.* **τήρει**
impv τηρέω. || **μηκ-έτι** *no longer.* **ὑδρο-πότει** impv -ποτέω 23
drink water (only), μηκέτι ὑδ. *stop drinking (nothing but)
water.* **οἶνος** *wine.* **ὀλίγος** *a little.* **χρῶ** (α + ου) impv
χράομαι *use.* **στόμαχος** *stomach.* **πυκνός** *frequent.* **ἀ-σθέ-**
νεια (ἀ- + σθένος[8] strength) *poor health.* || **τινῶν...τισίν** 24
(masc.) *of some...others...* **πρό-δηλος** *evident.* **προ-άγουσαι**
ptc fem. -άγω *pre-cede,* go ahead of. **ἐπ-ακολουθέω** τινί
follow sth ; subject is αἱ ἁμαρτίαι, lit. *the sins of some men
are evident, going ahead of them to judgement* (i.e. they are
already known), *while others* (i.e. other sinners, obj.)
they follow (come to light subsequently). || **ὡς-αύτως** 25
likewise. **ἄλλως** *otherwise,* ἅ. ἔχοντα (ptc) *which are otherwise* Ac 7:1 (ἔχω). **κρυβῆναι** aor[2] inf. pass. κρύπτω *hide* ;
one must understand aor. effective as *(cannot) be inde-
finitely suppressed.* || **ζυγός** *yoke.* **δεσπότης**[3] *master.* **τιμή** **6**
respect. **ἄξιος** *worthy.* **ἡγείσθωσαν** impv 3rd pl. ἡγέομαι
regard as, consider. **διδασκαλία** *Christian teaching.* **βλασ-**
φημῆται subj. pass. -φημέω *denigrate, speak ill of.* || **πιστός** 2
believing, i.e. Christian. **κατα-φρονείτωσαν** impv 3rd pl.
-φρονέω *look down on, despise* ; here, *think less of.* **ἀδελφοί**
i.e. *brothers* in Christ. **μᾶλλον** *all the more.* **δουλευέτωσαν**

impv -εύω serve, give good service. ἀγαπητός beloved, dear. εὐ-εργεσία a good work, work of kindness ; a benefit. ἀντι-λαμβανόμενοι ptc -λαμβάνομαι take hold of ; take in hand, take part in, help, benefit. ὅτι κτλ. supplies the motive for the extra service due to Christian masters : transl. either since they are believers and dear (to God, Rom 11:28) who take part in the good work (or works of kindness) ; or (as others who understand ἀντιλ. in a pass. sense) because those who are benefited by their (the slaves') good service are believers and dear (brothers).

3   διδασκε, παρακάλει impv. ‖ ἑτερο-διδασκαλέω teach something different. μή w. indic. in a real condition, only here in NT §440. προσ-έρχομαί τινι come up to ; adhere to. ὑγιαίνουσιν ptc dat. pl. ὑγιαίνω be healthy/sound. εὐ-

4 σέβεια piety, godliness ; κατ' εὐσέβειαν godly §130. ‖ τε-τύφωται pf τυφόομαι (pass.) be conceited, an alternative meaning for pf pass. being be foolish ; begins the apo-dosis. ἐπιστάμενος ptc -αμαι know. νοσῶν ptc νοσέω be ill ; v. περί τι met. be pining for sth. ζήτησις[a] investiga-tion ; debate. λογο-μαχία controversy. φθόνος envy. ἔρις[6] ἔριδος ἡ rivalry. βλασ-φημία slander. ὑπό-νοια suspicion.

5 πονηρός, in so far as dictated by ill-will. ‖ δια-παρα-τριβή (δια- to and fro + παρα-τρίβω rub against) mutual friction. δι-ε-φθαρμένων pf ptc pass. δια-φθείρω corrupt. νοῦς ὁ mind, τ. νοῦν acc. of respect §53. ἀπ-ε-στερημένων ptc pf pass. ἀπο-στερέω deprive one of sth. νομιζόντων ptc -ίζω consider, suppose, ptc causal, because they... πορισμός

6 profitable, way to make money, pred. ‖ αὐτ-άρκεια self-sufficiency, independence, i.e. of the contingent and super-

7 fluous. ‖ εἰσ-ηνέγκαμεν aor² -φέρω bring in §489. ὅτι: the difficulty of ὅτι = so that seems to be responsible for the var. (= Vulg.) ⟦ δῆλον ὅτι it is evident that (δῆλος clear).⟧

8 ἐξ-ενεγκεῖν aor² inf. ἐκ-φέρω take out. ‖ δια-τροφή sus-tenance ; means of subsistence. σκέπασμα[7] covering ; hence clothing, possibly also shelter. ἀρκεσθησόμεθα fut. pass. ἀρκέω be enough, pass. be satisfied/content, fut. we shall be content, or if standing for aor. subj. hort. let us be con-

9 tent §341. ‖ βουλόμενοι ptc βούλομαι want. πλουτεῖν inf. -τέω be rich. ἐμ-πίπτω fall into. πειρασμός temptation. παγίς[6] -ίδος ἡ snare. ἐπι-θυμία desire. ἀ-νόητος sense-less. βλαβερός (< βλάπτω harm) harmful. αἵ-τινες such as. βυθίζω sink (trans.), met. plunge. ὄλεθρος ruin. ἀπ-ώλεια

destruction. ‖ ῥίζα *root*. κακός *evil*, neut. as noun. φιλ- 10
αργυρία *love of money*. ἧς ref. ἀργύριον, *the goal* of φιλαργ.
ὀρεγόμενοι ptc ὀρέγομαί τινος *reach out* for sth. ἀπ-ε-
πλανήθησαν aor. pass. ἀπο-πλανάω *cause to wander away*;
pass. *wander away*. περι-έ-πειραν met. transl. freely
have been shot through, aor. περι-πείρω *put on a spit,
pierce*. ὀδύνη *pang*. ‖

ὦ w. voc. in NT emphatic §35. φεῦγε impv φεύγω τι 11
flee, shun sth. δίωκε impv διώκω *pursue*. ὑπο-μονή *fortitude*. πραϋ-παθία *gentleness*. ‖ ἀγωνίζου impv ἀγωνίζομαι 12
fight, struggle. ἀγών⁶ -ῶνος ὁ a *contest, fight* ; ἀγ. τῆς πίστεως
subjective gen., the fight which faith wages. ἐπι-λαβοῦ
aor² impv -λαμβάνομαί τινος *take hold* of sth, again the work
of faith. ἐ-κλήθης aor. pass. καλέω. ὡμο-λόγησας aor.
ὁμο-λογέω *confess, acknowledge*. ὁμο-λογία *accord* ; in NT
always *acknowledgement, confession*. μάρτυς⁶ -υρος ὁ *witness*. ‖ παρ-αγγέλλω *charge*. ζῳο-γονοῦντος ptc -γονέω *keep* 13
alive. μαρτυρήσαντος aor. ptc -ρέω τι *confirm, testify to*
sth. ‖ τηρῆσαι aor. inf. τηρέω, inf. obj. after παρ-αγγέλλω. 14
ἄ-σπιλος masc. and fem. *spot-less, un-stained*, ref. Timothy.
ἀν-επί-λημπτος *without reproach*. μέχρι *until*. ἐπι-φάνεια
manifestation, by act or appearance, of a divinity ; here
of Christ at his second coming. ‖ ἥν ref. Christ's appear- 15
ance. καιρὸς ἴδιος *his own* (good) *time* or *the proper time*.
δείξει fut. δείκνυμι *show*. μακάριος *blessed*. δυνάστης³ *po-
tentate*. βασιλευόντων ptc -εύω *reign*, ὁ β. *reigning mo-
narch, king*. κυριευόντων ptc -εύω *exercise lordship*, ὁ
κυριεύων *lord*. ‖ ἀ-θανασία *im-mortality*. οἰκῶν ptc οἰκέω 16
τι *dwell* in sth. ἀ-πρόσ-ιτος (< ἀ- + πρός + εἶμι (stem ἰ-)
go) *un-approachable*. ἰδεῖν aor² inf. ὁράω. τιμή *honour*.
κράτος⁸ *might*. ‖ πλούσιος *rich*. ὁ νῦν αἰών *the present age* 17
preceding the parousia. παρ-άγγελλε impv -αγγέλλω τινί
command, impress upon one. ὑψηλο-φρονεῖν inf. -φρονέω
be haughty. μηδέ *nor*. ἠλπικέναι *to set their hope*, pf inf.
ἐλπίζω *hope*. πλοῦτος *wealth*. ἀ-δηλότης⁶ -ότητος ἡ *uncertainty*. παρ-έχοντι ptc -έχω τινί *supply* one. πλουσίως
richly. εἰς *for*. ἀπό-λαυσις⁴ *enjoyment*. ‖ ἀγαθο-εργεῖν inf. 18
-εργέω *do good*. πλουτεῖν inf. -τέω *be rich*. εὐ-μετά-δοτος
(< εὖ *well* + μετα-δίδωμι *impart*) *generous*. κοινωνικός
ready to share. ‖ ἀπο-θησαυρίζοντας ptc -θησαυρίζω *treasure* 19
up. θεμέλιος *foundation, basis*. μέλλον ptc neut. μέλλω:
τὸ μ. *the future*. ἐπι-λάβωνται aor² subj. -λαμβάνομαι v.12.

20 ὄντως *really, truly.* ‖ παρα-θήκη (< παρα-τίθημι entrust)
   something entrusted, *trust, deposit.* φύλαξον aor. impv
   -άσσω *guard, keep.* ἐκ-τρεπόμενος ptc mid. -τρέπω τινά
   turn sth *aside* ; mid. *turn aside from, avoid* sth. βέβηλος
   godless. κενο-φωνία (< κενός empty + φωνή) *empty talk,*
   chatter. ἀντί-θεσις[4] *contradictions,* name for debates of a
   theoretical and technical kind. ψευδ-ώνυμος (< ψευδής[9]
21 + ὄνομα) *so-called (falsely).* γνῶσις[4] *knowledge.* ‖ ἐπ-αγγελ-
   λόμενοι ptc -αγγέλλομαί τι *promise ;* *make profession of* sth.
   πρός w. acc. *with regard to.* ἠ-στόχησαν aor. ἀ-στοχέω
   (< ἀ- + στόχος target) *be wide of the mark.* ‖

II TIMOTHY

κατά w. acc. perh. *with a view to, for.* **ἐπ-αγγελία** 1
promise. ‖ **ἀγαπητός** *beloved.* **ἔλεος**[8] *mercy.* ‖ 2
χάριν ἔχω τινί *I thank* one. **λατρεύω** τινί *serve, worship* 3
God. **πρό-γονος** *fore-bear, ancestor,* ἀπὸ πρ. *following my
forebears.* **καθαρός** *clean, pure.* **συν-είδησις**[4] *conscience.*
ὡς *when.* **ἀ-διά-λειπτος** *un-ceasing*; neut. as adv. *constantly.* **μνεία** *remembrance.* **δέησις**[4] *prayer, supplication.* **νυκτὸς καὶ ἡμέρας** *day and night,* gen. of time within
which. ‖ **ἐπι-ποθῶν** ptc -ποθέω τι *long for* sth. **ἰδεῖν** aor[2] 4
inf. ὁράω. **με-μνημένος** *having in mind,* pf ptc μιμνήσκομαί
τινος *remember* sth. **δάκρυον** *tear.* **χαρά** *joy*; gen. of
filling, *with joy.* **πληρωθῶ** aor. subj. pass. -ρόω. ‖ **ὑπό-** 5
μνησις[4] act. *reminder*; pass. *recollection.* **λαβών** aor[2] ptc
λαμβάνω. **ἀν-υπό-κριτος** masc. and fem. *un-feigned, sincere.* **ἥτις = ἥ,** or *such as.* **ἐν-ῴκησεν** aor. -οικέω *dwell
in.* **μάμμη** orig. "mother", later *grand-mother.* **πέ-πεισμαι**
I am convinced, pf pass. **πείθω** *persuade*; pf *convince.*
ὅτι sc. ἐνοικεῖ. ‖ **αἰτία** *cause, reason.* **ἀνα-μιμνήσκω** *re-* 6
mind. **ἀνα-ζω-πυρεῖν** inf. -πυρέω *rekindle.* **χάρισμα...ἐπι-**
θέσεως I Tim 4:14. ‖ **ἔ-δωκεν** aor. δίδωμι. **δειλία** *fearfulness,* 7
timidity. **σωφρονισμός** *moderation.* ‖ **ἐπ-αισχυνθῇς** aor. subj. 8
-αισχύνομαί τι *be ashamed of* sth. **μαρτύριον** *testimony,*
w. gen., act of *witnessing to.* **μηδέ** *nor.* **ἐμέ** *of me,* obj.
of ἐπαισχυνθῇς. **δέσμιος** (< δέω bind) *prisoner.* **συγ-**
κακο-πάθησον aor. impv -παθέω *take one's part in suffering.*
εὐ-αγγελίῳ *for the gospel,* dat. of advantage. **κατὰ δύναμιν**
θεοῦ *in the power of God.* ‖ **σώσαντος, καλέσαντος** aor. ptc 9
σῴζω, καλέω. **κλῆσις**[4] *vocation, calling.* **πρό-θεσις**[4] (< προ-
τίθημι propose) *purpose.* **δοθεῖσαν** aor. ptc pass. δίδωμι.
πρό *before.* **χρόνος** *time,* πρὸ χρ. αἰωνίων *before all eternity.* ‖
φανερωθεῖσαν aor. ptc pass. -ρόω *reveal.* **ἐπι-φάνεια** I Tim 10
6:14, here ref. first advent. **κατ-αργήσαντος** aor. ptc -αργέω
(render ἄ-εργος, inoperative) *bring to nothing, destroy.*
μέν...δέ II Cor 10:10. **φωτίσαντος** aor. ptc -ίζω τι *shed
light on* sth; *bring* sth *to light.* **ἀ-φθαρσία** *in-corruptibility*;

11 *immortality.* ‖ εἰς ὅ *to which,* ref. εὐαγγέλιον, i.e. preaching. ἐ-τέθην aor. pass. τίθημι *appoint.* κῆρυξ -υκος ὁ *herald.*

12 διδάσκαλος *teacher.* ‖ αἰτία v.6. πάσχω *suffer.* ἐπ-αισχύνομαι v.8. πε-πίστευκα pf -εύω: ᾧ πεπ. *in whom I have put my faith.* πέ-πεισμαι v.5. δυνατός *able.* παραθήκην

13 φυλάξαι (aor. inf.) I Tim 6:20. ‖ ὑπο-τύπωσις⁴ *model*; *norm.* ἔχε impv ἔχω. ὑγιαινόντων ptc -αίνω *be healthy/sound.*

14 ἤκουσας aor. ἀκούω τινός. ‖ φύλαξον aor. impv. ἐν-οικοῦν-

15 τος ptc v.5. ‖ 'Ασία Apoc 1:4. ἀπ-ε-στράφησαν aor² pass. -στρέφω *turn* sth *away,* pass. w. acc. *turn away from, turn*

16 one's *back on* one. ‖ δώη aor² opt. δίδωμι. ἔλεος v.2. οἶκος I Tim 5:4 ; was O. then dead ? his exclusion here and the separate prayer in v.18 leave us with this impression. πολλάκις *often.* ἀν-έ-ψυξεν aor. ἀνα-ψύχω *refresh, revive.* ἅλυσις⁴ *chain.* ἐπ-αισχύνθη aor. (wt aug.)

17 v.8. ‖ γενόμενος *when he came…he… aor²* ptc γίνομαι. σπουδαίως *promptly.* ἐ-ζήτησεν aor. -τέω. εὗρεν aor² εὑρίσκω. ‖ εὑρεῖν aor² inf. διηκόνησεν aor. διακονέω (aug-

18 mented as if cmpd vb) *minister to, serve,* ὅσα διηκ. *how many services he rendered.* βελτίων comp. of ἀγαθός, neut. βέλτιον as adv. *better,* here for positive *well,* or relative superl. *very well.* σύ emphatic. γινώσκω connoting personal knowledge. ‖

2   ἐν-δυναμοῦ impv pass. -δυναμόω *strengthen*; pass. *be*

2 *strong.* ‖ ἤκουσας aor. ἀκούω. μάρτυς⁶ -τυρος ὁ *witness,* διὰ πολλῶν μ. *before many witnesses* (able to corroborate where Paul's personal knowledge was wanting). παρά-θου aor² impv mid. -τίθημι *set before*; mid. *entrust.* πιστός *trustworthy.* οἵ-τινες *such as.* ἱκανός *sufficient,* ἱκ. …διδάξαι *capable of teaching.* ἔσονται fut. εἰμί. διδάξαι aor. inf.

3 διδάσκω. ἕτερος for ἄλλος §153. ‖ συγ-κακο-πάθησον aor. impv -παθέω *take one's share of suffering hardship.* στρα-

4 τιώτης³ *soldier.* ‖ στρατευόμενος *on active service,* ptc -ομαι *serve as a soldier.* ἐμ-πλέκεται pass. -πλέκω (ἐν- + πλέκω *weave*) *entangle,* pass. met. *be involved in.* βίος *daily life* I Tim 2:2. πραγματεία pl. *business, affairs.* στρατο-λογήσαντι *enlisting officer,* aor. ptc (-λογήσας) -λογέω *enlist.*

5 ἀρέσῃ aor. subj. ἀρέσκω τινί *satisfy* one. ‖ ἀθλῇ subj. ἀθλέω *compete* in a contest. στεφανοῦται pass. -νόω *crown.*

6 νομίμως *according to the rules.* ἀθλήσῃ aor. subj. ‖ κοπιῶντα *hard-working,* ptc -ιάω *labour.* γε-ωργός (< γῆ + ἔργον) *farmer.* καρπός *fruit, crop.* μετα-λαμβάνειν inf. -λαμβάνω

τινός *have a share of* sth. ‖ νόει impv νοέω *think about*;   7
grasp. δώσει fut. δίδωμι. σύν-εσις⁴ (< συν-ίημι *under-*
stand) *discernment, insight.* ‖ μνημόνευε impv -εύω τινός   8
(also τι) *remember.* ἐγηγερμένον pf ptc pass. ἐγείρω;
pass. intr. *rise* §230f. σπέρμα⁷ *seed, posterity.* ‖ ᾧ neut.   9
ref. (the preaching of) the gospel ; ἐν ᾧ *on account of which.*
κακο-παθέω *suffer.* μέχρι w. gen. *to the extent of, even.*
δεσμός a *bond,* pl. *chains, fetters.* κακ-οῦργος (< κακός +
ἔργω) *evil-doer, criminal.* δέ-δεται pf pass. δέω *bind,*
fetter. ‖ ὑπο-μένω *undergo, endure.* διά of final cause. ἐκ-   10
λεκτός *elect, chosen.* σωτηρία *salvation.* τύχωσιν aor² subj.
τυγχάνω τινός *attain* sth. ‖ πιστὸς ὁ λόγος I Tim 1:15.   11
συν-απ-ε-θάνομεν aor² -απο-θνῄσκω *die together with* (sc.
ἐκείνῳ). συ(ν)-ζήσομεν fut. -ζάω *live together.* ‖ συμ-βασι-   12
λεύσομεν fut. -βασιλεύω *reign together.* ἀρνησόμεθα fut.
ἀρνέομαι *deny, disown* ; εἰ w. fut. a concrete case §332.
κἀκεῖνος = καὶ ἐκεῖνος. ‖ ἀ-πιστέω *break faith, go back on*   13
one's word. ἀρνήσασθαι aor. inf. ‖

    ὑπο-μίμνῃσκε impv -μιμνήσκω *call to mind, remember.*   14
δια-μαρτυρόμενος ptc -μαρτύρομαι *adjure.* θεοῦ [[var. κυ-
ρίου]]. λογο-μαχεῖν inf. -μαχέω *fight/dispute over words.*
χρήσιμος *useful,* ἐπ᾽ οὐδὲν χρ. *serves no useful purpose,*
ἐπί final §129. κατα-στροφή (< κατα-στρέφω *overturn,*
destroy), *overthrow, ruin,* ἐπ᾽ οὐδὲν χρ., ἐπὶ κ. τ. ἀκουόντων
serves only to upset the listeners. ἀκουόντων ptc ἀκούω. ‖
σπούδασον aor. impv -άζω *be eager,* w. inf. *do one's utmost*   15
to. σε-αυτόν *your-self.* δόκιμος *approved.* παρα-στῆσαι aor.
inf. -ίστημι *present.* ἐργάτης³ *workman.* ἀν-επ-αίσχυντος
(ἀν- priv. + ἐπαισχύνομαι 1:8) *having nothing to be ashamed*
of. ὀρθο-τομοῦντα ptc -τομέω *cut* sth *straight* (sole oc-
currence in NT, LXX Prov 3:6 cut a direct way), here
impart the word of truth *without deviation, straight, un-*
diluted. ‖ βέβηλος *godless* I Tim 1:9. κενο-φωνία *empty*   16
talk, chatter. περι-ίστασο impv -ίσταμαί τι *go around,* so
avoid. πλείων neut. πλεῖον (comp. of πολύς) *more,* ἐπὶ πλ.
even more §70. προ-κόψουσιν fut. -κόπτω *progress, advance,*
ἐπὶ πλεῖον πρ. w. gen. *will make even further advances in...*
ἀ-σέβεια *un-godliness.* ‖ λόγος *teaching.* γάγγραινα *gan-*   17
grene. νομή *pasture,* met. ν. ἕξει (fut. ἔχω) transl. *will eat*
its way. ὧν *of their number, among whom.* ‖ οἵ-τινες = οἵ   18
§216. περί w. acc. *with regard to, over* the matter of.
ἠ-στόχησαν aor. ἀ-στοχέω *be wide of the mark.* ἀνά-στασις⁴

re-surrection. ἤδη *already*. γεγονέναι pf² inf. γίνομαι. ἀνα-
19 τρέπω *over-turn, upset*. ‖ μέντοι *however*. στερεός *firm,
solid*. θεμέλιος (< τίθημι) *foundation*. ἕστηκεν *stands*,
pf intr. (w. pres. sense) ἵστημι. σφραγίς⁶ -ῖδος ἡ *seal*, here
for an inscription. ἔ-γνω aor² γινώσκω, quotation from
LXX Num 16:5 ; constative aor. ὄντας ptc εἰμί: τούς
...αὐτοῦ *those who are his, his own*. ἀπο-στήτω aor² (intr.)
impv 3rd sg ἀφ-ίστημι *stand aloof / keep away from*. ἀ-
20 δικία *wickedness*. ὀνομάζων ptc -άζω *name*. ‖ σκεῦος⁸
utensil. χρυσοῦς -σῆ-σοῦν made *of gold*. ἀργυροῦς *of
silver*. ξύλινος *of wood*. ὀστράκινος *of earthenware*. ἁ μέν...
ἁ δέ *some...others*. εἰς *for*. τιμή *honour* = of special
value. ἀ-τιμία *dis-honour* = for humbler use (Rom 9:21). ‖
21 ἐκ-καθάρῃ aor. subj. -καθαίρω *purify*. ἡγιασμένον pf ptc
pass. ἁγιάζω *consecrate*. εὔ-χρηστος (< χράομαι use) *useful*. δεσπότης³ *master*. ἡτοιμασμένον *ready*, pf ptc pass.
22 ἑτοιμάζω *make ready*. ‖ νεωτερικός *youthful*. ἐπι-θυμία
desire. φεῦγε impv φεύγω *flee, shun*. δίωκε impv διώκω
pursue. μετά, ass. w. δίωκε rather than εἰρήνην. ἐπι-
23 καλουμένων ptc -καλέομαι *call upon*. καθαρός *pure*. ‖ μωρός
foolish. ἀ-παίδευτος *ignorant*. ζήτησις⁴ *speculation*. παρ-
αιτοῦ impv -αιτέομαι (mid.) *excuse oneself ; refuse, avoid*.
εἰδώς ptc pf-pres. οἶδα. γεννάω *bear*, met. *breed*. μάχη
24 *strife*. ‖ μάχεσθαι inf. μάχομαι *fight ; quarrel*. ἤπιος *kind*.
διδακτικός *with a gift for teaching*. ἀν-εξί-κακος (ἀνέξομαι
25 (fut. ἀνέχομαι bear + κακόν) *forbearing*. ‖ ἐν with §116.
πραΰτης⁶ -ύτητος ἡ *gentleness*. παιδεύοντα ptc -εύω *instruct*.
ἀντι-δια-τιθεμένους *opponents*, ptc. -τίθεμαι (mid.) *oppose
oneself to*. μή-ποτε ref. fut. (and so w. subj.) *lest ; μ.
δώῃ in case God may/intends to grant*... §345. δώῃ aor²
subj. δίδωμι. μετά-νοια *repentance*. εἰς *that leads to*. ἐπί-
26 γνωσις *knowledge*. ‖ ἀνα-νήψωσιν aor. subj. -νήφω (ἀνα-
again + νήφω be sober) *come to one's senses*. παγίς⁶ -ίδος
ἡ *snare*. ἐ-ζωγρημένοι pf ptc pass. ζωγρέω *capture and
keep alive* Lk 5:10. εἰς τό...θέλημα *for* (i.e. *to do*) *his will*.
ἐκεῖνος = αὐτός Tit 3:7.

3   γίνωσκε impv. ἔσχατος *last*. ἐν-στήσονται fut. -ίστα-
2 μαι *be imminent/at hand*. χαλεπός *difficult*. ‖ ἔσονται fut.
εἰμί. φίλ-αυτος *selfish*. φιλ-άργυρος *money-loving*. ἀλαζών
-όνος ὁ *boaster*. ὑπερ-ή-φανος *arrogant*. βλάσ-φημος *blasphemous*. γονεύς⁵ *parent*. ἀ-πειθής⁹ *dis-obedient, rebellious*. ἀ-χάριστος *un-grateful*. ἀν-όσιος *ir-religious* I Tim

1:9. ‖ ἄ-στοργος (ἀ- priv. + στοργή family affection) *devoid* 3
of natural affection, callous. ἄ-σπονδος (ἀ- + σπένδομαι
pour a libation) *implacable.* διά-βολος (< δια-βάλλω accuse) *slanderer.* ἀ-κρατής⁹ *in-temperate.* ἀν-ήμερος (un-
tamed) *savage.* ἀ-φιλ-άγαθος *unresponsive to good.* ‖ προ- 4
δότης³ *traitor.* προ-πετής⁹ (< πίπτω) *reckless.* τε-τυφωμένοι
pf ptc τυφόομαι (pass.) *be conceited.* φιλ-ήδονος *pleasure-
loving.* μᾶλλον ἤ here, *instead of*; the converse of §445.
φιλό-θεος *loving God.* ‖ μόρφωσις⁴ *form* in various senses, 5
here *appearance* opp. reality. εὐ-σέβεια *piety, godliness.*
ἠρνημένοι pf ptc ἀρνέομαι *deny.* ἀπο-τρέπου impv -τρέ-
πομαι *turn away from, reject.* ‖ ἐκ τούτων *among these/such.* 6
ἐν-δύνοντες ptc -δύνω *insinuate oneself, slip in.* αἰχμ-αλω-
τίζοντες ptc -ίζω (< αἰχμή spear + ἁλίσκομαι be captured)
hold captive ; here, *captivate.* γυναικάριον dim. w. sense
of *silly woman.* σε-σωρευμένα pf ptc pass. -εύω *heap/pile
up* ; σεσ. ἁμαρτίαις *loaded with sins.* ἀγόμενα ptc pass. ἄγω
lead. ἐπι-θυμία *desire.* ποικίλος *variegated* ; *of various
kinds.* ‖ πάν-τοτε *always.* μανθάνοντα ptc -θάνω *learn.* 7
καί *but* §455β. μηδέ-ποτε *never.* ἐπί-γνωσις 2:25. ἐλθεῖν
aor² inf. ἔρχομαι. δυνάμενα ptc δύναμαι. ‖ τρόπος *manner,* 8
way ; ὅν τρόπον advl phrase, *in the same way that, just as.*
ἀντ-έ-στησαν aor² ἀνθ-ίστημι *set against,* aor² w. sense of
mid. ἀνθ-ίσταμαί τινι *set oneself against one, oppose, defy.*
κατ-ε-φθαρμένοι *depraved,* pf ptc pass. κατα-φθείρω *corrupt.*
νοῦς νοός ὁ *mind* ; νοῦν and πίστιν ac. of respect, *with regard to/as* to §53. ἀ-δόκιμος *failing the test.* ‖ προ-κόψουσιν 9
ἐπὶ πλεῖον 2:16, οὐ... πλεῖον *they will not gain any further
ground.* ἄ-νοια *folly.* ἔκ-δηλος *evident.* ἔσται fut. εἰμί. ἡ
that sc. ἄνοια. ἐκείνων *of those* (*others*), i.e. J. and J.
ἐ-γένετο *came to be,* aor² γίνομαι. ‖

παρ-ηκολούθησας aor. -ακολουθέω *follow closely.* μου 10
emphatic. διδασκαλία *instruction.* ἀγωγή *way of life.* πρό-
θεσις⁴ (< προ-τίθημι set before) *resolve, aim.* μακρο-θυμία
patience. ὑπο-μονή (< ὑπο-μένω endure) *steadfastness.* ‖
διωγμός (< διώκω pursue) *persecution.* πάθημα⁷ (< πάσχω 11
suffer) *suffering.* οἷος *such as,* (2nd time) *such.* ἐ-γένετο
happened. ὑπ-ήνεγκα aor² (for -κον §489) ὑπο-φέρω *endure.*
ἐρ-ρύσατο aor. ῥύομαι *rescue.* ‖ εὐ-σεβῶς *devoutly,* εὐσ. ζῆν 12
to live a godly life. ζῆν inf. ζάω. διωχθήσονται fut. pass.
διώκω *persecute.* ‖ γόης⁶ γόητος ὁ *magician* ; here *charlatan.* 13
προ-κόψουσιν 2:16 ; πρ. ἐπὶ τὸ χεῖρον *go from bad to worse.*

χείρων[6] -ονος neut. χεῖρον comp. of κακός. πλανῶντες *deceivers*, ptc -νάω *lead astray, deceive.* πλανώμενοι *de-*
14 *ceived*, ptc pass. ǁ μένε impv μένω. ἐν οἷς = ἐν τούτοις ἅ §16. ἔ-μαθες aor[2] μανθάνω v.7. ἐ-πιστώθης aor. pass. πιστόω *put one's faith in* ; pass. *be sure/convinced.* εἰδώς
15 2:23. τίνων masc. ǁ καὶ ὅτι ass. w. εἰδώς. βρέφος[8] *infant.* γράμμα[7] *letter* of the alphabet, τὰ ἱερὰ γρ. *holy scripture(s).* δυνάμενα v.7. σοφίσαι aor. inf. -ίζω *make wise.* σωτηρία
16 *salvation.* ǁ πᾶς wt art. *all* (scripture) *as such* §189. γραφή *scripture.* θεό-πνευστος (< θεός + πνέω *breathe*) *God-inspired*, ϑ. καί... *being inspired by God* (*is*) *also* ... ὠφέλιμος *useful.* διδασκαλία v. 10. ἐλεγμός *refutation.* ἐπ-αν-όρθω-
17 σις[4] *correction.* παιδεία *discipline, training.* ǁ ἄρτιος *capable, fit.* ᾖ subj. εἰμί. ἐξ-ηρτισμένος *ready equipped*, pf ptc
4 pass. -αρτίζω *fit* (*out*), *equip.* ǁ δια-μαρτύρομαι *adjure.* μέλλοντος ptc μέλλω. ζῶντας ptc ζάω. ἐπι-φάνεια *appearing*, i.e. the parousia ; acc. after διαμαρτύρομαι *I ad-*
2 *jure* (*you*)...*by his appearing and by his reign.* ǁ κήρυξον aor. impv κηρύσσω *preach, proclaim.* ἐπί-στηθι *stand by, take your stand on*, aor[2] impv ἐφ-ίστημι *come upon* ; aor[2] and mid. *stand by.* εὐ-καίρως *timely, opportunely.* ἀ-καίρως *un-timely, in-opportunely.* ἔλεγξον aor. impv ἐλέγχω *admonish, advise.* ἐπι-τίμησον aor. impv -τιμάω *rebuke.* παρα-κάλεσον aor. impv -καλέω. μακροθυμία 3:10. διδαχή
3 *teaching.* ǁ ἔσται 3:9. ὑγιαινούσης ptc fem. -αίνω *be sound* or *healthy.* διδασκαλία *instruction.* ἀν-έξονται fut. -έχομαί τι cf II Cor 11:1, *put up with* sth, *tolerate* ; subject impers. "they". ἐπι-θυμία *desire.* ἐπι-σωρεύσουσιν fut. -σωρεύω *heap up* ; *load themselves with.* διδάσκαλος *teacher.* κνηθόμενοι ptc mid. κνήθω *scratch*, also *tickle*, κνηθ. τ. ἀκοήν
4 met. *having their ears titillated.* ἀκοή *hearing; ear.* ǁ μέν... δέ II Cor 10:10. ἀπο-στρέψουσιν fut. -στρέφω τί τινος† *turn* sth *away* from sth. μῦθος *fable.* ἐκ-τραπήσονται fut[2] pass. -τρέπω *turn* sth *aside* ; pass. in refl. sense *turn away from*, also *turn aside* (sc. from the right way) *to* (εἰς or
5 ἐπί) sth. ǁ νῆφε impv νήφω *be sober.* κακο-πάθησον *brave hardship*, aor. impv -παθέω *suffer.* ποίησον aor. impv ποιέω. εὐ-αγγελιστής[3] *evangelist.* διακονία *ministry, office.* πληρο-φόρησον aor. impv -φορέω = πληρόω *fulfil, ac-*
6 *complish.* ǁ ἤδη *already.* σπένδομαι pass. σπένδω *pour out* as a libation. ἀνά-λυσις[4] (ἀνα-λύω *depart*) *departure*, met. of *death.* ἐφ-έστηκεν *has come, is here*, pf -ίστημι v.2. ǁ

ἀγών⁶ -ῶνος ὁ *contest, fight.* ἠγώνισμαι pf ἀγωνίζομαι *fight.* 7
δρόμος (< δραμ- aor. stem of τρέχω run) *course.* τε-τέλεκα
pf τελέω *complete, finish.* τε-τήρηκα pf τηρέω. ‖ λοιπόν 8
transl. *now* in sense of *henceforth.* ἀπό-κειμαι *put away/on
one side* ; w. dat. *reserve for.* στέφανος *crown,* victor's
wreath. ἀπο-δώσει fut. -δίδωμι *give back* ; *give* sth due.
κριτής³ *judge.* ἠγαπηκόσι pf ptc ἀγαπάω, pf connoting
lasting effect considered from the standpoint of the last
judgement. ἐπι-φάνεια v.l. ‖

σπούδασον aor. impv -άζω *do* one's *best* to. ἐλθεῖν 9
aor² inf. ἔρχομαι. ταχέως (adj. ταχύς) *quickly.* ‖ ἐγ-κατ-έ- 10
λιπεν aor² -κατα-λείπω *leave alone, desert.* ἀγαπήσας aor.
ptc. ὁ νῦν αἰών *this world* opp. the world to come Tit
2:12. ἐ-πορεύθη aor. dep. -εύομαι *go.* Γαλατίαν [[var.
Γαλλίαν *Gaul*]]. ‖ ἀνα-λαβών aor² ptc -λαμβάνω *take* as com- 11
panion or *pick up* on the way. ἄγε impv ἄγω *bring.*
σεαυτοῦ *yourself, you.* εὔ-χρηστος *useful.* διακονία v.5. ‖
ἀπ-έ-στειλα aor. ἀπο-στέλλω. ‖ φαιλόνη *cloak.* ἀπ-έ-λιπον aor² 12,13
1st sg ἀπο-λείπω *leave behind.* ἐρχόμενος *when you come,*
ptc ἔρχομαι. φέρε impv φέρω *bring.* βιβλίον orig. dim.,
became the equivalent of βίβλος ἡ (form of βύβλος papyrus)
papyrus roll, book. μάλιστα superl. of μᾶλλον *above all,
chiefly.* μεμβράνα = Lat. *membrana, parchment.* ‖ χαλ- 14
κεύς⁵ *copper-smith.* κακόν τό *wrong, harm.* ἐν-ε-δείξατο
aor. -δείκνυμι *show,* ἐνδ. τι τινί *show/do* sth to one. ἀπο-
δώσει v.8. ‖ φυλάσσου impv mid. -άσσω *keep* ; mid. *keep* 15
oneself *clear (of).* λίαν *very* ; *strongly, violently.* ἀντ-έ-στη
aor² (intr.) ἀνθ-ίστημι in intr. tenses and mid. *oppose.*
ἡμέτερος *our.* ‖ ἀπο-λογία *defence.* παρ-ε-γένετο aor² παρα- 16
γίνομαι *be present* ; sts w. idea of help and support. ἐγκα-
τέλιπον v.10. λογισθείη aor. opt. pass. -ίζομαι *reckon,
count,* λ. τι τινί *count* sth *against* (sts also *credit*) one. ‖
παρ-έστη *stood by,* aor² -ίστημι *present* ; in intr. tenses 17
stand by, help, Rom 16:2. ἐν-ε-δυνάμωσεν aor. -δυναμόω
make strong, give strength/power to. κήρυγμα⁷ (κηρύσσω
preach) *preaching about Christ, gospel message.* πληρο-
φορηθῇ aor. subj. pass. -φορέω v.5. ἀκούσωσιν aor. subj.
ἀκούω. ἐρ-ρύσθην aor. pass. ῥύομαι *rescue.* λέων⁶ λέοντος ὁ
lion. ‖ ῥύσεται fut. ἔργον πονηρόν *evil* (= hostile) *action.* 18
σώσει fut. σῴζω. ἐπ-ουράνιος *heavenly.* ᾧ ἡ δόξα Phil
4:20. ‖

19,20   ἄσπασαι aor. impv ἀσπάζομαι *greet.* ‖ ἔ-μεινεν aor. μένω. ἀπ-έ-λιπον v.13. ἀ-σθενοῦντα ptc -σθενέω *be weak/in poor*
21   *health.* ‖ σπούδασον v.9. πρό *before.* χειμών⁶ -ῶνος ὁ
22   *winter* (avoiding storms at sea). ἐλθεῖν v.9. ‖ ὁ κύριος μετά... *may the Lord be with...* ‖

TITUS

κατά w. acc. perh. *with a view to, for,* II Tim 1:1. **1**
ἐκ-λεκτός *elect, chosen.* ἐπί-γνωσις[4] *knowledge.* εὐσέβεια
godliness, ἀλήθεια κατ᾽ εὐσέβειαν *truth in accordance with
religion,* signifying that based on or leading to genuine
religion. || ἐπί w. dat. ref. the basis, *in* the hope. ἐλπίς[6] **2**
-ίδος ἡ *hope.* ἐπ-ηγγείλατο aor. -αγγέλλομαι *promise.* ἀ-
ψευδής[9] *who knows no falsehood.* χρόνος *time.* || ἐ-φανέρω- **3**
σεν aor. -ρόω *reveal.* καιρὸς ἴδιος I Tim 6:15. κήρυγμα[7]
preaching, ἐν κ. wt art. stressing the manner §176. ἐ-
πιστεύθην aor. pass. -εύω τί τινι *entrust* one *with* sth ;
pass. *be entrusted with,* ὃ ἐπ. *with which I was entrusted*
§72. ἐπι-ταγή (< ἐπι- τάσσω order) *command.* || γνήσιος **4**
genuine, true. κοινός *common, shared,* κατὰ κ. πίστιν *in a
common faith.* χάρις καὶ εἰρήνη Rom 1:7. σωτήρ[6] -ῆρος ὁ
saviour. ||

χάριν w. gen. as adv. *for the sake of ; because of,* τούτου **5**
χ. *for this reason ;* τούτου ref. what follows §213. ἀπ-έ-
λιπον aor[2] ἀπο-λείπω *leave* (behind), intr. *remain.* λεί-
ποντα ptc -πω *leave ;* intr. *be lacking,* τὰ λ. *what remains*
(to be done). ἐπι-δι-ορθώσῃ aor. subj. mid. -ορθόω *set
right* (ὀρθός straight ; cf ἐπανόρθωσις II Tim 3:16), mid.
have / get sth *put right.* κατα-στήσῃς aor. subj. καθ-
ίστημι *appoint.* κατά distributive, κ. πόλιν *in each city.*
δι-ε-ταξάμην aor. mid. δια-τάσσω τινί *order, command* one. ||
ἀν-έγκλητος *ir-reproachable.* πιστός pass. *trustworthy ;* act. **6**
believing, τέκνα π. *children who are believers.* κατ-ηγορία
accusation, μὴ ἐν κ. w. gen. *not liable to a charge of.* ἀ-σωτία
(ἀ- priv. + σῴζω save, keep) *extravagance* often ass. w.
dissipation. ἀν-υπό-τακτος *in-sub-ordinate, rebellious.* || ἐπί- **7**
σκοπος *bishop* I Tim 3:1 (ἐπισκοπή). οἰκο-νόμος (< οἶκος +
νέμω manage) *steward.* αὐθ-άδης[9] *complacent ; arrogant.*
ὀργίλος *irascible.* πάρ-οινος *over-fond of wine.* πλήκτης[3]
pugnacious man. αἰσχρο-κερδής[9] *greedy for dishonest gain.* ||
φιλό-ξενος *hospitable.* φιλ-άγαθος *loving* (all that is) *good.* **8**
σώφρων[6] -ονος neut. σῶφρον *temperate.* ὅσιος *devout.* ἐγ-

9 **κρατής**⁹ *self-controlled.* ‖ **ἀντ-εχόμενον** ptc -έχομαί τινος *hold to, be faithful to* sth, ἀντεχ. ...λόγου *holding fast to the sure word in conformity with the doctrine.* **διδαχή** *teaching.* **πιστός** *sure,* v.6. **δυνατός** *able, competent.* ᾗ subj. εἰμί. **καί...καί** *both...and.* **παρακαλεῖν** inf. **ἐν** *with.* **διδασκαλία** *instruction.* **ὑγιαινούσῃ** ptc fem. -αίνω *be sound/healthy.* **ἀντι-λέγοντας** *opponents,* ptc -λέγω *contradict, oppose.* **ἐλέγχειν**

10 *refute,* cf II Tim 3:16 (ἐλεγμός). ‖ **ἀνυπότακτος** v.6. **ματαιο-λόγος** (μάταιος vain, empty) (*one spouting*) *wordy nonsense, wind-bag.* **φρεν-απάτης**³ (φρήν mind + ἀπατάω deceive) *one who deludes the mind.* **μάλιστα** superl. of μᾶλλον. **περι-τομή** *circum-cision,* οἱ ἐκ τῆς π. *those of*

11 *Jewish origin.* ‖ **ἐπι-στομίζειν** inf. -στομίζω *stop the mouth, silence.* **οἵ-τινες** *the kind who...* **ἀνα-τρέπω** *turn upside down, upset.* ἃ **μὴ δεῖ** *what they have no right to.* **χάριν**

12 v.5. **αἰσχρός** *base, disgraceful.* **κέρδος**⁸ *gain.* ‖ **τις ἐξ αὐτῶν** *one of them,* i.e. a Cretan. **ἴδιος αὐτῶν προφήτης** *a prophet of their own.* **Κρής Κρητός** ὁ *a Cretan.* **ἀεί** *always.* **ψεύ-στης**³ *liar.* **θηρίον** (*wild*) *beast,* κακὸν θ. *vicious brute.* **γαστήρ** -τρός ἡ (acc. -τέρα) *belly;* met. *glutton.* **ἀργός** (ἀ-εργός)

13 *idle.* ‖ **μαρτυρία** *testimony.* **ἀληθής**⁹ *true* (to fact). **αἰτία** *cause,* δι' ἥν αἰτ. *therefore.* **ἔλεγχε** impv ἐλέγχω *reprimand.* **ἀπο-τόμως** (< ἀπο- + τέμνω cut) *sharply, severely.* **ὑγιαίνω-σιν** subj. -αίνω v.9, ὑγ. ἐν τῇ πίστει *be sound in the faith.* ‖

14 **προσ-έχοντες** ptc -έχω (sc. τὸν νοῦν) *pay attention to.* **μῦθος** *fable, yarn.* **ἀπο-στρεφομένων** ptc mid. -στρέφω *turn* sth *away;* mid. in refl. sense, *turn away from,* hence *repu-*

15 *diate.* ‖ **καθαρός** *pure,* pred. **με-μιαμμένοις** pf ptc pass. μιαίνω *defile.* **ἄ-πιστος** *un-believing.* **με-μίανται** pf pass. **καί...καί** v.9. **νοῦς** *mind.* **συν-είδησις**⁴ *conscience.* ‖ **ὁμο-λογέω** *profess.* **εἰδέναι** inf. pf-pres. οἶδα. **ἀρνέομαι** *deny, repudiate.* **βδελυκτός** *abominable.* **ὄντες** ptc εἰμί. **ἀ-πει-θής**⁹ *in-tractable.* **ἀ-δόκιμος** (not passing the test) ἀδ. πρός τι *in-capable of, worthless for.* ‖

2 **λάλει** impv λαλέω. **πρέπει** τινί *befits,* here *is conso-*

2 *nant with* sth. **ὑγιαινούσῃ, διδασκαλία** 1:9. ‖ **πρεσβύτης**³ *an older man,* pl. *the older/elderly.* **νηφάλιος** *sober.* **εἶναι** *dependent* on λάλει, (tell)...*to be.* **σεμνός** *inspiring respect.* **σώφρων** 1:8. **ὑγιαίνοντας** ptc -αίνω *be sound.*

3 **ὑπο-μονή** *constancy.* ‖ **πρεσβῦτις**⁶ -ύτιδος ἡ *elderly woman.* **ὡσ-αύτως** *like-wise.* **κατά-στημα**⁷ (< καθίστημι 1:5) *bearing, behaviour.* **ἱερο-πρεπής**⁹ *reverent.* **διά-βολος** *slanderer, scan-*

dal-monger. **δε-δουλωμένας** *enslaved, addicted,* pf ptc pass. fem. -λόω τινί *be a slave* to one. **καλο-διδάσκαλος** a *teacher of what is noble and good.* ‖ **σωφρονίζωσιν** subj. -ίζω *train* 4 *in self-control.* **νέος** *young.* **φίλ-ανδρος, φιλό-τεκνος** *lover of/loving one's husband, children.* ‖ **σώφρων** 1:8. **ἀγνός** 5 *pure.* **οἰκ-ουργός** *house-keeper.* **ὑπο-τασσομένας** *submissive,* ptc pass. -τάσσω *subject*; pass. intr. *submit.* **βλασφημῆται** subj. pass. -φημέω *slander, speak ill of.* ‖ **νεώτερος** 6 comp. of νέος, as in Eng. freq. for positive §150. **ὡσαύτως** v.3. **παρα-κάλει** impv -καλέω. **σωφρονεῖν** inf. -νέω *be reasonable/sensible.* ‖ **σε-αυτόν** *your-self.* **περὶ πάντα** *in all res-* 7 *pects* ; according to punctuation of text ass. w. παρεχό-μενος rather than σωφρονεῖν. **παρ-εχόμενος** ptc -έχομαι **ἑαυτόν** τι *show oneself* (as)... **τύπος** *example.* **διδασκαλία** 1:9. **ἀ-φθορία** *absence of corruption, integrity.* **σεμνό-** **της**[6] -τητος ἡ *dignity* ; *probity, honour.* ‖ **ὑγιής**[9] *sound.* 8 **ἀ-κατά-γνωστος** (< κατα-γινώσκω condemn) *incontestable.* **ἐναντίος** *opposite* ; *opposed, hostile,* ὁ ἐξ ἐναντίας *the opponent.* **ἐν-τραπῇ** aor[2] subj. pass. -τρέπω *put to shame.* **φαῦλος** *worthless* ; μηδέν...λέγειν φ. *nothing bad to say.* ‖ **δεσπότης**[3] *master.* **ὑπο-τάσσεσθαι** inf. pass. v.5 ; inf. still 9 dependent on παρακάλει v.6. **εὐ-άρεστος** *pleasant, obliging.* **εἶναι** inf. εἰμί. **ἀντι-λέγοντας** *argumentative,* ptc -λέγω *contra-dict.* ‖ **νοσφιζομένους** ptc mid. -ίζω *set apart* ; mid. 10 *appropriate* for oneself, *pilfer.* **ἐν-δεικνυμένους** ptc mid. -νυμι *show,* mid. esp. *show* in oneself a quality. **πᾶσα πίστις ἀγαθή** *complete good faith* (i.e. honesty, trustworthiness). **διδασκαλία** 1:9. **κοσμῶσιν** subj. -μέω τι *adorn, bring honour* to sth. ‖ **ἐπ-ε-φάνη** aor[2] pass. ἐπι-φαίνω *show* ; pass. *appear.* 11 **σωτήριος** wt art. pred. *bringing salvation.* ‖ **παιδεύουσα** ptc 12 fem. -εύω *discipline, train.* **ἀρνησάμενοι** aor. ptc ἀρνέομαι *deny* ; *renounce.* **ἀ-σέβεια** *un-godliness.* **κοσμικός** *worldly.* **ἐπι-θυμία** *desire.* **σωφρόνως** *with moderation, responsibly.* **δικαίως** *uprightly.* **εὐ-σεβῶς** *devoutly.* **ζήσωμεν** aor. subj. ζάω. ὁ νῦν αἰών *this world* as opp. "the world to come" which Christ will inaugurate at his parousia. ‖ **προσ-** 13 **δεχόμενοι** ptc -δέχομαι *await.* **μακάριος** *blessed.* **ἐλπίς**[6] -ίδος ἡ *hope,* here, ref. the object of hope. **ἐπι-φάνεια** *appearing* ; lit. "the blessed hope and manifestation" ; καί perh. *namely, that is* §455ζ ; the single art. makes possible also "the hoped-for blessed manifestation" §184. **τοῦ...θεοῦ** **καὶ σωτῆρος...Χριστοῦ**: the one art. favours interpreting

14 the whole phrase of Christ, cf Eph 5:5 §185. ‖ ἔ-δωκεν aor. δίδωμι. ὑπέρ *for* = ἀντί *in place of* §91. λυτρώσηται aor. subj. mid. λυτρόω *redeem*. ἀ-νομία *wickedness*. καθαρίσῃ aor. subj. -ίζω *purify*. περι-ούσιος (περι-ουσία superiority) LXX transln of a Hebr. word for *special possession* Dt 7:6, and w. λαός Ex 19:5, 23:22, cf περι-ποίησις Eph 1:14, I Pt 2:9. ζηλωτής³ *enthusiast*, ζ. τινος *one eager*

15 *for* sth. ‖ λάλει v.1. παρακάλει v.6. ἔλεγχε 1:13. ἐπι-ταγή 1:3, here *authority*. περι-φρονείτω 3rd sg impv -φρο-νέω τινός *look down on* one. ‖

3 ὑπο-μίμνησκε impv -μιμνήσκω *recall to mind, remember*. ἀρχή a *ruler* ; supply "and". ἐξουσίαι *authorities*. ὑπο-τάσσεσθαι 2:9. πειθ-αρχεῖν inf. -αρχέω (= πειθόμενος τῇ

2 ἀρχῇ) *obey*. ἔτοιμος *ready*. εἶναι inf. εἰμί. ‖ βλασ-φημεῖν inf. -φημέω *defame, slander*. ἄ-μαχος *not quarrelsome, peaceable*. ἐπι-εικής⁹ *considerate*. ἐν-δεικνυμένους 2:10. πραΰ-

3 της⁶ -τητος ἡ *gentleness*. ‖ ἦμεν impf εἰμί. ποτέ (encl.) *at one time, once*. ἀ-νόητος *sense-less*. ἀ-πειθής⁹ *rebellious* against God. πλανώμενοι ptc pass. -νάω *lead astray, delude*. δουλεύοντες ptc -εύω τινί *serve* one. ἐπι-θυμία *desire*. ἡδονή *pleasure*. ποικίλος *variegated* ; *of different kinds*. κακία *malice*. φθόνος *envy*. δι-άγοντες ptc -άγω *spend* time, *lead* a life ; abs. *spend* one's *life*. στυγητός

4 *hateful*. μισοῦντες ptc μισέω *hate*. ‖ χρηστότης⁶ -τητος ἡ *kindness, goodness*. φιλ-ανθρωπία *love for man*. ἐπ-ε-φάνη

5 2:11. σωτήρ -ῆρος ὁ *saviour*. ‖ ἐξ *in consequence of*. ἔργα τὰ ἐν δικαιοσύνῃ *deeds of righteousness*. ἐ-ποιήσαμεν *we had done*, rel. past §290. ἡμεῖς nom. emphatic. κατά as result *of*. ἔλεος⁸ *mercy*. ἔ-σωσεν aor. σῴζω. λουτρόν *washing*, Eph 5:25. παλιγ-γενεσία *re-generation, re-birth*. ἀνα-καίνωσις⁴ *re-newal* ; ἀνακ. πνεύματος ἁγ. *renewal by the*

6 *Holy Spirit*. ‖ οὗ attracted from ὅ §16. ἐξ-έ-χεεν aor²

7 ἐκ-χέω *pour out*. πλουσίως *richly*. ‖ δικαιωθέντες aor. ptc pass. -αιόω *justify, show to be in the right, pronounce righteous* ; in Pauline thought a new creation. ἐκεῖνος = αὐτός. κληρο-νόμος (< κλῆρος lot + νέμω assign) *inheritor*. γενηθῶμεν aor² subj. pass. γίνομαι. ἐλπίς 2:13, κατ' ἐλπίδα

8 *in hope*, ass. w. κληρονόμοι. ‖ πιστὸς ὁ λόγος I Tim 1:15. βούλομαι *wish, want* ; *will*. δια-βεβαιοῦσθαι inf. -βεβαιόομαι *insist on, make a point of*. φροντίζωσιν subj. -ίζω *give one's mind* (φρήν) *to, be attentive/careful*. καλὰ ἔργα *good works*. προ-ΐστασθαι inf. -ίσταμαι (stand in front) *take the*

lead, rule ; w. gen. *make* sth *one's first concern, devote oneself to* sth. πε-πιστευκότες *those who have put their trust in God,* pf ptc -εύω τινί which must here = π. ἐπί *believe in,* cf Ac 18:8. ὠφέλιμος *useful, beneficial.* ‖ μωρός 9 *foolish.* ζήτησις⁴ *speculation.* γενεαλογία *genealogy* I Tim 1:4. ἔρις⁶ ἡ (usu. gen. -ιδος I Cor 1:11 but sts decliued like πόλις) *rivalry.* μάχη *strife,* pl. *wrangles.* νομικός *connected with/about the Law.* περι-ίστασο impv -ίσταμαί τι *go round, so avoid.* ἀν-ωφελής⁹ *use-less.* μάταιος sts used as fem. but I Cor 15:17, *pointless, futile.* ‖ αἱρετικός *fac-* 10 *tious,* αἱρ. ἄνθρωπος *a heretic,* meaning here *schismatic.* μία fem. of εἷς, cardinal for ordinal number Mk 16:2 = Lk 24:1. δεύτερος *second.* νου-θεσία (νοῦς + τίθημι) *warn-ing.* παρ-αιτοῦ impv -αιτέομαι *shun.* ‖ εἰδώς ptc pf-pres. 11 οἶδα, causal. ἐξ-έ-στραπται pf pass. ἐκ-στρέφω *turn inside out* ; *pervert.* τοιοῦτος *such a man, a man like that.* ἁμαρτάνω *sin.* ὤν ptc εἰμί. αὐτο-κατά-κριτος *self-condemned,* perh. meaning that what may have been unconscious error now becomes deliberate. ‖

ὅταν w. aor. subj. *when* ref. fut. πέμψω aor. subj. 12 πέμπω. σπούδασον aor. impv -άζω *make haste to.* ἐλθεῖν aor² inf. ἔρχομαι. κέκρικα pf κρίνω *judge; deem;* pf *have decided.* παρα-χειμάσαι aor. inf. -χειμάζω *spend the winter.* ‖ νομικός ὁ *lawyer.* σπουδαίως *with alacrity.* πρό-πεμψον aor. 13 impv -πέμπω *see* one *off, send on* one's *way* w. provision for the journey. λείπῃ subj. -πω *be lacking.* ‖ μανθανέτω- 14 σαν impv 3rd pl. -θάνω *learn.* ἡμέτερος *our,* οἱ ἡμ. *our people,* ?the Cretan Christians. προ-ίστασθαι inf. v.8. εἰς *for* (= to relieve). ἀναγκαῖος *essential.* χρεία *need.* ὦσιν subj. εἰμί. ἄ-καρπος *un-fruitful, unproductive* ; *idle.* ‖ ἀσπάζομαι *greet.* ἄσπασαι aor. impv. φιλοῦντας ptc *love* 15 *as friends.* ‖

PHILEMON

1   δέσμιος (< δέω bind) *prisoner*. ἀγαπητός *beloved*.
2 συν-εργός *fellow-worker*. ‖ ἀδελφή *sister*. συ(ν)-στρατιώτης³
fellow-soldier, comrade in arms. ἡ κατ' οἶκον...ἐκκλησία *the
community which meets in the house* of... ‖
4   εὐχαριστέω *give thanks, thank*. πάν-τοτε *always*. μνεία
remembrance, μν. ποιούμενος Eph 1:16. προσ-ευχή *prayer*. ‖
5 ἀκούων ptc ἀκούω. ἀγάπην...πρός, πίστιν...εἰς: *love for the*
6 *saints, faith in* Jesus. οἱ ἅγιοι I Thess 1:2. ‖ ὅπως w.
subj. *in order that*; here introducing the content of the
prayer. κοινωνία w. obj. gen. *sharing in* your faith or
subjective gen. *fellowship inspired by* your faith. ἐν-
εργής⁹ *operative, effective*. γένηται aor² subj. γίνομαι. ἐπί-
γνωσις⁴ *knowledge, realization*, ἐν ἐπίγ. ...Χριστόν perh. *in a
realization of our full capacity for good* (παντός...ἡμῖν) *in*
7 *the cause of* (εἰς) *Christ*. ‖ χαρά *joy*. ἔσχον I *derived/got*,
aor² ἔχω. παρά-κλησις⁴ *encouragement; consolation*. ἐπί w.
dat. indicating the basis for an emotion §126. σπλάγχνα τά
bowels as seat of emotions, Eng. *heart*. ἀνα-πέ-παυται *are
refreshed*, pf pass. -παύω *refresh*. ἀδελφέ voc. ‖
8   δι-ό *accordingly, so it is that*. παρ-ρησία *boldness, confidence*. ἔχων ptc (concessive). ἐπι-τάσσειν inf. -τάσσω
command. ἀν-ῆκον ptc -ήκει impers. *it is right/proper/one's
9 duty*. ‖ μᾶλλον παρακαλῶ I *prefer to* / I *would rather make
an appeal*, π. σε (v.10) I *appeal to you*. τοι-οῦτος ὤν (ptc
εἰμί) ὡς *being such as* (I *am*). πρεσβύτης³ *old man*; others
understand as parallel to δέσμιος (v.1) πρεσβύτης *an
ambassador, and now also a prisoner, of Jesus Christ*,
10 cf Eph 6:20. νυνὶ δέ *and now*. καί *also*. ‖ περί = ὑπέρ
11 §96. ἐ-γέννησα aor. γεννάω *beget*. δεσμός *bond*. ‖ ποτέ
(encl.) *at one time, once*. ἄ-χρηστος (< χράομαι use) *use-
less*. νυνὶ δέ *but now*. εὔ-χρηστος transl. *really useful*
(implying "not only in name" — ὀνήσιμος meaning "use-
12 ful"). ‖ ἀν-έ-πεμψα aor. ἀνα-πέμπω *send back*, i.e. with this
letter, epistolary aor. τοῦτ' ἔστιν *in other words*. σπλάγχνα
13 v.7. ‖ ἐ-βουλόμην impf -λομαι *want*, impf replacing class.

opt. w. ἄν for modest assertion, ὃν ἐβ. *whom I should have liked* §356. πρός w. acc. sts *by, beside*, Mk 2:2. κατ-έχειν *keep, hold on to.* ὑπὲρ σοῦ for ἀντὶ σοῦ *in your stead* §91. διακονῇ subj. διακονέω τινί *serve/attend to* one. δεσμός v.10. ‖ χωρίς *without.* σός *your* (sg). γνώμη *opinion* ; 14 *consent.* ἠθέλησα aor. θέλω. ποιῆσαι aor. inf. ποιέω. ἀνάγκη *necessity* ; *compulsion*, κατὰ ἀν. *under compulsion.* τὸ ἀγαθόν *good deed.* ᾖ subj. εἰμί. ἑκούσιος *willing*, κατὰ ἑκ. *voluntarily, of* one's own *free will.* ‖ τάχα (< ταχύς *quick*) 15 *possibly, perhaps.* διὰ τοῦτο *this was why* §112. ἐ-χωρίσθη aor. pass. -ίζω *divide, separate* ; pass. sts *go away*, cf Ac 18:1 (here euphemism for "ran away"). πρὸς ὥραν *for a time.* αἰώνιος, neut. as adv. *for ever.* ἀπ-έχῃς that *you might have him back*, subj. -έχω *receive* (as payment in full). ‖ οὐκ-έτι *no longer.* ὑπέρ w. acc. *above* ; *more than.* 16 ἀγαπητός v.1, ass. w. ἐμοί and σοί. μάλιστα superl. of μᾶλλον, here elative, (ἀγ.) μ. *exceptionally so.* πόσος exclamatory, *how much !* π. μᾶλλον (by) *how much more.* καί... καί *both...and.* ἐν σαρκί *as a man.* ἐν κυρίῳ i.e. *as a Christian* ; in the order of nature and in the order of grace. ‖ εἰ w. indic. a simple condition §303. ἔχω w. acc. and 17 pred. acc. *hold/regard...as* sth. κοινωνός *sharer, partner* (in the faith v.6). προσ-λαβοῦ aor² impv -λαμβάνομαι *welcome.* ‖ ἠ-δίκησεν aor. ἀ-δικέω *injure, wrong.* ὀφείλω *owe.* 18 ἐλ-λόγα impv ἐλ-λογάω τινί *put down to* one's *account.* ‖ ἔ-γραψα *I am writing*, (epistolary) aor. γράφω. ἀπο-τίσω 19 fut. -τίνω *repay, pay back.* ἵνα μὴ λέγω *not to mention* II Cor 9:4. σε-αυτόν *your own self.* προσ-οφείλω *owe besides* ; though often = simplex. ‖ ναί *yes.* ἀδελφέ v.7. 20 ἐγώ emphatic. ὀναίμην *let me have the pleasure of* sth from you, aor² opt. mid. ὀνίνημι *benefit, enjoy.* ἀνά-παυσον aor. impv. σπλάγχνα v.7. ‖ πε-ποιθώς *confident*, pf² ptc πείθω 21 *persuade.* ὑπ-ακοή *obedience*, here *compliance* (cf v.9). εἰδώς ptc pf-pres. οἶδα. ὑπέρ v.16. ποιήσεις fut. ποιέω. ‖ ἅμα *at the same time.* ἑτοίμαζε impv -άζω *prepare*, pres. 22 perh. *be getting* a room *ready for me.* ξενία *hospitality* ; here, *guest room*, cf Ac 28:23. ἐλπίζω *I am hoping.* προσευχή *prayer.* χαρισθήσομαι fut. pass. -ίζω *grant* a favour, here, *freedom* (Ac 3:14), i.e. *I shall be spared* to you. ‖

ἀσπάζομαι *greet.* συν-αιχμ-άλωτος *fellow prisoner* (Col 23 4:10). συν-εργός v.1. ‖

1   πολυ-μερῶς (adj. -μερής[9] of many parts) *bit by bit, gradually.* πολυ-τρόπως (τρόπος way) *in many ways.* πάλαι *of old, in time past.* λαλήσας aor. ptc λαλέω. τοῖς πατράσιν (dat. pl. of πατήρ) not to be confined to the patriarchs;

2 *our forefathers.* ἐν ?instr. *by*; better, *in.* ‖ ἔσχατος *last,* τὸ ἔ. *end*; ἐπ᾽ ἐσχάτου τ. ἡμερῶν being LXX expression for the future messianic age, τούτων introduces an eschatological note, as it were *in these last days*; on the underlying Sem. idiom §41. ἐ-λάλησεν aor. ἐν υἱῷ wt art. seemingly stressing sonship opp. prophets, cf 12:7 §176. ἔ-θηκεν aor. *set*; *appoint.* κληρο-νόμος (< κλῆρος lot + νέμω distribute) *inheritor.* ἐ-ποίησεν aor. ποιέω. οἱ αἰῶνες

3 pl. Hebr., *the created worlds* 11:3. ‖ ὤν ptc εἰμί. ἀπ-αύγασμα[7] (< αὐγή light) *radiance.* χαρακτήρ[6] -ῆρος ὁ *impress* as of a seal. ὑπό-στασις[4] (< ὑφ-ίστημι cause to exist) with the development of Christology became t.t. for "Person" opp. οὐσία but in earlier centuries freely used in the sense of *being, reality, substance.* φέρων ptc φέρω *carry, bear*; *uphold.* ῥῆμα[7] *word,* instr. dat.; ῥ. τῆς δυνάμεως αὐτοῦ "Hebr." gen. meaning "his all-powerful word" §41. καθαρισμός *purification.* ποιησάμενος aor. ptc mid. ποιέω; class. use of mid. where π. combines w. its obj. to express the same idea as the cognate vb (here = καθαρίσας) §227. ἐ-κάθισεν aor. -ίζω *make one sit*; intr. *take* one's *seat, sit down.* δεξιός *right* (opp. left), δεξιά (sc. χείρ) *right (hand).* μεγαλωσύνη *majesty,* here as name for God, also 8:1. ὑψηλός *high,* ἐν ὑψηλοῖς *on high,* i.e. in heaven. ‖

4 τοσοῦτος...ὅσος Lat. *tantus...quantus,* τοσούτῳ + comp. ...ὅσῳ Fr. *d'autant...que,* (by) *as much...as.* κρείττων -ονος neut. κρεῖττον (comp. from same root as κράτος[8] strength, might) used as comp. of ἀγαθός, *better.* γενόμενος aor[2] ptc γίνομαι. τῶν ἀγγέλων gen. of comp., *than the angels.* δια-φορώτερος (comp. of διά-φορος different) *excellent, distinguished.* κε-κληρο-νόμηκεν pf κληρο-νομέω *inherit.* παρά w. acc. may express comparison, *in comparison*

to, than Lk 3:13. V.4*b* balances 4*a*, τοσούτῳ: κρείττων: τῶν ἀγγέλων paralleled by ὅσῳ: διαφορώτερον: παρ' αὐτούς, lit. "having been made mightier (superior) : than (to) the angels : by as much :: as : he has inherited a name more distinguished : in comparison to them (than theirs)". ‖

ποτέ (encl.) *at any time, ever.* εἶ 2nd sg εἰμί. σήμερον **5** *today.* γε-γέννηκα pf γεννάω *beget.* ἔσομαι...ἔσται fut. εἰμί. εἰς πατέρα for nom. pred., = a cstr of Hebr. orig. ‖ ὅταν **6** δὲ πάλιν *and again when,* ὅταν w. subj. ref. fut. §335. εἰσ-αγάγῃ aor² subj. -άγω *bring into* (sc. at the parousia). πρωτό-τοκος (< τίκτω bear) *first-born.* οἰκουμένη (sc. γῆ) (inhabited) *world.* προσ-κυνησάτωσαν aor. impv 3rd pl. -κυνέω τινί *worship* one. πάντες ἄγγελοι wt art. signifying all angels as such §188. ‖ μέν...δέ (v.8) Lat. *quidem... autem,* roughly equivalent to *on the one hand...on the other hand, ...indeed but..., while...yet...* ποιῶν ptc ποιέω, w. double acc. *make* one sth. Like πνεύματα the orig. Hebr. word (Ps 104:4) may equally well mean *spirits* or *winds.* λειτ-ουργός (< λαός + ἔργον) *minister* whether in civil or divine service ; in NT always w. religious connotation. φλόξ φλογός ἡ *flame,* πυρὸς φ. *a fiery flame,* "Hebr." gen. §40. ‖ θρόνος *throne.* ὁ θεός art. w. nom. for voc. §34. **8** εἰς τόν...αἰῶνος *for ever and ever.* ῥάβδος ἡ *sceptre.* εὐθύ-της⁶ (< εὐθύς straight) -τητος ἡ *uprightness.* σοῦ ⟦var. αὐτοῦ ⟧. ‖ ἠγάπησας aor. ἀγαπάω. ἐ-μίσησας aor. μισέω *hate.* **9** ἀ-νομία *lawlessness, iniquity.* ἔ-χρισεν aor. χρίω *anoint* ; in Hebr. "anoint one with" is expressed in a double acc. ὁ θεός (1st time) could be voc., "for this reason, O God, thy God has anointed thee". ἔλαιον *oil.* ἀγαλλίασις⁴ *exhilaration.* παρά w. acc. v.4, *rather than,* Rom 1:25. μέτ-οχος (< μετ-έχω share) *associate,* pl. *fellows.* ‖ ἀρχή *beginning,* **10** κατ' ἀρχάς *in the beginning.* κύριε voc. ἐ-θεμελίωσας aor. -ιόω *lay the foundation of, found.* ‖ ἀπ-ολοῦνται fut. mid. **11** -όλλυμι. δια-μένω *remain.* ἱμάτιον *garment.* παλαιωθήσον-ται fut. pass. -αιόω *make old* ; pass. *grow old, wear out.* ‖ ὡσεί *as, like.* περι-βόλαιον (< περι-βάλλω throw round) **12** *cloak.* ἑλίξεις fut. ἑλίσσω *roll up.* ὡς ἱμάτιον ⟦var. om. w. Ps 102:27⟧. ἀλλαγήσονται fut² pass. ἀλλάσσω *make other* (ἄλλος) *than it is, change.* ὁ αὐτός *the same.* ἔτος⁸ *year.* ἐκ-λείψουσιν fut. -λείπω intr. *fail,* in sense of *come to an end.* ‖ εἴρηκεν pf λέγω. ποτέ v.5. κάθου *sit !* (class. **13** κάθησο) impv κάθημαι. δεξιά v.3, neut. pl. (sc. μέρη) the *right side*. θῶ aor² subj. τίθημι, here *make*. ἐχθρός *enemy*.

14 ὑπο-πόδιον *footstool*, pred. ‖ οὐχί interr. expecting the answer "Yes". λειτουργικός *ministering*, cf v.7 (λειτουργός). εἰς *for*. διακονία *service*. ἀπο-στελλόμενα ptc pass. -στέλλω. μέλλοντας ptc μέλλω : τοὺς μ. κληρονομεῖν (inf. v.4) *those who are destined to inherit*. σωτηρία *salvation*. ‖

2 περισσοτέρως *increasingly*. προσ-έχειν inf. -έχω (sc. τὸν νοῦν) *pay attention to, heed*. ἀκουσθεῖσιν aor. ptc pass. *to what we have heard*, i.e. *learnt*. μή-ποτε *lest*. παρα-ρυῶμεν aor² subj. pass. -ρέω *flow past* ; pass. met. *be carried/

2 drift away*. ‖ δι' ἀγγέλων: for the tradition cf Ac 7:53, Gal 3:19. λαληθείς aor. ptc pass. λαλέω. ἐ-γένετο aor² γίνομαι. βέβαιος *firm ; confirmed, valid*. πᾶσα wt art. *every*. παρά-βασις⁴ (< παρα-βαίνω) *transgression*. παρ-ακοή *dis-obedience*. ἔ-λαβεν aor² λαμβάνω. ἔν-δικος *just, deserved*. μισθ-απο-δοσία (μισθός *wage* + ἀπο-δίδωμι give back)

3 reward ; retribution*. ‖ ἐκ-φευξόμεθα fut. -φεύγω *escape*. τηλικ-οῦτος *so great*. ἀ-μελήσαντες aor. ptc -μελέω *take no notice of, ignore*, ptc conditional, *if we ignore*. σωτηρία 1:14. ἥ-τις *such (a salvation) as*. ἀρχή *origin*. λαβοῦσα aor² ptc fem., ἀρχὴν λ. *having received its origin*. λαλεῖσθαι *to be proclaimed*, inf. pass. λαλέω. ὁ κύριος w. art. in NT designating Jesus Christ. ἀκουσάντων aor. ptc ἀκούω: οἱ ἀκ. *those who heard, the listeners*. εἰς ἡμᾶς *to us*. ἐ-βε-

4 βαιώθη aor. pass. -αιόω *confirm, guarantee*. ‖ συν-επι-μαρ-τυροῦντος ptc -μαρτυρέω *bear joint witness* to (ἐπί) sth, *add one's testimony* ; gen. abs. τέρας τέρατος τό a *wonder*. ποικίλος *variegated ; various*. δύναμις⁴ pl. *works of great power*. μερισμός (μερίζω divide into parts ; share out) *distribution*, πνεύματος ἁγίου μ. *distributing (the gifts of) the Holy Spirit*. θέλησις⁴ strictly *exercise of the will*, opp. θέλημα *what is willed*, but the distinction cannot everywhere be pressed. ‖

5 ὑπ-έ-ταξεν aor. ὑπο-τάσσω *put under, subject* ; the author's point being the superiority of Christ as man over the angels. οἰκουμένη *world* 1:6. μέλλουσαν *to come*, ptc fem. μέλλω, having in mind less the time than the

6 character of the new age. ‖ δι-ε-μαρτύρατο aor. δια-μαρ-τύρομαι *affirm solemnly*. πού (encl.) *somewhere*. ὅτι causal, not = "because" but giving the reason why the question is asked : *since, seeing that* §420. μιμνήσκῃ 2nd sg

-σκομαι *remember.* ἐπι-σκέπτῃ 2nd sg -σκέπτομαι (ἐπί +
σκέπτομαι *inspect*) *visit* ; in NT always prompted by God's
mercy and good will. ‖ ἠλάττωσας aor. ἐλαττόω (ἐλάσσων 7
inferior) *bring low, humble.* βραχύς -χεῖα -χύ *short* ; βραχύ τι
for a short time. παρά 1:4. τιμή *honour.* ἐ-στεφάνωσας
aor. -νόω *crown* ; ἐστεφ. αὐτόν ⟦[var. add , καὶ κατέστησας αὐτὸν ἐπὶ τὰ ἔργα τῶν χειρῶν σου *and didst set him over the
works of thy hands* (κατ-έ-στησας aor² καθ-ίστημι *appoint*)]⟧. ‖
ὑπ-έ-ταξας v.5. ὑπο-κάτω w. gen. *under.* ὑπο-τάξαι aor. 8
inf. ἀφ-ῆκεν aor. -ίημι *leave.* ἀν-υπό-τακτος *not subject.*
οὔπω *not yet.* ὑπο-τε-ταγμένα *subject, in subjection to,* pf
ptc pass. ‖ ἠλαττωμένον pf ptc pass., τὸν δέ...ἠλ. *the one* 9
who ; in view of the definitive nature of the pf (§285) some
would understand βραχύ of degree : *a little* lower, cf v.7.
βλέπομεν 'Ιησοῦν *we see* (*to be*) *Jesus.* πάθημα⁷ *suffering,*
π. τοῦ θανάτου *suffering of,* i.e. (entailed by) *death,* gen.
epexeg. §45. As ἠλατ. expresses the beginning of the
incarnation διὰ τ. πάθ. τ. θαν. may be understood to indicate the end ; or, ass. w. what follows, as specifying the
purpose of Jesus's death. ἐ-στεφανωμένον pf ptc pass.
v.7. ὅπως w. subj. *in order that.* γεύσηται aor. subj.
γεύομαί τινος *taste* ; *experience.* ‖ ἔ-πρεπεν impf πρέπει τινί 10
impers. *it is fitting* for one. δι' ὅν...καὶ δι' οὗ *for whom*
(final cause)...*and through whom* (efficient cause) §113.
πολλούς not a limitation of παντός v.9 but dictated by the
thought that "all" are "many" Mk 10:45. ἀγαγόντα aor²
ptc ἄγω *bring* ; the acc. (instead of dat. agreeing w. αὐτῷ)
is a possible alternative since God (αὐτόν) is the subject
of the inf. τελειῶσαι §394. ἀρχηγός *prince, leader* ; *founder,
author,* here combining the ideas of divine author and
human leader, cf Ac 5:31. σωτηρία v.3. τελειῶσαι aor.
inf. -ειόω *consummate, perfect.* Lit. "it was fitting for
him (God)... in bringing many to glory, to perfect *through
suffering the author...*" ; Gk style would also allow for a
transposition of ptc and inf. so yielding "it was fitting
for him to bring many to glory, in perfecting..." §263,
cf I Tim 1:12. ‖ ἁγιάζων ptc -άζω *consecrate.* ἁγιαζόμενοι 11
ptc pass. ἐξ ἑνός *from one* (the Father, both of Jesus
and of the "many sons"). αἰτία *cause,* δι' ἣν αἰτίαν *for
which reason, that is why.* ἐπ-αισχύνομαι *be ashamed.* κα-
λεῖν inf. ‖ ἀπ-αγγελῶ fut. -αγγέλλω *declare.* ἐν μέσῳ (wt 12
art. when gen. follows §182) *in the midst of.* ἐκκλησία

assembly. ὑμνήσω fut. ὑμνέω τινά *sing praises* to one. ‖

13 ἔσομαι fut. εἰμί. πε-ποιϑώς pf ptc πείϑω *persuade*; pf² *be convinced/confident.* παιδίον *son, child.* ἔ-δωκεν aor. δί-

14 δωμι. ‖ ἐπεί *since.* κε-κοινώνηκεν pf -νέω τινός *share (in)* sth. καὶ αὐτός *he too.* παρα-πλησίως (< πλησίον *near*) *likewise.* μετ-έσχεν aor² -έχω *partake, share* sth along with others. τῶν αὐτῶν i.e. the flesh and blood of men. κατ-αργήσῃ aor. subj. -αργέω (κατ- + α- + ἔργος put out of action) *bring to nothing, destroy.* κράτος⁸ *might, power.* ἔχοντα ptc ἔχω. τοῦτ' ἔστιν *that is to say.* διά-βολος (δια-βάλλω *slander*)

15 *accuser,* the *devil.* ‖ ἀπ-αλλάξῃ aor. subj. -αλλάσσω *free.* φόβος *fear,* φόβῳ *in fear.* ζῆν inf. ζάω *live,* as noun : διὰ παντὸς τοῦ ζ. *during their whole life.* ἔνοχός τινος *liable*

16 or *subject to* sth. δουλεία *slavery.* ‖ οὐ γὰρ δήπου *for of course / as you know...not.* ἐπι-λαμβάνομαί τινος *take* sth *upon oneself* (mid.), *take on,* as in Eng. w. connotation of responsibility for ; ref. priestly work of Jesus and assuming the incarnation to have taken place (v.14) ; v.17 explaining the link between the two. σπέρμα⁷ *seed, descendants.* ‖

17 ὅ-ϑεν *hence, this being so.* ὤφειλεν *he had to,* impf ὀφείλω *owe*; w. inf. *ought.* κατὰ πάντα *in all respects, in everything.* ὁμοιωϑῆναι aor. inf. pass. ὁμοιόω τινά τινι *make one like* sth ; pass. *become like.* ἐλεήμων *merciful.* γένηται aor² subj. γίνομαι. πιστός *faithful* ; here, *worthy of all confidence* ; ἐλεήμων...καὶ π. recalling an ass. freq. in Psalms, e.g. 25:11. τά acc. of respect, τὰ πρὸς τ. θεόν *in what concerns God* §74. εἰς τό w. inf. final. ἱλάσκεσθαι inf. ἱλάσκομαί τι *make propitiation/expiation for* sth ; pres. continuous,

18 cf 7:25b. ‖ ἐν ᾧ *in that, because,* ἐν causal Rom 8:3 §119. πέ-πονϑεν pf² πάσχω *suffer.* αὐτός *he himself,* nom. emphatic. πειρασϑείς aor. ptc pass. -άζω *tempt.* πειραζο-μένοις ptc pass., τοῖς π. *those under temptation.* βοηϑῆσαι aor. inf. -θέω τινί *give help to/help* one. ‖

3 ὅϑεν 2:17. ἅγιος not primarily of personal holiness but as ref. what is consecrated to God opp. this world ; common term for Christians, so ἀδελφοὶ ἅγιοι = *brothers in Christ.* κλῆσις⁴ *calling.* ἐπ-ουράνιος *heavenly,* a calling from heaven to heaven Eph 1:3. μέτ-οχος (< μετ-έχω) *sharer, partner.* κατα-νοήσατε aor. impv -νοέω *reflect on, consider.* ὁμο-λογία *profession, confession,* τῆς ὁ. ἡμῶν *in*

2 that he is the obj. of our confession. ‖ πιστός 2:17. ὄντα ptc εἰμί. ποιήσαντι aor. ptc ποιέω *appoint.* ὡς καί M.

as M. also. [[var. om. ὅλῳ]] οἶκος *house, household.* αὐτοῦ i.e. God's. ‖ πλείων πλείονος neut. πλεῖον *more, greater.* 3 παρά w. acc. *than* 1:4. ἠξίωται pf pass. ἀξιόω τινά τινος *deem/consider sb* or *sth more worthy of sth.* καθ' ὅσον *inasmuch as.* τιμή *honour.* οἴκου gen. of comp. κατα-σκευάσας aor. ptc -σκευάζω *construct.* ‖ V.4 a parenthesis. κατα-σκευάζεται 4 pass. θεός pred. ‖ μέν...δέ (v.6) 1:7 ; Μωϋσῆς: θεράπων: 5 ἐν... opp. Χριστός: υἱός: ἐπί... πιστός, αὐτοῦ v.2. θεράπων responsible *assistant, officer,* in the service often of one highly placed. μαρτύριον *testimony,* εἰς μ. *for/as a testimony/evidence.* λαληθησομένων fut. ptc pass., τῶν λ. *what was to be said.* ‖ ἐάν-περ *supposing that, if only.* παρ- 6 ρησία (πᾶς + ῥῆσις speech) *freedom of speech,* so in general, *confidence,* τὴν π. *our confidence,* i.e. in God. καύχημα[7] *boast.* ἐλπίς[6] -ίδος ἡ *hope,* τῆς ἐ. *our hope,* i.e. of eternal salvation awaited in faith. κατά-σχωμεν aor[2] subj. κατ-έχω τι *hold fast to sth,* ἐάνπερ κ. *(always) supposing we have held firmly to/preserved* [[var. before κατάσχωμεν add μέχρι τέλους βεβαίαν (v.14)]]. ‖

δι-ό *therefore.* σήμερον *today.* ἀκούσητε aor. subj. 7 ἀκούω τινός. ‖ σκληρύνητε aor. subj. -ύνω *harden.* παρα- 8 πικρασμός (παρα-πικραίνω exasperate) *provocation* amounting to *rebellion.* κατὰ τ. ἡμέραν *in the day.* πειρασμός *trial, testing.* ἔρημος ἡ *desert.* ‖ οὗ temporal, *when.* ἐ-πεί- 9 ρασαν aor. -άζω *put to the test, make trial of.* δοκιμασία *examination, test.* ‖ τεσσεράκοντα = 40. ἔτος[8] *year,* acc. 10 of duration. προσ-ώχθισα aor. -οχθίζω τινί *be provoked/angry* with one. γενεά *generation.* ἀεί *always.* πλανῶνται pass. -νάω *lead astray,* pass. intr. *go astray,* err. τῇ καρδίᾳ dat. of respect §53. ἔ-γνωσαν aor[2] γινώσκω. ‖ ὤμοσα aor. ὀμνύω 11 *swear.* ὀργή *wrath.* εἰ εἰσ-ελεύσονται fut. -έρχομαι, lit. "if...they will enter", Sem. for *on no account shall they enter,* implying an oath, e.g. "May God do so to me if they...", Gen 14:23 etc. κατά-παυσις[4] *rest,* also *place of rest,* meaning either eternal life or heaven. ‖ Vanhoye 12 has shown how the author interprets this Psalm in terms of Num 14 where the people refused to enter the promised land because of unbelief. βλέπετε impv *take care!* μή-ποτε *lest.* ἔσται fut. εἰμί; fut. instead of subj. after βλέπετε §344. ἀ-πιστία *un-belief,* καρδία...ἀπ. an...unbelieving *heart,* "Hebr." gen. §40. ἀπο-στῆναι aor[2] (intr.) inf. ἀφ-ίστημι *make to stand away* ; *cause to revolt*; intr. tenses,

fall away, defect. ζῶντος ptc ζάω: θεὸς ζ. anarthrous
13 stressing God's nature § 176. ‖ παρα-καλεῖτε impv -καλέω.
ἐ-αυτούς for ἀλλήλους. κατά distributive, καθ' ἑκάστην
ἡμέραν *every day.* ἄχρι(s) *until* ; ἀ. οὗ here, *as long as.*
σήμερον v.7. καλεῖται pass. καλέω. σκληρυνθῇ aor. subj.
pass. v.8. ἀπάτη *deceit* ; in HGk, also *allurement,* instr.
14 dat. ‖ μέτ-οχος v.1. γε-γόναμεν pf γίνομαι. ἐάν-περ v.6.
ἀρχή *beginning.* ὑπό-στασις⁴ that which underlies, so
ground of hope, then *confidence, assurance,* II Cor 9 :4.
μέχρι w. gen. *until.* τέλος⁸ *end.* βέβαιος *firm.* κατά-σχω-
15 μεν v.6. ‖ ἐν τῷ λέγεσθαι (inf. pass. λέγω) *when it is said.*
ἀκούσητε aor. subj. ἀκούω τινός. σκληρύνητε, παραπικρασμός
16 v.8. ‖ ἀκούσαντες *when they heard,* aor. ptc. παρ-ε-πίκραναν
aor. -πικραίνω abs. *be rebellious* (sc. against God). οὐ
interr. *was it not* all...? ἐξ-ελθόντες aor² ptc -έρχομαι.
17 διὰ Μωϋσέως i.e. *under Moses' leadership.* ‖ τίσιν; interr.
προσ-ώχθισεν τεσσεράκοντα ἔτη v. 10. οὐχί interr. expecting the answer "Yes". ἁμαρτήσασιν aor. (for aor²) ptc
-τανω *sin.* κῶλα τά *corpses,* esp. as left unburied. ἔ-πεσεν
18 aor² πίπτω. ἔρημος v.8. ‖ ὤμοσεν, κατάπαυσις v.11. εἰσ-
ελεύσεσθαι fut. inf. -έρχομαι. ἀ-πειθήσεσιν aor. ptc -πειθέω
19 *dis-obey.* ‖ ἠδυνήθησαν aor. dep. δύναμαι, notion of impos-
sibility echoing Num 14:32f. εἰσ-ελθεῖν aor² inf. ἀ-
4 πιστία v.12. ‖ φοβηθῶμεν aor. subj. dep. φοβέομαι, hort. subj.
μή-ποτε *lest.* κατα-λειπομένης ptc pass. -λείπω *leave behind,*
pass. *remain,* gen. abs. *while a* promise *remains* (open).
ἐπ-αγγελία *promise.* εἰσ-ελθεῖν aor² inf. -έρχομαι. κατά-
παυσις 3:11. δοκῇ subj. δοκέω *think, suppose.* ὑστερη-
2 κέναι pf inf. -ρέω (< ὕστερος later) *come too late.* ‖ Vv. 2-10
illustrate how by lack of faith men exclude themselves
from the promise ; v.11 renews the exhortation in v.1.
καὶ γάρ *for in fact.* εὐ-ηγγελισμένοι pf ptc pass. -αγγελίζω
preach the good news, pass. *be evangelized, have the good
news preached to one.* καθ-ά-περ *just as.* κἀκεῖνοι = καὶ
ἐκεῖνοι. ὠφέλησεν aor. ὠφελέω τινά *benefit, do good to one.*
ἀκοή *hearing* ; *report, message* I Thess 2:13. συγ-κε-κερασμέ-
νους pf ptc pass. -κεράννυμί τινι *mix, blend with* sth, also
associate closely with one. ἀκούσασιν aor. ptc, ἐκείνους
μή...ἀκούσασιν *those not intimately united with the ones who
heard with faith* [[var. μὴ συγκεκερασμένος (ass. w. ὁ λόγος
τῆς ἀκοῆς) "the word not being blended with", i.e. *not
3 meeting with faith in those who heard*]]. ‖ οἱ πιστεύσαντες

aor. ptc, *we* (1st pers. known from the finite vb) *who have believed*. εἴρηκεν pf λέγω: καθὼς εἴρ. *as it* (Scripture) *says* ; pf because the words of Scripture remain, cf γέγραπται Mt 2:5 et passim. ὡς...μου 3:11. καίτοι w. ptc, *and yet*. ἀπό temporal. κατα-βολή (κατα- + βάλλω) *foundation*. γενηθέντων aor. ptc pass. γίνομαι, ptc concessive, gen. abs. i.e. God's work has been completed (and so his rest exists) since the foundation... ‖ πού encl. *somewhere*.   4
ἑβδόμη (sc. ἡμέρα) ἡ *the seventh day*. κατ-έ-παυσεν aor. κατα-παύω *cause to rest* ; intr. *rest*. ‖ ἐν τούτῳ *in this place/*   5
context. ‖ ἐπεί *since*. ἀπο-λείπεται pass. -λείπω *leave be-*   6
hind ; pass. impers. *there remains*, w. acc. + inf. *the fact remains that*. εἰσ-ελθεῖν v.1, *are to enter*. πρότερος *former*, neut. as adv. *before*. εὐ-αγγελισθέντες aor. ptc pass. v.2. ἀ-πείθεια *un-belief*. ‖ ὁρίζω (ὅρος *boundary*) *define,*   7
fix a day. σήμερον *today*. ἐν 1:1. τοσοῦτος *so great*, of time, *so long*. χρόνος *time*. προ-είρηται pf pass. -λέγω *say before*, καθὼς πρ. *as aforesaid*. σήμερον κτλ. 3:7f. ‖
Ἰησοῦς -οῦ = (Hebr.) *Joshua*. κατ-έ-παυσεν v.4, εἰ κατέπ. in   8
trans. sense, *if he had given rest to*, unfulfilled condition §313. ἐ-λάλει impf λαλέω: οὐκ ἄν...ἐλ. in apodosis, *he* (God) *would not have spoken*. περὶ ἄλλης...μετὰ ταῦτα ἡμέρας *of another time later on*. ‖ ἄρα *therefore*. ἀπο-λείπεται   9
there remains, v.6. σαββατισμός properly, *observance of the Sabbath*, so a rest, sc. in heaven. ‖ εἰσ-ελθών aor² ptc   10
v.6. κατάπαυσις v.1. καὶ αὐτός *he too*. κατ-έ-παυσεν v.4. ὥσπερ *as*. ‖ σπουδάσωμεν aor. subj. -άζω *be eager, do one's*   11
utmost. ὑπό-δειγμα⁷ *example*. ἵνα μή...τις = ἵνα μηδείς. πέσῃ aor² subj. πίπτω (here, *perish*). ἀ-πείθεια v.6. ‖ ζῶν   12
ptc ζάω. ἐν-εργής⁹ *active, effective*, a manifestation of life. τομώτερος comp. of τομός *cutting, sharp*. ὑπέρ w. acc. in comp. *than*, Lk 16:8 ; ὑ. πᾶσαν *than any*. μάχαιρα *sword*. δί-στομος (< δίς twice + στόμα) *two-edged*. δι-ϊκνούμενος ptc -ικνέομαι *pierce, penetrate*. ἄχρι *as far as, to the extent of*. μερισμός the act of *dividing, separation*. ἁρμός *joint* of the body. μυελός *marrow*, regarded as a basic, vital substance, pl. perh. indicating location in various parts of the body. κριτικός *critical, discerning*. ἐν-θύμησις⁴ *reflection, consideration*, often of a less speculative, abstract nature than ἔν-νοια *thought, idea*. ‖ κτίσις⁴   13
creation ; *creature*. ἀ-φανής⁹ (< φαίνομαι appear) *un-seen, not visible*. γυμνός *naked, bare*. τε-τραχηλισμένα pf ptc

pass. τραχηλίζω *break* one's *neck* (τράχηλος) by wringing or bending back ; pass. in rel. to sacrificial animals, *be laid open* to scrutiny. πρός w. acc. *in relation to, with.* λόγος *reckoning,* πρός...λόγος lit. "with whom the reckoning is to us (= ours)", i.e. *the reckoning with whom is (up) to us / is our responsibility.* ‖

14   ἔχοντες ptc ἔχω. δι-εληλυθότα pf² ptc -έρχομαι *pass through* ; as the high priest enters the Holy of holies on the Day of atonement. κρατῶμεν subj. (hort.) κρα-τέω τινός *hold fast* to sth, pres. durative, contrast 6:18.

15 ὁμο-λογία *confession.* ‖ γάρ ref. not to v.14 but to a possible objection, (e.g. without fear that he will prove aloof) *for...* δυνάμενον ptc δύναμαι. συμ-παθῆσαι aor. inf. -παθέω *sympathize.* ἀ-σθένεια (ἀ- + σθένος⁸ strength) *weak-ness,* i.e. such weakness as is inherent in human nature. πε-πειρασμένον pf ptc pass. -άζω *try, test* (here *not* "tempted" to sin) ; having triumphantly passed the test Jesus is for ever (pf) tried and tested. κατὰ πάντα 2:17. ὁμοιότης⁶ -τητος ἡ *likeness,* καθ' ὁμ. *likewise* (i.e. like us). χωρίς

16 *without.* ‖ προσ-ερχώμεθα subj. (hort.) -έρχομαι. παρ-ρησία *confidence.* θρόνος *throne.* λάβωμεν aor² subj. λαμβάνω. ἔλεος⁸ *mercy.* εὔρωμεν aor² subj. εὑρίσκω. εὔ-καιρος *op-*

5 *portune, timely.* βοήθεια *help.* ‖ πᾶς wt art. *every* §188. ἐξ ἀνθρώπων *from among men.* λαμβανόμενος *taken,* ptc pass. -βάνω. καθ-ίσταται pass. -ίστημι *constitute, appoint.* τὰ πρὸς τ. θεόν 2:17. προσ-φέρῃ subj. -φέρω *bring to, offer.* δῶρον *gift.* θυσία (θύω immolate) *sacrifice.* ὑπὲρ ἁμαρτιῶν

2 *for* (= in expiation of) *sins.* ‖ μετριο-παθεῖν inf. -παθέω τινί *moderate one's feelings* (e.g. anger, pain) *towards, deal gently with* one. δυνάμενος 4:15. ἀ-γνοοῦσιν ptc dat. pl. ἀ-γνοέω *be ignorant.* πλανωμένοις ptc pass. -νάω *lead astray* ; pass. intr. *go astray, err* ; sharing one art. w. ἀγνοοῦσιν perh. = *those who err through ignorance.* ἐπεί *since.* καὶ αὐτός *he too.* περί-κειμαι *have placed around* one, met. *be beset by* ; used as pf pass. περι-τίθημί τί τινι

3 *put sth around* one. ἀ-σθένεια 4:15. ‖ ὀφείλω *owe* ; hence ὀφείλει w. inf. one *ought/is bound to.* περί (twice) = ὑπέρ

4 §96. αὐτοῦ = ἑ-αυτοῦ. προσφέρειν inf. ‖ λαμβάνω *take.* τιμή *honour.* καλούμενος ptc pass. καλέω, understand a 2nd λαμβάνει in sense *receives it* : *not to himself does one take the honour but (receives it) as/when called by God.*

5 καθ-ὼς-περ *just as.* καί *also.* ‖ ἐ-δόξασεν aor. -άζω τινά

bring/show/do honour to one. **γενηθῆναι** aor. inf. dep.
γίνομαι: οὐχ ἑαυτὸν ἐδόξασεν γεν. *did not do himself the
honour of becoming.* **λαλήσας** aor. ptc **λαλέω**. **εἰ** 2nd sg
εἰμί. **σήμερον** *today.* **γε-γέννηκα** pf **γεννάω** *beget.* ‖ **ἑτέρῳ** 6
in another (place). **ἱερεύς**[5] *priest.* **εἰς τὸν αἰῶνα** *for ever.*
τάξις[4] (< **τάσσω** appoint) *order.* **Μελχισέδεκ** gen. i.e. *like
M.* 7:15. ‖ **σάρξ**, i.e. his life on earth. **δέησις**[4] *supplica-* 7
tion, prayer. **ἱκετηρία** *entreaty.* **δυνάμενον** 4:15. **σῴζειν**
inf. **σῴζω**. **κραυγή** *a cry.* **ἰσχυρός** *strong,* hence *loud.*
δάκρυον *a tear.* **προσ-ενέγκας** aor[2] ptc -**φέρω** v.l. **εἰσ-**
ακουσθείς aor. ptc pass. -**ούω** *listen to, hear* a prayer. **ἀπό**
causal, *because of, on account of,* cf Jn 21:6. **εὐ-λάβεια**
(**εὖ** + **λαμβάνω**) *fear of God, reverence, piety.* ‖ **καί-περ** *al-* 8
though. **ὤν** ptc **εἰμί**. **ἔ-μαθεν** aor[2] **μανθάνω** *learn.* **ἔ-παθεν**
aor[2] **πάσχω** *suffer.* **ὑπ-ακοή** *obedience.* ‖ **τελειωθείς** aor. 9
ptc pass. -**είοω** *perfect.* **ἐ-γένετο** aor[2] **γίνομαι**. **ὑπ-ακούου-**
σιν ptc -**ακούω** τινί *obey* one. **αἴτιος** *source.* **σωτηρία** *sal-*
vation. ‖ **προσ-αγορευθείς** aor. ptc pass. -**αγορεύω** *address* 10
one *as* sth ; *give* one *the title of, proclaim.* **τάξις** v.6. ‖

　　πολὺς ἡμῖν ὁ λόγος *we have much to say.* **δυσ-ερμή-** 11
νευτος (**δυσ-** hard + **ἑρμηνεύω** explain) *difficult to explain,*
δ. **λέγειν** *hard to explain in words.* **ἐπεί** v.2. **νωθρός**
sluggish ; of senses, *dull.* **γε-γόνατε** pf[2] **γίνομαι**. **ἀκοή**
hearing ; pl. *ears* as organs of hearing den. absorption
and understanding §118. ‖ **καὶ γάρ** *for indeed.* **ὀφείλοντες** 12
though you ought, ptc concessive, v.3 (2nd pers. pl. revealed
by vb **ἔχετε**). **διδάσκαλος** *teacher.* **διὰ τὸν χρόνον** *consider-*
ing the time, i.e. *by this time.* **πάλιν** *once again.* **χρεία**
need, χρ. **ἔχω** τινός *need* sth. **τινά** (encl.) *someone.* **στοι-**
χεῖον in pl. *elements of knowledge.* **ἀρχή** *beginning* ; *prin-*
ciple, the significance of the gen. is obscure. **λόγιον**
saying, τ. στοιχεῖα τ. ἀρχῆς τ. λογίων τ. θεοῦ *the elementary*
principles of God's oracles, perh. ref. OT scriptures, but
may ref. Christian teaching as a whole. **γε-γόνατε** w.
acc. ptc, "you have become" *people needing...,* **you are**
at the stage of needing. **γάλα** γάλακτος τό *milk.* **στερεός**
solid. **τροφή** (< **τρέφω** nourish) *food.* ‖ **πᾶς...ὁ** *all those* 13
who... §188. **μετ-έχων** ptc -**έχω** τινός *partake* of sth, here,
live on (a diet of). **ἄ-πειρος** (**ἀ-** + **πεῖρα** experience) *with-*
out experience. **λόγος δικαιοσύνης** in terms of the context could ref. "speaking correctly" but v.14b implies
teaching of uprightness or even Christian doctrine as a

14 whole. **νήπιος** *infant.* ‖ **τέλειος** *complete, perfect; adult;* gen. pl. pred., transl. *for adults.* **τῶν** ref. **τελείων.** **ἕξις**[4] *practice,* **διὰ τ. ἕξιν** *by practice/use.* **αἰσθητήριον** a *sense, faculty.* **γε-γυμνασμένα** pf ptc pass. **-άζω** *train.* **ἐχόντων** ptc **ἔχω.** **διά-κρισις**[4] a *distinguishing,* δ. **καλοῦ τε καὶ κακοῦ** *distinguishing between good and evil,* i.e. moral judge-

6 ment. ‖ **δι-ό** *so then.* **ἀφ-έντες** aor[2] ptc **-ίημι** *leave.* **ὁ λόγος τῆς ἀρχῆς** parallels 5:12, ref. elementary Christian teaching. **τελειότης**[6] **-ότητος** ἡ *perfection* ; *maturity.* **φερώμεθα** subj. pass. **φέρω,** subj. hort. *let us move on* (lit. "be borne along"). **θεμέλιος** *foundation.* **κατα-βαλλόμενοι** ptc **-βάλλομαι** *lay* (a foundation). **μετά-νοια** *change of mind, repent-ance.* **νεκρὰ ἔργα** are those not inspired by a supernatural

2 life. ‖ **βαπτισμός** *washing* as a ceremonial rite of purifica-tion ; here possibly *baptism* understood (like the rest of this v.) in close connection w. **διδαχή** *teaching,* **βαπτισμῶν δ.** will then = *catechetical instruction* ⟦var. **διδαχὴν** (appos. **θεμέλιον**)⟧. **ἐπί-θεσις**[4] *imposition, laying on.* **ἀνά-στασις**[4]

3 *re-surrection.* **κρίμα**[7] *judgement.* ‖ **τοῦτο** i.e. the step for-ward proposed in v.1. **ποιήσομεν** fut. **ποιέω** ⟦var. **ποιή-σωμεν** (aor. subj. hort.)⟧. **ἐάν-περ** *if, that is* 3:6,14. **ἐπι-**

4 **τρέπῃ** subj. **-τρέπω** *allow.* ‖ **ἀ-δύνατον** (*it is*) *impossible.* **ἅπαξ** *once.* **φωτισθέντας** aor. ptc pass. **-ίζω** *shine upon* ; met. *enlighten,* acc. as obj. of inf. **ἀνακαινίζειν.** **γευσαμέ-νους** aor. ptc **γεύομαί τινος** also **τινα** v.5, *taste, experience, enjoy.* **δωρεά** *gift.* **ἐπ-ουράνιος** *heavenly.* **μέτ-οχος** (< **μετ-έχω** share) *participator.* **γενηθέντας** aor. ptc dep. **γίνομαι.** ‖

5 **ῥῆμα**[7] *word.* **μέλλοντος** ptc **μέλλω:** τοῦ **μ.** αἰῶνος ref. the

6 era already introduced by Christ. ‖ **παρα-πεσόντας** aor[2] ptc **-πίπτω** *go astray* ; *fall away,* hence of apostasy. **ἀνα-καινίζειν** inf. **-καινίζω** *re-new.* **μετά-νοια** v.1. **ἀνα-σταυ-ροῦντας** ptc **-σταυρόω** *crucify anew.* **παρα-δειγματίζοντας** ptc **-δειγματίζω** *make a public example of* ; *expose to ridicule.* Vv. 4-6. The commonly accepted interpretation (as punctuated in our text) ass. **ἀδύνατον** w. **ἀνακαινίζειν** whose dir. obj. is the 3 ll. **τοὺς ἅπαξ...παραπεσόντας** and indir. obj. **μετάνοιαν,** a causal sense being attributed to **ἀνασταυροῦντες,** "it is impossible to renew to repentance those who have once...because they are crucifying again...". Recently Alonso Schökel and Proulx have revived a patristic interpretation which distinguishes the function of the anarthrous pres. ptcs (6*b*) (ref. the subject of **ἀνα-**

καινίζειν) from the definite aor. ptcs (4-6a) (obj. of ἀνα-
καινίζειν) and ass. εἰς μετάνοιαν w. ἀνασταυροῦντας (in
which case the comma printed after μετάνοιαν will instead
follow ἀνακ.). They point out that the right sequence is
(crucifixion), repentance, then renewal and not vice versa
(cf v.1 ; Ezek 36:25-27, Eph 4:22-24). On this interpretation the meaning will be, "As for those who have
once...and have apostatized, it is impossible to renew them
again, crucifying a second time for one's own ends the
Son of God with a view to repentance" : perhaps another
instance of the transposition of inf. and ptc noted in 2:10
§263 : "For it is impossible to crucify a second time the
Son of God for one's own repentance, so making a mock
of him, in order to renew again those who have once..." ‖
πιοῦσα aor² ptc fem. πίνω *drink.* ἐρχόμενον ptc ἔρχομαι. 7
πολλάκις *many times, often.* ὑετός *rain.* τίκτουσα ptc
τίκτω *bear, bring forth.* βοτάνη *plant.* εὔθετος (< εὖ +
τίθημι) *suitable, useful.* γεωργεῖται pass. -γέω *cultivate,
grow* (tr.). μετα-λαμβάνω τινός *share* in sth. εὐ-λογία *blessing.* ‖ ἐκ-φέρουσα ptc -φέρω *produce.* ἄκανθα *thorn(-bush).* 8
τρίβολος *thistle.* ἀ-δόκιμος opp. εὔθετος, *failing the test;
useless.* κατ-άρα a *curse,* opp. εὐλογία. ἐγγύς w. gen.
near, meaning perh. *threatened with.* τέλος⁸ *end, destiny.*
καῦσις⁴ *burning.* ‖ πε-πείσμεθα *we are sure of* (w. acc.), pf 9
pass. πείθω *persuade.* περὶ ὑμῶν *in your case.* ἀγαπητός
beloved. κρείσσων (or -ττων) -ονος neut. κρεῖσσον *better*
1:4. ἐχόμενα ptc mid. ἔχω ; mid. *adhere/belong to* ; ἐχ. τ.
σωτηρίας *relating to your salvation.* σωτηρία *salvation.* εἰ
καί *even though.* ‖ ἄ-δικος *un-just,* w. inf. consec. *unjust* 10
enough to..., so *unjust as to...* ἐπι-λαθέσθαι aor² inf. -λαν-
θάνομαί τινος *forget, overlook.* ἧς attracted from ἥν §16.
ἐν-ε-δείξασθε aor. mid. ἐν-δείκνυμι *show* ; mid. *show a
quality in oneself.* εἰς τὸ ὄνομα αὐτοῦ *for his sake.* διακονήσαντες...καὶ διακονοῦντες *when you served, and serve,*
aor. ptc, pres. ptc -νέω τινί *serve one.* οἱ ἅγιοι title of all
baptized believers. ‖ ἐπι-θυμέω *long for.* ὁ αὐτός *the* 11
same. ἐν-δείκνυσθαι inf. mid. σπουδή *eagerness, concern.*
πληρο-φορία *full assurance,* πρὸς τὴν πλ. τῆς ἐλπίδος *for the
realization of your hope.* ἐλπίς⁶ -ίδος ἡ *hope.* τέλος⁸ v.8,
ἄχρι τέλους *to the last,* i.e. *to the Parousia when hope will
be realized.* ‖ νωθρός *sluggish, slack.* γένησθε aor² subj. 12
v.4. μιμητής³ *imitator.* μακρο-θυμία (long temper) *for-*

bearance, patience. κληρο-νομούντων ptc -νομέω *inherit,*
pres. ?for obsolescent fut. ptc §282. ἐπ-αγγελία *promise.* ||
13 ἐπ-αγγειλάμενος aor. ptc -αγγέλλομαι *promise.* ἐπεί
since, as. εἶχεν impf ἔχω, w. inf. *can.* μείζων -ζονος neut.
μεῖζον comp. of μέγας. ὀμόσαι aor. inf. ὀμνύω κατά τινος
swear by sth. ὤμοσεν aor. Since the dominant idea is the
promise, this could be another instance of the transposition of ptc and finite vb (parallel to that of ptc and inf.
above and in 2:10) "swearing by himself (since...), God
made a promise to A. saying...", cf Rom 4:19 §376. ||
14 εἰ μήν strengthens an oath, *in very truth, surely.* εὐλογῶν
ptc -λογέω *bless.* εὐ-λογήσω fut., the combination of the
finite vb w. ptc (at other times w. cognate noun in the
dat.) is used to transl. a strongly emphatic Hebr. cstr
§60, 369. πληθύνων ptc -ύνω *multiply, increase.* πληθυνῶ
15 fut. || μακρο-θυμήσας aor. ptc -θυμέω *be patient ; wait pa-
tiently.* ἐπ-έ-τυχεν aor² ἐπι-τυγχάνω τινός *attain* sth. ἐπ-
16 αγγελία v.12. || μείζων, ὀμνύω κατά τινος v.13. ἀντι-λογία
contradiction ; controversy. πέρας -ατος τό *limit, end,* pred.,
subject being ὅρκος. εἰς *for (the purpose of).* βεβαίωσις⁴
17 *confirmation.* ὅρκος *oath.* || ἐν ᾧ causal (Aram.) *and so.*
βουλόμενος ptc βούλομαι *will, wish.* περισσότερος (comp.
of περισσός) neut. as adv. *even more (forcibly),* ass. w.
ἐπι-δεῖξαι aor. inf. -δείκνυμι *demonstrate.* κληρο-νόμος
inheritor 1:2. ἀ-μετά-θετος (ἀ- + μετα-τίθημι transfer, change) *un-changeable,* neut. as noun, *im-mutability.* βουλή
purpose. ἐ-μεσίτευσεν aor. -εύω *mediate,* ἐμ. ὅρκῳ *he
18 intervened with an oath.* || πρᾶγμα⁷ (< πράσσω do) *deed ;
a matter* or *thing.* ἀ-δύνατον v.4. ψεύσασθαι aor. inf.
ψεύδομαι *lie, say what is not true ;* subject θεόν. ἰσχυρός
strong. παρά-κλησις⁴ *encouragement, incentive,* obj. of ἔχωμεν subj. ἔχω. κατα-φυγόντες aor² ptc -φεύγω *flee,* aor.
effective, *we who had taken refuge (in him)* might have...
κρατῆσαι *to seize firm hold of,* aor. inceptive κρατέω τινός
hold fast to sth. προ-κειμένης ptc -κειμαι *lie before.* ἐλπίς
19 v.11. || ἄγκυρα *anchor.* ἀ-σφαλής⁹ (ἀ- + σφάλλω trip up)
safe, sure. βέβαιος *firm.* εἰσ-ερχομένην ptc -έρχομαι. ἐσώ-
τερος *inner,* τὸ ἐσ. *the inside.* κατα-πέτασμα⁷ *curtain,*
20 *veil.* || ὅπου *where.* πρό-δρομος (< πρό before + δραμ-
aor² stem of τρέχω run) *fore-runner.* τάξις v.11. γενόμε-
νος aor² ptc γίνομαι. εἰς τ. αἰῶνα *for ever.* ||

Σαλήμ gen. ἱερεύς⁵ *priest.* ὕψιστος *highest* ; of God, 7
Most High. συν-αντήσας aor. ptc -αντάω τινί (*go to*) *meet
one.* ὑπο-στρέφοντι ptc -στρέφω *return, come back.* κοπή
(κόπτω cut off) *slaughter.* εὐ-λογήσας aor. ptc 6:14. ‖
δεκάτη (sc. μερίς part) ἡ a *tenth.* ἐ-μέρισεν aor. -ίζω *divide,* 2
give a share. ἑρμηνευόμενος ptc pass. -εύω *translate* ;
ref. his name "M." ἔπ-ειτα *then.* ἐστίν = *means* Gal
4:25, Eph 4:9. ‖ ἀ-πάτωρ *without* (*recorded*) *father,* ἀ-μήτωρ 3
without mother (i.e. *unknown*). ἀ-γενεα-λόγητος *without
genealogy* ; i.e. Genesis is silent as to his origins for he did
not owe his priesthood to levitical origin. μήτε...μήτε
neither...nor. ἀρχή *beginning,* ἀ. ἡμέρων sc. of his life.
τέλος⁸ *end.* ἔχων, sc. in the biblical narrative. ἀφ-ωμοιω-
μένος *like,* pf ptc pass. -ομοιόω *make like.* δι-ηνεκής⁹
(δια- + φέρω carry through) *continuous* ; εἰς τὸ δ. *for ever.* ‖
θεωρέω *contemplate, look at* ; *see,* also w. the eyes of the 4
mind. πηλίκος *how great,* supply ἐστίν. ἔ-δωκεν aor. δίδωμι. ἀκρο-θίνιον (ἄκρος highest + θίς a heap) *first fruits* ;
choicest spoils of war. πατρι-άρχης³ *ruler of a clan* (πατριά),
patriarch, appos. Ἀβραάμ. ‖ Λευί gen. of Λευίς *Levi.* ἱερα- 5
τεία *priestly functions* ; *office of priest.* λαμβάνοντες ptc
-άνω: οἱ μέν...ὁ δέ *those* of the sons of L. who receive
the priesthood [all were eligible but not all exercised the
function] ...*but he* [Melchizedek] (v.6). ἀπο-δεκατοῦν inf.
-δεκατόω τινά *exact a tithe from* one. καί-περ *although.*
τοῦτ' ἐστιν *id est, that is* (*to say*). ἐξ-εληλυθότας pf² ptc
-έρχομαι. ὀσφῦς ὀσφύος ἡ *loins.* ‖ γενεα-λογούμενος ptc pass. 6
-λογέω *trace one's descent* ; pass. *be descended from.* δε-δεκά-
τωκεν pf -δεκατόω *tithe.* ἔχοντα ptc ἔχω. ἐπ-αγγελία *promise.* εὐ-λόγηκεν pf -λογέω *bless,* the pfs pointing to the
present reality inherent in the archetype. ‖ χωρίς w. gen. 7
without. ἀντι-λογία *contradiction,* χωρὶς δὲ πάσης ἀ. *un-
questionably.* ἐλάσσων (or -ττων) neut. -αττον *lesser, inferior,* τὸ ἔλ. *what is inferior* (neut.), thought being concen-
trated on quality wt ref. to persons ; a general proposition §141. κρείττων *better, superior* 1:4. εὐ-λογεῖται pass.
‖ ὧδε μέν...ἐκεῖ δέ *in this case...in the other.* δεκάτη v.2. 8
ἀπο-θνήσκοντες ptc pres. frequentative (that is always
happening) -θνήσκω: ἀ. ἄνθρωποι *men who die,* mortal
men. μαρτυρούμενος ptc pass. -ρέω: μ. ὅτι ζῇ *attested as
being alive.* ζῇ 3rd sg ζάω. ‖ ἔπος⁸ *word,* ὡς ἔ. εἰπεῖν 9
(aor² inf. λέγω) *so to speak.* δι' Ἀβραάμ (gen.) *through A.*

καὶ Λ. *even Levi.* λαμβάνων ptc, ὁ λ. *the receiver* of tithes
10 §371. δε-δεκάτωται pf pass. v.5. ‖ ὀσφῦς v.5. συν-ήντησεν
11 aor. v.1. ‖ εἰ μὲν οὖν...ἦν *if then...had been,* an "unfulfilled"
condition §313f. τελείωσις[4] *perfection.* ἱερωσύνη *priesthood.* ἐπ' αὐτῆς *on the basis of it* (the levitical priesthood). νε-νομο-θέτηται pf pass. -θετέω *make a law*; pass.
be given a law. χρεία w. acc. + inf. *need to.* τάξις[4] *order*
5:6. ἕτερος *different.* ἀν-ίστασθαι inf. -ίσταμαι *arise.*
ἱερεύς v.1. λέγεσθαι inf. pass. λέγω. Lit. "If then...
what need would there still be for a different priest to
arise according to the order of M. and not called accord-
12 ing to the order of Aaron?" οὐ w. inf. §440. ‖ μετα-τιθε-
μένης ptc pass. -τίθημι *transfer*; *change,* gen. abs. *when...
is changed.* ἀνάγκη *necessity,* ἐξ ἀ. *necessarily.* μετά-θεσις[4]
13 *change.* ‖ ἐφ' ὅν *about/of whom* (i.e. Christ). φυλή *tribe.*
μετ-έσχηκεν pf -έχω τινός *share* sth, φυλῆς μ. *belongs* (pf)
to a tribe. προσ-έσχηκεν pf -έχω τινί *devote oneself* to sth.
14 θυσιαστήριον *altar.* ‖ πρό-δηλος *clear, evident.* ἀνα-τέ-ταλκεν
pf -τέλλω *rise* (of the sun); met. *spring from.* εἰς *with
15 regard to, as to.* ἐ-λάλησεν aor. λαλέω. ‖ περισσότερον
(comp. -σῶς) ἔτι *still more.* κατά-δηλος *obvious.* ἐστίν, subject "it" = the statement in v.12. ὁμοιότης[6] -τητος ἡ
16 *likeness.* ἱερεύς v.1. ‖ σάρκινος *made of flesh, physical,*
ref. the law relating selection to physical descent. γέ-
γονεν pf[2] γίνομαι. ἀ-κατά-λυτος (κατα-λύω *demolish, abo-
17 lish*) *in-destructible,* hence *endless.* ‖ μαρτυρεῖται pass. *he
has witness borne to him*: ὅτι *as follows* = "... εἰς τ. αἰῶνα
18 *for ever.* ‖ ἀ-θέτησις[4] ἡ a *setting aside, annulment.* γίνεται
is made/effected. προ-αγούσης *preceding, previous,* ptc fem.
-άγω *bring before*; intr. *go before.* ἀ-σθενής[9] *weak,* τὸ ἀσ.
weakness §140. ἀν-ωφελής[9] *use-less,* τὸ ἀνωφ. *uselessness.* ‖
19 ἐ-τελείωσεν aor. -ειόω *bring to completion* or *perfection.*
But where the law failed a new hope proved effective:
ἐπ-εισ-αγωγή a *bringing in besides, introduction.* κρείττων
v.7. ἐλπίς -ίδος ἡ *hope.* ἐγγίζω *draw near* (ἐγγύς). ‖
20 καθ' ὅσον...κατὰ τοσοῦτο (v.22) *to the degree that...so* (*to
the same degree*). ὁρκ-ωμοσία (< ὅρκος *oath* + ὀμνύω *swear*)
swearing of an oath. οἱ μέν...ὁ δέ v.5. γε-γονότες pf[2] ptc
γίνομαι: εἰσίν...γεγ. periphrastic pf[2] γίνομαι = γεγόνασιν. ‖
21 διὰ τοῦ λέγοντος πρὸς αὐτόν *through the one who said to
him*; διά may denote principal cause §113. ὤμοσεν aor.
ὀμνύω *swear.* μετα-μεληθήσεται fut. dep. -μέλομαι *change*

one's *mind*. **εἰς τ. αἰῶνα** v.17. || **κατὰ τοσοῦτο** resuming 22
καθ' ὅσον v.20. **κρείττων** v.7. **δια-θήκη** *testament* ; in LXX
and NT freq. for συν-θήκη *covenant*. **γέ-γονεν** v.16. **ἔγ-
γυος** *surety*. A literal transln of vv. 20-22 would run:
"To the degree that it [the institution of the different
and eternal priest] was not without the swearing of an
oath — for those (others) without the swearing of an oath
have become priests but he *with* the swearing of an
oath by the One who said to him... '(v.21*b*)' — Jesus has
become surety of a covenant to that same degree supe-
rior." || **οἱ μέν...ὁ δέ** (v.24) v.5. **πλείων** πλείονος neut. 23
πλεῖον comp. of πολύς, comp. for positive, *numerous*, or
for elative superl. *in large numbers* §150, 147. **εἰσιν γε-
γονότες** v.20. **διὰ τό** w. inf. *because*. **θανάτῳ** dat. of
instr. **κωλύεσθαι** inf. pass. -λύω *prevent*, pres. frequentative. **παρα-μένειν** inf. -μένω *stay beside*, here *remain*
in office. || **μένειν** inf. μένω. **αὐτόν** (acc. as subject of inf.) 24
could have been omitted being subject also of ἔχει §393.
εἰς τ. αἰῶνα v.17. **ἀ-παρά-βατος** pred. adj. "which is not
passing" (away), i.e. *endless*, others understand "to an-
other" i.e. *inalienable* §142. **ἱερωσύνη** v.11. || **ὅ-θεν καί** 25
and hence, and so. **σῴζειν** inf. σῴζω. **παν-τελής**[9] *entire,
complete* ; εἰς τὸ π. *completely, totally*. **προσ-ερχομένους**
ptc -έρχομαί τινι. **πάν-τοτε** *always*. **ζῶν** ptc (causal) ζάω.
εἰς τὸ w. inf. of purpose. **ἐν-τυγχάνειν** inf. -τυγχάνω ὑπέρ
τινος *intercede* for one. || **τοι-οῦτος** *such*. **καί** *also*. **ἔ-πρεπεν** 26
impf πρέπω *be fitting*. **ὅσιος** *devout*. **ἄ-κακος** *guileless*.
ἀ-μίαντος *un-defiled*. **κε-χωρισμένος** *separated*, pf ptc χωρίζω
divide, separate, ref. ascended Christ, cf vv. 2:14, 17.
ἁμαρτωλός *sinner*. **ὑψηλότερος** comp. of ὑψηλός *high*. **οὐρα-
νῶν** gen. of comp., cf 4:14. **γενόμενος** aor[2] ptc γίνομαι. ||
καθ' ἡμέραν *every day*. **ἀνάγκη** v.12. **ὥσπερ** *like*. **πρότερος** 27
former, neut. as adv. τὸ πρ. *in the first* (strictly, "the former") *place*. **θυσία** *sacrifice*. **ἀνα-φέρειν** inf. -φέρω *offer
(up)*. **ἔπ-ειτα** *then, subsequently*. **τῶν** depending on ὑπέρ.
ἐ-ποίησεν aor. ποιέω. **ἐφ-άπαξ** *once for all*. **ἀν-ενέγκας**
aor[2] ptc ἀνα-φέρω. || **καθ-ίστημι** *constitute, appoint*. **ἔχοντας** 28
ptc ἔχω. **ἀ-σθένεια** *weakness*. **ὁρκ-ωμοσία** v.20, ὁ λόγος τ.
ὁρκ. *the word sworn on oath*. **υἱόν** opp. ἀνθρώπους, sc.
καθίστησιν. **τε-τελειωμένον** *perfect*, pf ptc pass. v.19. ||

    κεφάλαιον *main point, essence*. **λεγομένοις** ptc pass. 8
neut. λέγω: τοῖς λ. *what has been said*. **τοιοῦτος** *such*.

ἐ-κάθισεν aor. -ίζω *make one sit* ; intr. *take one's seat, sit.*
δεξιός *right* opp. left, ἐν δεξιᾷ (sc. χειρί) *at one's right*
(hand). θρόνος *throne.* μεγαλωσύνη *majesty* ; ἡ μ. a peri-
2 phrasis for God. ‖ τὰ ἅγια *the sanctuary.* λειτ-ουργός *mini-*
ster 1:7. σκηνή *tabernacle* as dwelling place of God. ἀληθινός *true, genuine.* ἔ-πηξεν aor. πήγνυμι *pitch* a tent ;
3 *erect* a tabernacle. ‖ εἰς τό w. inf. den. purpose. προσφέρειν inf. -φέρω *offer.* δῶρον *gift.* θυσία *sacrifice.* καθ-
ίσταμαι *be appointed.* ὅ-θεν *hence, this being the case.*
ἀναγκαῖον (sc. ἦν or ἐστίν) ἔχειν...καὶ τοῦτον *this one* (i.e.
high priest) *too had necessarily to have.* προσ-ενέγκῃ aor[2]
subj. -φέρω: τι...ὃ πρ. "something that he might offer" =
something to offer ; (the more usual cstr w. fut. ὅστις...
4 μεριμνήσει in Phil 2:20). ‖ μὲν οὖν *so.* εἰ...ἦν...οὐδ' ἂν ἦν *if*
he had been...he would not be, "unfulfilled" condition
and apodosis §313f. ὄντων (ptc εἰμί causal) τῶν προσφερόν-
των (ptc pres. frequentative) gen. abs., *since there are*
5 *those who offer...* ‖ οἵ-τινες *who* §216. ὑπό-δειγμα[7] *figure,*
emblem. σκιά a *foreshadowing.* λατρεύω *whether of priest*
or laity, worship. ἐπ-ουράνιος *heavenly* Eph 1:3, τὰ ἐπ.
the heavenly sanctuary. κε-χρημάτισται pf pass. -τίζω *do*
business (χρῆμα) ; of an oracle, *reply* ; esp. of God, *warn,*
instruct. μέλλων ptc, *(that he was) to.* ἐπι-τελεῖν inf.
-τελέω *complete* ; *perform* ; *erect.* σκηνή v.2. ὅρα impv
ὁράω ; before a command, *see (that)...* φησί 3rd sg φημί
say. ποιήσεις (impvl) fut. ποιέω. τύπος an *impress* ;
model, pattern. δειχθέντα aor. ptc pass. δείκνυμι *show.* ‖
6 νυν[ὶ] δέ *in fact.* δια-φορώτερος (comp. of -φορος *different)*
superior ; *excelling.* τέ-τυχεν *there has fallen to him,* i.e.
he has obtained from God, pf τυγχάνω τινός *obtain* by lot
or chance, *find* sth. λειτ-ουργία *sacred ministry,* cf v.2.
ὅσῳ *by as much as, in the same measure as.* κρείττων
better 1:4. δια-θήκη *covenant.* μεσίτης[3] *mediator.* ἥτις
seeing that §215. ἐπ-αγγελία *promise.* ἐπί w. dat. *on the*
basis of. νε-νομο-θέτηται *it* (the covenant) *has been drawn*
7 *up,* pf pass. νομο-θετέω *legislate.* ‖ εἰ...ἦν...οὐκ ἂν ἐζη-
τεῖτο cf v.4. ἄ-μεμπτος *fault-less;* so *perfect.* δεύτερος
second. ἐ-ζητεῖτο impf pass. ζητέω. οὐκ ἄν...τόπος "place
would not have been sought for a second", i.e. *there*
would have been no place (= occasion) *for a second* §316. ‖
8 μεμφόμενος ptc μέμφομαί τινα *blame, find fault with* one.
αὐτούς i.e. Israelites. καί (1st time) *when* §455δ. συν-

τελέσω fut. -τελέω *bring to an end, complete* ; *accomplish* ; σ. διαθήκην ἐπί τινα *make a covenant* with one (the choice of συντελέω which differs both from the Hebr. and the LXX seems to show that the author means to underline the perfection of the new covenant). **καινός** *new.* ‖ ἐ- 9 **ποίησα** aor. ποιέω. **πατράσιν** dat. pl. πατήρ. **ἐπι-λαβο-μένου** aor² ptc -λαμβάνομαί τινος *take hold* of one ; a Hebr. original may be responsible for this gen. cstr : "in the day of my taking them by the hand". **ἐξ-αγαγεῖν** aor² inf. -άγω *lead out* ; inf. final. **ὅτι** *because*, ref. need for a new covenant. **ἐν-έ-μειναν** aor. ἐμ-μένω *remain in, abide by.* **κἀγώ** = καὶ ἐγώ. **ἠ-μέλησα** aor. ἀ-μελέω τινός *over-look, neglect, pay no attention* to one, in this sense must be constative aor. or perh. *I lost interest in them*; in either sense, in appearance only. ‖ **ὅτι** *for.* **αὕτη** pred. **δια-** 10 **θήσομαι** fut. mid. -τίθημι *draw up, make* ; mid. for myself. **διδούς** ptc δίδωμι: the Hebr. equivalent of δίδωμι also means *put*, ptc stands for finite vb, here for fut. (parallel ἐπιγράψω) ; others explain otherwise. **διά-νοια** *mind, understanding.* **ἐπι-γράψω** fut. -γράφω *write on* or *in.* **ἔσομαι** fut. εἰμί: ἔ. εἰς for nom. pred., αὐτοῖς dat. of possession, *I shall be their God.* ‖ **διδάξωσιν** aor. subj. διδάσκω: οὐ μή 11 w. aor. subj. an emphatic neg. ref. future. **πολίτης³** *citizen*, Hebr. one's *fellow.* **γνῶθι** aor² impv γινώσκω; in the Bible the knowledge of God includes always a strong ethical element. **εἰδήσουσιν** fut. of pf-pres. οἶδα. **μικρός** *small*, or for superl., esp. ref. a category, *least* §146. ‖ **ἵλεως** -εω neut. -εων *merciful.* **ἀ-δικία** *wrong-doing* ; pl. 12 *wicked deeds.* **μνησθῶ** aor. subj. dep. μιμνήσκομαί τινος *remember* sth. **ἔτι** w. neg. *any more.* ‖ **ἐν τῷ λέγειν** *in* 13 *saying* §392. **καινός** v.8, the key word of the text cited. **πε-παλαίωκεν** pf -αιόω *make old, treat as old*; pass. *be old/outworn.* **ἡ πρώτη** (sc. διαθήκη), superl. for comp. §151. **δέ** *and.* **παλαιούμενον** ptc pass. **γηράσκον** ptc -άσκω *grow old* in years. **ἐγγύς** τινος *near* to sth. **ἀ-φανισμός** (ἀ- + φαίνω show) *disappearing*, i.e. on the point of becoming obsolete. ‖

εἶχε impf ἔχω. **ἡ πρώτη** 8:13. **δικαίωμα⁷** sth declared 9 to be just, a *righteous deed* ; *commandment, regulation.* **λατρεία** *service* of God, esp. *public worship.* **τὸ ἅγιον** *the sanctuary.* **κοσμικός** *which was earthly*, pred. adj. ‖ **σκηνή** 2 *tabernacle.* **κατ-ε-σκευάσθη** aor. pass. κατα-σκευάζω *con-*

struct. ἡ πρώτη, i.e. the outer one. λυχνία *lampstand* of Ex 25:31, *candelabrum.* τράπεζα *table.* πρό-θεσις⁴ (< προτίθημι set before) a *laying out,* ἡ π. τῶν ἄρτων *the setting out of the showbread* II Chr 13:11. ἥ-τις = ἥ §216. λέγεται *is called,* pass. λέγω. Ἅγια neut. pl. the *Holy Place.* ‖

3 μετά w. acc. of place, *behind.* δεύτερος *second.* καταπέτασμα⁷ *curtain, veil* ; the first hung at the entrance to the Holy Place, the second separating off the Holy of

4 holies. λεγομένη *called.* ‖ χρυσοῦς (gen. -σοῦ) -σῆ -σοῦν made of *gold.* ἔχουσα *containing,* ptc fem. ἔχω. θυμιατήριον (< θυμιάω burn incense) *censer* ; perh. understand as = θυσιαστήριον *altar of incense.* κιβωτός ἡ *ark.* διαθήκη *covenant.* περι-κε-καλυμμένην pf ptc pass. περι-καλύπτω *cover over.* πάντο-θεν *from all sides,* here *all over.* χρυσίον the metal *gold.* ἐν ᾗ ref. the ark, sc. ἦσαν. στάμνος ἡ *jar.* ῥάβδος ἡ *rod, staff,* symbol of priesthood. βλαστήσασα aor. ptc fem. -στά(ν)ω *sprout, bud.* πλάξ⁶ πλακός ἡ

5 *tablet.* ‖ ὑπερ-άνω *above,* adv. used as prep. §83. Χερουβὶν δόξης, the two cherubim which stood facing each other on top of the ark, their wings stretched over the mercy-seat. Together with the mercy-seat they were conceived as the throne of the divine Majesty Ex 25:17-22 ; δόξα signifying the divine presence. κατα-σκιάζοντα ptc -σκιάζω *overshadow.* ἱλαστήριον *mercy-seat,* sprinkled by the high priest on the day of Atonement w. the blood of sacrifices for expiation of sins. μέρος⁸ *part,* κατὰ μέρος distributive,

6 "bit by bit", *in detail.* ‖ κατ-ε-σκευασμένων pf ptc pass. κατα-σκευάζω v.2, gen. abs. μέν...δέ 1:7. σκηνή v.2. διὰ παντός *always.* εἰσ-ίασιν *are going in,* 3rd pl. εἴσ-ειμι (εἰς + εἶμι go) *go in,* pres. frequentative. ἱερεύς⁵ *priest.* λατρεία *worship,* pl. *acts of worship.* ἐπι-τελοῦντες *per-*

7 *form, carry out.* ‖ δεύτερος v.3. ἅπαξ *once.* ἐνιαυτός *year,* ἅπαξ τοῦ ἐν. *once a year,* gen. of time "within which". χωρίς w. gen. *without.* προσ-φέρω *offer.* ἀ-γνόημα⁷ *sin of*

8 *ignorance.* ‖ τοῦτο (obj. of δηλοῦντος) explained in the clause μήπω πεφανερῶσθαι ... ὁδόν. δηλοῦντος ptc δηλόω *show,* gen. abs. μήπω *not yet.* πε-φανερῶσθαι pf inf. pass. -ρόω *reveal.* τὰ ἅγια v.2, τὴν τῶν ἁ. (obj. gen.) ὁδόν (subject of inf.) *the way into the sanctuary.* στάσις⁴ *standing, station* (elsewhere in NT *dissension* ; *disturbance*) ἔτι... ἐχούσης (v.4) στάσιν gen. abs. *while the first tabernacle is*

9 *still standing,* i.e. *still exists.* ‖ ἥ-τις = ἥ (supply ἐστίν)

ref. all that is described in vv.6-8 ; fem. by attraction of
παρα-βολή (< παρα-βάλλω set side by side to compare) a
sign, symbol. εἰς *pointing to*. ἐν-εστηκότα *here present*,
pf ptc -ίστημι, pf intr. *have come*. καθ' ἥν *in conformity
with which, in which*. δῶρον *gift*. θυσία *sacrifice*. προσ-
φέρονται pass. v.7. δυνάμεναι ptc fem. δύναμαι. συν-είδησις⁴
(< σύν-οιδα be conscious) *moral consciousness, conscience*.
τελειῶσαι aor. inf. -ειόω *make perfect*. λατρεύοντα ptc
-εύω *worship*, ὁ λατρεύων *the worshipper*. ‖ μόνον ἐπί   10
w. dat. (make perfect)...*only on (the level of)*. βρῶμα⁷
(< βιβρώσκω eat) *food*. πόμα⁷ (< πίνω drink) *drink*. διά-
φορος *different*. βαπτισμός *ceremonial ablution*, cf 6:2,
Mk 7:4. δικαίωμα v.1, δ. σαρκός *regulations for external/
material things*. μέχρι w. gen. *until*. δι-όρθωσις⁴ a making straight, *putting right, reform*. ἐπι-κείμενα *imposed*,
ptc -κειμαι *lie upon ; be imposed*. ‖ παρα-γενόμενος aor² ptc   11
-γίνομαι *appear, come*. γενομένων *that with him have
come to be*, aor² ptc γίνομαι ⟦var. μελλόντων *to come*⟧.
μείζων -ονος neut. μεῖζον, comp. of μέγας. τελειότερος comp.
of -ειος *perfect*. χειρο-ποίητος *wrought/made by the hands
of men*, pred. adj., οὐ χ. opp. κοσμικός (v.1). τοῦτ' ἔστιν
id est, that is (to say). κτίσις⁴ *creation*, οὐ ταύτης τῆς κτ.
not of ordinary building. ‖ δι' αἵματος instr. *through blood   12
or, of circumstances, with blood*. τράγος *goat*. μόσχος
calf. ἐφ-άπαξ *once for all*. τὰ ἅγια v.2. αἰωνία fem. of
αἰώνιος (which freq. serves also for fem.). λύτρωσις⁴ *redemption*. εὐράμενος (for -όμενος §459) aor² ptc mid.
εὑρίσκω i.e. through his passion and death ; mid. signifying "by himself", cf use of τυγχάνω 8:6. ‖ ταῦρος *bull*.   13
σποδός *ashes*. δάμαλις⁴ *heifer*. ῥαντίζουσα ptc fem. -ίζω
sprinkle. κε-κοινωμένους pf ptc pass. -νόω *make common
either meaning share or (as in NT) make ceremonially un-
clean, defile*. ἁγιάζω *consecrate, render sacred*, in ceremonial sense = separate from all that is profane (κοινός).
καθαρότης⁶ -τητος ἡ *purity*. ‖ πόσος *how much!* exclama-   14
tory, πόσῳ μᾶλλον *how much more!* προσ-ήνεγκεν aor² -φέρω
v.7. ἄ-μωμος *un-blemished*. καθαριεῖ fut. -ίζω *purify*.
συν-είδησις v.9. ἡμῶν ⟦var. ὑμῶν⟧. λατρεύειν inf. v.9.
ζῶντι ptc ζάω. ‖ διὰ τοῦτο *consequently*. δια-θήκη v.4.   15
καινός *new*. μεσίτης³ *mediator*. ὅπως w. subj. *in order
that*. γενομένου aor² ptc γίνομαι, gen. abs. *having taken
place*. ἀπο-λύτρωσις⁴ w. gen. *redemption from*. ἐπὶ τῆ...

on the basis of, under, or temporal, *in the days of.* **παράβασις**⁴ (< παρα-βαίνω) *trans-gression.* **ἐπ-αγγελία** *promise.* **λάβωσιν** aor² subj. λαμβάνω. **κε-κλημένοι** pf ptc pass. καλέω. **κληρο-νομία** *inheritance,* gen. epexeg. of ἐπαγγελία: *the promise, namely the eternal inheritance = the promised*

16 *eternal inheritance.* ‖ **ὅπου** *where.* **διαθήκη** here in its more common sense (outside scripture) of *testament, will.* **ἀνάγκη** *necessity* (sc. ἐστίν) w. acc. + inf. *it is necessary that.* **φέρεσθαι** *be brought in, be involved,* inf. pass. φέρω *bring.* **δια-θεμένου** aor² ptc -τίθεμαι *draw up/make* one's

17 *will,* aor. ptc *testator.* ‖ **ἐπί** *on the basis of.* **νεκροί** *persons deceased.* **βέβαιος** *firm* ; of a will, *operative.* **ἐπεί** *since.* **μήποτε** w. indic. (HGk) *never.* **ἰσχύω** *be strong,*

18 hence *be valid/operative.* ‖ **ὅ-θεν** *hence.* **χωρίς** v.7. **ἐγ-κε-καίνισται** pf pass. -καινίζω *restore ; inaugurate,* pf highlighting the permanent significance of everything

19 contained in scripture. ‖ **λαληθείσης** aor. ptc pass. λαλέω, gen. abs. **πᾶσα ἐντολή** wt art. *each law.* **λαβών** aor² ptc λαμβάνω. **μόσχος, τράγος** v.12. **ἔριον** *wool.* **κόκκινος** *crimson.* **ὕσσωπος** ἡ *hyssop,* Jn 19:29. **βιβλίον** *book,* αὐτό τε τὸ β. *and the book itself.* **ἐ-ράντισεν** aor. v.13. ‖

20 **ἧς** attracted from **ἥν** §16. **ἐν-ε-τείλατο** aor. -τέλλομαι

21 *command, enjoin.* ‖ **σκεῦος**⁸ *vessel.* **λειτουργία** *sacred mini-*

22 *stry.* **ὁμοίως** *likewise.* ‖ **σχεδόν** *almost, nearly* ; ass. w. πάντα. **καθαρίζεται** pass. v.14. **χωρίς** v.7. **αἱματ-εκ-χυσία** (αἷμα + ἐκ + χέω *pour) shedding of blood.* **ἄφ-εσις**⁴ (< ἀφ-ίημι) *forgiveness.* ‖

23 **ἀνάγκη** (sc. ἦν) v.16. **μέν...δέ** 1:7. **ὑπό-δειγμα**⁷ *figure, emblem.* **τὰ ἐν τοῖς οὐρανοῖς** = τὰ ἐπουράνια *the heavenly sanctuary.* **τούτοις** *by these means.* **καθαρίζεσθαι** inf. pass. **κρείττων** *better* 1:4. **θυσία** v.9. **παρά** w. acc. after comp.

24 *than.* ‖ **χειρο-ποίητος** v.11. **ἀντί-τυπος** *resembling* ; as noun, *representation, image* as an impression mirrors the die itself, here *prefiguration.* **ἀληθινός** *true, genuine.* **ἐμ-φα-νισθῆναι** aor² inf. pass. -φανίζω *reveal* ; pass. w. dat. *appear* before one. ‖ **πολλάκις** *often.* **προσ-φέρῃ** subj. v.7. **ὥσ-**

25 **περ** *like.* **ἐνιαυτός** v.7, κατ' ἐνιαυτόν *yearly, year by year,* cf καθ' ἡμέραν 7:27. **ἐν** *with* §116. **ἀλλότριος** *of another,*

26 *not one's own.* ‖ **ἐπεί** *since (in that case).* **ἔδει** impf δεῖ w. acc. + inf., an "unfulfilled" apodosis wt ἄν: *it would have been necessary, he would have had to.* **παθεῖν** aor² inf. πάσχω. **ἀπό** temporal. **κατα-βολή** (κατα- + βάλλω) *founda-*

tion. **νυνὶ δέ** *but as it is.* **ἅπαξ** v.7. **συν-τέλεια** (συν-τελέω complete) *consummation,* σ. τ. αἰώνων *in the fullness of time, at the climax of history* (NEB). **εἰς** of purpose. **ἀ-θέτησις** *annulment, destruction of the power* of sin. **θυσία** v.9. **πε-φανέρωται** pf pass. -ρόω v.8. ‖ **καθ᾽ ὅσον** 3:3, here 27 *just as.* **ἀπό-κειμαι** *be stored away,* impers. ἀπόκειταί τινι w. inf. *it is one's destiny to...* (cf colloq. "to be in store for" one). **ἀπο-θανεῖν** aor² inf. -θνῄσκω. **κρίσις**[4] *judgement.* ‖ **προσ-ενεχθείς** aor. ptc pass. -φέρω. **εἰς τό** final. **ἀν-** 28 **ενεγκεῖν** aor² inf. ἀνα-φέρω *bear, take upon oneself.* **ἐκ δευτέρου** (v.3) *a second time.* **χωρὶς ἁμαρτίας** (this time) *apart from / not in relation to sin,* contrast sense in 4:15. **ὀφθήσεται** fut. pass. ὁράω; pass. intr. *appear.* **ἀπ-εκ-δεχομένοις** ptc -δέχομαι *await eagerly.* **σωτηρία** *salvation,* εἰς σ. *with a view to / for the purpose of salvation.* ‖ **σκιά** *fore-* **10** *shadowing.* **εἰκών**[6] εἰκόνος ἡ *image* in which the reality is reflected. **πρᾶγμα**[7] (< πράσσω do) *deed; matter; thing.* **ἐνιαυτός** *year,* κατ᾽ ἐνιαυτόν *yearly, year after year,* ass. w. προσφέρουσιν. **θυσία** *sacrifice,* ταῖς αὐταῖς θ. dat. instr. *by the same sacrifices.* **προσ-φέρω** *offer,* 3rd pl. impers. "they", often w. force of a pass. "which are sacrificed/offered" §1. **δι-ηνεκής**[9] (< δια-φέρω carry through) *continuous;* εἰς τὸ δ. *continually; for ever* (v.12). **οὐδέ-ποτε** *never.* **δύναται,** subject ὁ νόμος. **προσ-ερχομένους** ptc -έρχομαι *approach, draw near,* here, to God in worship. **τελειῶσαι** aor. inf. -ειόω *make perfect.* ‖ **ἐπεί** *for (in that case).* **οὐκ** interr. 2 expecting the answer "Yes". **ἐ-παύσαντο** aor. παύομαι (mid.) *cease, stop,* οὐκ ἂν ἐπ.; *would they* (i.e. the sacrifices) *not have stopped* being offered? ἄν indicating unfulfilled condition; protasis implied §313. **προσ-φερόμεναι** ptc pass. **διὰ τό** w. acc. + inf. *because, seeing that.* **ἔχειν,** subject τοὺς λατρεύοντας (9:9), obj. μηδεμίαν συνείδησιν. **ἔτι** after a neg. *any longer.* **συν-είδησις** 9:9. **ἅπαξ** *once.* **κε-καθαρισμένους** *once cleansed,* pf ptc pass. -ίζω *purify, make clean.* ‖ **ἐν αὐταῖς** (sc. θυσίαις) *in them* or *by them.* 3 **ἀνά-μνησις**[4] *remembrance* (sc. γίνεται *is made*). ‖ **ἀ-δύνατος** 4 *un-able, power-less,* neut. either agreeing w. αἷμα or impers. cstr w. acc. + inf. *it is impossible for...to...* **ταῦρος** *bull.* **τράγος** *goat.* **ἀφ-αιρεῖν** inf. ἀφ-αιρέω *take away.* ‖ **δι-ό** *so* 5 *it is that.* **εἰσ-ερχόμενος** ptc, a clue to the unexpressed subject of λέγει. **θυσία** v.1. **προσ-φορά** *offering.* **ἠ-θέλησας** aor. θέλω. **κατ-ηρτίσω** aor. mid. 2nd sg -αρτίζω *put into*

6 *order*; *prepare*, mid. for someone. ‖ ὁλο-καύτωμα⁷ *burnt sacrifice* (one in which the whole (ὅλος) is burnt (καίω)). καὶ περὶ ἁμαρτίας (sc. θυσίας) *and sin offerings*; περί = ὑπέρ 5:1 §96. εὐ-δόκησας aor. (not always augmented)

7 -δοκέω *consider good*, *like*, *approve* sth. ‖ εἶπον must be 1st sg because of ἥκω *I have come*. κεφαλίς⁶ -ίδος ἡ *scroll*. βιβλίον 9:19, gen. epexeg. §45. γέ-γραπται *it stands written*, pf pass. γράφω. τοῦ ποιῆσαι (aor. inf.) inf. final dependent

8 on ἥκω. ὁ θεός for voc. §33f. ‖ ἀνώτερον (comp. ἄνω *above*) *higher up*, ref. writings, *earlier*, *above*. ὅτι as follows = "... θυσία v.l. προσ-φορά v.5. αἵ-τινες *such as*,

9 *namely those which*. προσ-φέρονται pass. v.l. ‖ εἴρηκεν pf λέγω, on pf 4:3. ἀν-αιρέω *do away with*. δεύτερος *second*.

10 στήσῃ aor. subj. ἵστημι *confirm*. ‖ ἐν instr. §119, ἐν ᾧ θελήματι *by which will*, i.e. God's will. ἡγιασμένοι pf ptc pass. ἁγιάζω *make holy*, *consecrate*. ἐφ-άπαξ *once for*

11 *all*, ass. w. προσφορά. ‖ μέν...δέ 1:7. ἱερεύς⁵ *priest*. ἕστηκεν *stands*, pf (intr. w. pres. meaning) ἵστημι. καθ᾽ ἡμέραν *daily*, *every day*. λειτ-ουργῶν ptc -ουργέω *offer worship*. πολλάκις *often*. προσ-φέρων ptc v.l. αἵ-τινες *such as*. οὐδέ-ποτε v.l. περι-ελεῖν aor² inf. -αιρέω *take away / remove*

12 what surrounds (cf εὐπερίστατον ἁμαρτίαν 12:1). ‖ ὑπὲρ ἁμαρτιῶν 5:1. προσ-ενέγκας aor² ptc (for -κών §489) -φέρω. εἰς τὸ δι-ηνεκές v.l ; ass. w. προσενέγκας or (rather) ἐ-κάθισεν

13 ἐν δεξιᾷ cf 8:1. ‖ τὸ λοιπόν neut. of λοιπός *remaining*, as adv. *henceforth*. ἐκ-δεχόμενος ptc -δέχομαι *wait*. τεθῶσιν aor. subj. pass. τίθημι. ἐχθρός *enemy*. ὑπο-πόδιον *footstool*,

14 pred. ‖ τε-τελείωκεν pf τελειόω v.l. ἁγιαζομένους ptc pass.

15 v.10, pres. den. a continuous process. ‖ μαρτυρεῖ ἡμῖν *testifies to us*, w. dat. sts in this sense Apoc 22:18. εἰρη-

16 κέναι pf inf. λέγω: μετὰ τὸ εἰρ. *after saying*. ‖ V.16, see

17 8:10. ‖ ἀ-νομία *wickedness*, pl. *transgressions* of the law. οὐ μή w. aor. subj. (or fut. indic.) an emphatic neg. ref. future §444. μνησθήσομαι fut. dep. μιμνήσκω τινός *remember*

18 sth. ἔτι v.2. ‖ ὅπου *where*. ἄφ-εσις⁴ (< ἀφ-ίημι) *forgiveness*. οὐκ-έτι *no longer*. περί = ὑπέρ 5:1 §96. ‖

19 παρ-ρησία *confidence* 3:6, π. εἰς τ. εἴσοδον "confidence for the entering", i.e. to enter. εἴσ-οδος ἡ *entrance*, both in concrete sense and, as here, of the act of entering.

20 τὰ ἅγια the *heavenly sanctuary*. ‖ ἥν ref. εἴσοδον. ἐν-ε-καίνισεν aor. ἐγ-καινίζω *inaugurate*, *institute*. πρόσ-φατος *recent*, *new*. ζῶσαν ptc fem. ζάω, Christ being the way

and the life. κατα-πέτασμα⁷ *curtain, veil* 9:3. ὁδὸν πρόσφα-
τον...τῆς σαρκὸς αὐτοῦ either Christ's body likened to a
veil : *a new and living way through the veil which is his
flesh* (RSV, JB) or to a way : *a new and living way through
the veil, (the way) of his flesh* (NEB). ‖ ἱερεύς v.11. ‖   21
προσ-ερχώμεθα subj. hort. v.1. ἀληθινός *true, genuine.*   22
πληρο-φορία *assurance.* ῥε-ραντισμένοι pf ptc pass. -τίζω
(ἀπό) *sprinkle clear of* / *free from.* τὰς καρδίας acc. of
respect. συν-είδησις⁴ *conscience.* λε-λουσμένοι pf ptc pass.
(or mid.) λούω *wash,* prob. in baptism. καθαρός *pure.* ‖
κατ-έχωμεν subj. hort. -έχω *hold fast.* ὁμο-λογία *profession.*   23
ἐλπίς⁶ -ίδος ἡ *hope.* ἀ-κλινής⁹ (κλίνω bend) *un-wavering.*
πιστός *faithful, to be trusted.* ἐπ-αγγειλάμενος aor. ptc -αγγέλ-
λομαι *promise.* ‖ κατα-νοῶμεν subj. hort. -νοέω τινά *take*   24
notice, take knowledge of, study another. εἰς *for* (the purpose of). παρ-οξυσμός (< παρα- + ὀξύς sharp) *incitement,
spur.* ‖ ἐγ-κατα-λείποντες ptc -λείπω *abandon.* ἐπι-συν-   25
αγωγή *gathering, meeting.* ἑ-αυτῶν 3rd pl. for 1st ἡμῶν
αὐτῶν §209. ἔθος⁸ *habit.* παρα-καλοῦντες ptc -καλέω.
τοσοῦτος...ὅσος *as much...as,* τοσούτῳ + comp. ... ὅσῳ *by so
much the more...as, all the more that.* ἐγγίζουσαν ptc -ίζω
draw near (ἐγγύς). ‖ ἑκουσίως *deliberately,* in emphatic po-   26
sition. ἁμαρτανόντων ptc -τάνω *sin,* pres. continuous, gen.
abs. *if we continue to sin deliberately...* λαβεῖν aor² inf.
λαμβάνω: μετὰ τὸ λαβεῖν *after receiving.* ἐπί-γνωσις⁴ *knowledge.* οὐκ-έτι, περί v.18. ἀπο-λείπεται *is left,* pass. -λείπω
leave behind, intr. *remain.* ‖ φοβερός *terrifying.* ἐκ-δοχή   27
(< ἐκ-δέχομαι v.13) *expectation.* κρίσις⁴ *judgement.* ζῆλος
(ζέω boil) *ardour,* πυρὸς ζῆλος *raging fire.* ἐσθίειν inf.
ἐσθίω. μέλλοντος ptc μέλλω: ἐσθίειν μ. *ready to devour.*
ὑπ-εν-αντίος w. dat. *against,* οἱ ὑ. *the adversaries.* ‖ ἀ-θετή-   28
σας aor. ptc -θετέω *flout.* οἰκτιρμός *pity,* pl. is Hebr.
usage. ἐπί w. dat. *on the evidence of.* δυσί, τρισί dat.
δύο, τρεῖς. μάρτυς⁶ -υρος ὁ *witness.* ἀπο-θνήσκει *dies* ; in
accordance w. the court's sentence, pres. frequentative. ‖
πόσος; *how much?* δοκέω *be of opinion, think.* χείρων   29
-ρονος neut. χεῖρον (comp. of κακός) *worse.* ἀξιωθήσεται
fut. pass. -ιόω τινός *be worthy* ; *consider worthy* of sth.
τιμωρία *punishment.* κατα-πατήσας aor. ptc -πατέω *trample
underfoot* ; πόσῳ...κ.; lit. "how much worse punishment
think you will he be deemed to merit, who has trampled
underfoot... ?" διαθήκη *covenant* 7:22. κοινός *common to*

all ; *ordinary* ; *profane*. ἡγησάμενος aor. ptc ἡγέομαι *lead* ; *consider, regard*. ἐν instr. §119. ἡγιάσθη aor. pass. -άζω
30 *consecrate*. ἐν-υβρίσας aor. ptc -υβρίζω *insult, affront*. ‖ εἰπόντα aor² ptc λέγω. ἐμοί dat. of possession. ἐκ-δίκησις⁴ *vindication*. ἀντ-απο-δώσω fut. -δίδωμι *repay*. κρινεῖ fut. κρίνω. ‖
31 φοβερός v.27. ἐμ-πεσεῖν aor² inf. -πίπτω *fall into*. ζῶντος
32 ptc ζάω. ‖ ἀνα-μιμνήσκεσθε impv -μιμνήσκομαι *recall, remember*. πρότερον adv. *earlier*. φωτισθέντες aor. ptc pass. -ίζω *shine upon* ; met. *enlighten*. ἄθλησις⁴ *contest*, met. ἀ. παθημάτων *wrestling with suffering*. ὑπ-ε-μείνατε aor. ὑπομένω *endure, support*. πάθημα⁷ (< aor. stem παθ- of πάσχω
33 *suffer*) *suffering*. ‖ τοῦτο μέν...τοῦτο δέ, neut. advl, *sometimes* you were...*on other occasions* you made/showed. μέν...δέ 1:7. ὀνειδισμός *abuse, insult*, dat. instr. θλῖψις⁴ (< θλίβω press) *distress, trouble*, here prob. *persecution*. θεατριζόμενοι ptc pass. -ίζω *appear in a* θέατρον, *act* ; pass. *be publicly exposed*. κοινωνός *partner*, κ. γίνομαί τινων *make common cause, show solidarity* with. οὕτως *thus* (i.e. in ignominy and persecution). ἀνα-στρεφομένων ptc -στρέφομαι *live*. γενηθέντες aor. ptc dep. γίνομαι. ‖
34 καὶ γάρ *for in fact*. δέσμιος *prisoner*. συν-ε-παθήσατε aor. συμ-παθέω *sympathize; share the sufferings of*. ἁρπαγή *robbery, plundering* ?= confiscation. ὑπ-αρχόντων ptc -άρχω *exist, be*; ὑπ. τινί *belong to one*, τὰ ὑπάρχοντα *possessions, goods*. χαρά *joy*. προσ-ε-δέξασθε aor. -δέχομαι *welcome* ; *accept willingly*. ἑ-αυτούς 3rd pl. for 2nd pers., acc. as subject of ἔχειν. κρείττων *better, superior* 1:4. ὕπ-αρξις⁴ (ὑπ-άρχω) *existence* ; *means* of existence, *possession, property*. μένουσαν ptc fem. μένω: καὶ μ. *and a lasting one*. ‖
35 ἀπο-βάλητε aor² subj. -βάλλω *throw away* ; also *let go, lose*. παρ-ρησία v.19. ἥτις (a confidence) *which*. μισθ-απο-δοσία
36 *reward* 2:2. ‖ ὑπο-μονή *endurance*. χρεία *need*, χρ. ἔχω τινός *have need of/need* sth. ποιήσαντες aor. ptc ποιέω. κομίση-σθε aor. subj. mid. -ίζω *bring* ; mid. *take to oneself, receive*.
37 ἐπ-αγγελία *promise*. ‖ μικρός *little*, neut. as adv. *a little* (*while*). ὅσον (orig. exclamatory, *how much! how!*) *very*, μικρὸν ὅ. ὅ. *a very little while* (cf Eng. "much" less). ὁ ἐρ-χόμενος *he who is to come*, t.t. for Messiah. ἥξει *will be here*, fut. ἥκω *to have come* v.7. χρονίσει fut. -ίζω *delay*. ‖
38 ζήσεται fut. ζάω. ὑπο-στείληται aor. subj. mid. -στέλλω *draw back*. εὐ-δοκέω ἔν τινι v.6, *take pleasure* in someone. ‖
39 ἡμεῖς doubly emphatic, by position and by being expressed

at all (nom.). ὑπο-στολή a *shrinking back, timidity,* οὐκ
ἐσμὲν τῆς ὑπ. *we are not of those who shrink back.* ἀπ-ώλεια
destruction. περι-ποίησις[4] (περι-ποιέω acquire) a *securing,*
combining the meanings of "acquisition" and "possession" Eph 1:14, εἰς π. *to secure.* ψυχῆς obj. gen. *soul* or
life (eternal) ; cf Lk 17:33. ‖

ἐλπιζομένων *things hoped for, hopes,* ptc pass. -ίζω **11**
hope. ὑπό-στασις[4] (< ὑφ-ίστημι place under ; give substance to) *substance* 1:3, pred. πρᾶγμα[7] (< πράσσω do)
deed; a *matter; thing.* ἔλεγχος *proof.* βλεπομένων ptc
pass. neut. βλέπω: οὐ w. ptc where the combination expresses a single idea : *(things unseen).* ‖ ἐν ταύτῃ *on this* 2
account, for this. ἐ-μαρτυρήθησαν *they were testified to* /
attested, aor. pass. -ρέω τινί *testify* in favour of one, i.e.
they were noted for their faith. πρεσβύτερος (comp. of
πρέσβυς old) *older* ; pl. *men of the past.* ‖ πίστει causal dat. 3
because of / by faith §58. νοέω w. acc.+inf. *understand.*
κατ-ηρτίσθαι (κατα- + ἄρτιος perfect) aor. inf. pass. -αρτίζω
put into proper order, κ. τ. αἰῶνας *form the worlds,* incl.
subterranean and superterrestrial. ῥῆμα[7] *word.* εἰς τό
w. inf. consec. *so/in such a way that* §352. μὴ ἐκ φαινο-
μένων (ptc pass. φαίνω *show*) *not from things visible.*
γεγονέναι pf inf. γίνομαι *come into being* ; the verse generally understood as ref. creation ex nihilo. ‖ πλείων *more,* 4
comp. of πολύς: πλ. θυσία (10:1) *a greater sacrifice.* παρά
w. acc. after a comp. *than.* προσ-ήνεγκεν aor[2] -φέρω *offer.*
δι᾽ ἧς sc. θυσίας. ἐ-μαρτυρήθη v.2, δι᾽ ἧς ἐμ. εἶναι δίκαιος
(nom. in agreement w. the subject unexpressed since it is
subject also of ἐμαρτυρήθη) "by which he was attested as
being righteous", i.e. *which* (his sacrifice) *witnessed to his
righteousness.* μαρτυροῦντος ptc, μ. ἐπί = simple dat.
witnessing in favour of, *approving,* gen. abs. δῶρον *gift.*
αὐτοῦ τ. θεοῦ *God himself.* αὐτῆς i.e. his faith (shown in
offering sacrifice). ἀπο-θανών aor[2] ptc -θνήσκω, ptc concessive, *though dead.* ‖ μετ-ε-τέθη *was translated,* aor. pass. 5
μετα-τίθημι *remove* from one place to another. τοῦ w. inf.
consecutive §352. ἰδεῖν aor[2] inf. ὁράω. ηὑρίσκετο pass.
impf εὑρίσκω. δι-ότι *because.* μετ-έ-θηκεν aor., rel. past,
transl. *had translated* §290. πρό *before.* μετά-θεσις[4] *translation.* με-μαρτύρηται pf pass. εὐ-αρεστηκέναι pf inf.
-αρεστέω τινί *be pleasing* to, *please* one. ‖ χωρίς w. gen. 6
without. ἀ-δύνατον (sc. ἐστίν) w. inf. *it is impossible* to.

εὐ-αρεστῆσαι aor. inf. πιστεῦσαι aor. inf. dependent on δεῖ. προσ-ερχόμενον ptc -έρχομαί τινι *come to* one. ἔστιν (not encl.) *he exists*. ἐκ-ζητοῦσιν ptc dat. pl. -ζητέω *seek out* ; "seek God" w. biblical ethical connotation of devoting oneself to his service. μισθ-απο-δότης³ *one who rewards*

7 2:2 (-δοσία). ‖ χρηματισθείς aor. ptc pass. -ίζω *instruct* 8:5. μηδέπω *not yet*. βλεπομένων v.1. εὐ-λαβηθείς, transl. *took heed and...*, aor. ptc dep. -λαβέομαι *be concerned* ; *revere/fear God*. κατ-ε-σκεύασεν aor. κατα-σκευάζω *construct*. κιβωτός ἡ *ark*. σωτηρία *welfare, safety*. οἶκος *household*. κατ-έ-κρινεν impf κατα-κρίνω *condemn*. ἐ-γένετο aor² γίνομαι.

8 κληρο-νόμος *inheritor* 1:2. ‖ καλούμενος ptc pass. καλέω. ὑπ-ήκουσεν aor. -ακούω *obey*. ἐξ-ελθεῖν aor² inf. -έρχομαι. ἤμελλεν impf μέλλω: ἤμ. λαμβάνειν *he was to receive*. εἰς instead of pred. acc. §70. κληρο-νομία *inheritance*. ἐπιστά-μενος ptc ἐπίσταμαι *know*. ποῦ as indir. interr. *where*. ἔρχεται tense of direct speech, transl. *where he was

9 going* §346. ‖ παρ-ῴκησεν aor. -οικέω *come from home to live*. γῆ ἐπ-αγγελίας *land of promise*, "Hebr." gen. *promised land* §41. ἀλλότριος *belonging to another, not one's own*. σκηνή *tent*. κατ-οικήσας *made his home* in tents, aor. ptc -οικέω *live* ; *dwell*, aor. ptc ref. action contemporaneous w. main vb. συγ-κληρο-νόμος *fellow-heir*. τῆς ἐπαγγελίας τῆς

10 αὐτῆς *of the same promise*. ‖ ἐξ-ε-δέχετο impf ἐκ-δέχομαι *expect, look forward to*. θεμέλιος (< τίθημι) pl. *founda-tions*. ἔχουσαν ptc fem. ἔχω. τεχνίτης³ *craftsman* ; *builder*. δημι-ουργός (< δῆμος the people + ἔργον) *creator* ; τ. and δ.

11 pred. ‖ καί *even*. αὐτή proleptic prn §204. στεῖρα *barren*. κατα-βολή (< κατα- + βάλλω) *deposit*, δύναμιν εἰς κ. σπέρ-ματος if ref. Sarah can only mean *power to conceive*. σπέρμα⁷ *seed*. ἔ-λαβεν aor² λαμβάνω. καί *when* §455δ, or perh. *although* §452. παρά w. acc. *beyond, over*. ἡλικία *age*. ἐπεί *for*. πιστός *faithful, to be trusted*, pred. ἡγήσατο aor. ἡγέομαι *consider, believe*. ἐπ-αγγειλάμενον aor. ptc -αγγέλ-

12 λομαι *promise*. ‖ διό *so it was that*. ἐ-γεννήθησαν *were born*, aor. pass. γεννάω *bear*. καὶ ταῦτα *and (he) moreover*. νε-νεκρωμένου pf ptc pass. νεκρόω *put to death* ; pf ptc pass. *as good as dead*; here *impotent*, ref. ἑνός. ἄστρον *star*. πλῆθος⁸ *multitude*; πλήθει *in number*, dat. of respect §53. ἄμμος ἡ *sand*. παρά w. acc. *along*. χεῖλος⁸ *lip*, hence

13 *edge, shore*. ἀν-αρίθμητος *count-less*. ‖ κατὰ πίστιν *in faith*. ἀπ-έ-θανον aor² v.4. λαβόντες aor² ptc λαμβάνω. ἐπ-αγγελία

v.9. **πόρρω-θεν** *from afar.* **ἰδόντες** aor² ptc ὁράω. **ἀσπα-σάμενοι** ptc ἀσπάζομαι *greet, hail.* **ὁμολογήσαντες** aor. ptc -λογέω *confess.* **ξένος** as noun, *stranger, foreigner.* **παρ-επί-δημος** (παρα- from elsewhere + ἐπί with + δῆμος a people) *settler,* cf Eng. dialect "off-comer". || **τοιαῦτα** *such things,* οἱ λέγοντες τ. *those who speak so.* **ἐμ-φανίζω** *show plainly.* **πατρίς** -ίδος ἡ *homeland.* **ἐπι-ζητέω** *be in search of.* || **μέν...δέ**(v.16) 1:7. **ἐκείνης** (sc. πατρίδος). **ἐ-μνημό-νευον** impf -εύω τινός *have in mind, be thinking of* ; also *mention* (v.22) ; εἰ w. past tense and ἄν in apodosis, an unfulfilled condition §313f. **ἀφ'** (ἀπό) = ἐξ §88. **ἐξ-έ-βησαν** aor. ἐκ-βαίνω *go or come out.* **εἶχον** ἄν impf ἔχω; *if they had had in mind that (country) which they had left, they would have had...* **ἀνα-κάμψαι** aor. inf. -κάμπτω *return.* || **νῦν δέ** *instead.* **κρείττων,** neut. κρεῖττον *better* 1:4. **ὀρέγομαί** τινος *reach out for, aspire to* sth. **τοῦτ' ἔστιν** *id est, in other words.* **ἐπ-ουράνιος** *heavenly.* **δι-ό** *for which reason.* **ἐπ-αισχύνομαί** τινα *be ashamed of* one; here w. acc. of person and w. inf. **ἐπι-καλεῖσθαι** inf. pass. -καλέω *give another name to,* pass. *be also called,* Ex 3:15. **ἡτοίμασεν** aor. ἑτοι-μάζω *make ready* (ἕτοιμος). || **προσ-ενήνοχεν** pf -φέρω *bring to* ; *offer,* esp. in sacrifice ; pf appropriate to what, on the spiritual plane, was a completed act with lasting conse-quences, or due to the author's preference when ref. to whatever "stands written" in the sacred text as of per-manent significance (cf Rom 15:4). **πειραζόμενος** ptc pass. -άζω *put to the test.* **καί** *not only so.* **μονο-γενής**⁹ *only (begotten) son.* **προσ-έ-φερεν** impf conative, *he was on the point of offering | ready to offer.* **ἐπ-αγγελία** v.9. **ἀνα-δεξάμενος** *who had accepted,* aor. ptc -δέχομαι *accept.* || **ὅν** i.e. Abraham. **ἐ-λαλήθη** aor. pass. λαλέω. **ὅτι** = "... κληθήσεται** fut. pass. καλέω. **σοί** "ethical" dat. w. the suggestion of 'for' you, 'in your interest', not always translatable into Eng. **σπέρμα** v.11. || **λογισάμενος** aor. ptc λογίζομαι *reckon, judge.* **ἐγείρειν** inf. ἐγείρω. **δυνατός** *able, capable.* **ὅ-θεν** *hence,* i.e. *in this conviction.* **αὐτόν** = Isaac. **ἐ-κομίσατο** *he got him back,* aor. mid. -ίζω *bring* ; mid. *receive ; recover.* **ἐν παραβολῇ** (9:9) *in a type/symbol* (of the death and resurrection of Christ). || **περί μελλόντων** (ptc) *in connection with things to come.* **εὐ-λόγησεν** aor. -λογέω *bless.* || **ἀπο-θνήσκων** *when he was dying,* ptc -θνήσκω. **Ἰωσήφ** gen. **προσ-ε-κύνησεν** aor. -κυνέω *prostrate oneself,*

14

15

16

17

18

19

20

21

here, *bow down* in worship. ἐπί w. acc. (*leaning*) *on.*
22 ἄκρον *top.* ῥάβδος ἡ *staff.* ‖ τελευτῶν *at the end* (of his
life) ptc -τάω *come to an end, die.* ἔξ-οδος ἡ a *going out,
exodus* (cf εἴσοδος 10:19). ἐ-μνημόνευσεν aor. v.15. ὀστέον
23 *bone.* ἐν-ε-τείλατο aor. ἐν-τέλλομαι *give instructions.* ‖ γεννηθείς *when he was born,* aor. ptc pass. γεννάω *bear.* ἐ-
κρύβη aor² pass. κρύπτω *hide* (trans.) τρί-μηνος adj. *of 3
months* ; acc. of duration, *for 3 months.* οἱ πατέρες = οἱ
γονεῖς *his parents.* δι-ότι *because.* ἀστεῖος *beautiful, fine,*
pred. παιδίον (dim. of παῖς) *child.* ἐ-φοβήθησαν aor. dep.
24 φοβέομαι. διά-ταγμα⁷ (< δια-τάσσω ordain) *edict.* ‖ γενόμενος aor² ptc γίνομαι: μέγας γεν. *when he grew up.* ἠρνή-
σατο aor. ἀρνέομαι *deny* ; *refuse.* λέγεσθαι *to be called,*
25 inf. pass. λέγω. θυγάτηρ -τρός ἡ *daughter.* ‖ μᾶλλον...ἤ
...*rather than,* sts implying downright contradiction §445.
ἑλόμενος aor² ptc αἱρέομαι *choose.* συγ-κακ-ουχεῖσθαι inf.
pass. -ουχέομαι *endure hardship with.* πρόσ-καιρος *fleeting,
short-lived,* ref. ἀπόλαυσιν. ἔχειν inf. ἔχω. ἀπό-λαυσις⁴
26 *pleasure.* ‖ μείζων comp. of μέγας w. gen. of comp. πλοῦτος *wealth,* pred. ἡγησάμενος aor. ptc ἡγέομαι v.11.
θησαυρός *treasure.* ὀνειδισμός *insult* (10:33) ; ὀν. τ. Χριστοῦ
opprobrium/disgrace of Christ: that attached to the cause of
Christ or that which Christ himself suffered. ἀπ-έ-βλεπεν
impf ἀπο-βλέπω *look* (away) *to.* μισθ-απο-δοσία *reward* 2:2. ‖
27 κατ-έ-λιπεν aor² κατα-λείπω *leave.* φοβηθείς aor. ptc dep.
v.23. θυμός *anger, rage.* γάρ: what follows explains his
constancy. ἀ-όρατος *un-seen, in-visible* (sc. God). ὁρῶν
ptc ὁράω: ὡς ὁρ. *as if he saw* (him). ἐ-καρτέρησεν aor.
28 -ρέω *be steadfast/constant.* ‖ πε-ποίηκεν (pf) ποιέω, pf ref.
inauguration of a rite still observed ; ποιέω τὸ πάσχα *keep
the Passover.* πρόσ-χυσις⁴ (προσ- + χέω pour) *pouring ;
sprinkling.* ὀλοθρεύων ptc -εύω *destroy,* ὁ ὀλ. *the destroyer.*
πρωτό-τοκος *first born,* neut. pl. *the first-born of men and
29 animals.* θίγῃ aor² subj. θιγγάνω *touch.* ‖ δι-έ-βησαν aor²
δια-βαίνω *go through ; cross.* ἐρυθρός *red.* ξηρός *dry.* πεῖρα
experiment, trial ; experience (v.36). λαβόντες aor² ptc
λαμβάνω: πεῖραν λ. τινός *make trial of* sth. κατ-ε-πόθησαν
30 aor. pass. κατα-πίνω *swallow up.* ‖ τεῖχος⁸ *wall.* Ἰεριχώ
gen. ἔ-πεσαν (for -ον §489) aor² πίπτω. κυκλωθέντα *when
they had been encircled,* aor. ptc pass. -λόω *go round.* ἐπί
31 w. acc. instead of (simple) acc. of duration §80. ‖ πόρνη
prostitute. συν-απ-ώλετο aor² mid. -όλλυμι *destroy* one with

another, mid. *perish with*. ἀ-πειθήσασιν *unbelievers*, aor.
ptc dat. pl. -πειθέω *disbelieve*. δεξαμένη aor. ptc δέχομαι,
ptc causal. κατά-σκοπος *spy*. ‖ καί freq. precedes an interr. 32
§459. ἔτι *more*. λέγω subj. delib. ἐπι-λείψει fut. -λείπω
leave behind, w. obj. *fail* one. δι-ηγούμενον ptc -ηγέομαι
recount, tell, ptc conditional, *time will fail me if I tell
about...* χρόνος *time*. ‖ κατ-ηγωνίσαντο aor. -αγωνίζομαι 33
defeat, conquer. εἰργάσαντο (= ἠργάσαντο) aor. ἐργάζομαι
work; εἰρ. δικαιοσύνην *practised justice*, constative (global)
aor. ἐπ-έ-τυχον aor² ἐπι-τυγχάνω τινός *attain* sth. ἔ-φραξαν
aor. φράσσω *stop (up)*, *shut*. λέων⁶ λέοντος ὁ *lion*. ‖ ἔ-σβεσαν 34
aor. σβέννυμι *quench*. ἔ-φυγον *escaped*, aor² (effective)
φεύγω *flee*. μάχαιρα *sword*, στόμα μαχαίρης *edge of the sword*.
ἐ-δυναμώθησαν aor. pass. -μόω *empower, make strong*. ἀπό
= ἐκ "out of former state of". ἀ-σθένεια *weakness*.
ἐ-γενήθησαν aor² dep. (= ἐγένοντο) γίνομαι. ἰσχυρός
strong, powerful. πόλεμος *war*. παρ-εμ-βολή *army camp*;
armed forces. ἔ-κλιναν aor. κλίνω *bend*; *dent, break a
military formation*. ἀλλότριος *of another*, hence *foreign*. ‖
ἔ-λαβον aor² λαμβάνω. ἀνά-στασις⁴ (< ἀν-ίστημι) *re-surrec-* 35
tion. ἐ-τυμπανίσθησαν aor. pass. -ίζω *torture*. προσ-δεξά-
μενοι aor. ptc -δέχομαι *accept*, οὐ π. *not willing to accept*
the proffered release. ἀπο-λύτρωσις⁴ *release*. κρείττων
v.16. τύχωσιν aor² subj. τυγχάνω τινός *attain* to sth. ‖
ἔτεροι = ἄλλοι §153. ἐμ-παιγμός (< ἐμπαίζω ridicule) *jeer-* 36
ing. μάστιξ⁶ -ιγος ἡ *whip*, pl. *lashes*. πεῖρα v.29. ἔτι (cf
v.32) here, *even*. δεσμός (< δέω bind) pl. δεσμά τά *bonds*.
φυλακή (φυλάσσω guard) *prison*. ‖ ἐ-λιθάσθησαν aor. pass. 37
-άζω *stone*. ἐ-πρίσθησαν aor. pass. πρί(ζ)ω *saw* (in two)
⟦var. ἐπειράσθησαν *they were tempted* (aor. pass. πειράζω)⟧.
ἐν instr. φόνος *murder*. μάχαιρα v.34. ἀπ-έ-θανον aor²
ἀπο-θνήσκω: ἐν...ἀπέθ. "they died by murder (= being
murdered) by the sword". περι-ῆλθον aor² -έρχομαι *go
about*, aor. constative. μηλωτή *sheepskin*. αἴγειος *of a
goat*. δέρμα⁷ *skin*. ὑστερούμενοι *destitute*, ptc pass, -ρέω
be in want. θλιβόμενοι *oppressed*, ptc pass. θλίβω *press*.
κακ-ουχούμενοι ptc pass. -ουχέω *ill-treat*. ‖ ἄξιος *worthy*. 38
ἐρημία a *desert*. πλανώμενοι ptc pass. -νάω *cause to wander*,
pass. intr. *wander*. ὄρεσιν dat. pl. ὄρος⁸. σπήλαιον *cave*.
ὀπή *crevice*. ‖ μαρτυρηθέντες aor. ptc pass.; ptc conces- 39
sive, (although) *attested/approved*. ἐ-κομίσαντο aor. mid.
-ίζω v.19; mid. *take to oneself, receive*. ‖ κρεῖττον *better* 40

1:4. τι encl. *something.* προ-βλεψαμένου aor. ptc mid. -βλέπω *foresee*; mid. *provide.* χωρίς v.6. τελειωθῶσιν aor. subj. pass. -ειόω *bring to perfection*, pass. *reach perfection.* ||

12 τοι-γαρ-οῦν *consequently.* τοσ-οῦτος neut. -οῦτο or -οῦτον *so great.* ἔχοντες ptc ἔχω. περι-κείμενον ptc -κειμαι *have placed around* one, met. *be surrounded by* 5:2. νέφος[8] *cloud*, met. *multitude, host.* μάρτυς[6] -υρος ὁ *witness* (not only by word but by example, life, and death). ὄγκος *burden.* ἀπο-θέμενοι aor[2] ptc -τίθεμαι *put off* or *away, rid* oneself *of.* εὐ-περί-στατος (< εὖ *well* + περι- + ἵστημι) ? *easily besetting* (meaning uncertain). ὑπο-μονή *perseverance.* τρέχωμεν subj. τρέχω, hort. προ-κείμενον ptc -κειμαί τινι *be placed/lie before* one. ἀγών[6] ἀγῶνος ὁ *contest, race.* ||

2 ἀφ-ορῶντες ptc -οράω *look away from* (immediate surroundings) *to*, ἀφ. εἰς *fix* one's *eyes on.* ἀρχηγός *founder, inspirer.* τελειωτής[3] (< τελειόω *make perfect*) *one who perfects* or *completes* (not found elsewhere). ἀντί *for*, i.e. "in place of" or "for the sake of"; ἀ. τ. προκειμένης χαρᾶς either : *for* (i.e. to obtain as a prize) *the joy set before him endured...* or : *instead of the joy...endured* (i.e. chose to endure)... χαρά *joy.* ὑπ-έ-μεινεν aor. ὑπο-μένω *undergo, endure.* σταυ-ρός *cross.* αἰσχύνη *shame.* κατα-φρονήσας aor. ptc -φρονέω τινός *think nothing of/despise* sth. ἐν δεξιᾷ 8:1. θρόνος *throne.* κε-κάθικεν pf καθίζω *make one sit*, intr. *take* one's

3 *seat*, pf definitive. || ἀνα-λογίσασθε aor. impv -λογί-ζομαι *reckon; consider.* τοι-οῦτος *such*, ass. w. ἀντιλο-γίαν. ὑπο-με-μενηκότα pf ptc ὑπο-μένω, pf because like all Christ's acts its consequences are lasting. ὑπό = ἀπό = class. παρά *from.* ἁμαρτωλός *sinner.* ἀντι-λογία *contradiction*; also in deed, *opposition.* κάμητε aor[2] subj. κάμνω, if abs. *be weary/worn out*, if ass. w. ψυχαῖς *be sick at heart.* ἐκ-λυόμενοι ptc pass. -λύω *slacken*; pass. *grow faint, flag.* ||

4 οὔπω *not yet.* μέχρι(ς) w. gen. of degree, *to the point of.* αἷμα[7] here for *bloodshed.* ἀντι-κατ-έστητε aor[2] (intr.) -καθ-ίστημί τινα πρός τινα *set* one *against* another ; aor[2] (intr.) w. πρός *resist, refuse* sth. ἀντ-αγωνιζόμενοι ptc -αγωνίζομαι

5 *fight, struggle.* || ἐκ-λέ-λησθε pf ἐκ-λανθάνομαί τινος *forget* sth *completely.* παρά-κλησις[4] *exhortation.* δια-λέγομαί τινι *address* (words to) one. υἱέ voc. of υἱός. ὀλιγώρει impv -ρέω τινός (< ὀλίγος v.10 + ὤρα *care*) *make light of*, take *no notice of.* παιδεία *discipline.* μηδέ *and...not.* ἐκ-λύου impv -λύομαι. ἐλεγχόμενος ptc pass. ἐλέγχω *reprimand.* ||

παιδεύω *discipline.* μαστιγόω *scourge.* παρα-δέχομαι *re-* 6
ceive, accept. || εἰς indicating purpose, *for, as.* ὑπο-μένετε 7
impv v.2. προσ-φέρεται pass. -φέρω *bring to* ; pass. w. dat.
deal with/treat one. υἱός, πατήρ wt art. stressing quality :
"in the capacity of, *qua*" §179, τίς...υἱός; *what son is there*
whom a father...? || χωρίς *without.* παιδεία v.5. μέτ-οχος 8
(< μετέχω share) *sharer.* γε-γόνασιν pf² γίνομαι. ἄρα *in
that case, then.* νόθος *spurious,* ref. son, *bastard.* || εἶτα 9
then again. εἴχομεν impf ἔχω. παιδευτής³ *one who educates/
trains,* esp. by discipline (παιδεία). ἐν-ε-τρεπόμεθα pass.
ἐν-τρέπω *put to shame* ; pass. trans. *have regard for, respect.*
οὐ interr. expecting the answer "Yes". ὑπο-ταγησόμεθα
fut² pass. -τάσσω *subject* ; pass. *submit.* τῶν πνευμάτων
of our spirits. καί *so that,* final §455γ. ζήσομεν fut.
(= ζησόμεθα) ζάω. || οἱ μὲν γάρ...ὁ δέ *for they...but he.* 10
ὀλίγος *small* ; πρὸς ὀλ. ἡμέρας *for a short time.* δοκοῦν inf. of
impers. δοκεῖ τινι *it seems good* to one. ἐ-παίδευον impf
v.6. συμ-φέρον ptc neut. -φέρει *it is profitable/useful,* ἐπὶ
τὸ σ. *for our benefit.* εἰς τό w. acc. (here wanting) + inf. of
purpose. μετα-λαβεῖν aor² inf. -λαμβάνω τινός *share.* ἁγιότης⁶
-τητος ἡ *holiness.* || μέν...δέ 1:7. παρ-όν ptc -ειμι *be present,* 11
τὸ π. *the present time,* πρὸς τὸ π. *at the time.* χαρά v.2, χαρᾶς
εἶναι *to be matter for joy.* λύπη *grief.* ὕστερος *last,* neut.
as adv. *later on, afterwards.* καρπός *fruit,* lit. and met.,
ass. w. δικαιοσύνης. εἰρηνικός *peaceful* ; *peace-giving.* γε-
γυμνασμένοις pf ptc pass. -άζω *exercise, train.* ἀπο-δίδωμι
render ; ἀ. καρπόν *yield fruit.* || δι-ό *so, therefore.* παρ-ειμένας 12
drooping, listless, pf ptc pass. -ιημι *let fall by the side;
slacken.* παρα-λε-λυμένα *weak,* pf ptc pass. παρα-λύω *undo ;
enfeeble.* γόνυ -νατος τό *knee.* ἀν-ορθώσατε aor. impv -ορθόω
straighten again, brace up. || τροχιά (τρόχος wheel < τρέχω 13
run) *wheel-track; path.* ὀρθός *straight.* ποιεῖτε impv ποιέω.
ποσίν *with your feet,* dat. of instr. Pr 4:26. χωλός *lame,*
neut. *lame member* / *limb.* ἐκ-τραπῇ aor. subj. pass. -τρέπω
turn sth aside, hence pass. *be put out of joint.* ἰαθῇ aor.
subj. pass. ἰάομαι. *cure.* ||

διώκετε impv διώκω *pursue.* μετὰ πάντων ass. w. 14
εἰρήνην. ἁγιασμός *holiness.* οὗ χωρίς *without which.* ὄψε-
ται fut. ὁράω. || ἐπι-σκοποῦντες ptc -σκοπέω *observe,* w. μή 15
watch that...not. ὑστερῶν supply ᾖ (subj. εἰμί), ptc -ρέω
come late, so miss. ρίζα *root,* μή τις ρίζα depending on ἐπι-
σκοποῦντες, *...that* no bitter *root...* πικρία *bitterness*

("Hebr." gen. §40). ἄνω *above* ; *up.* φύουσα ptc fem. φύω *grow.* ἐν-οχλῇ subj. -οχλέω *trouble* (Lk 6:18), abs. *cause trouble.* μιανθῶσιν aor. subj. pass. μιαίνω *defile.* ‖

16 πόρνος *fornicator*, here *one leading an immoral life* I Cor 5:9. βέβηλος *godless* I Tim 1:9. ἀντί w. gen. *in exchange for.* βρῶσις[4] (βιβρώσκω eat) *eating* ; *food* ; βρ. μιᾶς *one dish* (of food). ἀπ-έ-δετο (HGk for -έδοτο, cf Mk 12:1 and parallels) aor. mid. ἀπο-δίδωμι v.11 ; mid. *sell.* πρωτο-τόκια

17 τά *birthrights of eldest son.* ‖ ἴστε class. (= οἴδατε). μετ-έπειτα *later on.* θέλων ptc θέλω. κληρο-νομῆσαι aor. inf. -νομέω *inherit.* εὐ-λογία *blessing.* ἀπ-ε-δοκιμάσθη aor. pass. ἀπο-δοκιμάζω *reject after testing.* μετά-νοια *change of mind/intention* (on the part of Isaac), LXX in same sense of God, e.g. I Sam 15:29, Joel 2:13. τόπος *place, occasion* 8:7. εὖρεν aor[2] εὑρίσκω. καίπερ w. ptc *although.* δάκρυον a *tear.* ἐκ-ζητήσας aor. ptc -ζητέω (ἐκ- successfully or to

18 the utmost) *seek*, glossed by JB as "pleaded for". ‖ προσ-εληλύθατε pf[2] -έρχομαι *come (up) to* οὐ γὰρ πρ. ... continued in v.22 ἀλλὰ πρ. κτλ. introducing the contrast of the new covenant. ψηλαφωμένῳ ptc pass. -φάω *touch* ; ptc pass. *tangible*, i.e. *material.* κε-καυμένῳ pf ptc pass. καίω *set alight* ; pass. *burn* (intr.). γνόφος *darkness.* ζόφος *gloom.*

19 θύελλα *whirlwind.* ‖ σάλπιγξ -πιγγος ἡ *trumpet.* ἦχος *sound* (masc. or neut, cf Lk 21:25). ῥῆμα[7] *word.* ἀκούσαντες aor. ptc ἀκούω τινός. παρ-ῃτήσαντο aor. -αιτέομαι w. inf., *beg* (παρα- w. force of "from"). προσ-τεθῆναι aor. inf. pass. -τίθημι *add* ; Eng. idiom prefers act., "not to add

20 another word". ‖ ἔ-φερον impf 3rd pl. φέρω *bear.* δια-στελλόμενον ptc pass. -στέλλομαι *give orders*, τὸ δ. *the order/command.* κἄν = καὶ ἐάν *if even.* θηρίον *beast* (in the wild). θίγῃ aor[2] subj. θιγγάνω τινός *touch sth.* λιθο-βοληθήσεται fut. pass. -βολέω (λίθος stone + βάλλω throw)

21 *stone*, impvl fut. ‖ φοβερός *awesome.* φανταζόμενον ptc pass. -άζω *make to appear*, τὸ φ. *the sight/spectacle.* ἔκ-

22 φοβος *terrified.* ἔν-τρομος *trembling.* ‖ ἀλλὰ προσεληλύθατε v.18. ζῶντος ptc ζάω. ἐπ-ουράνιος *heavenly.* μυριάς[6] -άδος ἡ *myriad.* παν-ήγυρις[4] (< πᾶς + ἄγυρις = ἀγορά) *con-*

23 *course, gathering.* ‖ πρωτό-τοκος *first-born*, of the first Christians as first to be made sons of God in Christ. ἀπο-γε-γραμμένων pf ptc pass. -γράφω *record* ; mid. *register oneself* ; pass. *be recorded/enrolled.* κριτής[3] a *judge.* πνεῦμα here as opp. embodied spirits of men on earth. τε-τελειω-

μένων pf ptc pass. -ειόω *make perfect.* ‖ δια-θήκη *covenant.* 24
νέος *new.* μεσίτης *mediator,* appos. Ἰησοῦ. ῥαντισμός a
sprinkling, αἷμα ῥαντισμοῦ "Hebr." gen. *sprinkled blood*
§40. κρείττων 11:16, neut. as adv. *better* ; here, *to more
purpose.* λαλοῦντι ptc λαλέω, neut. in agreement w.
αἵματι. παρά w. acc. after comp. *than.* ‖ βλέπετε impv, 25
βλ. μή *see that...not.* παρ-αιτήσησθε aor. subj. -αιτέομαί τινα
refuse, disregard one, contrast v.19 w. inf. (= beg that).
τὸν λαλοῦντα *the speaker,* i.e. Jesus whose blood "speaks"
(v.24). ἐξ-έ-φυγον aor² ἐκ-φεύγω *escape.* ἐπὶ γῆς ass. w.
χρηματίζοντα. παραιτησάμενοι *when they disregarded.* χρηματίζοντα ptc -ίζω *warn* 8:5. ἀπο-στρεφόμενοι ptc -στρέ-
φομαί τινα *turn away from* one. ‖ οὗ ἡ φωνή *whose voice.* 26
ἐ-σάλευσεν aor. -εύω *shake.* ἐπ-ήγγελται pf -αγγέλλομαι
promise, pf because still in force. ἔτι ἅπαξ *yet once more.*
σείσω fut. σείω *shake.* ‖ τὸ δέ marking a quotation, e.g. 27
"the words"... δηλόω *show, point to.* σαλευομένων ptc
pass., den. what belongs to this age. μετά-θεσις⁴ (< μετα-
change + τίθημι) *removal.* πε-ποιημένων *created,* pf ptc
pass. ποιέω. μείνῃ aor. subj. μένω. τὰ μὴ σαλευόμενα den.
what belongs to the age to come. ‖ δι-ό *therefore.* ἀ-σάλευ- 28
τος *un-shakeable.* παρα-λαμβάνοντες ptc -λαμβάνω *receive*
what is handed down or over. ἔχωμεν (subj. hort. ἔχω)
χάριν *let us be grateful,* Lk 17:9, I Tim 1:12. δι' ἧς (sc. the
act of thanksgiving). λατρεύωμεν subj. hort. -εύω *worship, serve.* εὐ-αρέστως τινι *acceptably, in a way pleasing*
to one. εὐ-λάβεια *reverence.* δέος⁸ *awe.* ‖ ὁ θεός sc. ἐστίν.
κατ-αναλίσκον ptc neut. -αναλίσκω *consume.* ‖

φιλ-αδελφία *brotherly love.* μενέτω impv 3rd sg μένω *con-* **13**
tinue, last. ‖ φιλο-ξενία *hospitality.* ἐπι-λανθάνεσθε impv 2
-λανθάνομαι *forget, neglect.* διὰ ταύτης *by this means.*
ἔ-λαθον aor² λανθάνω *escape notice,* here be *unaware/un-
conscious* of. ξενίσαντες aor. ptc -ίζω *entertain.* ‖ μιμνή- 3
σκεσθε impv -σκομαί τινος *remember* one or sth; *bear in
mind.* δέσμιος *prisoner.* ὡς *as if.* συν-δε-δεμένοι *fel-
low-prisoners,* pf ptc pass. -δέω *bind together.* κακ-ουχου-
μένων ptc pass. -ουχέω *ill-treat.* ὡς καὶ αὐτοὶ ὄντες (ptc
εἰμί) *as being also yourselves...* ἐν σώματι and so liable
to like treatment. ‖ τίμιος *precious ; honourable,* sc. ἔστω 4
impv εἰμί. γάμος *marriage,* art. generic. ἐν πᾶσιν if masc.
in the case of/for everyone ; if neut. *in every way.* κοίτη
marriage-bed. ἀ-μίαντος *un-defiled.* πόρνος 12:16. μοιχός

5 *adulterer*. **κρινεῖ** fut. κρίνω. || **ἀ-φιλ-άργυρος** *free from the love of money, without avarice*, sc. ἔστω. **τρόπος** *manner; way of life*. **ἀρκούμενοι** ptc pass. ἀρκέω *suffice*; pass. *be contented*; ptc w. impv force. **τοῖς παρ-οῦσιν** *with what is there*, i.e. *with what you have*, ptc dat. pl. -ειμι *be present*. **αὐτός** emphatic, *he himself*. **εἴρηκεν** pf λέγω. **οὐ μή** w. subj. an emphatic neg. ref. fut. §444 ; w. οὐδέ does not become affirmative. **ἀν-ῶ** aor² subj. -ίημι *relax* ; *give up* ; *fail*. **ἐγ-κατα-λίπω** aor²
6 subj. -λείπω *forsake*. || **θαρροῦντας** *undaunted*, ptc θαρρέω (= θαρσέω) *be courageous*, ptc acc. in agreement with subject of inf. **βοηθός** *helper*. **φοβηθήσομαι** fut. dep.
7 φοβέομαι. **ποιήσει** fut. ποιέω. || **μνημονεύετε** impv -εύω τινός *remember* one. **ἡγουμένων** ptc gen. pl. ἡγέομαι *lead*, οἱ ἡγούμενοι *your leaders*. **οἵ-τινες** *as those who*. **ἐ-λάλησαν** aor. λαλέω. **ἀνα-θεωροῦντες** ptc -θεωρέω *observe closely, consider*. **ἔκ-βασις**[4] *end; outcome, result*. **ἀνα-στροφή** (< ἀνα-στρέφομαι behave) *way of life* ; ὧν...τῆς ἀ. *the outcome of whose way of life*. **μιμεῖσθε** impv μιμέομαι *imitate*. ||
8 **ἐχθές** *yesterday*. **σήμερον** *today*. **ὁ αὐτός** *the same*. ||
9 **διδαχή** *doctrine*. **ποικίλος** *variegated* ; *various, diverse*. **ξένος** *strange*. **παρα-φέρεσθε** impv pass. -φέρω *divert, turn aside* ; pass. *be carried away* Eph 4:14. **καλόν** w. acc.+inf. *it is good...* **βεβαιοῦσθαι** inf. pass. βεβαιόω *confirm, strengthen*. **βρῶμα**[7] *food*. **ἐν** instr. *by (means of)* §119. **ὠφελήθησαν** aor. pass. -λέω τινά *be beneficial, be of use* to one; pass. *be helped/benefited*. **περι-πατοῦντες** ptc -πατέω ; ptc den.
10 *those who follow that way of life*. **θυσιαστήριον** *altar*. **φαγεῖν** aor² inf. ἐσθίω. **σκηνή** *tabernacle*, signifying the old
11 covenant. **λατρεύοντες** ptc -εύω τινί *worship*. || The cstr of v.11 thus : ὧν...ζῴων τὸ αἷμα...τούτων τὰ σώματα κατα-καίεται lit "of which animals the blood...of those the bodies are burnt", i.e. *those animals whose blood...have their bodies burnt...* **εἰσ-φέρεται** pass. -φέρω *bring in*; subject being τὸ αἷμα. **ζῷον** *animal*. **περί** = ὑπέρ 10:6. **τὰ ἅγια** *the sanctuary*. **διά** sts refers to the principal cause §113. **κατα-καίεται** pass. -καίω *burn (up)*. **ἔξω** w. gen.
12 *outside*. **παρ-εμ-βολή** *camp*. || **δι-ό** *therefore*. **ἁγιάσῃ** aor. subj. -άζω *consecrate*. **πύλη** *gate*. **ἔ-παθεν** aor² πάσχω *suffer*. ||
13 *fer*. **τοίνυν** *so then*. **ἐξ-ερχώμεθα** subj. hort. -έρχομαι.
14 ὀνειδισμός 11:26. **φέροντες** ptc φέρω *carry, bear*. || **μένουσαν** ptc fem. μένω v.l. **τὴν μέλλουσαν** ptc, *which is to come*.
15 ἐπι-ζητέω *search for* ; *look to*. || **ἀνα-φέρωμεν** subj. hort. -φέρω

offer (*up*). θυσία *sacrifice.* αἴνεσις⁴ *praise,* gen. epexeg. "consisting in praise". διὰ παντός *continually.* τοῦτ᾽ ἔστιν *i.e.,* that is (to say). χεῖλος⁸ *lip,* gen. pl. χειλέων (like ὀρέων Apoc 6:15 usu. uncontracted), contrast ἐθνῶν. ὁμολογούντων ptc -λογέω *confess, acknowledge* ; here may transl. Hebr. word for *praise.* ‖ εὐ-ποιΐα *well-doing,* esp. 16 acts of kindness. κοινωνία a *sharing* in common, *solidarity,* here of practical help. ἐπι-λανθάνεσθε v.2. τοι-οῦτος *such.* εὐ-αρεστεῖται pass. -αρεστέω *please.* ‖ πείθεσθε 17 impv pass. πείθω *persuade* ; pass. *be persuaded, believe,* w. dat. *obey* Gal 5:7. ἡγουμένοις v.7. ὑπ-είκετε impv -είκω τινί *submit, defer* to one. ἀγρ-υπνέω *be vigilant, keep watch* Eph 6:18. λόγος *account.* ἀπο-δώσοντες fut. ptc -δίδωμι *render,* fut. ptc (*who*) *must render* §282. χαρά *joy.* ποιῶσιν subj. ποιέω. στενάζοντες ptc -άζω *groan.* ἀ-λυσι-τελής⁹ (λυσι-τελής *worth the price*) *not worth while, not advantageous* ; litotes (see comment on Ac 1:5) instead of expressing positively the contrary : "detrimental, damaging"; pred. (subject being τοῦτο). ‖ προσ-εύχεσθε impv. 18 περί v.11. πειθόμεθα v.17. συν-είδησις⁴ *conscience.* ἐν πᾶσιν *in every way.* καλῶς *well,* i.e. *as we should,* ass. w. ἀναστρέφεσθαι. θέλοντες *seeing that we want* ptc causal θέλω. ἀνα-στρέφεσθαι inf. -στρέφομαι (pass. refl.) *conduct oneself, live.* ‖ περισσοτέρως *more than ever.* τοῦτο ποιῆσαι 19 (aor. inf.) ἵνα, i.e. to *pray that.* τάχιον comp. (but often positive in meaning) of ταχέως *quickly, soon.* ἀπο-κατα-σταθῶ aor. subj. pass. -καθ-ίστημι *restore.* ‖

ἀν-αγαγών aor² ptc -άγω *bring up.* ποιμήν⁶ -μένος ὁ 20 *shepherd.* πρόβατον *sheep.* ἐν causal §119. διαθήκη *covenant.* ‖ κατ-αρτίσαι aor. opt. -αρτίζω *fit together* ; *put into* 21 *proper order;* w. inf. *fit* one to... ; the opt. expressing a wish §355. εἰς τό w. inf. of purpose. ποιῶν ptc. εὐ-άρεστος *pleasing,* τὸ εὐ. *what is pleasing.* ἐνώπιον αὐτοῦ *in his sight;* closer to Hebr. idiom than simple dat. ‖ ἀν-έχεσθε impv -έχομαί τινος *endure* ; *bear with* sth. παρά- 22 κλησις⁴ *exhortation,* ὁ λόγος τ. π. den. this epistle. καὶ γάρ *for in fact.* διά (w. gen.) of manner. βραχύς -έως neut. βραχύ *brief, short,* διὰ βρ. *in few words, briefly.* ἐπ-έ-στειλα aor. ἐπι-στέλλω τινί *write* to one. ‖ γινώσκετε impv. ἀπο- 23 λε-λυμένον pf ptc pass. ἀπο-λύω *release, set free.* μεθ᾽ οὗ *in whose company.* τάχιον v.19. ἔρχηται subj. ἔρχομαι. ὄψομαι fut. ὁράω. ‖ ἀσπάσασθε aor. impv -άζομαι *greet.* 24

ἡγουμένους v.7. οἱ ἅγιοι title of all baptized believers. οἱ ἀπὸ τ. Ἰταλίας susceptible of two interpretations : "All here send you greetings from Italy" or "The Italians here send you greetings.". ‖

φυλή *tribe.* δοῦλος, not "brother". δια-σπορά (< δια- **1**
σπείρω scatter) ἡ δ. *dispersion* of the Jews, whether the
act, the displaced people, or the region. χαίρειν impvl
inf., the usual opening to a Greek letter, Ac 15:23 ; other
epistles have specifically Christian greetings. ||

χαρά *joy.* ἡγήσασθε aor. impv ἡγέομαι *lead* ; *regard,* **2**
consider, πᾶσαν χαρὰν ἡγ. *consider* (*it*) *all joy.* ὅταν w.
subj. *when* ref. fut. πειρασμός *trial.* περι-πέσητε aor[2]
subj. -πίπτω τινί *fall in with* ; *fall into.* ποικίλος *variegated* ;
various. || δοκίμιον τό *proof.* κατ-εργάζομαι *work out,* **3**
result in. ὑπο-μονή *fortitude.* || δέ *and,* introducing the **4**
climax. τέλειος *perfect.* ἐχέτω impv 3rd sg ἔχω. ἦτε
subj. εἰμί. ὁλό-κληρος (ὅλος + κλῆρος lot) *complete, whole.*
λειπόμενος ptc pass. λείπω *leave* ; pass. w. gen. *be lacking* ;
λείπομαι ἔν τινι *come short* in sth. || σοφία practical *wisdom.* **5**
αἰτείτω impv 3rd sg αἰτέω. διδόντος ptc δίδωμι. πᾶσιν
masc. ἁπλῶς (adj. ἁπλός simple, un-compounded) *simply* ;
without discrimination (so Hermas and Chrysostom).
ὀνειδίζοντος ptc -ίζω *reproach,* μὴ ὀν. here wt feeling con-
tempt for or without demeaning the recipient. δοθήσεται
fut. pass. δίδωμι, subject "it" (= σοφία). || δια-κρινόμενος **6**
ptc mid. -κρίνω (δια- (in mid.) to-and-fro + κρίνω judge)
distinguish ; mid. *doubt.* ἔ-οικα τινι pf-pres. *be like* sth.
κλύδων[6] -ωνος ὁ *wave, surf.* ἀνεμιζομένῳ ptc -ίζομαι (< ἄνεμος wind) *be moved about by the wind.* ῥιπιζομένῳ ptc pass.
-ίζω (< ῥιπίς fan) *toss about.* || οἰέσθω impv 3rd sg οἴομαι **7**
think ; pres. neg. *he must stop/not go on thinking...* λήμψε-
ται fut. λαμβάνω. || δί-ψυχος *of two minds, waverer.* ἀ-κατά- **8**
στατος *un-stable, ir-resolute.* ||

καυχάσθω impv 3rd sg -χάομαι *glory/take pride* in. **9**
ταπεινός *humble,* here "of humble station in life". ὕψος[8]
height, high position. πλούσιος *rich* (sc. καυχάσθω ὁ ἀδελ- **10**
φός v.9). ταπείνωσις[4] *down-grading, humiliation.* ἄνθος[8]
flower. χόρτος *grass* ; ἄνθος χ. *wild flower* rather than of
grass as such : an OT image of fragility Is 40:6, Ps 103:15.

11 παρ-ελεύσεται fut. -έρχομαι *pass by* or *away*. ‖ ἀν-έ-τειλεν aor. ἀνα-τέλλω *cause to rise* ; intr. of the sun, *rise*. The aorists of vv.11 and 24 are often explained as gnomic (proverbial) aors. appropriate to general statements ; they may also be viewed as proleptic aors. ; transl. by pres. tense. ἥλιος *sun*. καύσων⁶ -ωνος ὁ (< aor. (ἔκαυσα) of καίω burn) *scorching wind*. ἐ-ξήρανεν aor. ξηραίνω *dry up, wither*. ἐξ-έ-πεσεν aor² ἐκ-πίπτω *fall away* ; *fade*. εὐ-πρέπεια *beauty*. πρόσωπον *appearance*. ἀπ-ώλετο aor² mid. -όλλυμι. πορεία (< πορεύομαι) *journey* ; here of journey through life. μαρανθήσεται fut. pass. μαραίνω *quench* ; pass. *wilt, waste away*. ‖

12 μακάριος *happy, blessed*. ὑπο-μένω *stand up to, bear*. πειρασμός v.2. δόκιμος *approved*. γενόμενος aor² ptc γίνομαι. λήμψεται v.7. στέφανος *crown* ; τὸν σ. τῆς ζωῆς gen. epexeg. *that crown which is life* §45. ἐπ-ηγγείλατο aor. -αγγέλλομαι *promise*, sc. as subject, God. ἀγαπῶσιν

13 ptc -πάω. ‖ πειραζόμενος *when he is tempted*, ptc pass. -άζω *tempt*. λεγέτω impv 3rd sg λέγω, subject μηδείς. ὅτι = "... ἀπό most likely deliberately replacing ὑπό ; from motives of reverence to exclude efficient cause and signify source. πειράζομαι pass. ἀ-πείραστος *not subject to temptation*. κακός *evil*. αὐτός nom. emphatic, *he him-*

14 *self*. ‖ ἐπι-θυμία *desire*. ἐξ-ελκόμενος ptc pass. -έλκω *draw away, lure*. δελεαζόμενος ptc pass. -άζω *entice* by a

15 bait (δέλεαρ). ‖ εἶτα *then*. συλ-λαβοῦσα aor² ptc fem. συλλαμβάνω *conceive*. τίκτω *give birth to, bear*. ἀπο-τελεσθεῖσα *come to maturity*, aor. ptc pass. fem. -τελέω *complete*. ἀπο-κυέω *give birth*, but in met. senses *engender, bring into*

16 *being, produce*. ‖ πλανᾶσθε impv pass. -νάω *mislead* ; μὴ π.

17 *make no mistake!* ἀγαπητός *beloved*. ‖ πᾶς wt art. *every*. δόσις⁴ a *giving* ; *gift, favour*. δώρημα⁷ *gift*. τέλειος *perfect*. ἄνω-θεν *from above*. κατα-βαῖνον ptc -βαίνω. πατήρ i.e. creator. φῶς pl. here den. sun, moon, and stars. ἔνι = ἐν w. ἐστίν understood (= ἔνεστιν) *there is*. παραλλαγή (< παρα- + ἀλλάσσω change) *variation*. τροπή *change*. ἀπο-σκίασμα⁷ *shadow*, the author may have had

18 astronomical imagery in mind. ‖ βουληθείς *by an act of will, deliberately*, aor. ptc dep. βούλομαι *wish, will*. ἀπ-ε-κύησεν aor. -κυέω v.15. λόγος ἀληθείας = the gospel Col 1:5. εἰς τό w. acc.+inf. of purpose. ἀπ-αρχή *first-fruits* ; ἀπ. τινα a *kind of first-fruits*, i.e. the Jews who were

called before the gentiles. **κτίσμα**[7] *creation* (what is created). ||

ἴστε pres. indic. (class. = HGk οἴδατε) *this you know* ; 19 but more likely impv, *be sure of that!* **ἀγαπητός** v.16. **ἔστω** impv 3rd sg εἰμί. **ταχύς** *quick, prompt.* **εἰς** = *w. respect to* (inf. = noun) *prompt to listen, slow to speak.* **ἀκοῦσαι** aor. inf. ἀκούω. **βραδύς** -δεῖα -δύ *slow.* **λαλῆσαι** aor. inf. λαλέω. **ὀργή** *anger.* || **δικαιοσύνη** θεοῦ *justice* 20 *willed by God* or perh. *vindicative justice of God.* **ἐργά- ζομαι** *work* ; *accomplish, bring about.* || **δι-ό** *therefore.* 21 **ἀπο-θέμενοι** aor[2] ptc -τίθημι *put off* or *away, rid oneself of.* **ῥυπαρία** *filth,* esp. of avarice, transl. *smirch (of avarice).* **περισσεία** *excess, surplus,* hence *remains,* cf περισσεῦον Mt 14:20, 15:37. **κακία** *malice.* **ἐν** *with* of concomitant circumstances (sociative) §116. **πραΰτης**[6] -τητος ἡ *gentle- ness,* ἐν πρ. perh. *with good will/receptiveness.* **δέξασθε** aor. impv δέχομαι *accept,* aor. effective §252. **ἔμ-φυτος** (< ἐμ- φύω *implant*) *rooted in* (you). **λόγος** sc. ἀληθείας v.18. **δυνάμενον** ptc δύναμαι. **σῶσαι** aor. inf. σῴζω. **ψυχή** *soul.* || **γίνεσθε** impv γίνομαι, supplying impv for εἰμί. **ποιητής**[3] 22 *doer.* **ἀκροατής**[3] *listener.* **παρα-λογιζόμενοι** ptc -λογίζομαι *misconstrue, so deceive.* || **ἔοικεν** v.6. **κατα-νοοῦντι** ptc -νοέω 23 *take note of, consider, study.* **γένεσις**[4] *birth* ; *origin,* τὸ πρόσωπον τῆς γ. *the face nature gave him* (NEB). **ἔσ-οπτρον** *mirror.* || **κατ-ε-νόησεν: on** the aors. v.11. **ἀπ-ελήλυθεν** pf[2] 24 -ἔρχομαι: pf, *is off* or *away* ; or ? aoristic pf, in same sense as neighbouring aors. §289. **ἐπ-ε-λάθετο** aor[2] ἐπι-λαν- θάνομαι *forget.* **ὁποῖος** *of what kind,* i.e. *what he is like.* || **παρα-κύψας** aor. ptc -κύπτω *bend over* to *look more closely,* 25 *peer.* **τέλειος** v.17. **ἐλευθερία** *freedom.* **παρα-μείνας** transl. *and continues,* aor. ptc -μένω *remain beside* (here, "in this activity"). **ἐπι-λησμονή** *forgetfulness,* ἀκροατὴς ἐπ. a *forget- ful hearer* ; so also ποιητὴς ἔργου an *active doer,* "Hebr." gen. §40. **γενόμενος, μακάριος** v.12. **ποίησις**[4] *doing, ac- tion.* **ἔσται** fut. εἰμί. || **δοκέω** *think, suppose.* **θρησκός** 26 *religious.* **εἶναι** inf. εἰμί. **χαλιν-αγωγῶν** ptc -αγωγέω (< χα- λινός a bridle + ἄγω) *bridle, restrain.* **γλῶσσα** *tongue.* **ἀπα- τῶν** ptc -τάω *deceive.* **μάταιος** masc. and fem. (also -αία I Cor 15:17) *empty, futile.* **θρησκεία** *religion.* || **καθαρός** 27 *pure.* **ἀ-μίαντος** *un-defiled.* **παρά** w. dat. of pers. *with* ; *in the eyes/view of.* **αὕτη** ref. what follows §213. **ἐπι- σκέπτεσθαι** inf. -σκέπτομαι *visit* (here as in Hebr., in order to help). ὀρφανός *orphan*. χήρα *widow*. θλῖψις⁴ *distress*, whether grief or want. ἄ-σπιλος masc. and fem. *spotless, un-stained*. τηρεῖν inf. κόσμος *world* (as "worldy" = sinful). ||

2 ἐν *with* of concomitant circumstances (sociative) §116. προσωπο-λημψία *partiality, respect/favouring of persons* on the ground of social standing, wealth, or influence. μὴ ἔχετε (impv) *do not hold*. τοῦ κυρίου obj. gen. τῆς δόξης "Hebr." gen., *our glorious Lord* §40 or perh. appos. to κυρίου: *the glory* = šekinah, presence of God, an amplifi-
2 cation of "Lord of glory" I Cor 2:8. || γάρ introducing an illustration. εἰσ-έλθῃ aor² subj. -έρχομαι. συν-αγωγή in early times ref. also to a Christian meeting for worship. χρυσο-δακτύλιος (χρυσοῦς (of) gold + δακτύλιος ring) *with/ wearing gold rings*. ἐσθής⁶ -ῆτος ἡ *clothes*. λαμπρός *luxurious, expensive*. πτωχός *a poor man*. ῥυπαρός *dirty*. ||
3 ἐπι-βλέψητε aor. subj. -βλέπω *look at*, subj. dependent on ἐάν. φοροῦντα ptc φορέω *wear*. εἴπητε aor² subj. λέγω. κάθου impv καθίημι *be seated*. καλῶς *in a good place*; there is some evidence for use of καλῶς as Eng. "please". στῆθι *stand*, aor² (intr.) impv ἵστημι. ὑπο-πόδιον *footstool*,
4 ὑπὸ τ. ὑποπ. μου i.e. *at my feet*. || οὐ interr. expecting the answer "Yes". δι-ε-κρίθητε aor. dep. δια-κρίνομαι *doubt, hesitate* 1:6 ; *make a distinction, discriminate*. ἐν *between*. ἐ-γένεσθε aor² γίνομαι. κριτής³ *judge*. δια-λογισμός *reason-*
5 *ing*, δ. πονηρῶν *false standards of judgement*. || ἀκούσατε aor. impv -ούω. ἀγαπητός *beloved*. οὐχ interr. ἐξ-ε-λέξατο aor. ἐκ-λέγομαι *choose*, w. double acc., e.g. τινα πλούσιον *choose one to be rich*. πτωχός v.2. τῷ κόσμῳ ethical dat., *in the estimation of the world*, or dat. of respect, *in the things of the world*. πλούσιος *rich*. κληρο-νόμος *inheritor*. ἦς attracted from ἥν §16. ἐπ-ηγγείλατο aor.
6 -αγγέλλομαι *promise*. ἀγαπῶσιν ptc dat. pl. -πάω. || ἠ-τιμά-σατε aor. ἀ-τιμάζω (< τιμή honour) *treat without respect* or actively, *insult*. κατα-δυναστεύω τινός *oppress* one. αὐτοί nom. emphatic, *are not they the ones who...?* ἕλκω *drag,*
7 *hale*. κριτήριον *law-court*. || βλασ-φημέω *slander* men, *blaspheme* God. ἐπι-κληθέν aor. ptc pass. neut. -καλέω *give an additional name to, surname* one ; τὸ ἐπικ. ἐφ' ὑμῶν (name) *which has been given to you* ; the idea that God gives his name to his people dates from OT times Am 9:12
8 = Ac 15:17. || μέντοι *indeed, really*. τελέω *accomplish* ;

observe a law *fully.* **βασιλικός** *royal,* νόμος β. Mt 22:39=
Lev 19:18. **γραφή** *scripture.* **ἀγαπήσεις** fut. impvl -πάω.
πλησίον adv. *near,* ὁ πλ. one's *neighbour.* **σε-αυτόν** *your-*
self. **καλῶς** *well.* ‖ **προσωπο-λημπτέω** *show favouritism, dis-*   9
criminate (between people). **ἐργάζομαι** *work,* ἁμαρτίαν ἐρ.
commit sin. **ἐλεγχόμενοι** ptc pass. **ἐλέγχω** *convince, make*
one acknowledge ; pass. *be convicted.* **παρα-βάτης**[3] (< παρα-
βαίνω trans-gress) *transgressor.* ‖ **ὅσ-τις** w. subj. wt ἄν,   10
indef. *who-ever* §336. **τηρήσῃ** aor. subj. τηρέω. **πταίσῃ** aor.
subj. πταίω *stumble.* **ἐν ἑνί** *over one point.* **γέ-γονεν** pf[2]
γίνομαι. **πάντων** (the law) *as a whole.* **ἔν-οχος** (< ἐν-έχομαι
be held ; be liable) *liable to* ; *answerable for.* ‖ **εἰπών**   11
aor[2] ptc λέγω: ὁ εἰπών *he who said...* **μοιχεύσῃς** aor.
subj. -εύω *commit adultery.* **φονεύσῃς** aor. subj. -εύω
commit murder. ‖ **λαλεῖτε, ποιεῖτε** impv λαλέω, ποιέω. **διὰ**   12
νόμου *by a law* Rom 2:12. **ἐλευθερία** *freedom.* **κρίνεσθαι**
inf. pass. κρίνω : ὡς...μέλλοντες κ. *as those who will be judged.*
‖ **κρίσις**[4] *judgement.* **ἀν-έλεος** (gen. -ελέου) *without mercy.*   13
ποιήσαντι aor. ptc ποιέω. **ἔλεος**[8] *mercy.* **κατα-καυχάομαί**
τινος lit. *boast against* ; *over-ride* sth. ‖

　　ὄφελος (< ὀφέλλω increase) *advantage, use.* **λέγῃ** subj.   14
λέγω. **ἔργον** *work, action.* **ἔχῃ** subj. **μή** interr. expecting
the answer "No". **ἡ πίστις** that faith just referred to.
σῶσαι aor. inf. σώζω. ‖ **ἀδελφή** *sister* (i.e. a woman member   15
of the Christian community). **γυμνός** *naked.* **ὑπάρχωσιν**
subj. ὑπ-άρχω *be from the beginning* ; *exist* ; often simply *be.*
λειπόμενοι 1:4. **ἐφ-ήμερος** *for the day.* **τροφή** *food.* ‖ **εἴπῃ**   16
v.3. **ὑπ-άγετε** impv -άγω. **θερμαίνεσθε** *keep warm !* impv
mid. -αίνω *warm* ; mid. *warm oneself.* **χορτάζεσθε** *eat*
your fill ! impv pass. -άζω *satisfy with food,* Phil 4:12.
δῶτε aor[2] subj. δίδωμι, dependent on ἐάν (v.15). **ἐπι-τήδειος**
necessary ; τὰ ἐπιτ. τινος *the necessities for* sth. ‖ **ἔχῃ** v.14,   17
in sense *involve, entail.* **καθ' ἑαυτήν** *in itself.* ‖ **ἐρεῖ** fut.   18
λέγω: **ἀλλ' ἐρεῖ** τις normally introduces an objection.
δεῖξον aor. impv δείκνυμι *show.* **χωρίς** w. gen. *without.*
δείξω fut. ‖ **καλῶς ποιεῖς** *you do well* (to believe). **φρίσσω**   19
shiver, shudder. ‖ **γνῶναι** aor[2] inf. γινώσκω: θέλεις δὲ γνῶναι   20
do you want convincing? **ὦ** w. voc. in HGk is emphatic
§35. **κενός** *empty* ; ἄνθρωπε κενέ *you inane fellow!* **ἀργός**
(ἀ-εργός) *idle, use-less.* ‖ **οὐκ** interr. v.5. **ἐ-δικαιώθη** aor.   21
pass. -αιόω *justify* ; on this point seemingly contradicting
Paul, Rom 4:1ff. **ἀν-ενέγκας** aor[2] ptc (for -ενεγκών §489)

22 ἀνα-φέρω *offer* a sacrifice. θυσιαστήριον *altar*. ‖ συν-ήργει impf -έργω τινί *co-operate with* one. ἐ-τελειώθη aor. pass.
23 -ειόω *complete, perfect*. ‖ ἐ-πληρώθη aor. pass. -ρόω. γραφή v.8. λέγουσα ptc fem. ἐ-πίστευσεν aor. -εύω. ἐ-λογίσθη *reckon, count*. εἰς *as*, w. pred. a Hebr. §32. φίλος *friend*.
24 ἐ-κλήθη aor. pass. καλέω. ‖ δικαιοῦται pass. -αιόω. οὐκ ἐκ πίστεως μόνον: faith is necessary but to be operative must
25 be shown by deeds v.18. ‖ ὁμοίως *similarly*. πόρνη *prostitute*. οὐκ interr. ἐ-δικαιώθη v.21. ὑπο-δεξαμένη aor. ptc -δέχομαι *welcome, entertain a guest*, ptc causal. ἄγγελος *messenger*. ἐκ-βαλοῦσα aor² ptc -βάλλω *throw out*; also, as
26 here, *send away*. ‖ ὥσπερ...οὕτως (in the same way) *as...so*. χωρίς v.18. πνεῦμα *spirit* as synonymous w. life Lk 8:55, Ac 7:59. ‖

3   διδάσκαλος *teacher*. γίνεσθε impv γίνομαι: μὴ πολλοὶ διδ. γ. *not many should become teachers*. εἰδότες pf-pres. ptc οἶδα. μείζων neut. μεῖζον here, *severer*, comp. of μέγας.
2 κρίμα⁷ *judgement*. λημψόμεθα fut. λαμβάνω. ‖ πολλά acc. pl. as adv. (= much) intensifying the vb, *in many directions* or *many times*. πταίω *stumble*. ἅπαντες = πάντες. λόγῳ *in word/speech*. τέλειος *perfect*. δυνατός + inf. *able to, capable of*. χαλιν-αγωγῆσαι aor. inf. -αγωγέω *bridle*,
3 *restrain* 1:26. ‖ ἵππος *horse*, gen. dependent on στόματα. χαλινός *bit; bridle*. εἰς τό w. acc.+inf. *(in order) that*. πείθεσθαι inf. pass. πείθω *persuade*; pass. w. dat. *obey* one. καί introducing the apodosis. μετ-άγω *lead else-*
4 *where* (μετ-), *guide, steer*. ‖ τηλικ-οῦτος *so big*; τ. ὄντα (neut. pl.) *big as they are*. ἄνεμος *wind*. σκληρός *hard*; of wind, *rough, stiff*. ἐλαυνόμενα ptc pass. ἐλαύνω *drive*. μετ-άγεται pass. ἐλάχιστος superl. of ὀλίγος *small*, elative superl. *very small*. πηδάλιον *rudder*. ὁρμή *impulse*. εὐ-
5 θύνων ὁ *pilot, man at the helm*, ptc -θύνω *steer*. ‖ γλῶσσα *tongue*. μικρός *small*. μέλος⁸ *member*. αὐχέω τι *boast of* sth. ἡλίκος *of what size*, hence *how small!* or (2nd time) *how great!* ὕλη *wood* in same senses as Eng. incl. "fire-
6 wood", here *forest*. ἀν-άπτω *set alight*. ‖ πῦρ pred. ὁ κόσμος τῆς ἀδικίας *the world of wickedness*; or "Hebr." gen. *the wicked world*. It is not clear whether this phrase is appos. to γλῶσσα (as punctuated in our text) or pred. to καθίσταται ("constitutes/? shows itself (to be) the world of wickedness among (ἐν)...") and no convincing explanation of the expression in this context has yet been put forward.

καθ-ίσταται mid. or pass. -ίστημι *appoint* ; either mid. *make* (*oneself*), *become*, or pass. *be appointed*, *be made*. σπιλοῦσα ptc -λόω *stain, pollute*. φλογίζουσα ptc fem. -ίζω (< φλόξ ή flame) *set aflame*. τροχός *wheel*. γένεσις[4] *birth* ; *existence* ; τρ. τῆς γεν. an expression borrowed from the mystery religions, ref. the wheel or cycle of human life. φλογιζομένη ptc pass. γέεννα Hebr. *Gehenna, hell*, see Mt 5:22. ‖ φύσις[4] *nature*, freq. for *genus*, "kind". θηρίον 7 *large animal/beast* in the wild (not necessarily fierce). πετεινόν (< πέτομαι fly) *bird*. ἑρπετόν (< ἕρπω creep) *reptile*. ἐν-άλιον (< ἅλς ή sea) *marine life, sea creatures*. δαμάζεται pass. -άζω *subdue*. δε-δάμασται pf. ἀνθρώπινος *human*, ή φύσις ἀν. *humankind* (opp. ή φύσις θηρίων) : δαμάζεται καὶ δεδ. τῇ φύσει τῇ ἀνθρωπίνῃ *can be subdued and is subdued to that* (φύσει) *of man* (or *to humankind*) *or possibly, can be tamed and has been tamed by mankind* (dat. of agent §59). ‖ οὐδείς...ἀνθρώπων *no human being*. δαμάσαι aor. 8 inf. ἀ-κατά-στατος *rest-less* 1:8 or perh. *dis-orderly* (cf ἀκαταστασία v.16, στάσις Mk 15:7). κακόν τό *evil*, pred. μεστός *full*. ἰός *poison*. θανατη-φόρος "death-bearing", *deadly*. ‖ ἐν instr. §119. εὐ-λογέω *bless*. κατ-αράομαι *curse*. 9 ὁμοίωσις[4] *likeness*. γε-γονότας *made*, pf[2] ptc γίνομαι. ‖ ὁ αὐτός *the same*. εὐ-λογία *blessing*. κατ-άρα *cursing*. οὐ 10 χρή w. acc.+inf. *ought not*. γίνεσθαι inf. *to happen, to be*. ‖ μήτι interr. expecting the answer "No". πηγή a *spring of* 11 *water*. ὀπή *crevice, opening*. βρύω *gush with, pour out* (trans.). γλυκύς -κεῖα -κύ *sweet*, neut. (sc. ὕδωρ) *sweet/ drinking water*. πικρός *bitter*, neut. (sc. ὕδωρ) *water unfit to drink*. ‖ μή = μήτι. συκῆ *fig-tree*. ἐλαία an *olive*. ποιῆ- 12 σαι aor. inf. ποιέω *produce* fruit. ἄμπελος *vine*. σῦκον a *fig*. οὔτε = οὐδέ. ἁλυκός (< ἅλς ὁ salt) *salt(y)*. ‖

σοφός *wise, experienced*. ἐπι-στήμων -μονος neut. -μον 13 *understanding*. ἐν *among*. δειξάτω aor. impv δείκνυμι *show*. ἐκ *through, by*. ἀνα-στροφή (< ἀνα-στρέφομαι be-have) *way of life*. ἔργον *deed, action* ; here perh. *his achievements*, obj. of δειξάτω. πραΰτης[6] -τητος ή *unassuming-ness, unpretentiousness*. σοφία *wisdom*. ‖ ζῆλος (ζέω boil) 14 *zeal* ; *jealousy; opinionatedness*. πικρός v.11. ἐριθεία *ambition; party-spirit*. κατα-καυχᾶσθε impv -καυχάομαι *boast against* ; *over-ride* 2:13. ψεύδεσθε impv -δομαι κατά τινος here *belie, give the lie to*. ‖ αὕτη fem. of οὗτος. 15 ἄνω-θεν *from above*. κατ-ερχομένη ptc -έρχομαι *come down*.

ἐπί-γειος *earthly.* ψυχικός *natural* as opp. spiritual, *animal.*
16 δαιμονιώδης⁹ *diabolical.* ‖ ἀ-κατα-στασία *disorder.* φαῦλος
worthless, bad. πρᾶγμα⁷ *deed* ; *matter,* φαῦλον πρ. *malprac-*
17 *tice.* ‖ ἁγνός *pure.* ἔπειτα *then.* εἰρηνικός *peaceable.* ἐπι-
εικής⁹ *considerate.* εὐ-πειθής⁹ *obedient,* here *obedient to*
reason, reasonable. μεστός v.8. ἔλεος⁸ *mercy.* ἀ-διά-
κριτος (< ἀ- + διακρίνομαι 2:4) *impartial.* ἀν-υπό-κριτος
18 *without pretence, sincere.* ‖ σπείρεται pass. σπείρω *sow.*
ποιοῦσιν ptc dat. pl. ποιέω: τοῖς π. εἰρήνην *for* (or *by,* dat.
of agent §59) *peacemakers* (= those who behave peaceably
as well as make peace). ‖

4   πό-θεν; *from where?* sc. "come". πόλεμος *war.* μάχη
a *fight.* οὐκ interr. expecting the answer "Yes". ἐντεῦ-θεν
ref. place, *from here* ; ref. source, *hence, from this.* ἡδονή
pleasure. στρατευομένων met. *warring, at war,* ptc -εύομαι
2 *serve in the army.* μέλος⁸ *member.* ‖ ἐπι-θυμέω *desire.*
φονεύω *murder.* ζηλόω *covet.* ἐπι-τυχεῖν aor² inf. -τυγχάνω
attain. μάχομαι *fight.* πολεμέω *go to war.* διὰ τό w. acc.+
inf. *because.* αἰτεῖσθαι inf. mid. αἰτέω mid. *petition/pray*
3 *for.* ὑμᾶς subject of αἰτεῖσθαι. ‖ δι-ότι *because.* κακῶς
amiss, wrongly. δαπανήσητε aor. subj. -νάω *spend* (money). ‖
4 μοιχαλίς -ίδος ἡ *adulteress,* prob. ref. OT simile for Israel's
unfaithfulness Hos 9:1 ; Ezek 16:15ff. φιλία *friendship.*
ἔχθρα *enmity.* ὃς ἐάν (= ἄν) w. subj. *who-ever.* βουληθῇ
aor. subj. dep. βούλομαι *wish, will.* φίλος *friend.* ἐχθρός
5 *enemy.* καθ-ίσταται *constitutes himself* 3:6. ‖ δοκέω *think,*
suppose. κενῶς (adj. κενός *empty*) *without good reason.*
ἡ γραφή scriptural quotation only partially identifiable.
φθόνος *envy* ; *jealousy.* τὸ πνεῦμα ?subject or ? obj. of
ἐπι-ποθέω *long/yearn for.* κατ-ῴκισεν aor. -οικίζω *dwell* ;
cause to dwell. To understand God as subject and τὸ
πνεῦμα as obj. seems best to accord w. the context.   Taking πρὸς φθόνον as advl (for φθονερῶς) *with envy, jealously,*
Out of jealousy he longs for the spirit which he made to
dwell in us."   On the other hand, the many references in
LXX to the "jealous" love of God are always expressed
by ζῆλος and derivatives, not by φθόνος, cf also II Cor
11:2.   Others would punctuate so as to begin the quotation w. ἐπιποθεῖ "the scripture says with regard to envy" ;
but the v. ἢ δοκεῖτε...ἐν ἡμῖν may be punctuated and under-
6 stood in various ways. ‖ μείζων -ονος neut. μεῖζον comp.
of μέγας. δι-ό *therefore.* ὑπερ-ή-φανος *arrogant.* ἀντι-τάσ-

σομαι (range oneself against) *oppose.* ταπεινός *humble.* ‖
ὑπο-τάγητε aor² impv pass. -τάσσω *sub-ordinate* ; pass. 7
submit. ἀντί-στητε aor² impv ἀνθ-ίστημι *resist.* διά-βολος
(< δια-βάλλω *slander*) *accuser,* the *devil.* φεύξεται fut.
φεύγω *flee.* ‖ ἐγγίσατε aor. impv -ίζω *draw near.* ἐγγιεῖ 8
fut. καθαρίσατε aor. impv -ίζω *cleanse.* ἁμαρτωλός *sinner.* ἁγνίσατε aor. impv -ίζω *purify.* δί-ψυχος masc.
and fem., neut. -χον *of two minds,* ὁ δ. *waverer.* ‖ ταλαιπω- 9
ρήσατε *be wretched* or *miserable,* aor. impv -ρέω *be wretched.*
πενθήσατε aor. impv -θέω *mourn.* κλαύσατε aor. impv
κλαίω *weep.* γέλως⁶ -ωτος ὁ *laughter.* πένθος⁸ *mourning.*
μετα-τραπήτω aor² impv pass. 3rd sg -τρέπω *change* ; pass.
be turned into. χαρά *joy.* κατήφεια *gloom.* ‖ ταπεινώθητε 10
aor. impv pass. -νόω *humble* ; pass. sts *humble oneself.*
ὑψώσει fut. ὑψόω *lift up.* ‖

κατα-λαλεῖτε impv -λαλέω τινός *speak ill* of; μή w. 11
impv may indicate a general rule §246. κατα-λαλῶν ptc.
εἶ 2nd sg εἰμί. ποιητής³ *doer,* i.e. *keeper* of the law. κριτής³
judge. ‖ νομο-θέτης³ (< νόμος + τίθημι) *law-giver.* δυνά- 12
μενος ptc δύναμαι. σῶσαι aor. inf. σῴζω. ἀπ-ολέσαι aor.
inf. -όλλυμι *destroy.* τίς εἶ, ὁ κρίνων; ὁ κ. voc. §34, Eng.
idiom, *Who are you to judge...?* πλησίον 2:8. ‖

ἄγε νῦν *come now!* οἱ λέγοντες *you who say* §34. σήμερον 13
adv. *today.* αὔριον *tomorrow.* πορευσόμεθα fut. -εύομαι.
εἰς τήνδε τὴν πόλιν *to such-and-such* a *town.* ποιήσομεν fut.
ποιέω *spend* time. ἐνιαυτός a *year.* ἐμπορευσόμεθα fut.
-εύομαι *do business.* κερδήσομεν fut. -δαίνω *gain, make
money.* ‖ ἐπίσταμαι *know,* οἵτινες οὐκ ἐπίστασθε *you who* 14
are such that you do not know. τὸ τῆς αὔριον *what belongs
to* / *what will happen tomorrow.* ποῖος; *of what sort?* as
indir. interr. *what* your *life (will be) like.* ἀτμίς⁶ -ίδος ἡ
properly *steam* ; met. *vapour, mist.* ὀλίγος *little,* πρὸς ὀλίγον
for a short while. φαινομένη *seen,* ptc pass. φαίνω *show*
sth. ἔπ-ειτα *then.* ἀφ-ανιζομένη ptc pass. -ίζω *hide* sth
from sight, pass. *disappear.* ‖ ἀντὶ τοῦ λέγειν *instead of your* 15
saying. θελήσῃ aor. subj. θέλω. ζήσομεν, ποιήσομεν fut.
ζάω, ποιέω. Others would put the full point after ἀφανιζο-
μένη thus setting νῦν δὲ καυχᾶσθε in direct contrast to
v.15 instead of to v.13ff. ‖ νῦν δέ *but actually, as it is.* 16
καυχάομαι *boast.* ἀλαζονεία *ostentation,* pl. *airs of arro-
gance.* καύχησις⁴ *boasting.* τοι-οῦτος *such.* ‖ εἰδότι *to one* 17
who knows, dat. of εἰδώς pf-pres. ptc οἶδα. ‖ οὖν *so then.*

ποιεῖν inf. ποιέω. ποιοῦντι ptc, καὶ μὴ π. *and does not do (it).* ‖

5   ἄγε νῦν 4:13. πλούσιος *rich (man).* κλαύσατε 4:9, aor. inceptive §250. ὀλολύζοντες ptc -ύζω *howl.* ἐπί *over.* ταλαιπωρία *wretchedness,* pl. *miseries.* ἐπ-ερχομέναις ptc
2   -έρχομαι *come upon.* ‖ πλοῦτος *wealth.* σέ-σηπεν pf² σήπω *make rotten,* pf² *has rotted.* ἱμάτιον *outer garment, cloak,* pl. *clothes.* σητό-βρωτος (< σῆς moth + βιβρώσκω eat)
3   *moth-eaten.* γέ-γονεν pf² γίνομαι. ‖ χρυσός *gold.* ἄργυρος *silver.* κατ-ίωται pf² pass. -ιόω *cover with rust.* ἰός *poison* (cf 3:8); *rust.* εἰς instead of nom. pred. §32. μαρτύριον *evidence.* ἔσται fut. εἰμί. φάγεται fut. ἐσθίω *consume.* ἐ-θησαυρίσατε aor. -ίζω *store up treasure,* aor. constative, *you have stored...* ἐν *in* the last days (implying "already here") rather than *for* the last days. ἔσχατος *last.* ‖ μισθός
4   *wages.* ἐργάτης³ *workman.* ἀμησάντων aor. ptc ἀμάω *mow.* χώρα properly *region*; *country* as opp. town, pl. *fields.* ἀπ-ε-στερημένος pf ptc pass. ἀπο-στερέω *rob, deprive* one ; pass. of wages, *be kept back/witheld.* κράζω *call out,* met. *cry aloud.* βοή a *cry/shout.* θερισάντων *those who reaped,* aor. ptc -ίζω *reap.* οὖς ὠτός τό *ear.* Σαβαωθ
5   Hebr. *hosts, armies.* εἰσ-εληλύθασιν pf² -έρχομαι. ‖ ἐ-τρυφή-σατε aor. -φάω *live in luxury.* ἐπὶ τῆς γῆς implying another very different sphere elsewhere. ἐ-σπαταλήσατε aor. -λάω *be self-indulgent/pleasure-loving.* ἐ-θρέψατε aor. τρέφω *nourish.* καρδία seat not only of thought but of the emotions. σφαγή *slaughter* ; ἐν ἡμέρα σ. *in the day of (your)*
6   *slaughter,* either here and now or imminent. ‖ κατ-ε-δι-κάσατε aor. κατα-δικάζω *condemn.* ἐ-φονεύσατε aor. -νεύω *murder.* ἀντι-τάσσομαι mid. *oppose, resist.* ‖

7   μακρο-θυμήσατε aor. impv -θυμέω *be patient.* παρ-ουσία *coming* ; *presence* ; t.t. for Christ's *advent.* γεωργός (γῆ + ἔργον) *farmer,* ἰδοὺ ὁ γ. *for instance the farmer.* ἐκ-δέχομαι *wait for.* τίμιος *precious.* μακρο-θυμῶν ptc. ἐπ' αὐτῷ *over/ about it.* λάβῃ aor² subj. λαμβάνω, subject "the crop" understood. πρό-ϊμος *early* (in the year) (sc. ὑετός) *early rain* of November (the Jewish year beginning in the
8   autumn). ὄψιμος *late rain* of spring. ‖ στηρίξατε aor. impv -ίζω *stabilize* ; *make resolute.* ἤγγικεν *is near,* pf
9   ἐγγίζω *draw near.* ‖ στενάζετε impv -άζω *groan,* σ. κατ' ἀλλήλων here, *blame each other.* κριθῆτε aor. subj. pass. κρίνω. κριτής³ *judge.* πρό w. gen. *before,* π. τ. θυρῶν

at the gates. ἕστηκεν *is standing,* pf (intr. w. pres. sense) ἵστημι. ‖ **ὑπό-δειγμα**[7] *example, pattern,* pred. λάβετε aor[2] 10 impv λαμβάνω. **κακο-πάθεια** *endurance of or under hardship.* **μακρο-θυμία** *patience.* **προφήτας** obj. of λάβετε. **ἐ-λάλησαν** aor. λαλέω. ‖ **μακαρίζω** *call happy or blessed.* 11 **ὑπο-μείναντας** aor. ptc -μένω *endure, stand firm.* **ὑπο-μονή** *steadfastness.* **ἠκούσατε** aor. ἀκούω τι *hear of* sth. **τέλος**[8] *end, outcome,* τὸ τ. κυρίου (wt art.) *the ending brought about by (the) Lord,* i.e. God. **εἴδετε** *you have seen,* aor[2] ὁράω. **πολύ-σπλαγχνος** *full of pity.* **οἰκτίρμων** -μονος neut. -μον *compassionate.* ‖ **πρὸ πάντων** *above all.* **ὀμνύετε** impv 12 ὀμνύω τι *swear by* sth. **μήτε...μήτε** *neither...nor.* **ὅρκος** *oath,* cognate acc. *with* any other *oath.* **ἤτω** impv 3rd sg εἰμί: τὸ Ναὶ ναί...τὸ Οὖ οὔ (pred. anarthrous), *let your Yes be yes and your No, no.* **κρίσις**[4] *judgement,* here implying condemnation. **πέσητε** aor[2] subj. πίπτω. ‖ **κακο-** 13 **παθέω** *suffer hardship, be in trouble.* **προσ-ευχέσθω** impv 3rd sg -εύχομαι. **εὐ-θυμέω** *be in good spirits.* **ψαλλέτω** impv 3rd sg ψάλλω *play the harp; sing praises* (to harp accompaniment). ‖ **ἀ-σθενέω** *be delicate; be ill.* **προσ-** 14 **καλεσάσθω** aor. impv 3rd sg -καλέομαι *call to oneself.* **προσ-ευξάσθωσαν** aor. impv 3rd pl. -εύχομαι. **ἀλείψαντες** aor. ptc ἀλείφω *anoint.* **ἔλαιον** *olive oil.* ‖ **εὐχή** *prayer,* 15 εὐχὴ τ. πίστεως i.e. *prayer offered in faith.* **σώσει** fut. σώζω *make whole, cure.* **κάμνοντα** ptc κάμνω *be worn out / weary* Heb 12:3 ; hence *be ill.* **ἐγερεῖ** fut. ἐγείρω. **κἄν** = καὶ ἐάν. ᾖ subj. εἰμί. **πεποιηκὼς** pf ptc ποιέω: ἁμαρτίας εἰμὶ πεπ. periphr. cstr, *I have committed sin* §360. **ἀφ-εθήσεται** *it will be forgiven him,* fut. pass. -ίημι τινί τι *forgive* one sth. ‖ **ἐξ-ομολογεῖσθε** impv -ομολογέομαι 16 *confess.* **εὔχεσθε** impv εὔχομαι *pray.* **ὅπως** w. subj. final, *in order that.* **ἰαθῆτε** aor. subj. pass. ἰάομαι (mid.) *cure.* **ἰσχύω** (< ἰσχύς strength) *be able,* πολὺ ἰ. *is able* (*to accomplish*) *much.* **δέησις**[4] *petition.* **δικαίου** masc. **ἐν-εργου-μένη** *effective,* ptc -εργέομαι *be at work/effective* Col 1:29. ‖ **ὁμοιο-παθής**[9] *with the same feelings, of like nature.* **προσ-** 17 **ευχή** *prayer.* **προσ-ηύξατο** aor. -εύχομαι: προσευχῇ πρ. *he prayed earnestly;* an idiom common to Hebr., and relatively freq. in NT §60. τοῦ w. inf. taking the place of obj. inf., common in Lk e.g. 5:7, 17:1, Ac 27:1 etc. **βρέξαι** aor. inf. βρέχει impers. vb, *it is raining.* **ἔ-βρεξεν** aor. **ἐνιαυτός** *year;* the acc. of duration. **μήν** μηνός ὁ *month.*

18 ἔξ = 6. ‖ ὑετός *rain.* ἔ-δωκεν aor. δίδωμι. ἐ-βλάστησεν
19 aor. βλαστά(ν)ω *sprout* ; *produce.* ‖ πλανηθῇ aor. subj. pass.
   -νάω *lead astray* ; pass. *wander, stray.* ἐπι-στρέψῃ aor. subj.
20 -στρέφω *turn* sth, *turn* one *back.* ‖ γινωσκέτω impv 3rd
   sg -σκω. ἐπι-στρέψας aor. ptc, ὁ ἐπιστ. *one who turns*
   a sinner *back.* πλάνη *error.* ὁδός ἡ in ethical sense of
   "way of life". ψυχή *soul.* σώσει fut. σῴζω. καλύψει fut.
   καλύπτω *cover,* not conceal but rather as it were "overshadow, dominate" so as to smother the effect. πλῆθος[8]
   multitude. ‖

I PETER

ἐκ-λεκτός *chosen.* παρ-επί-δημος (παρα- from else- **1**
where + ἐπι- near + δῆμος a people) *settler,* cf Eng. dia-
lect "off-comer"; as those whose true homeland is in
heaven. δια-σπορά (< δια-σπείρω scatter) ἡ δ. *the disper-*
sion Jas 1:1, here in transferred sense of dispersed Christians in what is now Turkey. ‖ πρό-γνωσις[4] *foreknowledge* ; **2**
providence, ass. w. ἐκλεκτοῖς rather than ἀπόστολος.
ἁγιασμός *holiness.* πνεῦμα[7] almost certainly the Holy
Spirit, gen. of author : thus v.2 speaks of Father, Holy
Spirit, Son. εἰς *leading to.* ὑπ-ακοή *obedience.* ῥαντισμός
(< ῥαντίζω sprinkle) *sprinkling* ; a metaphor from the
covenant rite in which, after promising fidelity, the people
were sprinkled w. the blood of the sacrifice Ex 24:7-8.
πληθυνθείη aor. opt. pass. -ύνω *multiply, increase,* opt.
expressing a wish §355. ‖

εὐ-λογητός *blessed.* κατά *according* to the norm which **3**
is also the cause. ἔλεος[8] *mercy.* ἀνα-γεννήσας aor. ptc
-γεννάω *cause to be born again.* ἐλπίς[6] -ίδος ἡ *hope.*
ζῶσαν ptc fem. ζάω. ἀνά-στασις[4] *re-surrection.* ‖ κληρο-νομία **4**
inheritance. ἄ-φθαρτος (< ἀ- + φθείρω corrupt) *im-perish-*
able. ἀ-μίαντος (< ἀ- + μιαίνω defile) *undefiled.* ἀ-μάραν-
τος (< ἀ- + μαραίνομαι pass. wither) *unfading.* τε-τηρη-
μένην pf ptc pass. τηρέω. εἰς ὑμᾶς *for you* = ὑμῖν but the
prep. brings out God's expectation §51. ‖ ἐν local or instr. **5**
φρουρουμένους ptc pass. -ρέω *guard.* εἰς *until* or purposive,
for ; ass. w. φρουρ. σωτηρία *salvation.* ἕτοιμος *ready* (w.
inf. almost = μέλλων). ἀπο-καλυφθῆναι aor. inf. pass. -κα-
λύπτω *reveal.* ἔσχατος *last,* ἐν καιρῷ ἐ. *at the last,* but cf
v.20. ‖ ἀγαλλιάομαι *be jubilant, rejoice,* indic. (rather than **6**
impv) ἐν ᾧ ἀγ....εἰ *in which* or (causal) *and so you rejoice*
even if... Heb. 6:17. ὀλίγον *for a little while.* ἄρτι *now.*
δέον [ἐστίν] periphr. cstr = δεῖ. λυπηθέντες aor. ptc
pass. λυπέω *cause grief,* pass. *be distressed.* ποικίλος
variegated ; *various.* πειρασμός *trial.* ‖ δοκίμιον *proof.* **7**
Jas 1:3 ; inferring its *genuineness.* πολυ-τιμότερος comp.

of πολύ-τιμος *valuable*. χρυσίον the metal *gold*, gen. of comp. ἀπ-ολλυμένου *perishable*, ptc mid. -όλλυμι. δοκι-μαζομένου ptc pass. -άζω *try*, *test*, gen. abs. *yet tested*. εὑρεθῇ aor. subj. pass. εὑρίσκω: εὑρ. εἰς "may be found" i.e. *may prove to be for (your)*. ἔπ-αινος *praise*. τιμή *honour*. ἀπο-κάλυψις[4] *revelation* ; ἐν ἀπ. *at the revelation*. ‖

8 ἰδόντες aor[2] ptc ὁράω [[var. εἰδότες (ptc pf-pres. οἶδα)]]. ὁρῶντες ptc ὁράω: οὐκ ἰδόντες a plain statement of a matter of fact ; μὴ ὁρ: *though you may not see* you believe... §440. πιστεύοντες ptc -εύω. χαρά *joy*. ἀν-εκ-λάλητος *in-ex-pressible*. δε-δοξασμένη *glorious*, pf ptc pass. -άζω *glo-*

9 *rify*. ‖ κομιζόμενοι ptc mid. -ίζω *bring* ; mid. *receive*, usu. of that which is due or promised. τέλος[8] *end*, *consumma-tion*. σωτηρία *salvation*. ψυχῶν i.e. yourselves as living

10 persons. ‖ ἐξ-ε-ζήτησαν aor. ἐκ-ζητέω *research*. ἐξ-εραύνησαν aor. -εραυνάω *study*, *examine*. εἰς *destined for*. προφη-

11 τεύσαντες aor. ptc -εύω. ‖ ἐραυνῶντες ptc ; the simplex foll. so closely the cmpd has often the same force. εἰς (1st time) temporal, *at*. ποῖος as indir. interr. *what kind of*, *what*, εἰς τίνα ἢ ποῖον καιρόν *at what time and in what circumstances*. ἐ-δήλου impf δηλόω *declare* (subject, πνεῦμα Χριστοῦ). προ-μαρτυρόμενον ptc -μαρτύρομαι *testify before-hand*, *fore-tell*. εἰς (2nd time) v.10. πάθημα[7] (< ἔπαθον aor[2] πάσχω) *what is felt/experienced* ; esp. *suffering*. ‖

12 ἀπ-ε-καλύφθη aor. pass. ἀπο-καλύπτω v.5. ἑ-αυτοῖς *for them-selves*. διηκόνουν impf διακονέω τινί τι (augmented as if cmpd vb) *do a service* for someone. ἀν-ηγγέλη *has been announced*, aor[2] pass. -αγγέλλω *declare*. εὐ-αγγελισαμένων aor. ptc -αγγελίζομαί τινα *evangelize/bring the good news to* one. ἀπο-σταλέντι aor[2] ptc pass. -στέλλω. ἐπι-θυμέω *de-sire*, *long for*. ἄγγελοι wt art., possibly connoting "even such (exalted) beings as angels" §171. παρα-κύψαι aor. inf. -κύπτω *peer*, π. εἴς τι *look into* sth. ‖

13 δι-ό *therefore*. ἀνα-ζωσάμενοι aor. ptc mid. -ζώννυμι *gird up* the long flowing garment which impedes action Lk 12:35. ὀσφύς -ύος ἡ *loins*. διά-νοια *mind*. νήφοντες ptc νήφω *be self-controlled*. τελείως *completely*, *fully*. ἐλ-πίσατε aor. impv -ίζω *hope*, ἐλπ. ἐπί τι *fix one's hope on* sth. φερομένην ptc pass. φέρω *bring* ; ref. pres. or fut.

14 *being brought...* ἐν ἀποκαλύψει v.7. ‖ ὑπ-ακοή v.2 ; τέκνα ὑπακοῆς i.e. those characterized by obedience = *obedient* §43. συ(ν)-σχηματιζόμενοι ptc mid. or pass. -σχηματίζω

τί τινι *shape* sth *in accordance w.* a certain pattern ; mid.
conform (oneself) to ; μὴ σ. ταῖς...ἐπιθυμίαις *not in compliance
with your desires...* πρότερον *formerly.* ἄ-γνοια *ignorance.*
ἐπι-θυμία *desire.* ‖ καλέσαντα aor. ptc καλέω. καί *so.* αὐτοί 15
shown by 2nd pers. pl. vb to mean *yourselves.* ἀνα-
στροφή (way of) *life, behaviour.* γενήθητε aor. impv dep.
γίνομαι. ‖ δι-ότι *for.* γέ-γραπται *it stands written,* pf pass. 16
γράφω. ὅτι = "... ἔσεσθε fut. εἰμί, impvl. ὅτι (2nd time)
because. ἐγώ in emphatic position. ‖ The cstr of the long 17
sentence is clear : εἰ w. indic. introduces a simple (real)
condition, "if (as you do)..." ἐπι-καλέω *call upon, invoke.*
πατέρα (wt art.) is pred. of τὸν κρίνοντα, *as father.* ἀ-προ-
σωπο-λήμπτως *without respect of persons, impartially.* κρίνοντα ptc κρίνω. The apodosis begins w. ἐν φόβῳ (φόβος
fear, awe). παρ-οικία a *stay* in a foreign country. χρόνος
time, acc. of extent, *for/during the time...* ἀνα-στράφητε
aor[2] impv pass. -στρέφω *overturn* ; pass. refl. *live* in a certain way. ‖ εἰδότες see var. in v.8, the cstr. is ὅτι... 18
ἐλυτρώθητε...τιμίῳ αἵματι...Χριστοῦ. φθαρτός *perishable.*
ἀργύριον *silver.* χρυσίον *gold.* ἐ-λυτρώθητε aor. pass. λυτρόω
ransom. ματαία fem. of μάταιος masc. (and sts also fem.)
pointless, futile, useless. ἀναστροφή v.15. πατρο-παρά-δοτος
handed down, here from one's forebears, *inherited.* ‖
τίμιος *precious.* ἀμνός sacrificial *lamb.* ἄ-μωμος *without* 19
blemish. ἄ-σπιλος *without spot.* ‖ προ-ε-γνωσμένου pf ptc 20
pass. προ-γινώσκω *know beforehand,* of God implying "fore-
ordained". μέν...δέ = Lat. *quidem...autem,* roughly equivalent to *on the one hand...on the other hand, ...indeed,
but..., while...yet...* κατα-βολή (κατα- + βάλλω) *foundation.*
φανερωθέντος aor. ptc pass. -ρόω *reveal.* ἔσχατος *last,* ἐπ' ἐ.
τῶν χρόνων *in* (this) *last age* (inaugurated by the incarnation). δι' ὑμᾶς *on your account, for your sake.* ‖ πιστός 21
believing in God, *faithful,* τούς...π. appos. ὑμᾶς. ἐγείραντα
aor. ptc ἐγείρω. δόντα aor[2] ptc δίδωμι. ὥστε w. acc.+inf.
so that consec. ἐλπίς[6] -ίδος ἡ *hope,* under one art. w. πίστις:
so that your faith and hope are in God or *so that your faith
is also hope in God.* ‖ ἡγνικότες pf ptc ἁγνίζω *purify.* 22
ἐν instr. ὑπ-ακοή (v.2) τῆς ἀληθείας *obedience to the truth.*
εἰς *to* the point of. φιλ-αδελφία *brotherly love.* ἀν-υπό-κριτος
un-feigned, sincere. καθαρός *pure.* ἀγαπήσατε aor. impv
-πάω. ἐκ-τενῶς (< ἐκτείνω *stretch out*) *earnestly, whole-
heartedly.* ‖ ἀνα-γε-γεννημένοι pf ptc pass. -γεννάω v.3. 23

σπορά *sowing* of seed, hence *procreation* ; also *seed*. φθαρτός
v.18. ἄ-φθαρτος v.4. ζῶντος, μένοντος ptcs ζάω, μένω. ‖

24 δι-ότι v.16. πᾶσα σάρξ *all men,* σάρξ stressing man's frailty.
χόρτος *grass.* ἄνθος[8] *flower.* ἐ-ξηράνθη aor. pass. ξηραίνω
wither. ἐξ-έ-πεσεν aor[2] ἐκ-πίπτω *fall out* or *off* ; the aor.
(the tense wt limitation) is by nature suited to proverbs
and general statements ; known as gnomic aor. transl. by
25 pres. tense. ‖ ῥῆμα[7] *word.* εἰς τ. αἰῶνα *for ever.* εὐ-αγγελισθέν aor. ptc pass. neut. -αγγελίζω *announce good news,*
preach. ‖

2   ἀπο-θέμενοι aor[2] ptc mid. -τίθημί τι mid. *put off* or
away, rid oneself of sth. κακία here prob. in general sense
of *wickedness* (in particular = *malice*) πᾶσα κ. wt art.
connoting *every form of*... §188. δόλος properly a "bait",
so any *deceitful act,* also in abstract, *deceit.* ὑπό-κρισις[4]
hypocrisy, affectation, insincerity. φθόνος *envy.* κατα-λαλιά
2 *evil-speaking, backbiting.* ‖ ἀρτι-γέννητος *newborn.* βρέφος[8]
infant. λογικός *spiritual* rather than "rational". ἄ-δολος
un-adulterated, cf δόλος v.1. γάλα γάλακτος τό *milk,* art.
connoting that well known. ἐπι-ποθήσατε aor. impv
-ποθέω *long for.* ἐν instr. *by.* αὐξηθῆτε aor. subj. pass.
αὐξάνω τι (trans.) *increase* sth ; act. intr. and pass. *grow.*
3 σωτηρία *salvation.* ‖ ἐ-γεύσασθε aor. γεύομαι *taste ; experience.*
4 χρηστός *good* in the sense of kind. ‖ προσ-ερχόμενοι ptc.
λίθος *stone.* ζῶντα ptc ζάω. μέν...δέ 1:20. ἀπο-δε-δοκι-
μασμένον pf ptc pass. ἀπο-δοκιμάζω *reject* (after testing).
παρὰ θεῷ *with God, in the eyes of God.* ἐκ-λεκτός *choice.*
5 ἔν-τιμος *valuable ; honourable.* ‖ αὐτοί *you yourselves.* οἰκο-
δομεῖσθε impv pass. -δομέω *build.* πνευματικός *spiritual.*
εἰς = *so as to become.* ἱεράτευμα[7] *priesthood.* ἀν-ενέγκαι
aor[2] inf. (for -ενεγκεῖν §489) ἀνα-φέρω *offer* sacrifice. θυσία
sacrifice, πνευμ. θ. those inspired by the Spirit, cf Heb
6 13:15f. εὐ-πρόσ-δεκτος *acceptable.* ‖ δι-ότι *so.* περι-έχω
contain ; impers. *it says,* foll. by a quotation. γραφή a
writing, esp. *scripture.* ἀκρο-γωνιαῖος adj. *corner.* οὐ μή
w. aor. subj. an emphatic neg. ref. fut. §444. κατ-αισχυνθῇ
aor. subj. pass. -αισχύνω τινά *put* one *to shame* ; in Hebr.
one who is disappointed of his hope is said to be put to
7 shame. ‖ τιμή *honour* (as opp. "shame", looking back to
ἔντιμος and ultimately to ἱεράτευμα v.5). ἀ-πιστοῦσιν
un-believers, ptc -πιστέω *dis-believe.* ἀπ-ε-δοκίμασαν aor.
v.4. οἱ οἰκο-δομοῦντες *the builders.* ἐ-γενήθη aor. dep.

γίνομαι. εἰς in place of pred. acc. γωνία *corner*. ‖ πρόσ- 8
κομμα[7] *a cause of stumbling, obstacle*, λίθος προσκόμματος
"stone of stumbling", *occasion of falling* and *ruin*, ref.
Christ humble and humiliated. πέτρα *rock*. σκάνδαλον
trap ; hence *stumbling block, occasion of sin*. προσ-κόπτω
stumble. ὁ λόγος *the word* of the Christian gospel. ἀ-
πειθοῦντες *by disobeying*, ptc -πειθέω *dis-obey*. εἰς ὅ *to
which end*. ἐ-τέθησαν aor. pass. τίθημι *appoint*. ‖ γένος[8] 9
race, a *people*. ἐκ-λεκτός *chosen* (cf. v.4). βασίλειος *royal*.
ἱεράτευμα v.5. περι-ποίησις[4] *possession*, but see on Eph 1:14.
ὅπως w. subj. final, *in order that*. ἀρετή *virtue*; pl. freq.
ref. pagan gods, *glories, wonders*. ἐξ-αγγείλητε aor. subj.
-αγγέλλω *proclaim*. σκότος[8] *darkness*. καλέσαντος aor. ptc
masc. καλέω. θαυμαστός *marvellous*. ‖ ποτέ encl. *at one* 10
time. οὐ λαός *no people* (*of his*) Hos 1:9. ἠλεημένοι pf
ptc pass. ἐλεέω τινά *have mercy on* ; pass. *have mercy
shown* one, *receive mercy*. ἐλεηθέντες aor. ptc pass. ‖

    ἀγαπητός *beloved*. πάρ-οικος orig. a *neighbour*, later 11
one from elsewhere, stranger. παρ-επί-δημος 1:1. ἀπ-έχεσθαι
inf. -έχομαί (mid.) τινος *eschew, keep away from* ; παρακαλῶ
ὡς παροίκους...ἀπέχεσθαι leaves the obvious ὑμᾶς to be
understood. σαρκικός *sensual*. ἐπι-θυμία *desire*. αἵ-τινες
which are such that §215. στρατεύομαι *serve in the army*
(στράτευμα[7]), met. *war* against, *be at war* with. ψυχή
soul. ‖ ἀνα-στροφή (mode of) *life, conduct*. ἔχοντες ptc 12
impvl. §373. καλός *noble, honourable*. ἐν (sc. τούτῳ ἐν) ᾧ
in the matters for which, cf Rom 2:1. κατα-λαλέω τινός
speak ill of one. κακο-ποιός *evil-doer*. ἐπ-οπτεύοντες ptc
-οπτεύω *be a spectator*. δοξάσωσιν aor. subj. -άζω *glorify,
praise*. ἐπι-σκοπή *inspection, visitation, intervention* of God
in mercy or judgement, here perh. the time when the
gentiles will have received the gift of faith or at Christ's
second coming. ‖ ὑπο-τάγητε aor[2] impv pass. -τάσσω *sub-* 13
due ; pass. refl. *submit*. ἀνθρώπινος *human*. κτίσις[4] *creation* ; *institution*. διὰ τ. κύριον *for the Lord's sake*. εἴτε...
εἴτε *whether...or*. βασιλεύς here the Roman emperor.
ὑπερ-έχοντι ptc -έχω *be supreme*. ‖ ἡγεμών -μόνος ὁ *governor*. 14
δι' αὐτοῦ does not necessarily exclude the principal cause
§113. πεμπομένοις ptc pass. πέμπω *send*. ἐκ-δίκησις[4]
punishment. ἔπ-αινος *praise*. ἀγαθο-ποιός *well-doer*. ‖ οὕτως 15
a Hebr for τοῦτο. ἀγαθο-ποιοῦντας *in doing what is right*,
ptc -ποιέω *do good/what is right*. φιμοῦν inf. φιμόω

muzzle, silence. ἄ-φρων ἄφρονος neut. ἄφρον *silly.* ἀ-γνωσία
16 *ignorance* (wilful). ‖ ἐλεύθερος *free* nom., ass. w. ὑπο-
τάγητε v. 13. ἐπι-κάλυμμα⁷ *cover, pretext.* ἔχοντες ptc
17 ἔχω, transl. *making.* κακία v.1. ἐλευθερία *freedom.* ‖ τιμή-
σατε *show honour,* aor. impv τιμάω *honour.* ἀδελφότης⁶
-τητος ἡ *brotherhood,* in concrete sense of "brothers".
ἀγαπᾶτε, φοβεῖσθε, τιμᾶτε impv ἀγαπάω, φοβέομαι, τιμάω. ‖
18 οἰκέτης³ any *member of the household,* so *servant, slave* ;
οἱ οἰκ. for voc. ? §34. ὑπο-τασσόμενοι ptc pass. v.13 ; ptc
impvl, 3:1,7 §373. φόβος *fear, awe* ; ἐν παντὶ φ. *with
all due respect.* δεσπότης³ *master.* ἐπι-εικής⁹ *considerate.*
19 σκολιός *crooked* ; *perverse.* ‖ τοῦτο ref. what follows εἰ
§213. χάρις *a grace* ; or *a credit* cf Lk 6:32ff. συν-είδησις⁴
(< σύν-οιδα be conscious) *conscience, consciousness,* διὰ σ.
θεοῦ *in (full) consciousness of God* involving moral obligation, *with God in mind.* ὑπο-φέρω *undergo, bear.* λύπη
grief, sorrow. πάσχων ptc πάσχω *suffer.* ἀ-δίκως *un-justly.* ‖
20 ποῖος ; *what sort of?* κλέος⁸ *fame, glory, noteworthiness.*
εἰ w. (fut.) indic. a real condition "if...in fact..." §303.
ἁμαρτάνοντες ptc -άνω *do wrong.* κολαφιζόμενοι ptc pass.
-ίζω *give one a blow* with the fist (κόλαφος), ptcs temporal.
ὑπο-μενεῖτε fut. -μένω *endure* ; εἰ ἁμ. ...ὑπομενεῖτε *if when
you do wrong and get beaten you endure (it).* ἀγαθο-ποιοῦντες
21 v.15. παρὰ θεῷ v.4. ‖ ἐ-κλήθητε aor. pass. καλέω. ὅτι
καὶ Χριστός *since Christ also.* ἔ-παθεν aor² πάσχω. ὑπο-
λιμπάνων ptc -λιμπάνω τινί τι *leave* (behind) sth for one.
ὑπο-γραμμός *pattern, example.* ἐπ-ακολουθήσητε aor. subj.
-θέω *follow.* ἴχνος⁸ *footprint,* as obj. of vbs meaning "walk
22 in, follow", (pl.) *footsteps.* ‖ ἐ-ποίησεν aor. ποιέω. εὑρέθη
23 aor. pass. εὑρίσκω. δόλος v.1. ‖ λοιδορούμενος ptc pass.
-ρέω *abuse, insult.* ἀντ-ε-λοιδόρει impf ἀντι-λοιδορέω *return abuse/insults.* πάσχων v.19. ἠπείλει impf ἀπειλέω
threaten. παρ-ε-δίδου impf παρα-δίδωμι *hand over, commit,*
(understand as obj. himself and his cause). κρίνοντι ptc
24 κρίνω. δικαίως *justly, with justice.* ‖ ἀν-ήνεγκεν aor² ἀνα-
φέρω *take up.* ξύλον *wood,* of various wooden implements ;
gallows ; in NT *cross.* ἀπο-γενόμενοι aor² ptc -γίνομαι
depart, die. ζήσωμεν aor. subj. ζάω. μώλωψ⁶ μώλωπος ὁ
weal ; *wound* left by scourging, instr. dat. *by whose wounds.*
25 ἰάθητε aor. pass. ἰάομαι *heal.* ‖ ἦτε impf εἰμί. πρόβατον
sheep §482. πλανώμενοι ptc pass. -νάω *lead astray* ; pass.
wander, err. ἐπ-ε-στράφητε aor² pass. ἐπι-στρέφω *turn to,*

turn back, trans. and intr. ; pass. refl. in same sense. ποιμήν⁶ -μένος ὁ *shepherd*. ἐπί-σκοπος *over-seer* ; *guardian*. ψυχή v.11. ||

ὁμοίως *likewise*. ὑπο-τασσόμεναι ptc pass. -τάσσω *sub-**3** ordinate*, pass. refl. *sub-mit*, ptc impvl §373. ἵνα HGk w. fut. indic. §340. ἀ-πειθέω *dis-obey*, in scripture usu. of disobedience to God, in NT taking the form of disbeliev- ing the gospel. ὁ λόγος 2:8. ἀνα-στροφή *behaviour*, (way of) *life*. ἄνευ λόγου *without a word*. κερδηθήσονται fut. pass. -δαίνω *gain, win* (*over*). || ἐπ-οπτεύσαντες aor. ptc **2** -εύω τι *be a spectator of* sth. φόβος *awe, reverence*. ἁγνός *pure*, τήν...ὑμῶν transl. *the reverence and purity of your lives*. || ὧν fem. ἔστω impv εἰμί: ὧν ἔστω οὐχ *yours must not be*... ἔξωθεν *external, outward*, ἔ. ...κόσμος *outward adornment* of which ἐμπλοκῆς, περιθέσεως, ἐνδύσεως are gen. θερεχεg. *of* (or *such as*) *plaiting* ... *and wearing* ... *and dressing*.. ἐμ-πλοκή (< ἐν- + πλέκω weave) *plaiting*, cf I Tim 2:9 (πλέγμα). θρίξ τριχός ἡ *hair*. περί-θεσις⁴ (< περι- τίθημι put round or on) *wearing*. χρυσίον *gold* ; pl. and sts also sg, cf I Tim 2:9, *gold jewellery*. ἔν-δυσις⁴ (< ἐν- δύω clothe) a *putting on*. ἱμάτιον *outer garment, cloak*, pl. *clothes*. κόσμος *adornment*. || κρυπτός (< κρύ-πτω hide **4** (trans.)) *hidden* ; ὁ κ. τῆς καρδίας ἄνθρωπος gen. epexeg. *the hidden man, in other words the heart* §45. ἐν *in* = *with* (its). ἄ-φθαρτος 1:4, neut. as noun *imperishability*. πραΰς -αεῖα -αΰ *gentle*. ἡσύχιος *quiet*. πολυ-τελής⁹ *pre- cious*. || ποτέ (encl.) *once* (*on a time*). ἐλπίζουσαι ptc **5** fem. -ίζω *hope*. ἐ-κόσμουν impf κοσμέω *adorn*. ὑπο-τασ- σόμεναι v.l. || ὑπ-ήκουσεν aor. -ακούω τινί *obey* one, consta- **6** tive aor. καλοῦσα ptc fem. καλέω. ἐ-γενήθητε aor. dep. γίνομαι; if ἀγαθ. and φοβ. are understood as cond. ptcs, ἐγ. will be a proleptic aor. §257. ἀγαθο-ποιοῦσαι *women who do good* or cond. *if you do good*, φοβούμεναι ptcs fem. -ποιέω (2:15), φοβέομαι. πτόησις⁴ act. *intimidation* ; or pass. *terror*. || ὁμοίως v.l. συν-οικοῦντες ptc -οικέω *live with* in **7** marriage, ptc impvl v.l. γνῶσις⁴ *knowledge* that enlightens the Christian understanding. ἀ-σθενέστερος (comp. of -νής⁹) *weaker*. σκεῦος⁸ *utensil* ; *body* I Thess 4:4. γυναι- κεῖος *of a woman, feminine*. ἀπο-νέμοντες ptc -νέμω *ap- portion, assign* ; ptc impvl, *show* honour. τιμή *honour*. συγ-κληρο-νόμος *fellow-heir*. χάρις free *gift* of grace. ζωῆς gen. epexeg. (*consisting*) *in life* §45. εἰς τὸ μή w. acc.+inf.

so that...may not... ἐγ-κόπτεσθαι inf. pass. -κόπτω *block* ; *hinder.* προσ-ευχή *prayer.* ‖

8   τέλος⁸ *end* ; τὸ τ. advl acc. *finally* §74. ὁμό-φρων neut. -ρον *of one mind.* συμ-παθής⁹ *feeling for one another, sympathetic.* φιλ-άδελφος *having brotherly affection.* εὔ-σπλαγχνος *compassionate.* ταπεινό-φρων -φρον *humble-minded.* ‖

9   ἀπο-διδόντες ptc (impvl) -δίδωμι *repay.* κακόν τό *evil.* ἀντί w. gen. *for, in place of.* λοιδορία *insult.* τοὐναντίον = τὸ ἐναντίον advl acc. *on the contrary.* εὐ-λογοῦντες ptc (impvl) -λογέω *bless.* τοῦτο retrospective. ἐ-κλήθητε 2:21. εὐ-λογία a *blessing.* κληρο-νομήσητε aor. subj. -νομέω *inhe-*

10 *rit.* ‖ ἀγαπᾶν inf. ἰδεῖν aor² inf. ὁράω. παυσάτω aor. impv παύω *stop* ; *restrain.* γλῶσσα *tongue.* χεῖλος⁸ *lip.* τοῦ μή w. inf. = ἀπὸ τοῦ λαλῆσαι *from speaking,* aor. inf. λαλέω,

11 cf κατεῖχον...τοῦ μή... Lk 4:42. δόλος *deceit.* ‖ ἐκ-κλινάτω aor. impv -κλίνω *turn away.* ποιησάτω, ζητησάτω, διωξάτω

12 aor. impvs ποιέω, ζητέω, διώκω (*pursue*). ‖ ὀφθαλμοὶ κυρίου ἐπὶ δικαίους *the Lord watches over righteous men.* οὓς ὠτός τό *ear.* δέησις⁴ (δέομαι beg, beseech) *supplication, prayer.* πρόσωπον δέ...ἐπὶ ποιοῦντας (ptc) κακά (v.9) *but (the) face*

13 *of the Lord is against evil doers.* ‖ κακώσων fut. ptc κακόω *harm.* ζηλωτής³ *one ardent, enthusiast.* γένησθε aor²

14 subj. γίνομαι, supplying aor. for εἰμί. ‖ εἰ καί *even if.* πάσχοιτε opt. πάσχω *suffer* ; the opt. lifts the condition from a factual (εἰ w. indic.) onto a theoretical plane, *even if you were to suffer* §323. μακάριοι *blessed/happy are you!* φόβος *fear* ; cognate acc. of content ὁ φ. αὐτῶν obj. gen. §62. φοβηθῆτε aor. subj. dep. φοβέομαι: τόν...φ. *do not be afraid (with fear) of them.* ταραχθῆτε aor. subj. pass. τα-

15 ράσσω *disturb, trouble.* ‖ κύριον pred. *as Lord.* ἁγιάσατε aor. impv -άζω *make holy* ; *treat as holy, hallow.* ἕτοιμος *ready.* ἀεί *ever, always.* ἀπο-λογία *defence; rational explanation.* αἰτοῦντι ptc αἰτέω τινά τι *ask one for sth.* λόγος

16 a *reason.* ἐλπίς⁶ -ίδος ἡ *hope.* ‖ πραΰτης⁶ -τητος ἡ *gentleness.* φόβος *respect.* συν-είδησις 2:19, here, *conscience.* ἔχοντες ptc ἔχω, ptc impvl. ἐν (sc. τούτῳ ἐν) ᾧ *in the matter for which.* κατα-λαλεῖσθε pass. -λαλέω *speak ill of, disparage.* κατ-αισχυνθῶσιν aor. subj. pass. -αισχύνω *put to shame.* ἐπ-ηρεάζοντες ptc -ηρεάζω *slander, decry.* ἐν Χριστῷ Pauline expression, repeated 5:10,14. ἀναστροφή

17 v.l. ‖ κρείττων -ονος neut. κρεῖττον used as comp. of ἀγαθός: κρεῖττον...πάσχειν (inf. v.14) *it is better to suffer.*

ἀγαθο-ποιοῦντας *as well-doers*, ptc -ποιέω v.6, pred., acc. as ref. unexpressed subject of πάσχειν. θέλοι opt. θέλω if the will of God *should* (so) *decree*, cf v.14 (πάσχοιτε). κακο-ποιοῦντας *as evil doers*, ptc -ποιέω *do wrong*. ‖ καὶ Χριστός 18 *Christ also*, as the one in whom we live v.16. ἅπαξ *once*. περί = ὑπέρ *for* (= in expiation of) Heb 5:3, cf 1. ὑπὲρ ὑμῶν *for* (= on behalf of). ἔ-παθεν aor² πάσχω [[var. ἀπέ-θανεν (aor² ἀποθνήσκω)]]. ἄ-δικος *un-just*. προσ-αγάγῃ aor² subj. -άγω τινά τινι *bring* one *to* or *before* another. θανα-τωθείς aor. ptc pass. -τόω *put to death*. μέν...δέ 1:20. σαρκί dat. of respect, i.e. in the human sphere, of the earthly aspect of the Crucifixion. ζωο-ποιηθείς aor. ptc pass. -ποιέω *bring to life*. πνεύματι in the spiritual sphere: the act of God in the resurrection. ‖ ἐν ᾧ sc. πνεύ- 19 ματι. The translation of v.19 will vary with the understanding as to its point of reference : whether a descent into the underworld to preach the gospel to the souls of the departed or ref. the ascension to pronounce judgement on the fallen angels cf Gen 6:2. φυλακή (< φυ-λάσσω keep, guard) *prison*. πνεύματα: either *souls* (?Heb 12:23), or superhuman beings, i.e. *angels* or *spirits* (Mt 8:16, Lk 10:20). πορευθείς aor. ptc -εύομαι: ref. a descent (elsewhere καταβαίνω) into hades, or ref. ascension (v.22, Ac 1:10 and Jn 14 passim, 16:7,28). ἐ-κήρυξεν aor. -ύσσω in NT *preach the gospel*, in secular literature *make a procla-mation*, so *make proclamation of his victory* (v.22b). ‖ ἀ-πειθήσασιν aor. ptc -πειθέω v.1, qualifying πνεύμασιν. 20 ποτέ (encl.) *at some time, once*. ἀπ-εξ-ε-δέχετο impf -εκ-δέχομαι *wait*. μακρο-θυμία (long temper) *patience*. Νῶε *Noah*, indecl., here gen. κατα-σκευαζομένης ptc pass. -σκευάζω *build* ; gen. abs. κιβωτός ἡ *ark*. εἰς (i.e. by entering) *into* which a few...were saved. ὀλίγος *little*, pl. *few*. τοῦτ᾽ ἔστιν *id est, that is*. ὀκτώ = 8. ψυχαί *souls*, i.e. living persons. δι-ε-σώθησαν aor. pass. δια-σῴζω *save, bring to safety*. διά instr. *through* (= by means of) water (?baptism), cf I Tim 2:15. ‖ ὅ = ὕδωρ. ἀντί-τυπος *cor-* 21 *responding to/realizing exactly* sth foreshadowed in the "type" (model or symbol), neut. as noun, *replica, counter-part*, here ref. the water of baptism prefigured in the saving of Noah. (Contrast Heb 9:24 where ἀντίτυπος refers to an earthly representation or image of the eternal and perfect τύπος in heaven.) Either adjectival : (*that water*)

which, as baptism, corresponding exactly to the earlier
"type" *now saves you also,* or nominal : ...*which as counter-
part* of the "type", *I mean baptism, now...* βάπτισμα⁷
baptism. ἀπό-θεσις⁴ (< ἀπο-τίθεμαι 2:1) a *putting off* or
away, a *getting rid* of. ῥύπος *dirt,* gen. obj. συν-είδησις⁴
v.16, corresponding antithetically to ῥύπου, is also gen.
obj. ἐπ-ερώτημα⁷ *question* ; perhaps a *request* (Mt 16:1) ;
more likely *pledge, undertaking* (traditionally made by
question and answer), so Cyril of Alexandria (5th cent.),
a meaning attested by papyri of 2nd cent. onwards.
ἀνάστασις⁴ *resurrection,* through baptism is imparted the
saving effect of Christ's death and resurrection, see on
22 Rom 1:4. || δεξιός *right,* δεξιά ἡ (sc. χείρ) *right hand.*
πορευθείς v.19. ὑπο-ταγέντων aor² ptc pass. -τάσσω *subdue,
subject,* gen. abs. αὐτῷ for ἑαυτῷ §208. ||

4 παθόντος aor² ptc pass. πάσχω, gen. abs. [[var. add
ὑπὲρ ἡμῶν or ὑπὲρ ὑμῶν]]. ἔν-νοια (< ἐν + νοῦς mind)
thought, idea ; *frame of mind,* explained by ὅτι... ὁπλίσασθε
aor. impv mid. -ίζω *arm* ; mid. w. τι *arm oneself with* sth.
πέ-παυται pf pass. or mid. παύω τινά τινος *stop* one *from...* ;
mid. and pass. *cease* ; *break with* ; pf pass. possibly *be
free from* ; Christ's παθὼν σαρκί is mystically represented
in the Christian's death to sin in baptism ; this seems more
appropriate to the context than a ref. to physical suffer-
2 ing under persecution. || εἰς τό w. inf. final, ref. ὁπλίσασθε.
μηκ-έτι *no longer.* ἐπι-θυμία *desire,* dat. *for* (i.e. in satisfy-
ing) human *desires.* ἐπί-λοιπος *remaining.* βιῶσαι aor.
3 inf. βιόω *live.* χρόνος *time,* acc. of extent. || ἀρκετός
enough. παρ-εληλυθώς pf² ptc -έρχομαι *pass by,* ὁ π. χρόνος
the past. βούλημα⁷ *will, inclination* ; β. τ. ἐθνῶν *what the
gentiles want.* κατ-ειργάσθαι pf inf. -εργάζομαι *accomplish, do* ; ἀρκετός...κ. (*was*) *enough for doing...* πε-πορευ-
μένους pf ptc -εύομαι, like περιπατέω of "leading one's
life", *live.* ἀσέλγεια *debauchery.* οἰνο-φλυγία *drunkenness.*
κῶμος *orgy.* πότος *drinking bout.* ἀ-θέμιτος (< ἀ- + θέμις
4 *custom, law*) *forbidden.* εἰδωλο-λατρία *idolatry.* || ἐν ᾧ
by/at which. ξενίζονται pass. ξενίζω *entertain* a *guest ;
surprise,* ξενίζομαί τινι (v.12) or ἔν τινι *be surprised at*
or *by* sth. συν-τρεχόντων ptc -τρέχω *run* (*together*), gen.
abs. *when you do not rush...* εἰς τ. αὐτήν *into the same*
(sc. ? "as they do" or "as you used to do"). ἀ-σωτία (ἀ- +
σῴζω *save, keep*) *dissipation.* ἀνά-χυσις⁴ (< ἀνα-χέω *pour*

out) *out-pouring, flood.* βλασφημοῦντες ptc -φημέω *slander,
vilify* (sc. you). ‖ ἀπο-δώσουσιν fut. -δίδωμι *render.* λόγος 5
an *account.* ἐτοίμως *readily.* ἔχοντι ptc (masc., of God)
ἔχω; when combined w. adv. den. a state ἔχω = *be,* ἐτοίμως
ἔ. *be ready,* cf κακῶς ἔχω *be ill* Mk 1:32 etc. κρῖναι aor.
inf. κρίνω. ζῶντας ptc ζάω. ‖ εἰς τοῦτο *for this (reason),* 6
this is why. Perhaps an answer to contemporary bewilder-
ment at the death of Christians before the return of Christ,
cf I Thess 4:13-18. καὶ νεκροῖς *to the dead* (lit. "dead
men") *as well.* εὐ-ηγγελίσθη aor. pass. -αγγελίζομαι *preach
the gospel.* ἵνα supplying the content of τοῦτο: *so that
though as men* (or, *in men's eyes) they suffer* (the common
lot of) *condemnation to physical death, they may live in
the spirit with the life of God* (or, *in the eyes of God.*) κρι-
θῶσι aor. subj. pass. κρίνω *condemn* Jn 3:17f. μέν...δέ
1:20, prob. contains an implicit subordination of the μεν-
clause : *though they be condemned...they may live...* §452.
κατὰ ἀνθρώπους either *as men* or *in men's eyes.* σαρκί...
πνεύματι dat. of respect §53. ζῶσι subj. ζάω. ‖ τέλος⁸ 7
end. ἤγγικεν pf ἐγγίζω (< ἐγγύς *near) approach,* pf *be at
hand.* σω-φρονήσατε aor. impv -φρονέω *be of sound* (σῶς)
mind ; be sober-minded/reasonable. νήψατε aor. impv νήφω
be self-controlled. προσ-ευχή *prayer ;* εἰς πρ. *with a view to
your prayers,* i.e. so that you will be able to pray properly. ‖
πρὸ πάντων *above all.* ἑαυτούς for ἀλλήλους, also v.10. 8
ἐκ-τενής⁹ *eager, out-going.* ἔχοντες ptc impvl §373. καλύπτω κτλ. Jas 5:20, here too apparently ref. one's own
sins. πλῆθος⁸ *multitude.* ‖ φιλό-ξενος *hospitable.* ἄνευ w. 9
gen. *without.* γογγυσμός *grumbling.* ‖ ἔ-λαβεν aor² λαμ- 10
βάνω. χάρισμα⁷ *free gift* from God, a special grace given
to some for the service of the community. διακονοῦντες
ptc impvl -νέω *serve,* εἰς ἑαυτοὺς αὐτὸ δ. *use it in service
to one another.* οἰκο-νόμος *steward.* ποικίλος *variegated ;
diverse, multi-form.* ‖ λαλεῖ connoting the ministry of the 11
word. ὡς supply impv "let the purport be". λόγιον
saying, utterance, esp. *oracles* of God or words inspired by
him. ἰσχύς -ύος ἡ *power.* ἧς attracted from ἥν §16.
χορηγέω τι (provide the expenses of a χόρος) in general,
provide, supply sth. δοξάζηται subj. pass. -άζω *glorify,
praise.* κράτος⁸ *might ; sovereignty.* ‖

ἀγαπητός *beloved.* ξενίζεσθε impv pass. v.4 ; pres. 12
do not be surprised (as you are). πύρωσις⁴ *burning, trial*

by fire, lit. and met. πειρασμός *testing*. γινομένη ptc
γίνομαι. ὡς *as if*. ξένος *alien, strange*. συμ-βαίνοντος

13 ptc -βαίνω *happen*, gen. abs. || καθ-ό = καθὼς *in so far as*.
κοινωνέω τινί *share* in sth. πάθημα⁷ *suffering* 1:11. χαίρετε
impv χαίρω *rejoice, be glad*. ἀπο-κάλυψις⁴ *revelation*. χαρῆτε
aor² subj. dep. χαίρω. ἀγαλλιώμενοι ptc -ιάομαι *be jubilant*.

14 || ὀνειδίζεσθε pass. -ίζω *revile, insult*, εἰ ὀν. ἐν ὀνόματι
Χριστοῦ lit. *if you are reviled* (or perh. permissive : *if you
allow yourselves to be reviled*) *on account of the name of
Christ* (which, as "Christians", you bear v.16). μακάριοι
3:14. τὸ τ. δόξης [[var. add καὶ δυνάμεως]]. ἀνα-παύεται
pass. -παύω *give respite* to one, *make* one *take rest* ; pass.

15 intr. *rest*. || πασχέτω impv 3rd sg πάσχω v.1. φονεύς⁵
murderer. κλέπτης³ *thief*. κακο-ποιός *evil-doer*. ἀλλοτρι-
επί-σκοπος *one given to interference in the affairs of others* ;
here, as subject of legal proceedings, perh. *one who tres-
passes on the rights or duties of another, usurper, intri-*

16 *guer*. || αἰσχυνέσθω impv mid. 3rd sg -ύνω *put to shame* ;
mid. *be ashamed*. ἐν τ. ὀνόματι τούτῳ ?(precisely) *on the
ground of this name*. δοξαζέτω impv 3rd sg -άζω v.11. ||

17 ἄρξασθαι aor. inf. ἄρχομαι *begin*, ὁ καιρὸς τοῦ ἄ. *it is time
to begin*. κρίμα⁷ *judgement*. οἶκος *household*. πρῶτον ἀφ'
ἡμῶν *beginning from* (= *with*) *us*. τί; sc. ἔσται *what* (*will
be*)*?* τέλος v.7. ἀ-πειθούντων ptc -πειθέω *disobey* 3:1. ||

18 καὶ εἰ *and if*. μόλις *scarcely*. σῴζεται pass. σῴζω. ἀ-σεβής⁹ *god-less*. ἁμαρτωλός *sinner*. ποῦ; *where?* φανεῖται

19 fut. mid. φαίνω *show* ; *shine* ; mid. *appear*. || πάσχοντες ptc
πάσχω v.1. πιστός *faithful*. κτίστης³ *creator* (not so much
of physical as of new life). παρα-τιθέσθωσαν impv mid.
3rd pl. -τίθημί τινι *set* (esp. food) *beside* or *before* one ;
mid. *entrust* to one. ἀγαθο-ποιΐα *well-doing*. ||

5   ἐν *among*. ὁ συμ-πρεσβύτερος (*I*) *your fellow-elder*.
μάρτυς -υρος ὁ *witness*. πάθημα⁷ *suffering* 1:11. μελλούσης
ptc μέλλω. ἀπο-καλύπτεσθαι inf. pass. -καλύπτω *reveal*.

2 κοινωνός *participant, sharer*. || ποιμάνατε aor. impv (§492)
-μαίνω *tend, shepherd*. ἐν ὑμῖν *in your charge*. ποίμνιον
flock. ἐπι-σκοποῦντες ptc -σκοπέω *oversee*, combines the
senses of "superintend" and "watch over", authority and
care [[var. om.]]. ἀναγκαστῶς *under compulsion*. ἑκουσίως
spontaneously. κατὰ θεόν *in God's way* [[var. om.]]. αἰσχρο-
κερδῶς (adj. -κερδής⁹) *in greed for* dishonest *gain*. προ-

3 θύμως (adj. -θυμος) *eagerly, whole-heartedly*. || κατα-κυριεύον-

τες ptc -εύω τινός *domineer/lord it over* one. κλῆρος *lot, portion*, in this case that part of God's household (2:17) assigned to one's care. τύπος *model, pattern.* γινόμενοι ptc γίνομαι (pres. continuous). ‖ φανερωθέντος aor. ptc 4 pass. -ρόω *reveal*; pass. often = *appear*, gen. abs. ἀρχι-ποίμην⁶ -ποίμενος ὁ *chief shepherd.* κομιεῖσθε fut. mid. -ίζω *bring*; mid. *receive* 1:9. ἀ-μαράντινος *un-fading.* στέφανος *crown.* ‖ ὁμοίως *likewise.* νεώτερος (comp. of νέος new) 5 *younger.* ὑπο-τάγητε aor² impv pass. -τάσσω *subdue*; pass. refl. *submit.* ταπεινο-φροσύνη *humble-mindedness, humility.* ἐγ-κομβώσασθε aor. impv -κομβόομαι *tie sth round oneself, bind sth to oneself.* ὑπερ-ή-φανος *arrogant.* ἀντι-τάσσομαι (range oneself against) *oppose, resist.* ταπεινός *humble.* ‖ ταπεινώθητε aor. impv pass. -νόω *humiliate*; *make humble*; 6 pass. sts refl. *submit humbly to.* κραταιός *mighty.* ὑψώσῃ aor. subj. ὑψόω *exalt.* ἐν καιρῷ *in due time* (at his own time). ‖ μέριμνα *care* II Cor 11:28 (also in sense of "preoc- 7 cupation, anxiety" Lk 21:34). ἐπι-ρίψαντες aor. ptc -ρίπτω *throw onto.* μέλει τινί impers. *it is a care or concern to one,* αὐτῷ μ. περὶ ὑμῶν *he cares about / is concerned for you.* ‖ νήψατε 4:7. γρηγορήσατε *watch out!* aor. impv 8 (inceptive) -γορέω (vb formed from pf ἐγρήγορα of ἐγείρω) *be watchful.* ἀντί-δικος *opponent* in a law-suit, hence *adversary*; or adjectival, *accusing.* ὁ διά-βολος *the devil* Jas 4:7. λέων⁶ λέοντος ὁ *lion.* ὠρυόμενος ptc -ομαι *roar.* ζητῶν ptc ζητέω. κατα-πιεῖν aor² inf. -πίνω *swallow, de-vour.* ‖ ἀντί-στητε *resist,* aor² (intr.) impv ἀνθ-ίστημι *set* 9 *against.* στερεός *solid, firm, constant.* εἰδότες aor² ptc pf-pres. οἶδα. πάθημα⁷ v.1, τὰ αὐτὰ τῶν π. *the same kinds of suffering,* subject of inf. pass. ὑμῶν ἀδελφότης⁶ -τητος ἡ *your brotherhood.* ἐπι-τελεῖσθαι inf. mid. or pass. -τελέω *accomplish,* here, *perpetrate* on. ‖ καλέσας aor. ptc 10 καλέω. ὀλίγον *a little* (while). παθόντας *when you have suffered,* aor² ptc πάσχω *suffer*; acc. to the foll. vbs. κατ-αρτίσει fut. -ίζω *rehabilitate, restore.* στηρίξει fut. -ίζω *stabilize; make resolute.* σθενώσει fut. -νόω (< σθένος⁸ strength) *strengthen.* θεμελιώσει fut. -ιόω *establish* [[var. om.]]. ‖ κράτος⁸ *might.* 11

πιστός *faithful, trustworthy.* λογίζομαι *reckon, consi- 12 der, believe.* δι᾽ ὀλίγων 3:20 *in few (words) briefly,* cf ἐν ὀλίγῳ Eph 3:3. ἔ-γραψα aor. (epistolary Eph 6:22) γράφω. παρα-καλῶν ptc -καλέω. ἐπι-μαρτυρῶν ptc -μαρτυρέω w.

acc.+inf. *testify, declare that*... ἀληθής[9] *true*. **εἰς** for **ἐν**:
a confusion not found elsewhere in the epistles, but perh.
additional evidence that this conclusion is from the hand
of the apostle himself, cf II Thess 3:17, Gal 6:11ff. §111.
στῆτε aor[2] impv (or subj.) ἵστημι *cause to stand*, seemingly
13 for pf (intr.) ἑστήκατε *stand!* ‖ ἀσπάζομαι *greet*. ἡ (sc.
ἐκκλησία) ἐν Βαβυλῶνι *the church here...in Babylon* ; B. generally understood as cryptic ref. to Rome ? because ass.
w. exile or ? because worldly and hostile to God —
14 often so in Apoc. συν-εκλεκτός *likewise elect*. ‖ ἀσπάσασθε
aor. impv. φίλημα[7] *kiss*. ‖

II PETER

ἰσό-τιμος masc. and fem., *equally precious* faith or **1**
an equal privilege...faith. λαχοῦσιν aor² ptc dat. pl. λαγ-
χάνω *receive by lot*. ἐν *by, through*. σωτήρ -ῆρος ὁ *saviour*,
τοῦ θεοῦ κ. σ. 'I. Χρ. under one art., prob. indicating one
and the same Person §185. ‖ πληθυνθείη aor. opt. pass. **2**
-ύνω *multiply, increase*, opt. expressing a wish §355. ἐν
through. ἐπί-γνωσις⁴ *knowledge*. ‖

ὡς *as, since*, ref. vv.3-4, resumed (v.5) by καί w. impv. **3**
πάντα obj. of δεδωρ. θεῖος *divine*. αὐτοῦ i.e. of Christ.
πάντα...τὰ πρός *everything that contributes to* / *furthers*.
εὐ-σέβεια *piety, godliness*. δε-δωρημένης pf ptc δωρέομαι
bestow, gen. abs. but transl. *since his divine power has
bestowed on us*... καλέσαντος aor. ptc καλέω. ἀρετή *virtue, excellence*, when ref. God, sts *manifestation of power*,
dat. either *for* or (instr.) *by his own*... ‖ ὧν prob. ref. δόξῃ **4**
κ. ἀρετῇ (though πάντα also possible). τίμιος *precious*.
μέγιστος *sublime*, superl. (elative) of μέγας. ἐπ-άγγελμα⁷
promise. δε-δώρηται pf mid. διὰ τούτων *through these*
(ref. v.3 or the things promised). γένησθε aor² subj. γίνομαι. κοινωνός *sharer*. φύσις⁴ *nature*. ἀπο-φυγόντες aor² ptc
-φεύγω τινά (2:18), τινός perh. influenced by prefix, *escape*
ἐν (2nd time) causal, *because of*. ἐπι-θυμία *desire*, here,
evil desire. φθορά *corruption*. ‖ αὐτὸ τοῦτο advl acc. *for **5**
this very reason*. σπουδή *zeal, earnestness*. παρ-εισ-ενέγ-
καντες aor² (for -ενεγκόντες §489) ptc -εισ-φέρω *bring in
alongside, introduce* ; *bring to bear*. ἐπι-χορ-ηγήσατε aor.
impv -ηγέω *provide for in addition, add, supplement* sth
(ἔν τινι) *with* sth (τι), ἐπιχ. ἐν τῇ πίστει ὑ. τὴν ἀρετήν *to your
faith add virtue, supplement your faith with virtue*. γνῶσις⁴
knowledge. ‖ ἐγ-κράτεια *self-control*. ὑπο-μονή *endurance*. **6**
εὐσέβεια v.3. ‖ φιλ-αδελφία *brotherly affection*. ‖ ὑπ-άρχοντα **7,8**
ptc (conditional) -άρχω τινί *be, belong to* one. πλεονάζοντα ptc -άζω *multiply, increase*, ὑμῖν ὑπάρχοντα καὶ πλ.
if these virtues are increasingly yours. ἀργός (ἀ-εργός)
idle, use-less. ἄ-καρπος *fruit-less* ; litotes : a figure of

speech which expresses an idea by denying the opposite.
καθ-ίστημι *constitute, render, make*; sg after neut. pl.
9 subject. ἐπί-γνωσις⁴ v.2, εἰς...ἐπ. *for...knowledge.* ‖ ᾧ masc.
μή (not οὐ), (class.) in indef. rel. clause. πάρ-ειμι *be present*; πάρεστί τινι *one has.* τυφλός *blind.* μυωπάζων ptc
-άζω *be short-sighted*, here culpably, *closing his eyes.* λήθη
oblivion, forgetfulness. λαβών aor² ptc λαμβάνω, forming a
pass. λήθην λ. τινός *be oblivious* of sth. καθαρισμός *cleansing.*
10 πάλαι *long ago, in the past.* ‖ σπουδάσατε aor. impv -άζω
be zealous, do one's utmost. βέβαιος *firm, steadfast.* ὑμῶν
of you, obj. gen. κλῆσις⁴ (< καλέω) *vocation, calling.*
ἐκ-λογή *election*, (God's) *choice.* ποιεῖσθαι inf. mid. ποιέω,
see on Heb 1:3 (ποιησάμενος); here ἐκλογὴν ποιεῖσθαι
"make a choice" = ἐκ-λέγεσθαι "choose" §227. ποιοῦντες
in so doing, ptc. οὐ μή w. subj. emphatic neg. ref. fut.
πταίσητε aor. subj. πταίω *stumble.* ποτέ (encl.) *ever.* ‖
11 πλουσίως *richly, amply.* ἐπιχορηγηθήσεται *will be afforded*,
fut. pass., cf v.5. εἴσ-οδος ἡ *entrance, entry.* τοῦ κυρίου...
12 καὶ σωτῆρος v.1 (σωτήρ). ‖ δι-ό *so then.* μελλήσω fut.
μέλλω w. inf. forming a periphrastic fut. *I mean to.* ἀεί
always. ὑπο-μιμνήσκειν inf. -μιμνήσκω *remind.* καί-περ w.
ptc *although.* εἰδότας ptc pf-pres. οἶδα, agreeing w. ὑμᾶς.
ἐ-στηριγμένους *steadfast*, pf ptc pass. -ίζω *establish, confirm.*
παρ-ούσῃ ptc -ειμι v.9, τῇ π. ἀληθείᾳ "the truth present with
13 you" or "that has come to you". ‖ ἡγέομαι *consider*,
δίκαιον ἡγ. *I think it right.* ἐφ' ὅσον (sc. χρόνον) acc. of
duration, *for as long as.* σκήνωμα⁷ *tent*, of the body as
sheltering the soul. δι-εγείρειν inf. -εγείρω *rouse, wake
one up*, pres. iterative. ἐν *by, with.* ὑπό-μνησις⁴ *reminder.* ‖
14 εἰδώς v.12. ταχινός (< ταχύς quick) *imminent, near* (in
time). ἀπό-θεσις⁴ *a divesting*, ταχινή ἐστιν ἡ ἀπ. *it will
soon be time to divest myself* of... ἐ-δήλωσε aor. -λόω *show.* ‖
15 σπουδάσω fut. -άζω v.10. ἑκάσ-τοτε *at all times, always.*
ἔχειν w. inf. *be able to*, σπουδάσω...ἔ. ὑμᾶς...τὴν τούτων μνή-
μην ποιεῖσθαι "I shall do my utmost that after my death
you may bear in mind these things". ἔξ-οδος ἡ *departure*;
death. μνήμη *remembrance.* ποιεῖσθαι inf. mid. ποιέω, see
on I Thess 1:2. ‖
16 σε-σοφισμένοις *clever, subtle*, pf ptc pass. -ίζω *make
wise*; mid. *concoct* sth clever or subtle. μῦθος *myth.*
ἐξ-ακολουθήσαντες aor. ptc -ακολουθέω τινί *follow.* ἐ-γνω-
ρίσαμεν aor. -ίζω *make known.* παρ-ουσία *presence, coming.*

ἐπ-όπτης³ t.t. of the mystery religions, ref. an initiate, *spectator*, *eye-witness*. γενηθέντες *by having been made*, aor. ptc pass. γίνομαι or for mid. γενόμενοι *having been*. μεγαλειότης⁶ -τητος ἡ *majesty*. ‖ λαβών v.9 ; in the absence 17 of a finite vb one may translate "for he received". τιμή *honour*. ἐνεχθείσης aor. ptc pass. φέρω *carry, bring* ; φωνῆς ἐνεχ. gen. abs., *when a voice was borne*, i.e. *came* (action simultaneous §261). τοιόσδε fem. gen. τοιόσδε -άδε -όνδε *such as that*. μεγαλο-πρεπής⁹ *majestic*, μ. δόξα = God himself. ἀγαπητός *beloved*, so perh. *only*. εἰς ὅν for the usual ἐν ᾧ perh. pregnant cstr, presupposing a movement of contentment toward, and resting on, one §99. εὐ-δόκησα aor. -δοκέω (εὖ well + δοκέω consider) *be well pleased, approve* ; if not rendering a Sem. pf, cf Mt 3:17, the aor. must be constative. ‖ ἠκούσαμεν aor. ἀκούω. 18 ὄντες *when we were*, ptc pres. representing impf εἰμί. ‖ βεβαιότερος comp. of βέβαιος v.10, hardly "more reliable" 19 than the Transfiguration; perh. pred.: the prophet's word *to be all the more reliable* or (neut. as adv.) we hold the prophetic word *with greater certainty* (as a result of the Transfiguration). προφητικός *prophetic* ; in Jewish use applicable to any part of the OT. καλῶς ποιεῖτε w. ptc, *you do well* to. προσ-έχοντες ptc -έχω (sc. τὸν νοῦν) *pay attention to, heed*. λύχνος *lamp*. φαίνοντι ptc- νω intr. *shine*. αὐχμηρός *austere ; dark*. ἕως οὗ w. subj. *until* = ἕως τοῦ χρόνου ᾧ §17. δι-αυγάσῃ aor. subj. -αυγάζω *dawn*. φωσ-φόρος (lightbringing) *day-star* (Venus). ἀνα-τείλῃ aor. subj. -τέλλω *make to rise*, intr. *rise*. ‖ τοῦτο ref. ὅτι κτλ. πρῶτον *first* 20 *of all*. γινώσκοντες ptc -σκω. πᾶσα...οὖ Sem. *no*. προφη-τεία *prophecy* = prediction. γραφή *scripture*. ἴδιος *one's own, individual, personal*. ἐπί-λυσις⁴ *explanation, interpreta-tion*, ἰδίας ἐ. οὐ γίνεται *is not (a matter) of personal interpre-tation*. ‖ θελήματι ἀνθρώπου *at the will of a man*. ἠνέχθη 21 *was brought about*, aor. pass. φέρω v.17. ποτέ v.10. φερό-μενοι ptc pass. *borne along, moved*. ἐ-λάλησαν aor. λαλέω. ἀπὸ θεοῦ ⟦var. add ἅγιοι⟧. ‖

ἐ-γένοντο aor² γίνομαι. ψευδο-προφήτης³ *false pro-* 2 *phet* ; καί implying "as well as true prophets". ἐν *among*. ἔσονται fut. εἰμί. ψευδο-διδάσκαλος *false teacher*. οἵ-τινες *such as* §215. παρ-εισ-άξουσιν fut. -άγω *introduce*. αἵρεσις⁴ *system of thought*, usu. as opp. the (Christian) Way ; later esp. of subversive doctrines claiming to be Christian,

heresy ; also body of persons holding such views, *faction*.
ἀπ-ώλεια *destruction*, αἱρ. ἀπωλείας a "Hebr." gen. *disruptive
factions* or *disastrous heresies* §40. καί *even*. ἀγοράσαντα
aor. ptc -ράζω *buy*. δεσπότης[3] *master, lord*. ἀρνούμενοι
ptc ἀρνέομαι *deny, disown*. ἐπ-άγοντες ptc -άγω τινί *bring
2 on one*. ταχινός *swift*. ‖ ἐξ-ακολουθήσουσιν fut. -ακολουθέω
τινί *follow* sth. ἀσέλγεια *debauchery*. βλασ-φημηθήσεται
3 fut. pass. -φημέω *malign, defame*. ‖ πλεον-εξία (desire to
"have more") *unscrupulous greed, rapacity*, ἐν π. *prompted
by / from greed* §117. πλαστός (< πλάσσω form) *moulded ;
fabricated, sham*, π. λόγοις *fabrications*. ἐμπορεύσονται
fut. -εύομαι *do business* Jas 4:13 ; w. acc. *exploit*.
οἷς *for whom*. κρίμα[7] *condemnation*. ἔκ-παλαι *for a long
time* (past). ἀργέω (< ἄ-εργος) *be inoperative, lie idle*.
καί...αὐτῶν *a way of varying a rel*. phrase parallel to οἷς...
4 ἀργεῖ. νυστάζω *doze* ; met. *be sleeping*. ‖ ἁμαρτησάντων
aor. ptc (for ἁμαρτόντων §491) -τάνω *sin*. ἐ-φείσατο aor.
φείδομαί τινος *spare* one (from sth). σειρά *bond*, dat. to
παρέδωκεν ⟦var. σιροῖς (σιρός *pit*)⟧. ζόφος *gloom* of the
netherworld. ταρταρώσας aor. ptc -ταρόω *consign to hell*.
παρ-έ-δωκεν aor. παρα-δίδωμι. εἰς *for*. κρίσις[4] *judgement*.
5 τηρουμένους ptc pass. τηρέω. ‖ καί continues the condition introduced by εἰ (v.4) whose apodosis is delayed till
v.9f. ἀρχαῖος *ancient*. ὄγδοος *eight*. Νῶε indecl., here
acc. κῆρυξ[6] -υκος ὁ *herald ; preacher*. ἐ-φύλαξεν aor.
-άσσω *guard, protect*, "protected Noah, preacher of righteousness, as the eighth" (class. idiom = Noah and 7 others).
κατα-κλυσμός *deluge*. ἀ-σεβής[9] *god-less*. ἐπ-άξας aor. (for
6 -αγαγών §491) ptc -άγω τί τινι *bring* sth *upon* sth. ‖ Σόδομα
-μων τά Sodom, gen. epexeg. §45. τεφρώσας aor. ptc -ρόω
reduce to ashes. κατα-στροφή *ruin*. κατ-έ-κρινεν aor. κατα-
κρίνω *condemn*. ὑπό-δειγμα[7] *example*. μελλόντων ptc μέλλω.
If ἀσεβεῖν (inf. -βέω *be godless, commit impieties*) is to be
read, μελλόντων ἀσ. will form a periphrastic fut 1:12 ;
if ἀσεβέσιν (dat. pl. ἀσεβής) *of what is destined for the
7 impious*. τε-θεικώς pf ptc τίθημι. ‖ κατα-πονούμενον ptc
pass. -πονέω *oppress, wear down*. ἄ-θεσμος (ἀ- + θεσμός
law, custom) *un-principled*. ἀσέλγεια v.2. ἀνα-στροφή *life*
in sense of conduct. ἐρ-ρύσατο aor. ῥύομαι *rescue*. ‖
8 V.8 a parenthesis. βλέμμα[7] *sight*. ἀκοή *hearing*, βλέμματι
κ. ἀ. *at the sight and sound*. ἐγ-κατ-οικῶν ptc -οικέω *live
among*. ἡμέραν ἐξ ἡμέρας *day after day*. ἄ-νομος *lawless*,

wicked. ἐ-βασάνιζεν impf -ίζω *torture.* ‖ οἶδα w. inf. 9
know how to. εὐ-σεβής⁹ (< εὖ + σέβομαι worship) *devout.*
πειρασμός *trial*(s). ῥύεσθαι inf. ἄ-δικος *un-just, wicked.*
εἰς temporal, *until.* κρίσις v.4. κολαζομένους ptc pass.
-άζω *punish* ; either *keep under punishment till...* or (pres.
for fut. §283f.) *keep till the day...to be punished.* τηρεῖν
inf. ‖ μάλιστα (superl. of comp. μᾶλλον) *above all, especially.* 10
ὀπίσω adv. *behind* ; as prep. w. gen., πορεύομαι ὀ. τινός Hebr.
follow sth. ἐν *in, with* (ἐν of concomitant circumstances,
sociative §116). ἐπι-θυμία *desire.* μιασμός *pollution,* ἐπι-
θυμία μ. perh. "Hebr." gen. *depraved desire* §40. κυριότης⁶
-τητος ἡ *lordship, dominion,* here of the authority of God
or of the sovereignty which faith ascribes to Christ as
Lord (κύριος). κατα-φρονοῦντας ptc -φρονέω τινός *look down
on despise* sth. τολμητής³ a *bold-faced/insolent man.* αὐθ-
άδης⁹ *arrogant.* αἱ δόξαι things and persons in whom
shines the divine majesty, here, *the good angels.* τρέμω
tremble, hence (w. ptc) *be afraid* to. βλασ-φημοῦντες ptc
v.2. ‖ ὅπου *where,* in sense *whereas.* ἰσχύς -ύος ἡ *might,* 11
dat. of respect §53. μείζων comp. of μέγας. ὄντες ptc
εἰμί. φέρω *bring* ; φ. κρίσιν *pronounce judgement* (cf 1:17).
παρὰ κυρίου *on the part of / emanating from the Lord.*
βλάσφημος *defamatory.* ‖ ἄ-λογος *devoid of reason.* ζῷον 12
animal. γε-γεννημένα pf ptc pass. γεννάω *bear* ; pass.
be born. φυσικός *natural, of nature* ; ζῷα γεγεννημένα φ.
εἰς ἅλωσιν *creatures of instinct born for capture...* ἅλωσις⁴
capturing. φθορά *decadence* ; *destruction.* ἐν οἷς = ἐν τούτοις ἅ. ἀ-γνοέω τι *be ignorant of, not understand* sth.
φθαρήσονται fut² pass. φθείρω *corrupt* ; *destroy* ; either, *in
their decadence they will suffer decay* ; or, *in their* (of brute
beasts) *annihilation they* (those of v. 10) *will perish,*
i.e. they will meet the same end as the animals. ‖ ἀ- 13
δικούμενοι ptc pass. -δικέω *wrong, injure, inflict hurt on.*
μισθός *wage, reward.* ἀ-δικία *wrong-doing,* ἀδικούμενοι
μισθὸν ἀδικίας *hurt as retribution for hurt* (inflicted). ἡδονή
pleasure. ἡγούμενοι ptc ἡγέομαι *think, regard as.* ἐν ἡμέρᾳ
in the daytime. τρυφή *dissipation.* σπίλος *blot.* μῶμος
blemish. ἐν-τρυφῶντες ptc -τρυφάω *revel.* ἀπάτη *deception* ; HGk *enticement* Mk 4:19 [[var. ἀγάπαις *love-feasts*]].
συν-ευωχούμενοι *while they feast with you,* ptc -ευωχέομαί τινι
feast with one. ‖ ἔχοντες ptc ἔχω. μεστός w. gen. *full* 14
of, ὀφθαλμοὺς ἔ. μ. *with eyes for nothing* but. μοιχαλίς⁶

-ίδος ἡ *adulteress*. ἀ-κατά-παυστος w. gen. *not ceasing from,
incessant in*. δελεάζοντες ptc -άζω *entice*. ἀ-στήρικτος
(< στηρίζω fix, establish) *un-stable*. καρδίαν obj. of ἔχοντες. γε-γυμνασμένην *practised* (usu. τινί *in* sth, here w.
gen.) pf ptc pass. -νάζω *train*. πλεον-εξία v.3. κατ-άρα a
15 *curse*, τέκνα κ. "Hebr." gen. = *accursed* §43. || κατα-
λείποντες ptc -λείπω *leave, forsake*. εὐθύς -θεῖα -θύ *straight*.
ἐ-πλανήθησαν aor. pass. -νάω *mislead*; pass. *go astray*.
ἐξ-ακολουθήσαντες aor. ptc v.2. ἠγάπησεν aor. ἀγαπάω. ||
16 ἔλεγξις[4] *reproof*. ἔσχεν *received*, aor² ἔχω, aor. inceptive.
παρα-νομία *wrong-doing*. ὑπο-ζύγιον (under yoke) *beast of
burden*, esp. *ass* or *mule*. ἄ-φωνος *dumb* (= unable to
speak). ἐν instr. §119. φθεγξάμενον aor. ptc φθέγγομαι
utter; speak. ἐ-κώλυσεν aor. κωλύω *hinder*, aor. effective
prevent. παρα-φρονία (< παρα- + φρήν mind) (a word un-
17 known elsewhere) *aberration*. || πηγή a *spring*. ἄν-υδρος
water-less. ὁμίχλη *mist*. λαῖλαψ[6] -λαπος ἡ *wind-storm*.
ἐλαυνόμεναι ptc pass. -νω *drive*. οἷς *for whom*. ζόφος
v.4. σκότος[8] *darkness*. τε-τήρηται *is reserved*, pf pass.
18 τηρέω. || ὑπέρ-ογκος (< ὄγκος burden; bulk) *inflated,
boastful*. ματαιότης[6] -τητος ἡ *futility*, ὑπέρογκα ματαιότη-
τος *empty bombast*. φθεγγόμενοι ptc. δελεάζω *entice* v.14.
ἐν ἐπιθυμίαις σαρκός *with low desires / sensual passions*.
ἀσέλγεια v.2, without καί perh. a precision of ἐπιθυμίαις
σαρκός. ὀλίγως *barely, only just*. ἀπο-φεύγοντας ptc -φεύγω
τι (cf 1:4) *escape* sth (trans.). πλάνη *error*, esp. of paganism. ἀνα-στρεφομένους ǀ ptc -στρέφομαι *live* in a certain
19 way; obj. of ἀποφ. || ἐλευθερία *freedom*. ἐπ-αγγελλόμε-
νοι ptc -αγγέλλομαι *promise*. ὑπ-άρχοντες ptc -άρχω *be,
αὐτοὶ ὑπ. *whereas they themselves* (nominative, emphatic)
are... φθορά v.12. ἥττηται pf ἥττάομαι *be worsted/defeated*.
δε-δούλωται pf pass. -λόω *enslave*; ᾧ...τις...δεδ. "whatever
20 a man is defeated by, to that he is enslaved". || ἀπο-
φυγόντες aor² ptc -φεύγω. μίασμα[7] *corruption*. ἐπί-γνωσις[4]
knowledge, ἐν ἐπ. instr. *by/through a knowledge*. σωτήρ
-ῆρος ὁ *saviour*; on τοῦ κυρίου...καὶ σωτῆρος 1:1. τούτοις
neut. ἐμ-πλακέντες aor² ptc pass. -πλέκω *entangle; impli-
cate*. ἡττῶνται pres. γέ-γονεν pf² γίνομαι. ἔσχατος *last*,
τὰ ἔ. *the last state*. χείρων -ρονος neut. χεῖρον (comp.
κακός) *worse*. τῶν πρώτων gen. of comp. *than the first*
21 (state). || κρείττων -τονος neut. κρεῖττον used as comp.
of ἀγαθός. ἦν apodosis of an unfulfilled ("unreal") condi-

tion wt ἄν, *it would have been* Mt 26:9, 24, Heb 9:26. ἐπεγνωκέναι pf inf. ἐπι-γινώσκω *know.* ἐπι-γνοῦσιν aor² ptc
dat. pl. in agreement w. αὐτοῖς: μὴ ἐπεγνωκέναι...ἢ ἐπιγ. *not
to have known...than having known...* ὑπο-στρέψαι aor. inf.
-στρέφω *turn back.* παρα-δοθείσης aor. ptc pass. -δίδωμι. ‖
συμ-βέβηκεν pf -βαίνω *happen.* ἀληθής⁹ *true.* παρ-οιμία 22
(< πάροιμος by the way) *common saying, proverb,* τὸ τῆς...π.
that (which is found) in the proverb, cf Jas 4:14 (τὸ τῆς
αὔριον). κύ ων κυνός ὁ *dog.* ἐπι-στρέψας aor. ptc -στρέφω
trans. *turn* sth *to ;* intr. *return, turn back.* ἐξ-έραμα⁷
vomit. ὗς ὑός ὁ *pig* and ἡ *sow* (elsewhere in NT χοῖρος
§482). λουσαμένη aor. ptc mid. λούω *wash.* κυλισμός *rol-
ling, wallowing.* βόρβορος *mire, mud.* ‖

ἤδη *already, now.* ἀγαπητός *beloved.* δεύτερος *second.* 3
ἐπι-στολή *letter.* δι-εγείρω *rouse,* met. *stir* e.g. the mind.
ὑμῶν ass. w. διάνοια. ἐν *by, with.* ὑπό-μνησις⁴ *reminder.*
εἰλι-κρινής⁹ *sincere, pure.* διά-νοια *mind.* ‖ μνησθῆναι inf. 2
μιμνήσκομαί τινος *remember, recall* sth. προ-ειρημένων pf
ptc pass. -λέγω *say/speak beforehand.* ῥῆμα⁷ *word.* τοῦ
κυρίου...καὶ σωτῆρος 1:1; accumulation of gens., lit. "the
command of your apostles" (i.e. ? those who were sent
to you), *to remember...the apostolic command to you of
our Lord and saviour* §47. ‖ τοῦτο...γινώσκοντες 1:20. 3
ἐλεύσονται fut. ἔρχομαι. ἔσχατος *last,* ἐπ᾽ ἐ. τ. ἡμερῶν *in
the last days,* cf I Pt 1:20. ἐν *with* §117. ἐμ-παιγμονή (only
here) *mockery, jeering.* ἐμ-παίκτης³ *scoffer, jeerer.* ἐπι-
θυμία *desire.* πορευόμενοι ptc = περιπατέω *live, behave* ‖
ποῦ; *where?* ἐπ-αγγελία *promise.* παρ-ουσία *advent, com-* 4
ing. ἀφ᾽ ἧς = ἀπὸ τ. (ἡμέρας) ἣ by attraction of the rel.
§17. οἱ πατέρες *our forefathers.* ἐ-κοιμήθησαν aor. dep.
-μάομαι *be asleep,* aor. inceptive, *fell asleep,* i.e. died. δια-
μένω *remain, continue.* ἀρχή *beginning.* κτίσις⁴ *creation.* ‖
λανθάνω *escape notice,* λ. τί τινα sth *escapes the notice* 5
of one, or one *ignores* sth. θέλοντας ptc θέλω: λανθά-
νει...θ. ὅτι *they deliberately ignore* (the fact) *that.* ἦσαν
impf εἰμί. ἔκ-παλαι *from of old.* ἐξ ὕ. καὶ δι᾽ ὕδατος:
διά as effecting coherence of particles or exerting external
pressure. συν-εστῶσα pf ptc fem. -ίστημι *bring* or *put
together ;* in intr. tenses, *con-sist* (here closer to sense of
"exist" than of "compounded of"). τῷ...λόγῳ dat. instr.
by the word. ‖ τότε *then.* κατα-κλυσθείς aor. ptc pass. 6
-κλύζω *flood.* ἀπ-ώλετο aor² mid. -όλλυμι. ‖ τῷ αὐτῷ λόγῳ 7

by the same word. τε-θησαυρισμένοι pf ptc pass. -ίζω *pre-serve.* πυρί *for fire.* τηρούμενοι ptc pass. τηρέω. εἰς *until.* κρίσις⁴ *judgement.* ἀπ-ώλεια *destruction.* ἀ-σεβής⁹

8 *god-less, im-pious.* ‖ ἕν...τοῦτο *this one fact,* subject of λανθανέτω, ass. w. ὅτι. λανθανέτω impv v.5, μὴ λ. ὑμᾶς *let...not escape you, you must not ignore...* ἀγαπητός v.1.

9 χίλιοι -ιαι -ια = 1000. ἔτος⁸ *year.* ‖ βραδύνω *delay,* here w. gen. *be slow over sth, be slow in giving effect to.* βραδύτης⁶ -τητος ἡ *slowness.* ἡγέομαι *regard, think of.* μακρο-θυμέω (be long-tempered) *show patience.* εἰς ὑμᾶς *to you* [[var. δι' ὑμᾶς *on your account*]]. βουλόμενος ptc -λομαι *wish, want.* τις after a neg. *any.* ἀπ-ολέσθαι aor² inf. mid. v.6. μετά-νοια *change of mind, repentance.* χωρῆσαι

10 aor. inf. -ρέω *withdraw;* χ. εἰς *reach.* ‖ ἥξει *will arrive,* fut. ἥκω to *have come.* κλέπτης³ *thief.* ῥοιζηδόν adv. *with a loud noise* made by what is rushing upon or past one. παρ-ελεύσονται fut. -έρχομαι *pass by; pass away.* στοιχεῖον *element;* pl. *elements* from which the world is constituted. καυσούμενα ptc pass. -σόω *burn.* λυθήσεται fut. pass. λύω *loose;* pass. *fall apart, break up, dissolve.* εὑρεθήσεται fut. pass. εὑρίσκω; the vars. are poorly at-

11 tested and the sense of εὑρ. remains obscure. ‖ λυομένων ptc pass. (pres. for fut. §207) gen. abs. *since all these things are to be dissolved.* ποταπός *what kind of?* here exclamatory. ὑπ-άρχειν inf. -άρχω *be.* ἀνα-στροφή *life* in

12 sense of *conduct.* εὐ-σέβεια *piety.* ‖ προσ-δοκῶντας ptc -δοκέω τι *wait for* sth. σπεύδοντας ptc -δω *hasten.* παρ-ουσία v.4. δι' ἥν *because of / for which.* πυρούμενοι *on fire,* ptc pass. -ρόω *set on fire, burn.* τήκεται pass. τήκω

13 *melt* sth; pass. intr. *melt.* ‖ καινός *fresh, new.* ἐπ-άγγελμα⁷

14 *promise.* κατ-οικέω *dwell.* ‖ διό *therefore.* ἀγαπητός v.8. σπουδάσατε *make it your concern,* aor. impv -άζω *be eager/zealous.* ἄ-σπιλος *spotless.* ἀ-μώμητος *unblemished.* εὑρε-

15 θῆναι *be found to be,* aor. inf. pass. εὑρίσκω. ‖ μακρο-θυμία *patience.* σωτηρία pred. *salvation.* ἡγεῖσθε impv v.9, *con-sider/look* on sth as. δοθεῖσαν aor. ptc pass. δίδωμι.

16 σοφία *wisdom.* ἔ-γραψεν aor. γράφω. ‖ ἐπιστολή v.1. λαλῶν ptc λαλέω. τούτων ref. the Last Things. δυσ-νόητος (< δυσ- difficult + νοῦς mind) *hard to understand, obscure.* ἀ-μαθής⁹ (ἀ- + μανθάνω learn) *ignorant.* ἀ-στήρικτος 2:14. στρεβλόω *distort.* λοιπός *remaining.* γραφή *scrip-*

17 *ture.* ἀπ-ώλεια v.7. ‖ προ-γινώσκοντες ptc -γινώσκω *know*

beforehand. φυλάσσεσθε impv mid. -άσσω *guard,* mid. *be on* one's *guard.* ἵνα μή *lest, that...not.* ἄ-θεσμος *un-principled* 2:7. πλάνη *error,* dat. led *into error,* or instr. led away *by...* συν-απ-αχθέντες aor. ptc pass. -απ-άγω *lead away with* or *together.* ἐκ-πέσητε aor² subj. -πίπτω *fall away,* w. gen. *lose.* στηριγμός (< στηρίζω) *firmness, stability,* or concrete, *standing-place, ground, basis* i.e. for hope of salvation. ‖ αὐξάνατε impv -άνω *increase* ; intr. *grow.* 18 γνῶσις⁴ *knowledge.* τοῦ κυρίου...καὶ σωτῆρος 1:1. αἰ ών here, *eternity,* gen. epexeg. "that day which is eternity" §45 or subjective gen. "the day (of the Lord) where eternity begins". ‖

I JOHN

1 ἀρχή *beginning.* ἀκηκόαμεν pf ἀκούω. ἐωράκαμεν pf ὁράω, the pfs den. lasting effect ; testimony based on sight and hearing. ἐ-θεασάμεθα aor. θεάομαι *contemplate, look upon.* ἐ-ψηλάφησαν aor. -φάω *touch, feel.* ἡ ζωή in John that which is pre-eminently life, life par excellence ; περὶ τ. λόγου τ. ζωῆς appos. the preceding accusatives, safe-guards the "Word of life" (= divine life in the Person of Christ) from being misunderstood as ref. the gospel **2** message. ‖ ἐ-φανερώθη aor. pass. -ρόω *make evident/visible.* ἀπ-αγγέλλω *proclaim.* ἥτις = ἥ §216. πρὸς τὸν πατέρα w. acc. in HGk may = παρά w. dat. *beside/with* a person, though in John πρός often includes a dynamic sense of **3** personal relationship. ‖ κοινωνία *fellowship.* ἔχητε subj. **4** ἔχω. ἡμέτερος *our.* μετὰ τ. πατρός supply ἐστιν. ‖ ἡμεῖς nom. in HGk not invariably emphatic Jn 5:39, 15:16 §198 ⟦var. ὑμῖν⟧. χαρά *joy.* ἡμῶν ⟦var. ὑμῶν⟧. ᾖ subj. 3rd sg εἰμί. πε-πληρωμένη *complete,* pf ptc pass. -ρόω. ‖ **5** αὕτη: in Jn οὗτος often looks forward to what follows ; the latter commonly introduced by ὅτι or ἵνα. ἀγγελία *message.* ἀν-αγγέλλω *re-port ; declare.* σκοτία **6** *darkness.* ‖ εἴπωμεν aor² subj. λέγω. κοινωνία v.3. σκότος⁸ *darkness.* περι-πατῶμεν subj. -πατέω *walk,* here *behave, live* one's life. ψεύδομαι *tell an untruth, lie.* ποιοῦμεν τ. ἀλήθειαν *do the deeds that truth demands :* showing truth to be not so much sth to be grasped intellectually as **7** willed and realized in one's way of life. ‖ καθαρίζω **8** *cleanse.* ‖ ἐ-αυτούς 3rd for 1st pl. ἡμᾶς αὐτούς §209. **9** πλανάω *mislead, deceive.* ‖ ὁμο-λογῶμεν subj. -λογέω "say the same thing", *acknowledge, confess.* πιστός *faithful, to be trusted.* δίκαιος inasmuch as forgiveness has been promised by God and won by the blood of Christ. ἵνα den. content, *in forgiving.* ἀφ-ῇ aor² subj. -ίημι τινί τι *forgive* one sth. καθαρίσῃ aor. subj. -ίζω. ἀ-δικία *wicked-* **10** *ness.* ‖ εἴπωμεν aor² subj. λέγω. ἡμαρτήκαμεν pf ἁμαρτάνω *sin.* ψεύστης³ *liar.* ὁ λόγος αὐτοῦ *his word* which is the word of truth revealed as the norm for judgement and for action. ‖

τεκνίον dim. of τέκνον. ἁμάρτητε *that you may* not **2** *commit sin,* aor² subj. -τάνω 1:10 §251. παρά-κλητος *advocate, spokesman, intercessor.* πρός w. acc. of person, *with.* ‖ ἱλασμός *propitiation, expiation,* in which case abstract for **2** concrete ; but sts (and prob. here) *offering, sacrifice* offered as propitiation. περί for ὑπέρ §96. ἡμέτερος *ours.* ‖ ἐν τούτῳ *by this means,* taken up by ἐάν... 1:5. ἐ-γνώκαμεν **3** pf γινώσκω in sense of knowledge through personal relationship fruitful in a life conformed to its object. τηρῶμεν subj. τηρέω *observe, keep.* ‖ ὁ λέγων *a man who says.* **4** ὅτι = "... τηρῶν ptc. ψεύστης³ *liar.* ‖ τηρῇ subj. ἀληθῶς **5** (adj. -θής⁹) *truly.* ἐν τούτῳ (1st time) masc. *in him* ; (2nd time) neut. *by this,* i.e. by a Christ-like life. τε-τελείωται pf pass. -είόω *perfect.* ἐν αὐτῷ ἐσμεν *we are in* (intimate union with) *him* §116f. ‖ ὁ λέγων here virtually **6** "one who claims". ὀφείλω *owe,* w. inf. *ought.* καθὼς ἐκεῖνος...καὶ αὐτός "exactly as he (Jesus)...so he", i.e. *ought himself so to live as he* (Jesus) *lived.* περι-ε-πάτησεν aor. περι-πατέω 1:6, context revealing a constative (global) aor. §253. αὐτός nom. emphatic, *himself.* περιπατεῖν inf. depending on ὀφείλει. ‖

ἀγαπητός *beloved.* καινός *fresh, new.* παλαιός *old,* και- **7** νήν...παλαιάν (1st time) pred. *a commandment which is new...which is old.* εἴχετε impf ἔχω. ἀρχή *beginning,* here = when the gospel was first preached to them. ἠκούσατε aor. ἀκούω. ‖ πάλιν *again, at the same time* a **8** new commandment. ὅ *which fact* ref. to the foll. clause ὅτι κτλ. ἀληθής⁹ *true* in fact, *verified.* ὅτι *because,* explaining why it is new. σκοτία *darkness.* παρ-άγεται pass. -άγω *lead past* ; pass. intr. *pass (away).* ἀληθινός *true, genuine.* ἤδη *already.* φαίνω *show* ; *shine.* ‖ ἐν τ. φωτί **9** ass. w. εἶναι. μισῶν ptc μισέω *hate.* ἄρτι *now* ; ἕως ἄ. *up to now, still.* ‖ ἀγαπῶν ptc -πάω. σκάνδαλον *stumbling* **10** *block, occasion of sin,* σ. ...οὐκ ἔστιν possibly meaning "he does not constitute an occasion of sin to others", i.e. he does not make life difficult for them, but σκ. may also bear the meaning *fall(ing) into sin.* ‖ ποῦ as indir. interr. **11** *where.* ὑπ-άγω *go away,* here simply *go.* ἐ-τύφλωσεν aor. -λόω *blind.* ‖ τεκνίον v.l. ἀφ-έωνται pf pass. -ίημι 1:9. **12** διὰ τ. ὄνομα αὐτοῦ *for his name's sake,* the name represent-

13 ing the person himself. ‖ ἐ-γνώκατε v.3. τὸν ἀπ' ἀρχῆς
him who is from the beginning, 1:1. νεανίσκος young man.
νε-νικήκατε pf νικάω overcome. ὁ πονηρός the Evil One =
14 the Devil. ‖ ἔ-γραψα aor. γράφω, epistolary aor. Eph 2:22
(ἔπεμψα). παιδίον dim. of παῖς child. ἰσχυρός strong. ‖
15 ἀγαπᾶτε impv -πάω. τὰ ἐν τ. κόσμῳ the things of the world,
here esp. as distractions from the service of God, ὁ κ.
at times denoting the kingdom of sin actively hostile to
God, at others, secular society estranged from and ignor-
ing the kingdom of God. ἀγαπᾷ subj. ἡ ἀγάπη τοῦ πατρός
generalized gen. signifying the whole complex relation
between ἀγάπη and πατήρ: in Jn man's love for the Father
is grounded in the love with which he first loved us
16 §36. ‖ ἐπι-θυμία desire, appos. to πᾶν. σαρκός gen. subjective, ἐπιθυμία σ. sensual appetite. ἐπιθ. τ. ὀφθαλμῶν the
lustful eye (JB). ἀλαζονεία ostentation ; fostered by material things. βίος daily life ; means of subsistence, worldly
17 goods. οὐκ ἔστιν ἐκ does not come from. ‖ παρ-άγεται v.8.
αὐτοῦ of / for it, obj. gen. ποιῶν ptc ποιέω, pres. den.
habitually. εἰς τ. αἰῶνα for ever. ‖
18   παιδίον v.14. ἔσχατος last. ἠκούσατε v.7. ἀντί-χριστος
either enemy of (against) Christ or one who sets himself up as (in the place of) Christ. ἔρχεται transl. was
coming (Gk uses tense of dir. speech §346). γε-γόνασιν
have come, pf² γίνομαι. ὅ-θεν hence, from which fact. ‖
19 ἐξ-ῆλθαν aor² (for -ον §489) -έρχομαι. οὐκ ἦσαν ἐκ they did
not belong to §134. εἰ...ἦσαν unreal (unfulfilled) condition w. ἄν in apodosis §313. με-μενήκεισαν they would
have remained, plpf (wt aug.) μένω. ἀλλά understand
"they left" or "this happened". φανερωθῶσιν that they
might be clearly shown, aor. subj. pass. -ρόω make evident/
known ; or quasi-impvl, but they had to be shown in their
true colours §415. οὐκ εἰσὶν πάντες ἐξ ἡμῶν lit. "all are
20 not", i.e. none of them belong to us §446. ‖ χρῖσμα⁷ (< χρίω
anoint) unction, anointing, cf v.27 ; the grace of the
Holy Spirit or the gift of the Spirit himself indwelling
the faithful and by virtue of faith leading them into all
truth Ac 10:38, II Cor 1:21. ἀπὸ τ. ἁγίου from the Holy
One, i.e. God (cf Is 40:25) or rather, Christ (Jn 6:69).
καὶ οἴδατε πάντες and you all know (it) ⟦var. κ. οἶδ. πάντα
21 (neut. pl. acc.) and you know everything⟧. ‖ ἔ-γραψα aor.
γράφω: I have not written. ψεῦδος⁸ a lie, πᾶν ψ. ἐκ τ. ἀλη-

θείας οὐκ ἔστιν *no lie springs from the truth* §446. ‖ ψεύστης 22
v.4, w. art. = *the arch-liar.* ἀρνούμενος ptc ἀρνέομαι
deny, οὐκ is redundant but not uncommon w. vbs of denial and hindering, cf Lk 20:27, Ac 14:18. ὁ Χριστός *the
Anointed, Messiah.* ἀντίχριστος v.18. ‖ πᾶς ὁ ἀρνούμε- 23
νος...οὐδέ...ἔχει *no one who denies...has even...* v.21. ὁμο-
λογῶν ptc -λογέω *confess* 1:9. ‖ ὑμεῖς *as for you,* emphatic 24
as nom. and by position. ὃ ἠκούσατε ἀπ' ἀρχῆς v.7, subject of μενέτω impv 3rd sg. μείνῃ aor. subj. μένω. καί
then, introducing the apodosis. μενεῖτε fut. ‖ ἐπ-αγγελία 25
promise. ἐπ-ηγγείλατο aor. -αγγέλλομαι *promise.* ἡμῖν ‖var.
ὑμῖν‖. τὴν ζωήν... explains αὕτη. ‖ ἔ-γραψα v.21. πλανώντων 26
ptc -νάω *lead astray,* pres. conative τῶν πλ. *those who would*
(= are trying to) *mislead.* ‖ ὑμεῖς *in your case,* cf v.24, 27
highlighting the contrast of the readers' unique standing.
χρῖσμα v.20. ἐ-λάβετε aor² λαμβάνω. χρεία *need.* ἵνα for
inf. διδάσκῃ subj. -άσκω. ἀληθής v.8. ψεῦδος v.21. ἐ-δί-
δαξεν aor. -άσκω. μένετε impv or perh. pres. indic. ἐν
αὐτῷ sc. in Christ, cf v.28. ‖

τεκνία v.1. μένετε impv. φανερωθῇ aor. subj. pass. 28
-ρόω 1:2 pass. intr. *appear,* ἐάν sts approximating to ὅταν
in meaning Jn 12:32. σχῶμεν aor² subj. ἔχω, subj. hort.
παρ-ρησία (complete freedom of speech) *complete confidence*
(4 times in I Jn). αἰσχυνθῶμεν aor. subj. pass. -ύνω *put
to shame,* pass. w. ἀπό *shrink from* one *in shame.* παρ-ουσία
(< πάρ-ειμι be present ; to have come) *advent, coming.* ‖
εἰδῆτε aor² subj. οἶδα. ποιῶν v.17, ὁ π. δικαιοσύνην *who* 29
makes a practice of doing right. γε-γέννηται pf pass.
γεννάω *bear* ; pass. *be born.* ‖ ποταπός; orig. "from what 3
country ?" *of what sort?* exclamatory, *what! or how great!*
δέ-δωκεν pf δίδωμι. ἵνα w. subj. consec. for ὥστε w. inf.
§352. κληθῶμεν aor. subj. pass. καλέω. διὰ τοῦτο taken
up by ὅτι: *the reason why...is that.* ἔ-γνω aor² γινώσκω
2:3. ‖ ἀγαπητός *beloved.* οὔπω *not yet.* ἐ-φανερώθη *it has* 2
not *been revealed,* aor. pass. -ρόω *make evident/known.*
ἐσόμεθα fut. εἰμί. φανερωθῇ 2:28. ὅμοιος *like.* ὀψόμεθα
fut. ὁράω. ὅτι explains not our destiny but our recognition of it §420. ‖ πᾶς ὁ ἔχων *everyone who has.* ἐλπίς⁶ -ίδος 3
ἡ *hope.* ἐπ' αὐτῷ ass. w. ἐλπίδα. ἁγνίζω *purify.* ἁγνός
pure. ‖ ποιῶν 2:17. ἀ-νομία *lawlessness, wickedness,* prin- 4
ciple radically opp. δικαιοσύνη Rom 6:19 ; Heb 1:9, having eschatological associations II Thess 2:7 ; Mt 24:12.

5 καί (2nd time) *and (indeed).* ‖ ἐκεῖνος i.e. Christ. ἐ-φανερώθη *appeared,* v.2. ἄρῃ aor. subj. αἴρω. ἁμαρτία...οὐκ
6 ἔστιν *there is no sin.* ‖ ἁμαρτάνω *sin.* ἁμαρτάνων ptc pres.,
habitually. ἑ-ώρακεν pf ὁράω, here spiritually, by faith
(Jn 1:18), οὐχ ἑώρ. *is a stranger to* Christ. ἔ-γνωκεν pf
7 γινώσκω. ‖ τεκνίον 2:1. πλανάτω impv 3rd sg -νάω *mis-*
8 *lead, deceive.* ποιῶν 2:17. ‖ διά-βολος (< δια-βάλλω accuse)
the *devil.* ἀρχή *beginning,* ἀπ' ἀρχῆς ἁμ. Eng. idiom demands translⁿ "he has been sinning (i.e. a sinner) from
the start". εἰς τοῦτο explained by ἵνα... epexeg. §410.
9 ἐ-φανερώθη v.5. λύσῃ aor. subj. λύω *undo.* ‖ πᾶς...οὐ ποιεῖ
no one...does (commits), pres. perh. *makes a habit of...* γε-
γεννημένος pf ptc pass. γεννάω *bear* ; pass. *be born.* σπέρμα⁷
seed. ἁμαρτάνειν inf. pres. perh. *lead a sinful life*
(pres.) opp. aor. *commit a sin,* cf 2:1 §251. γε-γέννηται
10 2:29. ‖ τούτῳ elucidated in 10*b.* φανερός *evident.* ἐστιν
sg w. neut. pl. subject. τέκνον, like υἱός in met. sense
I Thess 5:5. ὁ...ποιῶν δικαιοσύνην 2:29. ἀγαπῶν ptc -πάω
cf Rom 13:9, Mt 22:40. ‖
11   αὕτη...ἵνα epexeg. *this is...(namely) that.* ἀγγελία *mes-*
sage. ἠκούσατε aor. ἀκούω. ἀπ' ἀρχῆς 2:7. ἀγαπῶμεν
12 subj. -πάω. ‖ ἐκ τ. πονηροῦ *(who was) on the side of the Evil*
One. ἔ-σφαξεν aor. σφάζω *slaughter.* χάριν τίνος ; "for
13 the sake of what ?" *why?* αὐτοῦ *his* (own). ‖ θαυμάζετε
impv -άζω *be surprised,* §264. μισέω *hate.* ὁ κόσμος 2:15. ‖
14 μετα-βε-βήκαμεν pf μετα-βαίνω *go/pass* from one place to
another. ὅτι *for* §420. ἀγαπῶμεν pres. indic. (same form as
subj. v.11). ἀγαπῶν v.10. ἐν τ. θανάτῳ in (the state of)
15 *death.* ‖ μισῶν ptc. ἀνθρωπο-κτόνος (< obs. κτείνω kill)
murderer. πᾶς...οὐκ ἔχει *no...has.* μένουσαν ptc fem. μένω. ‖
16 ἐν τούτῳ...ὅτι *this is how...(namely) that.* ἐ-γνώκαμεν v.6.
ψυχή *life.* ἔ-θηκεν aor. τίθημι *lay down.* ὀφείλω *owe,* w.
17 inf. *ought.* θεῖναι aor² inf. τίθημι. ‖ ἔχῃ subj. ἔχω. βίος
daily *life ; means* of livelihood, *worldly goods.* θεωρῆ subj.
-ρέω *see.* χρεία *need,* χρείαν ἔχοντα (ptc) *in need.* κλείσῃ
aor. subj. κλείω *shut,* w. ἀπό. σπλάγχνα τά *entrails* as
18 source of feelings = Eng. *heart, compassion.* ‖ τεκνίον
2:1. ἀγαπῶμεν subj. hort. -πάω. γλῶσσα *tongue,* μή...λόγῳ
μηδὲ τῇ γ. *not by mere word or speech.* ἔργον *deed.* ‖
19   ἐν τούτῳ ref. back to v.18. γνωσόμεθα fut. γινώσκω.
ἐκ v.12. ἔμ-προσθεν αὐτοῦ *in his* (God's) *presence,* i.e. in
judgement. πείσομεν fut. πείθω *persuade ; convince ;* re-

assure, π. τὴν καρδίαν ἡμῶν...ὅτι (v.20 2nd time)... either
we shall persuade/convince our hearts...that God is greater...
or *we shall reassure our hearts...for God is greater...* ‖ In   20
the intervening clause ὅτι ἐάν can best be understood as
ὅ-τι ἄν *whatever*. κατα-γινώσκῃ subj. -γινώσκω τινός τι
condemn one *for* sth, *whatever* (matter) *our heart condemns
us for.* ὅτι (2nd time) *that* or *for.* μείζων comp. of μέγας,
God being transcendent in knowledge, understanding, and
mercy, cf Rom 8:3. καρδίας gen. of comp. ‖ ἀγαπητός   21
v.2. παρ-ρησία *complete confidence*, π. πρός τινα *confidence
in* one. ‖ ὅ ἐάν (< ἄν) w. subj. *what-ever.* ἀρεστός (< ἀρέ-   22
σκω *please*) *pleasing.* ‖ ἵνα for inf. epexeg. (explaining   23
αὕτη) §410. πιστεύσωμεν aor. subj. -εύω. τῷ ὀνόματι =
εἰς τὸ ὄν., i.e. all that Jesus is : Son of God, Messiah, Kyrios.
ἀγαπῶμεν v.11. ἔ-δωκεν aor. δίδωμι. ‖ τηρῶν ptc τηρέω.   24
καὶ ἐν τούτῳ...ἐκ... *and by this we know...*(namely) *from...*
οὗ by attraction of the rel. ὅ §16. ‖

    ἀγαπητός *beloved.* πιστεύετε impv, π. τινί *believe* one   4
5:10. δοκιμάζετε impv -άζω *test*, pres. iterative. τὰ
πνεύματα inspirers of charisms. εἰ (as indir. interr.) ἐκ τ.
θεοῦ ἐστιν whether *they come from God.* ψευδο-προφήτης[3]
false prophet. ἐξ-ε-ληλύθασιν *have emerged/appeared*, pf[2] ἐξ-
έρχομαι. ‖ ἐν τούτῳ ref. what follows. πᾶς wt art. distri-   2
butive, *every* §188. ὁμο-λογέω *acknowledge, confess.* ἐν
σαρκί *in flesh* (excluding all tendencies to docetism). ἐ-
ληλυθότα *as having come*, pf[2] ptc ἔρχομαι. ‖ τοῦτο *the latter.*   3
τὸ τοῦ ἀντιχρίστου *that* (i.e. the spirit) *of antichrist.* ἀκη-
κόατε pf[2] ἀκούω. ἔρχεται *is coming* w. fut. force. ἤδη
already. ‖ ἐκ τ. θεοῦ *belong to God.* τεκνίον 2:1. νε-
νικήκατε pf νικάω *overcome.* μείζων comp. of μέγας. ‖   4
αὐτῶν ἀκούει *listens to, heeds them* (gen.). ‖ ἐκ τούτου *this*   5,6
is how. γινώσκομεν *we recognize.* πλάνη *error.* ‖

    ἀγαπητός v.1. ἀγαπῶμεν subj. hort. *let us love.* ἐκ τ.   7
θεοῦ ἐστιν *is of God.* ἀγαπῶν ptc. γε-γέννηται pf pass.
γεννάω *bear*, pass. *be born.* ‖ ἔ-γνω aor[2] γινώσκω. Note   8
how the knowledge of God is always practical and personal with the object of assimilation which however is
only attainable through a rebirth enabling man to
participate in the nature of Him who is love. ‖ ἐν   9
τούτῳ...ὅτι 3:16. ἐ-φανερώθη aor. pass. -ρόω *make clear/
known.* ἐν ἡμῖν parallel to simple dat. §120. μονο-γενής[9]
only (begotten). ἀπ-έ-σταλκεν pf ἀπο-στέλλω, pf, so w. per-

manent effect. ζήσωμεν aor. subj. ζάω (aor. perh. incep-
10 tive, *come to life*). ‖ ἠγαπήκαμεν *we love*, pf ἀγαπάω. ἠγάπησεν aor. -πάω. ἀπ-έ-στειλεν aor. ἀπο-στέλλω. ἱλασμός
11 2:2, pred. περί for ὑπέρ §96. ‖ καί *too*. ὀφείλω owe, w.
12 inf. *ought*. ἀγαπᾶν inf. -πάω. ‖ πώ-ποτε *ever, at any time*.
τε-θέαται pf θεάομαι *behold, look upon*. ἀγαπῶμεν subj.
τε-τελειωμένη pf ptc pass. -ειόω *make perfect*, forming w.
13 εἰμί periphr. pf tense, cf pf pass. in v.17, 2:5. ‖ ὅτι (1st
time) *that* ; (2nd time) epexeg. τούτῳ. ἐκ partitive *of*, in
modern Eng. preceded by "one" or "some" etc. where
appropriate, often untranslatable. δέ-δωκεν pf δίδωμι. ‖
14 ἡμεῖς John speaking as a witness 1:1, and Jn 1:14. ἀπ-έ-
15 σταλκεν v.9. σωτήρ[6] -ῆρος ὁ pred. *as saviour*. ‖ ὃς ἐάν
16 (= ἄν) *who-ever*. ὁμο-λογήσῃ aor. subj. -λογέω v.2. ‖ ἐ-
γνώκαμεν pf γινώσκω. πε-πιστεύκαμεν pf -εύω. ἐν ἡμῖν v.13;
? "the love poured into our hearts" Rom 5:5 §105. ‖
17 τε-τελείωται pf pass. cf v.12. παρ-ρησία *complete confidence*.
ἔχωμεν subj. ἔχω. καθώς...καί *such as...so* Jn 6:58, 14:27 ;
18 "such as he is so are we in this world". ‖ φόβος *fear*,
φ. οὐκ ἔστιν ἐν... *there is no fear in...* τέλειος *perfect*. ἔξω
out(*side*). κόλασις[4] (< κολάζω punish) *punishment*. ἔχω
19 here, *involve, entail* Jas 2:17. ‖ ἀγαπῶμεν indic. πρῶτος
(as in Eng.) for πρότερος (comp., of two) §151. ἠγάπησεν
20 v.10. ‖ εἴπῃ aor[2] subj. λέγω. ὅτι = "... μισῇ subj. μισέω
hate. ψεύστης[3] *liar*. ἀγαπῶν v.7. ἑώρακεν pf ὁράω. ἀγαπᾶν v.11 ⟦[var. πῶς δύναται ἀγαπᾶν;]⟧. ἀγαπᾷ subj. ‖

5   ὁ Χριστός pred., on art. §174. γε-γέννηται *has been
born* already, pf pass. γεννάω *bear* ; faith is not the
cause of rebirth but the effect. ἀγαπῶν 4:7. γεννή-
σαντα aor. ptc, τὸν γ. *his father*. γε-γεννημένον pf ptc pass.
2 γ. ἐξ αὐτοῦ and so his brother. ‖ ἀγαπῶμεν (2nd time)
subj. (after ὅταν), same form as indic. (v.2a). ποιῶμεν
3 subj. ‖ αὕτη...ἵνα for inf. epexeg. §410. τηρῶμεν subj.
4 τηρέω. βαρύς -εῖα -ύ *heavy, burdensome*. ‖ νικάω *conquer, overcome*. κόσμος 2:15 (τὰ ἐν τ. κ.). νίκη *victory*.
5 νικήσασα aor. ptc fem., aor. effective §252. ‖ νικῶν ptc. ‖
6   ἐλθών aor[2] ptc ἔρχομαι. διά resumed by ἐν, notion of
concomitant circumstances combined w. that of instrumentality. ὕδωρ and αἷμα represent baptism and the
cross, (prob. opp. Cerinthus) ; not only he who was baptized
was the Son of God but also he who was crucified. μαρτυ-
8 ροῦν ptc -ρέω. ‖ τὸ ὕδωρ κ. τ. αἷμα: by an extension of

the ass. w. baptism and the cross (v.6), water and blood,
here ref. Christian baptism and the eucharist (celebrating
Christ's death on the cross), are cited as witnesses.
εἰς τὸ ἕν εἰσιν *are united, are at one* ; εἰς prob. due to Hebr.
influence §32. ‖ μαρτυρία *testimony*. μείζων 4:4. ὅτι (1st   9
time) *for*. με-μαρτύρηκεν pf -ρέω. ‖ πιστεύω τῷ θεῷ   10
believe God, to be distinguished from -εύω εἰς τ. θεόν.
ψεύστης³ *liar*. πε-ποίηκεν pf ποιέω ; disbelief being tan-
tamount to an accusation of lying. αὐτόν i.e. God. πε-
πίστευκεν pf. ‖ ἔ-δωκεν aor. δίδωμι, by the incarnation   11
of the Son, cf Jn 3:16. ‖

    ἔ-γραψα *I am writing*, (epistolary) aor. γράφω 2:14.   13
εἰδῆτε aor² subj. of pf-pres. οἶδα. τοῖς πιστεύουσιν (ptc
dat. pl.) appos. to ὑμῖν. ‖ παρ-ρησία πρός τινα 3:21. ὅτι   14
explains αὕτη. αἰτώμεθα subj. αἰτοῦμαι *petition for, beg,
beseech*. ‖ ἐάν instead of εἰ w. indic. §331. ἀκούει ἡμῶν   15
listens to us. ὁ ἐάν (= ἄν) *what-ever*. αἴτημα⁷ *request*.
ἠτήκαμεν pf αἰτέω: w. cognate acc. αἰτέω αἴτημα ἀπό τινος
make a request to one. ‖ ἴδῃ aor² subj. ὁράω. ἁμαρτάνοντα   16
ptc -άνω *sin* : w. cognate acc. *committing sin*. πρὸς θάνατον
fatal, mortal Jn 11:4, ἁμαρτία π. θάνατον ?apostasy v.12,
(Heb 6:4-6, 12:16f.) or ?sin against the Holy Spirit (Mk
3:29). αἰτήσει fut. impvl αἰτέω, sc. as obj. "God". δώσει
fut. δίδωμι. τοῖς ἁμαρτάνουσιν (ptc dat. pl.) μὴ πρὸς θάνατον
(sc. *that is*) *to sinners not (guilty) of mortal sin*. ἔστιν
(not encl.) *there is*, i.e. "for mortal sin *exists* and about
that I do not say that one should pray." ἐρωτήσῃ aor.
subj. -τάω *ask*. ‖ ἀ-δικία *wrong doing*. καί *but* §455β.   17
ἔστιν v.16. οὐ transl. (*which is*) *not*. ‖ γε-γεννημένος v.l.   18
γεννηθείς aor. ptc pass. γεννάω, here of the Son begotten
of God, perh. opp. ὁ γεγεννημένος *the believer*. ὁ πονηρός
the Evil One, the devil. ἅπτομαί τινος *touch* one, here (as
sts in Eng.) with evil intent. ‖ ἐκ τοῦ θεοῦ ἐσμέν *we belong*   19
to God §134. κεῖται *lies*, used as pf pass. τίθημι: κεῖμαι
ἔν τινι *lie in the power of* one. ‖ ἥκω to *have come*. δέ-   20
δωκεν pf δίδωμι. διά-νοια *mind, understanding*. γινώσκωμεν
subj. -σκω. ἀληθινός *true, genuine, real*, τὸν ἀ. *him who
is reality*, better, *the true (God)*. οὗτος: as a climax to
vv. 18-20 the ref. is almost certainly to God the real, the
true, opp. paganism (v.21). ‖ τεκνίον 2:1. φυλάξατε aor.   21
impv -άσσω *guard, keep*. ἑαυτά (neut. as ref. τεκνία) for
ὑμᾶς αὐτούς §209. εἴδωλον (< εἶδος⁸ outward form) *image,
idol*. ‖

II JOHN

ἐκ-λεκτός *elect, chosen.* κυρία *lady,* met. ref. some
local church which John is warning to beware of certain
heretics. τέκνον i.e. member. ἐν ἀληθείᾳ either *in truth,*
i.e. sincerely. ἐ-γνωκότες pf ptc γινώσκω, who *have embraced* the truth, practically and not only intellectually
2 I Jn 2:3. ‖ μένουσαν ptc μένω, truth understood as a
force dwelling and active in man. ἔσται fut. εἰμί: μένουσαν...καί...ἔσται ptcl cstr disrupted by καί co-ord. §375.
3 εἰς τ. αἰῶνα *for ever.* ‖ ἔσται *there will be* : an assurance in
place of the usual wish. ἔλεος[8] *mercy.* ‖
4   ἐ-χάρην aor[2] dep. χαίρω. λίαν *much, greatly.* εὕρηκα
pf εὑρίσκω. ἐκ τῶν *some of,* Sem. for τις w. partitive gen.
Jn 1:24 §80. περι-πατοῦντας ptc -πατέω I Jn 1:6. ἐ-λάβομεν
5 aor[2] λαμβάνω. ‖ ἐρωτάω *ask.* κυρία v.1, here voc. καινός...
ἀπ᾽ ἀρχῆς I Jn 2:7. εἴχομεν impf ἔχω. ἀγαπῶμεν subj. -πάω. ‖
6 αὕτη...ἵνα for inf. epexeg. §410. περιπατῶμεν subj. ἠκούσατε
7 aor. ἀκούω. ‖ πλάνος *misleading* ; as noun, *deceiver.* ἐξῆλθον
εἰς... meaning "have emerged and are abroad in...". ὁμο-
λογοῦντες ptc -λογέω *acknowledge.* ἐρχόμενον ptc, ref. incarnation. ὁ πλάνος pred. w. art., "the" known and expected
8 §174. ἀντί-χριστος I Jn 2:18. ‖ βλέπετε impv. β. ἑαυτούς
(on ἑαυτ. I Jn 5:21) *look to yourselves, beware.* ἵνα μή
that...not, lest. ἀπ-ολέσητε aor. subj. -όλλυμι [[var. ἀπο-
λέσωμεν]]. εἰργασάμεθα *we have achieved,* aor. ἐργάζομαι
(trans.) *work for, undertake* sth. μισθός *reward.* πλήρης
full. ἀπο-λάβητε aor[2] subj. -λαμβάνομαι *receive* what is due
9 [[var. ἀπολάβωμεν]]. ‖ προ-άγων ptc -άγω *go ahead.* διδαχή
10 *teaching.* καί...καί *both...and.* ‖ φέρω *bring.* λαμβάνετε,
λέγετε impv ; pres. impv not "stop receiving..." but retaining pres. iterative force, *never receive him...never give
him a greeting,* cf I Tim 4:14. χαίρειν Gr formula of greet-
11 ing, *welcome !* ‖ κοινωνέω *share*/*take part in.* ‖
12   ἔχων concessive, *though I have.* ἐ-βουλήθην aor. dep.
βούλομαι *want,* perh. epistolary aor. *I do not want* (understand : *to do so*). διά w. gen. of manner, *with.* χάρτης[3]

papyrus, in use the equivalent of today's paper. **μέλας** -αίνη -αν *black* ; τὸ μέλαν *ink*. **γενέσθαι** aor[2] inf. γίνομαι: γ. πρός τινα *come to one*. **στόμα πρὸς στόμα** *face to face*. **λαλῆσαι** aor. inf. λαλέω. **χαρά** *joy*. **πε-πληρωμένη** pf ptc pass. -ρόω, w. ᾖ (subj. εἰμί) forming periphrastic cstr. ‖ **ἀσπάζομαι** *greet*. **τὰ τέκνα** v.l. **ἀδελφὴ ἐκλεκτή** a "sister" 13 community of Christians like ἡ κυρία ἐκλ. v.l. ‖

III JOHN

1,2   ἀγαπητός *beloved.* ἐν ἀληθείᾳ II Jn 1. ‖ ἀγαπητέ voc.
περὶ πάντων *in every way,* ass. w. εὐοδοῦσθαι. εὔχομαι =
προσεύχομαι. εὐ-οδοῦσθαι inf. -οδόομαι "be well led";
do well, succeed. ὑγιαίνειν inf. -αίνω *be in good health, be*
3   *well.* ‖ ἐ-χάρην aor² dep. χαίρω. λίαν *much, greatly.* ἐρχο-
μένων ptc, gen. abs. *when brethren* (Christians) *came.*
μαρτυρούντων ptc -ρέω τινί *testify* in favour of ; hence
μ. σου τῇ ἀληθείᾳ *brought good news of your* (life in) *truth.*
4   καθώς *as* (*in fact*). περιπατέω I Jn 1:6. ‖ μειζότερος comp.
of a comp. (μείζων; cf Eng. less-er) *greater.* χαρά *joy.*
τούτων...ἵνα ἀκούω gen. of comp. *than this news...that.*
περι-πατοῦντα ptc neut. pl. -πατέω I Jn 1:6. ‖
5   ἀγαπητέ v.2. πιστός *faithful,* πιστὸν ποιέω *do a work*
of faith. ὃ ἐάν (= ἄν) *all that.* ἐργάσῃ aor. subj. -άζω
work ; undertake, do work. εἰς *for.* καὶ τοῦτο *and espe-*
6   *cially, and...at that.* ξένος *strange, foreign.* ‖ ἐ-μαρτύρησαν
aor. v.3. καλῶς *well,* κ. ποιήσεις (fut. ποιέω) w. ptc =
Eng. *please.* προ-πέμψας aor. ptc -πέμπω *send on* one's
way, implying provision for the journey. ἀξίως *worthily,*
ἀ. τ. θεοῦ i.e. doing your best as in the service of God. ‖
7   ὑπέρ *for the sake of.* τὸ ὄνομα i.e. of Jesus = Jesus himself.
λαμβάνοντες ptc -βάνω. ἐθνικός (< ἔθνη gentiles) *pagan.* ‖
8   ὀφείλω *owe,* w. inf. *ought, we owe it* (*to them*) *to...* ὑπο-
λαμβάνειν inf. -λαμβάνω *welcome.* τοι-οῦτος *such* (*a one*).
συν-εργός *fellow-worker.* γινώμεθα subj. γίνομαι. τῇ ἀληθείᾳ
9   *in truth* or *for the truth,* i.e. the gospel. ‖ ἔ-γραψα aor.
γράφω. φιλο-πρωτεύων ptc -πρωτεύω τινός *like to take the*
lead/dominate one ; in common w. vbs of pre-eminence
foll. by gen. of comp., pl. according to the sense (church
members). ἐπι-δέχομαι *receive, accept.* ἡμᾶς perh. signify-
10   ing "my authority". ‖ διὰ τοῦτο *for this reason.* ἔλθω
aor² subj. ἔρχομαι: ἐάν w. subj. an eventual condition.
ὑπο-μνήσω fut. -μιμνήσκω τι *bring to mind ; bring up, raise*
a matter. φλυαρῶν ptc -ρέω τινά *talk nonsense about* one,
φ. λόγοις πονηροῖς *talk vituperative nonsense.* ἀρκούμενος

not *content with*, ptc pass. ἀρκέω *suffice*. ἐπὶ τούτοις
with that. βουλομένους ptc -λομαι *will, want*, τοὺς β.
those who are willing (sc. to receive them). κωλύω *prevent,
stop*. ἐκ-βάλλω *ex-pel*. ‖ μιμοῦ impv μιμέομαι *imitate*. ἀγαθο- 11
ποιῶν ptc -ποιέω *do good*. κακο-ποιῶν ptc *do evil*. ἑ-ώρακεν
pf ὁράω, οὐχ ἑ. in Jn meaning "is a stranger to God". ‖
μεμαρτύρηται *is attested*, pf pass. -ρέω v.3. αὐτὴ ἡ ἀλήθεια
the truth itself. μαρτυρία *testimony*. ‖

εἶχον impf ἔχω (when he started writing he "had"). 13
γράψαι aor. inf. v.9. διὰ μέλανος II Jn 12. κάλαμος
reed, so, *reed-pen*. ‖ ἐλπίζω *hope*. εὐθέως *very soon*. ἰδεῖν 14
aor² inf. ὁράω. στόμα πρὸς σ. II Jn 12. λαλήσομεν fut.
λαλέω. ‖ ἀσπάζομαι *greet*. φίλος *friend*. ἀσπάζου impv 2nd 15
sg. κατ' ὄνομα i.e. *individually*, κατά distributive. ‖

JUDE

'Ιούδας -δα *Judas, Jude*, ἀδελφός...'Ιακώβου but cf Lk
6:16, Ac 1:13. ἐν θεῷ = παρὰ θεῷ. ἠγαπημένοις pf ptc
pass. ἀγαπάω. τε-τηρημένοις pf ptc pass. τηρέω: τετ. 'I.
Χριστῷ *kept safe for Jesus Christ*, the pf envisaging the
lasting result of past action. κλητός (< καλέω) *called*. ||
2 ἔλεος[8] *mercy*. πληθυνθείη aor. opt. pass. 3rd sg -ύνω
multiply, increase ; opt. den. a wish.

3 ἀγαπητός *beloved*. σπουδή *haste* ; *eagerness*, σ. ποιοῦμαι
(mid.) = σπουδάζω see on Rom 13:14 (ποιεῖσθε) ; σπ.
ποιούμενος γράφειν pres. ptc representing impf §371, here,
as often, den. an action in progress when sth intervened
§275. κοινός *common, shared*. σωτηρία *salvation*. ἀνάγκη
necessity. ἔσχον aor² (inceptive) ἔχω. γράψαι aor. inf.
γράφω: ποιούμενος...γράψαι *I was anxious to write to you*
(pres. ptc and inf.) *about...when necessity arose* (lit. "I
acquired a necessity") *to write...* (aor. and aor. inf.). παρα-
καλῶν *urging (you)* ptc -καλέω. ἐπ-αγωνίζεσθαι inf. -αγω-
νίζομαι τινι *strive for/on behalf of*. ἅπαξ *once* (v.5), *once
for all*. παρα-δοθείσῃ aor. ptc pass. -δίδωμι. ἡ πίστις *the
4 deposit of faith*. || παρ-εισ-έ-δυσαν 3rd pl. of aor. -έδυσα or
of aor² -έδυν (like ἔγνων), pres. παρ-εισ-δύ(ν)ω *creep/steal in*,
the prefix παρ-εισ- connoting "unawares" Gal 2:4, II Pt
2:1. πάλαι *long ago*. προ-γε-γραμμένοι *pre-scribed, ordained*
(in writing), pf ptc pass. προ-γράφω *write beforehand*. τοῦτο
ref. what follows. κρίμα[7] *judgement, condemnation*. The
foll. vv. provide examples of the punishment of sinners
from OT. ἀ-σεβής[9] *god-less, im-pious*. χάριτα alternative
to χάριν acc. of χάρις, Ac 24:47. μετα-τιθέντες ptc -τίθημι
move sth from one place to another ; *transform*. ἀ-σέλγεια
debauchery, i.e. they pervert the freedom bestowed by
grace into licence. δεσπότης[3] *master*, of Christ (II Pt
5 2:1). ἀρνούμενοι ptc -νέομαι *deny, disown*. || ὑπο-μνῆσαι
aor. inf. -μιμνήσκω *remind*. βούλομαι *wish, want*. εἰδότας
ptc pf-pres. οἶδα: εἰδ. πάντα ὅτι... ptc concessive, *though
you know all about how...* ἅπαξ ass. w. σώσας aor. ptc σῴζω.

δεύτερος *second*, τὸ δ. *on the second occasion, the next time.*
πιστεύσαντες aor. ptc -εύω. ἀπ-ώλεσεν aor. -όλλυμι. ∥
τηρήσαντας aor. ptc τηρέω. ἀρχή *domain* over which 6
lordship was accorded them. ἀπο-λιπόντας aor[2] ptc -λείπω
abandon. οἰκητήριον *abode.* κρίσις[4] *judgement.* δεσμός a
bond, chain. ἀΐδιος (< ἀεί ever) *perpetual.* ζόφος *gloom*
of the underworld. τε-τήρηκεν pf. ∥ Σόδομα II Pt 2:6. 7
ὅμοιος *like.* τρόπος *manner*, ὅμοιον τ. τούτοις advl acc.
in the same way as these (v.6). ἐκ-πορνεύσασαι aor. ptc
-πορνεύω *commit fornication*, fem. as ref. πόλεις. ἀπ-ελ-
θοῦσαι aor[2] ptc -έρχομαι: ἀπ. ὀπίσω (Hebr.) σαρκὸς ἑτέρας
indulge in unnatural vice. πρό-κειμαι *be set before.* δεῖγμα[7]
(< δείκνυμι show) *sample ; evidence* i.e. of what happens
to such people ; pred. πυρός gen. epexeg. of δίκη *punishment.* ὑπ-έχουσαι ptc -έχω *undergo.* ∥ ὁμοίως *likewise.* 8
μέντοι *nevertheless.* οὗτοι = those of v.4. ἐν-υπνιαζό-
μενοι *in their sleep, dreaming*, ptc -υπνιάζομαι *dream* ; here
perh. meaning preferring their sensual imaginings to
(or mistaking their...for...) moral reality. μιαίνω *defile.*
κυριότης[6] -τητος ἡ *dominion.* ἀ-θετέω *flout.* αἱ δόξαι
things and persons in whom shines the divine majesty,
here, *the good angels.* βλασ-φημέω *malign, defame.* ∥ ἀρχ- 9
άγγελος *prince of angels, archangel.* διά-βολος (< διαβάλλω
accuse) *devil.* δια-κρινόμενος ptc mid. -κρίνω *differentiate* ; mid. *differ, dispute* ; also *debate with oneself, be of
two minds, waver* (v.22). δι-ε-λέγετο impf δια-λέγω (δια-
back and forth + λέγω) *debate, argue*, (related in the
Assumption of Moses). ἐ-τόλμησεν aor. -μάω *dare.* κρίσις
v.6, a *charge.* ἐπ-ενεγκεῖν aor[2] inf. ἐπι-φέρω *bring.* βλασ-
φημία *blasphemy* (sc. against the devil for claiming to be
lord of the material world) ; others would assimilate the
sense to that of II Pt 2:11 and understand as "Hebr."
gen., *a defamatory charge.* ἐπι-τιμῆσαι aor. opt. 3rd sg
-τιμάω *rebuke.* ∥ μέν...δέ with the connotation "on the 10
one hand...on the other...". φυσικῶς *by instinct.* ἄ-λογος
devoid of reason. ζῷον *animal.* ἐπίσταμαι *know* esp. by
practical experience. ἐν instr. *by.* φθείρονται pass. -ρω
corrupt ; destroy. ∥ οὐαί *alas (for) !* Κάϊν: Philo makes 11
him the type of the impious libertine. ἐ-πορεύθησαν aor.
dep. -εύομαι I Pt 4:3. πλάνη *error.* μισθός *wage*, gen. of
price, *for a reward.* ἐξ-ε-χύθησαν aor. pass. ἐκ-χέω *pour
out*, pass. *abandon oneself.* ἀντι-λογία *contradiction* ; re-

bellion, dat. instr. *by*. ἀπ-ώλοντο aor² mid. -όλλυμι. ‖
12 ἀγάπη *love-feast*, celebrated before the Lord's Supper as
a mark of mutual charity. σπιλάς⁶ -άδος ἡ *submerged
rock*; also = σπίλος *blot*. συν-ευωχούμενοι ptc -ευωχέομαί
τινι *feast with* one. ἀ-φόβως (adj. ἄφοβος *fearless*) here,
without scruple. ποιμαίνοντες ptc -μαίνω *mind* a flock
(ποίμνη), *lead to pasture* ; here, π. ἑαυτούς *looking after
themselves*. νεφέλη *cloud*. ἄν-υδρος *water-less*, *bringing no
rain*. ἄνεμος *wind*. παρα-φερόμεναι *driven*, ptc pass. -φέρω
carry away. δένδρον *tree*. φθιν-οπωρινός *autumnal*, *of autumn*, i.e. of the season of fruit-bearing. ἄ-καρπος *unproductive*, *barren*. δίς *twice*. ἀπο-θανόντα aor² ptc -θνή-
σκω: δὶς ἀπ. *doubly dead*. ἐκ-ριζωθέντα aor. ptc pass.
13 -ριζόω *uproot*. ‖ κῦμα⁷ *wave*. ἄγριος *wild*. ἐπ-αφρίζοντα ptc
-αφρίζω τι *foam* with sth. αἰσχύνη *shame*, plur. *deeds of
shame*. ἀστήρ⁶ -τέρος ὁ *star*. πλανήτης³ *wanderer*, ἀστέρες
πλ. *wandering stars*. ζόφος v.6. σκότος⁸ *darkness*. εἰς
αἰῶνα *for ever*. τε-τήρηται *is reserved*, pf pass. ‖ προε-
14 φήτευσεν aor. προφητεύω, instead of ἐ-προφ-, augmented as
if cmpd vb ; subject Ἑνώχ. ἕβδομος *seventh* in line. ἐν
sociative, *with* §116. μυριάς⁶ -άδος ἡ = 10,000, *myriad*. ‖
15 ποιῆσαι aor. inf. ποιέω. κρίσις v.9. ἐλέγξαι aor. inf.
ἐλέγχω *convict*. ἀ-σέβεια *im-piety*, ἔργον ἀσεβείας "Hebr."
gen., *impious deed* §40. αὐτῶν pleon. before ἠσέβησαν aor.
ἀ-σεβέω *commit impieties*. ὧν (twice) for ἅ by attraction
of rel. §16. σκληρός *hard*, neut. pl., here *defiant words*.
ἐ-λάλησαν aor. λαλέω. ἁμαρτωλός *sinner*. ἀ-σεβής v.4. ‖
16 γογγυστής³ *grumbler*. μεμψί-μοιρος (< μέμφομαι *blame* +
μοῖρα *fate, lot*) *disgruntled*. πορευόμενοι κατά τι *go the
way of* sth. ἐπι-θυμία *desire*. ὑπέρ-ογκος (< ὄγκος *burden,
bulk*) *inflated*, *excessive*, neut. pl. *bombast*. θαυμάζοντες
ptc -άζω τι *wonder at/admire* sth, θ. πρόσωπα *deferring to
people* or (as in OT) = λαμβάνοντες πρ. *showing favour/
partiality to*... Gal 2:6. ὠφέλεια *advantage, benefit*. χάριν
w. gen. *for (the sake of)*. ‖
17 ἀγαπητός v.3. μνήσθητε aor. impv dep. μιμνήσκομαι
remember. ῥῆμα⁷ *word*. προ-ειρημένων pf ptc pass. -λέγω
18 *say* or *speak beforehand*. ‖ ἔ-λεγον impf λέγω. ἔσχατος *last*.
χρόνος *time*, ἐπ' ἐσχάτου [τοῦ] χ. *in the last age*. ἔσονται
fut. εἰμί. ἐμ-παίκτης³ *scoffer, jeerer*. ἀ-σέβεια v.15, pl. =
ἔργα ἀσεβείας v.15, gen. governed by ἐπιθυμίας *desires*
19 *for*. ‖ ἀπο-δι-ορίζοντες ptc -ίζω (< ὅρος *boundary* + δια-

between + ἀπο-) *divide, create division.* ψυχικός *natural,*
as excluding the spiritual. ἔχοντες ptc ἔχω. ‖ ἐπ-οικο- 20
δομοῦντες ptc -δομέω *build up | establish* on. ἁγιώτατος
superl. (elative) ἅγιος. προσ-ευχόμενοι ptc -εύχομαι. ‖
τηρήσατε aor. impv -ρέω. προσ-δεχόμενοι ptc -δέχομαι 21
wait for. ἔλεος v.2. ‖ οὒς μέν...οὒς δέ...οὒς δέ *some...*
others...yet others. ἐλεᾶτε impv ἐλεάω = ἐλεέω τινά *have* 22
mercy on one. δια-κρινομένους v.9. ‖ σῴζετε impv. ἁρπά- 23
ζοντες ptc -άζω *snatch.* φόβος *fear,* ἐν sociative, *with*
fear, sc. lest they seduce you. μισοῦντες ptc μισέω *hate.*
καί *even.* ἐ-σπιλωμένον pf ptc pass. -λόω *stain, pollute.*
χιτών (*outer*) *garment.* ‖

　　δυναμένῳ ptc δύναμαι. φυλάξαι aor. inf. -άσσω *guard.* 24
keep. ἄ-πταιστος (< πταίω *trip up,* intr. *stumble*) *un-*
stumbling. στῆσαι aor. inf. ἵστημι. κατ-εν-ώπιον w. gen.
in the presence of §83. ἄ-μωμος *without blemish.* ἀγαλλία-
σις[4] *jubilation.* ‖ μόνος θεός (*the*) *only God.* σωτήρ[6] -ῆρος ὁ 25
saviour, σ. ἡμῶν i.e. *he who saves us.* μεγαλωσύνη *majesty.*
κράτος[8] *might.* In view of πρό...αἰῶνος perhaps supply
ἐστίν rather than ἔστω (a wish) ; or, understanding the
phrase as Sem. co-ord. for subord., "as it was before all
ages, so be it now and for ever". ‖

APOCALYPSE

1 ἀπο-κάλυψις[4] (< ἀπο-καλύπτω reveal) *revelation*. ἔ-δω-κεν aor. δίδωμι. δεῖξαι aor. inf. δείκνυμι *show*; inf. final. γενέσθαι aor[2] inf. γίνομαι. τάχος[8] *speed*; ἐν τ. *quickly, shortly*. ἐ-σήμανεν aor. σημαίνω *indicate, make known* §492. ἀπο-στείλας aor. ptc -στέλλω, graphic ptc §363; ἐσήμανεν

2 ἀπ. διά Hebr.-Aram. cf Mt 11:2 (πέμψαι). ‖ ἐ-μαρτύρησεν aor. -ρέω, epistolary aor. ἐμ. ...ὅσα εἶδεν *bears witness to all that he saw as being the word of God and...* μαρτυρία

3 *testimony*. ‖ μακάριος *blessed, happy*. ἀνα-γινώσκων ptc -γινώσκω *read*. ἀκούοντες ptc ἀκούω. προφητεία *prophecy*, τῆς π. *this prophecy*. τηροῦντες ptc τηρέω. γε-γραμμένα

4 pf ptc pass. γράφω. ἐγγύς *near*. ‖ Ἀσία the Roman province, now SW region of Turkey. ὤν ptc εἰμί: ὁ ὤν κτλ. treated as an indecl. name. ὁ ἦν indic. supplying for a durative past ptc; the fact that the whole "name" is undeclined after ἀπό adds the impression of immutability to that of eternity. ἐρχόμενος ptc ἔρχομαι: ὁ ἐ. Mk 11:9, Heb 10:37 ὁ ὤν...ἐρχ. *he who is and who was and who is to come*. ἑπτὰ πνεύματα in Jewish literature of the seven archangels who stand before (the throne of) God; others understand the Holy Spirit w. his sevenfold manifestation to the 7 churches, or again as one in name, yet

5 seven in power, cf Is 11:2. θρόνος *throne*. ‖ μάρτυς[6] -υρος ὁ *witness*; after Χριστοῦ the gen. is abandoned in spite of appos. §13. πιστός *faithful*. πρωτό-τοκος (< τίκτω bear) *first-born*, πρ. τ. νεκρῶν less in time than in worthiness and honour. ἄρχων[6] ἄρχοντος ὁ *ruler*. ἀγαπῶντι ptc -πάω. λύσαντι aor. ptc λύω *loose, free*. ἐν instr. §119. ‖

6 ἐ-ποίησεν aor. ποιέω: τῷ ἀγαπῶντι...καὶ λύσαντι...καὶ ἐπ.: καί co-ord. continuing the ptcpl cstr w. indic. cf II Cor 6:9 (καὶ ζῶμεν), II Jn 2 (καὶ ἔσται) §375. βασιλεία a people under the kingship of God or rather eschatological: *kingdom, dominion, sovereignty* 20:6, I Thess 2:12. ἱερεύς[5] *priest*. ὁ θεὸς καὶ πατήρ under one art., ref. the same Person §184. αὐτοῦ of Christ, ass. also w. θεῷ. κράτος[8]

might. εἰς τ. αἰῶνας *for ever.* ‖ νεφέλη *cloud.* ὄψεται fut. 7
ὁράω. οἵτινες = οἵ §216. ἐξ-ε-κέντησαν aor. ἐκ-κεντέω
pierce. κόψονται fut. mid. κόπτω *beat* ; mid. ἐπί τινα
beat the breast / mourn for one. φυλή *tribe.* ναί *yes,*
here emphasizing the foregoing, *so it shall be.* ‖ τὸ ᾽Αλφα 8
καὶ τὸ ᾽Ω the first and last letters of Gk alphabet, therefore the beginning and the end ; rabbinical expression
adapted to Gk by substitution of Ω for *tau.* ὁ ὢν κτλ. v.4.
παντο-κράτωρ⁶ -κράτορος *al-mighty, all-sovereign.* ‖

συγ-κοινωνός *fellow-sharer.* θλῖψις⁴ *distress, suffering.* 9
βασιλεία v.6. ὑπο-μονή *endurance, fortitude* : three ideas
which pervade the whole book, the three under one art.
§184, closely ass. w. Jesus. ἐν §118. ἐ-γενόμην aor² γίνομαι.
νῆσος ἡ *island.* καλουμένη *called,* ptc pass. καλέω. διά
w. acc. *on account of* seems to point to persecution as
the reason for his staying on the island. μαρτυρία v.2,
μ. ᾽Ιησοῦ (gen. obj.) *testimony to Jesus.* ‖ ἐν πνεύματι 10
state in which one is particularly sensitive to the Spirit's
influence ; ἐγενόμην ἐν πν. here, *I fell into a state of ecstasy.*
κυριακός *of the Lord.* ἤκουσα aor. ἀκούω. ὀπίσω *behind,*
adv., as prep. w. gen. §83. σάλπιγξ⁶ -ιγγος ἡ *trumpet.* ‖
λεγούσης ptc fem. γράψον, πέμψον aor. impv γράφω, πέμπω. 11
βιβλίον orig. dim., became equivalent of βίβλος ἡ (= βύβλος
papyrus) *papyrus roll, book.* ‖ ἐπ-έ-στρεψα aor. ἐπι-στρέφω 12
return, turn back or *round,* trans. and intr. βλέπειν inf.
final, β. τὴν φωνήν i.e. to see whose voice. ἥτις = ἥ §216.
ἐ-λάλει impf λαλέω. ἐπι-στρέψας *when I turned,* aor. ptc.
λυχνία *lampstand.* χρυσοῦς (gen. -σοῦ) -σῆ -σοῦν made
of *gold.* ‖ μέσος *middle,* ἐν μ. wt art. as often in prep. 13
phrases. ὅμοιος w. dat. *like* sth ; here mistakenly (as
in 14:14) cstr like ὡς which does not affect the case.
ἐν-δε-δυμένον pf ptc mid. ἐν-δύω *clothe* someone else ;
mid. *put on* (oneself), *wear.* ποδήρης⁹ sc. χιτών (*garment*)
reaching to the feet. περι-ε-ζωσμένον pf ptc mid. or pass.
περι-ζώννυμί τι *gird* one *with* sth ; mid. *gird oneself* (pf
wear) ; pass. *be girded with...* μαστός *breast,* πρὸς τ. μαστοῖς
round his chest, πρός w. dat. rare, Jn 18:16, 20:12. ζώνη
girdle. χρυσᾶν for -ῆν (? by parallel w. ἀργυρᾶν). ‖ θρίξ 14
τριχός ἡ a *hair.* λευκός *white.* ἔριον *wool.* χιών⁶ χιόνος ἡ
snow. φλόξ⁶ φλογός ἡ *flame.* ‖ χαλκο-λίβανος *bronze* ; exact 15
substance unidentified. κάμινος ἡ *furnace.* πε-πυρωμένης
pf ptc pass. fem. -ρόω *burn; refine* ; πεπ. fem. and gen.,

defies explanation as it stands, amendments are suggested
16 but these have poor MS support. || ἔχων wt grammatical
subject, logically ref. υἱόν ἀνθρώπου (v.13). δεξιός *right*,
ἡ δεξιά, w. or wt χείρ, *right hand*. ἀστήρ⁶ ἀστέρος ὁ
star. ῥομφαία *sword*. δί-στομος (δίς twice + στόμα) masc.
and fem., neut. -ον *two-edged*. ὀξύς ὀξεῖα ὀξύ *sharp*. ἐκ-
πορευομένη ptc -πορεύομαι *issue, come out*. ὄψις⁴ *face*.
ἥλιος *sun*. φαίνω *show*; intr. *shine*. ἐν τῇ δυνάμει αὐτοῦ
17 *with its (full) force*. || ἔ-πεσα aor² (for -σον §489) πίπτω:
π. πρὸς τ. πόδας τινός *fall at* one's *feet*. ἔ-θηκεν aor. τίθημι.
18 φοβοῦ impv φοβέομαι. ἔσχατος *last*. || ζ ῶν ptc ζάω. ἐ-γενό-
μην v.9. εἰς τοὺς αἰῶνας τ. αἰώνων *for ever and ever*. κλείς
κλειδός ἡ (acc. pl. class. κλεῖς, HGk κλεῖδας) *key*. ᾅδης³
hades, underworld, ἡ κλεὶς τ. ᾅδου here, the power of deli-
19 vering from or consigning to the lower world. || γράψον
20 v.11. μέλλει γενέσθαι (v.1) *is to come about*. || μυστήριον
mystery, hidden meaning; acc. of respect, *with regard to* /
as to the secret. ἀστήρ v.16. λυχνία, χρυσοῦς v.12; acc.
instead of gen. (after μυστήριον) under influence of εἶδες.
ἄγγελος explained in different ways, all of which from
"guardian angels" to "messengers from the churches"
are beset by difficulties. Probably the angels stand as
symbols of the spirit and outlook characterizing each
community. ||

2   γράψον aor. impv γράφω. τάδε *these things*, (class.
ref. what follows) opp. ταῦτα (class. ref. what precedes)
§213. κρατῶν ptc -τέω *hold*, esp. in one's power ἀστήρ,
δεξιός 1:16. περι-πατῶν ptc -πατέω. ἐν μέσῳ 1:13. λυχνία,
2 χρυσοῦς 1:12. || κόπος *labour, toil*. ὑπο-μονή *endurance,
fortitude*. δύνῃ 2nd sg δύναμαι (= class. δύνασαι). βαστά-
σαι aor. inf. -άζω *carry*; met. *tolerate, endure*. κακός *evil*,
masc. pl *evil men*. ἐ-πείρασας aor. -άζω *put to the test*.
τοὺς λέγοντας...καὶ οὐκ εἰσίν ptc cstr lapsing into indic.
w. καί co-ord. 1:6 §375. εὗρες aor² εὑρίσκω. ψευδής⁹
3 *false*. || ἐ-βάστασας aor. κε-κοπίακες (for -κας: ending as-
similated to aor. §489) pf κοπιάω *become weary* from hard
4 work. || τὴν ἀγάπην σου τ. πρώτην i.e. the (brotherly) love
you had at first. ἀφ-ῆκες aor. 2nd sg (for -ας §489) -ίημι
5 *leave*. || μνημόνευε impv -νεύω *remember*. πόθεν *whence,
from where*, implying "how far". πέ-πτωκας pf πίπτω.
μετα-νόησον aor. impv -νοέω *repent*. ποίησον aor. impv
ποιέω. εἰ δὲ μή *if not, otherwise*. ἔρχομαι w. fut. sense.

σοι = ? πρός σε or ? dat. of disadvantage. κινήσω fut. κινέω move ; remove, take away. λυχνία 1:12. μετα-νοήσῃς aor. subj. ‖ τοῦτο explained by foll. ὅτι. ἔχεις sc. "in 6 your favour". μισέω hate. κἀγώ = καὶ ἐγώ. ‖ οὓς ὡτός τό 7 ear. ἀκουσάτω aor. impv 3rd sg ἀκούω. τί as indir. interr. νικῶντι ptc νικάω conquer, be victorious ; in Apoc ὁ νικῶν has everywhere the sense of one who, in the power of Christ, has overcome sin and endured martyrdom ; αὐτῷ superfluous. δώσω fut. δίδωμι grant, allow. φαγεῖν aor² inf. ἐσθίω: δίδωμί τινι φ. ἐκ Mt 14:16. ξύλον wood, tree. παράδεισος word of Persian origin, garden ; here, home of the blessed, heaven. ‖

    γράψον, τάδε v.1. ἔσχατος last. ἔ-ζησεν came to life, 8 aor. (inceptive) ζάω §250. ‖ θλῖψις⁴ distress, affliction. 9 πτωχεία poverty, destitution. πλούσιος rich. βλασ-φημία slander. ἐκ on the part of. τῶν λεγόντων…καὶ οὐκ εἰσίν v.2. συν-αγωγή synagogue ; congregation. ‖ φοβοῦ impv φο- 10 βέομαι. πάσχειν inf. πάσχω suffer. διά-βολος the devil. ἐξ ὑμῶν (sc. τινές) some of you, a Hebr., II Jn 4 §80. φυλακή (< φυλάσσω guard, keep) prison. πειρασθῆτε aor. subj. pass. -άζω v.2. ἔξετε fut. ἔχω. θλῖψις here prob. in the form of persecution. ἡμερῶν gen. of time during which. δέκα = 10. γίνου be ! impv 2nd sg γίνομαι, for little used ἴσθι (εἰμί). πιστός faithful. ἄχρι until, unto. δώσω v.7. στέφανος crown. τῆς ζωῆς epexeg. namely eternal life §45. ‖ V.11a = 7a. νικῶν v.7. οὐ μή w. subj. 11 emphatic neg. ref. fut. ἀ-δικηθῇ aor. subj. pass. -δικέω injure, hurt. ἐκ from, by. δεύτερος second, θάνατος ὁ δ. 21:8. ‖

    γράψον, τάδε v.1. ῥομφαία, δίστομος, ὀξύς 1:16. ‖ 12 ποῦ as indir. interr. where. κατ-οικέω live, dwell. ὅπου 13 there where. ὁ θρόνος τ. Σατανᾶ: sanctuary of Asclepius with the serpent as its symbol, a famous centre for worship of pagan gods and the emperor in particular. κρατέω hold firmly, cf v.1. ἠρνήσω aor. 2nd sg ἀρνέομαι deny. καί (3rd time) even. 'Αντιπᾶς gen. -πᾶ: in Apoc proper names often left in nom. §13. μάρτυς (nom. appos. to 'Αντ.) one who testifies, a witness ; since under persecution this often meant death, μάρτυς acquired the new meaning of martyr ; Apoc 2:13 perh. the earliest known use in this sense. πιστός v.10. ἀπ-ε-κτάνθη aor. pass. -κτείνω. παρ' ὑμῖν i.e. in your town. ‖ ὀλίγος small, pl. 14

a few. κρατοῦντας v.1, (masc.) "people holding", *some who hold.* διδαχή *teaching.* Βαλαάμ the author's alias for the Nicolaitans (v.15). ἐ-δίδασκεν impf -σκω, here w. dat. βαλεῖν aor² inf. βάλλω. σκάνδαλον *stumbling block, occasion of sin.* φαγεῖν v.7, inf. hovering between final and consec. εἰδωλό-θυτος *sacrificed to an idol,* neut. *meat* so sacrificed. πορνεῦσαι aor. inf. -εύω *commit fornication.* ‖

15 ἔχεις καὶ σύ *you too have,* sc. as well as the Ephesians ?

16 v.6. ὁμοίως *likewise.* ‖ μετα-νόησον v.5. εἰ δὲ μή, ἔρχομαί σοι v.5. ταχύς -χεῖα -χύ *quick,* neut. as adv. *quickly, soon.* πολεμήσω fut. -μέω *do battle, attack.* ἐν instr. *with* §119.

17 ῥομφαία 1:16. ‖ ὁ ἔχων...αὐτῷ v.7. τοῦ μάννα partitive gen. *(a share) of the manna.* κε-κρυμμένου *hidden,* pf ptc pass. κρύπτω *hide.* ψῆφος ἡ *pebble, stone* used in voting : the black against, and the white in favour. λευκός *white.* καινός *new.* γε-γραμμένον pf ptc pass. γράφω. εἰ μή *except.* ‖

18 φλόξ⁶ φλογός ὁ *flame.* ὅμοιος *like.* χαλκο-λίβανος 1:15. ‖

19 διακονία *service.* ὑπο-μονή v.2. ἔσχατος v.8, standing for comp. *latter* §151. πλείων -ονος *greater,* comp. πολύς. πρῶτος

20 for comp. *former,* gen. of comp. ‖ ἀφ-εῖς 2nd sg -ίημι (in form -έω) *allow, tolerate.* ἡ λέγουσα for acc. (appos. to obj. of ἀφεῖς) §13f. προφῆτις -ιδος ἡ *prophetess.* καί coord. breaks in on ptcpl cstr. πλανάω *lead astray,* w. inf.

21 *lure...into.* πορνεῦσαι, φαγεῖν εἰδωλόθυτα v.14. ‖ ἔ-δωκα aor. δίδωμι. χρόνος *time.* μετα-νοήσῃ aor. subj. -νοέω v.5. μετα-νοῆσαι ἐκ *to repent of,* aor. inf. πορνεία *fornication,*

22 here, as often = idolatry. ‖ βάλλω αὐτὴν εἰς κλίνην *I shall make her take to her bed,* (Hebr. cf βεβλημένος "laid low, laid up" Mt 8:6, 9:2 ; Mk 7:30) ; pres. indic. possibly representing Hebr. pres. ptc which may equally ref. fut.

23 μοιχεύοντας ptc -εύω *commit adultery.* θλῖψις v.9. ‖ ἀπο-κτενῶ fut. -κτείνω. γνώσονται fut. γινώσκω. ἐραυνῶν ptc -νάω *search, examine* ; ἐραυνῶν...καὶ δώσω cstr similar to vv. 2, 9, 20. νεφρός pl. *kidneys,* supposed seat of the affec-

24 tions, ν. κ. καρδίας *affections and thoughts.* ‖ οἱ λοιποί *the others.* διδαχή v.14. οἵτινες *those who.* ἔ-γνωσαν aor². βαθύς -εῖα -ύ *deep,* τὰ β. *the deep things,* i.e. mysteries. βάλλω

25 *lay.* βάρος⁸ a *weight, burden.* ‖ πλήν *except, only.* κρατή-σατε aor. impv v.13. ἄχρι(s) v.10, ἄ. οὗ ἄν *until such time as* (= ἄ. τοῦ χρόνου ᾧ §17) ἥξω until *I come,* fut. or aor.

26 subj. ἥκω (only in pres. = *have come* I Jn 5:20). ‖ ὁ νικῶν

pendent nom. §25. τηρῶν ptc τηρέω. τέλος⁸ end. ‖ ποι- 27
μανεῖ fut. -μαίνω mind a flock, hence rule. ἐν v.16. ῥάβδος
ἡ rod. σιδηροῦς -ρᾶ -ροῦν of iron. σκεῦος⁸ vessel, pot.
κεραμικός of clay. συντρίβεται pass. -τρίβω smash, pres.
for fut. ‖ κἀγώ v.6. εἴληφα pf λαμβάνω. ἀστήρ 1:16. 28
πρωϊνός early ; ὁ ἀστὴρ ὁ π. the morning star (Venus), symbol of Christ 22:16. ‖ V.29 = v.7a. ‖

ἄγγελος 1:20. γράψον, τάδε 2:1. ἀστήρ 2:28. ὄνομα 3
ἔχεις ὅτι... you have the name of... ζῇς 2nd sg ζάω. ‖ γίνου 2
impv γίνομαι. γρηγορῶν ptc -ρέω be watchful/alert ; γίνου
γρ. periphr. (Aram.) to express continual watchfulness
§242. στήρισον aor. impv -ίζω stabilize, strengthen. λοιπός
(< λείπω leave) left, τὰ λ. what remains (sc. of your Christian life). ἔ-μελλον impf μέλλω. ἀπο-θανεῖν aor² inf.
-θνήσκω. εὕρηκα pf εὑρίσκω. πε-πληρωμένα pf ptc pass.
-ρόω fulfil, complete. ‖ μνημόνευε impv -εύω remember. 3
πῶς as indir. interr. εἴληφας pf λαμβάνω, pf meaning
have received (and still hold), but the form (aug. substituted for reduplication) lends itself to treatment as if
aor., cf 5:7, 8:5 §289. ἤκουσας aor. ἀκούω. τήρει impv
τηρέω, understanding as obj. "it" (i.e. what you still
hold). μετα-νόησον aor. impv -νοέω repent. γρηγορήσῃς
aor. subj. -ορέω. ἥξω I shall come 2:25. κλέπτης³ thief.
οὐ μή w. subj. emphatic neg. ref. fut. §444. γνῷς aor²
subj. γινώσκω. ποῖος ; what kind? also as indir. interr.
what ; acc. may den. a point of time Jn 4:52, Ac 10:3. ‖
ὀλίγος small, pl. a few. ὀνόματα (Hebr.) persons, people, 4
Ac 1:15. ἐ-μόλυναν aor. -ύνω defile. ἱμάτιον (outer) garment. περι-πατήσουσιν fut. -πατέω. λευκός white. ἄξιος
(< ἄγω draw down a scale, weigh) worthy. ‖ νικῶν ptc 5
νικάω conquer, be victorious 2:7. περι-βαλεῖται fut. mid.
-βάλλω put on or around one, mid. put on (oneself), here
w. ἐν (also 4:4) transl. shall be clothed in ... ἐξ-αλείψω
aor. subj. -αλείφω wipe out. βίβλος ἡ (= βύβλος papyrus)
roll, book. καί (2nd time) but §455β. ὁμο-λογήσω acknowledge, cf Mt 10:32. ‖ V.6 = 2:7a. ‖   6

γράψον, τάδε, 2:1. ἀληθινός true, genuine ; Hebr. true 7
to one's promise. κλεῖς κλειδός ἡ key : to hold the key
implying all authority. Δαυείδ indecl., here gen. ἀνοίγων
ptc. κλείσει fut. κλείω shut ; in ὁ ἀνοίγων καὶ οὐδεὶς κ.
the καί is consec. so that §455γ. ‖ δέ-δωκα pf δίδωμι in 8
Hebr. sense of set. θύρα door = an opening to spread

the gospel, I Cor 16:9. ἠν-εῳγμένην pf ptc pass. (w. triple aug.) ἀνοίγω. κλεῖσαι aor. inf. κλείω. αὐτήν redundant after ἥν Sem. §201. μικρός *little*. καί (1st time) *and yet* §455α. ἐ-τήρησας aor. τηρέω. ἠρνήσω aor. 2nd sg ἀρνέο-

9 μαι *deny*. ‖ διδῶ for δίδωμι §493 ; ἰδοὺ δ. literal Hebr. cstr "behold me granting, that...", i.e. *I will bring it about that...* ἐκ τ. συναγωγῆς: understand τινές before ἐκ (*some of those*) *from the synagogue* 2:10 §80. τῶν λεγόν-των...καὶ οὐκ εἰσίν 2:2. ψεύδομαι *utter an untruth, lie*. ποιήσω (v.12) αὐτοὺς ἵνα ἥξουσιν (v.3) consec. *I will make them come*, w. fut. (instead of subj.) foll. ἵνα §352, 340 ; proleptic prn Hebr. §207. προσ-κυνήσουσιν fut. -κυνέω τινί or (sts, e.g. 9:20, 13:8) τινά *prostrate oneself before, go down on one's knees to, worship* one. γνῶσιν v.3 ; dependent on ἵνα. ἠγάπησα aor. ἀγαπάω, possibly the aor. represents a Hebr. pf which in vbs den. a state may =

10 pres. Mk 1:11 (εὐδόκησα). ‖ ὑπο-μονή *constancy*, τὸν λόγον τῆς ὑ. μου *my call to constancy*. κἀγώ = καὶ ἐγώ. τηρήσω fut. πειρασμός *trial*. μελλούσης ptc μέλλω. οἰκουμένη (sc. γῆ) ἡ *the inhabited world*. πειράσαι aor. inf. -άζω *test*. κατ-οικοῦντας ptc -οικέω *live, dwell*, οἱ κ. ἐπὶ τ. γῆς *the*

11 *inhabitants of the earth*. ‖ ἔρχομαι ταχύ 2:16. κράτει impv κρατέω *hold fast*. λάβῃ aor² subj. λαμβάνω. στέφανος *crown*.

12 ‖ ὁ νικῶν v.5, pendent nom. resumed by αὐτόν §25. ποιήσω fut. ποιέω. στῦλος *pillar*. ναός *temple*. ἔξω *out*. οὐ μή v.3. ἐξ-έλθῃ aor² subj. -έρχομαι. ἔτι w. neg. *any more*. γράψω fut. γράφω. καινός *new*. κατα-βαίνουσα

13 ptc nom. appos. to noun in gen. §13. ‖ V.13 = 2:7α. ‖

14 γράψον, τάδε 2:1. ὁ ἀμήν *the Amen*, ref. Christ. πιστός *faithful*. ἀληθινός *true*. ἀρχή *beginning, origin, ultimate*

15 *source*. κτίσις⁴ *creation*. ‖ οὔτε...οὔτε *neither...nor*. ψυχρός *cold*. ζεστός (< ζέω *boil*) *hot*. ὄφελον particle introducing a wish unlikely to be realized, *would that ! if only !*

16 §355. ἧς impf 2nd sg εἰμί. ‖ χλιαρός *tepid, lukewarm*. ἐμέσαι aor. inf. ἐμέω *vomit, be sick*, μέλλω σε ἐμ. for fut.

17 *I will spit you out...* ‖ ὅτι (2nd time) = "... πλούσιος *rich*. πε-πλούτηκα pf -τέω *be rich*. χρεία *need*, οὐδὲν χ. ἔχω *I lack nothing*. ταλαίπωρος *wretched*, σὺ εἶ ὁ τ. *it is you who are the wretched one*. ἐλεεινός *pitiable*. πτωχός

18 *poor*. τυφλός *blind*. γυμνός *naked*. ‖ συμ-βουλεύω *counsel, advise*. ἀγοράσαι aor. inf. -άζω (< ἀγορά *market*) *buy*. παρ᾽ ἐμοῦ *from me*. χρυσίον (the metal) *gold*. πε-πυρω-

μένον pf ptc pass. -ρόω *refine* by fire. πλουτήσῃς aor. subj. ἱμάτιον, λευκός v.4. περι-βάλῃ aor² subj. mid. v.5. φανερωθῇ aor. subj. pass. -ρόω *reveal, show.* αἰσχύνη *shame.* γυμνότης⁶ -τητος ἡ *nakedness.* κολλ[ο]ύριον *eye-ointment.* ἐγ-χρῖσαι aor. inf. -χρίω *smear, apply* ointment. βλέπῃς subj. βλέπω. ‖ ἐάν = ἄν. φιλῶ subj. φιλέω *love.* ἐλέγχω *reprove.* παιδεύω *discipline.* ζήλευε impv -εύω = ζηλόω *envy*; abs. *be zealous/eager.* μετα-νόησον v.3. ‖ ἔστηκα *I stand,* pf (intr. w. pres. meaning) ἵστημι. ἐπί w. acc. *at,* Mk 2:14. θύρα v.8. κρούω *knock.* ἀκούσῃ aor. subj. ἀκούω. ἀν-οίξῃ aor. subj. -οίγω. εἰσ-ελεύσομαι fut. -έρχομαι. δειπνήσω fut. -νέω *dine*; δεῖπνον was the main meal, usually early in the evening. ‖ νικῶν v.5, pendent nom. resumed by αὐτῷ. δώσω fut. δίδωμι *grant.* καθίσαι aor. inf. -ίζω *make* one *sit*; also intr. ἐν here, *on.* θρόνος *throne.* κἀγώ v.10. ἐ-νίκησα aor. ἐ-κάθισα aor. ‖ V.22 = 2:7a. ‖

εἶδον, καὶ ἰδού Hebr. meaning "I had a vision of..." **4** θύρα *door.* ἠνεῳγμένη pf ptc pass. (w. triple aug.) ἀν-οίγω. φωνή like θύρα dependent on ἰδού. πρώτη for comp., the voice of 1:10. ἤκουσα aor. ἀκούω. σάλπιγξ⁶ -ιγγος ἡ *trumpet.* λαλούσης ptc fem. λαλέω. λέγων treated as if Hebr. (undeclinable). ἀνά-βα (= -βηθι) *come up!* aor² impv -βαίνω, cf Mt 17:20 (μετά-βα). δείξω fut. δείκνυμι *show.* γενέσθαι aor² inf. γίνομαι. ‖ ἐ-γενόμην ἐν πνεύματι 1:10. **2** θρόνος *throne.* ἔ-κειτο impf κεῖμαι (used as pf pass. τίθημι) *be placed/set,* hence *lie, stand.* καθήμενος *one seated,* ptc κάθημαι. ‖ ὅμοιος *like.* ὅρασις⁴ *sight,* dat. of respect, *in* **3** *appearance.* λίθος *stone.* ἴασπις⁶ -ιδος ἡ *jasper.* σάρδιον *cornelian.* ἶρις⁶ ἴριδος ἡ *rainbow*; ? *coloured halo.* κυκλό-θεν adv. *(from) round about*; as prep. w. gen. *around* §83. ὅμοιος (2nd time) masc. in spite of ἶρις, but ὁμοία v.6. σμαράγδινος *emerald.* ‖ καί supply εἶδον. εἴκοσι **4** τέσσαρες = 24. περι-βε-βλημένους pf ptc pass. περι-βάλλω *put on* or *around* one; pf pass. *wear.* ἱμάτιον (outer) *garment.* λευκός *white.* στέφανος *crown.* χρυσοῦς (gen. -σοῦ) -σῆ -σοῦν *of gold.* ‖ ἐκ-πορεύομαι *issue, go out.* ἀστραπή **5** *lightning,* pl. *flashes of lightning.* βροντή *thunder,* pl. *peals of thunder, thunder-claps.* λαμπάς⁶ -άδος ἡ *torch.* καιόμεναι ptc pass. καίω *set on fire*; pass. intr. *burn.* ‖ ὑάλινος (< ὕαλος glass) *of glass.* κρύσταλλος *crystal.* ἐν **6** μέσῳ 1:13. κύκλος *circle,* dat. κύκλῳ as adv. *in a circle,*

round about, like κυκλόθεν used as prep. w. gen. §83. τέσσαρες = 4. ζῷον *animal*, here *living creature* (Ezek 1:5f). γέμοντα ptc γέμω τινός *be full of* sth. ἔμπροσθεν
7 *in front*. ὄπισθεν *behind*. ‖ λέων⁶ λέοντος ὁ *lion*. δεύτερος *second*. μόσχος *calf*. τρίτος *third*. τέταρτος *fourth*.
8 ἀετός *eagle*. πετομένῳ ptc πέτομαι *fly*. ‖ ἓν καθ' ἕν *each* (one). ἀνά distributive, *each, apiece*. πτέρυξ⁶ -υγος ἡ *wing*. ἕξ = 6. κυκλόθεν adv. v.3. ἔσωθεν (*from*) *within/inside*. ἀνά-παυσις⁴ *rest*, ἀ. οὐκ ἔχουσιν...λέγοντες *they cry without ceasing*. ἡμέρας καὶ νυκτός (*by*) *day and* (*by*) *night*, gen. of time within which. ἅγιος pred. παντο-κράτωρ -κράτορος *al-mighty, all-sovereign*. ὁ ἦν...ἐρχόμενος
9 1:4. ‖ δώσουσιν fut. δίδωμι, fut. for subj. after ὅταν; together w. the 3 futs. in v.10, this fut. may represent a Hebr. impf (= pres.) *whenever...they give...* etc. τιμή *honour*. εὐχαριστία *thanksgiving*. καθημένῳ v.2. ζῶντι
10 ptc ζάω. εἰς τ. αἰῶνας τ. αἰώνων *for ever and ever*. ‖ πεσοῦνται fut. πίπτω. εἴκοσι τέσσαρες v.4. προσ-κυνήσουσιν fut. -κυνέω τινί *prostrate oneself before* one, *worship*. βα-
11 λοῦσιν fut. βάλλω. στέφανος v.4. ‖ ἄξιος *worthy*. ὁ κύριος voc. λαβεῖν aor² inf. λαμβάνω. ἔ-κτισας aor. κτίζω *create*. διά *by reason of*. ἦσαν *existed*. ἐ-κτίσθησαν aor. pass. ‖

5 δεξιός *right*, δεξιά (sc. χείρ) *right* (*hand*). καθημένου 4:2. βιβλίον *papyrus roll, book* 1:11. γε-γραμμένον pf ptc pass. γράφω. ἔσω-θεν (*from*) *inside*. ὄπισ-θεν (*from*) *behind, on the back*. κατ-ε-σφραγισμένον pf ptc pass. κατα-σφραγίζω (< κατα- perfective + σφραγίς) *seal up*. σφραγίς⁶
2 -ῖδος ἡ *seal*. ‖ ἰσχυρός *strong, mighty*. κηρύσσοντα ptc -ύσσω *proclaim*. ἄξιος 4:11. ἀν-οῖξαι aor. inf. -οίγω. λῦσαι
3 aor. inf. λύω *loose ; release*, hence *break* seals. ‖ ἐ-δύνατο impf δύναμαι. ὑπο-κάτω *below, underneath* ; used as prep.
4 w. gen. *under* §83. βλεπεῖν ?*to look inside it*. ‖ ἔ-κλαιον
5 impf κλαίω *weep*. εὑρέθη aor. pass. εὑρίσκω. ‖ εἷς for τις §155. κλαῖε impv. ἐ-νίκησεν aor. νικάω. λέων⁶ λέον-
6 τος ὁ *lion*. φυλή *tribe*. ῥίζα *root*. σφραγίς v.1. ‖ μέσος *middle*, ἐν μ. *in the middle*, repeated is Sem. for *between...and...* τέσσαρες = 4. ζῷον 4:6. ἀρνίον *lamb*. ἑστηκός *standing*, pf (intr. w. pres. meaning) ptc neut. ἵστημι. ἐ-σφαγμένον pf ptc pass. σφάζω *slaughter, slay*. κέρας κέρατος τό *horn*. ἀπ-ε-σταλμένοι pf ptc pass. ἀπο-
7 στέλλω. ‖ εἴληφεν pf λαμβάνω, aoristic pf 3:3 §289, sc. as
8 obj. "the book". δεξιὰ τοῦ καθημένου v.1. ‖ ἔ-λαβεν aor²

λαμβάνω. βιβλίον v.1. εἴκοσι τέσσαρες = 24. ἔ-πεσαν (for -ον §491) aor² πίπτω. κιθάρα *harp*. φιάλη *bowl*. χρυσοῦς -σῆ -σοῦν (*of*) *gold*. γεμούσας ptc γέμω τινός *be full* of sth. θυμίαμα⁷ *incense*. προσ-ευχή *prayer*. ‖ ᾄδω *sing*. ᾠδή *song*. 9 καινός *new*. ἄξιος 4:11. λαβεῖν aor² inf. λαμβάνω. ἀνοῖξαι v.2. σφραγίς v.1. ἐ-σφάγης aor² pass. 2nd sg σφάζω v.6. ἠγόρασας aor. ἀγοράζω *buy*. ἐν *with* Sem. for gen. of price. φυλή v.5, ἐκ...φ. wt (acc.) prn cf 2:10. γλῶσσα *tongue*, *language*. ‖ ἐ-ποίησας aor. ποιέω. βασιλεία 1:6. 10 ἱερεύς⁵ *priest*. βασιλεύσουσιν fut. -εύω *reign*. ‖ ἤκουσα 11 aor. ἀκούω. κύκλῳ, ζῷον 4:6. ἀριθμός *number*. μυριάς⁶ -άδος ἡ = 10,000. χιλιάς⁶ -άδος ἡ = 1,000. ‖ ἀρνίον, ἐσφαγ- 12 μένον v.6. λαβεῖν v.9. πλοῦτος *wealth*. σοφία *wisdom*. ἰσχύς -ύος ἡ *strength*, *might*. τιμή *honour*. εὐ-λογία *blessing*, *praise*. ‖ κτίσμα⁷ *creature*. ὑποκάτω v.3. καθημένῳ 13 v.1. κράτος⁸ *might*, *sovereignty*. εἰς τ. αἰῶνας τ. αἰώνων 4:9. ‖ τέσσαρες v.8. ἔ-λεγον impf λέγω. ἔ-πεσαν v.8. 14 προσ-ε-κύνησαν aor. 4:10. ‖

ἤν-οιξεν aor. ἀν-οίγω. ἀρνίον *lamb*. μία (fem. of εἷς) 6 here for ordinal, *first* (cf v.3 δευτέρα, v.5 τρίτη κτλ.). In HGk μία esp. prone to be used as ordinal, being paralleled in Hebr. idiom Mt 28:1. σφραγίς⁶ -ῖδος ἡ *seal*. ἤκουσα aor. ἀκούω. τέσσαρες = 4. ζῷον *animal* ; in Apoc *living creature* (Ezek 1:5f.). βροντή *thunder*, φωνὴ βροντῆς *sound of thunder*. ἔρχου impv ἔρχομαι. ‖ εἶδον καὶ ἰδού 2 4:1. ἵππος *horse*. λευκός *white*. καθήμενος ptc -ημαι: ὁ κ. ἐπ' (a horse) its *rider*. τόξον *bow* (weapon). ἐ-δόθη aor. pass. δίδωμι. στέφανος *crown*. νικῶν *victorious*, ptc νικάω *conquer*. νικήσῃ aor. subj. ‖ δεύτερος *second*. ‖ 3 πυρρός *red*. ἐ-δόθη (sc., e.g. ἐξουσία 13:5*b*) *authority was* 4 *given him* | *he was allowed to*. λαβεῖν aor² inf. λαμβάνω *take* (*away*). καί *that is* §455ζ. ἵνα for subject inf. §408. σφάξουσιν fut. σφάζω *slaughter*, fut. after ἵνα (instead of subj.) §340. μάχαιρα *sword*. ‖ ἤνοιξεν, σφραγίς v.1. τρίτος 5 *third*. μέλας (-ανος) μέλαινα μέλαν *black*. ζυγόν *a pair of scales*. ‖ ἐν μέσῳ 1:13. τέσσαρες v.1. χοῖνιξ⁶ -ικος ἡ *a* 6 measure of capacity = 1 quart (U.K.), a little over 1 litre ; about 1 day's ration of grain. σῖτος *grain*, esp. *wheat*. δηνάριον = Lat. *denarius*, a labourer's daily wage; gen. of price. κριθή *barley*. ἔλαιον (*olive-*)*oil*. οἶνος *wine*. ἀ-δικήσῃς aor. subj. ἀδικέω *harm*, *spoil*, i.e. they are to remain unaffected. ‖ τέταρτος *fourth* (ordinal). ‖ χλωρός 7,8 *yellow-green*; of a horse prob. *bay*; in 8:7 of grass. ἐπ-άνω adv. *above*; as prep. w. gen. *over, on* §83f. ᾅδης³ *hades, underworld*. ἠκολούθει impf ἀκολουθέω. τέταρτον *quarter*. ἀπο-κτεῖναι aor. inf. ἐν instr. §119. ῥομφαία *sword*. λιμός ὁ and ἡ *famine*. ὑπό foll. act. vb, ?the animals being regarded as agential instruments of a higher

9 power. θηρίον *wild beast*. ‖ πέμπτος *fifth*. ὑπο-κάτω adv. *under(neath)*, as prep. w. gen. §83. θυσιαστήριον *altar*. ἐ-σφαγμένων pf ptc pass. σφάζω v.4. διά *for*. μαρτυρία *testimony*. εἶχον impf ἔχω: for holding the same testi-

10 mony (teaching) as Christ had given. ‖ ἔ-κραξαν aor. κράζω *shout, cry out*. πότε; *when?* ἕως π.; *how long?* δεσπότης³ *master, lord*, ὁ w. nom. for voc. §33f. ἀληθινός 3:7. ἐκ-δικέω *vindicate*, ἐ. τι ἔκ τινος *avenge* sth *on* one.

11 κατ-οικούντων ptc -οικέω *dwell, live* 3:10. ‖ ἐ-δόθη v.2. στολή *long robe*. λευκός v.2. ἐρ-ρέθη aor. pass. λέγω: ἐρρ. αὐτοῖς ἵνα here w. fut. (normally subj.) for obj. inf. *they were told to* rest §407. ἀνα-παύσονται fut. mid. -παύω *cause to rest*; mid. *rest* (intr.). χρόνος *time*; χρ. μικρόν (3:8) *(for) a little while*, acc. of duration. πληρωθῶσιν aor. subj. pass. -ρόω *fulfil*; *complete* a period or number. σύν-δουλος *fellow-servants* (sc. of Christ). ἀπο-κτέννεσθαι inf. pass. -κτέννω (var. form of -κτείνω); μέλλοντες ἀποκτ.

12 *going to be killed*. ‖ ἕκτος *sixth*. σεισμός (< σείω v.13) *earthquake*. ἐ-γένετο aor² γίνομαι. ἥλιος *sun*. μέλας v.5. σάκκος = Hebr. *saq, sackcloth*, garment of mourning. τρίχινος (< θρίξ *hair*) *(made) of hair*. σελήνη *moon*. ‖

13 ἀστήρ⁶ -τέρος ὁ *star*. ἔ-πεσαν (for -ον §489) aor² πίπτω. συκῆ *fig-tree*. βάλλω here, *drop*. ὄλυνθος *late* (so unripe)

14 *fig*. ἄνεμος *wind*. σειομένη ptc pass. σείω *shake*. ‖ ἀπ-ε-χωρίσθη aor. pass. ἀπο-χωρίζω *separate*; pass. *be parted*. βιβλίον *scroll*. ἑλισσόμενον ptc pass. ἑλίσσω *roll up*, i.e. like the two halves of a split scroll rolled up and disappeared, Is 34:3. νῆσος *island*. ἐ-κινήθησαν aor. pass.

15 κινέω. ‖ μεγιστάν -ᾶνος ὁ *great man, magnate*. χιλί-αρχος (leader of 1000) properly a *military tribune*, here *high ranking officer, general*. πλούσιος *rich man*. ἰσχυρός *powerful*. ἐλεύθερος *free (man)*. ἔ-κρυψαν aor. κρύπτω *hide*. σπήλαιον *cave*. πέτρα *rock*. ὀρέων gen. pl. (rarely

16 contracted) ὄρος⁸, cf χειλέων Heb 13:15. ‖ πέσετε aor² impv πίπτω. κρύψατε aor. impv. θρόνος *throne*. ὀργή

wrath. ἀρνίον v.l. ‖ σταθῆναι *to stand,* aor. inf. pass. 17
(intr.) ἵστημι §231. ‖

τέσσαρες = 4. ἑστῶτας *standing,* pf² (intr. w. pres. 7
meaning) ptc ἵστημι. γωνία *angle, corner.* κρατοῦντας ptc
-τέω *hold fast; restrain.* ἄνεμος *wind.* πνέῃ subj. πνέω
blow. μήτε...μήτε *neither...nor,* μήτε ἐπὶ πᾶν (Sem.) *nor on
any* §446. δένδρον *tree.* ‖ ἀνα-βαίνοντα ptc -βαίνω *go up.* 2
ἀνα-τολή (< ἀνα-τέλλω rise) *rising of the sun.* ἥλιος *sun.*
ἔχοντα ptc ἔχω. σφραγίς -ῖδος ἡ *seal;* on absence of art.
§182. ζῶντος ptc ζάω. ἔ-κραξεν 6:10. ἐ-δόθη aor. pass.
δίδωμι (sc., e.g., ἐξουσία 13:5b), οἷς ἐδ. ...ἀδικῆσαι (aor. inf.
ἀ-δικέω 6:6) *who had been authorized to harm,* relative past
time §290. αὐτοῖς redundant after οἷς Sem. §201, 203. ‖
ἀ-δικήσητε aor. subj. ἄχρι w. subj. *until.* σφραγίσωμεν aor. 3
subj. -γίζω τι *set a mark or seal on* sth, to serve as protec-
tion as well as identification. μέτ-ωπον (< μετα- between
+ ὤψ face about the eye) *forehead.* ‖ ἤκουσα 6:1. ἀριθμός 4
number. ἐ-σφραγισμένων pf ptc pass. ἑκατόν = 100. τεσσεράκοντα τέσσαρες = 44. χιλιάς -άδος ἡ = 1000. φυλή *tribe.* ‖

εἶδον, καὶ ἰδοὺ 4:1. ὄχλος πολύς *a great crowd.* ἀριθ- 9
μῆσαι aor. inf. -μέω *number.* αὐτόν redundant after
ὅν cf v.2 (αὐτοῖς). ἐ-δύνατο impf δύναμαι. γλῶσσα *tongue.*
ἑστῶτες v.1, pl. according to the sense of ὄχλος. θρόνος
throne. ἀρνίον *lamb.* περι-βε-βλημένους pf ptc pass. (acc.
as if dependent on εἶδον) περι-βάλλω *put on or around*
one; pf pass. *wear.* στολή *long robe.* λευκός *white.* φοῖνιξ⁶
-ικος ὁ *palm tree; palm branch or leaf.* χερσίν dat. pl.
of χείρ. ‖ κράζω v.2. σωτηρία *salvation,* σ. τῷ θεῷ *salvation* 10
(*be ascribed*) *to God!* τῷ καθημένῳ *to him (who is) seated,*
ptc κάθημαι. ‖ εἱστήκεισαν plpf of pf-pres. (intr.) ἕστηκα 11
stand (ἵστημι). κύκλῳ *around* 4:6. τέσσαρες v.2. ζῷον
6:1. ἔ-πεσαν (for -ον §491) aor² πίπτω. προσ-ε-κύνησαν
aor. -κυνέω τινί *prostrate oneself before* one; *worship.* ‖
εὐ-λογία *blessing, praise.* σοφία *wisdom.* εὐχαριστία *thanks-* 12
giving. τιμή *honour.* ἰσχύς -ύος ἡ *might.* εἰς τ. αἰῶνας
τ. αἰώνων 4:9. ‖ ἀπ-ε-κρίθη aor. dep. ἀποκρίνομαι. εἷς 13
for τις §155. ἐκ for partitive gen. §80. περι-βε-βλημένοι,
στολή, λευκός v.9. πόθεν; *where from?* ‖ εἴρηκα pf λέγω, 14
aoristic pf §289. θλῖψις⁴ *distress, suffering.* ἔ-πλυναν aor.
πλύνω *wash.* ἐ-λεύκαναν pf -καίνω *make white* §492.
ἀρνίον v.9. ‖ διὰ τοῦτο *that is why.* θρόνος v.9. λατρεύω 15
τινί *serve, worship* God (esp. of corporate worship whether

by priest or laity). ἡμέρας κ. νυκτός 4:8. ναός heavenly *sanctuary*. ὁ καθήμενος v.10. σκηνώσει fut. -νόω (< σκηνή tent) *encamp*, hence *dwell* ; σκ. ἐπ' αὐτούς *his presence will rest over them*. ‖ οὐ...ἔτι *no more*. πεινάσουσιν fut. -νάω *be hungry*. διψήσουσιν fut. διψάω *be thirsty*. οὐδὲ μή
16 (like οὐ μή) w. subj., emphatic neg. ref. fut. §444. πέσῃ aor² subj. πίπτω. ἥλιος v.2. οὐδὲ πᾶν καῦμα⁷ *nor any heat*, οὐ...πᾶν rendering Sem. idiom §446. ‖ ἀνὰ μέσον *between*, here *in the middle*. ποιμανεῖ fut. -μαίνω *tend* sheep, *lead*
17 sheep *to pasture*, met. *care for*. ὁδηγήσει fut. -ηγέω *lead*. πηγή a *spring*. ἐξ-αλείψει fut. -αλείφω *wipe away*. πᾶν wt art. *every* §188. δάκρυον *tear*. ‖

8 ὅταν in HGk sts just *when*. ἤν-οιξεν aor. ἀν-οίγω. σφραγίς⁶ -ῖδος ἡ *seal*. ἕβδομος *seventh*. ἐ-γένετο aor² γίνομαι. σιγή *silence*. ὡς *about*, Jn 1:40, Ac 5:7. ἡμι-
2 ώριον (< ἥμισυ half + ὥρα) a *half-hour*. ‖ ἑστήκασιν pf (intr. w. pres. meaning) ἵστημι: οἱ ἐνώπιον τ. θεοῦ ἑ. Hebr. meaning *who serve God*. ἐ-δόθησαν aor. pass. δίδωμι.
3 σάλπιγξ -ιγγος ἡ *trumpet*. ‖ ἐ-στάθη *stood*, aor. pass. (intr.) ἵστημι (= ἔστη) §231. ἐπί w. gen. *at*. θυσιαστήριον *altar*. λιβανωτός (< λίβανος frankincense Mt 2:11) *incense* ; *censer*. χρυσοῦς -σῆ -οῦν (*of*) *gold*. θυμίαμα⁷ *incense*. δώσει fut. δίδωμι; fut. after ἵνα instead of subj. §340 ; understand "it" as obj. προσ-ευχή *prayer*, dat. of interest, "for",
4 transl. *with the prayers...* θρόνος *throne*. ‖ ἀν-έ-βη aor²
5 ἀνα-βαίνω. καπνός *smoke*. ‖ εἴληφεν *took*, (aoristic) pf λαμβάνω 3:3 §289. ἐ-γέμισεν aor. -ίζω *fill*. πῦρ i.e. *red-hot coals*. ἔ-βαλεν aor² βάλλω. ἐ-γένοντο v.1. βροντή, ἀστραπή 4:5. σεισμός 6:12. ‖
6 σάλπιγξ v.2. ἡτοίμασαν aor. ἑτοιμάζω (< ἕτοιμος ready) *prepare*. σαλπίσωσιν aor. subj. -ίζω *sound/blow a*
7 *trumpet*. ‖ ἐ-σάλπισεν aor. χάλαζα *hail*. με-μιγμένα pf ptc pass. μίγνυμι *mix* ; μ. τι τινί (15:2) or μ. τι ἔν τινι *mix* sth *with* sth. ἐ-βλήθη aor. pass. βάλλω. τρίτος *third*, τὸ τρίτον a *third* (*part*). κατ-ε-κάη aor² pass. κατα-καίω *burn* (*up*). δένδρον *tree*. χόρτος *grass*, πᾶς χ. *all grass* (wt art., grass
8 as a genus). χλωρός *green*. ‖ δεύτερος *second*. ὡς *as* (*though*), (*something*) *like*. καιόμενον *on fire*, ptc pass.
9 καίω *set on fire, burn* ; pass. intr. ‖ ἀπ-έ-θανεν aor² ἀπο-θνήσκω. κτίσμα⁷ *creature*. τὰ ἔχοντα (ptc ἔχω) for τῶν ἐχόντων (appos. κτισμάτων) §13. ψυχή *life*. πλοῖον *boat*.
10 δι-ε-φθάρησαν aor. pass. δια-φθείρω *destroy*. ‖ τρίτος, ἐσάλ-

πισεν v.7. ἔ-πεσεν aor² πίπτω. ἀστήρ⁶ -τέρος ὁ *star*. λαμ-
πάς -άδος ἡ *torch*. ποταμός *river*. πηγή a *spring*. ‖ λέγεται 11
pass. *is called*. εἰς for pred. nom. §32. ἄψινθος (Fr.
absinthe) *wormwood*, emblem of bitterness. ἐ-πικράνθησαν
aor. pass. πικραίνω *make* sth *bitter*. ‖ τέταρτος *fourth*. 12
ἐ-πλήγη aor² pass. πλήσσω *strike*. ἥλιος *sun*. σελήνη
moon. ἵνα final or perh. consec. §352. σκοτισθῇ aor. subj.
pass. -ίζω *darken*. φάνῃ aor² subj. φαίνω trans. *show*, intr.
shine. τὸ τρίτον αὐτῆς acc. of duration, lit. "for its third
part", i.e. *for a third of the time*. ὁμοίως *likewise*. ‖
ἤκουσα aor. ἀκούω. ἑνός for τινός. ἀετός *eagle*. πετο- 13
μένου ptc -ομαι *fly*. μεσ-ουράνημα⁷ *mid-heaven*, *zenith*,
ἐν μ. *high overhead*. οὐαί *alas* (*for*) *!* here w. acc. instead
of dat. κατ-οικοῦντας ptc -οικέω *inhabit*, *dwell*. ἐκ
after. οἱ λοιποί *the remaining*. σάλπιγξ v.2 ; φωνὴ σάλ-
πιγγος *blast of a trumpet*. μελλόντων ptc μέλλω. ‖ πέμπτος 9
fifth. ἐ-σάλπισεν aor. -ίζω *sound/blow a trumpet* (σάλπιγξ).
ἀστήρ⁶ -τέρος ὁ *star*. πε-πτωκότα *that had fallen*, pf ptc
πίπτω. ἐ-δόθη aor. pass. δίδωμι. αὐτῷ the star : ?a spirit.
κλείς κλειδός ἡ *key*. φρέαρ -ατος τό *well* ; of any hole resembling a well, here *shaft* leading to the abyss. ἄβυσσος ἡ
abyss, ref. Sheol. ‖ ἤν-οιξεν aor. ἀν-οίγω. ἀν-έ-βη aor² ἀνα- 2
βαίνω. καπνός *smoke*. κάμινος ἡ *furnace*. ἐ-σκοτώθη aor.
pass. -τόω *darken*. ἥλιος *sun*. ἀήρ⁶ ἀέρος ὁ *air*. ‖ ἀκρίς⁶ 3
-ίδος ἡ *locust*. σκορπίος *scorpion*. ‖ ἐρ-ρέθη aor. pass. λέγω : 4
ἐρρ. αὐτοῖς *they were told*. ἵνα for obj. inf. §407. ἀ-δική-
σουσιν fut. -δικέω *injure*, *harm* ; fut. for aor. subj. after
ἵνα §340. χόρτος *grass*. χλωρός *green*. δένδρον *tree*. εἰ μή
except ; in Aram. *ella* which also means *but* : the sense
required here. οἵ-τινες *such as*. σφραγίς -ῖδος ἡ *seal*.
μέτ-ωπον *forehead* 7:3. ‖ ἐ-δόθη v.1 ; (sc., e.g., ἐξουσία) 5
ἐδ. αὐτοῖς ἵνα μή...ἀλλ' ἵνα... *it was granted them not to...*
but to... ἀπο-κτείνωσιν aor. (or pres.) subj. -κτείνω. βασανισθήσονται fut. pass. -ίζω (< βάσανος orig. touchstone for
proving gold) *examine by torture*, hence generally *torture*.
μήν μηνός ὁ *month*. πέντε = 5. βασανισμός *torture*. παίσῃ
aor. subj. παίω *hit* ; of an insect, *sting*. ‖ ζητήσουσιν fut. 6
-τέω. οὐ μή εὑρήσουσιν (fut. εὑρίσκω) for aor. subj., emphatic negation of fut. action §444. ἐπι-θυμήσουσιν fut. -μέω
desire, *long*. ἀπο-θανεῖν aor² inf. -θνήσκω. φεύγω ἀπό *flee*
from, *elude*. ‖ ὁμοίωμα⁷ *appearance*, *form* ; τὰ ὁμ. τ. ἀκρίδων 7
(v.3) ὅμοια... *in form the locusts resembled...* ὅμοιος *like*.

ἵππος *horse.* ἡτοιμασμένοις *ready, prepared,* pf ptc pass. refl. ἑτοιμάζω *get ready, prepare.* πόλεμος *war.* στέφανος

8 *crown.* χρυσός *gold.* ‖ θρίξ τριχός ἡ a *hair.* ὀδούς⁶ ὀδόντος

9 ὁ *tooth.* λέων⁶ λέοντος ὁ *lion.* ‖ θώραξ⁶ -ακος ὁ *breast-plate.* σιδηροῦς -ρᾶ -ροῦν *of iron.* φωνή *sound.* πτέρυξ⁶ -υγος ἡ

10 *wing.* ἅρμα⁷ *chariot.* τρεχόντων ptc τρέχω *run.* ‖ οὐρά *tail.* ὅμοιος v.7. σκορπίος v.3. κέντρον *sting.* ἀ-δικῆσαι

11 aor. inf. v.4. μήν, πέντε v.5. ‖ ἐπ' αὐτῶν *over them.* βασι-λέα pred. *as king.* ἄβυσσος v.1. ὄνομα αὐτῷ "the name to him is", *his name is.* Ἑβραϊστί *in Hebrew/Aramaic.* Ἑλληνικῇ (sc. διαλέκτῳ) *Greek.* Ἀπολλύων *Destroyer,* ptc

12 ἀπόλλυμι. ‖ οὐαί *alas for! woe to!* ἡ οὐαί *the woe.* ἡ μία for πρώτη, cardinal for ordinal number, encouraged by Hebr. idiom Tit 3:10, Mk 16:2 §154. ἀπ-ῆλθεν *has passed.* ‖

13 ἕκτος *sixth.* ἐ-σάλπισεν v.1. ἤκουσα aor. ἀκούω. μίαν for τινά. τέσσαρες = 4. κέρας -ατος τό *horn.* θυσιαστήριον

14 *altar.* χρυσός v.7. ‖ λέγοντα (masc.) for λέγουσαν (appos. φωνήν). ὁ ἔχων for τῷ ἔχοντι §13. σάλπιγξ⁶ -ιγγος ἡ *trum-pet.* λῦσον aor. impv λύω *release, set free.* δε-δεμένους pf ptc pass. δέω *bind,* esp. as prisoner. ἐπί *at.* ποταμός

15 *river.* ‖ ἐ-λύθησαν aor. pass. ἡτοιμασμένοι v.7. εἰς *for.* μήν v.5. ἐνιαυτός *year.* ἀπο-κτείνωσιν v.5. τρίτον τό *a*

16 *third* (part). ‖ ἀριθμός *number.* στράτευμα⁷ *army;* also a *force* of troops. ἱππικός *cavalry.* δισμυριάς -άδος ἡ =

17 20,000. μυριάς = 10,000. ἤκουσα v.13. ‖ οὕτως εἶδον *this is how I saw…* ἵππος v.7. ὅρασις⁴ *sight; vision.* καθη-μένους ptc κάθημαι: οἱ κ. ἐπ' αὐτῶν *their riders.* ἔχοντας ptc ἔχω, transl. *with.* θώραξ v.9. πύρινος *red.* ὑακίνθινος *violet.* θειώδης⁹ (< θεῖον 17b) *yellow.* λέων v.8. ἐκ-πο-ρεύομαι *come out, issue.* καπνός v.2. θεῖον *sulphur.* ‖

18 τριῶν gen. of τρεῖς. πληγή (< πλήσσω strike) *wound;* met. *plague.* ἀπ-ε-κτάνθησαν aor. pass. ἀπο-κτείνω. τρίτον v.15.

19 ‖ ἐξουσία *power.* οὐρά v.10. ὄφις⁴ ὁ *snake.* ἔχουσαι ptc

20 ἔχω. ἐν instr. §119. ἀδικέω v.4, intr. *do injury.* ‖ λοιπός *left* (behind), οἱ λ. *the rest.* οὐδέ *not even,* perh. (here) *not even then.* μετ-ε-νόησαν aor. μετα-νοέω *change one's mind* (νοῦς), *repent,* foll. by ἐπί, ἀπό, or ἐκ *repent of.* τὰ ἔργα τ. χειρῶν namely, idols. ἵνα consec., ass. w. μετε-νόησαν, *in such a way that they no* (longer)… §352. προσ-κυνήσουσιν fut. -κυνέω τινί, sts τινά, *worship,* fut. for subj. §340. εἴδωλον *idol.* χρυσοῦς -σῆ -οῦν (*of*) *gold.* ἀργυροῦς (*of*) *silver.* χαλκοῦς *of bronze.* λίθινος (λίθος stone) *of*

stone. **ξύλινος** (ξύλον wood) *of wood.* ‖ **φόνος** *murder.* 21
φάρμακον *magic remedy, charm.* **πορνεία** *fornication.* **κλέμ-**
μα⁷ (< κλέπτω steal) *theft.* ‖

ἰσχυρός *strong.* **κατα-βαίνοντα** ptc. **περι-βε-βλημένον** pf 10
ptc pass. περι-βάλλω *put on* or *around* one ; pf pass. περι-
βέβλημαί τι *be clothed in* sth. **νεφέλη** *cloud.* **ἶρις**⁶ ἴριδος ἡ
rainbow. **ἥλιος** *sun.* **πούς** *here, leg.* **στῦλος** *pillar.* ‖ **καί** 2
co-ord. creating a break in the cstr. **βιβλαρίδιον** = βιβλί-
διον or βιβλάριον dim. *little scroll/book.* **ἠν-ε-ῳγμένον** *open,*
pf ptc pass. (w. triple aug.) ἀνοίγω. **ἔ-θηκεν** aor. τίθημι.
δεξιός *right,* opp. left. **εὐ-ώνυμος** "well-named", euphemism for ἀριστερός *left* (of bad omen). ‖ **ἔ-κραξεν** aor. 3
κράζω *shout, call* (out). **ὥσπερ** *as, like.* **λέων** 9:8. **μυκάο-**
μαι *roar.* **ἐ-λάλησαν** aor. λαλέω: ἐλ...τὰς ἑαυτῶν φωνάς
uttered their roar. **βροντή** *thunder.* ‖ **ἐ-λάλησαν** *had spo-*
ken, rel. past time §290. **ἤμελλον** *I was about to / on*
the point of, impf μέλλω. **ἤκουσα** aor. ἀκούω. **σφράγισον**
aor. impv -ίζω *seal up.* **γράψῃς** aor. subj. γράφω: μή...γ.
do not write. ‖ **ἑστῶτα** *standing,* pf² (intr. w. pres. meaning) 5
ptc ἵστημι. **ἦρεν** aor. αἴρω *raise.* **δεξιός** v.2, ἡ δεξιά (sc.
χείρ) *right hand.* ‖ **ὤμοσεν** aor. ὀμνύω *swear,* ὁ. ἔν τινι 6
Hebr. *swear by* sth or someone. τῷ ζῶντι (ptc) *him who*
lives. **εἰς τ. αἰῶνας...** 4:9. **ἔ-κτισεν** aor. κτίζω *create.*
ὅτι = "... **χρόνος** *time,* cf 2:21. **οὐκ-έτι** *no longer.* **ἔσται**
fut. εἰμί, i.e. *there shall be no more delay.* ‖ **φωνή** *sound,* 7
i.e. trumpet-call. **ἕβδομος** *seventh.* **ὅταν** w. subj. *when*
(ref. fut. action). **μέλλῃ** subj. μέλλω w. fut. force. **σαλπί-**
ζειν inf. 9:1 ; ἐν τ. ἡμέραις...σαλπίζειν *at the time of the call*
of the seventh angel when he comes to blow his trumpet.
καί (Hebr.) introducing the main clause after a temporal
clause ; may be indicated by "then" : *when he...then will*
have been accomplished... **ἐ-τελέσθη** aor. τελέω *complete,*
accomplish ; proleptic aor. §257. **μυστήριον** *secret purpose.*
εὐ-ηγγέλισεν aor. -αγγελίζω τινά *bring/make known good*
news to one. ‖ **ἤκουσα** v.4. **λαλοῦσαν...λέγουσαν** ptcs acc. 8
λαλέω, λέγω, perh. supply a second ἤκουσα. **ὕπ-αγε** impv
-άγω. **λάβε** aor² impv λαμβάνω. **βιβλίον** *papyrus roll, book.*
ἠνεῳγμένον v.2. **ἑστῶτος** v.5. ‖ **ἀπ-ῆλθα** for ἀπῆλθον §489. 9
δοῦναι aor² inf. δίδωμι. **βιβλαρίδιον** v.2. **κατά-φαγε** aor²
impv κατ-εσθίω *eat* (up), symbolic gesture (cf. Eng. "di-
gest" a book). **πικρανεῖ** fut. πικραίνω *make bitter* (predicting
sufferings). **κοιλία** *stomach.* **γλυκύς** -κεῖα -κύ *sweet* (bring-

ing good news to the faithful). μέλι -ιτος τό *honey*. ||

10 ἔ-λαβον aor². κατ-έ-φαγον aor². ἔ-φαγον rel. past time, *when I had eaten* it §290 ; a simplex foll. closely on a cmpd freq. retains the same force. ἐ-πικράνθη aor. pass. ||

11 προφητεῦσαι aor. inf. -εύω *prophesy*, i.e. in the light of the contents of the book he has now "eaten". ἐπί w. dat. (as w. gen.) *on the subject of, about.* γλῶσσα *tongue, language.* ||

11 ἐ-δόθη aor. pass. δίδωμι. κάλαμος *cane*, here for measuring. ὅμοιος *like.* ῥάβδος ἡ *staff.* λέγων wt subject. ἔγειρε impv (intr.) -ρω. μέτρησον aor. impv μετρέω *measure.* ναός *temple.* θυσιαστήριον *altar.* προσ-κυνοῦν-

2 τας *worshippers* 9:20. || αὐλή *courtyard.* ἔξωθεν adv. (from) *outside* ; as prep. w. gen. *outside.* ἔκ-βαλε aor² impv -βάλλω here, *reject, leave out.* μετρήσῃς aor. subj. πατήσουσιν fut. -τέω *trample.* μήν μηνός ὁ *month*, acc. of duration.

3 τεσσεράκοντα [καὶ] δύο = 42. || δώσω *I will assign*, fut. δίδωμι foll. by καί co-ord. here w. final force, *so that* §455γ. δυσίν dat. δύο. μάρτυς⁶ -υρος ὁ *witness.* προφητεύ-σουσιν fut. -εύω. ἡμέρας acc. of duration. χίλιοι = 1000. διακόσιοι = 200. ἑξήκοντα = 60. περι-βε-βλημένοι 10:1.

4 σάκκος *sackcloth* 6:12. || ἐλαία *olive*(-*tree*). λυχνία *lampstand.* ἑστῶτες *standing*, pf² (intr. w. pres. meaning) ptc

5 ἵστημι: masc. though appos. to λυχνίαι §13. || ἀδικῆσαι aor. inf. -κέω *damage.* ἐκ-πορεύομαι *come out, issue.* κατ-εσθίω *eat up, consume.* ἐχθρός *enemy.* θελήσῃ aor. subj. θέλω: εἰ w. subj. for ἐάν §330. ἀπο-κτανθῆναι aor.

6 inf. pass. -κτείνω. || κλεῖσαι aor. inf. κλείω *shut.* ὑετός *rain.* βρέχῃ subj. βρέχει *it is raining*, ὑετὸς β. *rain is falling.* ἡμέρας v.3. προφητεία *prophecy* ; *prophesying.* στρέφεω inf. -φω *turn sth*, σ. τι εἴς τι *turn sth into sth.* πατάξαι aor. inf. πατάσσω *strike.* ἐν instr. *with.* πληγή (< πλήσσω *strike*) *wound* ; met. *plague.* ὁσάκις ἐάν w. subj.

7 *as often as.* θελήσωσιν aor. subj. θέλω. || ὅταν w. subj. *when* ref. fut. action. τελέσωσιν aor. subj. τελέω *complete, finish.* μαρτυρία *testimony.* θηρίον *beast.* ἀνα-βαῖνον ptc neut. -βαίνω. ἄβυσσος ἡ *abyss.* ποιήσει fut. ποιέω; normal Gk usage would prefer mid. since the combination w. πόλεμος = πολεμέω; cf Rom 1:9 (μνεία) ; Phil 1:4 ; Heb 1:3 etc. §227. πόλεμος *war*, ποιέω π. μετά τινος *go to war with / make war on* one. νικήσει fut. νικάω *over-*

8 *come, defeat.* ἀπο-κτενεῖ fut. v.5. || πτῶμα⁷ (< πίπτω)

corpse. πλατεῖα (sc. ὁδός) fem. of πλατύς *broad* ; a *square,*
main street. ἥτις = ἡ. καλεῖται pass. καλέω. πνευματικῶς *spiritually* ; *symbolically.* ἐ-σταυρώθη aor. pass. -ρόω
crucify. ‖ ἐκ τ. λαῶν, sc. as subject τινές, (*men*) *from every* 9
people..., 2:10, Lk 21:16 §80. φυλή *tribe.* γλῶσσα 10:11.
ἡμέρας v.3. ἥμισυς -σεια -συ *half,* neut. ἥμισυ -σους as
noun, a *half.* ἀφ-ίουσιν (3rd plur. -ίω) = ἀφιᾶσιν (-ίημι)
allow. τεθῆναι aor. inf. pass. τίθημι. μνῆμα[7] *tomb, grave.* ‖
κατ-οικοῦντες ptc -οικέω *dwell, live* 3:10. εὐ-φραίνομαι 10
(< εὖ well + φρήν mind) *be glad.* δῶρον *gift.* πέμψουσιν
fut. πέμπω. ἐ-βασάνισαν aor. -ίζω *torture, torment* 9:5. ‖
ἐν = εἰς §99. ἔ-στησαν *they stood,* aor[2] (intr.) ἵστημι. 11
φόβος *fear.* ἐπ-έ-πεσεν aor[2] ἐπι-πίπτω *fall on.* θεωροῦντας
ptc -ρέω *look at* ; *see.* ‖ ἤκουσαν aor. ἀκούω. ἀνά-βατε 12
(for -βητε) aor[2] impv -βαίνω. ἀν-έ-βησαν aor[2]. νεφέλη
cloud. ἐ-θεώρησαν aor. ἐχθρός v.5. ‖ ἐ-γένετο aor[2] γίνομαι. 13
σεισμός (< σείω shake) *earthquake.* δέκατον *a tenth* (part).
ἔ-πεσεν *fell,* here *collapsed,* aor[2] πίπτω. ἀπ-ε-κτάνθησαν aor.
pass. v.5. ὄνομα = *person.* χιλιάς[6] -άδος ἡ *thousand* (considered as an entity) cf χίλιοι v.3 ; χιλιάδες ἑπτά "7 thou-
sands", 7000. οἱ λοιποί *the rest* 9:20. ἔμφοβος *terrified.*
ἔ-δωκαν aor. δίδωμι. ‖ οὐαί ἡ 9:12. δεύτερος *second.* τρίτος 14
third. ταχύς -χεῖα -χύ *quick,* neut. as adv. *shortly, soon.* ‖
   ἕβδομος *seventh.* ἐ-σάλπισεν aor. -ίζω *sound/blow a* 15
trumpet. λέγοντες masc. though appos. fem. φωναί §13.
βασιλεύσει fut. -εύω *reign.* εἰς τ. αἰῶνας... 4:9. ‖ εἴκοσι τέσ- 16
σαρες = 24. καθήμενοι *seated,* ptc κάθημαι. θρόνος *throne.*
ἔπεσαν...καὶ προσεκύνησαν τ. θεῷ 7:11. ‖ εὐ-χαριστέω *give* 17
thanks. κύριε voc. παντο-κράτωρ -κράτορος *al-mighty* ; ὁ
θεὸς ὁ π.: ὁ always w. nouns in appos. to one in voc. §33.
ὁ ὢν καὶ ὁ ἦν cf 1:4, this vision is eschatological (ἐγένετο
"the kingdom...has become...Christ's", v.15). εἴληφας pf
λαμβάνω. ἐ-βασίλευσας aor. -εύω *reign,* aor. inceptive,
thou hast assumed kingship. ‖ ὠργίσθησαν aor. pass. ὀργίζω 18
rouse to anger ; pass. intr. *be angry,* aor. inceptive *became/*
turned angry. ὀργή divine *wrath.* κριθῆναι aor. inf. pass.
κρίνω *judge,* ass. w. καιρός: *the time for the dead to be judged.*
δοῦναι aor[2] inf. δίδωμι. μισθός *reward.* φοβουμένοις ptc
φοβέομαι. μικρός *small.* δια-φθεῖραι aor. inf. -φθείρω
destroy. δια-φθείροντας ptc. ‖ ἠν-οίγη aor[2] pass. ἀν-οίγω. 19
ναός v.1. ὤφθη aor. pass. ὁράω. κιβωτός ἡ *ark.* δια-θήκη
testament, but in the bible usu. for συνθήκη *covenant.*

ἐ-γένοντο v.13. ἀστραπή, βροντή 4:5. σεισμός v.13. χά-λαζα hail. ‖

12 σημεῖον...ἐν τῷ οὐρανῷ a portent...in the sky. ὤφθη 11:19; sts appeared. περι-βε-βλημένη 10:1. ἥλιος sun. σελήνη moon. ὑποκάτω w. gen. under §84. στέφανος crown. ἀστήρ⁶

2 -τέρος ὁ star. ‖ γαστήρ -τρός ἡ belly, womb, ἐν γαστρὶ ἔχω be with child. κράζω cry out. ὠδίνουσα ptc fem. -ίνω suffer the pangs of childbirth, be in travail. βασανιζομένη in anguish, ptc pass. fem. -ίζω torture ; torment. τεκεῖν

3 aor² inf. τίκτω give birth. ‖ δράκων⁶ -κοντος ὁ dragon ; serpent. πυρρός red. κέρας -ρατος τό horn. δέκα = 10.

4 διάδημα⁷ diadem. ‖ οὐρά tail. σύρω drag. τρίτον τό a third (part). ἀστήρ v.1. ἔ-βαλεν aor² βάλλω. ἕστηκεν pf (intr. w. pres. meaning) ἵστημι here quite lit. stood in front of and not as in 8:2. μελλούσης about to, ptc fem. μέλλω. ὅταν w. subj. when ref. fut. τέκῃ aor² subj.

5 κατα-φάγῃ aor² subj. κατ-εσθίω devour. ‖ ἔ-τεκεν aor². ἄρσην -σενος neut. ἄρσεν male ; τὸ ἄ. a male (child), appos. υἱόν. μέλλει is destined to. ποιμαίνειν mind sheep, hence rule. ἐν instr. with. ῥάβδος ἡ staff, rod. σιδηροῦς -ρᾶ -ροῦν of iron. ἡρπάσθη aor. pass. ἁρπάζω seize and carry off. θρόνος

6 throne. ‖ ἔ-φυγεν aor² φεύγω flee. ἔρημος deserted, wild, ἡ ἐ. (sc. χώρα) desert, typifying Christian life uncompro-mised by worldly society. ἐκεῖ redundant after ὅπου, Hebr./Aram. §201, 202f. ἡτοιμασμένον pf ptc pass. ἑτοι-μάζω (ἕτοιμος ready) prepare. ἀπό possibly, "which God had had prepared", but prob. for ὑπό §90. τρέφωσιν subj. τρέφω nourish, feed, 3rd pl. impers. "they..." §1. ἡμέρας 11:3. χίλιοι = 1000. διακόσιοι = 200. ἐξήκοντα = 60. 1260 days = 42 months (11:2, 1:5) = 3¹/₂ years, v.14 (a period habitually ass. w. woes) during which the faith-ful will be subjected to onslaughts from the powers of this world and the supernatural powers of evil, vv. 7, 14, cf Dan 7:25, God's preservation is not from suffering but from sin and will be crowned by ultimate victory 14:1ff. ‖

7 ἐ-γένετο (of war) broke out, aor² γίνομαι. πόλεμος war. πολεμῆσαι aor. inf. -μέω make war, τοῦ π. μετὰ τοῦ δράκοντος (v.3) to fight against the dragon, prob. translating a Hebr. way of expressing purpose. ἐ-πολέμησεν aor. -μέω. ‖

8 ἴσχυσεν aor. -ύω be strong ; hence abs. prevail, be victorious. εὑρέθη was to be found, pass. εὑρίσκω Hebr. for there was no

9 place. ἔτι still, w. a neg., any longer. ‖ ἐ-βλήθη aor. pass.

βάλλω. ὄφις⁴ ὁ *snake, serpent*. ἀρχαῖος *of old*. καλούμενος ptc pass. καλέω. διά-βολος the *accuser*, the *devil*. πλανῶν ptc -νάω *lead astray*. οἰκουμένη (sc. γῆ) ἡ *the inhabited world*. ‖ ἤκουσα aor. ἀκούω. ἄρτι (*just*) *now*. ἐγένετο 10 *has come* v.7. σωτηρία *salvation*. κατ-ήγωρ -ήγορος ὁ (late) alternative to κατήγορος *accuser*. κατ-ηγορῶν ptc -ηγορέω *denounce*. ἡμέρας καὶ νυκτός 4:8. ‖ ἐ-νίκησαν aor. νικάω 11 *conquer, defeat*. διά w. acc. *because of*. ἀρνίον *lamb*. μαρτυρία *testimony*, i.e. to Jesus v.17. ἠγάπησαν aor. ἀγα-πάω. ἄχρι w. gen. of place, *as far as*, met. *unto, to the point of*. ‖ εὐ-φραίνεσθε impv 11:10. οἱ w. art. standing 12 for voc. §33f. σκηνοῦντες ptc -νόω (< σκηνή tent) *encamp*, hence *dwell*. οὐαί as in 8:13, w. acc. instead of dat. κατ-έ-βη aor² κατα-βαίνω. θυμός *rage, fury*. εἰδώς ptc pf-pres. οἶδα. ὀλίγος *small*, of time, *short*. ‖ ἐβλήθη v.9. ἐ-δίωξεν 13 aor. διώκω *pursue; persecute*. ἥτις = ἥ §216. ἔ-τεκεν v.5, *who had given birth to*, rel. past time §290. ἄρσην *male* (*child*) v.5. ‖ ἐ-δόθησαν aor. pass. δίδωμι. πτέρυξ⁶ -υγος ἡ 14 *wing*. ἀετός *eagle*. πέτηται subj. πέτομαι *fly*. ἔρημος v.6. ἐκεῖ after ὅπου redundant §202f. τρέφεται pass. τρέφω *nourish*. ἥμισυς 11:9, a time + 2 times (pl. for obs. dual) + one half of a time (cf 11:2, Dan 12:7). ὄφις ὁ v.9. ‖ ὀπίσω w. gen. *after*. ποταμός *river*. ποταμο-φόρητος 15 *swept away by a river*. ποιήσῃ aor. subj. ποιέω. ‖ ἐ-βοή- 16 θησεν aor. -θέω (< βοή + θέω *run* in response to *a call*) τινί *help* one. ἤν-οιξεν aor. ἀνοίγω. κατ-έ-πιεν aor² κατα-πίνω *swallow up*. ‖ ὠργίσθη 11:18 ; ὀργίζομαι ἐπί τινι *be* 17 *angry with* one. ποιῆσαι aor. inf. ποιέω, inf. final ; cf 11:7 (ποιήσει) §227f. πόλεμος v.7 ; ποιέω π. = πολεμέω (v.7 cf 11:7) μετά *fight against*. οἱ λοιποί *the rest* 9:20. σπέρμα⁷ *seed*, hence *progeny, offspring*. τηρούντων ptc -ρέω. μαρ-τυρία v.11, ἐχόντων τὴν μ. Ἰησοῦ *holding to their testimony to Jesus* ; testimony given by Jesus 6:9, cf Jn 18:37, and concerning Jesus 19:20, 20:4 §36. ‖ ἐ-στάθη *he stood*, aor. 18 pass. (intr.) for ἔστη aor² (intr.) ἵστημι ⟦var. ἐστάθην *I stood*⟧. ἄμμος ἡ *sand*. ‖

θηρίον (*wild*) *beast*. ἀνα-βαῖνον ptc neut. κέρας -ατος 13 τό *horn*. δέκα = 10. διάδημα⁷ *diadem*. βλασφημία lan-guage hostile or derogatory to God, *blasphemy, impiety* ; "Hebr." gen. *blasphemous* names §40f. ‖ ὅμοιος *like*. πάρ- 2 δαλις⁴ -λεως ἡ *leopard*. ἄρκος a *bear*. λέων λέοντος ὁ *lion*. ἔ-δωκεν aor. δίδωμι. δράκων⁶ -κοντος ὁ *dragon, ser-*

3 *pent.* Ϩρόνος *throne.* ‖ μίαν acc. depending on εἶδον? ἐκ τῶν for partitive gen. §80. ἐ-σφαγμένην pf ptc pass. σφάζω *slaughter* ; *attack, wound* in order to kill ὡς ἐσφ. εἰς Ϩάνατον "as if", i.e. *appeared to have had a fatal blow.* καί *but* §455β. πληγή (< πλήσσω strike) *blow, wound.* τοῦ Ϩανάτου *fatal,* "Hebr." gen. §41. ἐ-Ϩεραπεύϩη aor. pass. -εύω *heal.* ἐ-Ϩαυμάσϩη aor. dep. -άζω *wonder, marvel.* ὀπίσω w. gen. *behind* ; *after* ; by ἐϩαυ. ...ὀπίσω... must be 4 meant, *struck with astonishment followed...* ‖ προσ-ε-κύνησαν aor. -κυνέω τινί, sts τινά *prostrate oneself, do obeisance to, worship.* ἔ-δωκεν rel. past time, *had given* §290. Ϩηρίον 5 v.1. πολεμῆσαι aor. inf. -μέω *fight.* ‖ ἐ-δόϩη aor. pass. δίδωμι. λαλοῦν ptc neut. λαλέω: λ. μεγάλα *boast, talk big.* βλασφημία v.1. ποιῆσαι aor. inf. ποιέω : *to act* w. acc. of duration or *spend* w. obj. of time. μήν μηνός ὁ *month.* 6 τεσσεράκοντα [καὶ] δύο = 42. ‖ ἤν-οιξεν aor. ἀνοίγω. πρός w. acc. sts *against.* βλασ-φημῆσαι aor. inf. -φημέω *blaspheme.* σκηνή *tent, tabernacle, dwelling.* σκηνοῦντας ptc -νόω *encamp, dwell,* τούς...σ. as text stands, appos. σκηνήν. ‖ 7 πόλεμος *war* ; ποιῆσαι π. 11:7 §227f. νικῆσαι aor. inf. νικάω *conquer, defeat* [[var. om. v. 7a καὶ ἐδόϩη...αὐτούς]]. 8 φυλή *tribe.* γλῶσσα *tongue, language.* ‖ προσ-κυνήσουσιν fut. v.4, if fut. is understood as a Hebr. impf (= pres.) as in 4:9f. it makes better sense §281. κατ-οικοῦντες ptc -οικέω *dwell.* οὗ...τὸ ὄνομα αὐτοῦ *whose name* ; αὐτοῦ redundant after οὗ in Gk but not in Hebr./Aram. §201, 203. γέ-γραπται pf pass. γράφω. βιβλίον *scroll, book.* ἀρνίον *lamb,* gen. ref. βιβλίον. ἐ-σφαγμένου v.3. κατα-βολή (< κατα- + βάλλω) *foundation,* ἀπὸ κ. ... ?ass. w. γέγραπται 17:8 ; com-9 pare I Pt 1:19f. ‖ οὖς ὠτός τό *ear.* ἀκουσάτω aor. impv 10 3rd sg ἀκούω. ‖ εἰς *is* (destined) *for.* αἰχμ-αλωσία (< αἰχμή *lance* + ἁλίσκομαι *capture) captivity.* ἐν instr. μάχαιρα *sword.* ἀπο-κτανϩῆναι aor. inf. pass. -κτείνω (*is*) *to be killed,* inf. for fut. impvl. ὧδε *herein.* ὑπο-μονή *endurance,* 11 *fortitude.* ‖ Ϩηρίον ἀναβαῖνον v.1 ; ptc cstr taken up by καί co-ord. §375. εἶχεν impf ἔχω. κέρας v.1. ἀρνίον v.8. 12 ἐ-λάλει impf λαλέω. δράκων ?"a" *dragon,* wt art. ‖ πρῶτος *first,* for comp. πρότερον §151. ἐξουσίαν...ποιεῖ *wields authority.* ἐνώπιον αὐτοῦ *in his presence.* ποιεῖ...ἵνα expresses the causative form of Hebr./Aram. vbs, ποιεῖ τὴν γῆν...ἵνα *makes the earth...worship.* κατ-οικοῦντας v.8. προσ-κυνή-σουσιν v.8 ; fut. for subj. (after ἵνα). ἐ-Ϩεραπεύϩη ἡ πληγή

τ. θανάτου v.3. αὐτοῦ v.8 ; ref. πληγή. ‖ σημεῖον, as in Jn, 13 a *sign*, i.e. a *miracle*. ἵνα consec. ἵνα...ποιῇ (subj.) *such as making* §352. ‖ πλανάω *lead astray* ; *delude*. ἐ-δόθη 14 6:4, 7:2. ποιῆσαι v.5. λέγων *telling*. τοῖς κατοικοῦσιν v.8, *the inhabitants*. εἰκών -κόνος ἡ *image*. ὅς (masc.) because standing for antichrist. μάχαιρα v.10. ἔ-ζησεν *revived*, aor. ζάω. ‖ δοῦναι *to endow with*, aor² inf. δίδωμι; 15 inf. cstr resumed by καί co-ord. w. subj. ποιήσῃ. πνεῦμα *breath*, i.e. *life*. ἵνα = ὥστε *so that*. λαλήσῃ aor. subj. λαλέω. ποιήσῃ aor. subj., π. ἵνα...ἀποκτανθῶσιν (aor. subj. pass. v.10) *have* them *put to death* v.12. ὅσοι ἐάν (= ἄν) *all who*. προσ-κυνήσωσιν aor. subj. ‖ ποιεῖ πάντας...ἵνα cstr 16 as v.12. μικρός *small*. πλούσιος *rich*. πτωχός *poor*. ἐλεύ-θερος *free*. δῶσιν aor² subj. δίδωμι: ἵνα δ. αὐτοῖς "that they (impers.) give them", i.e. *that they be given* §1. χά-ραγμα⁷ (< χαράσσω engrave) *mark, stamp*. δεξιός *right* (opp. left). μέτ-ωπον *forehead*. ‖ καὶ ἵνα μή dependent on 17 ποιεῖ v.16. δύνηται subj. δύναμαι. ἀγοράσαι aor. inf. -άζω *buy* (in the ἀγορά). πωλῆσαι aor. inf. πωλέω *sell*. εἰ μὴ ὁ ἔχων "if not one possessing", *unless he had*. ἀριθμός *number*, ἀρ. τ. ὀνόματος i.e. sum of the numbers corresponding to the letters of his name. ‖ ἡ σοφία here, *the secret*, 18 *the answer*. νοῦς νοός ὁ *mind, intelligence*. ψηφίσατω aor. impv 3rd sg -ίζω (ψῆφος pebble) *count* (orig. w. pebbles). *reckon*. ἑξακόσιοι (χ') = 600. ἑξήκοντα (ξ') = 60 ⟦var. δέκα 10, i.e. in all 616⟧. ἕξ (ς') = 6. ‖

καὶ εἶδον καὶ ἰδού 4:1. ἀρνίον *lamb*. ἑστός *standing*, 14 pf (intr.) ptc neut. ἵστημι. ἑκατόν = 100. τεσσεράκοντα = 40. τέσσαρες = 4. χιλιάς 11:13. ἔχουσαι ptc fem. ἔχω agreeing w. χιλιάδες. γε-γραμμένον pf ptc pass. γράφω. μέτ-ωπον *forehead*. ‖ ἤκουσα aor. ἀκούω. φωνήν...πολλῶν 2 *roar of the ocean*. βροντή *thunder*. κιθαρῳδός (κιθάρα + ᾠδός singer) *harpist* who accompanies his own song. κιθαριζόν-των ptc -ίζω ἐν *play* (on) *the harp* ; ptc resumed by καί co-ord. w. indic. (v.3) §375. κιθάρα *harp*. ‖ ᾄδω *sing*. ὡς 3 if true reading here, *what seemed to be*. ᾠδή *song*. καινός *new*. θρόνος *throne*. ζῷον in Apoc. as in Ezek. *living creature*. ἐ-δύνατο impf δύναμαι. μαθεῖν aor² inf. μαν-θάνω *learn*. εἰ μή *except*. ἠγορασμένοι pf ptc pass. ἀγο-ράζω *buy* 13:17. ‖ ἐ-μολύνθησαν aor. pass. -ύνω *defile*. 4 παρθένος *virgin*. αὗτοι (2nd time) sc. εἰσίν. ἀκολουθοῦν-τες ptc -θέω τινί *follow* one. ἀρνίον v.1. ὅπου ἄν *wher-*

ever. ὑπ-άγῃ subj. -άγω *go away, go.* ἠγοράσθησαν aor. pass. *have been bought,* here *redeemed.* ἀπό *from among.* ἀπ-αρχή *first-fruits,* met. of the first to be conse-
5 crated to God in baptism. ‖ εὑρέθη aor. pass. εὑρίσκω pass. in Hebr. sense of *be* 12:8. ψεῦδος[8] a *lie.* ἄ-μωμος *without blemish.* ‖

6 πετόμενον ptc πέτομαι *fly.* μεσ-ουράνημα 8:13. ἔχοντα ptc ἔχω. εὐαγγέλιον αἰώνιον i.e. which does not change. εὐ-αγγελίσαι aor. inf. -αγγελίζω *preach* the gospel. καθη-μένους *sitting,* ptc κάθημαι; in Hebr. the same verb is commonly used for *dwell* : τοὺς κ. *those dwelling/living…*
7 φυλή, γλῶσσα 13:7. ‖ λέγων treated as indecl. (Hebr.) §14. φοβήθητε aor. impv dep. φοβέομαι. δότε aor[2] impv δίδωμι. κρίσις[4] *judgement.* προσ-κυνήσατε aor. impv 13:4.
8 ποιήσαντι aor. ptc ποιέω. πηγή *spring* of water. ‖ δεύτερος appos. to ἄγγελος *a second.* ἠκολούθησεν aor. v.4. ἔ-πεσεν aor[2] πίπτω. οἶνος *wine.* θυμός *rage, fury* ; also *passion* (cf v.10 and Eng. a "rage" and, colloq., a "rage for" sth). πορνεία *fornication,* θυμὸς τ. πορνείας αὐτῆς *her licentious passion,* "Hebr." gen. §40 ; in OT π. and πορνεύω freq. refer to idolatry. πε-πότικεν pf -ίζω *give*
9 *to drink.* ‖ τρίτος *third,* appos. ἄγγελος. θηρίον *beast.*
10 εἰκών[6] -κόνος ἡ *image.* χάραγμα[7] 13:16. μέτωπον v.1. ‖ καί introducing the apodosis. πίεται fut. πίνω *drink.* κε-κερασμένου pf ptc pass. κεράννυμι *mix* ; also, *add* to. ἄ-κρατος *undiluted.* ποτήριον *cup* ; transl. *he shall drink the wine of God's anger added* (i.e. *poured*) *undiluted into the cup of his wrath.* βασανισθήσεται fut. pass. -ίζω *torment.* ἐν instr. θεῖον *sulphur.* ἀρνίον v.1. ‖
11 καπνός *smoke.* βασανισμός *torment.* ἀνά-παυσις[4] *respite.* ἡμέρας κ. νυκτός foll. a neg. *day or night,* gen. of time "within which". προσ-κυνοῦντες ptc 13:4. ‖ ὧδε, ὑπο-
12 μονή 13:10. τηροῦντες ptc τηρέω, nom. for gen. (ref.
13 τῶν ἁγίων) §13. πίστις Ἰησοῦ *faith in Jesus.* ‖ ἤκουσα v.2. γράψον aor. impv γράφω. μακάριος *blessed, happy.* ἀπο-θνήσκοντες pres. ptc frequentative, οἱ ἀποθ. *who die.* ἀπ' ἄρτι *henceforth.* ναί *yes.* ἵνα impvl, *may* they / *let* them rest §415. ἀνα-παήσονται fut[2] dep. ἀνα-παύω *give rest* ; mid. *take rest, rest.* κόπος *toil, labour.* ἀκολουθέω v.4, ἀκ. μετά τινος *go along with* one. ‖
14 καὶ εἶδον… v.1. νεφέλη *cloud.* λευκός *white.* καθή-μενον v.6, acc. after εἶδον. ὅμοιος 1:13. υἱὸς ἀνθρώπου

"Hebr." gen. *a human being* §40. στέφανος *crown*. χρυσοῦς -σῆ -σοῦν *of gold*. δρέπανον *sickle*. ὀξύς ὀξεῖα ὀξύ *sharp*. ‖ ἄλλος cf vv. 6,8,9. ναός heavenly *sanctuary*. 15 κράζων ptc κράζω *call out*, *cry*. πέμψον aor. impv πέμπω. θέρισον aor. impv -ίζω *reap*. θερίσαι aor. inf. ἐ-ξηράνθη aor. pass. ξηραίνω *dry* sth; pass. intr. *dry up, wither*. θερισμός *harvest*. ‖ ἔ-βαλεν aor² βάλλω. ἐ-θερίσθη aor. 16 pass. ‖ ἐκ for ἀπό §87f. ὀξύς v.14. ‖ θυσιαστήριον *altar*. 17,18 ἐ-φώνησεν aor. φωνέω *call*. πέμψον v.15. τρύγησον aor. impv τρυγάω (Fr. récolter) *harvest*. βότρυς -υος ὁ *grape-cluster*. ἄμπελος ἡ *vine*, sts w. meaning of ἀμπελών *vineyard*. τῆς γῆς gen. epexeg. *vineyard of* (= *which is*) *the earth* §45. ἥκμασαν aor. ἀκμάζω *be ripe, ripen*. σταφυλή *bunch of grapes*. ‖ ἔ-βαλεν v.16 ἐ-τρύγησεν aor. ληνός 19 ἡ *wine-press*. θυμός v.10. τὸν μέγαν instead of fem. τὴν μεγάλην §13. ‖ ἐ-πατήθη aor. pass. πατέω *tread*. ἔξωθεν 20 (from) *outside*; used as prep. w. gen. §83. ἄχρι w. gen. *as far as*; *up to* (the height of). χαλινός *bridle*. ἵππος *horse*. στάδιον pl. -ια or -ιοι *stade*, measure of distance *c.* 600ft or 200m. ἀπό in HGk preceding the number expresses Eng. distance *away*, Jn 11:18. χίλιοι = 1000. ἑξακόσιοι = 600; 1600 stades = in round figures 300 km or 200 miles. ‖

θαυμαστός *marvellous*. ἔχοντας ptc ἔχω. πληγή (< πλήσ- **15** σω strike) a *blow*; *plague*. ἔσχατος *last*. ἐ-τελέσθη aor. pass. τελέω *end, complete*; proleptic aor. viewing the ultimate outcome as already achieved : *is consummated/ satisfied*. θυμός *wrath*. ‖ ὡς (something) *like*. ὑάλινος *of* 2 *glass*. με-μιγμένην pf ptc pass. μίγνυμι *mix*. νικῶντας *victors*, ptc -κάω *conquer*, ν. ἐκ connoting perh. *emerge victor over*. θηρίον *beast*. εἰκών⁶ -κόνος ἡ *image*. ἀριθμός *number*, ἀ. τοῦ ὀνόματος 13:17. ἑστῶτας *standing*, pf (intr.) ptc ἵστημι. ἔχοντας *holding* v.1. κιθάρα *harp*. ‖ καί co-ord. interrupting the ptc cstr. ᾄδω *sing*. ᾠδή 3 *song*. ἀρνίον *lamb*. κύριε ὁ θεός voc. παντο-κράτωρ⁶ -τορος *almighty;* appositions to a noun in voc. require art. §33. ἀληθινός *true*. ἐθνῶν [[var. αἰώνων]]. ‖ οὐ μή w. aor. subj. 4 ref. fut., emphasis diminished in interr. §444. φοβηθῇ aor. subj. dep. φοβέομαι. δοξάσει fut. (for subj.) -άζω *glorify, praise*. ὅσιος *holy*. ἥξουσιν *will come*, fut. ἥκω to *have come* 2:25. προσ-κυνήσουσιν fut. -κυνέω *prostrate oneself, do obeisance, worship*. δικαίωμα⁷ *just deed*. ἐ-φανερώθη-

5 **σαν** aor. pass. -ρόω *make clear, show, reveal.* ‖ **ἠν-οίγη** aor[2] pass. ἀν-οίγω. **ναός** *sanctuary.* **σκηνή** *tabernacle.* **μαρτύριον** *testimony,* σκηνὴ μ. where God reveals his will. ‖

6 **πληγή** v.1. **ἐν-δε-δυμένοι** pf ptc mid. ἐνδύω τινά *clothe* another ; mid. *put on* (oneself), *wear.* λίνον *linen.* **καθαρός** *clean.* **λαμπρός** *gleaming white.* **περι-ε-ζωσμένοι** pf ptc pass. περι-ζώννυμαί τι *gird oneself* w. sth. **στῆθος**[8] *breast,*

7 *chest.* **ζώνη** *girdle.* χρυσοῦς -σῆ -σοῦν *of gold.* ‖ **ἕν** for τι. **τέσσαρες** = 4. **ζῷον** 14:3. **ἔ-δωκεν** aor. δίδωμι. **φιάλη** *bowl.* **γεμούσας** ptc γέμω τινός *be full* of sth. **θυμός** v.1.

8 **ζῶντος** ptc (gen.) ζάω. **εἰς τ. αἰῶνας...** 4:9. ‖ **ἐ-γεμίσθη** aor. pass. -ίζω *fill.* **καπνός** *smoke.* **δόξα** *glory, sekina.* **ἐ-δύνατο** impf δύναμαι. **εἰσ-ελθεῖν** aor[2] inf. -έρχομαι. **ναός** v.5. **ἄχρι** w. subj. *until.* **τελεσθῶσιν** aor. subj. pass. τελέω v.1. ‖

16 **ἤκουσα** aor. ἀκούω τινός. **ναός** 15:8. **ὑπ-άγετε** impv -άγω. **ἐκ-χέετε** aor[2] impv -χέω *pour out.* **φιάλη** 15:7. **θυμός**

2 *wrath.* ‖ **ἐξ-έ-χεεν** aor[2]. **ἐ-γένετο** aor[2] γίνομαι. **ἕλκος**[8] *ulcer.* **κακός** *pernicious.* **ἔχοντας** ptc ἔχω. **χάραγμα**[7] *mark, stamp.* **θηρίον** *beast.* **προσ-κυνοῦντας** ptc -κυνέω 15:4.

3 **εἰκών** 15:2. ‖ **δεύτερος** *second.* **νεκροῦ** masc. *of one dead.* **ψυχὴ ζωῆς** "Hebr." gen. *living creature* §40. **ἀπ-έ-θανεν**

4 aor[2] ἀπο-θνήσκω. **τά** for ἡ. ‖ **τρίτος** *third.* **ποταμός** *river.*

5 **πηγή** *spring* of water. ‖ **ἤκουσα** v.1. **ὁ ὢν καὶ ὁ ἦν** 11:17. **ὅσιος** *holy.* **ἔ-κρινας** aor. κρίνω *judge, condemn,* ταῦτα ἔκρ. a Hebr. *you have pronounced these judgements* or *decreed*

6 *these punishments.* ‖ **ἐξ-έ-χεαν** (for -ον) aor[2] 3rd pl. ἐκ-χέω: ἐκ-χέω αἷμα *shed* blood. **καί** introducing the main clause after a subordinate one, Hebr. §457. [δ]**ἔδωκας** pf δίδωμι (ἔδ. aor.). **πιεῖν** aor[2] inf. πίνω. **ἄξιος** *worthy,*

7 ἄξιοί εἰσιν *this is their due, they deserve it.* ‖ **θυσιαστήριον** *altar.* **ναί** *yes.* **παντο-κράτωρ** 15:3. **ἀληθινός** *true.* **κρίσις**[4]

8 *judgement.* ‖ **τέταρτος** *fourth.* **ἥλιος** *sun.* **ἐ-δόθη** aor. pass. δίδωμι 7:2. **καυματίσαι** aor. inf. -ίζω *burn, scorch*

9 Mk 4:6. **ἐν** instr. ‖ **ἐ-καυματίσθησαν** aor. pass. **καῦμα**[7] *scorching heat,* cognate acc. **ἐ-βλασ-φήμησαν** aor. -φημέω *blaspheme.* **πληγή** *plague.* **καί** *but* §455β. **μετ-ε-νόησαν** aor. μετα-νοέω *repent.* **δοῦναι** aor[2] inf. δίδωμι, here consec.

10 ‖ **πέμπτος** *fifth.* **θρόνος** *throne.* **θηρίον** v.2. **ἐ-σκοτωμένη** *was in darkness,* pf ptc pass. -τόω *darken.* **ἐ-μασῶντο** impf μασάομαι *bite.* **γλῶσσα** *tongue.* **πόνος** *labour ; pain.*

11,12 **ἐκ** *with, because of.* ‖ **ἕλκος** v.2. ‖ **ἕκτος** *sixth.* **ποταμός**

v.4. ἐ-ξηράνθη aor. pass. ξηραίνω *dry* sth ; pass. intr.
dry up. ἑτοιμασθῇ aor. subj. pass. -άζω *prepare.* ἀνα-τολή
(< ἀνα-τέλλω rise) *rising* of the sun, i.e. the *east.* ἥλιος
v.8. ‖ δράκων⁶ -κοντος ὁ *dragon, serpent.* θηρίον v.2. 13
ψευδο-προφήτης *false prophet.* τρία, neut. of τρεῖς. ἀ-
κάθαρτος *un-clean.* βάτραχος *frog,* nom. instead of acc. ‖
ποιοῦντα ptc ποιέω. σημεῖον 13:13. ἐκ-πορεύομαι ἐπί τινα 14
go out to one. οἰκουμένη (*inhabited*) *world.* συν-αγαγεῖν
aor² inf. -άγω (for fut. ptc) *bring together* §282. πόλεμος
war. ἡ ἡμέρα ἡ μεγάλη = the day of the parousia and of
judgement. παντο-κράτωρ 15:3. ‖ κλέπτης³ *thief.* μακάριος 15
blessed, happy. γρηγορῶν ptc -γορέω be *watchful/alert.*
τηρῶν ptc τηρέω here *keep* one's clothes *on.* ἱμάτιον
(*outer-*) *garment* ; pl. *clothes.* γυμνός *naked.* περι-πατῇ
subj. -πατέω. βλέπωσιν subj. βλέπω, 3rd pl. impers. §1.
ἀ-σχημοσύνη *indecency* ; hence *private parts.* ‖ συν-ήγαγεν 16
aor². καλούμενον *called,* ptc pass. καλέω. Ἑβραϊστί *in*
Hebrew/Aramaic. ‖ ἕβδομος *seventh.* ἀήρ⁶ ἀέρος ὁ *air.* 17
ναός 15:8. γέ-γονεν pf² γίνομαι, *it is over, it is done.* ‖
ἀστραπή *lightning.* βροντή *thunder.* σεισμός *earthquake.* 18
οἶος *such as.* ἀφ' οὗ *since* (*the time*) *when.* ἄνθρωπος *man,*
mankind. ἐγένετο (3rd time) *came into existence.* τηλικ-
οῦτος *so big* ; τηλ. κτλ. redundant after μέγας οἶος...τῆς
γῆς §202f. ‖ ἐγένετο...εἰς τρία (v.13) *was split into three.*
μέρος⁸ *part.* ἔ-πεσαν aor² (for -ον §489) πίπτω. ἐ-μνήσθη 19
aor. pass. μιμνήσκομαι *remember,* ἐμν. ἐνώπιον τ. θεοῦ
"was remembered before God", i.e. *God remembered.* δοῦναι
v.9. ποτήριον *cup.* οἶνος *wine.* θυμός *fury.* ὀργή *wrath.* ‖
νῆσος ἡ *island,* πᾶσα ν. *every island* §188. ἔ-φυγεν aor² 20
φεύγω *flee.* ὄρη pl. of ὄρος. εὑρέθησαν aor. pass. εὑρίσκω:
οὐχ εὑρέθ. *were no more* (Hebr.). ‖ χάλαζα *hail.* ταλαντιαῖος 21
weighing a talent, i.e. of enormous weight. ἐβλασφήμησαν
v.9. ἐκ *because of.* πληγή v.9. σφόδρα *very,* μεγάλη...σφ.
very great indeed, i.e. *extremely severe.* ‖

εἷς ἐκ τ. ἀγγέλων for τ. ἀ. τις §155. ἐχόντων ptc ἔχω. 17
φιάλη *bowl,* 16:1. ἐ-λάλησεν aor. λαλέω. δεῦρο adv.
hither ; used as impv, *come here!* δείξω fut. δείκνυμι
show. κρίμα⁷ *judgement.* πόρνη *harlot, whore.* καθημένης
ptc -ημαι ἐπί, here perh. *dwell by* (same word in Hebr.). ‖
ἐ-πόρνευσαν aor. -εύω *commit fornication,* (as in OT) 2
signifying idolatry. καί = *who* §455e. ἐ-μεθύσθησαν *got*
drunk, aor. pass. μεθύσκω *intoxicate,* μεθ. ἔκ τινος Hebr.,

be drunk with sth. κατοικοῦντες ptc -οικέω *inhabit.*
3 οἶνος *wine.* πορνεία *fornication,* cf 14:8. ‖ ἀπ-ήνεγκεν aor²
ἀπο-φέρω *carry away.* ἔρημος ἡ (sc. χώρα) *desert.* θηρίον
(*wild*) *beast.* κόκκινος traditionally transl. *scarlet* but
perh. colour of cochineal, *crimson,* v.4 neut. noun, a
crimson garment. γέμοντα masc. (for neut.) ptc γέμω
τινός *be full* of sth, here w. acc. βλασ-φημία *blasphemy*
13:1. ἔχων masc. for fem. κέρας -ατος τό *horn.* δέκα =
4 10. ‖ περι-βε-βλημένη 10:1. πορφυροῦς -ρᾶ -ροῦν *purple,*
(sc. clothing). κε-χρυσωμένη pf ptc pass. -σόω *gild,* met.
adorn, deck out. χρυσίον *gold.* λίθος *stone.* τίμιος *precious.* μαργαρίτης³ *pearl.* ποτήριον *cup.* βδέλυγμα⁷ *de-
testable thing,* an *abomination,* in connection w. idolatry.
5 ἀ-κάθαρτος *unclean,* τὰ ἀκ. the *impurities/filth.* ‖ μέτ-ωπον
forehead. γε-γραμμένον *written,* pf ptc pass. γράφω. μυστή-
6 ριον a *secret.* πόρνη v.1. ‖ μεθύουσαν ptc fem. μεθύω *be
drunk.* μάρτυς⁶ -υρος ὁ 2:13. ἐ-θαύμασα aor. -άζω trans.
and intr. *marvel, be astonished (at).* ἰδών aor² ptc ὁράω.
θαῦμα⁷ a *wonder* ; *astonishment,* cognate acc., ἐθ. ...μέγα
7 *at the sight of her I was utterly astonished.* ‖ ἐρῶ fut. λέγω
tell. θηρίον v.3. βαστάζοντος ptc -άζω *carry.* ἔχοντος
8 ptc ἔχω. δέκα κέρατα v.3. ‖ ἄβυσσος ἡ *abyss,* ref. Sheol.
ἀπ-ώλεια *destruction, ruin.* θαυμασθήσονται fut. dep. κατ-
οικοῦντες 3:10, cf v.2 (trans.). ὧν...τὸ ὄνομα *whose name.*
γέ-γραπται pf γράφω. βιβλίον *scroll, book.* κατα-βολή 13:8.
βλεπόντων ptc βλέπω agreeing w. ὧν instead of w. οἱ κατοικοῦντες. τὸ θηρίον (acc.) ὅτι ἦν Sem. prolepsis §202. παρ-
έσται fut. -ειμι *be present* : ἦν καὶ κτλ. parody of the divine
9 title 1:4. ‖ νοῦς νοός ὁ *mind, understanding, intelligence.*
σοφία *wisdom.* ἐπ' αὐτῶν redundant after ὅπου §202f. ‖
10 πέντε = 5. ἔ-πεσαν aor² (for -ον §489) πίπτω. ἔστιν *exists*
(now). οὔπω *not yet.* ὅταν w. subj. *when* ref. fut. ἔλθῃ
aor² subj. ἔρχομαι. ὀλίγον a *short while,* supply "only".
11 μεῖναι aor. inf. μένω. ‖ ὄγδοος *eighth.* καὶ ἐκ τῶν ἑπτά
12 *and* at the same time *one of the seven.* ‖ δέκα κέρατα v.3.
οἵ-τινες = οἵ §216. οὔπω *not yet.* ἔ-λαβον aor² λαμβάνω.
13 μίαν ὥραν i.e. *for a short time.* ‖ γνώμη *intention, purpose*;
opinion, μίαν γ. ἔχω *be of one mind.* διδόασιν 3rd pl. δί-
14 δωμι. ‖ ἀρνίον *lamb.* πολεμήσουσιν fut. -μέω *go to war*
with. νικήσει fut. νικάω *defeat, conquer.* κλητός (< κα-
15 λέω) *called.* ἐκ-λεκτός *elect, chosen.* πιστός *faithful.* ‖ οὗ
16 *where.* πόρνη v.1. γλῶσσα *tongue, language.* ‖ δέκα κέρατα

v.3. μισήσουσιν fut. μισέω *hate.* ἠρημωμένην *desolate,* pf ptc pass. ἐρημόω *lay waste.* ποιήσουσιν fut. ποιέω: ἠρημωμένην π. αὐτήν *will leave her desolate.* γυμνός *naked.* φάγονται fut. ἐσθίω. κατα-καύσουσιν fut. -καίω *burn up, consume* (by fire). || ἔ-δωκεν aor. δίδωμι: ἔδ. εἰς τὰς καρδίας 17 Hebr. for *has put* (*it*) *into their hearts.* ποιῆσαι (aor. inf.) τὴν γνώμην (v.13) αὐτοῦ *to carry out his purpose.* ποιῆσαι μίαν γνώμην *act in concert.* δοῦναι aor² inf. δίδωμι. βασιλεία *sovereignty, sway.* ἄχρι *until.* τελεσθήσονται fut. pass. τελέω *accomplish.* ||

κατα-βαίνοντα, ἔχοντα, ptcs -βαίνω, ἔχω. ἐ-φωτίσθη aor. **18** pass. -ίζω *illuminate.* || ἔ-κραξεν aor. κράζω *call, cry.* 2 ἰσχυρός *strong.* ἔ-πεσεν aor² πίπτω. ἐ-γένετο aor² γίνομαι. κατ-οικητήριον *dwelling place, home.* φυλακή (< φυλάσσω *guard*) *prison.* πᾶς wt art. *every* §188. ὄρνεον *bird.* ἀ-κάθαρτος *un-clean.* θηρίον *beast.* με-μισημένον pf ptc pass. μισέω *hate.* || ἐκ τ. οἴνου...αὐτῆς 14:8. πέ-πωκαν pf 3 πίνω [[var. πεπτώκασιν (pf πίπτω) in which case ἐκ τ. οἴνου will mean *as a result of the wine*]]. ἐ-πόρνευσαν aor. -εύω *commit fornication* (as in OT signifying idolatry). ἔμ-πορος *merchant.* δύναμις: its Hebr. equivalent also *wealth,* here of degree. στρῆνος[8] *luxury.* ἐ-πλούτησαν aor. -τέω *become rich.* || ἤκουσα aor. ἀκούω. ἐξ-έλθατε aor² (for -ετε §489) 4 impv -έρχομαι. ὁ λαός for voc. §34. συγ-κοινωνήσητε aor. subj. -κοινωνέω *share in.* ἐκ τῶν... w. neg. *any of.* πληγή (πλήσσω *strike*) *blow, wound*; *plague.* λάβητε aor² subj. λαμβάνω. || ἐ-κολλήθησαν aor. pass. κολλάω *stick* sth, here 5 perh. *pile together.* ἄχρι w. gen. *up to.* ἐ-μνημόνευσεν aor. -εύω *remember.* ἀ-δίκημα[7] *crime; misdeed.* || ἀπό-δοτε 6 aor² impv -δίδωμι *give back, render.* ἀπ-έ-δωκεν aor. δι-πλώσατε aor. impv -λόω (to) *double,* δ. τὰ διπλᾶ *pay back double,* cf. Eng. *give twice as good as one gets.* διπλοῦς -λῆ -λοῦν *double.* ποτήριον *cup.* ἐ-κέρασεν aor. κεράννυμι *mix.* κεράσατε aor. impv. || ὅσος...τοσοῦτος *as great/ 7 much as...so great/much...,* the equivalent... ἐ-δόξασεν aor. -άζω *glorify, praise,* ἐδ. αὐτήν *she vaunted herself.* ἐ-στρηνίασεν aor. -άζω *live voluptuously.* δότε aor² impv δίδωμι. βασανισμός *torture, torment.* πένθος[8] *mourning.* ὅτι (2nd time) = "... βασίλισσα *queen,* καθ. β. *I sit* (*enthroned*) *as a queen.* χήρα *widow.* οὐ μή emphatic neg. ref. fut. §444. ἴδω aor² subj. ὁράω. || ἥξουσιν fut. ἥκω *arrive.* πληγή v.4. 8 θάνατος perh. *pestilence.* λιμός *famine.* κατα-καυθήσεται

fut. pass. -καίω *burn up*. ἰσχυρός v.2. κρίνας aor. ptc
9 κρίνω. ‖ κλαύσουσιν fut. κλαίω *weep*. κόψονται fut. mid.
κόπτω *beat* ; mid. κ. ἐπί τινα *beat the breast/mourn for* one.
πορνεύσαντες aor. ptc v.3. στρηνιάσαντες aor. ptc. βλέπωσιν subj. βλέπω. καπνός *smoke*. πύρωσις⁴ *burning*. ‖
10 μακρόθεν *far away* ; ἀπό redundant. ἑστηκότες *standing*,
pf (intr.) ptc ἵστημι. φόβος *fear*. βασανισμός v.7. οὐαί
alas ! ἡ πόλις for voc. ἰσχυρός v.2. μιᾷ ὥρᾳ *in one hour*.
11 κρίσις⁴ *judgement*. ‖ ἔμ-πορος *merchant*. κλαίω *weep*. πενθέω
mourn. γόμος *cargo; wares*. ἀγοράζω *buy*. οὐκ-έτι *any*
12 *longer*. ‖ χρυσός *gold*. ἄργυρος *silver*. λίθος τίμιος, μαργαρίτης 17:4. βύσσινος *fine linen*. πορφύρα *purple, purple
robe*. σιρικός *silk*. κόκκινος 17:3. πᾶς wt art. *every kind
of* §188. w. ξύλον *wood*, a change from gen. to acc.
θύϊνος *of citrus* (not lemon but a tree of African origin w.
fragrant wood). σκεῦος⁸ *vessel, utensil*. ἐλεφάντινος *of
ivory*. τιμιώτατος superl. (elative) τίμιος. χαλκός *brass* ;
13 *copper*. σίδηρος *iron*. μάρμαρος *marble*. ‖ κιννάμωμον
cinnamon. ἄμωμον an unidentified spice plant. θυμίαμα⁷
incense. μύρον *perfumed ointment*. λίβανος *frankincense*.
οἶνος *wine*. ἔλαιον *olive-oil*. σεμίδαλις⁴ *fine wheat flour*.
σῖτος *grain, wheat*. κτῆνος⁸ (< κτάομαι acquire) *beast of
burden*. πρόβατον a *sheep*, followed by two more changes
of case. ἵππος *horse*. ῥέδη a *chariot*. σῶμα a *slave* (cf
Eng. factory "hands"). ψυχαὶ ἀνθρώπων Ezek 27:13 *slaves*,
14 perh. differently but equally exploited. ‖ ὀπώρα *late sum-
mer* ; so *fruit*. ἐπι-θυμία *desire*, ἡ ὀπώρα...ψυχῆς *the fruit
your soul craved*. λιπαρός *sumptuous*. λαμπρός *splendid*,
τ. λιπαρὰ καὶ τ. λ. *all luxury and splendour*. ἀπ-ώλετο aor²
mid. -όλλυμι: ἀπό. ἀπὸ σοῦ *are lost to you*. οὐκ-έτι v.11.
οὐ μή v.7, here w. fut. εὑρήσουσιν fut. εὑρίσκω, impers.
15 pl., οὐ...εὑρ. *never will one find them again* §1. ‖ ἔμ-πορος
v.11. πλουτήσαντες *become rich*, aor. ptc -τέω *be rich*.
ἀπὸ μακρόθεν v.10. στήσονται fut. ἵσταμαι *stand*. φόβος,
16 βασανισμός v.10. κλαίοντες καὶ πενθοῦντες ptc v.11. ‖ οὐαί,
ἡ πόλις v.10. περι-βε-βλημένη pf ptc mid. περι-βάλλω
throw around, clothe another ; mid. *have on, wear*. βύσσινος
v.12. πορφυροῦς -ρᾶ -ροῦν *purple* (sc. clothing). κόκκινος
17 17:3. κε-χρυσωμένη χρυσίῳ...μαργαρίτῃ 17:4. ‖ ἠρημώθη aor.
pass. ἐρημόω *lay waste*. τοσοῦτος *so great*. πλοῦτος
wealth. κυβερνήτης³ *helmsman*. ἐπὶ τόπον *to this or that
place*, perh. *along the coast*. πλέων ptc πλέω *sail*. ναύτης³

sailor. **ὅσοι τ. θάλασσαν ἐργάζονται** *all who do business*
by sea, perh. by contrast implying those who take longer
journeys. **ἔ-στησαν** *stood*, aor^{2} (intr.) ἵστημι. || **ἔ-κραζον** 18
impf v.2. **βλέποντες...πυρώσεως** v.9. **ὅμοιος** *like*. || **ἔ-βαλον** 19
aor^{2} βάλλω. **χοῦς** χοός ὁ (acc. χοῦν) *dust*. **κλαίοντες,**
πενθοῦντες v.11. **ἐ-πλούτησαν** v.3. **τιμιότης**^{6} -ότητος ἡ
preciousness, value, ἐκ τ. *from high prices*. || **εὐ-φραίνου** 20
impv mid. -φραίνω *gladden, cheer* one ; mid. *be glad, re-*
joice. **οὐρανέ** voc. **οἱ** for voc. **ἔ-κρινεν** aor. (same form
as impf) κρίνω. **κρίμα**^{7} *judgement*, ἔκρινεν τὸ κ. ὑμῶν ἐξ
αὐτῆς *has given judgement for you against her*, i.e. *by pro-*
nouncing judgement against her God has vindicated your
cause. || **ἦρεν** aor. αἴρω. **εἷς** for τις. **μύλινος** *connected* 21
with a mill, λίθον ὡς μ. μέγαν *a stone like a great millstone*.
ὅρμημα^{7} (< ὁρμάω rush) *impetus*, ὁρμήματι *with a sudden*
onslaught. **βληθήσεται** fut. pass. βάλλω *throw down*. **οὐ**
μή...ἔτι *nevermore, never again*. **εὑρεθῇ** aor. subj. pass.
εὑρίσκω: οὐ μὴ εὑρ. ἔτι "shall nevermore be found", i.e.
shall be no more (Hebr.) cf 16:20. || **κιθαρ-ῳδός** *harpist* 22
who accompanies his own singing. **μουσικός** *connected w.*
music, ὁ μ. *musician*. **αὐλήτης**^{3} *flautist*. **σαλπιστής**^{3} *trum-*
peter. **ἀκουσθῇ** aor. subj. pass. ἀκούω: οὐ μὴ ἀ. ἔτι Ezek
26:13. **πᾶς...οὐ** *no...* **τεχνίτης**^{3} *craftsman*. **τέχνη** *craft, art,*
skill πάσης τ. w. neg. *of any craft*. **καί** after πᾶς οὐ, *nor*.
μύλος a *mill*. || **λύχνος** *lamp*. **φάνῃ** aor^{2} subj. φαίνω intr. 23
shine. **νυμφίος** *bridegroom*. **νύμφη** *bride*. **μεγιστάν**^{6} -ᾶνος ὁ
great man, magnate. **φαρμακεία** *magic, sorcery*. **ἐ-πλανή-**
θησαν aor. pass. -νάω *mislead*, pass. intr. *go astray, err*. ||
εὑρέθη aor. pass. εὑρίσκω. **ἐ-σφαγμένων** pf ptc pass. σφάζω 24
slaughter, slay. || **ἤκουσα** aor. ἀκούω. **ὄχλος πολύς** a *great* **19**
crowd. **ἀλληλου-ϊά** Hebr. impv *hall'lu Jah, praise God!*
σωτηρία *salvation*. **τοῦ θεοῦ** sc. εἰσίν. || **ἀληθινός** *true*. 2
κρίσις^{4} *judgement*. **ἔ-κρινεν** aor. κρίνω. **πόρνη** *prostitute,*
whore. **ἥτις** = ἥ §216. **ἔ-φθειρεν** aor. φθείρω *destroy* ; *cor-*
rupt. **ἐν** instr. **πορνεία** *fornication*. **ἐξ-ε-δίκησεν** aor.
ἐκ-δικέω τι ἔκ τινος *avenge* sth *on* one 6:10. **χείρ** often den.
power. || **δεύτερον** neut. as adv. a *second time*. **εἴρηκαν** 3
pf λέγω; aoristic pf §289. **καπνός** *smoke*. **εἰς τ. αἰῶνας**
4:9. || **ἔ-πεσαν** aor^{2} (for -σον §489) πίπτω. **εἴκοσι τέσσαρες** 4
= 24. **ζῷον** *living creature*. **προσ-ε-κύνησαν** aor. -κυνέω
τινί *prostrate oneself before, worship*. **καθημένῳ** ptc καθή-
μαι. **θρόνος** *throne*. ||

5 αἰνεῖτε impv αἰνέω τινά *praise* one ; here w. dat. (Hebr.).
6 μικρός *small.* ‖ ἤκουσα v.1. βροντή *thunder,* pl. *peals of thunder.* ἰσχυρός *strong,* here *loud.* λεγόντων for λέγουσαν. ἐ-βασίλευσεν aor. -εύω *reign,* aor. inceptive : *he has established his rule.* παντο-κράτωρ[6] -κράτορος *al-mighty.* ‖
7 χαίρωμεν, ἀγαλλιῶμεν subj. (hort.) χαίρω, ἀγαλλιάω *be jubilant.* δώσωμεν aor. subj. δίδωμι. γάμος *marriage.* ἀρνίον *lamb.* γυνή here *bride* rather than "wife". ἡτοίμασεν
8 aor. ἑτοιμάζω *make ready.* ‖ ἐ-δόθη aor. pass. δίδωμι: ἐδ. αὐτῇ (sc., e.g., ἐξουσία 13:5b) ἵνα... *she was allowed to...* περι-βάληται subj. mid. -βάλλω *put around* or *on* another ; mid. *put on oneself, wear.* βύσσινον τό *linen garment.* λαμπρός *gleaming white.* καθαρός *clean.* δικαίωμα[7] *righteous*
9 *deed.* ἐστίν = *is,* i.e. *signifies, stands for.* ‖ γράψον aor. impv γράφω. μακάριος *blessed, happy.* δεῖπνον *dinner,* here *marriage feast.* κε-κλημένοι pf ptc pass. καλέω *invite.* ἀληθινός v.2 ; οὗτοι subject, οἱ λόγοι ἀλ. τ. θεοῦ pred. ‖
10 ἔ-πεσα v.4. ἔμ-προσθεν adv. *in front,* as prep. w. gen. *before,* ἔπ. ἐ. τ. ποδῶν αὐτοῦ *fell at his feet.* προσ-κυνῆσαι aor. inf. v.4. ὅρα impv ὁράω, before a prohibition, *see* (*that*)...*not, take care that*...not ; ὅρα μή abs., Moulton compares Eng. *don't !* σύν-δουλός σου *fellow-servant of yours.* ἐχόντων ptc ἔχω. μαρτυρία *testimony,* τῶν ἐχόντων τὴν μ. Ἰησοῦ obj. gen. 12:17. προσ-κύνησον aor. impv. προφητεία *prophecy ;* τὸ πνεῦμα τ. πρ. may mean "the spirit inspiring (all) prophecy". ‖
11 ἠν-ε-ῳγμένον pf ptc pass. ἀν-οίγω. ἵππος *horse.* λευκός *white.* καθήμενος ptc, ὁ κ. ἐπ᾽ αὐτόν *its rider.* καλούμενος ptc pass. καλέω. πιστός *faithful.* ἀληθινός v.2, of Christ 3:14. ἐν sociative, *in the spirit of* §117. πολεμέω
12 *make war.* ‖ φλόξ φλογός ἡ *flame.* διάδημα[7] *diadem.* ἔχων masc. ref. back to ὁ καθήμενος. γε-γραμμένον pf ptc pass.
13 γράφω. εἰ μή *except.* ‖ περι-βε-βλημένος 18:16. ἱμάτιον *garment.* βε-βαμμένον pf ptc pass. βάπτω *dip, dye* ⟦var. ῥεραντισμένον *sprinkled* (pf ptc pass. ῥαντίζω)⟧. κέ-κληται pf pass. καλέω: *he was given* (and still bears, pf) *the name.* ‖
14 στράτευμα[7] *army.* ἠκολούθει impf ἀκολουθέω τινί *follow* one. ἵππος λευκός v.11. ἐν-δε-δυμένοι pf ptc mid. ἐν-δύω *clothe* another ; mid. *put on* (oneself), *wear.* βύσσινον
15 καθαρόν v.8. ‖ ἐκ-πορεύομαι *go out, issue.* ῥομφαία *sword.* ὀξύς ὀξεῖα ὀξύ *sharp.* ἐν instr. πατάξῃ aor. subj. πατάσσω *strike.* καὶ αὐτός introducing the principal clause (Hebr.)

he it is who... ποιμανεῖ fut. -μαίνω *mind* sheep, hence *rule.*
ῥάβδος ἡ *staff, rod.* σιδηροῦς -ρᾶ -ροῦν *of iron.* πατέω
tread. ληνός ἡ *wine-press.* οἶνος *wine.* θυμός *fury.* ὀργή
wrath 16:19. παντο-κράτωρ v.6. ‖ ἱμάτιον v.13. μηρός   16
thigh. γε-γραμμένον v.12. ‖ εἷς for τις. ἑστῶτα *standing,* 17
pf (intr.) ptc ἵστημι. ἥλιος *sun,* ἐν τῷ ἡλ. supposedly lit.
in the sun('s disk) and not "in the sun(light)". ἔ-κραξεν
aor. κράζω. ὄρνεον *bird.* πετομένοις ptc πέτομαι *fly.*
μεσ-ουράνημα[7] *mid-heaven, zenith,* ἐν μ. *high overhead.*
δεῦτε pl. of δεῦρο *hither* ; used as impv, *come !* συν-άχθητε
aor. impv pass. -άγω *bring together,* pass. w. refl. sense
come together, gather. δεῖπνον v.9. ‖ φάγητε aor[2] subj. 18
ἐσθίω. χιλί-αρχος (leader of 1000) *military tribune* ; here
in wide sense of *those in command.* ἰσχυρός v.6. ἵππων...
ἐπ᾽ αὐτῶν *of horses and of those who ride them* v.11 (καθήμενος). ἐλεύθερος *free man.* μικρός *small.* ‖ θηρίον *beast.* 19
στράτευμα v.14. συν-ηγμένα pf ptc pass. -άγω. ποιῆσαι
aor. inf. ποιέω: π. πόλεμον μετά 11:7. πόλεμος *war.* ‖
ἐ-πιάσθη aor. pass. πιάζω *seize.* ψευδο-προφήτης[3] *false pro-* 20
phet. ποιήσας aor. ptc, ὁ π. τ. σημεῖα *who had worked the
miracles,* rel. past §290. ἐν οἷς instr. *by which.* ἐ-πλάνησεν
aor. -νάω *lead astray* ; *delude* ; rel. past, *had led astray |
deluded* §290. λαβόντας *who had received,* aor[2] ptc λαμβάνω.
χάραγμα[7] *mark, stamp.* προσ-κυνοῦντας ptc -κυνέω τινί
worship sth; on pres. ptc §372. εἰκών -κόνος ἡ *image.*
ζῶντες *alive,* ptc ζάω. ἐ-βλήθησαν aor. pass. βάλλω. λίμνη
lake. καιομένης ptc pass. καίω *set on fire, burn* ; pass.
intr. *burn* ; fem. ref. λίμνη, perh. attracted into gen. by
πυρός §13. ἐν (2nd time) instr. *with.* θεῖον *sulphur.* ‖
οἱ λοιποί *the rest, the others.* ἀπ-ε-κτάνθησαν aor. pass. 21
ἀπο-κτείνω. ἐν instr. *by.* ῥομφαία v.15. ὁ καθήμενος ἐπί τ.
ἵππου v.11. ἐξ-ελθούσῃ aor[2] ptc -έρχομαι. ὄρνεον v.17.
ἐ-χορτάσθησαν aor. pass. -τάζω *satisfy with food* Phil 4:12. ‖

      κατα-βαίνοντα ptc -βαίνω. ἔχοντα ptc ἔχω. κλείς κλει- **20**
δός ἡ *key.* ἄβυσσος *abyss.* ἅλυσις[4] *chain.* ἐπὶ τ. χεῖρα
in his hand. ‖ ἐ-κράτησεν aor. -τέω *hold fast,* aor. *seize.* 2
δράκων -κοντος ὁ *dragon.* ὄφις[4] ὁ *serpent,* nom. although
appos. δράκοντα §13. ἀρχαῖος *of old.* διά-βολος (< δια-
βάλλω *accuse*) *accuser, the Devil.* Σα-τανᾶς -ᾶ of parallel
Hebr. derivation. ἔ-δησεν aor. δέω *bind.* χίλια neut. of
χίλιοι = 1000. ἔτος[8] *year.* ‖ ἔ-βαλεν aor[2] βάλλω. ἔ-κλει- 3
σεν aor. κλείω *shut.* ἐ-σφράγισεν aor. -ίζω *seal* ; sc. it (the

abyss). ἐπ-άνω adv. *above* ; as prep. w. gen. *over*. πλανήσῃ aor. subj. -νάω 19:20. ἔτι *still*, after a neg. *any longer*. ἄχρι (of time) *until*. τελεσθῇ aor. subj. pass. τελέω *accomplish, complete*. λυθῆναι aor. inf. pass. λύω *unleash, release*. μικρός *small* ; of time, *short*. χρόνος *time*. ‖

4 θρόνος *throne*. ἐ-κάθισαν *they sat*, aor. -ίζω *make to sit* ; also intr. *sit* (*down*) ; the subject is not identified. κρίμα[7] *judgement*. ἐ-δόθη *was entrusted*, aor. pass. δίδωμι. πε-πελεκισμένων pf ptc pass. πελεκίζω (< πέλεκυς ὁ axe) *behead*. μαρτυρία 'Ιησοῦ obj. gen. *testimony to Jesus* 12:17. προσ-ε-κύνησαν aor. -κυνέω here w. acc., ὅσοι οὐ προσεκ. *all who had not worshipped*, rel. past time §290, as also ἔ-λαβον aor[2] λαμβάνω. θηρίον, εἰκών, χάραγμα, μέτωπον, 14:9. ἔ-ζησαν *came back to life*, aor. (inceptive) ζάω. ἐ-βασίλευσαν aor. (constative) -εύω *reign*. ‖

5,6 οἱ λοιποί 19:21. ἀνά-στασις[4] *resurrection*. ‖ μακάριος *blessed, happy*. μέρος[8] *part*. ἐπί *over*. δεύτερος *second*. ἔσονται fut. εἰμί. ἱερεύς[5] *priest*. βασιλεύσουσιν fut. ‖

7 τελεσθῇ v.3. λυθήσεται fut. pass. λύω v.3. φυλακή

8 *prison*. ‖ ἐξ-ελεύσεται fut. -έρχομαι. πλανῆσαι aor. inf. -νάω *lead astray, delude*. τέσσαρες = 4, -αρσιν dat. pl. γωνία *angle, corner*. συν-αγαγεῖν aor[2] inf. -άγω *gather together, muster*. εἰς *for*. πόλεμος *war*. ἀριθμός *number*. αὐτῶν redundant w. ὧν, cf 7:2,9 ; 13:8 etc. §201, 203.

9 ἄμμος ἡ *sand*. ‖ ἀν-έ-βησαν aor[2] ἀνα-βαίνω. πλάτος[8] *breadth*, π. τῆς γῆς, OT expression Hab 1:6 ; meaning uncertain. ἐ-κύκλευσαν aor. -εύω *encircle, surround*. παρ-εμ-βολή *army camp* ; *armed forces* Heb 11:34. ἠγαπημένην pf ptc pass. ἀγαπάω, perh. ref. the new Jerusalem 21:2. κατ-έ-βη aor[2] κατα-βαίνω. ἐκ τ. οὐρανοῦ [[var. ἀπὸ τοῦ θεοῦ ἐκ τοῦ οὐρανοῦ]]. κατ-έ-φαγεν aor[2] κατ-εσθίω *eat up, consume*. ‖

10 διάβολος v.2. πλανῶν ptc. ἐ-βλήθη aor. pass. βάλλω. λίμνη *lake*. θεῖον *sulphur*. θηρίον v.4. ψευδο-προφήτης 19:20. βασανισθήσονται fut. pass. -ίζω *torture* 9:5. ἡμέρας κ. νυκτός (by) *day and* (by) *night*. εἰς τ. αἰῶνας ... 4:9. ‖

11 θρόνος v.4. λευκός *white*. τὸν καθήμενον (ptc κάθημαι) *the One seated*. οὗ ἀπὸ τ. προσώπου "from before whose face", i.e. *from his presence*. ἔ-φυγεν aor[2] φεύγω *flee*. εὑρέθη aor. pass. εὑρίσκω: τόπος οὐχ εὑρέθη αὐτοῖς 12 *there was no place for them*, cf 12:8 ; 14:5. ‖ μικρός v.3. ἑστῶτας pf[2] (intr w. pres. meaning) ptc ἵστημι. βιβλίον orig. dim., later = βίβλος v.15. ἠν-οίχθησαν aor. pass.

ἀν-οίγω. ἐ-κρίθησαν aor. pass. κρίνω. γε-γραμμένων pf
ptc pass. γράφω. ‖ ἔ-δωκεν aor. δίδωμι *give back, yield up.* 13
ᾅδης[3] *hades, underworld.* ‖ ἐ-βλήθησαν, λίμνη v.10. δεύτε- 14
ρος v.6. ‖ εὑρέθη v.11. βίβλος ἡ *papyrus roll, book.* ‖ 15
   καινός *new.* ἀπ-ῆλθαν aor[2] (for -ον §489) here, *disap-* 21
peared. ἔστιν thus accented, *exists.* ἔτι 20:3. ‖ κατα- 2
βαίνουσαν ptc -βαίνω. ἡτοιμασμένην pf ptc pass. ἑτοιμάζω
prepare. νύμφη *bride.* κε-κοσμημένη pf ptc pass. κοσμέω
adorn. ‖ ἤκουσα 19:1. θρόνος 20:11. σκηνή *tent, dwelling* 3
place. σκηνώσει fut. -νόω *encamp, dwell.* ἔσονται, ἔσται fut.
εἰμί. λαοί [[var. λαός]]. ‖ ἐξ-αλείψει fut. -αλείφω *wipe* 4
off/away. δάκρυον a *tear.* ἔτι v.1. πένθος[8] *mourning.*
κραυγή a *crying aloud.* πόνος *labour; pain.* ἀπ-ῆλθαν v.1. ‖
ὁ καθήμενος *the One seated,* ptc κάθημαι. καινός v.1. 5
γράψον aor. impv γράφω. πιστός *trustworthy.* ἀληθινός *true.* ‖
γέ-γοναν (for γεγόνασιν) pf[2] γίνομαι: *all has been brought to* 6
pass; it is done. τὸ Ἄλφα καὶ τὸ Ὠ 1:8. ἀρχή *beginning.*
τέλος[8] *end.* διψῶντι ptc διψάω *be thirsty.* δώσω fut. δίδωμι.
πηγή *spring.* δωρεάν adv. *freely, without payment.* ‖ ὁ 7
νικῶν *the victor* 2:7. κληρο-νομήσει fut. -νομέω (< κλῆρος a
lot + νέμω assign) *inherit,* opp. "earned". ἔσομαι, ἔσται
v.3. αὐτῷ θεός "God to him", *his God.* ‖ δειλός (< δείδω 8
fear) *cowardly ;* τοῖς δ. transl. *as for the cowards...* ἄ-πιστος *faithless.* ἐ-βδελυγμένοις pf ptc pass. -ύσσω *abominate,*
τοῖς ἐβδ. ?participants in pagan rites, cf 17:4 (βδέλυγμα).
φονεύς[5] *murderer.* πόρνος *fornicator.* φαρμακός *magician.*
εἰδωλο-λάτρης[3] *idolater* (εἴδωλον idol + λατρεύω worship)
idolater. ψευδής[9] *false ;* as noun, *liar.* μέρος[8] *part, lot,* sc.
ἔσται. λίμνη *lake.* καιομένη ptc pass. καίω *set on fire ;* pass.
intr. *burn.* θεῖον *sulphur.* δεύτερος *second.* ‖
   εἷς for τις §155. ἐχόντων ptc ἔχω. φιάλη *bowl.* γεμόν- 9
των ptc γέμω τινός *be full* of sth, gen. for acc. (ref. φιάλας)
§13. πληγή (< πλήσσω strike) *wound ; plague.* ἔσχατος
last. ἐ-λάλησεν aor. λαλέω. δεῦρο adv. *hither,* used as
impv, *come here!* δείξω fut. δείκνυμι *show.* νύμφη v.2.
ἀρνίον *lamb.* ‖ ἀπ-ήνεγκεν aor[2] ἀπο-φέρω *take away.* ὑψηλός 10
high. ἔ-δειξεν aor. κατα-βαίνουσαν v.2. ‖ ἔχουσαν ptc 11
ἔχω. φωστήρ[6] -ῆρος ὁ (< φῶς) *luminary ; brilliance.* ὅμοιος
like. λίθος *stone.* τιμιώτατος superl. τίμιος *precious.*
ἴασπις[6] -ιδος ἡ *jasper.* κρυσταλλίζοντι ptc -ίζω *shine like /*
be clear as crystal. ‖ ἔχουσα for ἔχουσαν; (1st time) = 12
indic. τεῖχος[8] *wall.* πυλών[6] -ῶνος ὁ *gate.* ἐπί *at.* ἐπι-γε-

γραμμένα pf ptc pass. ἐπι-γράφω *inscribe*, i.e. on the gates.
13 φυλή *tribe*. ‖ ἀνα-τολή *east* 16:12. βορρᾶς -ᾶ ὁ *north*. νότος
south. δυσμή (< δύνω of the sun, go down, set) *west*. ‖
14 ἔχων for ἔχον = indic. §13. θεμέλιος (< τίθημι) sc. λίθος,
foundation stone Eph 2:20, Heb 11:10. ἀρνίον v.9. ‖
15 λαλῶν ptc λαλέω, pres. ptc representing impf §371. εἶχεν
impf ἔχω. μέτρον *measure*. κάλαμος *reed*. χρυσοῦς -σᾶ
16 -σοῦν of *gold*. μετρήσῃ aor. subj. μετρέω *measure*. ‖ τε-
τράγωνος *quadr-angular*, *square*. κεῖται *is laid out*. μῆκος[8]
length. πλάτος[8] *width*. ἐ-μέτρησέν aor. μετρέω. ἐπί w.
gen. replacing acc. of extent. στάδιον pl. -ια or -ιοι
stade 14:20. χιλιάς[6] -άδος ἡ the number 1000. ὕψος[8]
17 *height*. ἴσος *equal*. ‖ ἕκατον τεσσεράκοντα τέσσαρες = 144.
πῆχυς[4] ὁ *forearm* ; *cubit* (c. 18 ins., not quite ½ metre).
μέτρον ἀνθρώπου ὅ ἐστιν ἀγγέλου perh. *a man's measure* (i.e.
scale of measurement = his forearm) *which is* (that) *of*
18 *an angel* ; one of several explanations. ‖ ἐν-δώμησις[4] *en-*
closure ; *incrustation*. ἴασπις v.11. χρυσίον the metal
gold. καθαρός *pure*, (2nd time) *clear*. ὅμοιος v.11. ὕαλος
19 *glass*. ‖ θεμέλιοι v.14. λίθος *stone*. τίμιος *precious*. κε-
κοσμημένοι v.2. δεύτερος v.8. τρίτος *third*. χαλκηδών[6]
-δόνος ὁ *chalcedony*, not precisely identified. τέταρτος
20 *fourth*. σμάραγδος *emerald*. ‖ πέμπτος *fifth*. ἕκτος *sixth*.
σάρδιον *cornelian*, one of the group classed as chalcedony ;
the remaining names are easily identifiable with their
Eng. equivalents. ἕβδομος *seventh*. ὄγδοος *eighth*. ἔνατος
ninth. δέκατος *tenth*. ἐν-δέκατος *eleventh*. δωδέκατος
21 *twelfth*. ‖ μαργαρίτης[3] *pearl*. ἀνά adv. distributive *apiece*,
ἀ. εἷς ἕκαστος τ. πυλώνων (v.12) ἦν ἐξ ἑνὸς μ. *each one of*
the gates was (formed) *of one pearl apiece*. πλατεῖα (sc.
ὁδός) fem. of πλατύς *broad* ; a *square*, also *wide* (main)
street. χρυσίον καθαρόν, ὕαλος v.18. δι-αυγής[9] (shining
22 through) *transparent*. ‖ ναός *temple*. παντο-κράτωρ -κράτορος
23 *almighty*. ἀρνίον v.9. ‖ χρεία *need*. ἥλιος *sun*. σελήνη
moon. ἵνα for inf. φαίνωσιν subj. φαίνω *show* ; intr. *shine*.
ἐ-φώτισεν aor. -ίζω τινά *illuminate*, *give light to*. λύχνος
24 *lamp*. ‖ περι-πατήσουσιν fut. -πατέω. διὰ τ. φωτὸς αὐτῆς *in*
25 *its light*, αὐτῆς fem., ref. πόλις. ‖ οὐ μή w. subj. emphatic
neg. ref. fut. §444. κλεισθῶσιν aor. subj. pass. κλείω *shut*.
26 ἡμέρας *by day* 14:11. γάρ = δέ *and* §473. ‖ οἴσουσιν fut.
φέρω *bring*. δόξα *splendour*. τιμή *honour* ; also *price*,
27 *value*, and so *wealth*. ‖ εἰσ-έλθῃ aor[2] subj. -έρχομαι. οὐ...

πᾶν *nothing.* κοινός *common* to all ; *ordinary* ; *profane* ; ceremonially *unclean.* ὁ ποιῶν (ptc) *anyone who commits.* βδέλυγμα⁷ *abomination* v.8. ψεῦδος⁸ *falsity, deceit,* ref. all opposition to truth. εἰ μή *except* instead of ἀλλά *but* (*only*) §470. γε-γραμμένοι, βιβλίον 20:12. || ἔ-δειξεν aor. 22 δείκνυμι *show.* ποταμός *river.* λαμπρός *shining.* κρύσταλλος *crystal.* ἐκ-πορευόμενον ptc -πορεύομαι *come,* here *flow out.* θρόνος *throne.* ἀρνίον *lamb.* || ἐν μέσῳ *in the* 2 *middle* (art. often dropped in prep. phrases). πλατεῖα 21:21. αὐτῆς i.e. τῆς πόλεως although not mentioned since 21:23. ἐντεῦ-θεν *hence.* ἐκεῖ-θεν *thence,* ποταμοῦ ἐντ. καὶ ἐκ. *this side and that of the river.* ξύλον *wood* ; *tree.* ποιοῦν ptc neut. ποιέω: π. καρπόν *bear fruit.* μήν μηνός ὁ *month.* ἀπο-διδοῦν ptc neut. -δίδωμι *give what is due.* φύλλον *leaf.* εἰς *for.* θεραπεία *healing.* || πᾶν...οὐ... 3 ἔτι *no...any more.* κατά-θεμα⁷ = ἀνάθεμα *curse.* ἔσται fut. εἰμί. λατρεύσουσιν fut. -εύω *worship.* || ὄψονται fut. ὁράω. 4 μέτ-ωπον *forehead.* || χρεία *need.* λύχνος *lamp.* ἥλιος *sun.* 5 φωτίσει fut. -ίζω 21:23, also intr. *shine.* βασιλεύσουσιν fut. -εύω *reign.* εἰς τ. αἰῶνας... 4:9. ||

πιστὸς καὶ ἀληθινός 21:5. ἀπ-έ-στειλεν aor. ἀπο-στέλλω. 6 δεῖξαι aor. inf. v.1. γενέσθαι aor² inf. γίνομαι. τάχος⁸ *speed,* ἐν τ. *speedily, in a short while.* || ταχύς -χεῖα -χύ 7 *quick* ; neut. as adv. *quickly, soon.* μακάριος *blessed, happy.* τηρῶν ptc τηρέω. προφητεία *prophecy.* βιβλίον 20:12. || κἀγώ = καὶ ἐγώ. ὁ ἀκούων κ. βλέπων either representing 8 impf, *was hearing and seeing,* or *the hearer and eye-witness.* ἤκουσα, ἔ-βλεψα aor. ref. rel. past, *I had heard, I had seen.* ἔ-πεσα aor² (for -ον §489) πίπτω: ἔμπροσθεν τ. ποδῶν αὐτοῦ 19:10. προσ-κυνῆσαι aor. inf. -κυνέω *worship.* δεικνύοντος ptc δείκνυμι. || ὅρα μή, σύν-δουλος 19:10. προσ-κύνησον aor. 9 impv -κυνέω τινί. || σφραγίσῃς aor. impv -ίζω *seal.* προ- 10 φητεία v.7. ἐγγύς *near.* || ἀ-δικῶν ptc ἀ-δικέω *do wrong.* 11 ἀ-δικησάτω aor. impv 3rd sg. ῥυπαρός *filthy, foul.* ῥυπαν-θήτω aor. impv pass. ῥυπαίνω *befoul, stain,* here with sin. δίκαιος *upright, just.* ποιησάτω aor. impv ποιέω 3rd sg. ἁγιασθήτω aor. impv pass. 3rd sg -ιάζω *make holy.* || ταχύ 12 v.7. μισθός *reward.* ἀπο-δοῦναι aor² inf. -δίδωμι v.2. || τὸ Ἄλφα καὶ τὸ Ω 1:8. ἔσχατος *last.* ἀρχή *beginning.* 13 τέλος⁸ *end.* || μακάριος v.7. πλύνοντες ptc πλύνω *wash.* 14 στολή *robe.* πλ. τ. στολὰς αὐτῶν ‖var. ποιοῦντες τὰς ἐντολὰς αὐτοῦ‖. ἔσται ἵνα (...καὶ εἰσέλθωσιν) : ἵνα w. fut. foll.

by subj. §342, ἵνα here final or perh. impvl, *may* their right *be* to the tree of life §415. ξύλον v.2. πυλῶν 21:12.

15 εἰσ-έλθωσιν aor² subj. -έρχομαι. ‖ ἔξω *outside* ?sc. ἔσονται. κύων κυνός *dog* (scavenger and so unclean). φαρμακός *magician*. πόρνος *immoral*. φονεύς⁵ *murderer*. εἰδωλολάτρης³ *idolater*. φιλῶν ptc φιλέω *love*. ποιῶν ptc ποιέω.

16 ψεῦδος⁸ 21:27. ‖ ἔ-πεμψα aor. πέμπω. μαρτυρῆσαι aor. inf. -ρέω *bear testimony*. ἐπί *on* the subject of, *about* 10:11. ῥίζα *root* ; in Hebr. the corresponding word also means *stock*. γένος⁸ *lineage*, *family*. Δαυίδ gen. ἀστήρ ἀστέρος ὁ *star*. λαμπρός v.1. πρωϊνός *early* ; ὁ ἀστήρ...ὁ πρ. 2:28. ‖

17 νύμφη *bride*. ἔρχου impv ἔρχομαι. εἰπάτω aor² (for -έτω §489) impv 3rd sg λέγω. διψῶν ptc διψάω *thirst*. ἐρχέσθω impv 3rd sg ἔρχομαι. λαβέτω aor² impv 3rd sg λαμβάνω.

18 δωρεάν 21:6. ‖ μαρτυρέω τινί *testify in favour of*, also *to* one Heb 10:15. ἀκούοντι ptc -ούω. προφητεία v.7. βιβλίον 20:12. ἐπι-θῇ aor² subj. -τίθημι ἐπί *add to* sth Mt 6:27; a play on words : *if anyone should add to them* : ἐπιθήσει fut. *God will strike him with | bring upon him*. πληγή

19 *wound* ; *plague*. γε-γραμμένας 20:12. ‖ ἀφ-έλῃ aor² subj. -αιρέω *take away*. ἀφ-ελεῖ fut. (for -αιρήσεται). μέρος⁸ *part*, *share*. ξύλον v.2. τῶν γεγραμμένων appos. to "tree

20 of life" and "holy city". ‖ μαρτυρῶν ptc -ρέω, here not of John as v.18, but Christ. ναί *yes*. ταχύ v.7. ἀμήν Hebr. a solemn confirmation, *so be it*. ἔρχου impv. κύριε

21 'Ιησοῦ voc. ‖ μετὰ πάντων ⟦var. μετὰ τῶν ἁγίων: other MSS μετὰ πάντων τῶν ἁγίων⟧. ‖

PARADIGMS OF VERBS
in Hellenistic forms

VERBS IN -ω

Active

TENSE	INDICATIVE		IMPERATIVE
PRESENT & IMPERFECT	*Present* λύ-ω -εις -ει -ομεν -ετε -ουσι(ν)	*Imperfect* ἔ-λυ-ον -ες -ε(ν) ἐ-λύ-ομεν -ετε ἔ-λυ-ον	 λῦ-ε λυ-έτω λύ-ετε λυ-έτωσαν
PERFECT & PLUPERFECT	*Perfect* λέ-λυ-κα -κας -κε(ν) λε-λύ-καμεν -κατε -κασι(ν)	*Pluperfect* (ἐ)-λε-λύ-κειν -κεις -κει -κειμεν -κειτε -κεισαν	
WEAK AORIST	ἔ-λυ-σα -σας -σε(ν) ἐ-λύ-σαμεν -σατε ἔ-λυ-σαν		 λῦ-σον λυ-σάτω λύ-σατε λυ-σάτωσαν
STRONG AOR. (βάλλω)	ἔ-βαλ-ον -ες -ε(ν) etc. as impf		 βάλ-ε βαλ-έτω βάλ-ετε βαλ-έτωσαν
FUTURE	INDIC. λύ-σω -σεις etc. conjugated as pres.		

Active

Subjunctive	Optative	Infinitive	Participle

λύ-ω
  -ῃς
  -ῃ
  -ωμεν
  -ητε
  -ωσι(ν)
	λύ-οιμι
	  -οις
	  -οι
	  -οιμεν
	  -οιτε
	  -οιεν
		λύ-ειν	λύ-ων
			(gen. -οντος)
			  -ουσα
			λῦ-ον

		λε-λυ-κέναι	λε-λυ-κώς
			(gen. -κότος)
			  -κυῖα
			  -κός

λύ-σω
  -σῃς
  -σῃ
  -σωμεν
  -σητε
  -σωσι(ν)
	λύ-σαιμι
	  -σαις
	  -σαι
	  -σαιμεν
	  -σαιτε
	  -σειαν
	(or -σαιεν)
		λῦ-σαι	λύ-σας
			(gen. -σαντος)
			  -σασα
			λῦ-σαν

βάλ-ω
  -ῃς
  -ῃ
  etc. as
pres. subj.
	βάλ-οιμι
	  -οις
	  -οι
	  etc. as
	pres. opt.
		βαλ-εῖν	βαλ-ών
			(gen. -όντος)
			  -οῦσα
			  -όν

Inf. λύ-σειν	Ptc λύ-σων, λύ-σουσα, λῦ-σον		

VERBS IN -ω

Middle and Passive

INDICATIVE		IMPERATIVE
Present	*Imperfect*	
λύ-ομαι	ἐ-λυ-όμην	
-η (or -ει)	ἐ-λύ-ου	λύ-ου
-εται	-ετο	λυ-έσθω
λυ-όμεθα	ἐ-λυ-όμεθα	
λύ-εσθε	ἐ-λύ-εσθε	λύ-εσθε
-ονται	-οντο	λυ-έσθωσαν
Perfect	*Pluperfect*	
λέ-λυ-μαι	(ἐ)-λε-λύ-μην	
-σαι	-λέ-λυ-σο	
-ται	-το	
λε-λύ-μεθα	-λε-λύ-μεθα	
λέ-λυ-σθε	-λέ-λυ-σθε	
-νται	-ντο	

Weak Aorist

Middle	*Passive*	*Middle*	*Passive*
ἐ-λυ-σάμην	ἐ-λύ-θην		
ἐ-λύ-σω	-θης	λῦ-σαι	λύ-θητι
-σατο	-θη	λυ-σάσθω	λυ-θήτω
ἐ-λυ-σάμεθα	-θημεν		
ἐ-λύ-σασθε	-θητε	λύ-σασθε	λύ-θητε
-σαντο	-θησαν	-σάσθωσαν	λυ-θήτωσαν

Strong Aorist

ἐ-βαλ-όμην	ἐ-τάγ-ην		
ἐ-βάλ-ου	-ης	βαλ-οῦ	τάγ-ηθι
-ετο	-η	βαλ-έσθω	ταγ-ήτω
etc. as	etc. as		
impf pass.	weak aor.	βάλ-εσθε	τάγ-ητε
	pass.	βαλ-έσθωσαν	ταγ-ήτωσαν

FUT. INDIC.	Mid. λύ-σομαι -ση (-σει) etc.
	Pass. λυ-θήσομαι -θήση (-θήσει) etc.

Middle and Passive

Subjunctive	Optative	Infinitive	Participle
λύ-ωμαι	λυ-οίμην		
-η	λύ-οιο		λυ-όμενος
-ηται	-οιτο	λύ-εσθαι	-ομένη
λυ-ώμεθα	λυ-οίμεθα		-όμενον
λύ-ησθε	λύ-οισθε		
-ωνται	-οιντο		
λε-λυ-μένος ὦ	-μένος εἴην		
ἦς	εἴης		λε-λυ-μένος
ἦ	εἴη	λε-λύ-σθαι	-μένη
λε-λυ-μένοι ὦμεν	λε-λυμένοι εἴημεν		-μένον

etc. with corresponding
tenses of εἰμί

Weak Aorist

Subjunctive		Optative	
Middle	*Passive*	*Middle*	*Passive*
λύ-σωμαι	λυ-θῶ	λυ-σαίμην	λυ-θείην
-ση	-θῇς	λύ-σαιο	-θείης
-σηται	-θῇ	-σαιτο	-θείη
λυ-σώμεθα	-θῶμεν	λυ-σαίμεθα	-θείημεν
λύ-σησθε	-θῆτε	λύ-σαισθε	-θείητε
-σωνται	-θῶσι(ν)	-σαιντο	-θείησαν

INF. { Mid. λύ-σασθαι PTC { Mid. λυ-σάμενος -σαμένη -σάμενον
{ Pass. λυ-θῆναι   { Pass. λυ-θείς (gen. -θέντος) -θεῖσα -θέν

Strong Aorist
(Mid.: βάλλω   Pass.: τάσσω)

βάλ-ωμαι	ταγ-ῶ	NT only	[ταγ-είην
-η	-ῇς	γέν-οιτο	etc. not
-ηται	-ῇ	(from	found in NT]
etc. as	etc. as	γίνομαι)	
pres. subj.	1st aor. subj.		

INF. { Mid. βαλ-έσθαι PTC { Mid. βαλ-όμενος -ομένη -όμενον
{ Pass. ταγ-ῆναι   { Pass. ταγ-είς (gen. -έντος) -εῖσα -έν

FUT. INF. { Mid. λύ-σεσθαι PTC { Mid. λυ-σόμενος } declined
{ Pass. λυ-θήσεσθαι   { Pass. λυ-θησόμενος } as pres.

VERBS IN -μι (Present Stem)
Active

INFINITIVE	INDICATIVE*	
	Present	*Imperfect*
εἶναι	εἰ-μί	ἤμην
	εἶ	ἦς (or ἦσθα)
	ἐσ-τί(ν)	ἦν
	ἐσ-μέν	ἦμεν (ἤμεθα)
	ἐσ-τέ	ἦτε
	εἰσί(ν)	ἦσαν
δι-δό-ναι	δί-δω-μι	ἐ-δί-δουν
	-ς	-δους
	-σι(ν)	-δου
	δί-δο-μεν	-δο-μεν
	-τε	-δο-τε
	δι-δό-ασι(ν)	-δο-σαν (ἐ-δί-δοῦν)
τι-θέ-ναι	τί-θη-μι	ἐ-τί-θην
	-ς	-θεις
	-σι(ν)	-θει
	τί-θε-μεν	-θε-μεν
	-τε	-θε-τε
	τι-θέ-ασι(ν)	-θε-σαν (ἐ-τί-θουν)
ἱ-έ-ναι	ἵ-η-μι †	[(ἥφ-)ιον †
	ἵ-η-ς (but ἀφ-εῖς)	for class.
	-σι(ν)	(ἀφ-)ί-ειν]
	ἵ-ε-μεν	
	-τε	
	ἱ-ᾶ-σι(ν)	
ἱ-στά-ναι	ἵ-στη-μι	ἵ-στη-ν
	-ς	etc.
	-σι(ν)	
	ἵ-στα-μεν	
	-τε	
	ἱ-στᾶ-σι(ν)	not found in NT

* FUT. of εἰμί pp. 12*f.; for FUT. and PF of the other
  verbs see pp. 10*f.
† In NT occurs only in compounds, ἀφ-ίημι, συν-ίημι
  etc. Exceptions to the paradigm are mostly from
  ἀφ-ίω, in impf treated as if uncompounded.

VERBS IN -μι (Present Stem)
Active

IMPERATIVE	SUBJUNCTIVE ‡	PARTICIPLE
ἴσθι ἔστω (ἤτω) ἔστε ἔστωσαν (or ἤτωσαν)	ὦ ἦς ᾖ ὦμεν ἦτε ὦσι(ν)	ὤν (gen. ὄντος) οὖσα ὄν
δί-δου δι-δό-τω δί-δο-τε δι-δό-τωσαν	δι-δῶ δι-δῷ-ς (or -δοῖς) δι-δῷ (-δοῖ) -δῶ-μεν -δῶ-τε -δῶ-σι(ν)	δι-δού-ς (gen. -δόντος) -δοῦ-σα -δό-ν
τί-θει τι-θέ-τω τί-θε-τε τι-θέ-τωσαν	τι-θῶ τι-θῇ-ς -θῇ -θῶ-μεν -θῆ-τε -θῶ-σι(ν)	τι-θεί-ς (gen. -θέντος) -θεῖ-σα -θέ-ν
-ει ἱ-έ-τω ἵ-ε-τε ἱ-έ-τωσαν	ἱ-ῶ -ῇ-ς -ῇ -ῶ-μεν -ῆ-τε -ῶ-σι(ν)	ἱ-εί-ς (gen. ἱ-έντος) ἱ-εῖ-σα ἱ-έ-ν
ἵ-στη ἱ-στά-τω not found in NT	ἱ-στῶ -στῇ-ς -στῇ -στῶ-μεν -στῆ-τε -στῶ-σι(ν)	ἱ-στά-ς (gen. ἱ-στάντος) ἱ-στᾶ-σα -στά-ν

‡ OPTATIVE: εἴ-ην -ης -η -ημεν -ητε -ησαν. The pres. opt. of the other verbs is not represented in the NT.

VERBS IN -μι (Present Stem)

Middle and Passive

INFINITIVE	INDICATIVE*	
	Present	*Imperfect*
δί-δο-σθαι	δί-δο-μαι	ἐ-δι-δό-μην
	-σαι	ἐ-δί-δο-σο
	-ται	-το
	δι-δό-μεθα	ἐ-δι-δό-μεθα
	δί-δο-σθε	ἐ-δί-δο-σθε
	-νται	-ντο
τί-θε-σθαι	τί-θε-μαι	ἐ-τι-θέ-μην
	-σαι	ἐ-τί-θε-σο
	-ται	-το
	τι-θέ-μεθα	ἐ-τι-θέ-μεθα
	τί-θε-σθε	ἐ-τί-θε-σθε
	-νται	-ντο
ἵ-ε-σθαι	ἵ-ε-μαι	ἱ-έ-μην
	-σαι	ἵ-ε-σο
	-ται	-το
	ἱ-έ-μεθα	ἱ-έ-μεθα
	ἵ-ε-σθε	ἵ-ε-σθε
	-νται	-ντο
ἵ-στα-σθαι	ἵ-στα-μαι	ἱ-στά-μην
	-σαι	ἵ-στα-σο
	-ται	-το
	ἱ-στά-μεθα	ἱ-στά-μεθα
	ἵ-στα-σθε	ἵ-στα-σθε
	-νται	-ντο

* For FUTURE and PERFECT PASS. see pp. 12*-13*

VERBS IN -μι (Present Stem)

Middle and Passive

IMPERATIVE	SUBJUNCTIVE	PARTICIPLE
δί-δο-σο δι-δό-σθω δί-δο-σθε δι-δό-σθωσαν	δι-δῶ-μαι δι-δῷ δι-δῶ-ται δι-δώ-μεθα δι-δῶ-σθε -νται	δι-δό-μενος δι-δο-μένη δι-δό-μενον
τί-θε-σο τι-θέ-σθω τί-θε-σθε τι-θέ-σθωσαν	τι-θῶ-μαι τι-θῇ τι-θῆ-ται τι-θώ-μεθα τι-θῆ-σθε τι-θῶ-νται	τι-θέ-μενος τι-θε-μένη τι-θέ-μενον
ἵ-ε-σο not found in NT	ἱ-ῶ-μαι	ἱ-έ-μενος ἱ-ε-μένη ἱ-έ-μενον
ἵ-στα-σο ἱ-στά-σθω ἵ-στα-σθε ἱ-στά-σθωσαν	ἱ-στῶ-μαι ἱ-στῇ ἱ-στῆ-ται ἱ-στώ-μεθα ἱ-στῆ-σθε ἱ-στῶ-νται	ἱ-στά-μενος ἱ-στα-μένη ἱ-στά-μενον

VERBS IN -μι (Verb Stem)

Aorist Active

INFINITIVE	INDICATIVE
δοῦ-ναι	(sg always 1st aor. ἔ-δω-κα etc. and commonly throughout) class. pl. ἔ-δο-μεν ἔ-δο-τε ἔ-δο-σαν
θεῖ-ναι	1st aor. ἔ-θη-κα -κας -κε ἐ-θή-καμεν -κατε ἔ-θη-καν
εἷ-ναι *	1st aor. ἧ-κα etc. conjugated like ἔθηκα
στῆ-ναι	ἔ-στη-ν -ς ἔ-στη ἔ-στη-μεν -τε -σαν

FUTURE δώ-σω; θή-σω; ἥ-σω; στή-σω
WEAK AOR. ἔ-δω-κα; ἔ-θη-κα; ἧ-κα; ἔ-στη-σα
PERFECT δέ-δω-κα; τέ-θει-κα (class. τέ-θη-κα); ἧ-κα (in cmpds); ἔ-στη-κα †

* In NT occurs only in compounds.
† PLPF: εἱ-στή-κειν; pf² inf. ἑ-στά-ναι (once 1st pf (ἐξ)-εστα-κέναι); pf ptc ἑστηκώς but more commonly pf² ἑστώς.

VERBS IN -μι (Verb Stem)

Aorist Active

IMPERATIVE	SUBJUNCTIVE	PARTICIPLE
δό-ς -τω -τε -τωσαν	δῶ δῷς (or δοῖς) δῷ (δοῖ, δώῃ‡) δῶ-μεν -τε -σι(ν)	δού-ς (gen. δό-ντος) δοῦ-σα δό-ν
θέ-ς -τω -τε -τωσαν	θῶ θῇς θῇ θῶ-μεν θῆ-τε θῶ-σι(ν)	θεί-ς (gen. θέ-ντος) θεῖ-σα θέ-ν
ἕ-ς (e.g. ἄφ-ες) -τω -τε -τωσαν	ὧ ᾗ-ς ᾗ ὧ-μεν ᾗ-τε ὧ-σι(ν)	εἵ-ς (gen. ἕ-ντος) εἷ-σα ἕ-ν
στῆ-θι (in cmpds sts -στα) στή-τω στῆ-τε στή-τωσαν	στῶ στῇ-ς στῇ στῶ-μεν στῆ-τε στῶ-σι(ν)	στά-ς (gen. στά-ντος) στᾶ-σα στά-ν

} all conjugated like verbs in -ω

‡ Distinguish aor² optative: δῴη (for δοίη). The verb ὀνίνημι forms aor² opt. ὀναίμην.

VERBS IN -μι

Aorist Middle

Infinitive	Indicative	
δό-σθαι	ἐ-δό-μην ἔ-δου ἔ-δο-το ἐ-δό-μεθα ἔ-δο-σθε -ντο	
θέ-σθαι	ἐ-θέ-μην ἔ-θου ἔ-θε-το ἐ-θέ-μεθα ἔ-θε-σθε -ντο	
ἕ-σθαι not found in NT		
1st aor. mid. στή-σασθαι	ἐ-στη-σάμην ἐ-στή-σω -σατο ἐ-στη-σάμεθα ἐ-στή-σασθε -σαντο	
Future of εἰμί ἔσ-ε-σθαι	ἔσ-ο-μαι -η -ται	ἐσ-ό-μεθα ἔσ-ε-σθε -ο-νται

Fut. { Mid. δώ-σομαι; θή-σομαι; στήσομαι
{ Pass. δο-θήσομαι; τε-θήσομαι; ἐ-θήσομαι; στα-θήσομαι
all conjugated like verbs in -ω.

VERBS IN -μι

Aorist Middle

IMPERATIVE	SUBJUNCTIVE	PARTICIPLE
δοῦ δό-σθω -σθε -σθωσαν	δῶ-μαι δῷ δῶ-ται δώ-μεθα δῶ-σθε -νται	δό-μενος δο-μένη δό-μενον
θοῦ θέ-σθω -σθε -σθωσαν	θῶ-μαι θῇ θῆ-ται θώ-μεθα θῆ-σθε θῶ-νται	θέ-μενος θε-μένη θέ-μενον
στῆ-σαι στη-σάσθω στή-σασθε στη-σάσθωσαν	στή-σωμαι στή-ση -σηται στη-σώμεθα στή-σησθε -σωνται	στη-σάμενος -σαμένη -σάμενον
		ἐσ-ό-μενος ἐσ-ο-μένη ἐσ-ό-μενον

WEAK AOR. PASS. ἐ-δό-θην; ἐ-τέ-θην ; -ἔ-θην (in cmpds,
for class. εἴ-θην); ἐ-στάθην
PERFECT PASS. δέ-δο-μαι; τέ-θει-μαι; ἕω-μαι (in cmpds, for
class. εἶ-μαι) but pf ptc pass. εἱ-μένος
all conjugated like verbs in -ω.

SOME RULES GOVERNING TENSE FORMATION

Tenses other than the present are formed directly from the verb-stem[1]. A "weak" tense relies on outside help to a greater extent than a "strong" tense which, if it is not formed directly from the verb-stem, relies solely on some modification in the elements composing it. The following notes will help to explain some otherwise unaccountable changes in spelling.

A. Vowel stems ending in -α, -ε, or -ο (e.g. τιμάω, ποιέω πληρόω) undergo the following contractions:

α + ε (or η) becomes ᾱ; ε + ε becomes ει; ο + ε (or ο) becomes ου;

α + ο (ω or ου) becomes ω; ε + ο becomes ου; ο + ω (or η) becomes ω;

α + ει (or η) becomes ᾳ; ε + long vowel is absorbed; ο + ει (η or οι) becomes οι.

The final vowel of the stem is regularly lengthened before tense endings: τιμάω τιμή-σω; ποιέω ἐποίη-σα; πληρόω πεπλήρω-κα.

B. Stems ending in a consonant. Consonants may be classified as below:

	voiced	voiceless	aspirate[2]
labials	β	π	φ (ph)
dentals	δ	τ	ϑ (th)
palatals	γ	κ	χ (ch as in *loch*)

λ, μ, ν, and ρ are known as "liquids". There remain σ and the "double" consonants ζ, ξ and ψ.

---

[1] Not directly deducible from the present indicative, e.g. εὑρίσκω (εὑρ-); πίνω (πι-); τίθημι (θε-).

[2] Not regarded as double consonants in Greek.

In any cluster of two consonants the first consonant is regularly assimilated to the order (voiced, voiceless, or aspirate) of the second, e.g. τρίβω τέτριπ-ται ἐτρίφ-θην; λέγω γέλεκ-ται ἐλέχ-θην; πλέκω ἐπλέχ-θην; βρέχω βέβρεκ-ται.

In accordance with the above and other rules, consonant stems are subject to modification :

before σ {
labials (β, π, φ) combine and are written ψ, e.g. βλέπω aor. ἔβλεψα

dentals (δ, τ, θ) drop out, e.g. πείθω fut. πεί-σω; ψεύδομαι aor. inf. ψεύ-σασθαι

palatals (γ, κ, χ) combine and are written ξ, e.g. ἀνοίγω fut. ἀνοίξω; ἄρχομαι aor. ἠρξάμην.
}

before τ or θ {
a labial + τ becomes ππ, e.g. γράφω pf γέγραπ-ται

a labial + θ becomes φθ, e.g. πέμπω aor. ptc pass. πεμφ-θείς

a dental becomes σ, e.g. πείθω aor. pass. ἐπείσ-θην

a palatal + τ becomes κτ, e.g. τάσσω (ταγ-) pf pass. τέτακ-ται

a palatal + θ becomes χθ, e.g. ἄγω fut. pass. ἀχ-θήσομαι.
}

before κ dentals drop out, e.g. ἐλπίζω (ἐλπιδ-) pf ἤλπι-κα.

before μ {
a labial becomes μ, e.g. θλίβω pf pass. τέθλιμ-μαι

a dental becomes σ, e.g. πείθω pf pass. πέπεισ-μαι

a palatal becomes γ, e.g. πλέκω pf pass. πέπλεγ-μαι.
}

Liquids : λ and ρ are not subject to modification but μ and ν show much irregularity.

A different principle is involved in the Perfect reduplication where a dis-similation takes place to avoid aspirates in successive syllables, e.g. φιλέω πε-φίληκα; θεάομαι τε-θέαμαι; χράομαι κέ-χρημαι. The same principle accounts for such changes as θάπτω aor. pass. ἐτάφην and τρέφω (θρεφ-) aor. ἔθρεψα.

ADDENDA ET CORRIGENDA
AD VOL. I

p. xxxi l. 2 from bottom : delete parenthesis after ἔρχομαι

Mt 2:23   delete the words between 1:22. and **Ναζωραῖος**
    6:27   after πῆχυς⁴ add ὁ ; so also Lk 12:25, Jn 21:8
    13:42 after κάμινος add ἡ
    14:20 after πλήρης add⁹, so also Lk 4:1
    23:16 ὀμόσῃ: for ὀμνύω read ὀμνύω
    23:33 after ὄφις⁴ add ὁ ; so also Lk 11:11, Jn 3:14

Lk 2:34   κεῖμαι before *destined* add *be*

Jn p. 287 left-hand heading : *for* 225 *read* 25

Ac 7:44   διετάξατο: *after* aor. *add* mid.
    11:24 after πλήρης for ⁸ read ⁹